Beginning SharePoint® Administration: Windows® SharePoint Services and SharePoint Portal Server

Göran Husman

WILEY

Wiley Publishing, Inc.

Beginning SharePoint® Administration: Windows® SharePoint Services and SharePoint Portal Server

Published by
Wiley Publishing, Inc.
10475 Crosspoint Boulevard
Indianapolis, IN 46256
www.wiley.com

Copyright © 2006 by Wiley Publishing, Inc., Indianapolis, Indiana

Published simultaneously in Canada

ISBN-13: 978-0-470-03863-5
ISBN-10: 0-470-03863-2

Manufactured in the United States of America

10 9 8 7 6 5 4 3 2 1

1B/RY/QZ/QW/IN

Library of Congress Cataloging-in-Publication Data is available from publisher upon request.

For general information on our other products and services please contact our Customer Care Depart- ment within the United States at (800) 762-2974, outside the United States at (317) 572-3993 or fax (317) 572-4002.

Beginning
SharePoint® Administration: Windows® SharePoint Services and SharePoint Portal Server

About the Author

Göran Husman is a true computer nerd who started his career as a computer programmer in 1978. After working as a C and Fortran developer for a medical university and later a large telecom company, he started his own consulting company in 1989. Due to market demands he soon switched his focus from Unix to the MS environment and from developing code to implementing large e-mail systems and building information systems. Göran has also been hired as a computer trainer since the beginning of 1980. In 1993 he became one of the first certified MS Certified Trainers (MCT) in Sweden, and he has regularly conducted MS courses ever since. He is also certified by MS as an MCP (with the number 2888) and an MSCE. His great engagement in e-mail systems awarded him status as Sweden's first MS Exchange MVP (Most Valuable Professional) by Microsoft. He switched focus to MS SharePoint in 2003, and in January 2006 Microsoft awarded him status as Sweden's first SharePoint Portal Server MVP. Göran has written a large number of training materials for the Swedish market over the years, and in 2001 his book *Exchange 2000 Server on Site* was released in the U.S. He is also frequently a speaker in conferences and seminars. Today Göran is dividing his time between consulting contracts, training, leading his company Human Data, and from time to time writing books. Oh, and he is also the proud father of six great kids from the ages of 5 to 27, which may be his greatest achievement in life.

Credits

Senior Acquisitions Editor
Jim Minatel

Development Editor
Kelly Talbot

Technical Editors
Phred Menyhert
Eli Robillard

Production Editor
Felicia Robinson

Copy Editor
Kim Cofer

Editorial Manager
Mary Beth Wakefield

Production Manager
Tim Tate

Vice President and Executive Group Publisher
Richard Swadley

Vice President and Executive Publisher
Joseph B. Wikert

Project Coordinator
Jennifer Theriot

Graphics and Production Specialists
Carl Byers
Jennifer Click
Carrie A. Foster
Joyce Haughey
Heather Ryan
Alicia South

Quality Control Technician
Laura Albert

Proofreading and Indexing
Techbooks

To all my kids—You are the true joy in my life!

Acknowledgments

When I started to write my own books, I also started to read the acknowledgments in different books I owned. This can be more interesting than one might first think. This is the place where the author really can say whatever he wants. But don't worry, I will not be *too* honest here. When I first told my wife that I was preparing to write this book, she questioned my sanity and her judgment in marrying me. It is good to have an honest wife, but.... Fortunately, she has actually stayed with me through the entire process. (Of course, I have not yet told her that I am planning to write a new book about SharePoint 2007; this will be a surprise for her.)

However, there are definitely a number of people who I really want to thank for helping me write this book. First is Jim Minatel, the Senior Acquisitions Editor at Wiley, who was brave enough to give me the chance to write this book. I also want to thank my great agent Neil J. Salkind at Studio B, who convinced me to start writing this book, and the great author Mitch Tulloc for getting me in contact with Neil! There are also some people at Wrox who have done a heroic job: Kelly Talbot, my Development Editor, who had to correct my bad grammar and sometimes totally confused descriptions (thanks Kelly—I really appreciate all your assistance!). Then I want to thank Phred Menyhert and Eli Robillard, both Technical Editors, for their great job of scrutinizing the technical part of the book. I was constantly amazed at your sharp eye for details and for your highly technical skills. I am solely responsible for the content of this book, but all the invaluable tips from Phred and Eli helped me write a book that is full of clear and valuable descriptions on how to perform important tasks in SharePoint.

During the writing of this book, I also got numerous tips and tricks from my colleagues, employees, and fellow SharePoint nerds on the Internet. I want to thank them all: Michael Jansson, Gustaf Westerlund, Kaj Sjöberg, Magnus Danielsson, James Milne, Siegfried Weber, and James Butler. You are all great guys, and your SharePoint expertise is outstanding, but I hope that as more women pursue careers as SharePoint professionals, the people I thank for my next book will be even more diverse!

Finally I want to thank my beloved wife Marina for her support and understanding; I know this hasn't always been easy, but sometimes a nerd's got to do, what a nerd's got to do. This is simply the life of a computer widow.

And to my fantastic kids, Anna, Thomas, Marielle, Alex, Beatrice, and Johan—I love you all!

Contents

Contents

Contents

Contents

Contents

Contents

Introduction

When I first started planning for this book, I took some time thinking about what challenges face a beginning SharePoint administrator. The many SharePoint courses I have conducted as a SharePoint trainer during the past four years have given me a good understanding of these challenges. All my SharePoint consulting has also been very helpful, because theory is one thing, but real-world experience is another. I also remember my own frustration and numerous questions when I myself was trying to learn what SharePoint was all about. I have written the book that I wished I had when I started to work with SharePoint. My hope is that you will find it full of practical and easy-to-follow instructions that will help you get your SharePoint environment up and running in no time.

The goal of this book is to be your practical guide when building your SharePoint environment. I have tried to be very clear and focus on the steps that you must understand to build a production environment. Because SharePoint is a very broad subject with lots of details, I had to make sure that the book contains information that you most likely will need to know, such as how to install SharePoint, how to administrate it, how to customize it, and how to do backup and restore procedures.

But administration is not the only important aspect of SharePoint. I know that most beginning SharePoint administrators also want to know what SharePoint is and what it can be used for. That is why the book also contains several chapters on how to use the features of SharePoint. As the administrator you will most likely be consulted by your users when they want to know how to get the most out of SharePoint.

Finally, the book has a lot of references and tips for smart add-ons and utilities that will enhance the functionality of SharePoint, such as better navigation, integrating with other systems, and workflow solutions. The book describes many free utilities and commercial third-party products. It also shows you where to find new utilities, because there is almost no other Microsoft product that has as many related new products and utilities constantly showing up.

Who This Book Is For

This book is intended for the beginning SharePoint administrator and for the administrator who has been working with SharePoint for some time but wants to know more about how it works. The book assumes that you have a basic understanding of the MS Windows operating system, including the Active Directory, as well as web applications in general. There is no need to be an expert in these areas, because the book explains everything you must know, but as always it helps to know the environment a product lives in. The book's main focus is planning, installation, configuration, and administration, but it also covers the basic information about customizing SharePoint—for example, how to create templates, how to build your own Site Definition, and how to use FrontPage for extending the look and feel of SharePoint.

The book covers the differences between SharePoint Portal Server (SPS) and Windows SharePoint Services (WSS) and helps you decide if you need only WSS or if you should also implement SPS. Regardless of your choice, the book describes how to use that environment in an optimal way. If you already have a SharePoint installation up and running, you can either skip Chapter 2 for WSS installation and Chapter 4 for SPS installation, or you can explore them to get a better understanding of how your SharePoint environment was set up.

What This Book Covers

This book covers Windows SharePoint Service 2003 (WSS) and SharePoint Portal Server 2003 (SPS). It does not describe how to migrate from the 2001 version of these products, because that task must be very carefully tailored to your specific needs. The last chapter of this book tells you what to expect from SharePoint 2007, also known as "Windows SharePoint Server 3.0" and "Microsoft Office SharePoint Services." You will also get several tips about what to avoid in customizing SharePoint 2003 in order to make the upgrade process to SharePoint 2007 easy.

This book also covers how to use SharePoint 2003 together with MS Office 2003, including MS Outlook 2003. It shows you how these products work together to solve typical situations for information workers (users working with projects, document management, and meetings).

You will also find an introduction to FrontPage 2003 and how to use it for extending and customizing SharePoint sites (for example, how to display information in external databases, how to add your own buttons and menus, and how to create blog sites in SharePoint).

How This Book Is Structured

The book begins with an introductory chapter to give you a sense of what SharePoint can do. It then continues with four more chapters of detailed instructions on how to install and configure WSS and SPS, along with explanations of what you must think of when selecting the type of MS SQL database for your SharePoint server. These chapters include information that describes how to configure specific features of WSS and SPS, such as how to control what the users can do in SharePoint, how to work with intranet news pages, and how to set up Active Directory synchronization. In Chapter 5 you will also find information on how to customize SPS, including how to change the colors, menus, logos, and the general look-and-feel of the portal site.

The remaining chapters are independent of each other, so you can read whatever interests you, but the book is written to encourage reading from the beginning to the end. Some of the content is hard to understand if you have skipped previous chapters, so I suggest that you read it from the beginning, and skip parts that do not interest you at this time. Later, you might find that you need to understand those parts; you can go back to them then. Following is more information about these chapters.

Chapter 6 focuses on advanced administration, mainly for the SPS environment, such as managing the search feature, creating audience groups, managing user security, handling site definitions, creating templates, and more. Even if you are mainly focusing on WSS, you will still find some interesting information here about important SPS features and how using SPS differs from WSS.

Chapter 7 compares WSS and SPS. You will see how they differ and what features are similar or identical. It will help you understand how these two product versions work and why some things just are different in WSS than SPS.

Chapter 8 tells you all you need to know about web parts, the basic building blocks of SharePoint sites. It explains the default web parts that come with SharePoint (for both WSS and SPS), what other interesting free (and not so free) web parts you can find on the Internet, and how to get the most out of them.

In Chapter 9 you will find a lot of tips on how to use SharePoint with MS Office for better file and document management. The chapter covers the ways you can configure and customize document libraries, such as activating version history, custom properties, and custom views. It also explains what document workspaces are used for and how to achieve workflow functionality in SharePoint 2003.

Chapter 10 is another very down-to-earth part of the book; it tells you how to use SharePoint 2003 together with MS Outlook to get better management of meetings and their information.

Chapter 11 shows you a practical way of building an intranet with either WSS or SPS and how they differ from each other. This chapter will summarize a lot of features described in the earlier chapters, and will help you understand how to use SharePoint 2003.

Chapter 12 describes how to use FrontPage 2003 for customizing SharePoint sites and extending their functionality. You do not need any previous FrontPage knowledge to get important information from this chapter.

One of the most important parts in the book is Chapter 13, which discusses how to make backups and do restores of your SharePoint environment. Sooner than you may think, this SharePoint server will become business-critical, because it will contain lots of important documents, lists, and contacts. You don't want to lose that information. Make sure to read Chapter 13 to understand how to restore your SharePoint environment.

Finally, in Chapter 14 you will see what new developments SharePoint 2007 brings. This chapter contains a long list of new features and how they differ from SharePoint 2003. This chapter also lists the different ways you can upgrade from SharePoint 2003.

What You Need to Use This Book

This book is full of practical step-by-step instructions. To get the most out of this book, you should run SharePoint so you can test these instructions. If you don't have a SharePoint environment, the book tells you how to find either the full WSS version or the evaluation version of SPS and install it. You will also need a Windows 2003 Server up and running, preferably in an Active Directory domain, to install SharePoint. A tip is to use an MS Virtual PC or VMWare environment for building your test environment.

Some of these instructions and examples require you to run other programs, such as MS Office 2003, MS Outlook 2003, MS InfoPath 2003, or FrontPage 2003. You can follow many, but not all, of the instructions if you have MS Office 2000 or 2002/XP, instead of MS Office 2003. If you use MS Office 2007, some of these instructions will not be completely accurate, but the difference is not that big, and you will probably understand how to do these steps anyhow.

Conventions

To help you get the most from the text and keep track of what's happening, we've used a number of conventions throughout the book.

Try It Out

The *Try It Out* is an exercise you should work through, following the text in the book.

1. They usually consist of a set of steps.
2. Each step has a number.
3. Follow the steps through with your copy of the database.

> **Boxes like this one hold important, not-to-be forgotten information that is directly relevant to the surrounding text.**

Tips, hints, tricks, and asides to the current discussion are offset and placed in italics like this.

As for styles in the text:

❑ We *highlight* new terms and important words when we introduce them.

❑ We show keyboard strokes like this: Ctrl+A.

❑ We show URLs and code within the text like so: `persistence properties`.

❑ We present code in two different ways:

```
In code examples we highlight new and important code with a gray background.
```

```
The gray highlighting is not used for code that's less important in the present
context, or has been shown before.
```

Source Code

As you work through the examples in this book, you may choose either to type in all the code manually or to use the source code files that accompany the book. All of the source code used in this book is available for download at `http://www.wrox.com`. Once at the site, simply locate the book's title (either by using the Search box or by using one of the title lists) and click the Download Code link on the book's detail page to obtain all the source code for the book.

Because many books have similar titles, you may find it easiest to search by ISBN; this book's ISBN is 0-470-03863-2 (changing to 978-0-470-03863-5 as the new industry-wide 13-digit ISBN numbering system is phased in by January 2007).

Once you download the code, just decompress it with your favorite compression tool. Alternately, you can go to the main Wrox code download page at http://www.wrox.com/dynamic/books/download.aspx to see the code available for this book and all other Wrox books.

Errata

We make every effort to ensure that there are no errors in the text or in the code. However, no one is perfect, and mistakes do occur. If you find an error in one of our books, like a spelling mistake or faulty piece of code, we would be very grateful for your feedback. By sending in errata you may save another reader hours of frustration and at the same time you will be helping us provide even higher quality information.

To find the errata page for this book, go to http://www.wrox.com and locate the title using the Search box or one of the title lists. Then, on the book details page, click the Book Errata link. On this page you can view all errata that has been submitted for this book and posted by Wrox editors. A complete book list including links to each book's errata is also available at www.wrox.com/misc-pages/booklist.shtml.

If you don't spot "your" error on the Book Errata page, go to www.wrox.com/contact/techsupport .shtml and complete the form there to send us the error you have found. We'll check the information and, if appropriate, post a message to the book's errata page and fix the problem in subsequent editions of the book.

p2p.wrox.com

For author and peer discussion, join the P2P forums at p2p.wrox.com. The forums are a web-based system for you to post messages relating to Wrox books and related technologies and interact with other readers and technology users. The forums offer a subscription feature to e-mail you topics of interest of your choosing when new posts are made to the forums. Wrox authors, editors, other industry experts, and your fellow readers are present on these forums.

At http://p2p.wrox.com you will find a number of different forums that will help you not only as you read this book, but also as you develop your own applications. To join the forums, just follow these steps:

1. Go to p2p.wrox.com and click the Register link.

2. Read the terms of use and click Agree.

3. Complete the required information to join as well as any optional information you wish to provide and click Submit.

4. You will receive an e-mail with information describing how to verify your account and complete the joining process.

You can read messages in the forums without joining P2P but in order to post your own messages, you must join.

Once you join, you can post new messages and respond to messages other users post. You can read messages at any time on the web. If you would like to have new messages from a particular forum e-mailed to you, click the Subscribe to this Forum icon by the forum name in the forum listing.

For more information about how to use the Wrox P2P, be sure to read the P2P FAQs for answers to questions about how the forum software works as well as many common questions specific to P2P and Wrox books. To read the FAQs, click the FAQ link on any P2P page.

Introduction to SharePoint 2003

In this chapter you learn about the two versions of SharePoint 2003 — Windows SharePoint Services (WSS) and SharePoint Portal Server (SPS) — their history, and what differs between them. You will see several examples of how the built-in features of SharePoint work and how easy it is to use them. You also get an introduction to how SharePoint integrates with other products, such as MS Word and MS Outlook. The objective in this chapter is to show you why SharePoint is such an interesting product and to give you some ideas of what you can do after installing SharePoint.

What Is SharePoint?

The PC-based software industry today is about 30 years old. But if you look carefully at all the products that have been released, you will soon find that most of them are just different variations of a basic theme. For example, consider the most popular word processor today, MS Word. It still basically does the same thing WordStar did in 1978 — that is, it allows you to write text documents. Yes, MS Word is much more advanced than WordStar, but most of the documents you write today could have been created with WordStar as well. Or think about MS Excel, which is just a fancy (some would even say "sexy") version of VisiCalc, released in 1978. I could go on, but I think you get the idea. Not much is really new in the software industry.

Nevertheless, you will now and then see truly groundbreaking and innovative software products released, such as the web browser and personal search engines. The focus today is more on making all this sophisticated software interact with each other. For example, you can create a table in MS Excel and link it into an MS Word document, or you can create MS PowerPoint presentations that you send by e-mail (which is, itself, simply a fancier version of the File Transfer Protocol, or FTP). So you have all these nice software applications that you use to create and manage all kinds of files and information — the problem is that they all are stored in different places and in different formats, and that can make them hard to use.

What SharePoint does is help you gather this information together, regardless of what type of file or information it is. SharePoint also helps you find information, even when you don't know where it is stored; and SharePoint helps you keep track of updated information. In other words, SharePoint does not invent any new information type; instead, it helps you get the right information when you need it without spending lots of time. Even more importantly, all this information is easily shared between users, such as project teams, departments, or even large organizations. This truly is a new software concept!

Microsoft has performed a thorough analysis of how people work in a computer environment. It has a very good picture of what the problems are and what things need to be changed or removed. One of its findings indicates that people tend to become frustrated when they need help from the administrator or Help Desk to do simple things. Users want to have more power to do what they want, when they want, and exactly how they want. This concept is sometimes referred to as *self-service* and is a new trend in the computer business. For example, you can find applications that allow the user to reset her password, change her properties in the Active Directory (AD), and so on.

SharePoint is built around this concept, and the main idea is to allow the ordinary user to create web sites for projects and other activities without any support from the server administrator or Help Desk. This requires some training for the SharePoint user, but SharePoint is straightforward and easy to learn. Your role, as the SharePoint Server administrator, is to install, maintain, and configure SharePoint. You are also the person people contact when they need help understanding how do things in SharePoint, such as creating sites and managing lists of information. That's why this book tells you how to do these things and gives you tips and hints to make things easier for you and your users. I am sure you will like it for your own personal use, too—SharePoint is simply a fantastic application with enormous potential, if you know how to use it correctly!

Following is a short list of things you can do in SharePoint 2003:

❑   Create an intranet that targets news and information to specific groups.

❑   Build local intranets for departments.

❑   Search for documents, files, e-mail, and news regardless of where they are stored.

❑   Create a personal web site for each user that displays targeted information.

❑   Create web sites for managing projects, customers, and activities.

❑   Extend the functionality in MS Office with document management.

❑   Create web sites with MS Outlook to keep track of your meetings.

❑   Create alerts that will notify you by e-mail when something is changed.

The History of SharePoint

Around 2000, Microsoft unveiled an application called a Digital Dashboard. This web-based application used web parts, which are rectangular areas on a web page that display some type of information, such as a list of contacts, links, or documents. This was innovative because the user could now arrange the web parts on the web page herself, without any help from an HTML programmer.

In 2001, Microsoft released its first two SharePoint products. One was SharePoint Team Services (STS), and the other was SharePoint Portal Server (SPS). Most organizations did not use them, nor had they even heard about them, which was a pity. STS was a web-based product used for collaboration. You could use it to share contacts, calendar events, and documents within teams and small departments. The information was stored in an MS SQL database. It was a nice application, but it did not have any document-management features, and it was not built for creating intranet solutions for larger organizations.

SPS was a separate product, initially made as an MS Exchange 2000 public folder application (under the beta name Tahoe). However, during the beta phase of Tahoe, Microsoft got a loud and clear message from the customers: "Do not mess with our Exchange system!" So Microsoft finally released the SPS using a built-in MS Exchange 2000 server database (which made more than one SharePoint administrator wonder why on earth the SharePoint server event log contained messages from the Exchange Information Store). This new SPS had built-in document-management features, such as document versioning, checkout/check-in, and document workflow. One serious problem with SPS 2001 was the quality of its performance and the limited number of documents it could manage. And it did not have some of the nice collaboration features that STS had. In fact, the two products were competing with each other, to some extent, which is not a good way of convincing the customer to invest in SharePoint technology.

In October 2003, Microsoft released its new SharePoint solution. The old STS, now renamed Windows SharePoint Services, was basically a fancier version of STS (internally, Microsoft referred to it as STS version 2). SPS kept its name, SharePoint Portal Server, but that was about all that was kept from the previous SPS version. No longer did SPS have its own MS Exchange database, and no longer was SPS a separate product! Now it was an add-on to the WSS application. Finally, Microsoft had one integrated SharePoint solution, completely based on the MS SQL Server database.

> **This book describes the features and functionality of SharePoint 2003 with Service Pack 2, released in October 2005.**

The Future of SharePoint

Microsoft's version of WSS and SPS released in 2006 (called SharePoint 2007) is an easy upgrade from the previous version, as long as you have avoided modifying SharePoint's basic structure, such as the file structure that describes the default SharePoint configuration and the stored procedures in the SQL database. This book gives you instructions and tips on what to do — and what to avoid — in order to make the upgrade process easy for you.

Because this is just the beginning of the book, you will probably not understand a detailed description of the coming features. So here is just a general overview of the most important ones. As you read the chapters, you will see more detailed descriptions of these, when relevant. But for now, I just want to give you an idea of what to expect in the new version:

❑   Better navigation features and tree views.

❑   Easier to modify many existing sites by changing the template.

❑   Built-in workflow for documents and other types of lists.

❑   A recycle bin so you can undelete files.

❑   Item-level security on more types of objects.

❑   More advanced search functionality.

❑   Support for reading information on mobile devices.

❑   Gantt charts for project tasks.

❑   Better support for non-Microsoft web browsers.

❑   Support for Document lifecycle policies and Records Management.

❑   Configurable limited number of version history.

❑   Integration of Microsoft Content Management Server features.

❑   Better support for multilingual user interfaces.

❑   Two-way synchronization between SharePoint and Outlook.

❑   Support for creating Wiki and blog sites.

❑   Many enhancements for the developer.

Differences between WSS and SPS

When thinking of WSS and SPS, the important thing to understand is that WSS is the foundation and SPS is an optional add-on. In fact, you cannot install SPS by itself. If you try to do this, your computer will request that you install WSS first. So the question is: What else differs between WSS and SPS? Although some of these answers are hard to understand if you have never seen SharePoint before, give it a try anyhow. The following chapters further flesh out the following points.

Windows SharePoint Services 2003

Windows SharePoint Services 2003 has the following characteristics:

❑   Is a web-based application.

❑   Stores all information in an MS SQL database.

❑   Displays information using web parts.

❑   Has basic document-management features.

❑   Has a number of list types that you can use for storing all kinds of information.

❑   Is perfect for simple, but effective, intranet solutions.

❑   Is ideal for collaboration on project data, meetings, social events, and such.

❑   Is a free add-on to MS Windows 2003 Server (any edition).

In other words, WSS is the perfect place to collect information for your projects, your customers, and your meetings. You can copy all documents from your file system into WSS and by doing so get access to the simple but powerful document-management features. It is also a very good solution when you need local intranets for teams or departments. And all this is free when you run Windows 2003 Server!

But there are things that WSS does not offer. For example:

- ❏ Search functionality across sites and for external documents. Search is only available within a site.

- ❏ Advanced intranet features, such as targeted information and organizing information based on topics.

- ❏ Easy navigation features.

This is where SPS comes in.

SharePoint Portal Server 2003

This optional add-on to WSS includes the following characteristics:

- ❏ Must be installed on top of WSS.

- ❏ Makes it possible to target information to one or more user groups.

- ❏ Makes it possible to search for information, regardless of where it is stored.

- ❏ Makes it possible to collect information on one page, regardless of where it may be stored.

- ❏ Gives each SharePoint user a personal web site, for both private and public use.

- ❏ Is licensed both per server and per user.

These characteristics make SPS a very good solution for building global intranets that are smart enough to show the right information to the right people. SPS is also a good solution when you want to collect links to information (such as documents, contacts, and people) under a common topic when this information is stored in different places, including in SharePoint, on the file system, or on public Internet web sites.

> **To help you determine whether you should use WSS with or without SPS, consult Chapter 7, "Comparing WSS and SPS."**

What You Need to Run SharePoint

This section provides general information about what you need to install and run SharePoint, both WSS and SPS. It also has general guidelines on the hardware configuration and some tips for building a test environment. Chapters 2 and 4 provide the exact steps on how to do the actual installation.

Software Requirements

Because SharePoint is a web application, you need to have a web server. The only version supporting SharePoint is Internet Information Server version 6 (IIS 6), which runs on Windows 2003 Server. You can use any edition of Windows 2003 Server, including the cheaper Web Edition.

You also need to install the Microsoft ASP.NET web development platform, as described in Chapter 2. If you can write programs using ASP.NET, you can write your own SharePoint components. Installing ASP.NET also automatically installs some other web components, as you will see in Chapter 2.

The last, but not least, component you need is an MS SQL–based database. You have two choices: the free Microsoft SQL 2000 Server Desktop Engine (MSDE) or the MS SQL 2000/2005 Server. These two choices give you different features, as listed in the following table:

Feature	MSDE	MS SQL 2000/2005
Full text indexing of data	No	Yes
Limited database size	Yes (2 GB maximum)	No
Can run on a separate server	No	Yes
Includes management tools	No	Yes
License type	Free	Per CPU or per user

However, the story is a bit more complicated than this! If you use WSS alone, you have a special version of MSDE referred to as Windows MSDE (WMSDE). This version does not have any size limitations, which means that you can run WSS using a WMSDE database in a production environment—and all the software is free when running on Windows 2003 Server! But if you install SPS, you get the size-limited version of MSDE. This means that you cannot use SPS with MSDE in a production environment; rather, you must use the MS SQL 2000/2005 Server.

Please also note the difference regarding on what server the database can run. If you choose the MSDE or WMSDE database, it must run on the same server as SharePoint. Only MS SQL 2000/2005 gives you an option of choosing what server to use for storing all the data. Only by using SQL Server can you keep SharePoint and the database on separate servers, which will provide improved performance and scalability. This is known as a *small server farm* configuration.

Hardware Requirements

In addition to all the software requirements, the server hardware must also be configured properly. For a test environment, you can get by with 512 MB of memory and at least 2 GB of free disk space. This type of requirement is easily met by using virtual server software, such as MS Virtual PC. The CPU type is not important in a test environment; in a production environment you will want a high-speed single or multiple-CPU configuration. You learn more about this in Chapters 2 and 4.

Building a Test Environment

Using a virtual server, such as MS Virtual PC, makes it possible to build and test SharePoint on your ordinary MS Windows XP client. It also makes it possible to test and play with different configurations and scenarios. And if (or, more likely, when) things go wrong, you can simply use the undo feature of MS Virtual PC. Another option with virtual servers is to make a copy of the virtual server environment and, if necessary, restore that copy in case your test environment is messed up beyond repair!

I recommend that you use a virtual server for testing everything detailed in this book. It will make it much easier for you in case something goes wrong, and you won't have to worry about testing and playing around. Once you know how SharePoint works, you can then go on to use your own production environment.

Integrating with MS Office 2003

Given that you are reading this book, the chance that you use MS Office for creating documents, spreadsheets, and presentations is rather high. Therefore, this section is important for you. SharePoint will not change the way you are working with Office documents, but it will enhance the functionality, making many things a lot easier than they are without using SharePoint. What features you can expect depends on what version of MS Office you are using.

The story is this: MS Office was released together with SharePoint 2003 in October 2003. They were built to be integrated. Any previous versions of MS Office do not know about SharePoint, so they lack this integration capability. Do not expect Microsoft to release an update for previous versions of MS Office, though. It would most likely be too much to modify, and frankly Microsoft wants you to upgrade to Office 2003.

So what do you get if you have a previous version of MS Office, such as Office 2000 or Office XP?

❑ **File Save Integration:** Microsoft Office 2000 integrates with Windows SharePoint Services. Users can open and save files stored on SharePoint sites. They can also receive alerts in Outlook 2000.

❑ **Basic Data Integration:** Microsoft Office XP provides for data integration with SharePoint sites. Users can view properties and metadata for files stored on SharePoint sites. They can also export list data to Microsoft Excel 2002.

❑ **Contextual Integration:** SharePoint integrates fully into the business tasks that users perform every day with Microsoft Office 2003 Editions.

Microsoft produced a white paper describing Office integration called "Good, Better, Best." *Good* means the functionality achieved by MS Office 2000, *Better* is what you get with MS Office XP, and *Best* requires you to run Office 2003. Note that there is no technical problem in using SharePoint in a mixed MS Office environment, but it will place an extra burden on the Help Desk and the support team. A more detailed comparison among the three MS Office versions from the white paper has been modified and presented in the following table:

Feature	Office 2000	Office XP	Office 2003
Save and open files from SharePoint sites	Yes	Yes	Enhanced (Office plus FrontPage, InfoPath, OneNote, Microsoft Project, Publisher, Visio)
Create new documents in web browser	No	Yes (Excel, FrontPage, PowerPoint, Word)	Yes (Excel, FrontPage, InfoPath, PowerPoint, Microsoft Project, Publisher, Word)
Collect document columns automatically	No	No	Yes

Table continued on following page

Feature	Office 2000	Office XP	Office 2003
Change document columns in both Office and the web browser	Data stored, but not displayed	Yes	Enhanced (Excel, FrontPage, InfoPath, PowerPoint, Visio, Word)
Track document versions	No. Use web browser to view and manage document versions.	No. Use web browser to view and manage document versions.	Enhanced (Excel, PowerPoint, Visio, Word)
Check out and check in documents	No. Use web browser to manually check out and check in documents.	No. Use web browser to manually check out and check in documents.	Enhanced (Excel, PowerPoint, Visio, Word). Use web browser to manually check out and check in other types of documents.
Upload multiple documents	No	No	Yes
Use Inline discussions	Yes	Yes	Yes
Use Microsoft Office Components for SharePoint	No	No	Yes
Person Names Smart Tag	No	No	Yes
Create Document Workspace	No	No	Yes
Create Meeting Workspace	No	No	Yes (Outlook 2003)
Synchronize calendar and contact list sites	No	No	Yes (Outlook)
Alert integration with Outlook	No	No	Yes (Outlook)

Built-In Features of SharePoint

So what features can you expect in SharePoint? The answer depends on what version you implement: SPS or WSS. Following is a list of everyday scenarios showing you how SharePoint can make things easier for you and your users. Chapters 9 and 10 provide more detailed steps on how to create a SharePoint environment that solves these problems.

Alerts (WSS and SPS)

One feature that both WSS and SPS offer is something Microsoft refers to as alerts. An alert is a request you create in SharePoint to be notified by e-mail when SharePoint content changes (for example, when a document is updated, a contact is deleted, or a News item is added). Using alerts, you can be sure to keep yourself updated about changes to information that is important to you! SharePoint will send you an e-mail to notify you what has happened. The following information types are examples of what can be watched by alerts:

❑ Single documents and files in a document library.

❑ Document libraries.

❑ Picture libraries or single pictures.

❑ Contact lists or single contacts.

❑ Link lists or single links.

❑ News lists or single news items.

❑ Event lists or single events.

Alerts can watch a lot more places and types of information, as you will see in Chapters 9 and 10. This is extremely useful — you will no longer miss any important updates!

File and Document Management (WSS and SPS)

Today you organize your files by using a folder structure and giving your files descriptive names so that they are easy to find. But you also know that after some time, it gets harder and harder to find the file when you need it. And even worse, you may have several copies of different versions of the same file. How can you be sure you're looking at the right version? If you are looking for a file that somebody else created, it gets even harder because the folder structure may not be as intuitive as you would like it to be and the filenames may not be as descriptive as they should be.

This is where SharePoint comes in. All files and documents in SharePoint are stored in document libraries. This is very similar to a folder in the file system, but on steroids! The document library has lots of new features that will help you organize and find the files you are looking for. The key features are as follows:

❑ **Document Columns:** Add your own columns to describe the files and documents, such as Document Type, Customer Name, Project Name, or Status.

❑ **Document Views:** Create your own view on how the files should be presented. For example, you could create a view that shows only documents of the type Contract for the customer Volvo, sorted by status.

These features make it easier for you to name your documents. You no longer need files with names like `Contract_Volvo_version05.doc`. And more importantly, you can force the writers of documents to enter information in these columns when they save their files.

There are many other interesting features in SharePoint regarding document management. In this book, you will see and try most of the important features.

Project Management (WSS)

This section's title indicates that this functionality only works in WSS, but this is not actually true. However, in a real production environment you should avoid using SPS for project management. The reason for this is related to security. WSS allows you to set individual access settings per document library and other lists of information, whereas SPS allows you to set access settings only per web page, regardless of what types of document libraries and lists are displayed.

Think about projects. What type of information is related to a standard project? Although it depends on the project, you will still find that most projects share the following types of information among the project members:

- ❑ **Documents:** Examples include MS Word files, Excel spreadsheets, text files, and PowerPoint presentations.
- ❑ **Members:** A list of all the members in the project.
- ❑ **Calendar:** A list of events, such as meetings, conferences, and project milestones.
- ❑ **Contacts:** A list of external contacts, such as vendors, partners, consultants, and other resources.
- ❑ **Tasks:** A list of things to do, assigned to project members.
- ❑ **E-mail:** Questions, status, and comments regarding the project.

The problem today is that this information is stored in several places. Documents and files are stored in a file share; members exist in an e-mail distribution list; calendar events, contacts, and tasks are stored in an Outlook public folder; and e-mail is, of course, stored in each member's personal inbox. Another way to describe this is organized chaos. Each project member needs to know and remember exactly where each type of information is stored. If he does not do so, valuable time is wasted searching for the information. To make things worse, if a new member joins the project you must explain to her where everything is stored and how it works. To make sure the new member understands what has been going on, you must forward a copy of all mail related to this project—if you can find it. The new member then faces the challenging task of reading all this e-mail and understanding what it contains.

Do you recognize the situation? Everyone does! To solve this problem, you need something that can store all this information in a single place—or at least make all the information available through a single place. This is exactly what SharePoint does! Here is how you do it:

1. Create a SharePoint web site for the project.
2. Add the members to the site. SharePoint sends the members an e-mail with an invitation to the site.
3. Create a document library to store all files and documents, and copy all existing files to this document library.
4. Create another document library to store all e-mail, and copy all project-related e-mail to this document library.
5. Create a calendar, a task list, and a contact list, and then use these lists for the project data.

Chapter 2 gives detailed steps on how to create this type of web site and all its lists and fill it with data. You will also learn how easy it is to design the page to make it easy to use.

Managing Meetings (WSS)

If there is one thing that practically all employees agree on, it is that meetings are most of the time a huge pain! Why? The usual complaints are that they are a waste of time, boring, and too long; that meeting participants are unprepared; and that it's hard to follow up on tasks and activities after the meeting. That indicates that even a small step forward to make meetings more effective is important. With SharePoint, you will be able to change many things into something more positive.

In a typical meeting, the planners use Outlook to invite participants, as well as to reserve resources such as the conference room (you *have* left the Stone Age, right?). A meeting is an event where the following steps occur:

1. A number of people are invited.
2. The invitees come together.
3. While together, they discuss a number of topics.
4. The discussion results in a number of actions and decisions.

The Typical Meeting Process

The meeting organizer creates an agenda and describes the meeting objective. (Have you noticed how many meetings don't have a clear objective?) The meeting organizer then estimates the length of the meeting and sends an invitation to all participants. Some documents, with information needed for the meeting, may be attached to the invitation.

Later, the actual meeting takes place. Each participant has his own copy of the agenda and the attached documents. Well, actually, some participants forgot the agenda and need to print a copy; somebody else did not see the attached document, so he also needs to print a copy. About 15 minutes after the meeting should have started, everyone is ready to proceed. Because there is no clear indication as to how long each agenda point should take to discuss, the meeting takes 20 minutes longer than expected. This makes some people stressed because they have other appointments after this meeting.

During the meeting, someone takes notes about all the activities agreed upon, the tasks assigned, and the decisions made. This information is later listed in the meeting minutes. One more person also takes notes because, after this meeting, she will be the person appointed to check the minutes.

One week later, the meeting minutes are created and checked and sent to all participants by e-mail. A few of these participants actually read the minutes, some just take a quick glance at them, and some do not have time to even open the document. The next time this team has a meeting, only a few participants have read the previous minutes, and many have missed that they were assigned tasks. And the story goes on.

Using SharePoint for Effective Meetings

The preceding story might not be true for every organization, of course, but I am sure you are familiar with the ways meetings can go wrong. So what can SharePoint do to make this process both more effective and more interesting? Thanks to the integration of Outlook 2003 and SharePoint 2003, you can now simultaneously send a meeting invitation and create a *meeting workspace*, a web site where you can host all information regarding the meeting, including the following:

❑ **Agenda:** A list of all the items you will discuss during the meeting, including who is responsible for each one, how long it will take, and any comments regarding the items.

❑ **Participants:** SharePoint automatically creates a list of all invited participants. This list is automatically updated with the status of each participant so that everyone can see who will come or why someone declined the invitation.

❑ **Tasks:** A list of all the tasks agreed upon during the meeting.

❑ **Decisions:** A list of all the decisions agreed upon during the meeting.

❑ **Document Library:** Contains any document with information that will prepare the participants for the meeting, as well as documents created as a result of the meeting.

All this information is available to the participant directly when she receives the invitation. This means that she can see the agenda, maybe add some extra items to it, and get access to any document with information related to the meeting. If needed, the participant can add her own documents.

When the actual meeting takes place, you use a video projector that displays the meeting workspace. No one needs a printed copy of the meeting agenda because it is listed on the meeting workspace. All documents are listed in the document workspace—if there is a discussion about what a document contains, the organizer can quickly open the document for everyone to see.

Any activities, tasks, or decisions that are agreed upon during the meeting are directly entered into the list. Everyone can see this, so there is no need for anyone to check the meeting minutes afterwards. The effect is that everyone will be involved in whatever decision is made. This makes the meeting more interesting and engaging. Because the agenda clearly states the amount of time it should take to discuss each item, the participants can focus on that subject and try to stay within the estimated time.

Because everything is recorded directly during the meeting, you don't need any meeting minutes at all! If a participant afterwards needs to see what was decided in the meeting, she can simply go back to the meeting in the Outlook calendar and click the link to open the meeting workspace again.

In Chapter 10, you will see how to create a meeting workspace, configure what lists it contains, and fill it with data. You will also see that repeated meetings can be linked to the same meeting workspace, giving you one page for each meeting instance and making it very simple to go back and see what you discussed in a previous meeting.

Keeping Your Organization Updated (SPS)

For many years now, organizations have used an intranet to make sure that everyone has access to general information, such as company news, information from the Human Resources department, or a list of all employees and their contact information. SharePoint is a great tool to help you create an intranet. With SharePoint, you often refer to the intranet as "the portal site," or simply "the portal."

Using SharePoint for your intranet has many advantages. It is fast, it can support organizations with millions of users, and it has several interesting features, such as the following:

❑ **Targeting:** Helps you make sure that your news, links, and other information are visible to only a certain group of people, which is also referred to as an "audience."

- ❑ **Active Directory synchronization:** Makes it possible to present relevant information about your users, such as e-mail addresses, departments, phone numbers, pictures, descriptions, and so on. SharePoint stores this information in its profile database.

- ❑ **Topics:** Allows you to group links and actual documents under a given topic, regardless of what type of information it is or where it is stored. This makes it very easy to find frequently requested information.

- ❑ **Areas:** Allows you to create new pages on the intranet that may be used for a local department, such as Human Resources or IT. Each page may have its own news listing and other relevant information.

- ❑ **Site Directory:** Displays a list of existing web sites, including their names, descriptions, owners, and other properties. This makes it easy for a user to quickly find a specific web site.

- ❑ **My Site:** A personal site for each user that typically is used for displaying personal information, such as news, links, e-mail, and calendars, as well as document and picture libraries. There is also a public view of this site that displays information about the user, such as e-mail address, phone numbers, department, and a general description.

In addition, you will find that the News list allows you to define when to display and remove the news from the list. News is never automatically deleted; instead, items are archived and will still be possible to find using the search feature in SharePoint. You can link pictures to your news, and you can make the news item show up in several places, such as on the organization-wide intranet and on a local intranet for a given department.

An intranet based on SharePoint Portal Server will also have automatic links to the web sites you create for your projects, meetings, and other shared team sites. The intranet also allows you to create any type of list, including document libraries, contacts, and events. If you decide to go with both SPS and WSS, it is hard to find a good reason why you should use an additional product only for the intranet. Doing this will not only make things harder for you to support and manage (backup and restore!), but it will also force your organization to pay two server licenses rather than one.

Now take a look at an intranet scenario. Say your organization has three departments: sales, IT, and Human Resources. You also have some special groups: the executive team, a project team, and an external sales force. Your task is to make sure each of them gets the right information, in an easy and intuitive way. Your CEO requires a common intranet where all important information regarding the company, its customers, and its employees are presented. Each department requires its own intranet. The IT folks tell you they are sick and tired of all the sales info, and the sales guys asks you politely if there is a way to filter out everything except the sales-related information. And all of them say they want a fast and easy way to find the right web site where all the information is stored for the projects, meetings, customers, and so on. And by the way, the executive group wants an easy way of finding all contracts, regardless of where they are stored. How do you solve this?

One solution would be to do this:

1. Install SPS and WSS.

2. Create a common intranet portal for the organization.

3. Create a separate area page on the intranet for each department, with its own news listing, document workspace, and contact lists. The area pages are:

   ❑ Sales

   ❑ IT

   ❑ HR

4. Create these audiences:

   ❑ Sales Team

   ❑ IT Team

   ❑ HR Team

   ❑ Executive Team

   ❑ Project Team

   ❑ External Sales Team

5. Instruct your general news authors how to target their news items to a specific audience so that each audience only sees information targeting their group.

6. Instruct local news authors in the departments on how to create news items only for their own areas.

7. Use the Site Directory in SPS to create new web sites for each project, team site, and so on. This ensures that all web sites are listed in the site directory and are therefore easy to find.

8. Create a Topic in SharePoint named Contract. Tell the salespeople that whenever they create a new contract document to make sure it also is submitted to this topic.

9. Make sure every user has updated information in the Active Directory (AD), such as phone numbers, department, company name, and e-mail address. Then synchronize the AD with SharePoint. Make sure each user profile in SharePoint links to a photo. Instruct everyone that whenever they see a name listed, they can simply click it to get more information about that user.

Finding Your Information Faster (SPS)

How often do you search for information? I would guess at least once every day. Assume the average user spends 10 minutes every day searching for information. If you have 200 users, this would be about 2000 minutes, or 33 hours per day. You could also put it this way: Your organization pays for 200 employees, but it only gets the efficiency of 196 (4 people times 8 working hours = 32 hours in total per day). What this means is that even small improvements in efficiency may lead to big results. And not just for the owners of the company — the employees will be happy too because they can concentrate on doing their jobs instead of searching for information.

SharePoint Portal Server has its own built-in search and indexing engine, but Windows SharePoint Services does not have any built-in search feature. The only way of activating any type of searching in WSS is by using the Full Text Indexing feature that comes with MS SQL Server. And that type of searching is limited to the web site you are in when searching. Thus, this section discusses the search and indexing features of only SPS.

A number of client-based search tools are available, such as MSN Search and Google Search. At the time of this writing, these tools are not made for searching SharePoint information, so you need to implement

SPS in order to get a real search engine. But this is not just any search engine; it is a very sophisticated tool that enables you to search for any type of data in SharePoint, regardless of where it is stored. You can also instruct the index engine to make information outside the SharePoint database searchable, including these information sources:

❑ Every web site in the SharePoint environment (including all SPS and WSS sites).

❑ Any file server in your IT environment (including older NT 4 and Windows 2000 servers).

❑ Your MS Exchange database (such as all public folders or role-based mailboxes such as Help Desk).

❑ Any Lotus Notes database you may have.

❑ Other internal web sites (such as your old intranet, your public web site, or similar sites).

❑ External web sites (such as your partner's web site; and why not your competitor's?).

What File Types Can You Search?

The type of information you can search is almost anything! Of course you can search in any MS Office file format, such as MS Word and MS Excel, but you can also search in text files, standard file formats (such as HTML and RTF), and TIFF files.

Isn't that an image file type, you might ask yourself? You are absolutely right! The TIFF file type is often used for pictures and other images. But TIFF is also used to store scanned documents and incoming fax documents. And this is what SharePoint's index engine can help you with: to make scanned documents and faxes searchable. Everything you need comes with the SPS package. However, this feature is not activated by default. You can find more information about this feature using this link: http://support.microsoft.com/?kbid=837847&FR=1.

What about other common file types, such as PDF, ZIP, and CAD files? In order to explain this, I have to tell you a little more about the indexing process:

1. When the scheduled task for indexing starts, the search engine looks into every place you have instructed it to look in.

2. When it finds a file, it looks at the file type (for example, DOC).

3. It checks a list in SharePoint where you have specified what file types you want indexed. In this example, DOC is a file type that should be indexed.

4. The index process now needs a program that understands how to read DOC files. Such programs are referred to as Index Filters (IFilters, for short). Every file type needs its own IFilter, including DOC files.

5. The IFilter opens the file and starts scanning it. Whenever it finds some text, it stores this text in a separate file, called the Index File. The IFilter is smart enough to skip binary data and white noise (words like yes, no, one, and two and numerals like 1, 2, or 3).

6. When all the text in the file is read, the IFilter closes the file, and the process starts again with step 2.

So if you want to make file types like PDF searchable, you need to do two things: Configure SharePoint to look for PDF files and install an IFilterIFilter for the PDF file type. The search engine does not include this by default. You may wonder why Microsoft has not added common file types such as PDF or ZIP. The answer is simple: At the time SPS 2003 was released, Adobe owned the PDF format, so Microsoft did not want to include an IFilterIFilter for it. So Adobe is making the IFilterIFilter for the PDF — and the good news is that Adobe is giving it away for free to encourage people to use the PDF format for storing all kinds of content. In Chapter 6, you learn how to find and install common IFilters, including the PDF version.

What Type of Searching Can You Do?

The default configuration of the SharePoint search engine allows you to search for whole words and their stemmers only. For example, you can search for "write" and you will also find files with "writing" and "wrote." However, if you search for the word "Admin" you will not find "Administrator" because it is not a stemmer. This default behavior can be changed, as the following article at the www.msd2d.com site describes: http://msd2d.com/Content/Tip_viewitem_03.aspx?section=SharePoint& category=Development&id=e1982261-c9e0-4668-984a-69c94dc61a7c.

You can also search for document properties, also referred to as metadata, such as author, title, and file size. The list of properties is different for different types of documents. For example, if you want to see what properties a standard MS Word document has available, you can do this:

1. Open any Word file with the file extension .DOC.

2. Choose File⇨Properties.

3. Switch to the Summary tab. Here you will find all the standard properties for Word documents.

4. Switch to the Custom tab. Here you will find other, less common properties, including any properties automatically imported from columns in SharePoint's document libraries.

All the standard properties on the Summary tab are searchable. You can also make combinations, such as searching for all documents containing the word "Viking" with the attribute "Author" equal to "Göran Husman." This is satisfactory for most search scenarios. But sometimes you want to search for a document that matches your own column value. You may recall that you can add any number of columns to a document library, for example "Doc Type" or "Status." As you learn in Chapter 6, even these column properties can be searchable if you configure SharePoint properly.

If your SharePoint search engine has indexed many documents, you may want to limit the search to a given area. This is made possible by configuring search scopes. For example, you can create one search scope for MS Exchange, another for files on the file system, and so on. This reduces the number of search results, but it requires that you know in what search scope your document belongs.

Finally, you can define keyword best bets. This feature helps your users to find frequently requested information. For example, suppose that when you talk with the sales manager, she tells you that members in her team often need access to the product specifications. The problem is that these products have several names. The best-selling product is article X2025A, but most customers refer to this as the "Super Gadget"; to add to the problem, the internal name used by the sales team is the "Money Maker." She wants her team to be able to search for any of these terms and still find the product specification for the X2025A. With the keyword best bet feature in SharePoint, this is an easy fix. You simply need to create a list of each alias for the keyword X2025A and then link this keyword to the proper document. When someone later searches for any of these words, that person will find the product specification for X2025A at the top of the search results. Below it, he will find all other documents that match this search criterion.

Accessing SharePoint over the Internet

Very soon after you start working with SharePoint, you find that it contains more and more of your business-critical data. You also become aware of the fact that you need online access to the SharePoint server in order to work with the documents, projects, and everything else stored in the SharePoint database. So you start thinking, "How do I access this information when I am not at the office?" The answer is clear: You can make your SharePoint information accessible over the Internet, in a secure way, while still getting good performance. You have to plan this carefully and configure SharePoint and the other modules involved, such as the firewall.

How You Do It

Because SharePoint is a web application running on top of IIS 6, it is very easy to make SharePoint accessible from outside your organization. You simply open up your firewall so that it allows connections to the SharePoint server from the outside. But this is not a good solution from a security perspective. This leaves your SharePoint server wide open to the world, and there are lots of threats for this server that could destroy it or even the other servers on your network. Another big problem with this simple solution is that your password and user account could be transferred over the Internet unencrypted, depending on what type of authentication method you use. Someone listening in on your communication could learn your password and be able to log on as you!

A better solution is to install a Secure Socket Layer (SSL) certificate on your IIS 6 and demand that every access to the SharePoint server use SSL-encrypted connections. That is, the user must enter the Uniform Resource Locator (URL) address to the SharePoint server starting with `https://`. The effect of this is that your log-on credentials are protected. There is no longer any risk that someone will see your password.

The best solution is to prohibit the external users from accessing the SharePoint server directly from the outside, combined with the SSL-encrypted connection. Instead, your users would access something that looks like the SharePoint server but in reality is an image. This type of image is known as an application proxy server. Microsoft's solution is its product called Internet Security and Acceleration Server, also known as the MS ISA server. With this solution, things works like this:

1. The external user connects to the SharePoint web address over the Internet, using an SSL connection such as `https://intranet.contoso.com`. This is the exact same address for users on the inside, except for the `https://` part (internally, you would use `http://` instead).

2. The user is passing through the firewall but is directed to the MS ISA server instead.

3. The MS ISA server looks at the requested URL address, checks its rules, and if everything is okay, connects to that URL and retrieves the page. This page is then sent back to the user.

4. The user sees the requested URL. He clicks a link, and, once again, the MS ISA server gets a request for a new URL, repeating step 3.

The nice thing with this solution is that the user never gets access to anything more than the MS ISA server, which normally is installed on the Demilitarized Zone (DMZ) segment of the network. This segment is where you put all your publicly available servers, such as your public web site. You can use the rules in the MS ISA server to control exactly what the user can see and do. For example, in some organizations, users have different levels of access, depending on where they are situated at the moment. Inside the network, they have full access; on the Internet, they have access to only some part of SharePoint. This is something that only the MS ISA server can help you deploy because SharePoint itself cannot distinguish access to its information in this way. Another bonus effect is that frequently requested pages are cached on the MS ISA server, meaning that these pages will be displayed more quickly for the users.

Allowing External Partners Access

Now you know the general steps in configuring the SharePoint environment for access over the Internet. But what about partners and other users living outside your organization? If there is a need to give them limited access to your SharePoint server, it can be done! Before you do this, you must understand how SharePoint controls what the user can do with its access control feature.

Every user who is granted access to SharePoint must belong to a site group. The site group defines exactly what type of access you have. By default, WSS has these site groups configured and ready for use:

❑ **Reader:** Allows the user to open and read information, including documents, pictures, and list content. The user will not be able to create, modify, or delete information in SharePoint.

❑ **Contributor:** Allows the user to do everything a Reader can do, plus create, modify, and delete information, including news, documents, contacts, and so on.

❑ **Web Designer:** Allows the user to do everything a Contributor can do, plus create new document libraries, lists, document columns, and document views, as well as change the layout of the web site by adding or moving web parts.

❑ **Administrator:** Has full access to the site. Can do everything, including adding and deleting members and changing their access.

These site groups are not specifically used for intranet scenarios; site groups are used for controlling access to any part of SharePoint, regardless of user access.

First, look at how you can allow access internally. Assume that you hire a person named Anna. She needs access to your intranet, and she will only read information. You add Anna's user account to the site group Reader on the intranet portal site. Later, Anna comes back to you and says that she needs both read and write access to a given project site; now you add Anna's user account to the site group Contributor for this particular project site. Anna now belongs to different site groups in different sites of the SharePoint environment. Whenever she is accessing SharePoint, it will validate her user account and check what site group she belongs to.

If you want to allow access to a user outside your organization, he needs to be authenticated. In other words, he needs to log on so that SharePoint can see what access he is granted. This will be a problem with external users because they don't have a user account in your network. The only practical way to solve this is to create a user account for them. Now you can assign the user membership in any site group you like. The external user must remember to log on with the account you created. So everyone is happy now.

Problems with This Solution

But this solution is far from perfect. It works, this is true, but what happens if this external person goes to another company? For example, suppose that John works for the company ABC. John is involved in a project in your organization, Contoso, and needs access to the SharePoint site where all the project information is stored. You create a user account for John, grant him the proper access, and tell him the URL for the project site and that his logon is `Contoso\John`. He starts working with the project, and everything works as expected. One month later, John leaves ABC, and starts working for its competitor, XYZ. You don't have an agreement with XYZ, so its employees are not allowed access to your project site. You need to disable the account `Contoso\John`. But how will you know that John has left his old company, ABC? There is no automatic process that will inform you about this. Hopefully, someone at ABC tells you this, or somebody in the project team gets this information and tells you. Clearly, this situation will be very hard to handle if you have 10 or more external partners. But at the moment, this is how things work.

ADFS

However, there is some light at the end of the tunnel. Starting with Release 2 of Windows 2003 Server, Microsoft released a new feature called Active Directory Federation Service (ADFS). The objective of ADFS is to resolve precisely this type situation (that is, letting two completely separate organizations share access to web applications like SharePoint without the need to create local accounts for the remote organization). The idea is rather simple and easy to understand, but the technique beneath is advanced and worth its own book.

The basic idea of ADFS is to make it possible for an organization to use its own user accounts to get access on a remote web application. For example, assume that you have two companies, A and B. User Bob works for B, and he needs access to a SharePoint site in A. Bob talks to the administrator for the site in A, which then grants the `B\Bob` account access to the requested site.

The magic in this scenario is managed by adding extra servers to your Active Directory domain, one in each organization. The primary ADFS server is referred to as the *federation server* and hosts the federation service component. Its primary task is to route incoming requests from the Internet to the web site a user is trying to access. It is also responsible for creating a security token that will be passed on to the web application. The process that validates the external user is the ADFS Web Agent, which runs on the web server (in this case, the SharePoint server).

Most organizations do not want their federation server exposed to the Internet. You can protect it by installing an optional federation proxy server. This proxy relays federation requests from the outside world to your internal federation server, meaning that your federation server is no longer exposed directly to the outside world.

> *ADFS is based on the standard Security Assertion Markup Language (SAML), which means that that the external company need not be running MS Windows.*

Summary

In this chapter you learned the following:

- ❑ SharePoint is a web-based application that helps users share and collaborate with any type of data and information.

- ❑ The user of today requires more control and power to create and modify whatever she needs.

- ❑ SharePoint lets the ordinary user create sites and document libraries in a secure and controlled manner.

- ❑ The previous versions of SharePoint were STS (SharePoint Team Services) and SPS 2001 (SharePoint Portal Server). STS was replaced by WSS (Windows SharePoint Services) and SPS 2001 was replaced by SPS 2003.

❑ It is very easy to upgrade to SharePoint 2007 if you avoid modifying SharePoint's own system files and stored procedures in SQL Server.

❑ WSS is the SharePoint base module. It is used to create sites for managing and sharing information, such as projects, customer data, meetings, and local intranets.

❑ SPS is the optional add-on package. It enhances WSS with several new features in a special web site called "the portal site." Features include advanced global searching, advanced intranet features, including targeting of information, personal web sites, and topics for collecting references to information stored anywhere in SharePoint or any other computer.

❑ To install SharePoint, the server needs Windows 2003 Server with IIS and ASP.NET activated.

❑ SharePoint can use two types of SQL databases: MS SQL 2000/2005 Server and MSDE.

❑ MSDE must be installed on the same computer as SharePoint.

❑ MS SQL 2000/2005 Server can be installed on a separate computer if required.

❑ WSS has a special version of MSDE, named WMSDE.

❑ SharePoint 2003 (WSS and SPS) is best integrated with MS Office 2003.

❑ You can use Office 2000 or Office XP, but you will not be able to access everything that SharePoint offers.

❑ You can use SharePoint to build intranets for the complete organization, for the department, or for any local groups of teams, if requested.

❑ The index and search functionality in SPS 2003 are very good! It makes it possible to search anywhere and in practically any file type.

❑ WSS has no search functionality at all. But you can use the MS SQL 2000/2005 Server's Full Text Indexing feature in WSS. If you use the WMSDE, you will not have any way of searching for data.

❑ You can use SPS to index new file types by installing an IFilter (Index Filter).

❑ You can search for content in both files and properties, such as Author, Title, and Size.

❑ You can configure SharePoint to make your own library columns searchable.

❑ You can define keyword best bets for frequently requested information.

❑ SharePoint requires every user to have an account in order to authenticate. You can use local sever accounts or domain accounts, but no other types, such as MS Passports.

❑ If external users such as partners or customers need access, you must create an account for them in your environment.

❑ A new way of allowing users in remote organizations access to your SharePoint server is to install the Active Directory Foundation Service (ADFS).

❑ The access granted to a user is controlled by the site group she belongs to (for example, Reader, Contributor, or Administrator).

By now, you have a general idea of what SharePoint is and how you can use it. In the next chapter, you learn how to install and configure Windows SharePoint Services.

Installing Windows SharePoint Services

In this chapter, you learn how to prepare and install the Windows SharePoint Server (WSS) system with both types of available database configurations. You also learn how to prepare for the installation and understand the different types of system user accounts involved in this action. After the installation is done, you learn how to check that everything is okay. You also learn basic troubleshooting techniques.

> **WSS can run in either an NT 4 or Active Directory domain. It also runs in a work-group environment (for example, a stand-alone server). The instructions in this chapter use an Active Directory domain.**

This chapter is organized by initial sections describing what you are about to do and why, then a step-by-step description on how to do it, and finally some more information on the steps involved, including any tips and tricks based on real-world scenarios.

> **To help you determine whether you should use WSS with or without SPS, consult Chapter 7, "Comparing WSS and SPS."**

Preparing to Install WSS

WSS is the base module of SharePoint 2003, and it can use one of two available database types:

- ❑ Windows MSDE (WMSDE).
- ❑ MS SQL 2000 or 2005 Server.

> **The WMSDE database engine has no size limit, and only WSS can use WMSDE.**

SharePoint also needs some user accounts in order to work, and it is your job to decide what accounts are to be used. You should think about what WSS will be used for and who the users will be.

You should really think twice before making the choice to install WSS without SPS. It has a lot of benefits, not the least of which is that it comes free with Windows 2003 Server, but it also has its drawbacks. You should analyze what problems you are trying to solve with SharePoint. If you later decide to upgrade to SPS, it can be done, but you will have to complete several manual steps in order to make it work. So the best course of action is to be sure that you have the right version installed from the beginning.

> **The previous version of WSS was named SharePoint Team Services (STS). The STS acronym is still used in today's version of WSS, and even in WSS 3.0. Whenever you see something that begins with "STS," such as** STSADM **and** STS_Config**, think "WSS."**

Think about what needs and problems you want to solve with your SharePoint installation. Most likely you cannot answer this question on your own; you must talk with your end users because they are the ones who will use SharePoint. Talk with people in your organization and ask questions like the ones in the following table:

Question	People to Ask	Comment
Do you need an intranet for the whole organization?	Top management, people re-sponsible for managing organization-wide information	For a small company with fewer than 50 users, WSS may be sufficient. But if there is a lot of information, SPS will better suit your needs.
Do you need a local intranet for your depart-ment or team?	Middle management, team leaders	WSS is a good choice if the department or team is working with the same type of information.
Do you need an easy and fast way of navigating to your information, regard-less of its storage location?	Subject-matter experts, project leaders, power users, end users	SPS offers *topics* to solve this need. You canbuild similar functionality in WSS, but it requires much more work. See also Chapter 11.
Do you want to be able to search for information across sites or external to SharePoint?	All types of users	Only SPS offers global search functionality.
Is searching inside SharePoint enough for your needs?	All types of users	This is a complementary question to the previous one; if the answer is yes, you could fulfill this need by using WSS and MS SQL Server together.
Do groups of users need to share and update different information?	All types of users	If the answer is yes, this need is fulfilled with WSS. If only a few people need to update the information, an option is to use SPS areas. See also Chapter 11.
Do you need a way of presenting more information than just the e-mail address and phone num-ber for some or all of your users?	Middle management, team leaders, project leaders	SPS has the "My Site" feature, which presents much more information about users than the typical "Employee List."

> **In addition to asking these questions, be sure to check how much money an SPS-based solution will cost.**

If you get one or more answers that indicate an SPS solution is preferable, you must think carefully about what version to install. Sometimes, a requested functionality is not worth the investment that SPS requires. You should always have a follow-up question ready when your users, especially the managers, tell you that they need an SPS-only feature: "Is this feature worth the investment of X number of dollars?" It has happened more than once that these users then say, "No! Let's start with WSS only." If so, let them know that an upgrade will take time and money and it is easiest to start with SPS if this is what they will need in the end — maybe this will change their mind again.

If the results of your investigation suggest a solution based on WSS, you have two options: If you need basic search functionality, you must use an MS SQL Server, not a WMSDE database, engine. And if you use MS SQL Server, you can use a locally installed database or a remote database server; maybe one that is used for other applications but has the available resources for your WSS environment.

> **With Service Pack 2 for SharePoint, you can use MS SQL 2000 or MS SQL 2005 as your database engine. If possible, go with MS SQL 2005, which is faster and has more options!**

Types of WSS Configurations

In this section, assume your SharePoint solution will be based on WSS alone. (To see configurations for the SharePoint solution that includes SPS, see Chapter 4.) Now you must answer the following question: What database configuration should you use? The following table describes the options you have:

Database	Local Database Engine	Remote Database Server
WMSDE	Yes	Not supported
MS SQL 2000/2005 Server	Yes	Yes

Each solution has its own pros and cons:

❑ The WMSDE database is free, whereas MS SQL Server is not.

❑ A local database engine has the following characteristics:

    ❑ It requires no network communication, and therefore is very fast.

    ❑ No extra server is necessary, so it will be easier to install and maintain.

    ❑ However, the hardware requirements are higher when you want to run both WSS and the database on the same server.

If you are just building a simple test environment, you will most likely be happy with a local WMSDE database, unless you want to test the search capability. To make sure you understand all the different options, following is a summary of each configuration.

Single-Server Configuration with Local WMSDE

This is the preferred configuration for a small WSS environment where collaboration, sharing information, and document management are requested. It is free, and you do not have to pay any extra license for the WSS or WMSDE software. You can get this type of configuration up and running within 15 minutes, because most of the settings for getting WSS and WMSDE to communicate with each other are automatically configured. Microsoft refers to this type of configuration as *single-server*, because it has both SharePoint and the database engine on the same physical server.

There are no limitations regarding the number of users or the size of the database. It has all the functionality that you would find in a WSS and MS SQL Server environment, except for one important thing: There is no search capability! If you can live without this, then this is a very attractive solution.

If you purchase the MS Small Business Server 2003 Standard Edition, you will find this type of combination (WSS and WMDE) along with MS Exchange 2003 and MS Shared Fax Solution.

Single-Server Configuration with Local MS SQL Server

This configuration is perfect for the small organization or department that wants a very good platform for intranet, information sharing, and collaboration, as well as search capability. The cost is higher than the previous configuration because you need an MS SQL Server, which is not free. But if you already have invested in the MS SQL Server and it has free capacity available, you could install WSS on the same server; this would make a great solution.

> *You need one MS SQL Server Client Access License (CAL) for each WSS user. Make sure your current license agreement covers all the WSS users.*

Again, there are no limitations regarding the number of users or the size of the database, and thanks to the built-in functionality of Full-Text Indexing in MS SQL Server, you are able to search for information in your SharePoint database. However, your search is by default limited to information that belongs to the current site. In other words, if you have a number of sites, you must know exactly in what site the information is stored to be able to find it. There is a free solution from CorasWorks that allows you to search subsites as well, as you will learn in Chapter 8. If you purchase the MS Small Business Server 2003 Premium Edition, you will get this type of SharePoint environment, along with an MS Exchange server, MS ISA server, and FrontPage 2003.

Small Farm: WSS with a Separate MS SQL Server

The last configuration is where you install WSS on one server and MS SQL Server on another server. This is something Microsoft refers to as a *small farm*. This increases the number of users supported, and you have all the functionality of the previously described configuration. Once again, this would not be a free installation, because you need the MS SQL Server, but if you have such an installation already somewhere in your IT environment, it may be no extra cost. This depends on the type of license you have for this existing MS SQL Server, as described previously.

There is no added WSS functionality with this solution, aside from the increased number of users supported. However, you could use this configuration with a clustered MS SQL 2005 Server environment, with up to eight nodes, thus giving you both fault tolerance and higher availability.

There is no version of MS Small Business Server that supports this type of configuration as of this writing.

Hardware Requirements

SharePoint is an application that works best when it gets lots of memory and CPU resources. However, you may be surprised when finding out how little SharePoint actually requires to get started. For example, a standard low-budget server with 512 MB of memory will happily support an organization with several hundred users, as long as you have the disk capacity to store all data needed; see the next section for more details.

There are several things you must understand when planning your WSS server:

❏ SharePoint is a web application! There is no permanent connection between the client browser and the SharePoint server. Every time you open a link or a document, the browser connects, gets what you requested, and closes the connection immediately after that, regardless of how long the user looks at that information.

❏ The number of users in the organization is not the same as the number of simultaneous users.

❏ Different activities in SharePoint require different resources; for example, displaying a project site normally generates a very light load on the server, whereas indexing the database generates a much higher load.

Calculating the Number of OPS Required

There is a general, well-proven formula that you can use for calculating the load, or the *operations per second* (OPS), on the SharePoint server. From that you can estimate the number of supported users, given a certain hardware configuration. The formula requires you to find out or estimate a number of values:

$$\frac{A \times B \times C \times D}{360,000 \times E} = \text{Operations per second (OPS)}$$

Given the following estimated data that you must supply:

❏ A = The number of users.

❏ B = The percentage of active users on a typical day.

❏ C = The number of operations per active user per day.

❏ D = The peak factor.

❏ E = The number of working hours per day.

Two of these estimated parameters need to be explained in more detail. The peak factor is a value between 1 and 10, which is used to indicate the peak hours during the work hours. For example, if the organization works from 9 a.m. to 5 p.m., it is a safe bet that most workers start their day by opening their SharePoint environment, because there is where all the information can be found; after that you will probably have an even load. Then directly after lunch, you would get another peak again. A peak factor of 1 means "no peak load at all." A factor of 10 means "a peak load all day." A typical organization would get a peak factor value of 5. If you want to be on the safe side, use a higher value of 7.

The other estimated parameter is the number of operations per active user per day, which has to do with how much your SharePoint environment will be utilized per day. This is also a value between 1 and 10, where 1 means your users access SharePoint for almost no time at all and 10 means your users work all day with SharePoint. For a typical organization you would get something close to 10 for this value.

Example 1: An Organization with 200 Very Active Users

Your organization has 200 employees (A). The percentage of active users in a typical day is 80 (B). The number of operations per active user is 10 (C). The number of working hours for the organization as a whole is 12 hours (E). You estimate the peak factor (D) to be 10, to be on the safe side. The formula for this organization will look like this:

$$\frac{200 \times 80 \times 10 \times 10}{360,000 \times 12} = 0.37 \text{ Operations per second (OPS)}$$

Example 2: An Organization with 4,500 Normal Users

Your organization has 4,500 employees (A). The percentage of active users in a typical day is 50 (B). The number of operations per active user is 10 (C). The number of working hours for the organization as a whole is 12 hours (E). You estimate the peak factor (D) to be 5. The formula for this organization will look like this:

$$\frac{4,500 \times 50 \times 10 \times 5}{360,000 \times 12} = 2.60 \text{ Operations per second (OPS)}$$

Now you have a good idea of the load your system will generate. The next step is to use this information to calculate the hardware you need. In the following table are some typical configurations and the estimated operations per second they support:

Server Configuration	Estimated OPS Supported
A single-server with both WSS and WMSDE, configured with 1 GB memory and a 2.8 GHz CPU	35 OPS
One WSS server and one SQL 2000, both configured with 1 GB memory and a dual 2.8 GHz CPU	65 OPS
One WSS server and one SQL 2000, both configured with 1 GB memory and a dual 3.06 GHz CPU	105 OPS

From this table you can learn three important things:

- ❑ You don't need a large server to run WSS.
- ❑ Separating the WSS server and the MS SQL Server improves the OPS throughput.
- ❑ CPU is the most important resource. Notice the difference between 2.8 and 3.06 GHz CPUs.

In fact, using the figures in the more extreme organization from the previous Example 1, the first server configuration in the preceding table can support an organization of close to 20,000 users!

Calculating the Disk Space Needed

The disk space that WSS requires is less than 50 MB, so the important part is the database where SharePoint stores all its information. The database application itself requires about 100 MB for its binary files. It does not matter whether you are using the WMDE engine or the MS SQL Server; you still need to follow this simple but important rule:

> **You must always have at least 50 percent free space on your database disk!**

If not, you will not be able to perform database maintenance and troubleshooting, because these activities may need to make a copy of the database in order to perform their tasks. So what will require most space in the database? The answer is simply: Your documents! They will not be compressed, so a 1-MB Word file will require 1 MB of database disk space. The other things you store will of course also take some space, but they will most likely not generate anything near as much as the files you store. And a SharePoint site itself will require less than 200 KB of database space.

So to estimate the disk space needed for your database, start by estimating the number of files it will contain. For example, assume you estimate that it will contain about 50,000 files with an average of 500 KB; in total this will require 25 GB. Add to that 5 GB for the other types of information you will store, and you get 30 GB in total. Following the preceding rule, you must have at least a 60-GB disk for the database alone.

Remember that if you implement a small farm configuration (one WSS server and one MS SQL Server), you only require the 60-GB disk on the database server. The WSS server itself requires very little disk space.

Software Requirements

As you may recall from the previous chapter, SharePoint is a web application, and it requires Internet Information Services 6.0 (IIS 6), which in turn requires you to run MS Windows 2003 Server. SharePoint also requires that ASP.NET and its supporting components are installed. The easiest way to get this configuration right for a SharePoint server, with nothing more and nothing less than needed, is to follow these steps:

> *If you previously have installed .NET Framework 2.0, IIS will default to use ASP.NET 2.0, which may prohibit a successful installation of SharePoint. If so, make sure that SharePoint will use ASP.NET 1.1 by opening the IIS Manager, opening the properties for the virtual server used by SharePoint, and switching to the ASP tab (which will only be displayed if you have more than one ASP.NET version installed). Then continue with the following steps.*

1. Log on to your Windows 2003 Server as the administrator.
2. Choose Start⇨Control Panel.
3. Select Add/Remove Programs.
4. Click the Add/Remove Windows Component button.
5. Select the Application Server and click Details.
6. Make sure everything is cleared, including Internet Information Services (IIS).
7. Check the ASP.NET box, and it will automatically check all the components it needs.
8. Click OK to save this configuration and then click Next. Note that you may be asked to supply the Windows 2003 Server installation disk at this point.

Remember that you can use any edition of Windows 2003 Server for the WSS installation, but if you choose the Web Edition of Windows 2003 Server, you must install a separate MS SQL Server, because this edition does not support local databases.

The IIS Virtual Server

In the old days each web application required its own physical web server, which is clearly not the most economical solution. Microsoft solved this by allowing its IIS to create and manage virtual web servers, for example, the Default Web Site. Each web application running on top of IIS 6 needs its own virtual server. This makes it possible to run several web applications on the same physical server. In order to make it possible to separate each virtual server, they must differ in at least one of the following: the IP number, the Port number, or the Host Header name.

But that solution created a new problem: If one web application crashed, it also killed all other web applications running on the same IIS. Microsoft's solution was to invent the *application pool*, which gives a private virtual address space and security context for each web application. One virtual web server is linked to one application pool. However, each application pool can be linked to more than one virtual server, thus sharing address space and security context.

> **IIS 6 supports up to 9 virtual IIS servers with individual application pools or 99 virtual IIS servers sharing the same application pool.**

When installing SharePoint you need to be sure about these two things:

❏   What virtual IIS server SharePoint will be installed on.

❏   What user account the linked application pool will use.

The application pool security context can be a built-in account, typically the network service. As an alternative, you can configure the application pool to use a user account; if so, make sure this account is granted permission as database creator in the MS SQL Server.

Sharing the same application pool among several virtual IIS servers makes it possible for the other web applications to access the SQL database! Microsoft recommends that you use a separate application pool for the virtual IIS server that WSS will run in.

In addition to the application pool used by the virtual IIS server for the WSS sites, there is also a separate application pool for the web-based administration tool that comes with SharePoint. This must be a separate application pool. It should not share the same application pool as the WSS virtual server.

Minimum and Recommended Configurations

To summarize the previous hardware and software requirement sections, you can use the following table, which lists Microsoft's minimum and recommended configurations. Remember that for a pilot installation you can actually get away with even less than the given minimum memory size in this table:

Item	Minimum Requirement	MS Recommends
Operating System	Any edition of Microsoft Windows Server 2003	Any edition of Microsoft Windows Server 2003
CPU	1 CPU running at 550 MHz	2 CPUs running at least 1 GHz
RAM	512	1 GB or more

Item	Minimum Requirement	MS Recommends
Disk space	500 MB	500 MB / SharePoint Site
File System	NTFS	NTFS
IIS version	6.0 with ASP.NET (in Worker Process Isolation Mode)	6.0 with ASP.NET (in Worker Process IsolationMode)
Database engine	WMSDE or SQL Server 2000 with Service Pack 3a	A separate SQL Server 2005 and its latest Service Pack
Internet Browser	IE 5.01 with SP2 or later	IE 6 or later, with the latest Service Pack

Installing WSS

By now you have the necessary information to start the installation of WSS. The following section describes the exact steps required to install WSS in all three possible combinations. Before you start following these steps, make sure nobody is using this server for anything else, at least not during the installation. If you have other applications installed on the same server, please make a backup before you start, to be prepared for the unlikely possibility that something goes wrong and the server gets messed up beyond repair!

During the installation of WSS, you are asked to *extend* the virtual IIS server. This term means that the virtual IIS server gets configured in such a way that WSS can use it. You cannot install WSS unless the virtual server is extended. In simple scenarios, such as installing WSS and WMSDE together, the setup program for WSS automatically extends the virtual server. In more complex scenarios, such as a separate server for WSS and MS SQL Server, you have to extend the virtual server manually. It is not complicated; the steps are listed in the following sections.

The Config and Content Databases

WSS uses two types of databases, the *configuration database* and the *content database*. During the installation of WSS, you (or the setup program) will create these, depending on how complex the installation scenario is. These two database types contain the following information:

❑ **Configuration Database:** Maintains all the connections between all WSS servers (if more than one) and the SQL databases (if more than one). There is always only one configuration database, regardless of the number of WSS and SQL databases. For WSS installations using the MS SQL Server (not WMSDE), you name this `config database`.

❑ **Content Database:** This database contains all data and information that belongs to the WSS web sites, such as news lists, document libraries, and the web site itself. It also includes management data, such as user names and permission settings. Initially you have one content database, but you can create as many as you need. Large organizations can have more than a thousand content databases. The first WSS content database gets a name beginning with STS followed by the server name and then the number 1. For example, if the server is named SPSRV your first content database will be named `STS_SPSRV_1`. You will name any new content database that you add.

Following you will find all three possible configurations of WSS. Each configuration is completely described, including detailed steps on how to perform this type of installation. Many of these steps are identical in two or all of the installation scenarios. I recommend that you focus on the type of installation that is most interesting to you at this moment. Later, you can come back to this chapter when you need to perform another type of installation.

Installing a Single-Server with the WMSDE Database

Installing a WSS using a WMSDE database is very straightforward and easy. You can do it within 10 minutes without much hassle. You can either use an installation CD with WSS or download it from Microsoft's web site. Follow these steps to download and install both the WSS application and the WMSDE database on the same server:

Try It Out	Install WSS and WMSDE on a Single-Server

1. Log on as an administrator to the Windows 2003 Server you will use for your WSS and WMSDE installation.

2. Make sure Windows 2003 Server has the latest service packs and security patches installed by going to Start⇨All Programs⇨Windows Update.

3. Download the latest version of WSS from Microsoft's web site: Go to www.microsoft.com/ downloads and search for STSV2.EXE. Select the download link for WSS including the latest service pack (SP 2 as of this writing). On the following page, you should see a Download button. Before clicking this button, make sure you have the right WSS language.

   There are more than 30 languages and the default is English; if you want another language, use the change language drop-down menu and select the language you need; then click the Change button. This will take you to a localized download page. The following steps assume you are downloading the English version!

   Select to download the STSV2.EXE file to a folder on your server, such as C:\Install. The file is about 40 MB and will take some time to download, depending on your Internet connection and the load on the MS download server.

4. Verify that you have ASP.NET installed, as previously described in the section "Software Requirements."

5. Start the installation by running the STSV2.EXE file you downloaded.

6. The first dialog page is about the license agreement. If you agree, select "I accept the terms in the license agreement" and click Next.

7. The next page is important. Here you select if you want to use the WMSDE database Typical Installation or the MS SQL Server database Server Farm, as shown in Figure 2-1.

8. On the next page, you see a summary of the installation options. If it is correct, click the Install button to start the installation. If not, click Back and do the necessary modification.

   The installation takes a few minutes; shortly after that, WSS starts an automatic configuration that sets up the IIS virtual server and connects to the WMSDE database, and finally creates the first SharePoint web site.

9. When you see the new web site, the installation is done. Now you can start using it directly.

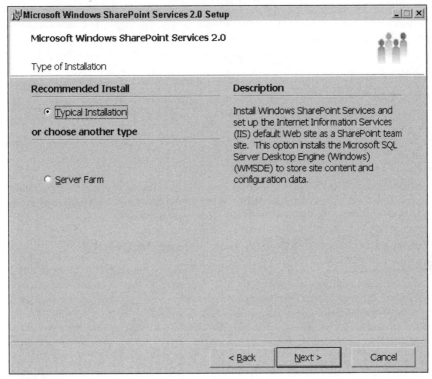

Figure 2-1

Checking the Installation

Before going on, it is a good idea to investigate what new things were installed on the server:

1. Start by opening the IIS manager: Start⇨Administration Tools⇨Internet Information Service (IIS) Manager.

2. Expand the Web Sites node. Note that you have two IIS virtual servers here:

    ❑ **Default Web Site:** Used by SharePoint for all user web sites, such as project sites, team sites, and so on.

    ❑ **SharePoint Central Administration:** Used by SharePoint for the administration web site.

3. Right-click Default Web Site and select Properties.

4. Switch to the Home Directory tab; note what application pool name this virtual server is using. The default is StsAppPool1. Close the properties for the Default Web Site.

5. Expand the Application Pools node in the left-hand column of the IIS Manager.

6. Right-click the application pool that the Default Web Site is using (StsAppPool1) and switch to the Identity tab. Note what security account this application pool is using. By default it is the predefined Network Service.

Do the same with the SharePoint Central Administration web site:

1. Right-click on its node.

2. Check the Home Directory tab to see its application pool (which should be the StsAdminAppPool).

3. Open the properties for that application pool and check that its security account on the Identity page also is the same predefined Network Service account.

This security account is granted access to the WMSDE database, and it is used by WSS whenever it needs to read or write to the database.

To summarize this, WSS uses two virtual IIS servers: one for the web sites that your SharePoint users utilize and one for the administration of SharePoint. These two virtual servers use separate application pools. Both these application pools use the same security account.

How to Avoid Installing WSS into the Default Web Site

As you can see, this installation method automatically chooses the IIS Default Virtual Site, regardless of whether you have more virtual servers installed. In fact, even if you have some other web application using this Default Web Site, SharePoint still selects it and configures it for its own use. Any previously installed web application on that virtual server might then stop working! If you need to install WSS on another virtual IIS server, you must use a special installation routine, as described in the next section.

Try It Out   Install WSS in a Given Virtual IIS Server

The STSV2.EXE file that you downloaded before is a compressed file. You can expand it and run the setup program SETUPSTS.EXE manually. This is necessary if you want to control exactly which virtual server WSS will use. Use the flag Provision=No to avoid the setup that automatically creates the first web site, thus leaving it to you to later select whatever virtual server you like for this.

If you have a CD with WSS, you will probably see the expanded files, including SETUPSTS.EXE instead of STSV2.EXE. If so, you don't need to do steps 2 and 3 in the following list.

Follow these steps to do it:

1. Create the virtual IIS server you want to use instead of the Default Web Site for the WSS web sites; in this example it is referred to as VS2.

2. Open a command prompt and switch to the folder where the STSV2.EXE file is located.

3. Run STSV2 with the /T flag to select the folder the expanded files will be stored in, and use /C to tell STSV2 that you only want to expand the files, instead of running the normal setup procedure. In the following example, STS expands the files into the path C:\WSS:

```
STSV2 /T:C:\WSS /C
```

4. Go to the folder with the expanded files. Start the installation by using the following:

```
SETUPSTS Provision=No
```

5. You will see the same type of pages during the installation as for the standard installation method. The first is the End-User License Agreement. Check I Accept if you do, and click Next.

6. On the next page you have a choice to install either a Typical Install or a Server Farm. In this example you install everything on the same server, including the WMSDE database, so choose a Typical Install and click Next.

7. The next and last page before the installation is a summary of your choices. Click Install to start the installation. Note that it is a bit hard to know when the installation is done. You simply have to wait some time until there are no more popup windows telling you what is going on.

When the installation is done, you will not see any changes to the virtual IIS servers or the application pools. The reason is that you must manually perform the last configuration steps that STSV2 performed for you before.

8. Open a command prompt and go to the following folder in your WSS server:

```
C:\Program Files\Common Files\Microsoft Shared\web server extensions\60\BIN
```

9. There you will find a number of utilities that SETUPSTS has installed. There is one special utility, the STSADM.EXE, which you will use to configure WSS to use a given virtual IIS server. Enter the following line of code to create the virtual IIS server SharePoint Central Administration for the WSS administration site and an application pool named StsAdminAppPool with the security account Network Service:

```
STSADM -o CreateAdminVS -admapcreatenew -admapidname StsAdminAppPool ⤶
-admapidtype NetworkService
```

10. You will get a notification that this WSS installation may use Kerberos authentication, instead of the standard Integrated Windows Authentication (IWA, also known as NTLM authentication). If you want to switch between Kerberos and IWA, you can use the scripts described in Microsoft's support article 832769. By default, IWA will be used.

Make sure the newly created virtual server SharePoint Central Administration and its StsAdminAppPool have been created. Check its setting as described before in the section "Checking the Installation." You should also find a newly created link to the web site for WSS administration in Start⇨All Programs⇨Administrative Tools⇨SharePoint Central Administration.

11. The next step is to reset IIS to activate the new settings. Open a command prompt window and run the command iisreset. Then open the Service Manager: Start⇨All Programs⇨ Administrative Tools⇨Services and make sure that MSSQL$SHAREPOINT is running.

12. With this administrative web site, you can go on and create the configuration database that WSS will need to store all configuration settings. You can do this by using the newly created administrative web site, or at the command prompt. The first method is to start the new SharePoint Central Configuration utility, and it will automatically take you to the page where you enter the database server name, the instance name for SharePoint (for example E2K3BASE\SharePoint), and the name you want for your config database. Click OK. The second method requires you to type in the following command to create a config database named sts_config in the E2K3BASE server:

```
STSADM -o setconfigdb -ds E2K3BASE\SharePoint -dn sts_config
```

13. The last step is to select the virtual IIS server you want for the WSS user web sites. For example, assume you have a new virtual IIS server named VS2 that you want to use. Then you would create this web site like this:

The following steps can also be used in case you installed WSS the normal way and later decide to add or change a virtual IIS server for a new WSS environment.

a. Start the WSS Administration web site by clicking the newly created link in Start⇨ All Programs⇨Administrative Tools⇨SharePoint Central Administration.

b. Select Extend or upgrade virtual server. The term Extend means that WSS will add extra features and configurations to it, in order to host the WSS user web site.

c. You should now see all available virtual servers that WSS has not yet extended. If not, you must create the virtual IIS server first and then return to this page. Click the virtual server VS2.

d. Click the option Extend and create a content database shown in Figure 2-2.

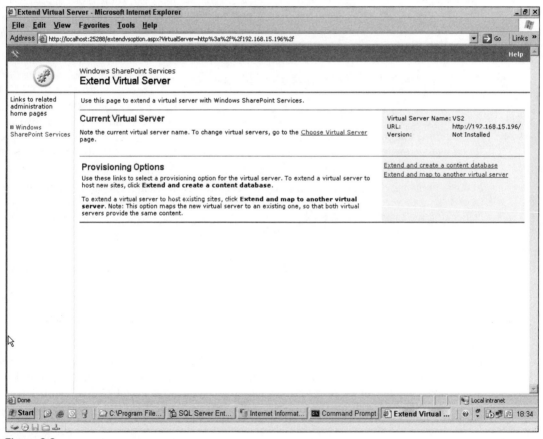

Figure 2-2

e. On the following page you have lots of important options; make sure to fill in the correct values in these sections:

❑ **Application Pool:** If you want to use an existing application pool, such as the DefaultAppPool, you must use the drop-down menu. You can also create a new application pool. If so, you must give it a name and select the security account it will use. For a WSS environment with a WMSDE database, you should use the built-in Network Service account.

❑ **Site Owner:** Enter the user account and e-mail address that will be the owner of this WSS environment and therefore have full control of it. Avoid personal user accounts; choose a role-based account if possible.

❑ **Database Information:** If you want to use a separate content database or database server for this new WSS environment, uncheck the Use default content database server and enter the name for the server and the content database.

❑ **Security Configuration:** Select what type of authentication mechanism you want to use. Note that the default is Kerberos, which requires that you have configured your Kerberos settings; if not you will not be able to run this new WSS environment. Change to NTLM if you are not sure you want to run Kerberos! You will in fact be warned if you select Kerberos, just to make sure you don't select it by mistake.

❑ **Custom URL:** Enter the URL address to this new WSS. It will be relative to the virtual server. For example, if the virtual server is referred to as vs2 and you enter the value **/home**, you will then reach this WSS environment by the URL http://vs2/home. Note that you can leave this field as it is; this will result in the URL address http://vs2 alone.

❑ **Quota Template:** You can configure this WSS environment to limit its maximum disk size by selecting a disk quota template. Because this is a new WSS installation, you will not have any template and must accept the default No Quota.

❑ **Site Language:** As mentioned before, WSS is available in more than 30 different languages. If you have installed any extra WSS language packs, you can now choose what language the first web site will use. By default you will only see the language of your WSS setup package, English.

Click OK when ready to save this configuration. This will start the creation of the new WSS environment for the virtual server (VS2 in this example).

f. When the process is done, you will get to the page Virtual Server Successfully Extended. Click OK to continue.

g. The next page is where you configure this new WSS virtual server. You learn more about this in the next chapter. Test your new WSS virtual server by using a browser and going to the URL for this site (http://e2k3base in this example). If you then see a page where you are requested to select a template for the new web site, you have successfully managed your mission to create a new WSS environment in the virtual IIS server of your choice.

h. If you want to see the new (and first) user web site, choose any site template and click OK to open it. Figure 2-3 shows the Team Web Site opened.

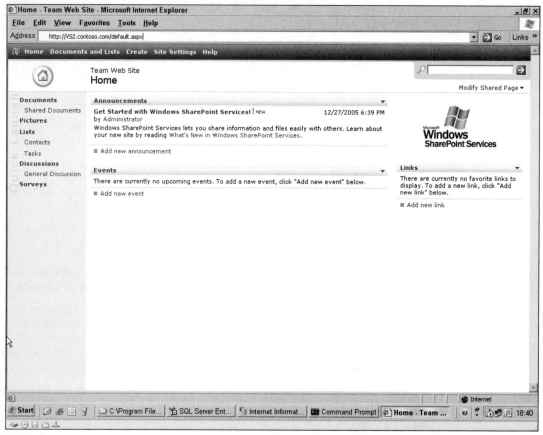

Figure 2-3

Installing a Single-Server with a Local MS SQL Database

You may recall that previous sections mentioned that the WMSDE does not have any support for index-ing, whereas MS SQL does. Another reason for choosing MS SQL is that it has powerful management tools for configuration, security settings, and backup procedures.

The following sections describe how to install both the WSS application with Service Pack 2 and the MS SQL database on the same server. Note that for the MS SQL 2000 version you must install Service Pack 3a or later before using it for WSS. You can also use the new MS SQL 2005 Server, as long as you have installed at least Service Pack 2 for WSS.

Make sure you have the MS SQL Server installed and running before performing the following steps. In order to get the indexing and search functionality to work in WSS, you must also make sure that the MS SQL Server has the Full-Text Search option installed.

Install WSS and MS SQL on a Single-Server

1. Log on as an administrator to the Windows 2003 server you will use for your WSS and MS SQL installation.

2. Make sure Windows 2003 Server has the latest service packs and security patches installed by going to Start➪All Programs➪Windows Update.

3. Download the latest version of WSS from Microsoft's web site: Go to www.microsoft.com/ downloads and search for STSV2.EXE. Select the download link for WSS including the latest service pack (SP 2 as of this writing). On the following page, you should see a Download button. Before clicking this button, make sure you have the right WSS language.

There are more than 30 languages and the default is English; if you want another language, use the change language drop-down menu and select the language you need; then click the Change button. This will take you to a localized download page. The following steps assume you are downloading the English version.

Select to download the STSV2.EXE file to a folder on your server, such as C:\Install. The file is about 40 MB and will take some time to download, depending on your Internet connection and the load on the MS download server.

4. Verify that you have ASP.NET installed, as previously described in this chapter under the section "Software Requirements."

5. Verify that your MS SQL Server is installed and running, including its latest service pack.

6. Start the installation by running the STSV2.EXE file you downloaded.

7. The first dialog page is about the license agreement. If you agree, select "I accept the terms in the license agreement" and click Next.

8. The next page is important. You must change the selected installation type to Server Farm in order to install WSS without the WMSDE database. Later, you will manually connect WSS to the MS SQL Server. Click Next to continue.

9. On the next page, click Install to start the installation. This will take a few minutes to complete.

10. When the installation is done, start the SharePoint Central Administration tool. Because you selected to install a server farm, you will have more configuration settings compared to the previous configuration, which was using a local WMSDE database.

The first page is the Configure Administrative Virtual Server:

❑ **Application Pool:** Choose what application pool this administrative web site will use. You can use the existing StsAdminAppPool, created by the WSS installation process, or you can create a new application pool and at the same time choose the security account it will use. If this is your choice, you must also decide if you want to use a built-in account such as the Network Service (if the MS SQL Server is installed on the same server as SharePoint) or an account that you have created. Note that whatever security account you will use, it must be granted access to the SQL Server by making it a member of the SQL roles Database Creators and Security Administrators. Later this account will create all the databases WSS needs and make itself the database owner for these databases. In this example use StsAdminAppPool.

❑ **Security Configuration:** Choose what type of security mechanism to use. By default it will say Kerberos, but that requires you to configure your domain to use Kerberos. The recommendation is to use the NTLM. If you later need to change this mechanism, you can do it by following the steps in MS Support article 832769. This example uses the NTLM.

Click OK to save these settings and continue. This opens up the Set Configuration Database Server page; however, before you continue you must make sure the account used by StsAdminAppPool has permission to configure the SQL Server, as described in the following step.

11. The security account you defined for the administrative application pool must be granted access to the MS SQL Server, including built-in accounts like the Network Service account. Follow these steps to add the account to MS SQL with the proper permissions:

   a. Open the management tool for SQL by navigating to Start⇨All Programs⇨Microsoft SQL Server⇨Enterprise Manager.

   b. Expand the local SQL Server; then expand the Security node.

   c. Right-click Logins and select New Login.

   d. Enter the name and domain for the user, as illustrated in Figure 2-4. (For the Network Service account, you must type the full name: **NT AUTHORITY\NETWORK SERVICE**.)

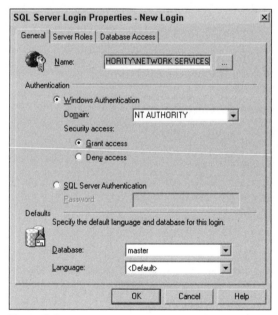

Figure 2-4

   e. Switch to the Server Roles tab and check the two options Security Administrators and Database Creators, as shown in Figure 2-5.

   f. Click OK to save this.

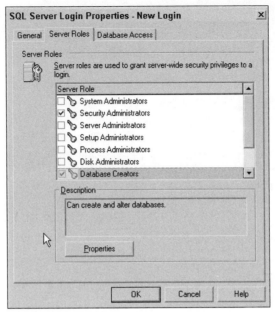

Figure 2-5

12. Go back to the Set Configuration Database Server page (see Figure 2-6). Here you will define what server is running MS SQL, the name you want for the configuration database, security settings, and more.

- ❏ **Database Server:** Enter the name of the local server (in this example **E2K3BASE**).

- ❏ **SQL Server Database Name:** Enter the name for the configuration database (in this example **WSS_Config**).

- ❏ **Database Connection Type:** Choose the authentication method. By default it will be Windows Authentication. It is not recommended to use SQL Authentication because it is less secure.

- ❏ **Connect to existing configuration database:** For the first WSS server, this is always unchecked! As you will learn later, you can have more than one WSS server using the same database; these servers will check this box, but not this time.

- ❏ **Active Directory Account Creation:** This is a one-time configuration setting! If you later want to change from one setting to another, you must reinstall completely. Make sure you understand this important setting. For any standard WSS installation that you will use for your domain users, stick with the default "Users already have domain accounts." The other option, "Automatically create active directory accounts for users of this site," is used when you want to enable each user who is a SharePoint site administrator to invite any user to that site, using their e-mail address; this automatically creates a user account in the domain, unless the invited user already has an account. Though this may sound like a good idea, it requires lots of planning. Never choose this option for a standard WSS implementation in a normal Active Directory domain; you normally will create a separate organizational unit (OU) in the domain for this purpose. The main purpose for this option is to enable WSS in an environment where you want self-provisioning (where the site administrators can create new user accounts). This could be a public WSS site or similar situation where the security requirements are not the highest priority.

Click OK to continue to the next page.

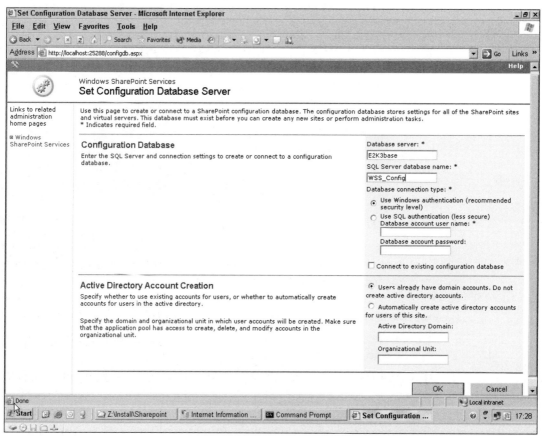

Figure 2-6

13. The config database is now created. (You can find it under Databases in the SQL Enterprise Manager.) The next step is to extend the virtual IIS server to prepare it for hosting all WSS user web sites. You can use the Default Web Site, or you can create a new virtual IIS server. In this example you will use the Default Web Site.

You should now see the Windows SharePoint Services Central Administration page. It contains many links, but you just need one of them at this time: Click the Extend or upgrade virtual server link.

14. On the following page, you will see all non-extended virtual IIS servers. Click Default Web Site to go on to the next page.

15. Look at the Provisioning Options section. Click Extend and create a content database.

16. On the following page you have lots of important options for the content database you are about to create; make sure to fill in the correct values in these sections:

❑ **Application Pool:** If you want to use an existing application pool, you must use the drop-down menu. The recommendation is to create a new application pool so that you can avoid conflict with any other web application on this server. If so, you must give it a name, for example WSSAppPool, and select the security account it will use. If you want you can use the built-in Network Service account or any another user account you might prefer. This account does not need access into the SQL Server database, because this is done by the security account defined for the administrative application pool.

❑ **Site Owner:** Enter the user account and e-mail address that will be the owner of this WSS environment, and therefore have full control of it. Avoid personal user accounts; choose a role-based account if possible, such as WSS_Admin. If so, remember to create that account before completing this page!

❑ **Database Information:** If you want to use a separate content database or database server for this new WSS environment, uncheck "Use default content database server" and enter the name for the server and the content database. The default is to use the same server as for the configuration database.

❑ **Security Configuration:** Select what type of authentication mechanism you want to use. Note that the default is Kerberos, which requires that you have configured your Kerberos settings; if not you will not be able to run this new WSS environment. Change to NTLM if you are not sure you want to run Kerberos! You will in fact be warned if you select Kerberos, just to make sure you don't select it by mistake.

❑ **Custom URL:** Enter the URL address to this new WSS. It will be relative to the server name; for example, if your server is referred to as E2K3Base and you enter the value **/home**, you will then reach this WSS environment by the URL http://E2K3Base/home. Note that you can leave this field as it is; this will result in the URL address http://E2K3base alone.

❑ **Quota Template:** You can configure this WSS environment to limit its maximum disk size by selecting a disk quota template. Because this is a new WSS installation, you will not have any template and must accept the default No Quota.

❑ **Site Language:** As mentioned before, WSS is available in more than 30 different languages. If you have installed any extra WSS language packs, you can now choose what language the first web site will use. By default you will only see the language of your WSS setup package (English).

Click OK when ready to save this configuration. This will complete the creation of the new WSS content database.

17. When the process is done, you will get the page Virtual Server Successfully Extended. Click OK to continue.

18. On the next page you will find a number of general configuration settings for this new WSS server. You learn more about these in the next chapter.

19. Test your new WSS virtual server by using a browser and go to the URL for this site: `http://E2K3Base` in this example. If you are logged on to the WSS server, you can also use the URL `http://localhost`.

The first time you go to this URL, you will see a page where you are requested to select a template for the new web site. You will learn a lot more about this later, but for now it is enough to know that a web site template defines the initial look and feel of this new WSS user web site. For now, select the Team Site template and click OK to open the new site to see what it looks like.

Installing a Single-Server Using a Remote MS SQL Database

Most of the steps in this configuration are similar or identical to the previous configuration with a local MS SQL Server. The reasons for using a remote MS SQL Server are these:

❑ **Increased performance:** The WSS server can handle many more users.

❑ **Fault-tolerance:** It is possible to connect WSS to an MS SQL cluster.

❑ **Better economy:** You can use a previously installed MS SQL Server.

The following sections describe how to install the WSS application with Service Pack 2 on one computer named E2K3Base and connect to an existing MS SQL database on a server named TOR. Both of these servers are members of the domain Contoso.

Make sure you have the MS SQL Server installed and running before performing the following steps. In order to get the indexing and search functionality to work in WSS, you must also make sure that the MS SQL Server has the Full-Text Search option installed.

Try It Out   Install WSS and MS SQL on Separate Servers

1. Log on as an administrator to the Windows 2003 server you will use for your WSS installation.

2. Make sure Windows 2003 Server has the latest service packs and security patches installed by going to Start⇨All Programs⇨Windows Update.

3. Download the latest version of WSS from Microsoft's web site. Go to `www.microsoft.com/downloads and search for STSV2.EXE`. Select the download link for WSS including the latest service pack (SP 2 as of this writing). On the following page, you should see a Download button. Before clicking this button, make sure you have the right WSS language.

There are more than 30 languages and the default is English; if you want another language, use the change language drop-down menu and select the language you need; then click the Change button. This will take you to a localized download page. The following steps assume you are downloading the English version.

Select to download the `STSV2.EXE` file to a folder on your server, such as `C:\Install`. The file is about 40 MB and will take some time to download, depending on your Internet connection and the load on the MS download server.

4. Verify that you have ASP.NET installed, as previously described in this chapter under the section "Software Requirements."

5. Verify that your MS SQL Server is installed and running, including its latest service pack.

6. Start the installation by running the STSV2.EXE file you downloaded.

7. The first dialog page is about the license agreement. If you agree, select "I accept the terms in the license agreement" and click Next.

8. The next page is important. You must change the selected installation type to Server Farm in order to install WSS without the WMSDE database. Later, you will manually connect WSS to the MS SQL Server. Click Next to continue.

9. On the next page, click Install to start the installation.

10. When the installation is done, WSS will start its administrative web page. The first thing to do is to create a configuration database for your WSS server. There is only one configuration database, regardless of the number of web sites or content databases.

The first page is Configure Administrative Virtual Server:

❑ **Application Pool:** Choose what application pool this administrative web site will use. You can use the existing StsAdminAppPool, created by the WSS installation process for this very purpose. Or you can create a new application pool and at the same time choose the security account it will use. If this is your choice, you must also decide if you want to use a built-in account like the Network Service or an account that you have created. Note that whatever security account you will use, it must be granted access to the SQL Server by making it a member of the SQL roles Database Creators and Security Administrators. Later this account will create all the databases WSS needs and make itself the database owner for these databases. In this example use the StsAdminAppPool.

❑ **Security Configuration:** Choose what type of security mechanism to use. By default it will say Kerberos, but that requires you to configure your domain to use Kerberos. The recommendation is to use NTLM. If you later need to change this mechanism, you can do it by following the steps in MS Support article 832769. This example uses NTLM.

Click OK to save these settings and continue.

11. The security account you defined for the administrative application pool must be granted access to the MS SQL Server, including built-in accounts like the Network Service account. Follow these steps to add the account to MS SQL with the proper permissions:

a. Open the management tool for SQL by navigating to Start⇨All Programs⇨Microsoft SQL Server⇨Enterprise Manager.

b. Expand the local SQL Server; then expand the Security node.

c. Right-click Logins and select New Login.

d. Enter the name and domain for the user you defined for the application pool, as illustrated in Figure 2-7. (For the Network Service account, you must type the full name: **NT AUTHORITY\NETWORK SERVICE.**)

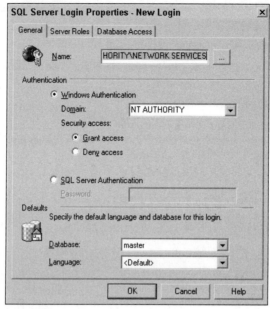

Figure 2-7

e. Switch to the Server Roles tab and check the two options Security Administrators and Database Creators, as shown in Figure 2-8.

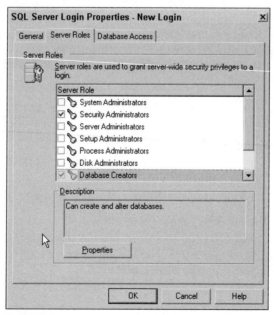

Figure 2-8

      f.   Click OK to save this.

12. On the next page you are requested to reset the IIS. Choose Start⇨Run, type **IISRESET**, and press Enter. Wait until it is done, and then click OK.

13. The next page is Set Configuration Database Server (see Figure 2-9). Here you will define what server is running MS SQL, the name you want for the configuration database, security settings, and more.

- ❑ **Database Server:** Enter the name of the local server; in this example **Tor**.

- ❑ **SQL Server Database Name:** Enter the name for the configuration database; in this example **WSS_Config**.

- ❑ **Database Connection Type:** Choose the authentication method. By default it will be Windows Authentication. It is not recommended to use SQL Authentication because it is less secure.

- ❑ **Connect to existing configuration database:** For the first WSS server, this is always unchecked! As you will learn later, you can have more than one WSS server using the same database; these servers will check this box, but not this time.

- ❑ **Active Directory Account Creation:** This is a one-time configuration setting! If you later want to change from one setting to another, you must reinstall completely. Make sure you understand this important setting. For any standard WSS installation that you will use for your domain users, stick with the default "Users already have domain accounts." The other option, "Automatically create active directory accounts for users of this site," is used when you want to enable each user to automatically create a user account in the domain. Though this may sound like a good idea, it requires lots of planning. Never choose this option for a standard WSS implementation in a normal Active Directory domain; you normally will create a separate organizational unit (OU) in the domain for this purpose. The main purpose for this option is to enable WSS in an environment where you want self-provisioning (where the site administrators create new user accounts). This could be a public WSS site or similar situation where the security requirements are not the highest priority.

14. The config database is now created. (You can find it under Databases in the SQL Enterprise Manager.) The next step is to extend the virtual IIS server to prepare it for hosting all WSS user web sites. You can use the Default Web Site, or you can create a new virtual IIS server. In this example you will use the Default Web Site.

You should now see the Windows SharePoint Services Central Administration page. It contains many links, but you just need one of them at this time: Click the Extend or upgrade virtual server link.

15. On the following page, you will see all non-extended virtual IIS servers. Click Default Web Site to go on to the next page.

16. Look at the Provisioning Options section. Click Extend and create a content database.

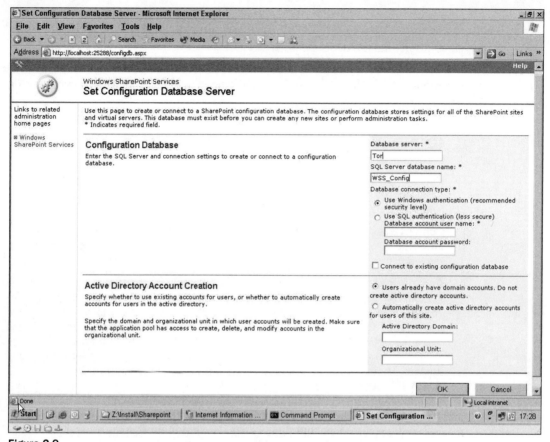

Figure 2-9

17. On the following page you have lots of important options for the content database you are about to create; make sure to fill in the correct values in these sections:

❑ **Application Pool:** If you want to use an existing application pool, you must use the drop-down menu. The recommendation is to create a new application pool, so that you can avoid conflict with any other web application on this server. If so, you must give it a name, for example WSSAppPool, and select the security account it will use. If you want you can use the built-in Network Service account, or any another user account you might prefer. This account does not need access into the SQL Server database, because this is done by the security account defined for the administrative application pool.

❑ **Site Owner:** Enter the user account and e-mail address that will be the owner of this WSS environment, and therefore have full control of it. Avoid personal user accounts; choose a role-based account if possible, such as WSS_Admin. If so, remember to create that account before completing this page!

❑ **Database Information:** If you want to use a separate content database or database server for this new WSS environment, uncheck "Use default content database server" and enter the name for the server and the content database. The default is to use the same server as for the configuration database.

❑ **Security Configuration:** Select what type of authentication mechanism you want to use. Note that the default is Kerberos, which requires that you have configured your Kerberos settings; if not you will not be able to run this new WSS environment. Change to NTLM if you are not sure you want to run Kerberos! You will in fact be warned if you select Kerberos, just to make sure you don't select it by mistake.

❑ **Custom URL:** Enter the URL address to this new WSS. It will be relative to the server name; for example, if your server is referred to as E2K3Base and you enter the value **/home**, you will then reach this WSS environment by the URL `http://E2K3Base/home`. Note that you can leave this field as it is; this will result in the URL address `http://E2K3base` alone.

❑ **Quota Template:** You can configure this WSS environment to limit its maximum disk size by selecting a disk quota template. Because this is a new WSS installation, you will not have any template and must accept the default No Quota.

❑ **Site Language:** As mentioned before, WSS is available in more than 30 different languages. If you have installed any extra WSS language packs, you can now choose what language the first web site will use. By default you will only see the language of your WSS setup package (English).

Click OK when ready to save this configuration. This will complete the creation of the new WSS content database.

18. When the process is done, you will get the Virtual Server Successfully Extended page. Click OK to continue.

19. On the next page you will find a number of general configuration settings for this new WSS server. You learn more about these in the next chapter.

20. Test your new WSS virtual server by using a browser and going to the URL for this site: `http://E2K3Base` in this example. If you are logged on to the WSS server, you can also use the URL `http://localhost`.

The first time you go to this URL, you will see a page where you are requested to select a template for the new web site. You will learn a lot more about this later, but for now it is enough to know that a web site template defines the initial look and feel of this new WSS user web site. For now, select the Team Site template and click OK to open the new site to see what it looks like.

Upgrading WMSDE to MS SQL Server

Many organizations start investigating what WSS can do by installing WSS using a local WMSDE database. The idea is often to run a pilot project. More often than not, this pilot project then incidentally turns into a production environment, with lots of important data that cannot be discarded. I am sure you don't belong to such an organization, but you probably know somebody else who does, right? Well, you can tell your friend that it is possible to move up from the WMSDE database to the MS SQL Server, so there is no need to worry.

Chapter 2

You have two types of possible upgrade scenarios:

❑   An in-place upgrade of WMSDE to a local MS SQL Server.

❑   Moving from WMSDE to a separate MS SQL Server.

The first scenario is straightforward: Simply run the MS SQL Server to upgrade WMSDE. The other scenario are more complicated, but not impossible. You might remember from earlier sections in this chapter that a remote SQL Server gives you better performance and also makes it possible to build a fault-tolerant MS SQL Server cluster. You will find all the steps for each upgrade scenario in the following sections.

Preparing to Upgrade Your WMSDE

The first and most important thing to remember is to back up your current WSS data. You are about to perform a very sensitive operation, and if something goes wrong, you must be sure you can go back to the previous version.

If it is a simple server configuration with just the WSS and the WMSDE database, you can of course perform a full Windows 2003 Server backup, including the System State (the local Registry, the IIS Metabase, and the Boot files). The other option is to make a backup of the Content database alone to make sure you have all data intact in case the upgrade to MS SQL for some reason does not work as expected.

Doing a Full Server Backup

The first option, doing a full server backup, is always a good idea even if you will do a separate database backup later. This option ensures that you can do a complete restore of the Windows 2003 Server, including the WSS environment and all its data. You can use the backup utility that comes with Windows 2003 Server for this operation, if you want. See the following steps:

Try It Out   Do a Full Server Backup

1.   Log on as an administrator to the WSS server. Make sure no one will use this server during the backup procedure.

2.   Choose Start⇨All Programs⇨Accessories⇨System Tools⇨Backup.

3.   This starts the backup program in Wizard mode (unless you previously have unchecked that option), which is fine for your purpose this time. Click Next.

4.   Make sure the following page has the following option selected: Backup files and settings. Click Next.

5.   On the page What to back up, make sure you select the option All information on this computer. Note that this makes a complete backup of all data on this disk. It also creates a system recovery disk that makes it possible to restore all data in case of a major failure. Click Next.

6.   On the page Backup Type, Destination and Name, choose where to store this backup file and give it a proper name, such as Full WSS Server Backup; click Next to go on.

You need a diskette to complete this backup operation. With this diskette you can later boot up the server and it will do a complete restore of the server!

7. On the next page you see a summary of your options. If it is okay, click Finish to close this page and start the backup procedure.

Of course you can use whatever backup routine you normally run for your computers instead of this procedure. Just make sure it is a complete backup, including the System State.

There is one drawback to this type of backup procedure: You will only be able to do a complete restore, if necessary. For example, you cannot just restore the WSS content database. That is why the second backup option is interesting.

Doing a File Backup of the WSS Databases

Once again, you have two options for this. You can simply stop the WMSDE database and make a file copy of all the database files, or you can use the STSADM tool that comes along with WSS for backing up parts or the entire content database.

There are lots of good and very cheap backup applications for all types of MS SQL databases, including WMSDE. For example, check out www.simego.com *and* www.msde.biz. *You can also use a local copy of the MS SQL Enterprise Manager.*

Try It Out   Copy All WSS Database Files Manually

To make a simple file copy, do this:

1. Stop the service MSSQL$SHAREPOINT (choose Start⇨Administrative Tools⇨Services).

2. Copy the files in C:\Program Files\Microsoft SQL Server\MSSQL$SHAREPOINT\Data. (There may be more than one database in WMSDE; if you just want to copy the WSS config and content databases, look for all files starting with STS_.)

3. Start the MSSQL$SHAREPOINT service again.

If you need to restore these database files after a failed MS SQL upgrade procedure, make sure to have a working WSS and WMSDE installation and then copy the STS_ files back to the original file location.

Doing a Backup of the Content Database

This method is very fast and selective. You will only back up the content for the WSS environment. The result will be files that can be used to migrate into any WSS or even SPS environment. The tool you must use here is STSADM.EXE. It is stored deep down in the file system, or to be exact, in this folder:

```
C:\Program Files\Common Files\Microsoft Shared\web server extensions\60\BIN
```

This is a command-based tool that you need to run in a command window. You will often need to access STSADM and other tools in this folder, and instead of entering the full path to these tools every time, it is easier to configure Windows to search in this folder directly. If you are old enough to remember when MS-DOS ruled the computer world, you might recollect there is a system variable named PATH. When you enter a program name in a command window, Windows looks for that file in all file paths defined in this variable. This is how to add the path to STSADM to this system variable:

Try It Out   **Update the PATH System Variable**

1. Start Windows Explorer and navigate to the path for the STSADM as given previously. Right-click the file path in the Address field and select Copy.

2. Click Start to see the Windows start menu.

3. Right-click My Computer and select Properties.

4. Switch to the Advanced tab and click its Environment Variables button.

5. In the lower pane named System Variables, locate PATH and click Edit.

6. Go to the end of the current list in Variable value (use the End key or the right arrow on the keyboard). Type in a semicolon (;) as a separator, and paste the path you copied in step 1. Then click OK three times to save this modification and close all dialog boxes.

7. Test it by opening a command window (Start⇨Run and type **Cmd**); type **STSADM** in this command window. If you get a long list of options, you did it right. If not, repeat these steps and make sure to do it exactly as described.

By now you have access to STSADM and the other tools in the same folder, regardless of where you are in the folder tree. But before you can perform your backup, you must know how it works. Every web site you create in WSS is either a top site or a subsite. Top sites are the start of a tree with any number of nested subsites, much like a top folder and subfolders in a file system. STSADM will help you back up a given top site, including all its subsites.

When you first installed WSS, the first top site was automatically created. Later, you will learn how to create new top sites and subsites for each of these top sites. To make it simple, say you only have one top site, with five subsites. The URL address for this top site is `http://e2k3base`, and you want to back up this complete site structure to a file named `WSS-back.bak` in the folder `C:\Bkup`. To do this, follow these steps:

Try It Out   **Use STSADM to Back Up a Site Structure**

1. Log on to the WSS server as an administrator.

2. Open a command window, type in the following text, and press Enter:

```
Stsadm -o Backup -url http://e2k3base -filename c:\bkup\wss-back.bak
```

3. When the backup is done, you will see the file `wss-back.bak` in the folder `C:\bkup`.

Upgrading WSS to a Local MS SQL Server

By now you have your WSS environment backed up. It is time to upgrade your WMSDE database to the full MS SQL 2005 Server. As said before, this is a very straightforward process. The only thing is to make sure no one is using the system before you start to upgrade. Follow these steps to upgrade the database:

Try It Out   **Upgrade WSS to a Local MS SQL 2000 Server**

1. Log on to the WSS server as an administrator.

2. Make sure no one is using the WSS system.

   Make sure the Windows 2003 Server is updated with Service Pack 1 or later if you want to upgrade to MS SQL Server 2005!

3. Mount the MS SQL 2000 Server CD. You automatically see a dialog box where you can start the installation or start the SETUP program directly from the CD.

4. Select to install MS SQL on a Local server, and click Next.

5. Select the option "Upgrade, Remove, or Add Components to an Existing Instance of SQL Server" and click Next.

6. Make sure the Instance Name is SharePoint and click Next.

7. You see a summary of your selected actions. Make sure the option Upgrade your existing installation is set and then click Next to go on.

8. Check the box that says "Yes, Upgrade my programs" and click Next.

9. Choose your type of license model. Then click Next.

10. Click Yes to install additional components like the Enterprise Manager and Full Text Search. Click Next two times to start the actual upgrade and installation process.

11. When the installation is done, restart the server if requested to do so.

12. Finally, install the latest service pack for the MS SQL Server from MS SQL home page: `http://www.microsoft.com/sql/download`.

13. Check your WSS environment. Make sure it works like before. You should see no differences, except possibly better performance. Open the MS SQL Server Enterprise Manager, and take a look at the databases for the local server. You should see two databases beginning with STS. If so, you are done with this upgrade from WMSDE to MS SQL Server. If not, something is wrong, in which case you must restore the WMSDE environment and retry this upgrade process.

Migrating WSS to a Remote MS SQL Server

This is the most complicated upgrade process, because you need to reconfigure WSS to use another computer as the database server. Actually, this is more of a migration process than an upgrade process. Before starting this process it is very important to make sure you have a working backup! This is a very long and complicated process that requires you to run scripts as well as configure the SharePoint and MS SQL environment. Use the following Microsoft article to get the complete instructions: `http://www.microsoft.com/resources/documentation/wss/2/all/adminguide/en-us/stsf17.mspx?mfr=true`.

Uninstalling WSS

The final section of this chapter is about removing WSS. You can select to remove just WSS, or WSS and the databases. If the databases remain, you can later reinstall WSS and reconnect to these databases.

Uninstalling WSS but Leaving the Database Files

This process removes WSS from a given virtual IIS server, but it does not remove the binary files from the server. For example, you may have a test environment using one virtual IIS server and a production WSS using another virtual IIS server on the same physical Windows 2003 Server.

To remove the test environment, follow these steps:

1. Restart SharePoint Central Administration.

2. Click the link Configure virtual server settings.

3. Click the virtual server used by WSS.

4. Click the link Remove Windows SharePoint Service from Virtual Server.

5. Select Remove without deleting content databases.

   This step is very important to do properly. If you accidentally delete the content databases, the only way to get them back is by performing a restore of the database!

6. Click OK.

The virtual IIS server is now free to use for other web applications. If you have another virtual IIS server that is configured (Expanded) for WSS, it will continue to work.

Removing WSS Completely

A more drastic method is to remove WSS completely from the Windows 2003 Server. This does not actually remove the database, be it the WMSDE or the MS SQL Server. If you want to remove these database engines, you must do this separately.

To remove WSS completely from a Windows 2003 Server, follow these steps:

1. Select Start⇨Control Panel⇨Add or Remove Programs.

2. Click the Microsoft Windows SharePoint Services 2.0 and then click the Remove button.

3. Complete the removal process. WSS is now gone!

4. Check to see if there are other WSS-related applications that also should be removed (for example, Office 2003 Web Parts or any third-party add-on).

5. If you also want to remove the database engine, locate its name and click Remove.

Note that there is no way to automatically remove both the WSS and the WMSDE database engines at the same time, although they were automatically installed in the same process.

When you remove WSS, you also remove the virtual IIS server used by the WSS administrative web site, along with its application pool. However, the Default Web Site remains after the installation, along with its application pool.

Summary

In this chapter you learned the following:

- ❏ STS was the previous version of WSS. You will still today find lots of references to the acronym STS, although it actually refers to WSS.

- ❏ Make sure you know what SharePoint edition you need: stand-alone WSS or WSS with SPS.

- ❏ Make sure you know what database engine you need: WMSDE or MS SQL Server (2000 or 2005).

- ❏ WSS needs Service Pack 2 or later to install MS SQL Server 2005.

- ❏ There are three types of WSS configurations:

  - ❏ WSS with a local WMSDE database.

  - ❏ WSS with a local MS SQL Server database.

  - ❏ WSS with a remote MS SQL Server database.

- ❏ Using WSS with WMSDE needs no special Client Access License besides the usual Windows 2003 Server CALs.

- ❏ The term *single server* means a SharePoint installation with a local database.

- ❏ The term *small farm* means one SharePoint server and a separate MS SQL Server.

- ❏ MS Small Business Server Standard Edition comes with one WSS and WMSDE.

- ❏ MS Small Business Server Premium Edition comes with one WSS and MS SQL Server.

- ❏ With at least 512 MB of memory you can actually set up a WSS production environment for at least 100 people.

  - ❏ There is a formula you can use to calculate the number of OPS (operations per second).

  - ❏ A single server with WSS and WMSDE on a 1-GB server and a 2.8-GHz CPU may be used for up to an organization with 20,000 users.

- ❏ It is the documents and files that fill up the main part of the database. The other data types are small in comparison. Make sure to always have at least 50 percent free disk space on the database disk.

- ❏ You need IIS and ASP.NET on a Windows 2003 Server to install WSS.

- ❏ Application pools are private virtual areas that the web application uses for its needs. If something goes wrong with the web application, it does not affect applications in other application pools.

- ❏ IIS 6.0 supports up to 9 virtual IIS servers with individual application pools or 99 virtual servers sharing the same application pool.

❑ WSS uses two types of databases: the config and the content databases.

    ❑ The config database stores configuration settings and connections between the WSS and the SQL database server. There is always only one config database. Its default name is STS_Config.

    ❑ The content database stores all the data, including all documents, web pages, and more. One content database may support more than 15,000 web sites, and you can have as many content databases as you need. The default name for the first database is STS_<server name>_1.

❑ The file STSV2.EXE is the complete WSS installation package. It can be downloaded from Microsoft's web site.

    ❑ You can expand the STSV2.EXE package. It results in a number of files, including the true installation file for WSS, named SETUPSTS.

    ❑ By default, WSS always installs into the virtual IIS server Default Web Site.

    ❑ Use SETUPSTS Provision=No if you need to control exactly how WSS will be installed.

❑ The tool STSADM.EXE comes with WSS and can be used for many things, including creating web sites and application pools.

❑ Starting from Service Pack 2 for WSS, you can select between Kerberos or NTLM authentication. The recommendation is to use NTLM unless the Kerberos system is fully configured in your system.

❑ Each application pool uses a security account that regulates what the web applications using this application pool can do. You can use any user account or built-in accounts such as Network Service.

❑ The application pool security account needs to be a member of the Security Administrators and the Database Creators role in the MS SQL Server.

❑ Upgrading a WMSDE database engine to a local MS SQL Server is very easy. Simply perform an in-place upgrade.

❑ Upgrading WMSDE to a remote MS SQL Server is very complex. Avoid it if you can by planning your server needs before installing WSS in the first place.

❑ There are several ways of performing a backup procedure for a WMSDE database. You can use tools like STSADM, install the SQL Server Client Tools to get the Enterprise Manager, or purchase third-party backup tools.

❑ To completely uninstall WSS from a computer, use Add or Remove Programs. But this will not remove any database engines.

❑ To remove the database engine, such as WMSDE or the MS SQL Server, you must use Add or Remove Programs separately.

In the next chapter you learn more about how to configure Windows SharePoint Services.

Configuring and Managing Windows SharePoint Services

In the previous chapter you learned the different installation scenarios available and how to set up WSS to work with either a WMSDE or MS SQL Server. In this chapter you learn more about configuring and managing an installed WSS, including how to activate and configure the search feature. In order to successfully manage the WSS environment, you need to understand important concepts, such as web sites, site collections, and the security model. The objective in this chapter is to give you the knowledge needed to set up the WSS environment so that it will match the needs of your users.

Before you start configuring WSS, check to see if your server has the Internet Explorer Enhanced Security Configuration setting activated, because this may cause a strange problem. You will find this setting in the Windows Components Wizard (see Figure 3-1), accessed via the Add or Remove Programs applet in the Control Panel.

If this setting is active, you may have problems performing SharePoint administrative tasks on the WSS server itself, depending on how your Internet Explorer is configured. If the WSS virtual server is defined as something other than the zones Local Sites or Trusted Sites, you will not be able to run scripts or execute code necessary for some parts of the SharePoint administration. The effect will be that on remote clients you can do everything, whereas on the WSS server itself you will experience problems. You can solve this in two ways:

❑　Uninstall Internet Explorer Enhanced Security.

❑　Define the URL to the virtual IIS server that WSS uses as a Trusted Site in Internet Explorer.

The last option is the most secure. By default, your WSS virtual server should be listed as a trusted site. If it isn't, you can adjust that by following these steps:

1.　Open Internet Explorer.

2.　Go to Tools⇨Internet Options⇨Security.

3.　Click Trusted Sites and the Sites button.

4.　Add the URL address for your virtual server (for example, `http://e2k3base`) as a trusted site.

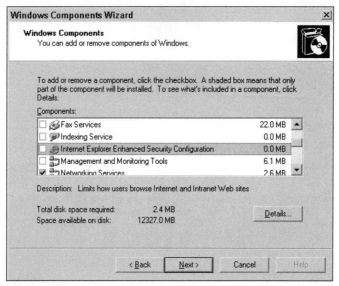

Figure 3-1

> If the WSS sites don't use SSL encryptions, you must first uncheck "require server
> verification (https:) for all sites in this zone."

Important Concepts

WSS is a web application. It uses web sites and web-related concepts to do its job. Some of these terms
and functionality may be well known to you already. But some have very specific meanings in the
SharePoint environment. You may recall from previous chapters that WSS is the basic foundation for
SharePoint and that there is an optional extension called SharePoint Portal Server (SPS). Even if you
implement WSS and SPS together, you will still need the information in this chapter to understand how
the WSS part works.

> To help you determine whether you should use WSS with or without SPS, consult
> Chapter 7, "Comparing WSS and SPS."

Administrative Web Sites and User Web Sites

SharePoint has two types of web sites:

❑   The administrative web site is used for more advanced configuration and management
of WSS.

❑ The user web site (also known as the team site, project site, and meeting workspace) contains the actual information that is shared between users, such as documents, lists, and images. There can be as many of these web sites as needed.

One important distinction between these two types of web sites is that only a SharePoint administrator will use the administrative web site, whereas everyone will use the user web sites. As you may remember from Chapter 2, these two web sites use two different virtual IIS servers:

❑ **SharePoint Central Administration:** Used by the administrative web site and runs in its own application pool (default name: StsAdminAppPool).

❑ **Default Web Site:** Used by the user web site and runs in a separate application pool (default name: StsAppPool1). Note that the name for this virtual server may be different if you created a separate virtual server for this use.

If you, for any reason, need to stop all users from accessing the WSS environment, just stop the Default Web Site (or whatever virtual IIS server the user web site uses) by using the IIS Manager tool in the Start⇨Administrative Tools program folder.

The Administrative Web Site

You have already used the administrative web site in Chapter 2. This web site allows the administrator to do more advanced administration and configuration of the WSS environment, such as extend a virtual server, configure the content databases, and define what database server to use. In this chapter you learn about all the important configuration settings available in this web site and how to make the most out of your WSS environment.

SharePoint has its own security system that makes sure only users with the proper permissions are able to access the administrative web site. As an extra security feature, this web site uses a randomly selected port number, known as the *administrative port*, that you must know in order to access it. This port number is set during the installation but can be changed later by following these steps:

Try It Out   **Change the TCP Port Number for the Admin Site**

1. Log on as an administrator to the WSS server.

2. Open the Internet Information Services Manager.

3. Expand the Web Sites node.

4. Right-click Central SharePoint Administration and select Properties.

5. Look at the Web Site tab in the TCP Port box. It should display a number higher than 1023, as shown in Figure 3-2.

6. Change the number to any port number above 1023. Click OK to save and close.

7. Update the link to the SharePoint Central Administration tool with the new port number.

    a. Choose Start⇨Administrative Tools.

    b. Right-click SharePoint Central Administration.

    c. Select Properties.

    d. Change the port number in the URL field.

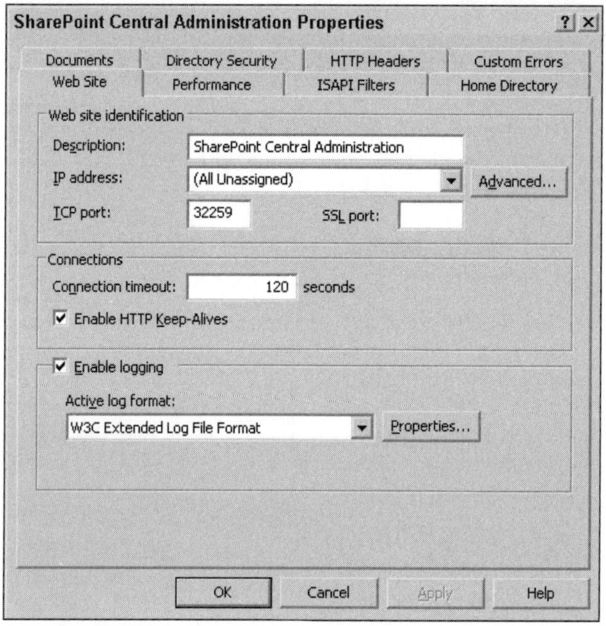

Figure 3-2

You have several ways of accessing this administrative web site, assuming that you have the proper permission. The easiest way is to use the Windows 2003 startup folder, Start⊅Administrative Tools, and click SharePoint Central Administration. Another way is to open this web site directly by using a browser. This requires that first you know the administrative port. Assuming that the port number is 32259 (as in Figure 3-2), you can open the web site using the URL address `http://localhost:32259`, as shown in Figure 3-3.

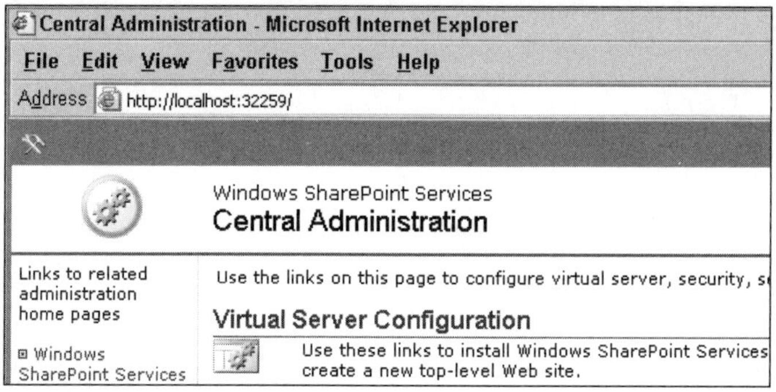

Figure 3-3

Be sure to protect this administrative web site. If a malicious user can access it, that user can remove content or even remove WSS from the virtual IIS server. But to do this, the malicious user would have to both learn the administrative port number and get access to the web site.

> Use Secure Socket Layer (SSL) to protect the administrative site if you need Internet access. If you don't need Internet access to this site, configure your firewall to prohibit access to the administrative port.

The User Web Sites

This is where the action is! These web sites are the foundation for creating shared web pages, team collaborations, departmental intranets, project sites, and so on. When you installed WSS using the default installation method (as described in Chapter 2), your first user web site was created automatically. It should look like the one in Figure 3-4.

The name of this default site, which is ready to be used, is Team Web Site. The only user who can access this site now is the user account you used when installing WSS. But you can grant access to any number of users or groups, each with individual permission settings, if required.

Note the URL address displayed in the Address field of Figure 3-4:

```
http://e2k3base/default.aspx.
```

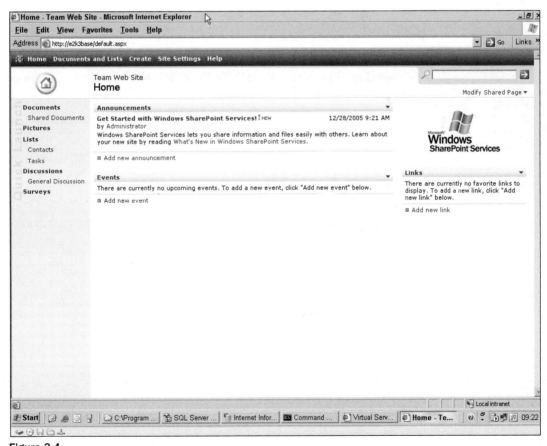

Figure 3-4

In this example, the WSS server name is E2K3Base. The suffix .aspx indicates that this is an ASP.NET application. On the top of the web page is a blue menu bar, with links to different parts of this web site:

❑ **Home:** Takes you to the start page for this web site (that is, the page in Figure 3-4).

❑ **Documents and Lists:** Shows a web page with all created document libraries, lists, and subsites.

❑ **Create:** Shows a web page where you can create new document libraries, lists, and subsites.

❑ **Site Settings:** Shows you the local administration page for this web site (see Figure 3-5).

Note that the local administration page is not equal to the administrative web site mentioned earlier in this chapter. The local administration page is where you configure access to this site, change its description, and work with templates, just to mention a few things. This type of administration is covered in detail in Chapters 9, 10, and 11.

> **Whatever page you are looking at, click Home to go back to the start page.**

On the left side of the home page is the *quick launch bar*, which contains links to lists and libraries in this web site. Later, you will learn how to use and configure the quick launch bar.

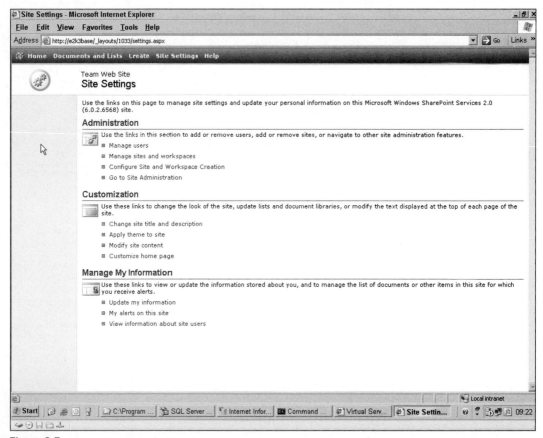

Figure 3-5

The home page shows some information directly, such as lists named Announcements, Events, and Links. It also shows a picture of the WSS logotype. All of these elements (and many more) are referred to as *web parts*. A web part is the basic building block for designing SharePoint sites. A typical web part is a rectangular area that displays some information, such as contact lists, a list of documents, or an external web site. You learn a lot more about web parts in Chapter 8.

At the upper right, just under the blue menu bar, is the Modify Shared Page menu. This menu has several options for modifying the look and feel of the home page, including adding new web parts to suit your needs. Chapter 8 explains in detail how to use this feature when designing this web page.

Top Sites, Subsites, and Site Collections

For each WSS installation, you have at least one *top site* like the one you just investigated. Under this top site, you can create new sites, referred to as *subsites*. Each subsite may, in turn, have its own subsite, creating a tree similar to a file system in which the top site is the root. If you need more than one top site, you can create a new one using the WSS administration web site, which creates the root for a new site tree. Figure 3-6 shows an example with two top sites that have several subsites each.

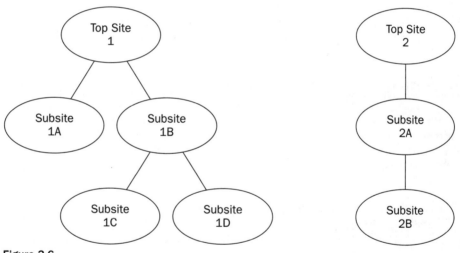

Figure 3-6

Each top site, including any optional subsites, is referred to as a *site collection*. There can be only one top site in each site collection, but there can be any number of subsites. Some configuration settings are special for given site collections, such as the following:

❑   Inheritance of permission settings.

❑   Site groups.

❑   Ownership and full access to all subsites.

❑   Creation and use of templates for web sites, lists, and web parts.

❑   Usage statistics.

❑   Site hierarchy.

You can copy some things (such as templates) from one site collection to another, but you should think of each site collection as an isolated island. For example, you could be the administrator in site collection A but still have no access whatsoever to site collection B. This is often exactly what different departments require: "We want our own SharePoint environment, without any possibility that someone belonging to another department can access our information!"

SharePoint uses the term *web site* for each web page within a site collection. Another term you will see is *workspaces*. The only difference between the two is the layout. You still have the same features and administration as with any other web site.

The reason for these two names is interesting. The development team for WSS has used the term "web site" since the beginning. However, when Office 2003 was released, it was designed to be integrated with WSS. One new feature in MS Office 2003 was that it could create web sites for working with documents, and MS Outlook 2003 could create web sites for meetings. But the MS Office team did not find the term "web site" very descriptive and intuitive, so they chose the new term "workspace" instead. So whenever you see the term "workspace," understand that it is "a web site created by MS Office."

The Security Mechanism

SharePoint keeps track of its own security settings. However, you still manage security by controlling how access is granted to different accounts. You need to be concerned with two types of security settings: user web sites and administrative web sites.

Security Settings for User Web Sites

You can grant any individual user account, from a domain or a local server account, access to all or parts of SharePoint. You can also grant access to security groups (domain or local). You can even grant access to distribution groups. Because distribution groups are used as mail groups, though, they cannot be used for security settings; so whenever you add such a group, SharePoint expands the group and adds its members instead.

> **If you later modify the distribution group membership, it will not affect SharePoint's access settings.**

Each user or group must belong to a *site group* in SharePoint in order to get access. It is possible to add a user without making her a member of a site group but she will not get access. By default, you will find the following site groups in WSS:

❑ **Reader:** Can read, copy, and print documents, files, and list content in a user web site.

❑ **Contributor:** Can also create, modify, and delete documents, files, and list content.

❑ **Web Designer:** Can change the color of the page, add and modify web parts, and create new document libraries and lists, plus everything the Contributor can do.

❑ **Administrator:** Has full access to everything, including security settings and local management of the web site.

Later in this chapter you learn how to change these default site groups as well as create new ones.

Security Settings for the Administrative Web Site

The previous section described how the user web site works. But how do you modify the inner guts of WSS? You may remember that the account used during the installation may also be the only account that can access the administrative web site. But this is not completely true!

Assume that Anna is the only user who can access the administrative web site. In other words, she is the SharePoint Goddess. By mistake, you happen to delete her user account. Before anyone notices, you create a new one, with the exact same name and password. Will Anna still be able to use the administrative web site? No! Because you have created a new account, you also have a new *Security ID* (SID), although with the same name. But SharePoint has granted administrative access to the old SID for Anna, so she cannot come in.

How do you solve this? Well, you can't unless you do a restore of the user account. Is there an easier way? Yes! Your escape route out of this misery is the fact that every user who is a member of the WSS server's local Administrators group automatically has full and unlimited access to all of WSS! The solution is to add Anna to this group.

The important thing for you to understand that everyone — every user and every member of a domain group — who is also a member of the local Administrators group is a SharePoint God or Goddess. And by default, the domain group Domain Admins is always a member of every computer in the domain. This results in the fact that every member of Domain Admins has full access to every part of SharePoint, including all user web sites. Is this really what you want?

> Make sure that the local Administrators group contains only users and groups that should have full access to all parts of SharePoint!

But there is also another way of granting administrative access to WSS. You can create a security group and grant this group administrative access by using the SharePoint Central Administration tool, using the following steps:

Try It Out   Define the SharePoint Administrative Group

1.   Log on as an administrator to the WSS server.

2.   Open the SharePoint Central Administration tool (in Start⇨Administration Tools).

3.   Click Set SharePoint Administration Group in the Security Configuration.

4.   Enter the group account name and click OK.

This group can do most (but not all) of the things a full SharePoint administrator can do. For example, this group cannot do the following:

❏   Extend a virtual IIS server to host WSS sites.

❏   Remove WSS from a virtual IIS server.

❏   Configure managed paths (that is, what URL paths WSS owns).

❏   Change the SharePoint Administrative Group.

❏   Change the Configuration database settings.

Chapter 3

- ❑ Manage the database server or the content database.

- ❑ Enable full-text searching.

- ❑ Configure the virtual IIS server SharePoint Central Administration.

- ❑ Use the STSADM.EXE tool.

But this group *can* perform administrative actions, such as using the administrative web site to view and manage all available web sites in this WSS environment, including reading any document, changing list content, and creating new content. Because this group can also create new sites and delete any web site, it is a very powerful group. You should think hard about what people you want to be members of it.

Beginning SharePoint Administration

This section describes the most common tasks you will perform as a full administrator for a fresh WSS installation. You also learn the basics of how the security works for sites and content. The objective here is to give you the basic information needed to set up a fully functional WSS environment. At this moment, it does not matter whether you've chosen a WMSDE or MS SQL database, or whether it is a local or remote database engine.

Creating Your First Sites

The first thing you most likely want to do is to create new sites. After all, this is where all files, lists, and other information will be stored.

You got your first top site and, therefore, the first site collection when you installed WSS. This top site is called the team web site, and its URL address is http://E2K3Base/default.aspx (that is, the name of the Windows 2003 server). The suffix /default.aspx is simply the page you are looking at now, in this web site.

You can create a subsite to this team web site by using the following steps:

Try It Out	Create a Subsite

1. Log on to any computer in the network as a SharePoint administrator. (The Administrator account is the only user account that has access to the team web site at the moment. Later in this chapter, you will see how to add more users.). Start the web browser and open the URL address to your new SharePoint site (for example, http://E2K3Base).

2. Click Create on the blue menu bar. This gives you a page that shows all types of objects you can create for this web site, including document libraries, contact lists, and subsites.

3. Click Web Pages to the left. This takes you to the end of this long page (or you can scroll down manually, if you prefer).

4. Click Sites and Workspaces.

5. The next page is a web form where you define the new subsite, as you can see in Figure 3-7. Fill in the following fields:

   - ❑ **Title:** Enter the title for this site. Spaces and any Unicode characters, such as Å and Ü, are okay here. You can change this text later, if necessary.

❑ **Description:** Enter a description of the site. It will be displayed on the web page. You can change this text later.

❑ **URL name:** Enter the web URL address for this site. Note that the prefix is inherited from the parent of this subsite and cannot be changed; in this example, it's `http://e2k3base/`. Although it is okay to use blank spaces and 8-bit characters here, you should avoid using them to prevent problems or strange URL addresses later on. For example, if you create an URL with the name `http://E2K3Base//räksmörgås` it will actually be listed as the URL `http://spsrv1/r%C3%A4ksm%C3%B6rg%C3%A5s`. It is also a good thing to keep the name of this URL as short as possible, while still making it descriptive. This will make it easier for you to later type in this address manually, if you want to.

❑ **User Permissions:** This option allows you to inherit the user permissions from the parent web site (that is, the team web site), which also is the default. You can also choose to use unique permission settings for this web site. The advantage of inherited permissions is that, if you later modify the permission settings for the top site, these new settings will also be used in the subsite. Whatever you choose, you can later switch it to the other option.

Click Create to start the process to create this site. This is normally complete in a matter of seconds.

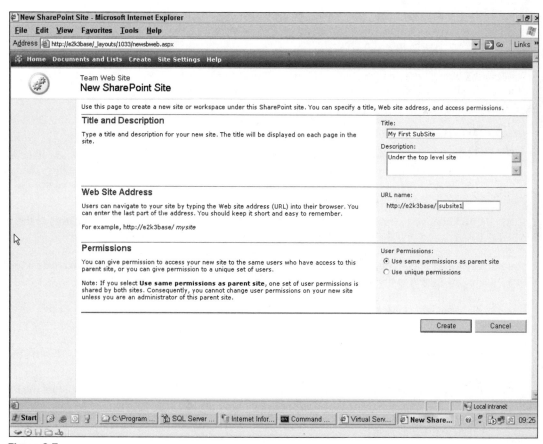

Figure 3-7

6. At this moment, the web site is actually created, but it does not yet have its appearance. The page you see now gives you a list of different styles; in SharePoint terms, these are referred to as *site templates*. There are initially eight templates, but you can (and later will) create new templates with the exact look you need.

   Select Team Site for this site and click OK to see how this site template looks.

Take a look at this new subsite. Does it not look very similar to the top site? It has the same color, the same web parts, and the same lists. It *should* look exactly like the other web site because it is built on the same site template! Look at the top-right corner of the page: It says Up to Team Web Site. From this, you can tell that the current site is a subsite and its parent is the Team Web Site. Another indication that this is a subsite is the URL address: `http://e2k3base/subsite1` (again, you skip `/default.aspx` because this is the web page you are looking at right now). When you understand how to read the URL address, you can directly see where in the site tree a given web site is situated.

Click Up to Team Web Site to go back to the parent (and in this case top) site. Look carefully to understand which site you are looking at. Check the URL: `http://e2k3base`. This is the proof you need that you are at the top site again.

But how can you go back down to the subsite? Well, one of the shortcomings of SharePoint 2003 is that — remarkably — it does not come with a site tree view! But this problem is easy to fix. Several very good web parts can give you a site tree view; some are free, some aren't. In Chapter 8 you learn how to install and manage web parts, including the site tree view.

By default you must follow these few steps to list and go to subsites:

Try It Out   List and Go to a Subsite

1. On the top site, click Documents and Lists in the blue menu bar.

2. On the left of the following page, click Sites under the heading See also. You now see all subsites directly under the current site. At the moment, you have only your single subsite there, named "My First SubSite." If you hover your cursor over it, you can see its URL address: `http://e2k3base/subsite1`. Click it to go to this subsite now.

3. Check that you actually are looking at the subsite now. You have two clear indicators of this: the URL address and the name at the top of the web site page.

You need an easier way to find this subsite from the top site. One way of solving this is to create a link to this subsite and store it in the top site, like this:

1. Right-click the URL address `http://e2k3base/subsite1/default` and select Copy.

2. Go back to the top site by clicking the link Up To Team Web Site.

3. In the Team Web Site you can find a web part with the name Links; under it, click the link that says Add new link.

4. In the resulting form (see Figure 3-8), right-click the URL field and select Paste to store the full URL address to the subsite. Enter a description (such as My First SubSite), and then click Save and Close.

5. Test the new link My First SubSite; it should take you directly to the subsite.

If you need to create a subsite under the current subsite, you do it in exactly the same way you did the first time. You can have any number of levels in your site collections, and each level can have any number of sites in parallel, as long as you give sites in the same level unique URL names. Remember that the names must be meaningful — if your users cannot easily find the site they need at the moment, something is wrong with either your structure or the way these sites are accessed.

Figure 3-8

Creating a New Top Site

Now that you know how to create subsites, the next step is to learn to create new top sites. This is a bit trickier because there is no easy-to-use link for this, but this problem can also be solved. In this section, you first see how to create a site using the SharePoint Central Administration (SCA) tool, and then learn how to display a link on the first top site that will allow anyone with the proper permission to create new top sites.

Creating a Top Site Using the SharePoint Central Admin Tool

Initially, this is the only way of creating a new top site in WSS. You must be an administrator (that is, a member of the local Administrators group on the WSS server) or a member of the SharePoint Administrators Group, if it exists. Follow these steps to create a new top site:

Try It Out   **Create a New Top Site Using the SCA Tool**

1. Start the SCA tool (Start⊅Administrative Tools⊅SharePoint Central Administration).

2. Click Create a Top-level Web site in the Virtual Server Configuration section.

3. Click the virtual IIS server for this WSS environment (usually the Default Web Site).

4. On the following web form (see Figure 3-9), you can define the URL name and owners for the new top site. There are several important settings here. Some can be changed afterward, and some cannot:

   ❑ **Web Site Address:** Cannot be changed. You can choose to give this new top site a URL under the first top site by selecting the option "Create site under this URL." For example, if you give the new top site the name top2, its complete URL address is then `http://e2k3base/sites/top2`. Note that the URL path designation "sites" is automatically added as a string that separates the first top site from any other top sites. This is known as a *wildcard inclusion URL path.* In other words, if you ever find a site with the URL address `http://e2k3base/sites/sales`, you know that this is a top site with the name "sales" and it was created after the first top site.

You can create other intrinsic URL paths, if needed, by clicking the Define Managed Paths link in the text to the left. (Note that this will take you away from the current page. You may want to right-click that link and select "Open in new window" to avoid leaving this page.) On this page, you can define new included URL paths of wildcard inclusion and explicit inclusion types.

The other option for the web site address is "Create site at this URL" with the URL path of "(root)." This option will not be valid unless you have created a new URL path of the explicit inclusion type. For example, if you have an explicit inclusion URL path named "Saturn," you can create a new top site with a URL address that begins with `http://e2k3base/Saturn`. SharePoint uses explicit inclusions to define the URL paths that it controls in case there are other web applications on this server. By using wildcard inclusions you can tell SharePoint that all URL addresses below a given address will be SharePoint sites. For example, the wildcard inclusion `http://E2K3Base/sites/*` says that every URL that starts with `http://E2K3Base/Sites` will point to a SharePoint site.

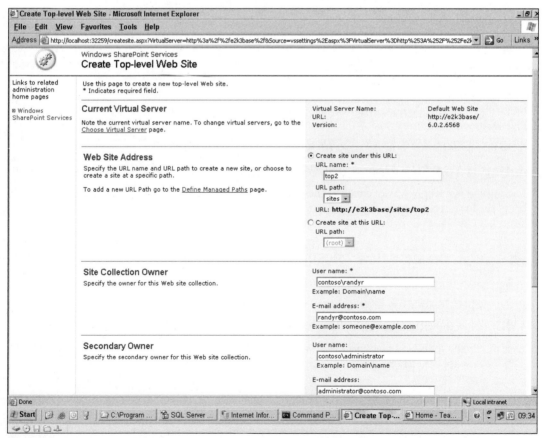

Figure 3-9

❑ **Site Collection Owner:** Can be changed later. Enter the user account and e-mail address for the owner of this top site. This will also affect all subsites in this site collection. You cannot prohibit a top site owner access to any of its subsites, regardless of the permission settings.

❑ **Secondary Owner:** Can be changed later. This is an optional owner, who, like the first owner, also has "divine" access to all sites in this site collection. Enter the user account and e-mail address, if any, for this secondary owner. In Chapter 6 you will see how WSS can help you clean up unused web sites by sending an e-mail to the owners and offering to remove these sites. If you have two owners, the chance is much higher that one of them will read this e-mail and can take the appropriate actions.

❑ **Quota Template:** Can be changed later. Use this setting to configure a size limit for this complete site collection. If your WSS environment is fresh, you do not have any quota template defined yet. If you want to define one, right-click the Manage Quota Template link to the left to create what you need, and then go back to the first page and click Refresh to see the new template in the pull-down menu.

❑ **Site Language:** Cannot be changed. By default, you will have only the language of the installed WSS pack (for example, English) available here. But if you install new WSS language template packs, you will be able to select between them. Later, you learn where to find these language packs and how to install them.

Click OK to save your settings.

5. The next page is just a confirmation that the site has been created successfully. If it hasn't, you will see the reason why here. You can click OK to go back to the central administration page or click the URL link to open your new top site in a new browser window.

6. The first time you view this new site, you will be requested to select the site template you want to apply to the new top site. Choose the one you need and click OK.

Creating a Top Site Using the WSS User Web Site

If users need an easy way to create top sites without asking you as an administrator to do it for them, it can be done. There is a special configuration setting in WSS called Self-Service Site Creation that regulates this. Note that you can still control which users will be able to create top sites because these users must be granted the Use Self-Service Site Creation permission.

When you activate this self-service feature, you see a new message show up in the Announcement list for the first top site in your WSS environment. This message contains a link to the ASP.NET script that creates the top sites; the name for this script is `scsignup.aspx`. You can later create your own link to run that script, as you can see in the following steps where you activate this feature:

Try It Out   **Activate Self-Service Site Creation**

1. Log on as an administrator to the WSS server.

2. Start the SharePoint Central Administration tool (SCA).

3. Click Configure Virtual Server Settings in the Virtual Server Configuration section.

4. Click the virtual IIS server used by WSS.

5. Click Configure Self-Service Site Creation in the Automated Web Site Collection Management section.

6. On the following page (see Figure 3-10), you can switch self-service on or off. By default, it is off; select On. The second configuration option on this page is the Require secondary contact box. If this box is checked, every top site will require a secondary owner (that is, another user account). This could be a very good feature if you later turn on the automatic clean-up of unused sites, because all owners of the top sites will get an e-mail from WSS asking whether the site should be deleted. This secondary owner is commonly a role-based user, such as Helpdesk, Support, or something similar. Set this option and click OK to save and close this page.

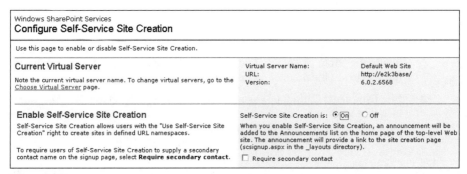

Figure 3-10

The self-service site creation feature is now turned on. Open the first top site in your WSS and check the Announcements list. You should see a new item here, as in Figure 3-11.

Figure 3-11

The link in this announcement takes you to the web form for creating new top sites. But this is not the best place to store such a link. Later on, there may be many new announcements, and it may be hard to find this one. One easy solution is to create a link in the Links list (see the following instructions).

Try It Out **Create a Top Site Using the scsignup.aspx Page**

1. Go to the home page of your first top site (`http://e2k3base` in this example).

2. In the new announcement, highlight the complete link `http://e2k3base/_layouts/1033/scsignup.aspx`; right-click it and select Copy Shortcut.

3. Under the Links list, click Add new link.

4. Right-click the URL box and select Paste. It should now show the previously copied link.

5. Enter a descriptive name for this link in the Description box (for example, **Create New Top Site**, as in Figure 3-12).

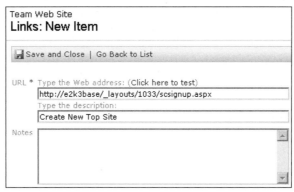

Figure 3-12

6. Click Save and Close. You will now return to the Home page.

7. Test the new link by clicking Create New Top Site.

8. You will now see the web form where you create new top sites (see Figure 3-13). Note that it is slightly different from the one you can activate using the WSS administration tool. For example, the URL address for this top site will always be under the /sites/ path.

- ❑ **Title:** Enter the title for this web site. This title shows up on the Home page.

- ❑ **Description:** Enter a description of this top site.

- ❑ **URL name:** Enter the URL address for this top site. Note that it automatically has a prefix of http://e2k3base/sites if your server is named e2k3base.

- ❑ **E-mail Address:** Enter your e-mail address. Because you create this top site, you are also the primary owner and, therefore, have full control of this complete site collection. The e-mail account is used if WSS needs to tell you anything about this site collection.

- ❑ **Secondary Owner User name:** Enter the user account for the secondary owner, including the domain name (for example, **Contoso\support**). It may be smart to use a role-based user account (or group) as the secondary owner in case the primary owner leaves the company or will be away for a long period of time.

- ❑ **Secondary Owner E-mail Address:** Enter the e-mail address for the secondary owner. The secondary owner's e-mail account receives copies of any messages that WSS sends out regarding this site collection.

Click Create to save and close this page.

9. In the next and final page, select what site template to use for this new site. Choose any you like and click OK. The new site opens.

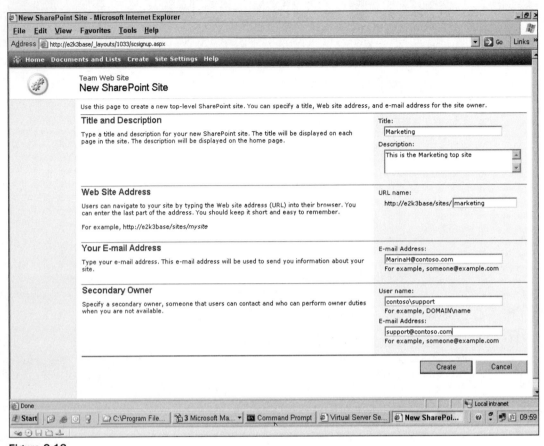

Figure 3-13

Configuring WSS to Use an SMTP Mail Server

Before progressing any further, you need to configure WSS to use an SMTP mail server. The reason is that WSS needs to send messages in several different situations, for example:

❑   Error messages to the owner of the site collection.

❑   Warning messages whenever the size of the site collection is near the quota template limit.

❑   Notifications to a user that she has been granted access to a site.

To set up WSS to use a specific mail server, in this case the local MS Exchange 2003 server, use the following instructions:

Try It Out — Configure WSS to Use a Mail Server

1. Log on as an administrator to the WSS server.

2. Start the SharePoint Central Administration tool.

3. Click Configure default e-mail server settings in the Server Configuration section.

4. In the following web form (see Figure 3-14), enter the e-mail settings.

   ❑ **Outbound SMTP server:** Enter the full name for the mail server, also known as the *Fully Qualified Domain Name* (FQDN). It does not have to be an MS Exchange server; it can be any SMTP server, remote or local. However, you must make sure this server allows WSS to send mail to your users; if not, the mail server may need extra configuration settings to allow it to relay messages. This is seldom a problem when using the internal mail servers in your network, but it may be a problem when using external mail servers located at an Internet service provider (ISP).

   ❑ **From address:** The virtual sender of these WSS messages. Note that this e-mail address does not need to exist! It can be any e-mail address.

   ❑ **Reply-to address:** If a user replies to a WSS message, it will go to this address. This address must exist. Avoid using a personal e-mail address here; instead, use a role-based address, such as helpdesk@contoso.com.

   ❑ **Character set:** Defines what character set WSS will use for its e-mail messages. There is very seldom a reason for changing this from the default 65001 (Unicode UTF-8) unless you have a very old or strange SMTP mail server that will be receiving these messages.

   Click OK to save these settings.

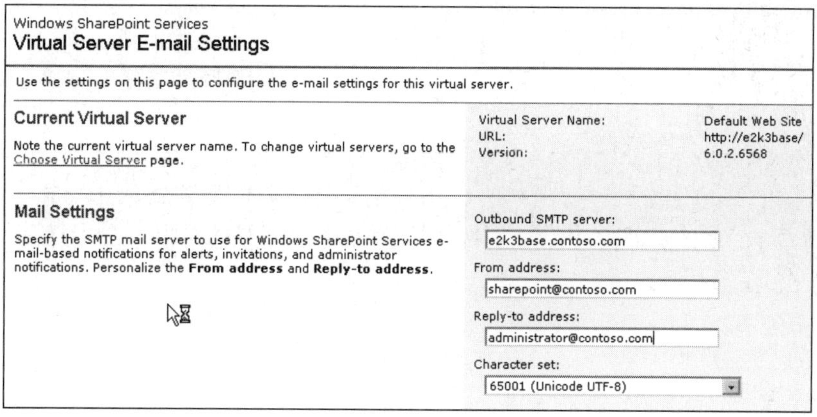

Figure 3-14

Managing Access Control of Web Sites

By now, you know how to create sites. The next logical step is to learn to configure the access to these sites. Although this is something the creator of the site normally will do without any assistance from the SharePoint administrator, it's still important for you to learn this aspect, too.

You may remember from previous sections that any security object, such as local or domain user accounts or security groups, may be granted access to WSS sites. These objects must be a member of one or more Site Groups, such as the Reader or Contributor group. For example, say you have two users: Randy Reader (Contoso\RandyR) and Candy Contributor (Contoso\CandyC). You want to add them as a Reader and a Contributor, respectively. Follow these steps to add these users to you first top site:

Try It Out   **Add Users to Your Web Site**

1. Log on as an administrator to any computer with network access to the WSS server.

2. Open Internet Explorer and enter the URL address **http://E2K3base**.

3. Click Site Settings on the blue menu bar to open the local administration page for this site.

4. Click Manage Users to open the page where you add, delete, and modify users and groups to this site.

5. Click the Add Users button.

6. The next page is a web form where you add the new users or groups (as Figure 3-15 shows). Notice that even though it says Add Users, you actually can add groups as well. In the Users box, you enter one or more users or groups. However, you can only select one site group for these users (or groups). Because in this example you want to add two users in two different site groups, you must do this twice! Start by adding the first user.

   Enter the name **contoso\RandyR** and check the site group Reader. Then click Next.

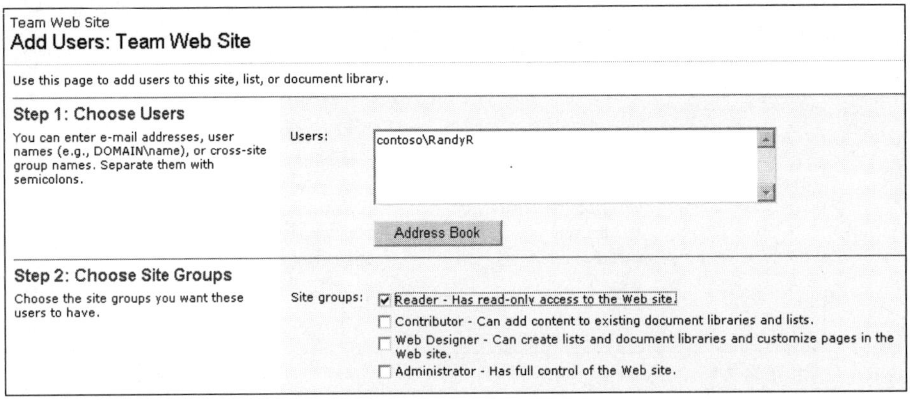

Team Web Site
Add Users: Team Web Site

Use this page to add users to this site, list, or document library.

Step 1: Choose Users

You can enter e-mail addresses, user names (e.g., DOMAIN\name), or cross-site group names. Separate them with semicolons.

Users: contoso\RandyR

Address Book

Step 2: Choose Site Groups

Choose the site groups you want these users to have.

Site groups: ☑ Reader - Has read-only access to the Web site.
☐ Contributor - Can add content to existing document libraries and lists.
☐ Web Designer - Can create lists and document libraries and customize pages in the Web site.
☐ Administrator - Has full control of the Web site.

Figure 3-15

7. The following page is very useful. If this user has an e-mail address known to the Active Directory, you will now be able to send an e-mail to Randy, telling him the good news about being granted access to this site as a reader. You do not need to enter the URL address, and you

actually don't even need to say what site group he belongs to; SharePoint will do this for you! Just fill in some text in the Body (see Figure 3-16) and click Finish to send the message. See Figures 3-16 and 3-17.

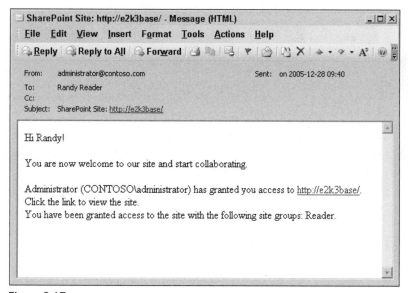

Figure 3-16

Figure 3-17

8. You will be returned to the Manage Users web page. Repeat steps 5–7 to add the user Candy as a Contributor and send an e-mail to her.

Alternatively, instead of entering the user accounts manually (as described in step 6), you can click the Address Book button on the same page. If you have a mail client, such as MS Outlook, you then see its global address list, and you can select one or more names to add to SharePoint (see Figure 3-18).

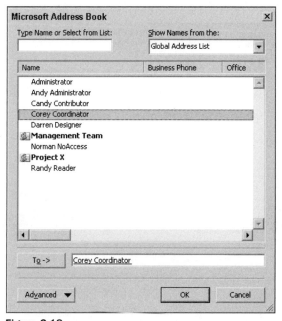

Figure 3-18

If you want to add a security group in the Active Directory, you can type it in manually, as in step 6. To add a mail distribution group, simply select it from MS Outlook's global address list, or enter its name manually. However, because distribution groups are not security groups, SharePoint cannot grant this group access. So it will instead expand the group and add all its members.

> **Note that if a distribution group is added and later modified, it will not affect the list of users who have been granted access previously!**

More Advanced WSS Administration

Now you know the basics of sites and how to control them. In this section, you learn the details about site groups, anonymous access, site templates, and how to activate the search feature in WSS.

Site Groups

Previously, you learned that a user must be a member of one or more site groups before he can access anything in SharePoint. The default site groups are Reader, Contributor, Web Designer, and Administrator.

Each site has its own set of site groups; in other words, the modifications you make in one site will not show up in another site, not even if the sites are in the same site collection. However, if a subsite inherits its permission settings, and you modify the sites groups in the parent site, this modification will also be valid for the subsite. You can view and modify the detailed permissions granted to these site groups by following these steps:

Try It Out   **Managing Site Groups**

1.   Log on as a SharePoint administrator and start a web browser.

2.   Open the site you want to work with (for example `http://e2k3base`).

3.   Go to Site Settings⇨Site Administration⇨Manage Site Groups.

4.   On the resulting page, you see all available site groups for this particular WSS site (see Figure 3-19).

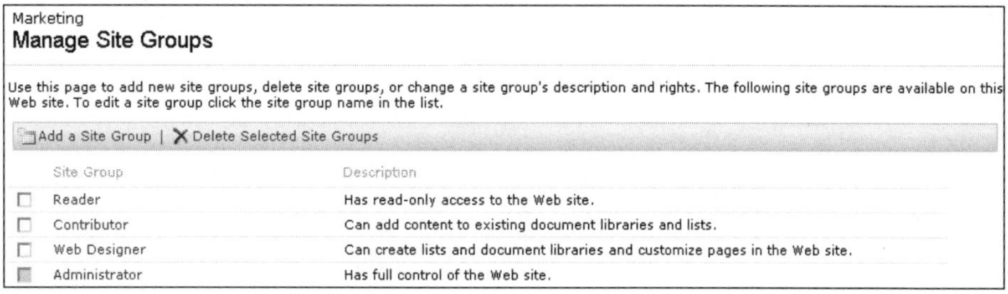

Marketing
Manage Site Groups

Use this page to add new site groups, delete site groups, or change a site group's description and rights. The following site groups are available on this Web site. To edit a site group click the site group name in the list.

🗋 Add a Site Group | ✕ Delete Selected Site Groups

	Site Group	Description
☐	Reader	Has read-only access to the Web site.
☐	Contributor	Can add content to existing document libraries and lists.
☐	Web Designer	Can create lists and document libraries and customize pages in the Web site.
▨	Administrator	Has full control of the Web site.

Figure 3-19

5.   Click Reader. This takes you to a page where all current members of this site group are listed (initially, of course, this is empty). Click the Edit site group permission link to view exactly what this Reader site group is allowed to do. By default, the rights are View Items, View Pages, and Use Self-Service Site Creation.

6.   If you need to modify the rights for this particular group, just add or remove whatever you need. Notice that if you add some rights, such as Manage Lists Permissions, it automatically adds the dependent rights for these particular rights (in this example, Manage Lists).

Click OK to save the modifications, or click Cancel to close this page without saving any changes.

In the following tables, you can see all the default site groups and their settings. Knowing this information can be useful if you start changing these site groups and want to restore the default settings. Unfortunately, there is no such thing as a Restore Default button.

Reader	Description
View Items	View items in lists, view documents in document libraries, view web discussion comments, and set up e-mail alerts for lists.
View Pages	View pages in the current web site.
Use Self-Service Site Creation	Create a top web site using Self-Service Site Creation.

Contributor	Description
Add Items	Add items to lists, documents to document libraries, and Web discussion comments.
Edit Items	Edit items in lists, edit documents in document libraries, edit Web discussion comments in documents, and customize web part pages in document libraries.
Delete Items	Delete items from a list, documents from a document library, and web discussion comments in documents.
View Items	View items in lists, view documents in document libraries, view web discussion comments, and set up e-mail alerts for lists.
Browse Directories	Browse directories in a web site.
View Pages	View pages in a web site.
Manage Personal Views	Create, change, and delete personal views of lists.
Add/Remove Private Web Parts	Add or remove private web parts on a web part page.
Update Personal Web Parts	Update web parts to display personalized information.
Create Cross-Site Groups	Create a group of users that can be granted access to any site within the site collection.
Use Self-Service Site Creation	Create a top web site using Self-Service Site Creation.

Web Designer	Description
Manage Lists	Approve content in lists, add or remove columns in a list, and add or remove public views of a list.
Cancel Check-Out	Check in a document without saving the current changes.
Add Items	Add items to lists, documents to document libraries, and web discussion comments.
Edit Items	Edit items in lists, edit documents in document libraries, edit web discussion comments in documents, and customize web part pages in document libraries.
Delete Items	Delete items from a list, documents from a document library, and web discussion comments from documents.
View Items	View items in lists, view documents in document libraries, view web discussion comments, and set up e-mail alerts for lists.
Add and Customize Pages	Add, change, or delete HTML pages or web part pages, and edit the web site using a Windows SharePoint Services–compatible editor.
Apply Themes and Borders	Apply a theme or borders to the entire web site.

Web Designer	Description
Apply Style Sheets	Apply a style sheet (.CSS file) to the web site.
Browse Directories	Browse directories in a web site.
View Pages	View pages in a web site.
Manage Personal Views	Create, change, and delete personal views of lists.
Add/Remove Private Web Parts	Add or remove private web parts on a web part page.
Update Personal Web Parts	Update web parts to display personalized information.
Create Cross-Site Groups	Create a group of users that can be granted access to any site within the site collection.
Use Self-Service Site Creation	Create a top web site using Self-Service Site Creation.

Administrator	Description
Manage List Permission	Grant, deny, or change user permissions to a list.
Manage Lists	Approve content in lists, add or remove columns in a list, and add or remove public views of a list.
Cancel Check-Out	Check in a document without saving the current changes.
Add Items	Add items to lists, documents to document libraries, and web discussion comments.
Edit Items	Edit items in lists, edit documents in document libraries, edit web discussion comments in documents, and customize web part pages in document libraries.
Delete Items	Delete items from a list, documents from a document library, and web discussion comments in documents.
View Items	View items in lists, view documents in document libraries, view web discussion comments, and set up e-mail alerts for lists.
Manage Site Groups	Create, change, and delete site groups, including adding users to the site groups and specifying which rights are assigned to a site group.
View Usage Data	View reports on web site usage.
Create Subsites	Create subsites such as team sites, Meeting Workspace sites, and Document Workspace sites.
Manage Web Site	Grant the ability to perform all administration tasks for the web site as well as manage content and permissions.
Add and Customize Pages	Add, change, or delete HTML pages or web part pages, and edit the web site using a Windows SharePoint Services–compatible editor.

Table continued on following page

Administrator	Description
Apply Themes and Borders	Apply a theme or borders to the entire web site.
Apply Style Sheets	Apply a style sheet (.CSS file) to the web site
Browse Directories	Browse directories in a web site.
View Pages	View pages in a web site.
Manage Personal Views	Create, change, and delete personal views of lists.
Add/Remove Private Web Parts	Add or remove private web parts on a web part page.
Update Personal Web Parts	Update web parts to display personalized information.
Create Cross-Site Groups	Create a group of users that can be granted access to any site within the site collection.
Use Self-Service Site Creation	Create a top web site using Self-Service Site Creation.

Taking some time to study the preceding tables will help you understand what site group a user needs to be a member of. Also notice that only the Administrator site group is allowed to create new subsites in an existing top site. Some organizations request that a member of the site group Contributor be able to create subsites. This is easy to fix: Simply modify the Contributor site group and add the right Create Subsite to it.

However, this might not be such a brilliant idea, after all. Imagine that six months after this modification, a new SharePoint administrator joins your team. She notices that several users can create subsites, although they are just members of the Contributor group. Because she knows that this group does not have the right to do this, she starts to troubleshoot the WSS environment. You get the idea, right? Changing default and well-known site group rights is just asking for confusion later. Or worse, imagine some administrator adding the Add Item ability to the Reader group! This would then give the members of the Reader site group the permission to create new items, such as documents and contacts, although the name Reader implies only read access. This could easily confuse administrators later on.

The proper method is to create a new site group. Fortunately, there is a way to copy existing group settings (including members, if needed), so adding extra site groups is an easy task. For example, say that you want to create a new Contributor group that has the Create Subsite right. To do so, follow these steps:

Try It Out   Create a New Site Group

1. Log on as an administrator or the owner for a web site.

2. Open the site where the new group should be created, such as `http://e2k3base/sites/marketing`.

3. Choose Site Settings⇨Site Administration⇨Manage Site Groups.

4. Because the new group should be an extension to the Contributor site group, click that particular group.

5. Click Edit Site Group Permissions. You will see all detailed rights for the Contributor group.

6. Scroll down to the bottom of the resulting web page. Click the Copy Site Group button.

7. The new page will have all the rights copied from the Contributor group. Enter the following values:

❑ **Site Group Name:** Enter a name that indicates what this group does, such as **Site Creating Contributors**.

❑ **Description:** Enter a description of what this group is used for.

❑ **Copy users from "Contributor":** If you check this box, the new site group will have a copy of the current membership of the Contributor site group. If the Contributor group is later changed, this will not affect the new group.

❑ **Rights:** Make the modifications you need. In this example, you check the appropriate Create Subsites.

Click Create Site Group. You will return to the page where all the site groups are listed, including the one you just created. You are done!

Test the group by adding a user account to this new site group, as you learned to do earlier. The new site group Site Creating Contributors is now listed on the page where you add users (see Figure 3-20).

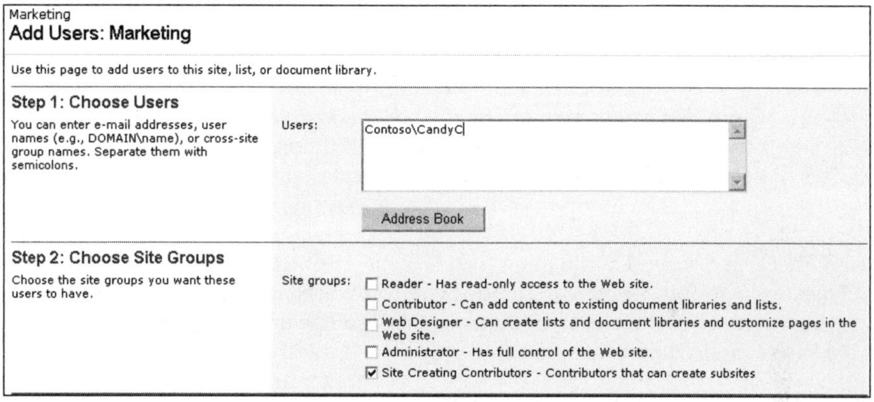

Marketing
Add Users: Marketing

Use this page to add users to this site, list, or document library.

Step 1: Choose Users

You can enter e-mail addresses, user names (e.g., DOMAIN\name), or cross-site group names. Separate them with semicolons.

Users: Contoso\CandyC

Address Book

Step 2: Choose Site Groups

Choose the site groups you want these users to have.

Site groups:
☐ Reader - Has read-only access to the Web site.
☐ Contributor - Can add content to existing document libraries and lists.
☐ Web Designer - Can create lists and document libraries and customize pages in the Web site.
☐ Administrator - Has full control of the Web site.
☑ Site Creating Contributors - Contributors that can create subsites

Figure 3-20

Log on as this user and open the web site with the new site group. You should be able to create new items, such as announcements, links, and events. You should also try to create a subsite in order to make sure the added right actually works.

Cross-Site Groups

When it comes to security, managing groups of users is much easier than managing individual user accounts. For this reason, you can create groups in, for instance, the Active Directory. But in large organizations, you will often find a particular group of network administrators that controls the creation of groups and other tasks in the AD. Some refer to this admin group as the "Active Directory Nazis" because it has the power (and the will) to prohibit you from creating new groups in the AD. If you work in such an environment, you know what I am talking about. These people will not allow the creation of a group simply because you need one — forget that! So what do you do? The answer is to create your own group in SharePoint.

These types of homebrewed groups are called *cross-site groups* in SharePoint. They work just like any other AD group except that they exist only within SharePoint. You can add any user account, local account, domain account, or existing group from the AD. The only catch is that you can use these cross-site groups only within a given site collection (a top site and its subsites).

You can use cross-site groups like any ordinary AD group or user account; add them as a member to any site group, such as the Reader group. If you add a new member to an existing cross-site group, this member will have access to all places in SharePoint where this cross-site group is added.

Create a cross-site group by following these steps:

Try It Out   Create a Cross-Site Group

1. Log on as an administrator or owner of a site collection.

2. Open any site in that site collection. You don't need to be at the top site to perform the following steps.

3. Choose Site Settings⇨Site Administration⇨Manage Cross-site Groups.

4. Click New Cross-Site Group.

5. Enter the following information for the new cross-site group:

    ❑ **Name:** Give it a name that indicates what type of group it is, such as **Managers**.

    ❑ **Description:** Enter a description for this cross-site group.

    ❑ **Cross-Site group owner:** Use this section to define who can modify membership of this cross-site group. The options are yourself (the creator of this group), someone else (use the Select button to choose a user that can modify this group), or to allow members of this cross-site group to add and remove site users.

    Click Create when finished.

6. The next page allows you to add members. You (the creator) are automatically added. Click Add Members and select the user accounts and AD groups that will be members. Note that another cross-site group cannot be a member!

7. The next page shows you the selected users or groups. Click Finish to confirm.

8. You will return to the page where the members are listed. If you want to add more users, you can do that now. If not, you are finished.

The next step is of course to test the cross-site group. Select any web site in this site collection and add this group, using the same steps as adding a user:

1. Open a web site in this site collection.

2. Choose Site Settings⇨Manage users.

3. Click Add Users.

4. Enter the name of the cross-site group. Note that you cannot use the address button for this; you must enter the name manually. If you forgot the names for the cross-site groups, go to the same page where you created them.

5. Click Next. You will now be able to send an e-mail to all members of this cross-site group.

6. Click Finish to save and close.

Anonymous Access

In some situations, you need to allow anonymous users access to a web site. You should think hard about this before you open up SharePoint—or anything else, for that matter—to everyone. Or perhaps you want to open WSS for all users in your organization, which is different from opening it up to anonymous users. In the following section you will find the steps on how to perform both of these configurations.

Opening WSS Sites for Every User in Your Organization

The important thing to understand here is that all users log on; that is, they all have user accounts. Windows Server has several special groups; one of these groups is called Everyone, and another is called Authenticated Users. The difference between them is that the Authenticated Users group contains only members that actually have logged on, using an ordinary user account, whereas the group Everyone also contains any type of connected session that does not require explicit log on, also known as a *NULL session*. In other words, it is safer to grant the group Authenticated Users access to SharePoint. To do this, follow these instructions:

Try It Out	Open WSS to All Authenticated Users

1. Log on as the WSS administrator.

2. Open the web site you want to open for all authenticated users. Note that this setting will only affect the current site (and all subsites that inherit permission settings from it). This setting can be used on every web site that has unique permission settings, not just the top site.

3. Choose Site Settings⇨Site Administration.

4. Click Manage Anonymous Access.

5. On the resulting web form, select Allow all authenticated users to access this site. Select the site group (that is, what rights these users will have) using the pull-down menu "Assign these users to the following site group". You will be able to choose between only the Reader or Contributor site group.

6. Click OK to save and close this page.

You could also do this by adding the group Authenticated Users like any other group or user. The difference between this method and the one described in the preceding steps is that when you add Authenticated Users, you can make it a member of any site group, not just Reader or Contributor. You will need this to be the case if you ever decide to grant all users special rights, using a custom-made site group.

Opening WSS Sites for Anonymous Access

So now you are really sure that you want to give everyone access to your WSS site, regardless of who they are. You can do this by making the WSS environment available to the Internet. Most likely, such a WSS environment would not contain sensitive information or anything not meant for public access. You could use three typical scenarios when exposing a WSS server to the Internet:

- ❑ **Connect WSS directly to the Internet:** Bad idea! It will not survive for long before someone hacks it. Do not connect any server directly to the Internet!

- ❑ **Protect the WSS server behind a firewall:** Better idea. Many organizations find this an acceptable solution—if the firewall is properly configured.

❑ **Protect the WSS behind an MS ISA server, which in turn may be protected by the ordinary firewall:** This is a very good — and safe — solution. Users on the Internet will never access the WSS directly; they will instead be directed to the MS ISA server, which in turn connects to the WSS server, grabs the information the user requests, and sends it back to the user.

The WSS server in the last scenario is so well protected that you may choose to allow external access to parts of the same WSS server you use for internal access. It is up to you whether you want a separate WSS server or you accept to run a single server for all WSS information.

If you need to open all or parts of WSS for anonymous access, follow these steps to do it:

Try It Out   Open WSS for Anonymous Access

1. Open the virtual IIS server for anonymous access. If you forget this step, the anonymous access settings are grayed out in WSS.

   a. Start the IIS Manager: Start⇨Administrative Tools⇨Internet Information Service (IIS) Manager.

   b. Right-click the virtual IIS server used by WSS (for example, Default Web Site) and select Properties.

   c. Switch to the Directory Security tab.

   d. In the Authentication and access control section, click the Edit button.

   e. Check Enable anonymous access. Note that the account IUSR_E2K3BASE (assuming that the server is named E2K3BASE) will be listed in the User name box. This account will be used by IIS whenever someone tries to access anything in this virtual IIS server. If you prefer, you can use your own account instead. The IURS_E2K3BASE user is a member of the built-in Active Directory group Guest but is not a member of Authenticated Users.

   f. Click OK until all pages are closed. Note that if you have web applications other than WSS active on the same virtual IIS server, you will be asked whether you want to apply the settings of anonymous access to their virtual directories. If this happens, just click OK again to close, without selecting any virtual directory in that dialog box.

   g. Close the IIS Manager. You do not need to reset IIS!

2. Open the WSS web site you want to open for anonymous access.

3. Choose Site Settings⇨Site Administration⇨Manage anonymous access. You will see a web form like the one in Figure 3-21.

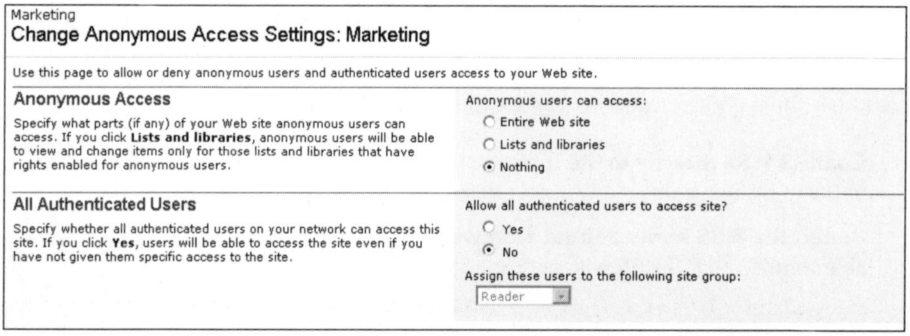

Marketing
Change Anonymous Access Settings: Marketing

Use this page to allow or deny anonymous users and authenticated users access to your Web site.

Anonymous Access	Anonymous users can access:
Specify what parts (if any) of your Web site anonymous users can access. If you click **Lists and libraries**, anonymous users will be able to view and change items only for those lists and libraries that have rights enabled for anonymous users.	○ Entire Web site ○ Lists and libraries ◉ Nothing
All Authenticated Users	Allow all authenticated users to access site?
Specify whether all authenticated users on your network can access this site. If you click **Yes**, users will be able to access the site even if you have not given them specific access to the site.	○ Yes ◉ No Assign these users to the following site group: Reader

Figure 3-21

4. Select what rights the anonymous users will have on this site. You have the following options:

    ❏ **Entire Web site:** Can access every part of this particular WSS site, including all lists and libraries and their contents.

    ❏ **Lists and libraries:** Can access any list or library on this WSS site that has enabled anonymous access. Cannot view the pages in this web site, such as the Home page, so users must have a direct link that opens the particular list or library that they are allowed to view.

    ❏ **Nothing:** The default choice. Nothing is accessible.

5. Click OK to save and close this web folder. This setting will immediately be active.

To make this last part complete, you need to know how to open specific lists for anonymous access. The second option in step 4, Lists and libraries, allows anonymous users to view, modify, or add information in any list open for anonymous access. To set this access, follow these steps:

Try It Out   Open a List or Library for Anonymous Access

1. Log on as a site owner or SharePoint administrator.

2. Open a web site based on the Team Site template. It contains a document library named Shared Documents, which you will open for anonymous access in this example.

3. Click Shared Documents.

4. Click Modify settings and columns.

5. Click Change permissions for this list.

6. Click Change anonymous access.

7. Check what type of access anonymous users will have in this particular list (or library):

    a. In Lists, anonymous users can be granted full access (that is, they can view, add, and modify). However, these users will not be able to delete information.

    b. In Libraries, anonymous users can be granted view-only access.

8. Click OK to save and close this page. This setting will be effective immediately.

What Happens When Access Is Denied

As you may recall, SharePoint has its own security system, which keeps track of what users can do. But it is the Internet Information Service that executes these rights! Whenever users try something they are not allowed to do, IIS will notice and generate an "Error 401 – Access denied" message in the IIS log files. IIS will then prompt the user for new log-on credentials. The user will see this as a log-on prompt. Most people will think that WSS lost their current user information and will therefore enter their user account and password again. It will, of course, not work this time either, so IIS will prompt the user once again. The user thinks he mistyped something and tries again. After the user's third log-on attempt, IIS will signal to WSS that this user is trying to access a forbidden page or action, and WSS will then do one of two things, depending on the site settings for this particular site collection (which can be set at Site Settings⇨Site Administration⇨Manage Access Requests):

❏ Show a page saying access is denied.

❏ Show a page where you can send a request to the owner of this site, asking to get access.

The last option is, of course, much more user-friendly, and it solves a common problem: When you create a new site, it is easy to forget to add some users who actually should have access. Now these users can simply fill in this request form and the owner will get an e-mail describing who the user is and what site he or she is trying to get access to.

There is no way in WSS to change the number of logon prompts. IIS will do this three times no matter what.

Working with Custom Site Templates

By now you have a rather good understanding of the basics in WSS. You know how to create sites and subsites, add users and groups, create custom site groups and cross-site groups, and enable anonymous access. But there is more — a lot more!

Wouldn't it be nice to control exactly what new sites look like right from the beginning? For example, assume that you have been asked to create 10 web sites for an upcoming project and that they all must look the same. You know that the look and feel of each web site can be designed by adding and modifying web parts to the site's home page, and you want happy users, so you start working on the design. After some time, you have created the first web site and it looks good; you check with the future users of these sites, and they are happy, too. Now you only have nine more web sites to create, with the exact same layouts and web parts, and then you are done.

But wait — there is a smarter way of doing this. The work process looks like this:

1. Create the first web site. Make sure it really looks like the users expect it to!

2. Save the site as a Site Template.

3. Create the second web site, using this new site template.

That's all there is to it — very easy to create and use!

Creating Custom Site Templates

You can take any existing web site, including a subsite, and save it as a custom site template. A template can also contain actual data, such as documents and list content. You can create as many site templates as you need. All site templates can be used anywhere in this site collection. If you want to use a site template in another site collection, you can do it by exporting the template from the content database to a file in a file system, and then importing that file back to the database into the other site collection.

However, there are some important limitations:

❑ You cannot modify an existing template. You can, however, delete the old template and create a new one with the same name and description.

❑ Any site that has been created using a custom template will not be affected if the template is re-created. Make sure that the template is perfect before you create new web sites based on it.

❑ Site templates are language dependent. If you create a site template from a Swedish web site, it cannot be used when creating English web sites. (In fact, it will not even be visible for sites based on languages other than the template's language.)

❑ The content included in the site template cannot be larger than 10 MB.

The Canadian company KWizCom offers a free language type converter for SharePoint templates. Using this you could take an English site template and convert its language type to German. Note that you still need to change the text labels manually. Download this excellent tool from this address: http://www.kwizcom.com.

Only top site administrators and full SharePoint administrators can create and apply custom templates. If you want to create a template using a subsite, you must be an administrator on both the current subsite and the top site. All custom templates are stored as STP files, which is a SharePoint-specific file format for templates. These STP files are stored in the content database, not in the ordinary file system, but you can export them to the file system. These templates are all collected into something SharePoint calls *Site Template Galleries,* and you can view, import, and delete custom site templates using these galleries. There is only one gallery per site collection, and it is only available from the top site of this site collection. To create a custom site template, follow these steps:

Try It Out   Create a Custom Site Template

1. Log on as a SharePoint administrator, the owner of the site collection, or the local administrator for the top site, including the site used to create the template.

2. Design the look and feel of the site you want to use as a template. Make sure that you have created all the lists, document libraries, and web parts you need for this site template. When you are sure it is what you want, choose Site Settings⇨Site Administration.

3. Click Save site as template. You will see web form requesting information about this new template (see Figure 3-22).

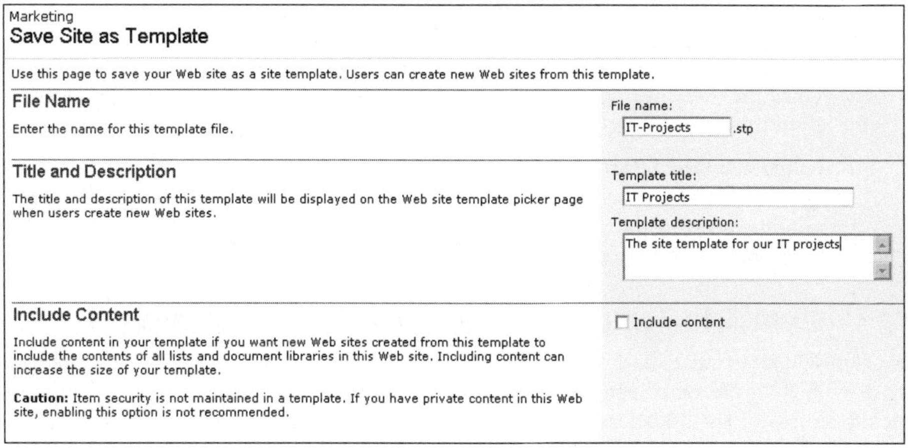

Marketing
Save Site as Template

Use this page to save your Web site as a site template. Users can create new Web sites from this template.

File Name
Enter the name for this template file.

File name:
`IT-Projects` .stp

Title and Description
The title and description of this template will be displayed on the Web site template picker page when users create new Web sites.

Template title:
`IT Projects`

Template description:
`The site template for our IT projects`

Include Content
Include content in your template if you want new Web sites created from this template to include the contents of all lists and document libraries in this Web site. Including content can increase the size of your template.

Caution: Item security is not maintained in a template. If you have private content in this Web site, enabling this option is not recommended.

☐ Include content

Figure 3-22

4. Fill in the template information:

❑ **File name:** Enter the name of this template file. (As mentioned previously, it will not be stored in the file system!)

❑ **Template title:** Enter a short description for this template. This will be listed along with all other templates later.

- ❏ **Template description:** Enter more information about this template (for example, what it is used for, who should use it, and what it contains). This information will also be visible on the template list.

- ❏ **Include content:** Use this check box if you want to store current content in the site template. Note that the maximum size for this content is 10 MB.

Click OK to save and close this web form.

5. The next page shows you whether the template was successfully created. If it was successful, you see a link to the Site Template Gallery. If you want to list all site templates now, click that link. If not, you can click OK to close this page.

If you want to return to the Site Template Gallery, choose Site Settings⇨Go to Site Administration⇨ Go to Top-level Site Administration⇨Manage site template gallery. If you cannot successfully create the site template, check that you have administrative rights for both the top site in this site collection and the current site!

Now you must test it to make sure it works:

1. Make sure that you are logged on as a user with administrative permissions for the current site, enabling you to create a new subsite. Note that this can be anywhere in the site collection tree; it does not have to be under the site you used to create this custom template!

2. Choose Create⇨Web Pages⇨Sites and Workspaces.

3. Enter the Title, Description, and URL address for this new site, as described earlier in this chapter. Select the type of user permissions you want (either Use same permissions as parent site or Use unique permissions). Click Create to save and close this page.

4. On the next page, select the site template. You should now see your newly created template at the end of the list. Click one time on your site; you now see its description under the picture to the left of this page. Click OK to select this template and complete the creation of the new site.

5. Inspect the new site. Make sure that everything looks the same as the template: the same lists and libraries, the same color scheme, and the same web parts and layout. The only things that should differ are the heading and description for this site, as well as permission settings. This is something you may want to update.

Copying Custom Site Templates to Other Site Collections

You now know how to create and use the site templates. Suppose that you show your template to your colleague, who is the owner of a separate site collection, and he is so impressed that he demands a copy of your site template! The question is how to copy the template to the other site collection. The general steps are as follows:

1. Go to the site template gallery where the template is located.

2. Save the template to a file on the file system.

3. Go to the template gallery for the other site collection.

4. Import that file to this gallery.

The detailed steps are also quite straightforward and easy. To copy your site template, just follow these steps:

Copy a Site Template to Another Site Collection

1.   Log on as a site collection administrator.

2.   Open the top site where the site template is currently stored.

3.   Choose Site Settings⇨Go to Site Administration.

4.   Click Manage site template gallery. You will see a list of all site templates for this site collection.

5.   Click the name for the site collection you want to copy (for example, IT-Projects).

6.   Choose to Save this file, and select a folder to save the file in. Keep the file name (IT-Projects.stp) unless you want to change it, and click the Save button. Then click Close to close this dialog box.

7.   Open the top site in the other site collection. Make sure that you are logged on as a local administrator for this site.

8.   Choose Site Settings⇨Site Administration⇨Site template gallery. You now see all templates for this site collection.

9.   Click Upload Template. Use the Browse button to select the template file you saved in step 6; click Open and then Save and Close. The template is now copied to this site collection.

10.   Test by creating a new subsite in this site collection using the copied template. Everything should look exactly as in the first site collection.

Adding a Site Template to the Global Site Template Gallery

The templates you have been working with up to this point have all been limited to a given site collection. But what happens when you create a new top site, and thus a new site collection? How do you make your own site templates available to these new sites?

Doing this is actually something that requires extra help, because WSS does not allow you to do it with the ordinary web-based administrator tool. Once again, you must call upon the STSADM.EXE (backups and restore, remember?). If you followed the instructions in Chapter 2 on how to add the path to this tool to the system environment path, you will find this to be very easy to do.

Add Site Templates Using STSADM

1.   Log on to the WSS server as a SharePoint administrator.

2.   Start up a command prompt (Start⇨Run, then enter **Cmd** and press Enter).

3.   Use steps 1 to 6 of "Try It Out: Copy a Site Template to Another Site Collection" to save the site template you want to add to the global site template gallery. For this example, you can assume that the file is c:\tmp\it-project.stp.

4.   Type the following command and press Enter:

```
STSADM -o AddTemplate -Filename C:\tmp\it-projekt.stp -Title "My Template" ⤶
-Description "This is a site template copied using Stsadm"
```

If you get a list of all available options now, you have misspelled something. Check your spelling and repeat the steps.

5. You must now reset the IIS. While still at the command prompt, type **IISReset** and press Enter.

6. When the command is finished, test by creating a new top site. Go to http://e2k3base (or whatever your first top site is called), and use its previously added link to create a new top site. You should see the new template in the list of templates (see Figure 3-23, where the new template is named "My Template").

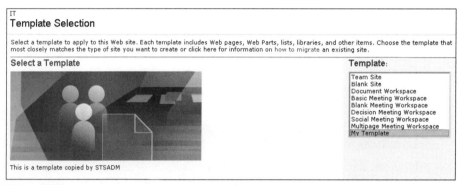

Figure 3-23

How Custom Site Templates Really Work

While you still have the command prompt window open, you can try some more things. For example, if you want to see what global site templates are installed, type this command:

```
STSADM -O EnumTemplates
```

It will show all that you have added manually. But what about those default site templates, such as the Team Site and the Blank Site? They are listed along with your own templates when creating the new site, but they are not listed here. Well, they are a bit special. You will not see them listed here because they are part of the actual site definition. When you created your custom templates, you told WSS to save the modifications to the site compared to its basic design — nothing more. In other words, the template file you copied to the file system is not a complete site definition! For example, if you try importing this file into another WSS installation that for some reason does not have the same basic site definition, it will fail!

In Chapter 6, you learn how to create your own site definitions. Using that technique, you will be able to make modifications to a site definition, and all existing web sites, based on this site definition, will be updated.

Importing Custom Site Templates from External Sources

As you have seen, creating custom site templates and exporting them to other WSS environments is easy. It will work as long as the receiving WSS server has the same basic site definition installed, based on the same WSS language pack. This is something you could use, for example, to make nice templates to distribute to others.

Microsoft has made a number of ready-to-use site templates that it gives away for free. These are really good and you are free to modify them as you wish. Microsoft does not actually call them custom site templates but *WSS Applications*. The easiest way to find them is by going to `http://www.microsoft.com` and searching for "Applications for Windows SharePoint Services." Or you can try this link: `http://www.microsoft.com/technet/prodtechnol/sppt/wssapps/default.mspx`.

Here you will find more than 30 site templates; following are just a few of them:

- ❑ **Absence and Vacation Schedule:** Use this web site to make vacation requests, see when your team members are away, and find links to job sites if you want to help others.

- ❑ **Board of Directors:** Use this web site to track tasks required by the board, keep member information, manage a calendar of meetings and activities, and store mission and business meeting minutes.

- ❑ **Classroom Management:** A teacher can use this web site to store all information regarding a single class, such as lesson plans, assignments, tasks, and grading.

- ❑ **Helpdesk Dashboard:** Use this web site to assist the Help Desk or customer support in managing requests from customers and to improve team communication. It contains an issue tracker, a document library for storing scripts, knowledge-base articles, how-to guides, and more.

- ❑ **Project Team Site:** Use this web site as a central place to store all information regarding a project. It will help the project manager and the team to collaborate and keep track of issues, tasks, and deadlines.

Using these templates is easy, but remember that they are based on the default site definition, using the English language (language code: 1033). If you want to use these templates, you must create an English web site! Follow these steps to download and install one of these applications:

Try It Out   Install a WSS Application from Microsoft

1. Download an application from Microsoft (for example, the Helpdesk Dashboard).

2. Use the Windows Explorer to locate the downloaded file. Double-click it to expand its three files: two custom site templates (you will recognize the STP file type) and one `Readme.txt` file.

   Now you have two types of this Helpdesk application: one using the basic look and feel of the standard WSS team site, and one that is much more elaborate, with nice background pictures and attractive colors. To see the difference between these two templates, you must install both of them.

3. Log on as an administrator for a top site. Then open that top site with the Internet Explorer.

4. Choose Site Settings➪Go to SharePoint Administration➪Manage site template gallery.

5. Click Upload Template.

6. On the following page, click Upload Multiple Files. Note that you must have Office 2003 installed on the local machine because your computer will try to activate an ActiveX component that comes with Office 2003.

7. Locate the two STP files from step 2. In this example, they are `Helpdesk_Basic.STP` and `Helpdesk_Custom.STP`. Check them both, because you want to install them both. Then click Save and Close to start uploading them.

8. You will now see both of these custom site templates in this gallery. They are ready to be used.

9. Create a new subsite using the first template. Go to Create⇨Web Pages⇨Sites and Workspaces, and enter a name, description, and URL for this subsite that indicates it is the basic version. Click Create.

10. On the next page, select the basic version of this application and click OK to complete the creation.

11. View the new site. It should look like the one in Figure 3-24.

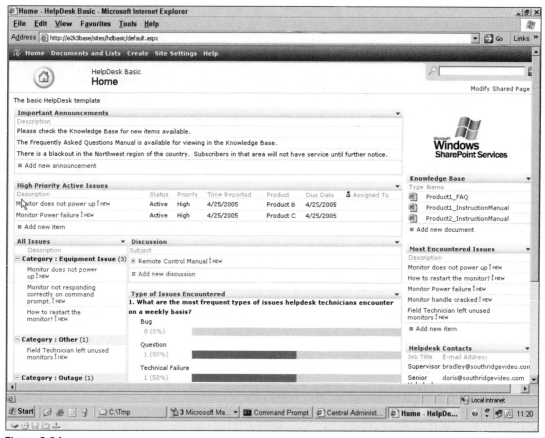

Figure 3-24

12. Create a second subsite using the other custom site template (in this example, `Helpdesk_Custom.STP`). It should look like the one in Figure 3-25.

As you can see, the second template is much nicer and easier for the user to work with. For example, if you want to add users to this site, choose SiteSettings⇨Add users. For some custom templates, it may be harder for users to find the standard links, such as Site Settings, because the links may be moved away from the usual spot. But the links are still there if the user looks carefully.

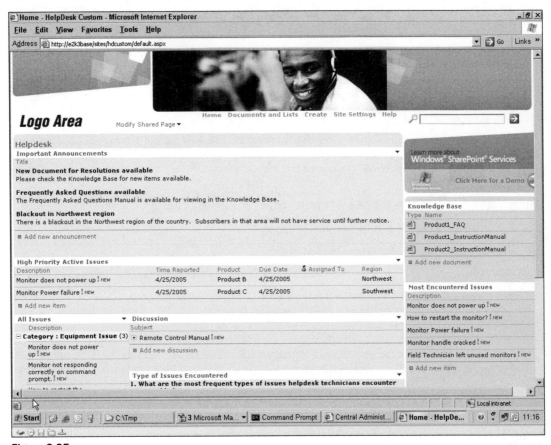

Figure 3-25

Removing User Accounts

As you know by now, all users must be members of site groups in order to access any part of SharePoint. In most organizations, these domain user accounts are stored in the Active Directory. This section describes what happens when these user accounts are deleted from the AD. You might assume that SharePoint automatically cleans up when someone is removed from the AD. But if you do, you are wrong!

A related situation is when someone is moving from one department to another, making it necessary for his or her rights to be updated accordingly. In the following sections are some of the most common scenarios in which a user account would need to be removed and how you should act in each situation.

Removing Single User Accounts

Say that the owner of user account `Contoso\Michael` has decided to leave the company. He has been a very active user in WSS and has individual access with different levels of access to different parts of the SharePoint environment. For example, he is a member of the Reader site group in two site collections; he is also the owner of one site collection and an administrator of five subsites. Now you remove his user account from the Active Directory — what happens next?

Because SharePoint is not directly dependent on the AD or even Windows NT, there is no automatic synchronization between SharePoint and the AD. If you remove a user account in the AD, the only thing that will happen in the AD is that the user account will no longer be able to be used for accessing SharePoint. But the name of this account will still be listed everywhere, which is annoying, to say the least.

One way of solving this problem is to remove this account in every place it is listed. But unless you have a very small WSS environment, doing this is a very labor-intensive task. To easily remove a user from a given site connection, just follow these steps:

Try It Out   Remove a User Account from a Site Collection

1. Log on as the site collection administrator.

2. Open the top site for this site collection.

3. Choose Site Settings⇨Site Administration⇨View site collection user information.

4. Check the user account you want to remove and click Remove Selected User. This user is now removed from every instance in this site collection, including any cross-site groups.

Okay, that was easy. But what do you do if there are lots of site collections? Well, you will not like this answer: You must remove the user account from each site collection individually. If you know the URL to each top site in your WSS environment, however, your job becomes a little easier (see the following steps).

Try It Out   Remove a User Account from Any Site Collection

1. Log on as the SharePoint administrator.

2. Open the SharePoint Central Administration tool.

3. Click Manage web site users.

4. The resulting web form is not the most user-friendly one you can find. Here's how it works:

   a. In the top box, enter the URL for the first site collection (such as **http://e2k3base**), and then click View.

   b. In the box at the bottom (labeled Account name, in the Change Existing User section), enter the name, including the domain (for example, **contoso\darrend**) and click View User. Note the top of the web form; if it says (in red) "User cannot be found," you entered the wrong user account or domain.

    c.   If the user name is correct, click Delete User.

    d.   The user is now removed from this site collection. Go back to step b to remove any other user from this site collection, or to step a if you want to switch to another site collection.

Removing a Domain Security Group

This is no different from how you remove a user account. Both methods previously described will work when removing security groups.

Removing the Owner of a Site Collection

This is a bit tricky because the ownership of site collections does not show up in the ordinary lists where users and groups are displayed with their site group membership. You might remember that there can be up to two owners of a site collection. You can see the ownership by following these steps:

| Try It Out | List Owners of a Site Collection |

1.   Log on as the site administrator or the full SharePoint administrator.

2.   Open the SharePoint Central Administration tool.

3.   Click Manage site collection owners.

4.   In the Web Site URL, enter the address to the top site for this site collection (for example, **http://e2k3base/sites/it**) and click View.

5.   You will now see one or two names that are defined as owners for this site collection. They have all permissions, regardless of what the security settings there may be.

6.   If you remove the secondary owner, he or she will still be listed as a user for this site collection. If you want to change either of these two owners, simply type in the new user name, including the domain name, thus replacing the old owner name. Click OK to save any modifications.

Owners of site collections also get the role Site Collection Administrators. In other words, if you see a user with the permission Site Collection Administrator, you know this is a site owner. Test this on your site collection:

1.   Go to the top site for this site collection.

2.   Choose Site Settings➪View information about site users.

3.   Click the name of the secondary owner. Note that it says on the following page that this user account is a Site Collection Administrator. If you try to edit this user and remove the check box for the site collector administrator, you will get an error message saying that you cannot take away this right because this user account is an owner.

If you remove a user from the site collection, his account will still be listed as an owner. You must manually remove that account as previously described.

Summary

In this chapter you learned the following:

❏ Be careful with the Internet Explorer Enhanced Security. It can give you trouble if your browser does not recognize WSS as a trusted or local site.

❏ SharePoint uses two types of sites: administrative sites and user sites.

   ❏ The administrative site is used only by SharePoint administrators (that is, members of the Local Administrators group of the WSS server or members of the SharePoint Administrator Group).

   ❏ Members of the SharePoint Administrative Group do not have all the permissions that the full administrator does.

❏ You can change the TCP port number to control the access to the administrative web site.

❏ The user sites are where the users create team sites, meeting workspaces, project sites, and so on.

❏ Every user site has a Home page. This is where the user accesses the lists and libraries.

   ❏ The Home page contains one or more web parts.

   ❏ A web part is a window inside the Home page that displays information. This information may come from a different part of this site, from a different site, or even from an external database.

❏ Sites are organized in site trees. On top is the top site; below are its subsites.

   ❏ The top site, including all its subsites, is referred to as a site collection.

   ❏ Many features (such as inheritance, ownership, templates, and more) are limited to one given site collection.

❏ The term *workspace* means the same as a *web site*.

❏ SharePoint uses local server or domain user accounts and group accounts to grant permissions.

❏ Each permission is controlled by site groups, such as Reader, Contributor, and so on.

   ❏ You can create your own site groups with special settings.

   ❏ If you cannot create groups in the Active Directory, you can create cross-site groups to be used in SharePoint.

   ❏ Cross-site groups contain other users or domain groups, just like any other group. However, you cannot make a cross-site group a member of another cross-site group.

❏ To create a new top site, you can use the SharePoint Central Administration tool.

❏ You can also configure WSS to enable self-service site creation, which displays a link to a page where you can create top sites using the user web site instead of the administrator tool.

❑ SharePoint does not come with an easy navigation between sites in the site tree. This is easily solved by installing one of many free or low-priced web parts that do exactly this.

❑ You must configure WSS to communicate with any SMTP server before alerts, errors, and other messages can be sent from WSS.

❑ You can enable anonymous access to all or part of WSS.

❑ MS ISA Server is easy to configure to make itself look like a SharePoint server for the users. It will grab whatever information the user requests and send it back to the user.

❑ When a user tries to access something he isn't allowed to use, IIS prompts him three times and then WSS either tells him that access is denied or offers to send a message to the administrator for this object (site, list, library, and so on) and request access.

❑ Creating custom site templates makes it easier to create several sites with the exact same look and feel.

    ❑ You can save content along with the site template, as long as it is less than 10 MB in size.

    ❑ A site template will only be visible within its own site collection.

    ❑ Site templates are always built for a given language. You cannot use French templates for a German site, for example, unless you use the STP Language Converter tool.

    ❑ You can copy site templates to other site collections by saving the template to a file.

    ❑ You can add site templates to the global template gallery using the STSADM tool.

    ❑ Custom site templates are not complete templates. They contain the differences compared to a given site definition.

    ❑ If you create many sites using a site template and later want to change the template, changing it will not affect existing sites.

❑ When removing a user account from the Active Directory, it will not automatically be removed from SharePoint.

    ❑ You can remove a user account from a complete site collection, but there is no feature to remove the user from all site collections at once.

    ❑ If you remove a user account from a site and that user is an owner for this site collection, he or she will still have full access. You must remove the user from the owner list manually if this account will still exist in the Active Directory.

❑ You can use the SharePoint Central Administration tool and its Manage site collection owner to control and modify the owner for a given site collection.

Now you know how to create sites and do general administration of WSS. In the next chapter, you learn how to install and configure SharePoint Portal Server 2003.

Installing SharePoint Portal Server

In this chapter you learn how to install SharePoint Portal Server (SPS) with both types of available database configurations. You also learn how to prepare for the installation and to understand the different types of system user accounts involved in this action. After the installation is complete, you learn how to check that everything is okay and some basic troubleshooting tips.

This chapter is organized by initial sections describing what you are about to do and why, then a step-by-step description follows on how to do it, and finally some more information, including any tips and tricks based on real-world scenarios.

> To help you determine whether you should use WSS with or without SPS, consult Chapter 7, "Comparing WSS and SPS."

Preparing for SPS

In Chapter 2 you learned how to install the stand-alone version of Windows SharePoint Services (WSS). When installing SPS you also install WSS, and the administration you learned to do in Chapter 3 is still valid. When running an SPS environment, it is common to refer to the WSS part as the *team sites*, and this name is also used in this and following chapters. The procedure to install SPS is very similar, but there are several important differences, such as the following:

- ❑ More system user accounts to define and plan for.
- ❑ Two more types of databases.
- ❑ New SharePoint service roles.
- ❑ A different type of MSDE database.

The effect is that you must plan more carefully when installing SPS compared to WSS. But you also gain many new and enhanced features, which enable you to build better solutions for sharing information between users and for more effective personal use.

In Chapter 2 you saw that WSS is the foundation for SPS. It is simply impossible to install SPS without WSS, and the setup program does it for you, so your SharePoint environment consists of one or more SPS portal sites and any number of WSS sites. Everything you learned about WSS in the previous chapter is still valid when running SPS and WSS together, including the option of running SPS in a non-domain environment.

Just as with WSS, you can choose between two database types: the Microsoft SQL Server 2000 Desktop Engine (MSDE) and the MS SQL 2000 or 2005 Server. One thing you must learn right away is that the MSDE version that comes with the stand-alone version of WSS is not the same as the MSDE version that comes with SPS! The difference is that the WSS version of MSDE, also known as the WMSDE, is unlimited in size and the number of concurrent sessions. (The MSDE that comes with SPS is limited to 2 GB of data and five concurrent sessions). This is very confusing, and one can only speculate about the reason behind this decision. Maybe Microsoft thinks that if you invest in SPS, you should also invest in the full SQL Server database engine.

When Do You Need SPS?

Because WSS comes free with Windows 2003 Server and SPS is not free, you must evaluate the need your users have. Chapter 2 has a more complete list, but the following table lists just the SPS features. If you need one or more of these, you must install SPS. These questions should probably be answered by users in your organization. Make sure to explain to them why it is so important they think hard before answering these questions:

Question	People to Ask	Comment
Do you need an intranet that allows you to target information to certain groups?	Top management, people responsible for managing organization-wide information.	Only SPS allows targeting of news and lists of information.
Do you need an easy and fast way to navigate to your information, regardless of its storage location?	Subject-matter experts, project leaders, power users, end users.	SPS offers *topics* to solve this need. You can build similar functionality in WSS, but it requires much more work.
Do you want to be able to search for information stored both inside and outside SharePoint?	All types of users.	Only SPS offers global search functionality.
Do you need a way of presenting more information than just the e-mail address and phone number for some or all of your users?	Middle-management, team leaders, project leaders.	SPS has its "My Site" feature, which presents much more information about users than the typical "Employee List."
Is there a need to integrate non-Microsoft applications into the SharePoint environment?	Top management, people responsible for managing organization-wide information.	SPS has a feature called "Single Sign-On," which allows you to write code that displays information stored in other applications, such as SAP.

The license model for SPS is based on the number of SPS servers and the number of SPS users. If a user is just reading information, she still needs one SPS user license. The exact cost for SPS installation depends on your type of software agreement with Microsoft and the number of users. If you have many users, you will pay less per user license, compared to a few users. You need to contact your license distributor to get the exact price.

SPS allows you to choose between the free, but limited, MSDE database and the full and unlimited MS SQL 2000 or 2005 Server. Because the MSDE size limit of 2 GB is so low, in practice you must choose the full MS SQL Server for a production environment. Note that it does not have to be an exclusive MS SQL Server for SPS; if you have an existing MS SQL Server and it has available capacity, you can use it.

Using SQL 2005 works only with WSS with Service Pack 2.

Three Database Combinations

Two types of databases and two types of locations are possible. However, one of these options is not supported, so there are in total three types of configurations. The following table describes the options you have for SPS and its database engine:

Databases	Local Database Engine	Remote Database Server
MSDE	Yes	Not supported
MS SQL 2000/2005 Server	Yes	Yes

Even though MSDE comes free with SPS, it is very hard to imagine this combination in a production environment because of the space limitation of MSDE. Still, it may be relevant in some cases, and you will find more information about how to install it in the next section.

Single-Server Configuration with a Local MSDE

This is an installation of both SPS (including WSS) and MSDE on the same computer. Microsoft sometimes refers to this configuration as a stand-alone server. The typical scenario for this kind of configuration is when doing a pilot or evaluation of SharePoint. You should think twice before using this configuration in a production environment because of the limitations of the MSDE database.

You cannot install MSDE on an Active Directory domain controller.

SPS has its own search and index module that is independent of the MS SQL database. Even when using the MSDE database, you have access to the advanced search features in the portal site.

Single-Server Configuration with a Local MS SQL Server

This configuration is known as the single-server configuration and is perfect for the small- to medium-sized organization. It is also a very good solution for larger departments or subsidiaries of larger companies that need a very good intranet solution with advanced search capabilities, as well as a team collaboration platform. The cost is higher than the previous configuration, because it requires both an SPS license and an MS SQL Server license.

You need one SPS Client Access License (CAL) and one MS SQL Server CAL for each SPS user.

This database engine allows you to build an SPS solution for many thousands of users because there are no size limitations. Note that you do not need to activate the full-text search feature in MS SQL. SPS has its own search engine and does not rely on MS SQL Server for searching.

A Small Farm: SPS with a Separate MS SQL Server

As with WSS you can choose to install SPS including WSS on one server and MS SQL on another server. Microsoft calls this a *small farm*, just like the combination of WSS and MS SQL on two separate servers. The term *farm* simply means you have two or more servers, regardless of the type of SharePoint installation.

Using a farm offers the following main advantages:

❑   Better performance (it can support more users).

❑   Possibility to build clustered SQL Servers (requires the Enterprise edition of MS SQL Server).

   Clusters require the Enterprise version of SQL Server.

It is possible to build SPS solutions with more than one SPS server for load balancing and fault-tolerance. Microsoft calls such installations *medium* or *large farms*, depending on how many SharePoint servers you use. To understand how these medium and large farms work, you must learn about the different roles in SPS, known as the front-end server roles, and what databases SPS is using.

The Databases in SPS

Because SPS is more advanced than WSS, it also needs more types of databases to perform its tasks. Two of these types are the same as in a WSS environment, and two are exclusive for SPS installations:

❑   **Configuration database:** (Used by WSS and SPS.) Contains SharePoint configuration settings, such as front-end and back-end servers, mail servers, and portal site names. The name suffix for this database is _Config_DB.

❑   **Content database:** (Used by WSS and SPS.) Contains the actual data, stored in the portal site and the team sites. Name suffix: _SITE.

❑   **User Profile database:** (Used by SPS.) Contains properties about every SharePoint user and definitions of audiences. Name suffix: _PROF.

❑   **Service Database:** (Used by SPS.) Contains data for the indexing and search service, plus information about alert settings in the portal site. This is also known as the component database. Name suffix: _SERV.

You can create a new content database when needed, but the other three types must exist in one copy only. In addition to these four databases, you can create a fifth one when installing the Single Sign-On function into SPS. That database will be named by the administrator (for example, "SSO" for single sign-on).

The Front-End and Back-End Roles

SharePoint Portal Server has more built-in functionality than WSS. To accomplish this, SPS is divided into four different services, known as front-end roles. These roles are as follows:

❑   Web Service

❑   Search Service

❑   Index Service

❑   Job Service

All these service roles can be configured to run on one SPS server or separated into several servers. In addition to these front-end service roles, there is also the term back-end server, which simply means the server that runs the SQL database engine.

By dividing the SPS functionality into different roles, you can build solutions that match the requirements you have. For example, small and medium organizations with up to 10,000 users may be satisfied with a small farm consisting of one front-end server running all SPS roles and one back-end server running MS SQL. Another organization may require fault-tolerance and build a solution with multiple front-end servers running the Web and Search roles, one more front-end server running the Index and Job roles, plus one back-end server.

The number of possible combinations is very large, so Microsoft decided to limit the number of supported farm configurations. After all, they are the ones who need to provide support, and even their support team consists of human beings. Later in this chapter you learn more about these farm configurations and how you can configure them.

The Web Service Role

This front-end role actually runs on both SPS and stand-alone WSS installations. It is responsible for answering any request from users who connect to the SharePoint server. In other words, this role shows the user the web site pages and content. This Web role will constantly read and write to the back-end server to do whatever the user requests.

The basic action in any web application is very simple: a web client requests a web page by entering a URL address or clicking a link. This is known as a GET request and results in a connection to the web server, asking the web server to find the requested page and send it back using the HTML format. After that, the session between the client and the server is disconnected. When the user clicks another link, a new connection is established. After the new page is sent back to the client, the session is disconnected again. There is nothing that requires that the exact same web server to be used for all the connected sessions from a web client. If you have another web server with access to the same information, it may answer the next connection from this web client. This is known as a *stateless connection*.

SharePoint's Web role uses stateless connections. If you install the Web role on several servers, it is possible to divide the client load between them. But you need to solve two problems first. One is to make sure all web servers have access to the same information. You do this by using a common back-end database for all of them. The second thing to solve is that all of these web servers must look like one single SharePoint server; otherwise the web clients must select a particular web server to communicate with. Using the Windows 2003 Network Load Balancing (NLB) service solves the second issue. The NLB service is a feature in Windows 2003 Server that allows up to 32 physical web servers to share a virtual server name; for the client all these servers will then look like one. This is known as a *web farm* (or a web cluster); however, SharePoint only supports up to eight servers running the web service role.

To summarize: Use the NLB service when you need to create a web farm with two or more SharePoint servers running the Web role. It will automatically direct a new client session to the Web role that is available with the least load. If a Web role server goes down, clients will be directed to another Web role server. The result is both load balancing and fault-tolerance.

For more information about using NLB for SharePoint farms, go to http://www.microsoft.com/technet/prodtechnol/sppt/reskit/c1261881x.mspx.

The Search Service Role

The second SharePoint role exists only for SPS installations; WSS alone does not have this. The responsibility for this role is to answer to search queries entered by the client. For example, when a user searches for the phrase "Viking," this happens:

1. The user enters the phrase in the search field in SPS.

2. This request is received by the Web service.

3. The Web service sends the request to the Search service.

4. The Search service looks for this phrase in its indexing files.

5. The result (no match, or a list of matching documents, files, and pages) is returned in XML format to the Web service.

6. The Web service converts the result to HTML format and sends this information back to the client.

This raises several questions: What are index files, where do they come from, and where are they stored? The answers are these: An index file consists of thousands of words and phrases, with a pointer to all the places and documents where these words or phrases will be found. These index files are created by the Index service and replicated to each server running the Search service. These index files are stored locally on the server running the Search service, by default in the folder C:\Program Files\SharePoint Portal Server\Data. By default there are two index types: Portal Content and Non-Portal Content.

You can install more than one SPS server running the Search service, but the maximum number is four. Because this service is using local index files, it is not dependent on other servers or roles to do its job. It is possible to combine the Search service with other services; this makes it possible to use the Search role on the same server that is running the Web role, even in web farm scenarios, as long as each Search role server has identical copies of the index files. That would result in load balancing and fault-tolerance for the search feature in SPS.

The Index Service Role

The third SharePoint service is also exclusive for SPS installations only. This service is responsible for building the index files by crawling content sources. The SharePoint administrator configures what content sources this service will index. The index files created by the crawling process are automatically copied by the Index service to all search servers, in case you have a configuration with a separate index and search servers. Note that this service does not crawl the portal site or the people in the user profile database; this is done by the Job role, as described in the next section.

You can configure this role to index the following content sources:

- ❑ Any file server in your network.
- ❑ Your MS Exchange server (including public folders).
- ❑ Any Lotus Notes database.
- ❑ Any other web application internally.
- ❑ Any external web site on the Internet.

For example, you can configure the Index service to scan and index all files and documents on your file server, all public folders in your MS Exchange server, and your partner's public web sites. When the users later search for information, they will find it, as long as it is stored in any of these content sources, including any part of the SharePoint database.

The Index service is very resource intensive regarding CPU and disk access. By separating this service from the Web and Search service, many more users will be supported in the SharePoint environment. The indexing activity can be split between up to four different SharePoint servers. There is no fault-tolerance built into this role, so if one index server goes down, no other will take over the indexing crawling that server is configured to do. But you can load-balance by dividing the content sources to be indexed between the index servers. You can have up to four different Index role servers in one SPS farm.

Only one Index server can crawl a given content source.

The Job Service Role

The final SharePoint service role is the Job service, and it is an exclusive SPS role. There can be only one server running the Job service in a farm, and it must be configured to run together with the Index service. The reason is that the Job role is responsible for managing the indexing of the portal site and all users listed in the User Profile database. The Job service relies upon the Windows Scheduler service, which defines when these indexing processes will run. Following is a list of the tasks that the Job service is responsible for:

- ❑ Managing user-defined alerts.
- ❑ Importing user profiles from Active Directory.
- ❑ Compiling audience membership.
- ❑ Crawling and indexing the portal site.
- ❑ Crawling and indexing the User Profile database.
- ❑ Hosting the single sign-on administration web pages.

Medium and Large Farms

Previously in this chapter you learned that a configuration with one SPS server and one MS SQL Server is referred to as a small farm and is designed to support up to 15,000 users. If you need to support more users or need to ensure high availability, you need to build configurations with more than one SPS server and maybe even more MS SQL Servers.

The first option is to build a medium farm, which will support up to 50,000 users, depending on the configuration. Microsoft supports these two medium farm configurations:

❑ Medium farm configuration:

  ❑ One or two SPS front-end servers with both the Web and the Search role.

  ❑ One SPS front-end server with both the Index and Job role.

  ❑ One or more MS SQL back-end servers.

❑ Medium farm in a clustered environment:

  ❑ A Windows 2003 cluster with two nodes, running active/passive mode. Each node runs the SPS front-end Web and Search roles, plus the back-end MS SQL Server.

  ❑ One SPS front-end server with both the Index and Job role.

The second option is to build a large farm configuration that may support more than a million users, depending on the exact configuration and the hardware settings for the servers. Microsoft supports these large farm configurations:

❑ Two to eight servers running SPS assigned the Web role.

❑ Two to four servers running SPS assigned the Search role.

❑ One to four servers running SPS assigned the Index role, one of which *must* be assigned the Job server role.

❑ One or more servers running MS SQL Server.

Hardware Requirements

SharePoint Portal Server is no different from WSS when it comes to hardware requirements. As long as there is at least 1 GB of memory, the speed and the number of CPUs will affect performance most. Just as with WSS, if you want to set up a demo environment or do a simple pilot installation, you will get far with 512 MB of memory and a single CPU server. But be careful — there has been more than one pilot installation that suddenly became regarded as a production environment. If you suspect that this could happen to you, I recommend installing the pilot on a server that has the requirements for the production environment or is easy to upgrade with more CPU and memory.

Important things to keep in mind when planning the production environment include the following:

❑ SharePoint is a web application! There is no permanent connection between the client browser and the SharePoint server. Every time a user opens a link or a document, the browser connects, gets what the user requested, and closes the connection immediately after that, regardless of how long the user looks at that information.

❑ The number of users in the organization is not the same as the number of simultaneous users.

❑ Different activities in SharePoint require different resources; for example, displaying a project site normally generates a very light load on the server, whereas indexing the database generates a much higher load.

Calculating the Number of OPS Required

You may recall the exact figures for calculating the operations per second (OPS) from Chapter 2, but here is the formula again for calculating the load on the SharePoint Portal Server. This information is used for estimating the number of supported users, given a hardware configuration:

$$\frac{A \times B \times C \times D}{360,000 \times E} = \text{Operations per second (OPS)}$$

Given the following estimated data that you must supply:

- ❑ A = The number of users
- ❑ B = The percentage of active users in a typical day
- ❑ C = The number of operations per active user per day (1–10, typically 8)
- ❑ D = Peak factor (1–10, typically 5)
- ❑ E = The number of working hours per day

For more details about these parameters, see Chapter 2.

Example: An Organization with 15,000 Normal Users

Your organization has 15,000 employees (A). The percentage of active users on a typical day is 50 (B). The number of operations per active user is 7 (C). The number of working hours for the organization as a whole is 12 hours (E). You estimate the peak factor (D) to be 10. The formula for this organization will look like this:

$$\frac{15,000 \times 50 \times 7 \times 10}{360,000 \times 12} = 12 \text{ Operations per second (OPS)}$$

Now you have a good idea of the load your system will generate. Next step is to use this information to calculate the hardware you need. In the following table are some typical configurations and the estimated operations per second they support:

Server Configuration	Estimated OPS Supported
Small farm: One SPS server and one SQL 2000, both configured with 1 GB memory and a dual 2.8 GHz CPU	65 OPS
Small farm: One SPS server and one SQL 2000, both configured with 1 GB memory and a dual 3.06 GHz CPU	105 OPS
Medium farm: Two web & search servers, one Index and Job plus 1 MS SQL Server with 1 GB memory and 2 x 3.06 CPU	110 OPS

As you can see from the preceding table, there is no need to install anything other than a small farm; notice that increasing the CPU speed makes a dramatic improvement of the number of OPS supported.

Calculating the Disk Space Needed

When planning for the required disk space, you do not have to worry about the SPS binary files, because they are small compared to other files. More important are the index and database files. Remember that with SPS you get the free MSDE database that is limited to 2 GB in size. Very few SPS installations have less than this limit, so you will normally end up using MS SQL. Regardless of the database type, you still need to follow this important rule:

> **You must always have at least 50 percent free space on your database disk!**

The reason for this is that some database troubleshooting utilities need to make a copy of the database to perform their tasks. If you don't have the required space, you may get into a situation where you cannot fix a problem.

There is no difference between SPS and WSS when it comes to estimating the required volume of data for your SharePoint environment. The documents, files, and pictures are responsible for more than 90 percent of the total database volume. To estimate the disk space needed for your database, start by estimating the number of files it will contain. For example, assume you estimate that it will contain about 100,000 files and documents, with an average of 400 KB; in total this will require 40 GB. Add to that 10 GB for the other types of information you will store and you get 50 GB in total. Following this rule, you must have at least a 100-GB disk for the database files alone.

Software Requirements

Because SharePoint Portal Server is a web application, it requires Internet Information Services 6.0 (IIS 6), running on MS Windows 2003 Server. SPS also requires that ASP.NET and its supporting components are installed. The easiest way to get this configuration right for a SharePoint server is to follow these steps:

Try It Out   **Prepare Windows 2003 for SPS 2003**

1.   Log on to your Windows 2003 Server as the administrator.

2.   Choose Start⇨Control Panel.

3.   Click the Add/Remove Windows Component button.

4.   Select the Application Server and click Details.

5.   Make sure everything is cleared, including the Internet Information Service (IIS).

6.   Check the ASP.NET box, and it will automatically check all the components it needs.

7.   Click OK to save this configuration.

SPS 2003 requires .NET 1.1 Frameworks. If you have previously installed ASP.NET 2.0 on this server, it will have .NET 2.0 Frameworks, which is not supported by SPS 2003. If so, make sure to configure the virtual servers in IIS used by SharePoint to not use ASP.NET 2.0 and .NET 2.0.

You can use any edition of Windows 2003 Server for an SPS installation. However, the Windows 2003 Server Web Edition does not allow a local database installation; in that case you must use a remote MS SQL Server.

The IIS Virtual Server

Chapter 2 presented the background to the development of Internet Information Server (IIS), its virtual web servers, and the application pools. SharePoint Portal Server has the same requirements as WSS in this respect. It also uses two different virtual IIS servers to start with: one for the user web sites (the portal sites and the team sites) and one for the administrative web site. Each of these two virtual IIS servers uses a separate application pool that is created during the setup of SPS:

❑ **The user web site:** By default uses the Default Web Site and the MSSharePointPortalAppPool.

❑ **The administrative site:** By default uses the SharePoint Central Administration site and the CentralAdminAppPool.

Each virtual IIS server can host only one portal site, including its team sites. If you need more than one SPS portal site, you need to create new virtual IIS servers for each one. It is possible to share the same application pool between multiple virtual IIS servers and therefore portal sites. IIS supports up to nine virtual IIS servers with individual application pools. Because the administrative web site uses one application pool, you may have up to eight portal sites with individual application pools. You can also use one single application pool that is shared with up to 99 virtual IIS servers (in effect, 98 portal sites).

When installing SPS you need to be sure about these two things regarding the user web site:

❑ Which virtual IIS server SharePoint is used for its portal and team sites.

❑ The security account used by the application pool for this virtual IIS server.

Each application pool uses something called the Security Account, which defines the security context for the application pool and its web sites. This can either be a built-in account (typically the Network Service) or a standard user account (if so, make sure this account is granted permission as Database Creators and the Security Administrators in the MS SQL Server).

When using a separate MS SQL Server, select a user account as the application pool security account, because it is easier to grant MS SQL roles.

In general, you should avoid creating a lot of service accounts because the more you have, the harder they are to manage. Because the same service account can be used by several application pools, you should create a separate user account, for example SP_Service, and use it as the security account for both SharePoint application pools.

Service Accounts for SPS

SharePoint Portal Server is more advanced than WSS and therefore needs more service accounts (user accounts used for specific services). Depending on how complex your SharePoint installation is, you might need more or fewer service accounts. You should create these accounts before starting the installation, but remember that you can use the same user account for more than one service if you want to keep the number of service accounts to a minimum.

Avoid using the standard Administrator account as a service account, because you need to update each SPS service every time you change the password.

During the installation of SPS, you need two or more of the following service accounts, depending on how complex your environment will be. For example, the single-server SPS installation with an MSDE database only requires the Default Content Access Account to create the portal; the rest is preconfigured but can be changed later. Some of these service accounts are requested when you activate special features later, even for a single-server installation of SPS. Use the following table as a reference for all service accounts in SharePoint Portal Server installations and configurations:

Service Account	Description	Recommendations
Application Pool Security Account	This account defines the security context for the web server connected to this application pool. It is also used when SPS communicates with the database server. It needs to be a member of the Security Administrator and Database Creators role in MS SQL Server.	For Single-Server installations, use the Network Service account. For SPS farms, use a separate service account for all application pools.
Default Content Access Account	This account is used when the Index role crawls locations outside SharePoint's databases. This account must have read access in these locations to do its job, but you can configure SharePoint to use a special user account for given locations.	Use an account with read access to most of the locations that will be indexed. Members of the Domain Admin group have this access.
Configuration Database Account	This account is used by SPS when communicating with the configuration database. You can use a local account or a domain account. It must be a member of the local server's Power User group or the local Administrators group.	This account will only be requested when using a full MS SQL Server. In most installations it is okay to use the same account as for the Application Pool security account.

If you use separate user accounts for Default Content Access Account and Application Pool Security Account, it may help you better understand error messages when they occur.

Minimum and Recommended Configurations

To summarize the previous hardware and software requirement sections, you can use the following table, which lists Microsoft's minimum and recommended configurations. Remember that for a pilot installation you can actually get away with even less than the given minimum memory size in the table:

Item	Minimum Requirement	MS Recommends
Operating System	Any edition of Microsoft Windows Server 2003	Any edition of Microsoft Windows Server 2003
CPU	1 CPU running at 550 MHz	2 CPUs running at least 1 GHz
RAM	512	1 GB or more
Disk space	500 MB	500 MB/SharePoint Site

Item	Minimum Requirement	MS Recommends
File System	NTFS	NTFS
IIS version	6.0 with ASP.NET (in Worker Process Isolation Mode)	6.0 with ASP.NET (in Worker Process Isolation Mode)
Database engine	WMSDE or SQL Server 2000 with Service Pack 3a	A separate SQL Server 2005 and its latest Service Pack
Internet Browser	IE 5.01 with SP2 or later	IE 6 with the latest Service Pack, or later IE versions

Installing SPS

By now you have the necessary information to start the installation of SPS. The following section describes the exact steps required to install SharePoint Portal Server. If you have other web applications installed on the same server, please make a backup before you start, to be prepared for the unlikely possibility that something goes wrong and the server gets messed up beyond repair!

Contrary to WSS installations, you have a choice of which virtual IIS server to use for the portal and team sites. When you select this virtual server, it is automatically extended, and you do not need to do this manually.

> *In the following sections are three complete step-by-step instructions on how to install SPS. You have to read the description only for the particular type of installation you are about to do. To get the SPS 2003 installation CD, you typically order it from your favorite software vendor.*

Installing a Stand-Alone Server with the MSDE Database

Installing an SPS using a local MSDE database is very straightforward and easy. You can do it within 10 minutes without much hassle. Remember that you cannot perform this type of installation on a domain controller, because it will not allow the MSDE database! Follow these steps to install both the SPS application and the MSDE database on the same server:

Try It Out   Install SPS and MSDE on a Stand-Alone Server

1. Log on as an administrator to the Windows 2003 Server you will use for your SPS and MSDE installation.

2. Make sure Windows 2003 Server has the latest service packs and security patches installed by going to Start⇨All Programs⇨Windows Update.

3. Verify that you have ASP.NET installed, as previously described in the section "Software Requirements." If not, you can cancel the installation of SPS now and install ASP.NET. You need the Windows 2003 CD, but you do not have to reboot the server.

4. Start the installation by mounting the SPS CD-ROM and selecting the option Install Microsoft Office SharePoint Portal Server 2003 Components in the start page that will be displayed. You can also choose to start the SETUP.EXE on the CD-ROM directly.

5. The first page displays what software is required to install SPS and WSS; notice that the MSDE database is listed as May Be Required, because you may choose to run the MS SQL Server instead. But in this installation you will use the MSDE database. Click Next to continue the installation.

6. The next page warns that the setup process needs to stop IIS and other web services; click OK to go on. You will not see a progress bar that shows the status of the installation of WSS and then SPS, so you will have to wait until the next page shows up.

7. The next page is the MS Office SPS 2003 Setup Wizard. Click Next. Note that this step may take several minutes to complete.

8. The next page is the End User License Agreement. Read it carefully, and if you agree check the box "I accept all of the terms in this license agreement" and click Next.

9. The next page is where you enter the Product Key. For some editions of SPS, this number is entered automatically. Click Next to go on.

10. On the next page you select whether to use the MSDE database "Install with database engine" or the full MS SQL Server "Install without database engine." Make sure to select the first option to get the MSDE database.

Notice also the Destination file locations; this is where you define where the binary and data files will be stored. The MSDE database will use the data path, and it is good practice to avoid using the C: drive for data files because of the paging file in Windows. If possible, use another local drive or SAN disk if available. Click the Browse button to change either of these two paths.

Click Next. This starts the installation of the SPS files. After that you will see a progress bar indicating the installation of the MSDE database engine. These steps may take several minutes to complete.

11. The next page shows the status. All three modules (the WSS, SPS, and MSDE engine) should now be marked as Installed. Click Next and then Finish to complete the installation.

12. The SharePoint Portal Server Central Administration tool starts up automatically. This is where you configure some of the service accounts used by SPS.

Go back to SharePoint's administrative page; the parameters asked for on this page are shown in Figure 4-1. For more details see the previous section about the service accounts.

❑ **Contact E-mail Address:** This address is used by SharePoint whenever it reads an external site, while indexing it. The address is registered in a log file at that server. If the external administrator needs to contact you, he may use this address.

❑ **Default Content Access Account:** This account is used when the Index role crawls external files (for example, your file server, MS Exchange, or external web sites). The default value is the Network Service. You may want to change that to a service account created in your domain. If so, check the Specify account box and enter the full account name, including the domain (for example, contoso\sp_service), and its password twice. Note that this account must exist to be accepted.

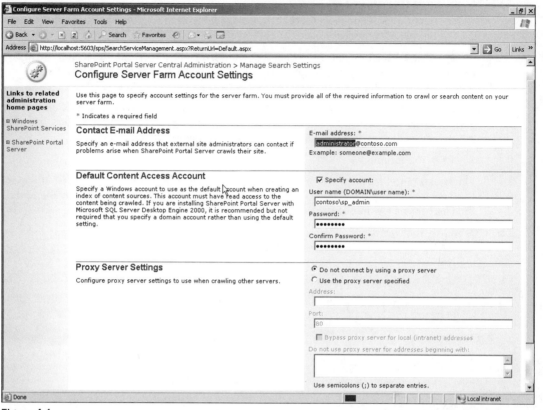

Figure 4-1

❑ **Proxy Server Settings:** The last part of this page is about connecting to the Internet. If you want SPS to crawl external web sites, you may have to pass a proxy server, such as MS ISA, to get out. This part is where you tell SPS how to make this connection through the proxy. If you don't have a proxy or if you do not want to crawl external web sites, you can leave this field as is.

Click OK to continue configuring SPS.

13. The next page is where you create the first portal site. At this moment there is no portal site. This is what you create next. You can choose what virtual IIS server to use for that portal site; you can use the existing Default Web Site or create a new virtual IIS server. The same rule for running multiple virtual servers in WSS also applies here: Multiple virtual servers must be distinct in some way, by having separate IP addresses, TCP Port numbers, or Host Header Names. If you want a special virtual server for the portal sites, make sure to create it now. When you know what virtual IIS server to use for the portal, go back to SharePoint's administrative page.

❑ **Portal Creation Options:** Make sure the option "Create a portal" is selected.

❑ **Site Name:** Enter the name for this portal. This name can be changed later.

❑ **Site URL/Virtual server:** Select the virtual IIS server for this portal site, including its team sites. If you have more than one available virtual server, use the pull-down menu to select the one to be used. The standard option is Default Web Site.

❑ **Site URL/URL:** This is the default URL address for this portal. By default it will be the server name. If you change it, make sure to create an alias record in the DNS server that points to this server.

❑ **Owner/Account name:** This user will have full access to all parts of SharePoint, including administrative rights. The best practice is to use a role-based account, such as "sp_admin," instead of an ordinary user account. See the example in Figure 4-2.

Click OK to continue.

14. On the next and final step, you are asked to confirm the creation of the new portal. If you want to change something, click the Back button. If all is fine, click OK to start creating the portal. This may take a few minutes to complete.

15. If you see the web page in Figure 4-3, you are done! The portal is created and ready to be used. Click the Home page link to see the results of your hard work.

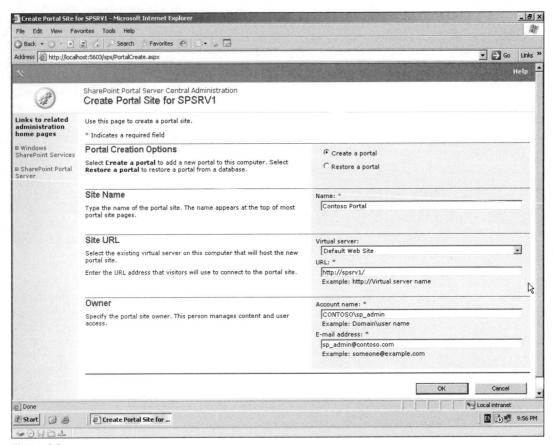

Figure 4-2

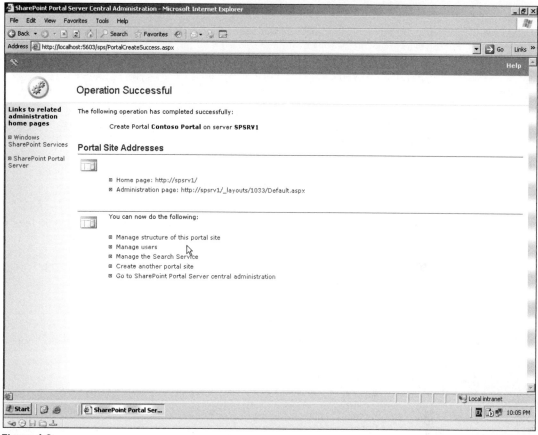

Figure 4-3

After the Installation of the Stand-Alone Server

There are many things to do directly after the installation, but some of these need immediate attention, and other things will be taken care of when appropriate. For a single-server installation of SPS, you should now do these two things:

❑ Download and install the latest service pack for SPS and WSS. You start by installing the WSS service pack and then the SPS service pack. A good place to start looking for these service packs is http://www.microsoft.com/windowsserver2003/technologies/sharepoint/default.mspx for WSS service packs and http://www.microsoft.com/office/sharepoint/prodinfo for SPS service packs.

❑ Do a full backup of the SharePoint Portal Server environment with the backup utility that comes with SPS (see the end of this chapter) or your ordinary backup program, if it is SharePoint-aware.

Checking the New Folder and Applications

The portal site is now up and running, and you will very soon check it out. But first take a look at what has changed in the Windows 2003 Server. You have several new file directories used by SPS and the underlying WSS environment:

❑ `C:\Program Files\Common Files\Microsoft Shared\web server extensions\60` — This folder has several new directories, including a Bin directory where several tools for WSS are stored. All these files and folders are identical to a pure WSS installation.

❑ `C:\Program Files\SharePoint Portal Server` — This has folders and files specific for the SPS application. There is a Bin directory that contains all the dll files plus the backup utility for SPS. In the Data folder you will find index files, and in the Log folder are installation log files and other log files that you can view from within the SPS administrative tool.

❑ `C:\Program Files\Microsoft SQL Server\MSSQL$SHAREPOINTPORTAL` — This folder structure stores the MSDE information; the Data folder stores the actual SQL database files; the Log folder stores the MS SQL transaction log files and error log files.

There are also new application links listed in the Start⇨All Programs⇨SharePoint Portal Server node. By default you will see four entries there:

❑ **SharePoint Central Administration:** This is the administrative tool for SharePoint. This is simply a link to the web site in the virtual IIS server "SharePoint Central Administration." You can start this tool from within the user portal site and its Site Settings link, as you will see more of in the next chapter.

❑ **SharePoint Portal Server's Administrative Guide:** This is the online help manual for SharePoint. You can also find help inside the user portal site almost anywhere.

❑ **SharePoint Portal Server Data Backup and Restore:** This starts the SPS backup program with a graphical interface. The same program can also be started using a command prompt, which makes it easy to create a backup script.

❑ **SharePoint Portal Server Single Sign-on Administration:** This is a special tool for managing the single sign-on feature in SPS. This tool is used to store user accounts and passwords for accessing external applications from within SPS.

Checking the New Virtual IIS Server Settings

Finally you will find that the virtual IIS server you selected for hosting the portal site has been extended (see Chapter 2 for more information about extending virtual servers). By default this will be the Default Web Site, unless you selected another virtual server. Start by opening the IIS Manager: Start⇨ Administration Tools⇨Internet Information Service (IIS) Manager.

Expand the Web Sites node. Note that you have two IIS virtual servers here:

❑ **SharePoint Central Administration:** Used by SharePoint for the administration web site. This virtual server was created during the initial phase of the SPS installation, before the portal site was created.

❑ **Default Web Site:** This is the virtual server that hosts the portal sites, team sites, and other WSS-based sites.

Right-click Default Web Site and select Properties. Switch to the Home Directory tab; note the application pool name this virtual server is using. You may recall from earlier in this chapter that this virtual server was using `DefaultAppPool` before the installation of SPS, but now it has changed to the `MSSharePointPortalAppPool`. The other virtual IIS server, SharePoint Central Administration, will by default use the `CentralAdminAppPool`. Expand the Application Pools node (located directly above the Web Sites node), right-click either of the application pools used by SharePoint's virtual servers, and switch to the Identity tab. Note that the security account this application pool is using is the built-in Network Service account, which is fine because this is a local database.

To summarize: WSS uses two virtual IIS servers, one for the web sites that your SharePoint users utilize and another for the administration of SharePoint. These two virtual servers use separate application pools. Both these application pools use the same security account.

Installing a Single-Server with a Local MS SQL Database

One of the most common installation scenarios for small and medium-sized organizations is a single-server with both SPS and MS SQL Server. Many of the following steps are identical to the previous installation scenario using a local MSDE database, except for these important things:

❑   You need to install the MS SQL 2000 Server with Service Pack 3 or later, before the installation of SPS. Note that as of this writing, SPS 2003 cannot use MS SQL 2005 Server.

❑   You will need to define more service accounts. An example is the user account that SPS will use when communicating with the MS SQL Server (the Application Pool Identity account).

Follow these steps to install both MS SQL 2000 and SPS 2003 on the same server:

Try It Out   **Install MS SQL Server 2000 and Service Pack 4**

1.   Log on as an administrator to the Windows 2003 Server you will use for your SPS and MS SQL installation.

2.   Make sure Windows 2003 Server has the latest service packs and security patches installed by going to Start➪All Programs➪Windows Update.

3.   Verify that you have ASP.NET installed, as previously described in this chapter in the section "Software Requirements."

4.   Mount the CD with the MS SQL 2000 Server. On the Welcome page, click Next.

5.   On the Computer name page, select Local Computer and click Next.

6.   On the Installation Selection page, select Create a new instance of SQL Server, or install Client Tools; then click Next.

7.   On the User Information page, enter the registered owner of this SQL 2000 license and click Next.

8.   On the Software license agreement page, read the agreement and if you accept it, click Yes to continue.

9.   On the Installation Definition page, select Server and Client Tools and click Next.

10.   On the Instance page, make sure the Default option is checked and click Next.

11. On the Setup Type page, choose the option Typical and click Next.

12. On the Service Account page, accept the default option Use the same account for each service. Auto start SQL Server Service. Then select the user account that will be used by the SQL services. For a local installation you can select the option User the Local System account. If you select another account, make sure it is a member of the computer's local Power Users group. Click Next to continue.

13. On the Authentication Mode page, accept the default Windows Authentication Mode and click Next.

14. On the Start Copying Files page, click Next to continue.

15. On the Choose License Mode page, select the type of license you have and click Continue to start the actual installation.

16. After the installation you will get the Setup Complete page. Click Finish to complete the installation of MS SQL Server 2000.

17. The next step is to install the service pack for MS SQL Server 2000. SharePoint requires at least Service Pack 3, but you should install Service Pack 4 or later. You can get this service pack from the following URL: `http://www.microsoft.com/technet/prodtechnol/sql/2005/downloads`. Look for the latest service pack for MS SQL Server 2000. Download it and expand it. Then start the installation file `Setup.bat`.

18. On the Welcome page, click Next.

19. On the Software License Agreement page, read it and if you accept it, click Yes to continue.

20. On the Instance Name page, click Next.

21. On the Connect to Server page, accept the default option "The Windows account information I use to log on to my computer with (Windows authentication)" and click Next.

22. On the SA Password Warning page, enter a password for the SQL account SA. Make sure to store it in a safe place and then click OK.

23. On the SQL Server 2000 Service Pack 4 Setup page, check the option "Upgrade Microsoft Search and apply SQL Server 2000 SP4 (required)"; then click Continue.

24. On the Error Reporting page, if you want to activate this feature, check this box. Click OK.

25. On the Start Copying Files page, click Next. This step will take several minutes to complete.

26. When the installation is done, you will see a dialog box reminding you to make a backup. Click OK and then Finish to complete the installation of this service pack.

The SQL Server service MSSQLSERVER has not started at this point; you will have to start it manually or restart the server before installing SPS.

This concludes the MS SQL Server 2000 installation. Because you are configuring a single-server installation, the next step will be to install SPS on the same server. During this installation you will be asked about several service accounts for SharePoint. One of these is the Configuration database administration user account. Make sure this account exists and has been granted the necessary rights in the SQL Server. If you miss this, the installation will fail in step 14 in "Try It Out: Install SPS 2003 on a Stand-Alone Server" when installing SPS! Follow these steps to grant this user the necessary rights in the MS SQL Server:

Try It Out   **Add the Configuration Database Account to SQL**

1. Log on as an administrator to the MS SQL Server.

2. Start the SQL management tool by going to Start⇨All Programs⇨Microsoft SQL Server⇨Enterprise Manager.

3. Expand the nodes Microsoft SQL Servers⇨SQL Server Group⇨(local) (Windows NT).

    A red dot at the server icon indicates that the SQL Server service is not yet started. If so, right-click the server node and select Start now.

4. Expand the Security node. Right-click Logins and select New Login.

5. This will bring you a form page where you enter the user account name. Make sure to include the domain name (for example, Contoso\sp_service). Accept the other default values on this page. Click Server Roles in the left pane. Check the following roles: Security Administrators and Database Creators. Click OK to save and close.

6. Close the SQL Server Enterprise Manager.

SQL Server is now ready for SharePoint Portal Server. Follow these steps to install SPS:

Try It Out   **Install SPS 2003 on a Stand-Alone Server**

1. Log on as an administrator to the Windows 2003 Server you will use for your SPS and SQL Server installation.

2. Make sure Windows 2003 Server has the latest service packs and security patches installed by going to Start⇨All Programs⇨Windows Update.

3. Verify that you have ASP.NET with .NET 1.1 Framework installed, as previously described in the section "Software Requirements." If not, cancel the installation of SPS now and install ASP.NET. You need the Windows 2003 CD, but you do not have to reboot the server.

4. Start the installation by mounting the SPS CD-ROM and selecting the option Install Microsoft Office SharePoint Portal Server 2003 Components in the start page that will be displayed. You can also choose to start the SETUP.EXE on the CD-ROM directly.

5. The first page displays what software is required to install SPS and WSS. Notice that the MSDE database is listed as May Be Required. Don't choose to install that database, because you will use the MS SQL Server instead. Click Next to continue the installation.

6. The next page warns that the setup process needs to stop the IIS and other web services; click OK to go on. You will not see a progress bar that shows the status of the installation of WSS and then SPS; you simply have to wait for the next page to show up.

7. The next page is the MS Office SPS 2003 Setup Wizard. Click Next.

8. The next page is the End User License Agreement. Read it carefully, and if you agree check the box "I accept all of the terms in this license agreement" and click Next.

9. The next page is where you enter the Product Key. For some editions of SPS, this number is entered automatically. Click Next to go on.

10. On the next page you select whether to use the MSDE database "Install with database engine" or the full MS SQL Server "Install without database engine." Make sure to select the second option because you will use the MS SQL Server.

Notice also the Destination file locations; this is where you define where the binary and data files will be stored. The best practice is to avoid using the C: drive for data files because of the paging file in Windows. Click the Browse button to change either of these two paths.

Click Next. This starts the installation of the SPS program files. This step may take several minutes to complete.

11. The next page prompts you for a user account name and password for the database configuration administration account. SPS will use this account when communicating with the configuration database in MS SQL Server. This user must be a member of the local server's Power Users group or the Administrators group, but it does not need to be a Domain Admin member! See Figure 4-4.

When selecting a user account, it will automatically be granted the following rights: Replace a process level token; Adjust memory quotas for a process; and Log on as a service. The best practice is to use the same user account here as for the Application Pool Security such as SP_Service. Click Next to continue.

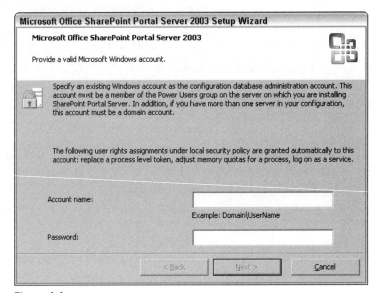

Figure 4-4

12. The next page shows the status. Only the two modules WSS and SPS should be marked as Installed. The MSDE database should be listed as Not Required. If not, you chose the wrong database type in step 10. Click Next and then Finish to complete the installation.

13. The SharePoint Portal Server Central Administration tool starts up automatically. This is where you configure two of the service accounts used by SPS; see Figure 4-5.

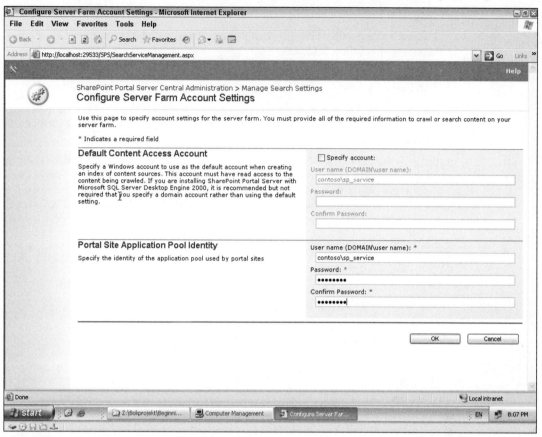

Figure 4-5

Remember that you have more details about each service account in the earlier section "Service Accounts for SPS."

Default Content Access Account: This account is used by the Index role when it crawls external content sources (for example, your file server, MS Exchange, or external web sites). The default value is the account defined as the Config user database account. The account that is used here needs read access to the external content sources to do its job. A tip here is to enter a user account that is a member of the Domain Admin group.

Portal Site Application Pool Identity: This account is used by the virtual server hosting the portal site and its team sites. You can use the same account as the for the Configuration user database account.

Click OK to continue the configuration of SPS.

14. The next page is the Specify Configuration Database Settings for <server name>. See Figure 4-6.

❑ **Database Connections:** Because this is the first and only SPS server, you must select Create configuration database.

❑ **Configuration Database Server:** The name for this server is automatically listed in the Database server field. Do not change this.

❑ **Configuration Database Name:** You can enter a name for this database or use the default name SPS01_Config.db. Unless you have a special reason, accept the default name. Click OK to continue.

15. The next page is the Configure Server Farm Account Settings. Enter the e-mail address for the responsible person for this SPS server. This address will be used by SPS when it crawls external source content, like public web sites on the Internet. The address will be registered in the remote web server's log file. The best practice is to use a role based e-mail address instead of a specific user to avoid problems if this person later leaves the company.

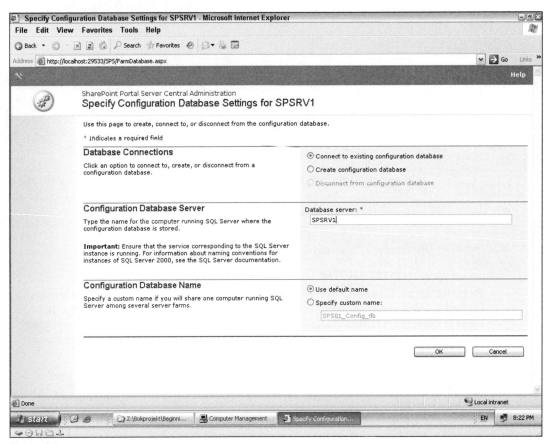

Figure 4-6

The second part on this page is about how SPS will connect to the Internet. If there is a proxy server that SPS needs to use, enter its address and port number. Click OK to continue.

16. The next page is the Configure Server Topology. The first time you look at this page, you might panic when you see the bottom of the page, which tells you all the problems with this SPS server, as Figure 4-7 shows.

But don't despair. It simply says that this SPS installation is not yet configured! Start by clicking the Change Components button at the bottom of this page. This will open the new page Change Components Assignments; here you set the front-end roles for this SPS server. Because this is a single-server configuration, it must have all the roles. Check the three boxes for Web, Search, and Index. The Job server role is almost hidden; use the pull-down menu and select the only option you have: the name of this server (see Figure 4-8). At the end of this page is a section called Document Library Server Component. This part is only used if you use SPS 2003 in an SPS 2001–compatible mode. If you do not need this, leave this section empty! When done, click OK to return to the previous page.

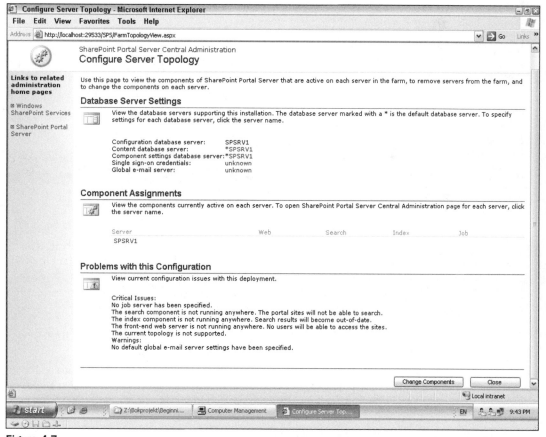

Figure 4-7

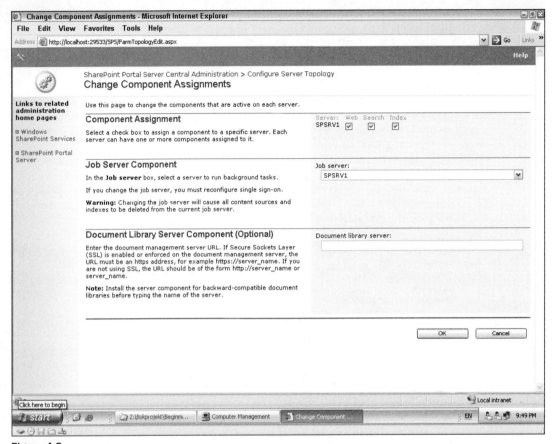

Figure 4-8

17. The number of warnings is now considerably fewer. The only complaint is that there is no e-mail server configured yet. So fix that now: Click the link Unknown to the right of the Global e-mail server in the Database Server Settings, and you will get a new page, as displayed in Figure 4-9.

The options are as follow:

❑ **Outbound SMTP server:** Enter any SMTP server that will accept e-mail from this server. It does not have to be an MS Exchange Server.

❑ **From e-mail address:** This is a fake sender address that will appear as the sender of messages from SharePoint. It does not have to exist! Give it a descriptive name, such as **SharePointNotification@contoso.com**, or simply **SharePoint@contoso.com**.

❑ **Reply-to e-mail address:** This must be a valid address, because it will be used in case any user will reply to the message from SharePoint.

❑ **Character Set:** In the Western world, the default 65001 (Unicode UTF-8) will be fine. For other parts of the world, check with your mail administrator for what to use.

Click OK to go back to the previous page.

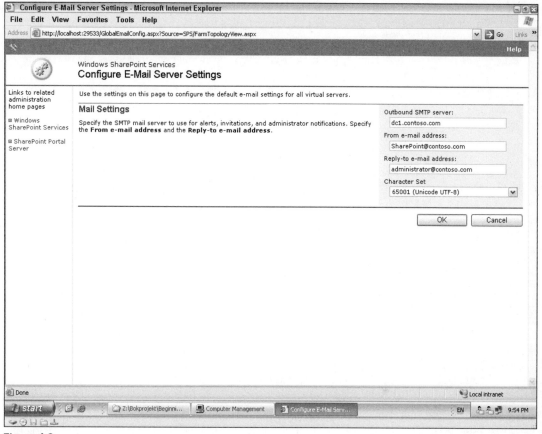

Figure 4-9

18. Notice the message at the bottom of this page. There are no issues at this time. Your farm is fine. So be happy and click Close to continue.

19. It is now time to create your first portal site. Click the link Create a portal site. On the following page you create the first portal site by following these directions:

❑ **Portal Creation Options:** Make sure the option "Create a portal" is selected.

❑ **Site Name:** Enter the name for this portal. This name can be changed later.

❑ **Site URL/Virtual server:** Select the virtual IIS server for this portal site (including any team sites). If you have more than one available virtual server, use the pull-down menu to select the one to be used.

❑ **Site URL/URL:** This is the default URL address for this portal. By default it is the server name. If you change it, make sure to create an alias record with this name in the DNS server that points to this server.

❑ **Owner/Account name:** This user has full access to all parts of SharePoint, including administrative rights. The best practice is to use a role-based account, such as "sp_admin," instead of an ordinary user account.

Click OK to continue.

20. On the next and final step you are asked to confirm the creation of the new portal. If you want to change something, click the Back button. If all is fine, click OK to start creating the portal. This may take a few minutes to complete.

21. The portal is created and ready to be used. Click the Home page link to see the portal site.

After the Installation of the Single-Server with a Local MS SQL

Two things you should do immediately after the installation of SPS 2003 has completed:

❑ Download and install the latest service pack for SPS and WSS (SP2 as of this writing). You start by installing the WSS service pack and then the SPS service pack. Download these service packs from `http://www.microsoft.com/windowsserver2003/technologies/sharepoint/default.mspx` for WSS service packs and `http://www.microsoft.com/office/sharepoint/prodinfo` for SPS service packs.

❑ Do a full backup of the SharePoint Portal Server environment with the backup utility that comes with SPS (see the next section) or your ordinary backup program, if it is SharePoint-aware.

Checking the New Folder and Applications

The portal site is now up and running. Take a look at what has changed in the Windows 2003 Server. You have several new file directories used by SPS and the underlying WSS environment:

❑ `C:\Program Files\Common Files\Microsoft Shared\web server extensions\60` — This folder has several new directories, including a Bin directory where several tools for WSS are stored. All these files and folders are identical to a pure WSS installation. These tools will also be used with an SPS installation in some situations.

❑ `C:\Program Files\SharePoint Portal Server` — This has folders and files specific for the SPS application. There is a Bin directory that contains all the dll files plus the backup utility for SPS. In the Data folder you will find index files, and in the Log folder are installation log files and other log files that you can view from within the SPS administrative tool.

❑ `C:\Program Files\Microsoft SQL Server\MSSQL` — This folder structure stores the MS SQL Server information; the Data folder stores the actual database files; the Log folder stores the MS SQL transaction log files and error log files.

There are also new application links listed in the Start➪All Programs➪SharePoint Portal Server node. By default you will see four entries there:

❑ **SharePoint Central Administration:** This is the administrative tool for SharePoint. This is simply a link to the web site in the virtual IIS server SharePoint Central Administration. You can also start this tool from within the user portal site and its Site Settings link, as you will see more of in the next chapter.

❑ **SharePoint Portal Server's Administrative Guide:** This is the online help manual for SharePoint. You can also find help inside the user portal site almost anywhere.

❑ **SharePoint Portal Server Data Backup and Restore:** This starts the SPS backup program with a graphical interface. The same program can also be started using a command prompt, which makes it easy to create a backup script.

❑ **SharePoint Portal Server Single Sign-on Administration:** This is a special tool for managing the single sign-on feature in SPS. This tool is used to store user accounts and passwords for accessing external applications from within SPS.

Checking the New Virtual IIS Server Settings

Finally, you will find that the virtual IIS server you selected for hosting the portal site has been extended (see Chapter 2 for more information about extending virtual servers). By default this will be the Default Web Site, unless you selected another virtual server. Start by opening the IIS Manager: Start⇨ Administration Tools⇨Internet Information Service (IIS) Manager.

Expand the Web Sites node. Note that you have two IIS virtual servers here:

❑ **SharePoint Central Administration:** Used by SharePoint for the administration web site. This virtual server was created during the initial phase of the SPS installation, before the portal site was created. Right-click this virtual server and select Properties; switch to the Home Directory tab. You can see what application pool this virtual server is using; by default it is the CentralAdminAppPool.

❑ **Default Web Site:** This is the virtual server that hosts the portal sites, team sites, and other WSS-based sites. Open the properties for this virtual server; look at the Home page, and you will find that the application pool it uses is the MSSharePointPortalAppPool.

Expand the Application Pools node, right-click the application pool CentralAdminAppPool, and switch to the Identity tab. Note that the security account used by this application pool is the account you entered in step 13 in the previous Try It Out. Then look at the Identity tab for the other application pool, the MSSharePointPortalAppPool, and you will find the same account name.

To summarize: SPS uses two virtual IIS servers, one for the portal sites and team sites and another for the administrative web site. These two virtual servers each use separate application pools. These two application pools should use the same security account and must be granted access to the SPS databases in the MS SQL Server. This is taken care of by the setup process.

Installing SPS in a Small Farm

This type of configuration uses one server for the SPS and a second server for the MS SQL. Note that the SQL Server doesn't need to be exclusive for SPS; it is perfectly okay to use an existing SQL Server that is used by other applications, as long as it will handle the extra load generated by SPS. Most of the steps in this configuration are similar, or identical, to the previous configuration with a local MS SQL Server. The reasons for using a remote instead of a local MS SQL Server are these:

❑ **Increased performance:** The SPS server can handle many more users.

❑ **Fault-tolerance:** It is possible to connect SPS to a MS SQL cluster.

❑ **Better economy:** Use a previously installed MS SQL Server.

This section describes how to install the SPS application with Service Pack 2 on one server named SPSrv2, and connect to an existing MS SQL 2000 database on a server named TOR.

Make sure you have the MS SQL 2000 Server with Service Pack 3 or later installed and running before performing the following steps. The system account you plan to use as the "Configuration database administration user" account must be granted permissions to the MS SQL Server before you can complete the installation of SPS. If you miss this, the installation will fail in step 14 when installing SPS! Follow these steps to add the user account and grant it the necessary SQL rights:

Try It Out   Add the Configuration Database Account to SQL

1.   Log on as an administrator to the MS SQL Server.

2.   Start the SQL management tool by going to Start⇨All Programs⇨Microsoft SQL Server⇨ Enterprise Manager.

3.   Expand the nodes Microsoft SQL Servers⇨SQL Server Group⇨(local) (Windows NT).

A red dot at the server icon indicates that the SQL Server service is not yet started. If so, right-click and select Start now.

4.   Expand the Security node. Right-click Logins and select New Login.

5.   This will bring you a form page where you enter the user account name; make sure to include the domain name (for example, Contoso\sp_service). Accept the other default values on this page. Click Server Roles in the left pane. Check the following roles: Security Administrators and Database Creators. Click OK to save and close.

6.   Close the SQL Server Enterprise Manager.

SQL Server is now ready for SharePoint Portal Server. Follow these steps to install SPS:

Try It Out   Install SPS and Configure a Small Farm

1.   Log on as an administrator to the Windows 2003 Server you will use for your SPS installation.

2.   Make sure Windows 2003 Server has the latest service packs and security patches installed by running Start⇨All Programs⇨Windows Update.

3.   Verify that you have ASP.NET installed, as previously described in the section "Software Requirements" earlier in this chapter. If not, cancel the installation of SPS now and install ASP.NET. You need the Windows 2003 CD to install it, but you do not have to reboot the server.

4.   Start the installation by mounting the SPS CD-ROM and selecting the option Install Microsoft Office SharePoint Portal Server 2003 Components in the start page that will be displayed. You can also choose to start the SETUP.EXE on the CD-ROM directly.

5.   The first page displays what software is required to install SPS and WSS; notice that the MSDE database is listed as May Be Required. You will not choose to install that database, because you will use the MS SQL Server instead. Click Next to continue the installation.

6.   The next page warns that the setup process needs to stop IIS and other web services; click OK to go on. You will not see a progress bar that shows the status of the installation of WSS first and then SPS, so you will have to wait until the next page shows up.

7.   The next page is the MS Office SPS 2003 Setup Wizard. Click Next.

8.   The next page is the End User License Agreement. Read it carefully, and if you agree check the box "I accept all of the terms in this license agreement" and click Next.

9.   The next page is where you enter the Product Key. For some editions of SPS, this number is entered automatically. Click Next to go on.

10.   On the next page you select whether to use the MSDE database "Install with database engine" or the full MS SQL Server "Install without database engine." Make sure to select the second option because you will use the MS SQL Server.

Notice also the Destination file locations; this is where you define where the binary and data files will be stored. The best practice is to avoid using the C: drive for data files because of the paging file in Windows. Click the Browse button to change either of these two paths.

Click Next. This starts the installation of the SPS program files. This step may take several minutes to complete.

11. The next page prompts you for a user account name and password for the database configuration administration account. See Figure 4-4 earlier in the chapter. SPS will use this account when communicating with the configuration database in MS SQL Server. This user must be a member of the local server's Power Users group or the Administrators group; but he does not need to be a Domain Admin member.

When selecting a user account, it will automatically be granted the following rights: Replace a process level token; Adjust memory quotas for a process; and Log on as a service by the setup program. The best practice is to use the same user account here as for the Application Pool Security, such as SP_Service. Click Next to continue.

12. The next page shows the current status. Only the two modules, WSS and SPS, should be marked as Installed. The MSDE database should be listed as Not Required. Click Next and then Finish to complete the installation.

13. The SharePoint Portal Server Central Administration tool starts up automatically, displaying the Configure Server Farm Account Settings page. See also Figure 4-5. This is where you configure two of the service accounts used by SPS.

> **Remember that you have more details about each service account in the earlier section "Service Accounts for SPS."**

- ❑ **Default Content Access Account:** This account is used by the Index role when it crawls external content sources (for example, your file server, MS Exchange, or external web sites). The default value is the account defined as the configuration user database account. The account that is used here needs read access to the external content sources, like the file system, to do its job. A user that is a member of the Domain Admin group will be able to read most file shares, but if you need maximum security, you should create a separate account for this purpose that only is granted read access to the content sources.

- ❑ **Portal Site Application Pool:** This account is used by the virtual server hosting the portal site and its team sites. You can use the same account as the for the configuration user database account.

Click OK to continue the configuration of SPS.

14. The next page is the Specify Configuration Database Settings for <server name>. (See Figure 4-10.)

- ❑ **Database Connections:** Because this is the first and only SPS server, you must select Create configuration database.

- ❑ **Configuration Database Server:** The name for this server is automatically listed in the Database server field. Make sure to change this to the SQL Server name (which in this example is the server TOR).

- ❑ **Configuration Database Name:** You can enter a name for this database or use the default name SPS01_Config.db. Unless you have a special reason, accept the default name. Click OK to continue.

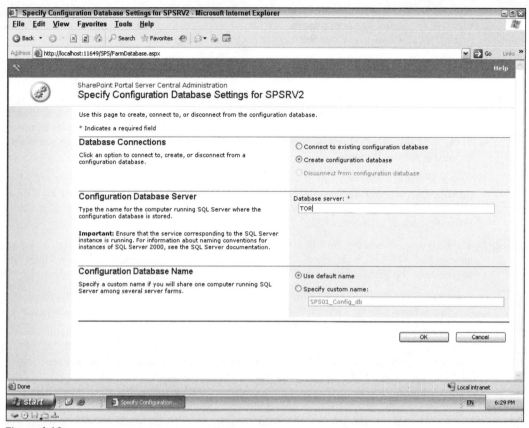

Figure 4-10

15. The next page is the Configure Server Farm Account Settings. Enter the e-mail address for the person responsible for this SPS server. This address will be used by SPS when it crawls external content source, such as public web sites on the Internet. The address will be registered in the remote web server's log file. It is a good idea to use a role-based e-mail address instead of a specific user to avoid problems if this person later leaves the company.

The second part on this page is about how SPS will connect to the Internet. If there is a proxy server that SPS needs to use, enter its address and port number. Click OK to continue.

16. The next page is Configure Server Topology. The first time you look at this page, you might panic when you see the bottom of the page, which tells you all the problems with this SPS server, as Figure 4-11 shows.

But don't despair. It simply says that this SPS installation is not yet configured! Start by clicking the Change Components button at the bottom of this page. This will open the Change Components Assignments page; here you set the front-end roles for this SPS server. Because this is a small farm configuration, it must have all the roles. Check the three boxes for Web, Search, and Index. But wait! You must set the Job server role too. Use the pull-down menu and select the only option you have: the name of this server. See also Figure 4-8. At the end of this page is a section called Document Library Server Component. This part is only used if you use SPS 2003 in an SPS 2001–compatible mode. If you do not need this, leave this section empty! When done, click OK to return to the previous page.

17. The number of warnings is now considerably fewer. The only complaint is that there is no e-mail server configured yet. So fix that now: Click the Unknown link to the right of the Global e-mail server in the Database Server Settings, and you will get a new page, as displayed previously in Figure 4-10.

The options are as follows:

❑ **Outbound SMTP Server:** Enter any SMTP server that will accept e-mail from this server. It does not have to be an MS Exchange Server.

❑ **From e-mail address:** This is a fake sender address that will appear as the sender of messages from SharePoint. It does not have to exist! Give it a descriptive name.

❑ **Reply-to e-mail address:** This must be a valid address, because it will be used in case any user will reply to the message from SharePoint.

❑ **Character Set:** In the Western world, the default 65001 (Unicode UTF-8) will be fine. For other parts of the world, check with your mail administrator for what to use.

Click OK to go back to the previous page.

18. Notice the message at the bottom of this page. There are no issues at this time. Your farm is fine. So be happy and click Close to continue.

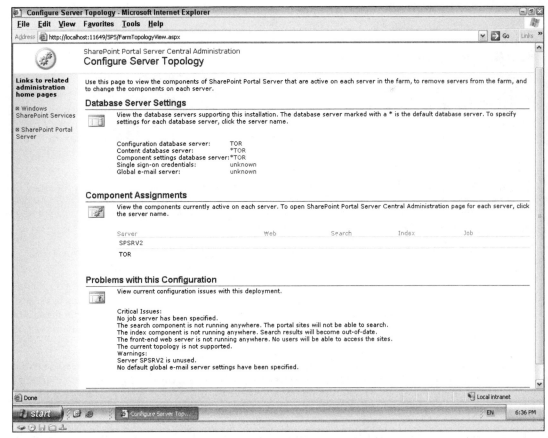

Figure 4-11

19. It is now time to create your first portal site. Click the "Create a portal site" link under the Portal Site and Virtual Server Configuration section. On the following page you create the first portal site by following these directions:

❑ **Portal Creation Options:** Make sure the option "Create a portal" is selected.

❑ **Site Name:** Enter the name for this portal. This name can be changed later.

❑ **Site URL/Virtual server:** Select the virtual IIS server for this portal site (including any team sites). If you have more than one available virtual server, use the pull-down menu to select the one to be used.

❑ **Site URL/URL:** This is the default URL address for this portal. By default it is the server name. If you change it, make sure to create an alias record with this name in the DNS server that points to this server.

❑ **Owner/Account name:** This user has full access to all parts of SharePoint, including administrative rights. It is recommended to use a role-based account, such as "sp_admin," instead of an ordinary user account.

Click OK to continue.

20. On the next and final step you are asked to confirm the creation of the new portal. If you want to change something, click the Back button. If all is fine, click OK to start creating the portal. This may take a few minutes to complete.

21. The portal is created and ready to be used. Click the Home page link to see the portal site.

After the Installation of a Small Farm

Two things you should do immediately after the installation of SPS 2003 has completed:

❑ Download and install the latest service pack for SPS and WSS (SP2 as of this writing). You start by installing the WSS service pack and then the SPS service pack. Download these service packs from `http://www.microsoft.com/windowsserver2003/technologies/sharepoint/default.mspx` for WSS service packs and `http://www.microsoft.com/office/sharepoint/prodinfo` for SPS service packs.

❑ Do a full backup of the SharePoint Portal Server environment with the backup utility that comes with SPS (see the next section) or your ordinary backup program, if it is SharePoint-aware.

Checking the New Folder and Applications

The portal site is now up and running. Take a look at what has changed in the Windows 2003 Server. You have several new file directories used by SPS and the underlying WSS environment:

❑ `C:\Program Files\Common Files\Microsoft Shared\web server extensions\60` — This folder has several new directories, including a Bin directory where several tools for WSS are stored. All these files and folders are identical to a pure WSS installation. These tools will also be used with an SPS installation, in some situations.

❑ `C:\Program Files\SharePoint Portal Server` — This has folders and files specific for the SPS application. There is a Bin directory that contains all the dll files plus the backup utility for SPS. In the Data folder you will find index files, and in the Log folder are installation log files and other log files that you can view from within the SPS administrative tool.

There are also new application links listed in the Start⇨All Programs⇨SharePoint Portal Server node.

By default you will see four entries there:

❑ **SharePoint Central Administration:** This is the administrative tool for SharePoint. This is simply a link to the web site in the virtual IIS server SharePoint Central Administration. You can also start this tool from within the user portal site and its Site Settings link, as you will see more of in the next chapter.

❑ **SharePoint Portal Server's Administrative Guide:** This is the online help manual for SharePoint. You can also find help inside the user portal site almost anywhere.

❑ **SharePoint Portal Server Data Backup and Restore:** This starts the SPS backup program with a graphical interface. The same program can also be started using a command prompt, which makes it easy to create a backup script.

❑ **SharePoint Portal Server Single Sign-on Administration:** This is a special tool for managing the single sign-on feature in SPS. This tool is used to store user accounts and passwords for accessing external applications from within SPS.

Checking the New Virtual IIS Server Settings

Finally, you will find that the virtual IIS server you selected for hosting the portal site has been extended (see Chapter 2 for more information about extending virtual servers). By default this will be the Default Web Site, unless you selected another virtual server. Start by opening the IIS Manager: Start⇨Administration Tools⇨Internet Information Service (IIS) Manager.

Expand the Web Sites node. Note that you have two IIS virtual servers here:

❑ **SharePoint Central Administration:** This is used by SharePoint for the administration web site. This virtual server was created during the initial phase of the SPS installation, before the portal site was created. Right-click this virtual server and select Properties. Switch to the Home Directory tab. You will see what application pool this virtual server is using; by default it is the CentralAdminAppPool.

❑ **Default Web Site:** This is the virtual server that hosts the portal sites, team sites, and other WSS-based sites. Open the properties for this virtual server; look at the Home page, and you will find that the application pool it uses is the MSSharePointPortalAppPool.

Expand the Application Pools node, right-click the application pool CentralAdminAppPool, and switch to the Identity tab. Note that the security account used by this application pool is the account you entered in step 13 in the previous Try It Out. Then look at the Identity tab for the other application pool, the MSSharePointPortalAppPool, and you will find the same account name.

To summarize: SPS uses two virtual IIS servers, one for the portal sites and team sites and another for the administrative web site. These two virtual servers each use separate application pools. These two application pools should use the same security account and must be granted access to the SPS databases in the MS SQL Server. This is taken care of by the setup process.

Backing Up SPS 2003

The obvious thing to do after a successful installation is to back up the SharePoint Portal Server. You will read a lot more about backing up and restoring in Chapter 8. However, because you have just completed an SPS installation, you are probably anxious to know how to protect your work with a backup, so the basics of backing up SPS are covered here.

SPS 2003 comes with the program SPSBACKUP.EXE. It allows you to make a complete backup of your SPS environment, including any team sites you may have. Regardless of whether the SQL Server is local or remote, the backup program needs to connect to the database and use the SQL Server Client Tools installed on the SPS server. These client tools contain the necessary applications that the SPSBACKUP.EXE needs to communicate with the SQL Server.

You must run the SPSBACKUP.EXE *program on the front-end Web server.*

Follow these steps to back up your new SPS server:

Try It Out   Do a Backup of Your SPS Server

1. Log on to the SPS server as an administrator.

2. If you are using an MSDE database, you must start with installing the SQL 2000 client tools. The detailed steps are listed earlier in the section "Installing a Single-Server with a Local MS SQL Database," except for some small changes, as listed here:

   a. Mount the MS SQL 2000 Server CD or start its Setup.exe program.

   b. Select SQL Server 2000 Components.

   c. Select Install Database Server. (Don't worry. You will only install the client tools.)

   d. Click Next five times, until you see the Installation Definition page.

   e. Select Client Tools Only and click Next.

   f. On the Select Components page, you can uncheck some of these options, such as the Books Online and Query Analyzer to save disk space. Click Next.

   g. On the next page, click Finish to complete the installation.

   h. Run MS SQL Server 2000 Service Pack 3 or later to update the client tools.

   i. Click Next to accept the default answers on the following pages until you see the page with the Finish button. Click this button to complete the installation of the service pack.

3. Verify that you can read the database:

   a. Start the SQL Server Enterprise Manager (in Start⇨All Programs⇨Microsoft SQL Server).

   b. Expand the nodes Microsoft SQL Server⇨SQL Server Group.

   c. If you can see your database server now, your client tools work as expected.

   d. Close the Enterprise Manager.

4. Select a shared disk resource where you can store the backup files; for example \\TOR\NTBackup. Make sure your current logon account has write permission to that share.

   If you create a new file share in Windows 2003, it will by default set the permission for the group Everyone = Read. This will prohibit even administrators from writing to that share. Add the administrator user account to that share and grant it Write permissions, or grant the group Backup Operators Write permission.

5. Start the backup program: Start⇨All Programs⇨SharePoint Portal Server⇨SharePoint Portal Server Data Backup and Restore.

6. On this page (see Figure 4-12), enter the following:

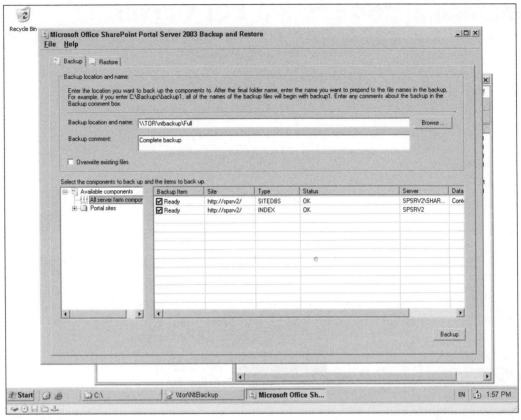

Figure 4-12

a. **Backup location and name:** Enter the server and share name, followed by a prefix. All files that belong to this backup session will have this prefix. For example, \\bkupsrv\sps\full-backp will set the prefix "full-backup" to all backup files stored in the "sps" share on the server "bkupsrv."

b. **Backup comment:** Enter a short comment to this backup session.

c. In the left pane, expand the nodes Available components⇨Portal sites⇨http://spsrv2 (which is the SPS server name). You now see two lines in the right pane. Both of these should have the Ready box checked.

d. Click the Backup button. This starts the backup procedure. When done, close the backup application.

7. Open the file location where the backup files are stored. Note that there are five files, all beginning with the file prefix you entered in step 6.

Now you have a complete backup of all data, including any index files and user profile data. You do not need to run a SQL backup. You have everything you need to perform a full restore if you lose data.

Running SPSBACKUP will not back up the file structure of SharePoint, IIS settings, or domain user accounts. To restore data with SPSBACKUP, you must have an SPS installation with the same settings as when you run the backup process. Otherwise you may not be able to restore everything!

Upgrading MSDE to MS SQL Server

If you for any reason chose to install SPS 2003 with a local MSDE database and later find out you need to upgrade it to the MS SQL 2000 Server, you have two choices:

❑   An in-place upgrade of MSDE to a local MS SQL Server. This is easy.

❑   Moving from MSDE to a separate MS SQL Server. This is a complicated process.

This section describes the first option only: an in-place upgrade. If you want to move from a local database to a remote database server, you can follow the steps listed in this Microsoft article `http://support.microsoft.com/?id=894164#3`.

Preparing to Upgrade to MS SQL Server

The most important thing to do before starting the upgrade process is to back up your current SPS database. You are about to perform a very sensitive operation, and if something goes wrong, you must be sure you can go back to the previous version. The previous section described how to back up your database.

During this upgrade process, no one can use the SPS server. Make sure to pick a time when no one is using the server. Because the MSDE version that comes with SPS only allows up to 2 GB of data, this upgrade process should be fairly quick, depending on your server hardware, but plan for at least two hours to be on the safe side.

Upgrading SPS to a Local MS SQL Server

As mentioned before, this is a very straightforward process. Make sure no one is using the system before you start to upgrade, because they may lose information during this process. The best practice is to schedule this upgrade process at a specific date and inform all affected users when this will happen. In step 3 in the following list, you need to have the SQL 2000 Client Tools installed on the server. Make sure you install these tools and SQL 2000 Server Service Pack 4 before starting this upgrade process. Follow these steps to upgrade the database:

Try It Out   Upgrade MSDE to a Local MS SQL 2000 Server

1.   Log on to the SPS server as an administrator.

2.   Make sure no one is using SPS at the moment.

3.   Start the SQL Enterprise Manager tool. Expand the nodes until you see the name of this server. Note the text after the server name; this is the Instance Name that the SharePoint installation has on this SQL Server. By default it is SHAREPOINTPORTAL. Write down this instance name, because you will need it when upgrading this MSDE database. Close the Enterprise Manager before continuing.

4.   Mount the MS SQL 2000 Server CD. You will automatically see a dialog box where you can start the installation by selecting SQL Server 2000 Components. You can also start the SETUP.EXE program directly from the CD.

5.   Select to Install Database Server.

6.   On the Welcome page, click Next.

7.   Select to install MS SQL on the Local server and click Next.

8. On the Installation Selection page, select the option Upgrade, Remove, Or Add Components To An Existing Instance of SQL Server and click Next.

9. On the Instance Name page, clear the check box next to Default and use the pull-down menu at the Instance name. Make sure to select the same instance name as in step 3 (by default, SHAREPOINTPORTAL).

10. On the Existing Installation page, make sure the choice "Upgrade your existing installation" is set and click Next.

11. On the Upgrade page, check the box for Yes, upgrade my programs, and click Next.

12. On the Choose License Mode page, set your type of SQL Server license. Then click Continue.

13. You get a dialog box that says Do you want to install additional components. Normally you select No, but if you want to add some extra SQL components to this installation you can do it. In this example, choose No.

14. Finally you get the Setup Complete page. Click Finish to complete this upgrade process.

At this moment, your MSDE database is updated to MS SQL 2000. However, it is important to install the latest service pack before you start using this SPS server. Continue with these steps.

15. Mount the latest service pack for SQL 2000. Start its `Setup.bat` script.

16. Click Next two times.

17. On the Instance Name page, make sure it is the correct instance name from step 3. Click Next to continue.

18. On the Connect to Server page, make sure to select the option "The Windows account information I use to log on to my computer with (Windows authentication)". Then click Next.

19. The Password Warning page is shown if the SQL user SA has a blank password. This is a high security risk, and you should enter a non-blank password here. Make sure to store that password in a safe place in case you need it later. Click OK when ready.

20. On the Error reporting page, if you want SQL to send error messages automatically to Microsoft, check the box "Automatically send fatal error messages to Microsoft". This will help the SQL development team to understand problems better, so they can build better products. Click OK to go on.

21. On the Start Copying Files page, click Next.

22. When the installation is done, you get a dialog box saying you should back up the databases, because the database format is modified. This is not only a good idea, it is mandatory, because you cannot use the previous backup sets any longer because of the modified format. Go back to the previous section describing how to take a backup and do it now! Click OK.

23. The next and final step is that the Setup program wants to restart the computer. Make sure you don't have anything unsaved in other programs and accept to reboot the server.

Check your SPS environment. Make sure it works like before. You should see no differences, except possibly better performance. Open the MS SQL Server Enterprise Manager and take a look at the databases for the local server. You should see the same databases as before, using the same instance name.

Do not remove the MSDE database from the SPS server! It is used by the upgraded MS SQL Server and contains the actual databases.

Post-Installation Tasks

The first thing to do after an installation or upgrade is to test SharePoint. Log on as an administrator, start Internet Explorer, enter the URL for the SPS portal, and enjoy. You may notice that it takes a long time to display the SPS portal site the first time, but later it will be much faster. This is due to how SharePoint works. It is based on the programming technique called ASP.NET, in which web applications are not fully compiled. The first time an ASP.NET application runs, it is converted into executable code that also is cached. The result is that the first time you start SharePoint it takes a long time; the second time it goes very fast. There is nothing you can do about this—just accept it as a fact of life, like death and taxes. Note that this cache is emptied every time you restart the server, execute the command IISRE-SET, or restart the IIS using the IIS Manager.

You may recall from earlier in this chapter that there are at least four databases used by SharePoint portal server. Microsoft does not want you to modify them in any way other than running SharePoint's web sites and administration sites. However, there is some interesting information hidden in these databases, as described in the following sections.

The Configuration Database

The purpose of the configuration database is to store SharePoint's configuration settings, such as what front-end servers exist, their role, and what back-end server is used. There is only one configuration database for all SharePoint servers in the farm. It coordinates how all the SharePoint servers know each other and their roles.

If you need to expand the SharePoint farm with a new front-end server, you install SPS on it and during the configuration you tell it to connect to the existing configuration database. This is very similar to how a new domain controller is added to an existing Windows domain. If you need to remove a SharePoint server, you simply disconnect it from the configuration database. Refer back to Figure 4-10 for the administrative page for this configuration setting:

The default name of this SQL database is SPS01_Config_db. The owner of this database in SQL, also known as the dbo role, must be the same account used by the application pool used by the virtual server that is hosting the SharePoint web sites (by default the MSSharePointPortalAppPool). This database contains a lot of interesting information regarding your SharePoint environment. For example, you can look into the tables of the configuration database to see what portal site it belongs to.

> *Never change the SQL tables unless specifically instructed to do so by Microsoft Support. If you make a mistake, it can corrupt the database!*

Try It Out   Check the Configuration Database Tables

1. After the SPS is installed, log on as a SQL administrator.
2. Open the SQL Enterprise Manager.
3. Expand the nodes Microsoft SQL Server⇨SQL Server Group⇨<SQL Server name>.
4. Expand the Databases folder and the configuration database SPS01_Config_db.
5. Click Tables to see all tables in this database.
6. Right-click the PortalZoneUrls table and select Open Table⇨Return all rows.

7.   This will open the table; look for the column named Url. It will list the default URL address to this portal.

8.   Now check some more tables, while you are here:

   a.   Right-click the VirtualServers table and select Open Table⇨Return all rows. Look at the Name column; it shows the name of the virtual IIS server used by this portal site.

   b.   Open the Databases table in the same way. In the Name column you see all other databases used by this SPS farm. In the SiteCount column you can see the current number of site collections. This value is especially interesting for content databases, because there is a maximum limit of site collections for each database.

   c.   Open the Sites table. In the UrlPath column you see all top-level sites. LastModified shows when the top site was created, and LastModifiedUser shows by whom.

Remember, never change the SQL tables unless instructed to do so by Microsoft Support. If you make a mistake, it can corrupt the database!

The Content Database

All data stored in the SharePoint portal site or any of its WSS sites is contained in the content database. By default the name for this database is the first eight characters from the portal name, then the number 1, followed by _SITE. For example, the portal name E2K3BASE has its first content database named E2K3BASE1_SITE.

This database will grow as your SharePoint environment is used by users. It is possible to create more than one content database, but the first one is by default limited to 15,000 site collections. You will not hit that limit immediately in most organizations. Note that it is the number of site collections that counts, not individual sites. In reality that could mean 10 or 100 times more sites in total, all stored in the same content database. All sites belonging to the same site collection must reside in the same content database; it is not possible to split a large site collection over several content databases!

If you have more than one MS SQL Server, you can create new content databases on these other SQL Servers. This works well when you have a distributed organization and the network connections between the different locations are low bandwidth (for example, less than 1024 Kb/s). By using locally placed SQL Servers with content databases, the performance is much better for the user who needs to work with documents and other information in the WSS sites. This may sound easy, but in reality it is rather difficult to achieve.

When you create a new top site (a new site collection), you cannot select what content database to use. There is a setting in SharePoint's administrative tool that defines the default content database. The rules that SharePoint follows when selecting the content database are these:

1.   You create a new site collection.

2.   SharePoint looks at all available content databases and checks whether they are online ("Ready"), or not ("offline"). It also looks at the current number of site collections and the maximum number of site collections.

3.   SharePoint selects the content database with the most space available that is online.

For example, assume you have two content databases, A and B. Both are online. Both Database A and B can host 1,000 sites. The current number of sites in A is 500 and in B is 600. A new site collection is created; it will be stored in the A, because it has 500 sites left, whereas B has only 400 left.

If you have full control over the creation process of the site collections, you can take all content databases offline, except one. You can then create the new site collection, and it will be stored in that content database. The exact steps for this procedure are covered in detail in Chapter 5.

The User Profile Database

SharePoint Portal Server can run in a Windows NT 4 or Windows 2000/2003 domain environment. If you have been in the IT business for some time, you may remember that the information about user accounts in Windows NT 4 was sparse, to say the least. It just contained the user account name and a description; no information about departments, phone numbers, e-mail addresses, and so on. Because one of the prime objectives in SharePoint is to make it easier for users to find information, SharePoint needs to store a lot of properties about each user. Microsoft solved this by creating the User Profile database.

This database is exclusive for SPS; you do not find it in a pure WSS environment. The default name for it is the first eight characters for the portal name, a number, and the suffix _PROF. For example, a portal named E2K3BASE has a user profile database named E2K3BASE1_PROF. The size of this database depends on the number of users. A large organization may have several hundred megabytes but still it will be a very small database compared to the content database.

The information in this database can be entered manually by the SharePoint administrator and to some extent by the user, or it can be automatically imported if the users belong to an Active Directory domain. The last option requires that the Active Directory is updated with all the user properties you want to import into the user profile.

In the next chapter you get all the details about how to configure this importing process and how to control what properties to import from the Active Directory. You also learn how to define what properties the users are allowed to change.

The user profile also stores information about SharePoint's Audiences. This term refers to groups of SharePoint users, like all Salespeople, or all Brain Surgeons, or New Employees. You can filter the information displayed on the portal site to only show information targeted to this audience group. In the next chapter you learn how to create and manage audiences.

The Service Database

This database is also exclusive for SPS only; it does not exist in a pure WSS environment. The Service database is also referred to as the Component Settings database. It contains the following types of information regarding the portal site:

❑   Data used by the Search and Index service, such as the status of the latest index process (also known as the Gatherer Log).

❑   Data used by the Alerts service, such as what alerts are defined and by whom.

This is normally a very small database compared to the content database. Using the MS SQL admin tools you can find some interesting pieces of information here, such as the name and e-mail address of all users who have an active alert defined in the portal site. Just follow these steps:

Try It Out   **Check the Component Database Tables**

1.   After the SPS is installed, log on as a SQL administrator.

2.   Start the SQL Enterprise Manager.

3.   Expand the nodes Microsoft SQL Server⇨SQL Server Group⇨<SQL Server name>.

4.   Expand the folder Databases and the configuration database <Portal>1_SERV.

5.   Click Tables to see all tables in this database.

6.   Right-click the table Sub_SubscriptionInfo and select Open Table⇨Return all rows.

7.   This opens the table. Look for the column name DeliveryChannelsXml. It will list the all defined alerts in the portal, along with the receiving e-mail address for these alerts.

> Note that alerts for WSS sites are still managed the same way as in a pure WSS environment; for more details about these alerts, see Chapter 3.

Uninstalling SPS

The final section of this chapter is about removing SPS. Remember that when installing SPS you also install WSS. You can select to remove just SPS and WSS, or SPS, WSS, and the databases. If the databases remain, you can later reinstall SPS and WSS and reconnect to these databases again.

Uninstalling SPS but Leaving the Database Files

This removes the SPS portal site and its team sites from a given virtual IIS server, but it does not remove the binary files from the server. For example, you may have a test environment using a separate virtual IIS server, and you might also have a production SPS using another virtual IIS server on the same physical Windows 2003 Server.

To remove the test environment, follow these steps:

1.   Start SharePoint Central Administration tool: Start⇨All Programs⇨SharePoint Portal Server.

2.   Click the link List and manage portal sites.

3.   You see the name of the portal site. Click to the right of that name. This brings a drop-down menu; select Delete portal site.

4.   On the next page, make sure the Delete all databases option is unchecked, and click OK. This starts the removal of the portal site and its team sites from the virtual IIS server. The databases will still be there in case you want to use them in a new portal site.

All binary files for SPS and WSS are still there; you can now create a new portal in the same virtual IIS server or another one. If you want to do this, look at the earlier sections in this chapter where the steps for creating portal sites are described.

Removing SPS Completely

A more drastic method is to remove SPS completely from the Windows 2003 Server. This does not actually remove the database, be it the WMSDE or the MS SQL Server. If you want to remove these database engines, you must do this separately after you uninstall SPS.

To remove SPS and WSS binary files completely from a Windows 2003 Server, follow these steps:

1. Start Add or Remove Programs in the Control Panel.

2. First you must remove SPS. Locate the line Microsoft SharePoint Portal Server 2003 and click the Change button. This starts the Setup Wizard for SPS; click Next.

3. On the Maintenance Mode Options page, select the option "Remove the server components of Microsoft Office SharePoint Portal Server 2003"; click Next.

4. You get warnings about removing SPS; click Yes and then OK to start the removal process.

5. The next step is to remove WSS. Select Microsoft Windows SharePoint Services 2.0 and click the Remove button.

6. You will be warned about removing WSS; click Yes. Wait for the removal process to complete. WSS is now gone!

7. Check to see if there are other WSS-related applications that also should be removed (for example, Office 2003 Web Parts or any third-party add-on).

8. If you also want to remove the database engine, locate its name, and click Remove.

There is no way of automatically removing both SPS and WSS at the same time, although they were automatically installed in the same process. You must remove them manually.

When you remove SPS, you also remove the virtual IIS server used by the SharePoint administrative web site, along with its application pool. The Default Web Site, however, remains after the installation, along with its application pool.

Summary

In this chapter you learned the following:

❑ SPS is more advanced (and, therefore, more complicated to install) than WSS.

❑ SPS has a different type of MSDE database compared to WSS, which is limited to 2 GB.

❑ SPS features:

    ❑ Targeting of information on the portal site.

    ❑ Organize information stored anywhere with the help of topics in SPS.

    ❑ Global searching, both inside SharePoint and outside.

    ❑ My Site is used both as a personal web site for the user, and to describe the users properties, such as e-mail address, phones, department, picture, and much more.

❑ License model for SPS is based on the number of SPS servers and clients that can access SPS.

❑ Even if you only read information in the portal site, you will need a separate Client Access License.

❑ SPS cannot use MS SQL Server 2005 as of this writing — but WSS 2003 can!

❑ SPS can use a local or remote database. It can be either MSDE or the MS SQL Server 2000.

❑ Definitions:

  ❑ **Stand-alone:** SPS with a local MSDE.

  ❑ **Single-server:** SPS with a local MS SQL Server 2000.

  ❑ **Front-end server:** A server that has SPS binaries installed and are running one or more of the SPS roles.

  ❑ **Back-end server:** A server running MS SQL, used by SPS for storing data.

  ❑ **Small farm:** SPS with a remote MS SQL Server 2000.

  ❑ **Medium farm:** An SPS configuration with one or two SPS servers running the Web and the Search role; then one SPS server running the Index and Job role; then one or more SQL Servers.

  ❑ **Large farm:** Two to eight servers running the Web service; two to four servers running the Search role; one to four servers running the Index role (one of which must be running the Job role); and one ore more SQL Servers.

  ❑ **The Web service:** Responsible for the contact with the user client.

  ❑ **The Search service:** Responsible for answering any search queries from the client.

  ❑ **The Index service:** Responsible for crawling and indexing information.

  ❑ **The Job service:** Responsible for several things, including alerts, importing from Active Directory, and compiling audience groups. Only one server in a farm can have the Job role!

❑ There are four different databases in SPS: Configuration, Content, User, and Component.

  ❑ If you implement the Single Sign-On feature of SPS, it creates a fifth database type.

  ❑ There may be any number of Content databases, but only one each of the other types.

❑ Hardware requirements for SPS are the same as for WSS.

❑ Use the formula for calculating the operations per second (OPS) to find out the load for a given user population.

❑ Even a small farm supports more than 20,000 users in a typical organization.

❑ Make sure the SQL Server always has at least 50 percent free disk space for its maintenance utilities.

❑ SPS requires ASP.NET with .NET 1.1 Framework.

❑ SPS also uses two virtual IIS servers, by default using one application pool each, just like WSS.

❑ The security account for the application pool is used when communicating with the database.

- ❑ The following service accounts will be required when installing SPS:
    - ❑ Application Pool security account
    - ❑ Default content access account
    - ❑ Configuration database user account
- ❑ Stand-alone version of SPS is very easy and fast to install; it does not ask about the application pool security account or the configuration database user account.
- ❑ The installation of SPS must be followed by an installation of the latest service pack.
- ❑ Three new file directory trees are created during the SPS installation:
    - ❑ `C:\Program Files\Common Files\Microsoft Shared\web server extensions\60` (for WSS)
    - ❑ `C:\Program Files\SharePoint Portal Server` (for SPS binaries)
    - ❑ `C:\Program Files\Microsoft SQL Server\MSSQL$SHAREPOINTPORTAL` (for a local MSDE Server) or `C:\Program Files\Microsoft SQL Server\MSSQL` (for a local SQL Server 2000).
- ❑ You get four new program links in Start⇨All Programs⇨SharePoint Portal Server:
    - ❑ SharePoint Central Administration
    - ❑ SharePoint Portal Servers Administrative Guide
    - ❑ SharePoint Portal Servers Data Backup and Restore
    - ❑ SharePoint Portal Server Single Sign-On Administration
- ❑ SPS asks for a SMTP mail server. It does not have to be MS Exchange; it can be any SMTP server that accepts e-mail from SharePoint.
- ❑ Use the SharePoint Portal Server Data Backup and Restore tool for complete backups of all data including all portal sites, all team sites, and index files.
- ❑ You can upgrade a local MSDE database to MS SQL Server 2000. This is a straightforward process.
- ❑ It is possible to migrate from a local MSDE database to a remote MS SQL Server, but it is a complicated process. Read Microsoft's knowledgebase article 894164.
- ❑ You can uninstall SPS in several ways:
    - ❑ Remove the portal site but not the binaries.
    - ❑ Remove the binaries but not the databases.
    - ❑ Remove everything.
- ❑ When removing SharePoint completely, you must start by removing SPS, then WSS, and then the database, if you used a local database.

In the next chapter, you learn more about managing and configuring the portal site in SPS.

Configuring and Managing SharePoint Portal Server

In this chapter you learn how to configure and manage the SharePoint Portal Server 2003. You learn about customization, portal areas, how to import user properties from the Active Directory, and how to target information for different groups of users. Even if you do not plan to implement SPS at this time, this chapter may still interest you because it describes the features that are specific to the portal site, compared to the pure WSS environment. This will help you understand the differences, and when using WSS with SPS is a better choice than using WSS alone.

> To help you determine whether you should use WSS with or without SPS, consult Chapter 7, "Comparing WSS and SPS."

You may recall from previous chapters that SPS is an optional add-on to the WSS platform. It will enable you to build one or more portal sites on top of the WSS team sites for easier navigation and sharing information within the whole organization. The objectives for the portal site are different than for the team sites. (In fact, each product has its own development team at Microsoft, which shows how different SPS and WSS are.) You could say that the portal site is the place where a few people create and manage information directed to many, whereas the team sites are the places where many people create and manage information that is directed to many.

The portal site is built upon the same structure as the WSS team sites, but sometime uses different terms. In the following table you can see how these terms are used in WSS and SPS and how they relate to each other:

SPS Terms	Corresponding WSS Terms
Portal Site: A site collection with a top site named Home and a number of subsites called *areas*.	**Team Sites:** A site collection with a top site that you define and with zero or more subsites.
Areas: These are subsites displayed as a page in the portal site (for example, News and Topics).	**Subsites:** These are the web sites under the top web site.
Area Content: Because each area is basically a WSS site, they all have their own content and security settings.	**Site Content:** All sites, including the top site and the subsites, have their own content and security settings.

This chapter focuses on the portal site and how it works. To follow the instructions in this chapter you will need at least one portal site. Use the instructions in Chapter 4 to create this portal site.

Changing the Look and Feel of the Portal Site

It is easy to create a new portal site, but most organizations want to customize its look and feel; this is sometimes referred to as *branding*. Some of this customization is very easy to do, whereas other modifications require extensive knowledge of HyperText Markup Language (HTML) and general web design expertise. This chapter gives you the basic information needed to change the design of the portal. Chapter 12 teaches you more about how to use MS FrontPage 2003 for customizing of both the portal and team sites. The default portal site looks like Figure 5-1.

Before you can modify any part of SharePoint, you must have the proper permissions, which means being a SharePoint Administrator or a member of the Web Designer site group. In Chapter 3 you learned how to add users to sites groups in WSS. In SPS you use the same technique, which is described in the section "Managing Access to the Portal Site" at the end of this chapter.

Modifying the Portal Site

The easiest parts to customize in a portal are things like the logo type, portal name, and the description. You can do this with a web browser on any computer, as long as you have the proper permission. You need to be a SharePoint Administrator or a member of the Web Designer site group to perform modifications of this type. The following table explains the things you can easily customize:

Object	Displayed	Comment
Portal site name	At the top of every area page and the Site Settings administration page on the portal site	Limited to 80 Unicode characters such as å, ö, and ü, except for these: \ / : * ? " < > | Warning: Very long names will move the "Site Settings" link and the other links further to the right of the page!
Portal site description	Not displayed	Only visible to users who are allowed to use the Site Settings page. Limited to 200 Unicode characters.

Object	Displayed	Comment
Logo file	At the top of every area page on the portal site	By default: SITELOGO.GIF File formats: GIF, BMP, JPEG, and PNG (TIFF is not supported). The default logo type is 225w x 26h pixels with a 96 dpi resolution. Use any reasonable size; the banner will adjust itself, but avoid pictures with more than 50 pixels in height, because this will make the banner too dominant on the page.

It is especially the logo file that most organizations want to replace. As previously described, you should avoid very large pictures, because it will reduce the available area for the rest of the page. It is okay to use animated GIF pictures, but you should really make sure it looks good, and not only fun, the first time you see it.

> *You can find lots of free animated GIF images on the Internet. Use your favorite search engine and look for "animated GIF".*

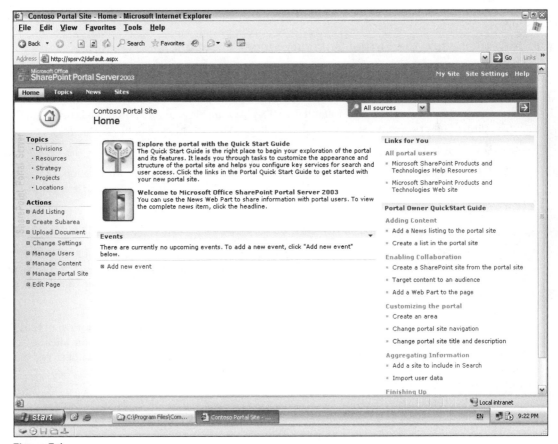

Figure 5-1

To modify any of these three properties, follow these steps:

Try It Out   Modify the Portal Site Properties

1. Log on as a web designer or administrator to any computer with access to the portal site.

2. Open the Home page of the portal site.

3. Click the link Site Settings and then Change portal site properties and SharePoint site creation settings.

4. On the following page you can see the Portal Name, Portal Description, and Location of logo file. Change them according to your needs. There are two other fields in this page, but leave them for now.

5. Click OK to save and close this page. Any changes to the portal name or logo will be effective immediately.

Note that the default path to the logo file is /_layouts/images/sitelogo.gif. This is a virtual IIS directory that in turn points to a physical file location on the SPS server. To see where it points to, follow these steps:

Try It Out   View the Virtual Directory Folder Location

1. Log on to the SPS server as an administrator.

2. Open the Internet Information Service Manager.

3. Expand the node Web Sites/Default Web Site/_layouts (if your SPS portal site is using another virtual IIS server, make sure to use that virtual server instead of Default Web Site).

4. Right-click the "images" virtual directory and select Properties.

5. On the Virtual Directory tab, look at the Local path. It will point to this file location: <disk>:\ Program Files\Common Files\Microsoft Shared\Web Server Extensions\60\ template\images.

6. Close this dialog box.

If you want to add your own logo file, Microsoft recommends that you create a new subfolder under the images folder. For example, assume you want to use the custom logo file My_Logo.gif. Create the new subfolder Custom and put the My_Logo.gif there. Then set the Location of the logo file to /_layouts/ images/custom/My_Logo.gif.

The folder path you found in step 5 is part of a large folder structure used by SPS for storing all files that describes how the portal site looks and behaves. It also contains the files for the WSS team sites, as well. Note that all documents, files, and other information users create inside SharePoint are not stored here; they are all stored in the content database in the SQL Server used by SharePoint. Use the Windows Explorer and navigate to this path:

```
<disk>:\Program Files\Common Files\Microsoft Shared\Web Server ⊃
Extensions\60\template
```

This is the start of all SharePoint folders and files; see Figure 5-2.

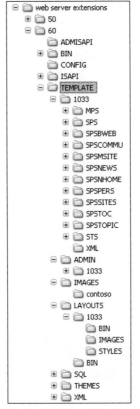

Figure 5-2

SharePoint's Folder Tree

SharePoint keeps a number of files in these folders, most commonly ASP.NET files (.aspx) and XML files (.xml). These files describe exactly how a given area page will look, including its menus, icons, links, and lists. For example, if you want to move the logo on the Home page to the far right instead of its current left position, you would modify the .aspx file for that particular page. Later in this chapter you will see several examples of how to do this type of modification. Most of these files can be modified with an editor, such as Notepad, but you should think twice before changing them. Some of them may be replaced when you apply the next service pack, and improper modifications may corrupt the portal site. In the following table is an explanation of the most interesting folders under the Template folder for the U.S. English version of SharePoint (1033) and what is inside them:

Template Folders	Used by	Comments
1033	SPS & WSS	Language-specific template files for both SPS and WSS sites. The folder 1033 is a *Language Code Identifier* (LCID) for U.S. English, indicating this is a U.S. English version of SharePoint. See the next table for a complete LCID list.
1033\SPS	SPS	The Home area page of the portal site, including its lists and configuration settings.
1033\SPSCOMMU	SPS	The Community area page of the portal site, including its lists and configuration settings.
1033\SPSMSITE	SPS	The My Site home page of the portal site, including its lists and configuration settings.
1033\SPSPERS	SPS	The team sites under My Site on the portal site, including their lists and configuration settings.
1033\SPSNEWS	SPS	The News area page of the portal site, including its lists and configuration settings.
1033\SPSNHOME	SPS	The News home page of the portal site, including its lists and configuration settings.
1033\SPSSITES	SPS	The Site Directory page of the portal site, including its lists and configuration settings.
1033\SPSTOC	SPS	The Topics home page of the portal site, including its lists and configuration settings.
1033\SPSTOPIC	SPS	The area pages under the Topics home page of the portal site, including their lists and configuration settings.
1033\STS	WSS	The template files for all WSS team sites, including their lists and configuration settings.
1033\MPS	WSS	The template file for all multi-page team sites, including their lists and configuration settings.
1033\XML	SPS & WSS	This folder contains files that you configure when you add any new site/area templates into WSS and SPS.
ADMIN	SPS & WSS	Contains all pages for the SharePoint Central Administration. Avoid modifying these pages.
IMAGES	SPS & WSS	Contains all icons and images used by SharePoint for its portal site and team sites. Create a subfolder under Images if you want to add your own pictures. Avoid modifying this folder.
LAYOUTS\1033	SPS & WSS	Contains all pages required for standard site administration. Do not modify these files.
LAYOUTS\1033\ STYLES	SPS	Contains Cascading Style Sheets (CSS) that control how the portal area pages will look.
LAYOUTS\1033\ IMAGES	SPS & WSS	Contains the images used by SPS and WSS in the administration pages.

Template Folders	Used by	Comments
SQL	SPS & WSS	Contains SQL scripts that are used when creating configuration and content databases. Do not change these files.
XML	SPS & WSS	Contains configuration files. The DOCICON.XML file is used when you need to map icons to new document file types.

SharePoint Portal Server 2003 is available in 25 different languages. After the installation you cannot change the language of the portal site, but you can install extra language template packs for the team sites (the WSS part of this SharePoint installation). There are 35 different language template packs for WSS, and you can install one or more of these. This will make it possible to create team sites with different languages, but again, the portal will not change. If you install any optional language templates for WSS, you will find corresponding LCID folders in the Template and Layouts folder. For example, if you add the Swedish template pack, it adds the new folder 1053, as Figure 5-3 shows. Compare this to Figure 5-2 with its default folders.

Figure 5-3

The complete LCID table is not so easy to find, but in the following table you will find all the locales currently supported by Microsoft:

LCID	Locale	LCID	Locale
5121	Algeria	6145	Morocco
11274	Argentina	5129	New Zealand
3081	Australia	19466	Nicaragua
15361	Bahrain	1044	Norway
16394	Bolivia	8193	Oman

Table continued on following page

LCID	Locale	LCID	Locale
1046	Brazil	1056	Pakistan
3084	Canada1	6154	Panama
4105	Canada2	15370	Paraguay
13322	Chile	2052	Peoples Republic of China
9226	Colombia	10250	Peru
5130	Costa Rica	1045	Poland
1029	Czech Republic	16385	Qatar
1030	Denmark	1049	Russia
7178	Dominican Republic	1025	Saudi Arabia
12298	Ecuador	4100	Singapore
3073	Egypt	1051	Slovakia
17418	El Salvador	1060	Slovenia
-2	European Union1	7177	South Africa
-1	European Union2	1053	Sweden
4106	Guatemala	2055	Switzerland
18442	Honduras	10241	Syria
3076	Hong Kong SAR	1028	Taiwan
1038	Hungary	1054	Thailand
1081	India	7169	Tunisia
1065	Iran	1055	Turkey
2049	Iraq	14337	UAE
1037	Israel	2057	United Kingdom
1041	Japan	1033	United States
11265	Jordan	14346	Uruguay
1042	Korea	8202	Venezuela
13313	Kuwait	1066	Vietnam
12289	Lebanon	9217	Yemen
4097	Libya	8193	Oman
2058	Mexico		

Go to http://www.microsoft.com *and search for "Language Template Pack" to add new language templates for the WSS team sites. Note that there is a special update for these language templates you should install if you are running Service Pack 2!*

Branding the Portal Site

All the files and folders mentioned in the previous section are the key to understanding how and what to modify when branding the portal site. So now start with a common request: Modifying the layout of the portal banner (the dark blue header at the top of every portal area page). This example describes how you move the Home, News, Topics, and Sites links to the top of the page. Now also move the My Site and Site Settings links to the same level as the other links.

This requires that you understand exactly what file to modify and what part in that file needs to be changed. You will find lots of information about customizing and branding SharePoint in the SharePoint Products and Technologies Software Development Kit (SPPT SDK) that you will find at http://msdn.microsoft.com. The following are just some examples that show you some of the easy things you can do. All the following folder references start at \Program Files\Common Files\Microsoft Shared\Web Server Extensions\60\template.

Start by modifying the page banner, changing its size, and removing the default logo. The file that controls how the Home area page looks is located at Template\1033\SPS\Default.aspx. Open this file with Notepad and locate this part:

```
<tr> <td colspan="3" width="100%">
    <SPSWC:PageHeader id="PageHeaderID" runat="server" PageContext="SitePage"
    ShowTitle="false" />
    <div class="ms-phnav1wrapper ms-navframe"> <SPSWC:CategoryNavigationWebPart
     runat="server" id="HorizontalNavBar" /> </div>
</td> </tr>
```

The SPSWC:PageHeader and the SPSWC:CategoryNavigationWebPart are SharePoint server controls that tell SharePoint how and where to display the header and the links on this page. To achieve the goal in this example, you must replace the complete code in the previous box with this:

```
<!-- NEW HEADER -->
<tr>
  <td colspan="3" width="100%">
    <table width="100%" cellpadding=0 cellspacing=0 border=0 >
      <tr>
        <td width="0%" nowrap>
          <div class="ms-phnav1wrapper">
          <SPSWC:CategoryNavigationWebPart runat="server"
            id="HorizontalNavBar"

          DisplayStyle="HorizontalOneLayer" />
          </div>
        </td>
        <td width="100%" class="CustomNavBar" nowrap align="left"
         valign="top">
          <a href="http://spsrv2">Contoso</a>
        </td>
        <td width="0%" class="CustomNavBar" nowrap align="left"
         valign="top">
          <SPSWC:PageHeader id="PageHeaderID" runat="server"
          PageContext="SitePage"
          ShowTitle="false" HelpID="NavBarHelpHome"
          mode="LinksOnly"/>
```

```
          </td>
        </tr>
      </table>
    </td>
  </tr> <!-- NEW HEADER -->
```

This will result in a portal site that looks like Figure 5-4.

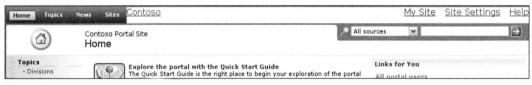

Figure 5-4

As you can see, the logo is gone and the header is much smaller.

You need to add the logo back again and move it all the way to the right while you are at it. The problem now is that the new code will not care about the file you entered previously in the Location of logo file text box. So you have to write some code that loads and displays the logo file. This example uses the logo file `Contoso_logo.gif`, but you can use whatever logo you want. Make sure to store it in the Custom subfolder. The new code that does all this is inserted into the previous code segment, and the result looks like this:

```
<!-- NEW HEADER -->
<tr>
  <td colspan="3" width="100%">
    <table width="100%" cellpadding=0 cellspacing=0 border=0 >
      <tr>
        <td width="0%" nowrap>
          <div class="ms-phnav1wrapper">
          <SPSWC:CategoryNavigationWebPart runat="server"
            id="HorizontalNavBar"

          DisplayStyle="HorizontalOneLayer" />
          </div>
        </td>
        <td width="100%" class="CustomNavBar" nowrap align="left"
         valign="top">
          <a href="http://spsrv2">Contoso</a>
        </td>
        <td width="0%" class="CustomNavBar" nowrap align="left"
         valign="top">
          <SPSWC:PageHeader id="PageHeaderID" runat="server"
           PageContext="SitePage"
           ShowTitle="false" HelpID="NavBarHelpHome"
           mode="LinksOnly"/>
        </td>
      </tr>
    </table>
```

```
<table width="100%" border="0" cellspacing="0" cellpadding="0">
    <tr>
      <td width="100%">
      </td>
      <td width="150" align="right">
        <img src="/_layouts/images/custom/contoso_logo.gif"
        alt="Contoso">
      </td>
    </tr>
  </table>
</td>
</tr>
<!-- NEW HEADER -->
```

The result now looks like Figure 5-5. The logo is visible and located at the far right side of the header.

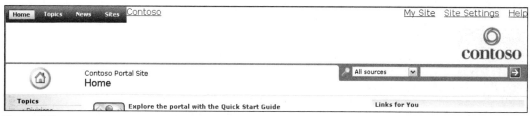

Figure 5-5

But still it does not look very good! Some parts remain dark blue, and some links such as My Site and Site Settings are of a different font and size than the rest of the text in the header. To change this, you need to apply a style sheet, which is described in the next section.

And there are other things you need to fix. For example, open the News page. It still has the default design! This indicates clearly that you need to change each and every page individually. The modifications you did on the `Default.aspx` file for the Home page must be repeated for all pages in the portal site. Unfortunately, they all are independent so you must modify each `Default.aspx` file in every folder under Template that begins with SPS, meaning these files:

❑ `[lcid]\SPS\Default.aspx`

❑ `[lcid]\SPSCOMMU\Default.aspx`

❑ `[lcid]\SPSMSITE\Default.aspx`

❑ `[lcid]\SPSPERS\Default.aspx`

❑ `[lcid]\SPSNEWS\Default.aspx`

❑ `[lcid]\SPSNHOME\Default.aspx`

❑ `[lcid]\SPSSITES\Default.aspx`

❑ `[lcid]\SPSTOC\Default.aspx`

❑ `[lcid]\SPSTOPIC\Default.aspx`

There are more files to modify if you want every page to use the same header look. For example, there is a page that shows the search results, another page when you request more information about a document, and so on. Make sure to do the same modifications on these files too:

❑   [lcid]\SPS\Txtlstvw.aspx

❑   [lcid]\SPS\Search.aspx

❑   [lcid]\SPS\Moreinfo.aspx

❑   [lcid]\SPS\DMFramesetTopFrame.aspx

❑   [lcid]\SPSSITES\LISTS\SITELST\Summary.aspx

❑   LAYOUTS\[lcid]\PortalHeader.aspx

The last file, `PortalHeader.aspx`, is especially interesting. SharePoint has a property called `AlternateHeader`. It is used by team sites in SPS environments to display another header instead of the default WSS header by pointing to the `PortalHeader.aspx` file. That is why you need to modify this file: to make sure team sites use the same header as the portal site.

Changing the CSS File

The look of a web page, including its color, fonts, and font size, can be set directly in the code. But this would make a complex web application very hard to adjust. For example, if you wanted to change all text that uses Times New Roman to Arial on all web pages, it would require you to manually edit every web page. A much smarter way is to use labels for each part of the web page, like the header, text block, and tables; then define what colors, fonts, and size to be used for each part in a separate file. This is called a *style sheet*. If you later want to change the header from blue to green, you identify the label for the header and change its color settings in the style sheet.

SharePoint is indeed a complex web application with lots of pages, and it uses style sheets to control the appearance of these pages. SharePoint actually uses several style sheets, which are read one after another, and the settings in the last style sheet have precedence over any other setting for the same object. This is called a *Cascading Style Sheet*, or *CSS*. The following table lists the CSS files used by SPS:

Style Sheet File Name	Description
SPS.CSS	SharePoint Portal Server Styles
OWS.CSS	Windows SharePoint Services styles
MENU.CSS	The styles used to create the drop-down menus
OWSMAC.CSS	The styles used to render pages for the Apple Macintosh
OWSPERS.CSS	The style used for the My Site page

Most CSS files for other web applications are rather short, but not SharePoint's CSS files. They contain more than 1,000 lines of definitions, and it is hard to understand exactly what each line does without some help. One good source of information is this document:

    http://msdn.microsoft.com/library/default.asp?url=/library/⊃
    en-us/odc_sp2003_ta/html/ODC_SPSCustomizingSharePointSites3.asp

If you want to change just parts of the web page, you can add your own custom CSS files or you can change the original CSS files. Note that a new service pack or update may overwrite these standard CSS files, so make sure to back up your modified files in case you need to restore them.

Try It Out   Change the Portal Site Header

In this example, you create a custom CSS file that will contain the modifications needed to make the new header look nice, with a green background color. You will create an empty CSS file with the name `MyStyle.CSS` and save it with the other CSS files in the folder `\LAYOUTS\1033\STYLES`. This file will override the default CSS settings. Follow these steps:

1. Log on to the SharePoint server as an administrator.

2. Create the file `MyStyle.CSS` in the STYLES directory.

3. Open the portal site and click the Site Settings link.

4. Click the link Change portal site properties and SharePoint site creation settings.

5. At the bottom of this page, in the "Location of cascading style sheet file" text box, enter **/_layouts/1033/styles/MyStyle.css** and click OK. You have just told SharePoint where to find your custom CSS file, and the order of priority is now as follows:

    a. OWS.CSS (lowest priority)

    b. SPS.CSS

    c. MyStyle.CSS (highest priority)

6. Previously you modified the position for the custom class `CustomNavBar`, which is the part of the header that contains the links My Site, Site Settings, and Help. You want to set its background color to green and change the font to Tahoma, using white bold text and 70% in size; continue with these steps.

    Use Notepad to add the following code to your `MyStyle.CSS` file:

```css
.CustomNavBar
{
    border-top: 1px green solid;
    background-color: green;
    padding-left: 10px ;
    padding-top: 3px;
}
.CustomNavBar a
{
    background-color: green;
    font-family: Tahoma;
    font-size: 70%;
    font-weight: bold;
    color: white;
    text-decoration: none;
}
.CustomNavBar a:hover
{
    text-decoration: underline ;
}
```

7. Save the file (but leave `MyStyle.CSS` open in Notepad). Refresh your portal page by pressing F5. It should now reflect the new settings and the header should look like Figure 5-6.

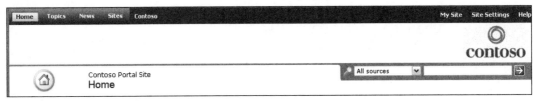

Figure 5-6

8. How do you know how to define the color green? And what if you want to use another color? The answer to that is to learn how to define colors using the standard Cascading Style Sheets Level 2 (CSS2) color codes. You can learn a lot more about this in any HTML development book, but you get a quick summary in the following table, which shows the ways to define a standard green color. Use whatever method you want; the point is that you have a number of options for defining a specific color, and some of them give you much more control over the exact color tone, if this is needed.

Method	Example	Explanation
HTML 4.0 color names	Green	Use the HTML 4.0 standard names, like Black, Red, Green, Olive, Yellow, and so on
RGB 3 digits	#080	First character is Red, then Green, then Black, with hexadecimal values between 0 and F.
RGB 6 digits	#008000	First two characters is Red, next two is Green and last two is Black, with hexadecimal values between 00 and FF.
RGB Triples	rgb(0,128,0)	First number is Red, next Green and last is black, with decimal values between 0 and 255.
RGB Triples	rgb(0%,50%,0%)	Same as above, but with values between 0 and 100%

> **You will find more information about color setting on this site:** `http://www.w3.org/TR/REC-html40/types.html#idx-color`.

You must now fix the remaining part of the header that is still dark blue. This part is known as the SharePoint class `CategoryNavigationWebPart`. You need only to define the difference between the default color settings for this class and your new green look. To make sure the box around the current area name stands out (for example Home), you want a black frame around it, and you want the text in the box to be green as well.

Add the following code segment at the end of your `MyStyle.CSS` file:

```
.ms-phnav1wrapper {
    background-image: none;
    border-top: 1px green solid;
    background-color: green;
    BACKGROUND-REPEAT: no-repeat;
}
.ms-phnavmidc1sel, .ms-phnavmidc0sel
{
    BORDER-top: black 1px solid;
    BORDER-left: black 1px solid;
    BORDER-right: black 1px solid;
    BORDER-bottom: black 1px solid;
}
.ms-phnavmidc1sel a, .ms-phnavmidc0sel a
{
    color: green;
}
```

The page should now look like Figure 5-7.

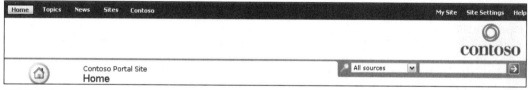

Figure 5-7

9. Almost done; all that is left is to change the blue color around the search box and the title area frame line.

   Add the following code segment to the end of your `MyStyle.CSS` file:

```
Div.ms-titleareaframe
{
    border-top: 3px solid green;
}
.ms-sbtable
{
    background-color: green;
}
```

   Did you notice that the rounded corners on the search box are still blue? They are actually built up by two images (`Cornerbl.gif` and `Cornertop.gif`), and you need to change them separately, as in the following steps.

10. Make a copy of the original files in the `Templates\Images` and store them in the same location as your previously custom-made logo files (`Templates\Images\Custom`).

11. Use an image tool and give them the same green color as the header.

12. Then reload these images by adding this code segment to the end of your `MyStyle.CSS` file:

```
.ms-sblbcorner
{
    background-image: url(/_layouts/images/custom/cornerbl.gif);
}
.ms-sbtopcorner
{
    background-image: url(/_layouts/images/custom/cornertop.gif);
}
```

The page should now look like Figure 5-8.

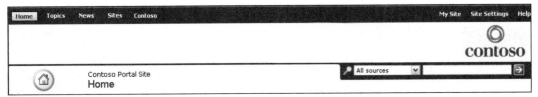

Figure 5-8

Now it looks good, right? As you can see, you can make it look however you want, as long as you know what to modify. Make sure to study the software development kit for SharePoint described earlier; you will also find tons of tips and examples on the Internet on what you can do to customize your portal site.

Now you will end this customization part by adding a breadcrumb trail to the pages. You may remember the old and rather cruel story about the two kids left alone in the woods by their father. To make sure they found their way back home, the boy secretly dropped breadcrumbs on their way out to the woods. Unfortunately for the kids, all the breadcrumbs where eaten by birds; but that's another story.

In web applications, breadcrumb trails are a way of indicating for the user what pages she used to get to this particular page. Breadcrumbs are shown as a series of web pages, and you can jump to any of these previous pages by clicking on them. SharePoint does not have breadcrumb trails, but you can add them easily. Not all area pages in the portal will benefit from these breadcrumbs, but the Topics page will, because it can have a number of subareas. Follow these steps to add this to the Topics subareas (SPSTOPICS):

Try It Out   **Add Breadcrumb Trails**

1. Open this file with Notepad: `SPSTOPIC\Default.aspx`.

2. Locate the following code segment (note that it may be hard to find if the files are not using indented lines, but look carefully and you will find it):

```
<tr>
    <td ID="onetidPageTitle" class="ms-pagetitle">
        <SPSWC:CategoryProperty runat="server" Property="Name" />
    </td>
</tr>
```

3. Directly after that part you add this code segment:

```
<tr>
   <td>
      <SPSWC:BreadCrumbTrail runat="server" id="NewBreadCrumbTrail"
      LeadInText=""
      VerticalMode="false" FrameType="None" />
   </td>
</tr>
```

4. Save and close this `Default.aspx` file.

Test the new breadcrumb trails. Open the portal site, go to the Topics area, and select any subarea (for example, Sales). It should look like Figure 5-9.

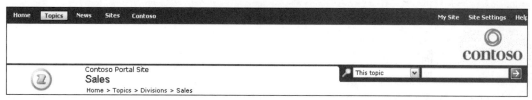

Figure 5-9

Click any link in the breadcrumb trail, and it will take you back to that particular page. Now that was nice, wasn't it? By now you have a basic understanding about what you can do and how it is done. It is not hard, as long as you know what to modify, but that is the trick, of course.

Managing Portal Areas

Now is a good time to look more closely at the different pages in the portal site. You may remember from the beginning of this chapter that each page is called an area, and every area is in fact a separate site. The top-level site in SPS is by default the Home area; all other areas are subsites. By default every new portal site will contain these area pages:

❑ **Home:** The start page and top-level area for the portal. This page contains both local information, such as links and a calendar, and information that is stored in other pages, such as a news list and a topics list.

❑ **Topics:** A subarea that is used to group information together, regardless of where this information may be stored. Use this page to make it easy for users to navigate to the information they are looking for. There are a number of subareas under this page.

❑ **News:** A subarea that is used to list news and information (for example, about the organization and its customers). By default there are three subareas used for categorizing the news listings.

❑ **Sites:** A subarea that lists all team sites (WSS sites) directly under the portal site. Use it to make it easy for users to find the team site they are looking for.

Few organizations implementing SPS are completely satisfied with the default portal site. But the good news is that all of these area pages can be changed in almost any way you want. And most changes do not require anything other than the web client browser (and the permission to do it, of course). Now look more closely at these area pages and what you can do with them.

The Home Area Page

The start page lists locally stored information and mirrors the News and Topics page content. This area page is most often used to display information of general interest and to ease the navigation to other parts. You can adjust the Home page in many ways (for example, to display news lists from several area pages).

News Listings

Now start with the news listing (see Figure 5-1 at the beginning of the chapter). There are two news listings by default: "Explore the portal with the Quick Start Guide" and "Welcome to the Microsoft Office SharePoint Portal Server 2003"; each has a picture next to it. Now switch to the News page. You find the exact same news here. So how does this connection work? Check it out with these steps:

Try It Out   View the News List Connection in the Home Area

1. Log on as a SharePoint administrator.

2. Open the Home page using a web browser.

3. Under Actions, click Edit page. This will switch the page to edit mode. Choose Modify Shared➪ Design This Page. Now all web part headers display an arrow that opens a drop-down menu with a number of options.

4. On the header for the News list web part, click the arrow at the far right; then select Modify Shared web part. This will open an edit pane to the right of the page.

5. At the top of this edit pane, note that it says Home > News. This is the connection you are looking for. It can be modified so the news list of the Home page mirrors the news list of any area page you want!

6. The best way to understand this connection between the news list and what it displays is to test it. For example, say you want to display a second news list on the Home page, and that list should contain news items stored on the Topics page. Start by creating the new News web part that will be the source for the News listing on the Home page. Switch to the Topics area page.

7. Under Actions, click Edit page to open this page in edit mode.

8. On the upper-right part of the page, choose Modify Shared Page➪Add Web Parts➪Browse. This will open a list of web part galleries and their web parts for this particular page.

9. Make sure that the Contoso Portal Site Gallery is selected. In the Web Part List you are looking for the News web part. You will see the first 10 web parts; click Next to list the next 10, and the News web part should be visible. If not, you are in the wrong web part gallery.

10. Select the News web part and drag it to any web part zone (for example, the Middle Left Zone). (Or use the drop-down menu on the bottom of this page, select Middle Left Zone, and click Add.) Click the Topics link to close the web part list and end the edit mode. You should now see an empty news list on the Topics page, as depicted in Figure 5-10.

     This news list is completely independent of any other news list, and you can enter news listings in it that will not show up in any other news list, if necessary. The next step is to create a news list on the Home page that connects to this list.

11. Switch back to the Home page.

12. Under Actions, click Edit page.

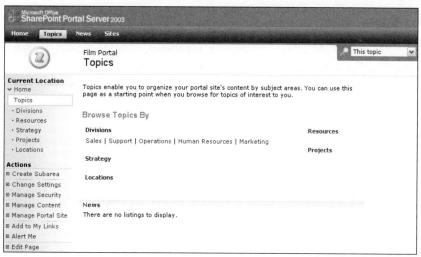

Figure 5-10

13. Choose Modify Shared Page⇨Add Web Parts⇨Browse to open the web part gallery list.

14. Locate the same web part as in step 10 (the News web part) and drag it to any web part zone (for example, the Top Zone). The new News web part will now be visible in that zone.

15. On the new News web part header, click its arrow to open a menu, and then select Modify Shared Web Part. It will open the configuration pane for this web part.

16. At the top of the pane, click Change location. A new window opens; select Topics and click OK to save and close that window. Now this web part is connected to the Topics news web part. While you are here, change the name of this listing:

    a.   Expand the Appearance section at the bottom of the pane.

    b.   Change the Title from News to Topic News.

    c.   Click OK to close the configuration of this News web part (and refresh the page, if necessary). You should now see this empty News listing, but because Microsoft wants you to be sure it is empty, it automatically adds the text "There are no listings to display." Very nice of them!

So far, so good. The final test is to create a news listing for the Topics news web part and see if it shows up on the Home page, as expected. But how should you enter the news item? Well, by default the portal site only has this link on the News page, which is rather logical if you think about it.

17. Switch to the News area page.

18. Under Actions, click Add News. This will display a web form where you define a news item, its title, its text, its description, when it should be displayed and archived, its image, and in what news listing it is to appear. You learn more about this form in the next section, but for now enter the following text:

    a.   **Title:** "This is news in the Topics area."

    b.   **Description:** "This is a test."

    c.   **Content:** Select the option Add news listing by entering text.

    d.   **Location:** Click Change Location to open a dialog box; Make sure to remove the check box from the News and check the Topics. Click OK to save and close the dialog box.

When you return to the previous form, make sure the location is Home > Topics. Click OK to save and close this News item.

19. You are returned to the News area. Note that the news item is not listed on this page. Switch to the Topics area, and make sure the news item is visible here.

20. Switch to the Home area page and you will see the news item listed in the Topics News web part.

21. In order to prepare for the next test, you should add one or more news items to all three subareas of the News page: Company News, Press Announcements, and External News. Repeat step 18 and make sure to change the Location in step 18d to point only to each of these three subareas, respectively.

In other words, you can create any number of News web parts in any portal area and use the Home area as a front page, much like a newspaper. This connection feature actually works with any area page, not only the Home page, except for the Sites area, which does not allow you to add any web parts.

Another very interesting web part that relates to this discussion is the News Area. This web part lists all news titles for all areas with a News web part. For instance, in the preceding example you created a News web part in the Topics area. The news in that web part automatically shows up in the News Area web part. Test it and see:

> **Note that the specific results shown here are based on having also completed the previous Try It Out on viewing the News list connection in the Home area.**

Try It Out   The News Area Web Part

1. Open the Home area page.

2. Under Actions, click Edit page.

3. Choose Modify Shared Page⇨Add Web Parts⇨Browse to open the web part gallery list.

4. Locate the News Areas web part; drag it to any web part zone (for example, the Top Zone). It will directly display news from both the News area and the Topics area, because they both have a News web part.

5. But there is more to this web part, as you will see. Open its configuration settings by clicking the blue arrow to the right and select Modify Shared Web Part.

6. Modify the Subarea Layers field from 1 to 2. Click OK to save and close.

7. Refresh this page. Like magic you now see news listings from at least two other areas that you did not even know had any news listings.

These new listings come from subareas under Topics (for example, Projects and Divisions). When you configured the Subarea Layer to 2, it instructed the News Area web part to display all top areas, including every second-level area. Both the Topics and News area have subareas, but only Projects and Divisions under Topics have any news listings by default. If you added news listings to any other subareas, they will also show up now. Figure 5-11 shows news listings from five subareas: Company News, News, Projects, Divisions, and Topics.

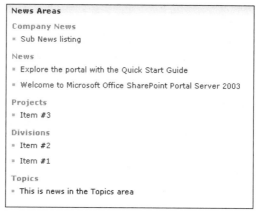

Figure 5-11

Switch to the Topics area, then Projects, and you will see the news listing Item #3 that was listed in Figure 5-11. Figure 5-12 displays the Projects area.

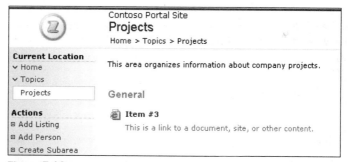

Figure 5-12

But look more closely at this Projects area. Is this really a news listing? Yes, it actually is! But it is slightly different from the news listing in the News area. You can see this more clearly if you hover the mouse over the action Add Listing. Do it and look at the status bar in the bottom of the page. It says something like `http://spsserver/Projects/_layouts/1033/spnewlisting.aspx?CatID`. Then switch to the News area and hover the mouse over the action Add News and the status bar will be the same, except for the extra string `Mode=News`. This extra string is the reason that the form you fill in for News items prompts for dates to start displaying and to remove the item from the list, as opposed to Add Listing, which does not ask for these dates.

In other words, all subareas under Topics contain news listings, except they are not called news; they are just called listings. That is why they all show up in the News Areas web part.

Topics Listings

In addition to the News listings, there is also one other connected list displayed on the Home area page. It is the Topics list that you can see on the left side of the Home page. See Figure 5-13.

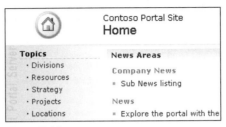

Figure 5-13

This listing shows all topics directly under the Topics area and makes it very easy to open a particular topic. It is faster to use than first switching to the Topics area and then opening a topic. This listing cannot be modified like the News listing, because it's not a web part. This listing simply shows all the main topics that exist on the Topics area page. Whenever you change the Topics page, this list reflects the changes.

If you don't use the Topics feature, you probably do not want this list to show up on the Home page. You can change this list in a number of ways:

❑ Remove the Topics area page.

❑ Remove all topic listings and hide the Topics area.

❑ Remove the access to the Topics area page and to its area listing.

❑ Change the code that displays this list.

The first option from the preceding list is to remove the Topics area completely. After this, no one will be able to use topics. Therefore, avoid this method this unless you are very sure you will never use the Topics feature! This is how you do it:

Try It Out   Remove the Topics Area Completely

1. Open any main area on the portal, for example the Home area.

2. Under Actions, click Manage Portal Site. This lists all area pages listed on the top menu bar.

3. Point to Topics in that list. Use the arrow to the right to see the drop-down menu. Select Delete from that menu list. The Topics area and it listing on the Home page are now gone!

If you do not want to remove the page completely, you can hide it instead. But to make sure the Topics listing is removed from the Home page as well, you also need to remove these topics. This method is much more secure, because it allows you to enable the Topics feature later on when you finally discover that it is indeed a cool feature. This is how you do it:

Try It Out   **Hide the Topics Area and All Topics Listings**

1. Open any main area on the portal, for example the Home area.

2. Under Actions, click Manage Portal Site. This lists all area pages listed on the top menu bar.

3. Locate Topics in that list and click the + sign to expand all its topics; by default there are five topics.

4. For each of these topics, point the mouse to the right of the topic name (for example, Divisions) and click the arrow to display the drop-down menu. Select Delete and then OK two times to remove it.

5. When all topics are removed, you must now hide the Topics page itself. Click to the right of the Topics name and select Edit.

6. Switch to the Display tab, check "Exclude from portal site navigation," and click OK. The Topics page is now hidden and no topics are listed on the Home page.

The third method is the one that will allow some users to use topics. You remove the rights for a group of users to see the Topics area and all its listings. For example, say that you want to remove the Topics feature for the site group Reader only and allow all other site groups to still use Topics. This is how you do it:

Try It Out   **Hide the Topics for Some Users**

1. Open the Topics area page.

2. Under Actions, click Manage Security.

3. Check the Reader site group and click Remove Permissions. This hides the Topics area page for any user that belongs to the Reader group. Still, they would see the Topics listing on the Home page, so you need to do one thing more.

4. In the text at the top of this page, you can see a link embedded that says "Only show to users with View Area right." Click that link and the text will change to "Show to all users."

That's it. Test this by opening the portal site as a user with Reader membership. There should be no trace of topics anywhere.

Finally, there is a way of changing the code so the Topics listing is removed for everyone, regardless of whether they have access to the Topics page. Follow these steps to do it:

Try It Out   **Remove the Topics Listing from the Home Area**

1. Log on to the SharePoint server as an administrator.

2. Open the `Default.aspx` file with Notepad, located in this folder (assuming you have a U.S. English version of SPS): `C:\Program Files\Common Files\Microsoft Shared\web server extensions\60\TEMPLATE\1033\SPS`.

3. Locate the following line. Note that there is a similar line with the `id="HorizontalNavBar"`; be sure to modify the correct line!

```
<SPSWC:CategoryNavigationWebPart runat="server" id="VerticalNavBar"
DisplayStyle="VerticalOneLayer" />
```

4. Remove that line completely. Better still, make it a comment so you can restore it later, if necessary. A good idea is also to add some text to your comment explaining why you did this so you won't become confused later and delete it. To make it a comment, enter the following strings before `<!--` and after `-->` so it looks like this:

```
<!--  <SPSWC:CategoryNavigationWebPart runat="server" id="VerticalNavBar"
DisplayStyle="VerticalOneLayer" />  -->
```

5. Save the `Default.aspx` file.

6. Refresh the Home area page. The Topics listing is now gone.

Other Listings on the Home Page

By default you will see some other information on this area page. This is local information, not connected or displayed in any other area:

❑ **Events:** Located under the News web part. This is a calendar type web part that can be used to display general events and meetings for every portal user. This web part is connected to a list with the same name; click its name and you will see a separate page for this list, including all its bookings and configuration links.

❑ **Links for you:** Located to the right on this page. This is actually a News web part that is configured to display only the titles; these items point to help files stored in the file system, for example `/_vti_bin/help/1033/sps/html/HelpResources.htm` (where `/ _vti_bin` points to `C:\Program Files\Common Files\Microsoft Shared\web server extensions\ 60\ISAPI`).

❑ **Portal Owner QuickStart Guide:** Located to the right on this page. This is a special web part not listed in any web part gallery; if you remove it, you will lose it. The purpose of this web part is to give you a list of links to locations inside the portal where you do things such as adding portal users and news; see Figure 5-14.

Portal Owner QuickStart Guide

Adding Content
- Add a News listing to the portal site
- Create a list in the portal site

Enabling Collaboration
- Create a SharePoint site from the portal site
- Target content to an audience
- Add a Web Part to the page

Customizing the portal
- Create an area
- Change portal site navigation
- Change portal site title and description

Aggregating Information
- Add a site to include in Search
- Import user data

Finishing Up
- Give users access to the portal
- Remove this Web Part

Figure 5-14

This last web part, the Portal Owner QuickStart Guide, is too good to just throw away. It has some special features that you can use for your own purpose. It allows you to enter HTML code into a special property named LinkHTML that displays custom links. This web part then uses your code to enable these features:

❑ Render the text line for each link.

❑ Open the link when the user clicks it.

❑ Create extra popup links for help and information.

Before you continue playing with this web part, save it and then import it to the general web part gallery. Follow these steps:

Try It Out   **Save the Portal Owner QuickStart Guide Web Part**

1. Open the Home page.

2. Click Edit Page (under Actions).

3. Click the menu arrow, to the right of this web part header. Select Export. In the following dialog box, click Save and store the file on the disk. Now you have a copy of this web part. The next step is to import it to the web part galley.

4. Choose Site Settings⇨Manage security and additional settings⇨Manage Web Part gallery. This displays a long list of all web parts existing on this portal site.

5. Click Upload Web Part. Use the Browse button to locate the file you saved in step 3. You may want to specify your own group value (for example, "Imported web parts"). Click Save and Close when ready with this form. Now this web part is available anywhere in this portal site.

Because you now have a copy of this web part installed in the web part gallery, it is okay to play with its settings and see what it does:

1. On the Home page, switch to Edit Page mode and click the menu arrow on the existing web part.

2. Click Modify Shared Web Part to view its configuration pane.

3. Expand the Miscellaneous section at the bottom of this pane. There is the magic thing in this web part; the HTML for links.

4. Click anywhere in that text block and a new button with three dots will appear to the right; click that button. This will open the Web Page Dialog where the HTML code is stored. It is not formatted, so it's almost impossible to see exactly what it does; following is this code in a much more easy-to-read style:

```
<TABLE class="ms-ls">
    <TR>
        <TD colspan=2 style="padding-top: 6px;" class="ms-smallheader">
        <SPAN class="ms-announcementtitle">Adding Content</SPAN>
        </TD>
    </TR>
    <TR>
        <TD valign=top>
        <IMG SRC="%LSTBULETGIF%" alt="">
        </TD>
        <TD width="100%" valign=top class="ms-lsmin ms-vb">
```

```
        BEGINPOPUP
        _vti_bin/help/%LCID%/sps/html/QsAddaNewsItemtothePortal.htm
        ENDPOPUP
        BEGINNAVIGATE
        /_layouts/%LCID%/spnewlisting.aspx?Mode=News&Focus=PQSG&CatID=%NEWSID%
        ENDNAVIGATE
        BEGINTEXT
        WP_Home_QuickStart_AddNewsItem_Title
        ENDTEXT
        </TD>
    </TR>
    <TR>
        <TD valign=top>
        <IMG SRC="%LSTBULETGIF%" alt="">
        </TD>
        <TD width="100%" valign=top class="ms-lsmin ms-vb">
        BEGINPOPUP
        _vti_bin/help/%LCID%/sps/html/QsCreateaListinthePortal.htm
        ENDPOPUP
        BEGINNAVIGATE
        /_layouts/%LCID%/spscreate.aspx
        ENDNAVIGATE
        BEGINTEXT
        WP_Home_QuickStart_CreateAList_Title
        ENDTEXT
        </TD>
    </TR>
    <TR>
        <TD colspan=2 style="padding-top: 6px;" class="ms-smallheader">
        <SPAN class="ms-announcementtitle">Enabling Collaboration
        </SPAN>
        </TD>
    </TR>
    <TR>
        <TD valign=top>
        <IMG SRC="%LSTBULETGIF%" alt="">
        </TD>
        <TD width="100%" valign=top class="ms-lsmin ms-vb">
        BEGINPOPUP
        _vti_bin/help/%LCID%/sps/html/qsCreateaSharePointSitefromthePortal.htm
        ENDPOPUP
        BEGINNAVIGATE
        /SiteDirectory
        ENDNAVIGATE
        BEGINTEXT
        WP_Home_QuickStart_CreateATeamSite_Title
        ENDTEXT
        </TD>
    </TR>
    <TR>
        <TD valign=top><IMG SRC="%LSTBULETGIF%" alt="">
        </TD>
        <TD width="100%" valign=top class="ms-lsmin ms-vb">
```

```
            BEGINPOPUP
            _vti_bin/help/%LCID%/sps/html/QsTargetContenttoanAudience.htm
            ENDPOPUP
            BEGINNAVIGATE
            /_layouts/%LCID%/Audience_list.aspx
            ENDNAVIGATE
            BEGINTEXT
            WP_Home_QuickStart_TargetContent_Title
            ENDTEXT
            </TD>
    </TR>
    <TR>
        <TD valign=top>
        <IMG SRC="%LSTBULETGIF%" alt="">
        </TD>
        <TD width="100%" valign=top class="ms-lsmin ms-vb">
        BEGINPOPUP
        _vti_bin/help/%LCID%/sps/html/QsAddawebparttothePage.htm
        ENDPOPUP
        BEGINNAVIGATE
        /default.aspx?Mode=Edit&PageView=Shared
        ENDNAVIGATE
        BEGINTEXT
        WP_Home_QuickStart_AddAwebPart_Title
        ENDTEXT
        </TD>
    </TR>
    <TR>
        <TD colspan=2 style="padding-top: 6px;" class="ms-smallheader">
        <SPAN class="ms-announcementtitle">Customizing the portal
        </SPAN>
        </TD>
    </TR>
    <TR>
        <TD valign=top><IMG SRC="%LSTBULETGIF%" alt="">
        </TD>
        <TD width="100%" valign=top class="ms-lsmin ms-vb">
        BEGINPOPUP
        _vti_bin/help/%LCID%/sps/html/QsCreateaCategory.htm
        ENDPOPUP
        BEGINNAVIGATE
        /_layouts/%LCID%/spnewcategory.aspx?Focus=PQSG
        ENDNAVIGATE
        BEGINTEXT
        WP_Home_QuickStart_CreateACategory_Title
        ENDTEXT
        </TD>
    </TR>
    <TR>
        <TD valign=top><IMG SRC="%LSTBULETGIF%" alt="">
        </TD>
        <TD width="100%" valign=top class="ms-lsmin ms-vb">
        BEGINPOPUP
        _vti_bin/help/%LCID%/sps/html/QsChangePortalNavigation.htm
        ENDPOPUP
```

```
            BEGINNAVIGATE
            /_layouts/%LCID%/CatMan.aspx
            ENDNAVIGATE
            BEGINTEXT
            WP_Home_QuickStart_ChangePortalNavigation_Title
            ENDTEXT
            </TD>
    </TR>
    <TR>
            <TD valign=top><IMG SRC="%LSTBULETGIF%" alt="">
            </TD>
            <TD width="100%" valign=top class="ms-lsmin ms-vb">
            BEGINPOPUP
            _vti_bin/help/%LCID%/sps/html/QsChangetheLogoonthePortalsite.htm
            ENDPOPUP
            BEGINNAVIGATE
            /_layouts/%LCID%/PortalProperties.aspx
            ENDNAVIGATE
            BEGINTEXT
            WP_Home_QuickStart_ChangePortalProperties_Title
            ENDTEXT
            </TD>
    </TR>
    <TR>
            <TD colspan=2 style="padding-top: 6px;" class="ms-smallheader">
            <SPAN class="ms-announcementtitle">Aggregating Information
            </SPAN>
            </TD>
    </TR>
    <TR>
            <TD valign=top><IMG SRC="%LSTBULETGIF%" alt="">
            </TD>
            <TD width="100%" valign=top class="ms-lsmin ms-vb">
            BEGINPOPUP
            _vti_bin/help/%LCID%/sps/html/qsAddaSiteLinktothePortal.htm
            ENDPOPUP
            BEGINNAVIGATE
            /SiteDirectory
            ENDNAVIGATE
            BEGINTEXT
            WP_Home_QuickStart_AddASiteToIncludeInSearch_Title
            ENDTEXT
            </TD>
    </TR>
    <TR>
            <TD valign=top><IMG SRC="%LSTBULETGIF%" alt="">
            </TD>
            <TD width="100%" valign=top class="ms-lsmin ms-vb">
            BEGINPOPUP
            _vti_bin/help/%LCID%/sps/html/QsImportUserData.htm
            ENDPOPUP
            BEGINNAVIGATE
            /_layouts/%LCID%/ProfMain.aspx
            ENDNAVIGATE
```

```
        BEGINTEXT
        WP_Home_QuickStart_ImportUserData_Title
        ENDTEXT
        </TD>
    </TR>
    <TR>
        <TD colspan=2 style="padding-top: 6px;" class="ms-smallheader">
        <SPAN class="ms-announcementtitle">Finishing Up
        </SPAN>
        </TD>
    </TR>
    <TR>
        <TD valign=top><IMG SRC="%LSTBULETGIF%" alt="">
        </TD>
        <TD width="100%" valign=top class="ms-lsmin ms-vb">
        BEGINPOPUP
        _vti_bin/help/%LCID%/sps/html/QsGiveUsersAccessToThePortal.htm
        ENDPOPUP
        BEGINNAVIGATE
        /_layouts/%LCID%/user.aspx
        ENDNAVIGATE
        BEGINTEXT
        WP_Home_QuickStart_GiveUsersAccessToThePortal_Title
        ENDTEXT
        </TD>
    </TR>
    <TR>
        <TD valign=top><IMG SRC="%LSTBULETGIF%" alt="">
        </TD>
        <TD width="100%" valign=top class="ms-lsmin ms-vb">
        BEGINPOPUP
        _vti_bin/help/%LCID%/sps/html/QsRemoveThisWebPart.htm
        ENDPOPUP
        BEGINNAVIGATE
        /default.aspx?Mode=Edit&PageView=Shared
        ENDNAVIGATE
        BEGINTEXT
        WP_Home_QuickStart_RemoveWebPart_Title
        ENDTEXT
        </TD>
    </TR>
</TABLE>
```

So exactly what does this code do? Try it to understand how it works. Click the first link, "Add a News listing to the portal site." Two things happen: You get to the portal form where you define news items, and a help window opens up at the same time. How is this done? Analyze this link and take a closer look at the code that makes it work. The first line of codes shows this table row (the lines between `<TR>` and `</TR>`):

```
<TR>
    <TD colspan=2 style="padding-top: 6px;" class="ms-smallheader">
    <SPAN class="ms-announcementtitle">Adding Content</SPAN>
    </TD>
</TR>
```

This part creates the first header, "Adding Content," on its own row, using the class ms-announcementtitle.

The next code segment starts a new row, using the HTML code <TR>. The first thing in this line is a bullet icon that will show up in front of the link, using the variable %LSTBULETGIF%. This variable points to the file lstbulet.gif, which is stored in the same Template\Images folder you have looked at several times before in this chapter:

```
<TR>
    <TD valign=top>
    <IMG SRC="%LSTBULETGIF%" alt="">
    </TD>
```

Note that this is the same icon used by all the standard lists in SharePoint. You can modify this file, but it will affect every list, so think hard before you do this.

After this icon you will find code that does several things. To start with, the help text that will pop up in a separate window when you click this link is stored in the file QsAddaNewsItemtothePortal.htm as this code segment shows:

```
BEGINPOPUP
_vti_bin/help/%LCID%/sps/html/QsAddaNewsItemtothePortal.htm
ENDPOPUP
```

This file is stored in the folder \ISAPI\help\1033\sps\html, next to the \Template folder.

When you click this link, the following code will execute the spnewlisting.aspx form that lets you enter a news item:

```
BEGINNAVIGATE
/_layouts/%LCID%/spnewlisting.aspx?Mode=News&Focus=PQSG&CatID=%NEWSID%
ENDNAVIGATE
```

This is the same form that you can open if you click the Add News link on the News area page. This aspx file is stored under the \Template folder tree.

The actual text string for this link is in the last part of this table row, which starts with the label BEGINTEXT, as in this code:

```
BEGINTEXT
WP_Home_QuickStart_AddNewsItem_Title
ENDTEXT
```

Exactly what the WP_Home_QuickStart_AddNewsItem_Title link does is not documented by Microsoft, but this a good example of what you can do with SharePoint's web part without using a Visual Studio .NET environment, and it contains a link to interesting documentation for the SharePoint administrator. You can still use this web part and its link in several ways:

❑ Move this Quick Start Guide to another area page, along with other tips and tricks for the portal owner. This requires that you export this web part before removing it from the Home area.

❑ Learn from this web part how you can activate commonly used aspx pages; for example, how to use the Add News aspx link to add this link to a button for making it easier to add news to any area page that has a local News web part.

The Topics Area Page

The purpose of the Topics area page on the portal site is to allow easy navigation to information regardless of where it is stored. For example, say you have a sales department in your organization. The sales personnel need a quick link to a lot of information, such as the following:

❑ Document templates for quotations, contracts, and invoices.

❑ Help and support information.

❑ Price lists.

❑ Product information.

❑ Information about competing products.

❑ Contact information for the sales manager and other sales resources.

All this information may be stored anywhere; some is stored in the file system, some in Outlook's public folder, and some in SharePoint itself. Some information may even exist on external web sites, such as a supplier's web site. Because all this information may be used by several different groups, you cannot move it. You need an easy way of collecting the information without moving it. This is exactly what the Topics area page helps you to do.

By default you will find a number of topics, including some subtopics. Remember that all topics are in fact areas, which in turn are web sites. These default topics are there just go give you an indication of what you can do. You probably will want to modify or remove them and create new topics. To do this, you need to understand how to add information to each Topics area, including how to define the security settings. This is described more in detail in the following sections. Figure 5-15 shows the default topics.

Figure 5-15

Removing, Modifying, and Creating Topics Areas

You may recall from the previous section that there is a page that displays the portal area tree. This page is used for adding new areas and modifying or deleting existing areas. Because Topics also are areas, this page is what you need.

For example, say you want to remove the default Strategy topic; this is how you would do it:

Try It Out   Remove a Topic

1. Open the Topics area page.

2. Under Actions, click Manage Portal Site. This displays the complete area tree, with Home as the top area.

3. Under Topics you see five main topics, named Divisions, Resources, Strategy, Projects, and Locations. Locate the topic to be removed, Strategy, and open its edit menu (hover the mouse over its name and click the arrow to the right of the name). Select Delete. You will be prompted whether you want to continue; answer OK and this topic will be deleted.

4. When the deleting operation is done, you will see a status page, hopefully telling you that the operation was successful. Click OK to close this page and return to the area tree.

To confirm that this worked as expected, click the Topics link on the top menu bar (next to Home). This page should now display just the four remaining main topics.

The next thing to learn is how to modify existing topics. For example, say that you want to change the topic Projects to Activities; this is how you would do it:

Try It Out   Modify an Existing Topic

1. Open the Topics area page.

2. Under Actions, click Manage Portal Site to see the area tree.

3. Use the edit menu for the topic Projects. Select Edit. This displays the configuration page for this topic.

4. Change the Title from Projects to Activities. But wait; there are at least two things more you want to modify when changing the topic name: the URL name and the Description. Change the URL name to Activities and update the description to something like "This area organizes information about company activities." Click OK at the end of this page.

   On this page you will see a comment about changing URL names. If there are other pages or links that refer the old URL, they will break when you change the URL name. Be sure to update any link pointing to the old URL name.

Open the Topics area; it will list the Activities topic. Click its name to open that area page. Note that its URL address is `http://spsserver/activities` and that the description you entered is displayed on this page.

You will also discover that there is a link on this page with the name Item #3. This is just a demo link added to the Projects area by default. This link points to the URL address `http://www.example.com`, which is a special site name reserved by the Internet authorities in the standard document RFC 2606. This site is used for test and demonstration purposes, which is exactly why Microsoft added this link.

Finally, you need to know how to create new topics. You can select to enter a main topic, which will be listed on the Topics list at the Home page, or a subtopic. Open the Topics area page again and look at the topic Divisions; under it you will see these subtopics: Sales, Support, Operations, Human Resources, and Marketing. These topics will not be displayed on the Home page.

For example, say that you want to add one new main topic named HelpDesk and two subtopics under it named IT and Sales. There are two ways to do it, and you will learn both of them:

Try It Out **Create New Topic**

1. Open the Topics area page.

2. Under Actions, click Manage Portal Site to see the area tree.

3. When creating a main topic, it must be located directly under the Topics area. Use the edit menu for Topics; select Create Subarea. This displays a form where you enter the information for this new topic:

   a. **Title:** HelpDesk.

   b. **Description:** This area is used to organize HelpDesk issues for different departments.

   c. **Publishing dates:** Do not change these default settings because they are fine.

   d. **Location:** Make sure it says Home > Topics for all main Topics areas like this one.

   e. Click OK to save and close this page.

4. You are returned to the area tree; the new HelpDesk topic should be listed now.

   The new HelpDesk topic is now ready to be used. But in this example you also wanted to create two subtopics, so continue with these steps.

5. Use the edit menu for the HelpDesk topic and select Create subarea. Use the same steps as before and enter the title **IT** and the description **HelpDesk issues for the IT department**. Then click OK to save and close.

6. You could do the exact same steps to add the second subtopic, but there is another way of doing this without using the area tree. So to add the Sales topic, you instead click the Topics link on the top menu bar (next to Home) to display the page with all topics. Then click HelpDesk to view its page.

7. On the HelpDesk area, notice the hierarchical tree view in the left pane of the page. It shows that there is one subarea called IT under HelpDesk. To create the second one, click Create Subarea under the Actions menu. It will open the same web form as in step 3. Enter the following settings:

   a. **Title:** Sales

   b. **Description:** HelpDesk issues for the Sales department

   c. **Publishing dates:** Do not change these default settings because they are fine.

   d. **Location:** Do not change it because the location is correct by default.

   e. Click OK to save and close this page.

You now have one main topic (HelpDesk) with two subtopics (IT and Sales). Open the Topics area page; it shows these three new topics and their relationship to each other. The next step is to add information to these Topics areas.

Adding Information to Topics Areas

Remember that the purpose of Topics areas is to collect or gather information related to a given subject in order to make it easier for users to quickly find what they need to accomplish their tasks. This information can be of many different types, but it is important to understand that it does not have to be locally stored. For example, you can add the following to a Topics area page:

Type	Example	Description
Links to team sites	http://sps/sites/sales	Makes it easy for users to find all sites related to a specific subject.
Links to lists	http://sps/sites/sales/orders	Makes it possible to collect a list of all lists for a specific subject, regardless of their location.
Links to files in SharePoint	http://sps/sites/sales/orders/Volvo.doc	Makes it easy to find important documents and files in SharePoint. You can link to any type of file, including doc, xls, mp3, and zip.
Links to external files or folders	\\Fileserver1\Public\Pictures	Makes it easy to find files and folders stored in other servers on the network.
Links to web sites	http://www.microsoft.com	Makes it easy to find other web sites, locally or on the Internet, which relate to a specific subject.
Links to ftp sites	ftp://ftp.microsoft.com	Points to FTP sites used anywhere in this particular subject.
Links to people	Contoso\Anna	Makes it easy to find information about people related to this subject.
Local info	Sales Statistics.xls	Displays files that are stored on this particular topic page. These can be any types of files that SharePoint accepts, for example doc, xls, pdf, and wmi files.

In other words, you can collect any type of information, regardless of where it may be stored. Can you imagine how much easier it is for your users when they have only one page to visit to find all the information regarding a given subject? It is not only faster; it is the correct version! No more hassle with hunting down a file, just to discover that it was an old version. Say that each user saves 10 minutes per day (a very modest number) and there are 600 users in your organization: this would save the company 6,000 minutes in total or 100 hours per day. If each person is paid $30 per hour, you have just saved the company $3,000 per day, or $15,000 per week! Of course, things are not always that simple, but the general idea is definitely correct. You can save a lot of money by making users more effective, and you can help them avoid a lot of frustration at the same time.

To continue with the HelpDesk example, you can make all information related to HelpDesk issues easier for users to find. If you just installed this SPS server, you will not have all the locations and places mentioned in this example, so before you start adding links, create a team site that you can use for this example. Note that this is a quick demo; you will learn better ways to do these things later.

Try It Out   **Create a Demo Team Site**

1. Open the Home area page on the portal.

2. Locate the Portal Owner QuickStart Guide; click its link Create a SharePoint site from the portal site (or click the Sites area page).

3. Click Create Site under Actions. Enter this information:

    ❑ **Title:** HelpDesk Team Site

    ❑ **URL name:** Enter the name "hd" to make the complete URL: `http://spsrv2/sites/hd`

    ❑ Make sure the E-mail address is correct.

4. Click Create; then on the following page click OK and then OK again. Now you have created a team site. This site will now open.

5. Click Create on the top menu and select Discussion Board; give it the Name "FAQ" and click the Create button.

6. This opens the new list. Now enter some information in it. Click New Discussion and enter the following information:

    ❑ **Subject:** Why is my monitor black?

    ❑ **Text:** Make sure you have power on.

    Click Save and Close.

7. Click Create on the top menu and select Issues. Give it the Name "Issues" and click the Create button. You have just created a list for users to report issues. (Isn't this easy?)

8. Click Home to display the start page for this team site. Click Contacts in the left pane. Click New Item and in the following web form enter the following:

    ❑ **Last name:** Ballmer

    ❑ **First name:** Steve

    ❑ **E-mail address:** steveb@microsoft.com

    ❑ **Company:** Microsoft

    Click Save and Close.

9. The demo team site is now ready to be used in the example; click Up to Contoso Portal Site in the far upper right on the page to return to the portal site.

Now you have information stored in a separate team site that you can use when experimenting with the topics links. The portal site in this example has the following URL: `http://spsrv2`. Just to make sure it works, start off by entering three simple links, not using any fancy features. Follow these steps to add links to the topics page:

Try It Out   **Add Links to a Topic**

1. Open the HelpDesk Topics area page.

2. Assume you have a SharePoint site named "Help Desk" with the URL address `http://spsrv2sites/hd` where most of the information regarding helpdesk issues is stored. Now you want to make it easier for users to find this type of information:

   a. Click Add Listing under Actions; this opens a web form where you define this link.

   b. Enter the Title **The HelpDesk Team Site**, the Description **This is where most HelpDesk related information is located**, and the Address **http://spsrv2/sites/hd**. Accept the default settings for the rest of this page.

   c. Click OK to save and close.

3. You also want to link to a list of Frequently Asked Questions (FAQs) that is stored on the HelpDesk team site. The name of this list is Frequently Asked Questions:

   a. Click Add Listing under Actions.

   b. Enter the Title **Frequently Asked Questions**, the Description **Check this list before you report issues**, and the Address **http://spsrv2/sites/hd/lists/faq**.

   c. Click OK to save and close.

4. Next, you want to add a list to contacts that can help answer questions. There is a list in the HelpDesk team site where all these contacts are stored. Add this list to the HelpDesk topic:

   a. Click Add Listing under Actions.

   b. Enter the Title **Support Contacts**, the Description **This list contain contact info to vendors and support personnel that may help you solve your problem**, and the Address **http://spsrv2/sites/hd/lists/contacts**.

   c. Click OK to save and close.

   Links to information stored on the portal do not need to contain the default URL address to the portal itself. For example: instead of "http://spsrv2/sites/hd" you can enter "/sites/hd". This will in fact happen automatically if you enter a complete URL address. The reason for this is that you now can change the server URL (`http://spsrv2`) without breaking the links.

Inspect the HelpDesk Topics area now. You should see three links, all collected under the headline General, as Figure 5-16 shows. Test them and make sure they all work as expected.

By now you probably have several questions, like these:

❑ How do I edit a link? For example, if I misspelled the title or the link?

❑ Is it possible to change the icon displayed next to the link?

❑ Is it possible to add and modify group headlines?

❑ Can I hide a link for certain people?

Figure 5-16

The answer to all these questions is Yes! You can do it. The last bullet about hiding will be described later, when you know more about audiences. But the first three are described in more detail in the following sections.

Try It Out	**Editing an Existing Link**

1. Open the Topics area page containing this link.

2. Click Edit page under Actions. This switches the whole page over to edit mode. All lists now have an edit menu, where you can do things such as editing (or course), deleting, or moving this link. Choose any link on this page. Hover the mouse over the name, and you will see a frame around the link. Click in this frame to display the menu and select Edit.

3. This displays a web form with four tabs, General, Publishing, Display, and Search:

   ❏ **General:** You can change the title, description, or link address. You can also move this link to any area page (for example, to another topic). Note that you cannot split a link here so it shows up in two or more places. If you want to do this, you must enter all areas when creating the link.

   Publishing: You can change when this link will be displayed and archived (removed but not deleted; you can still search for it). This tab is also used to approve or reject ... if this feature is activated.

   Display: You can define the group headline for this link, any image or icon to be displayed, and what audience (group of people) will see this link.

   ❏ **Search:** You can control if this link will be searchable or not.

   Make whatever changes you need and click OK to save and close this web form.

   When returned to the area page, it will still be in edit mode, which is fine if you want to do some more editing. To exit the edit mode click View page under Actions, or click the topic name.

The next question on the bullet list was about changing the icons displayed to the left of each link. The default icon for any link is the standard HTML document link. If you add a link to a specific file, for example a .doc or .mp3 file, you will see the default icon for that particular type of file. It is easy to change the default icon for any link, but you need a suitable image for the icon to make it look good: It should be an image of size 16 to 32 pixels, and it must be stored in a location available for all users. You have several options when selecting such a location:

❑ One such place is the default location used by SharePoint for its icons: `C:\Program Files\ Common Files\Microsoft Shared\web server extensions\60\TEMPLATE\IMAGES`. SharePoint has a virtual IIS directory that points to this location: `/_layouts/images`. You can create a subdirectory or store your images directly in this folder. If you are using several SharePoint servers, make sure to save these extra image files on all SharePoint servers running the Web role.

❑ You can save all images in an Image Library in SharePoint. This is a list specifically made for storing images of all sorts. Because this library is stored in the SQL database, it will be available to all SharePoint servers without any special configuration. The URL address depends on where you create this image library. The shortest address will be for libraries stored in the Home area.

❑ You can also save these images in any file server or other location that is available for all users (for example, your general file server to which all users have been granted at least read access).

In the following example you use some of SharePoint's own icons to be listed next to the Contact link on this page. Then you learn how to create an image library on the Home area.

Try It Out   Enter a Custom Icon for a Link

1. Open the Topics area page containing this link.

2. Click Edit page under Actions. Click to the right of the Support Contacts link and select Edit from the popup menu.

3. Switch to the Display tab.

4. For the Icon field, enter the path to the new icon. In this example you will use an icon named `LTContct.gif` that is stored in SharePoint's default image folder: `/_layouts/images/ LTContct.gif`.

5. Click OK to save and close this form.

6. Repeat steps 2–5 for the Help Desk Team Site link and add this icon file: `/_layouts/images/ cenadmin.ico`.

By now you should see three links, two with custom icons. Next you learn how to create a new image library on the Home area and use it for these link icons instead.

Try It Out   Create an Image Library and Use It for Icons

1. Open the Home area page.

2. Click Manage Content under Actions. This opens a page where all current lists and libraries for this area are displayed. By default you see a number of existing lists, such as Document Library, Image Library, and Contacts. So there actually exists one image library already. But you want to play a little, so you create a new one by following these steps:

a. Click Create high on this page.

b. Click Picture Library.

c. Give it the name Icons and the Description "Images to be used as icons."

d. Click Create to save and close this page. This takes you to the newly created library.

3. The next step is to add some images to this library. For this example, copy one image file from the same folder you used before (just to save you from creating your own picture this time):

a. Still on the Image picture library page, click Add Picture.

b. Click Browse and locate the file `Newspg.gif` in `C:\Program Files\Common Files\ Microsoft Shared\web server extensions\60 \TEMPLATE\IMAGES`.

c. Click Save and Close.

4. The image file is now visible in the picture library. Before you use this file as an icon or anywhere else in SharePoint you must be aware that you normally enter the path to pictures manually; that is, there is no browse functionality. So the next thing to do is to copy the URL for this address. Remember the tip you got before: links do not have to contain the initial portal server address (for example, `http://spsrv2`).

a. Click the picture to open it.

b. Right-click the picture and select Copy Shortcut. This is the URL address you will need later on.

5. Go back to the HelpDesk topics area. Use the steps you learned in the previous example to open the edit page for the Frequently Asked Questions link; switch to the Display tab, and paste the copied URL address into the Icon field. Remove the first part of the address so you only have this left: `/Icons/newspg.gif` (of course, you could also use the complete URL address if you want). Click OK to save.

If you create a library with the name "Images," SharePoint will give it the URL "Images1" because SharePoint has reserved the name "Images."

The benefit of storing pictures and images in a picture library is that it is easy to view, use, and modify. Still, you can use whatever location for your images as you see fit. Your three links on the HelpDesk area should now look like Figure 5-17.

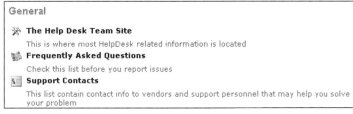

Figure 5-17

The third question listed previously was about the groups. For example, why are all these links grouped together under General? The simple answer is because you said so. The story is this: By default SharePoint has three group headlines defined:

❑ **General:** The default value for all links.

❑ **Highlight:** A special group for important links.

❑ **Expert:** The default group for links to people.

It is easy to change the group setting for links, and you can also add, delete, or modify groups. For example, make sure the Topic page is in edit mode, then right-click the link Frequently Asked Questions, and select Highlight. The link is now listed under Highlight instead of General.

So what is really going on here? The answer is that you are working with a special type of web part: the Grouped Listings. This list is similar to the News web part, in the way that it lists items with headlines and descriptions (and icons if you want). But it always points to something, such as a document, folder, or site.

This web part is configured to sort its content based on the groups previously mentioned. If you open the properties for the web part, you can play with its settings:

1. On the HelpDesk topic page, click Edit Page.

2. Click Modify Shared Page, then Design this Page to enter the design mode.

3. Click the Edit menu for the Grouped Listings web part (click the arrow on its headline) and select Modify Shared Web Part. You now see the properties for this web part.

   There are several special settings for this web part, and some of the most interesting are these:

   ❑ **Current Area Override:** None. This is exactly the same setting as for the News web part displayed on the Home page, if you remember. None means that this web part should list information on this page. You could click Change Location and make this web part show content from another area. That remote area is called the anchor area. There is also a setting on this page to Ignore Listings in Anchor Area that may be of interest to you, if you change the area location.

   ❑ **Maximum Number of Listings:** = 0. This setting displays an unlimited number of link items per group; in other words, all existing links for each group. If you change this value to 3, it will show three items for each existing group.

   ❑ **Subarea Layers:** = 0. This setting says how many subtopics are to be displayed in this web part. For example, if you change this to 2, it will also list all link items two layers down. You could use this to list all links under a given Topics area, regardless of where they actually are stored. If you try it now, it will not show any extra links because there are no links in the subareas. Create one in the IT or Sales area and it will show up here. In Figure 5-18, the link IT Managers is actually located in the IT Subarea.

   ❑ **Group By:** Group. This setting is what makes this web part display the list items organized into groups. You can change this setting to Area, Creation Date, or several other settings.

   ❑ **Display Columns:** 1. This setting controls how many columns to use when displaying links.

   ❑ **Highlights Visibility:** All Listings. This setting controls what links to display. You can select between All Listings, Highlight Listings Only, and Non-highlight Listings Only.

Figure 5-18

As you can see, the Highlight group is treated a bit special. Although you can change the name for this group, it is inadvisable because you would always have to remember which group had originally been Highlight, because there are property settings referring to this name.

It is time for you to learn how to manage these groups. For example, say you want to create one new group named Public Info and you also want to change the group Experts to Geeks. This is how you would do it:

Try It Out   Add and Modify Groups

1. Open the HelpDesk area page and click Edit Page.

2. Under the group listings, click the link Manage Grouping and Ordering. This displays all current links and the groups they belong to.

3. Click Add Group and enter the title **Public Info**; click OK to return to the previous page.

4. Click Add Listing and enter these settings for the new link:

    a. **Title:** MS Support.

    b. **Description:** Search MS Support site.

    c. **Address:** http://support.microsoft.com.

    d. **Group:** Public Info.

    e. Click OK to save and return to the previous page.

5. The new link is now listed under the new group name.

6. To modify an existing group, you must click Manage Groups under Actions; this displays a list of all existing groups. Note that there is a list of Position from Top. This list controls in what order the groups will be listed on the Topics page. To change the name of the Expert group, click its name, type **Geek**, and click OK. You are returned to the previous page. Just for testing, change the position for Public Info to 2; then click Return to Grouping and ordering page.

7. Click HelpDesk in the left pane to view the new settings.

To complete this discussion on links and groups, you must learn how to add links to people. After all, one of the most common requests is to find a particular person. And very often this person is searched for because she is responsible for a given area or is a subject-matter expert, such as a sales manager or an MS Office expert. SharePoint lets you create links to people and place them next to the other links discussed previously. It is very logical to have all relevant links regarding a subject on the same page.

For example, say you have one Office expert named Anna and you want to list her name on the HelpDesk page. Follow these steps to do it:

Try It Out   Create a Link to a Person

1. Open the HelpDesk area page.

2. Click Add Person under Actions. This displays a web form where you enter the user name for this person. You can type the complete name (including the domain name), such as **Contoso\Anna**, or click Select a person and search the directory.

3. Enter a description, such as **Subject Matter Expert on MS Office**.

4. Make sure the group is "Geek" (or "Expert" if you did not change its name previously).

5. Click OK to save and close this web form.

Note that you could not select an icon for this link. By default it will always be a special icon with an image of a person. You cannot change this icon, even if you try. There is actually an icon link setting in the properties for this person link, but SharePoint will ignore anything you type in there. If you followed all the preceding examples, your HelpDesk area should now look like Figure 5-19.

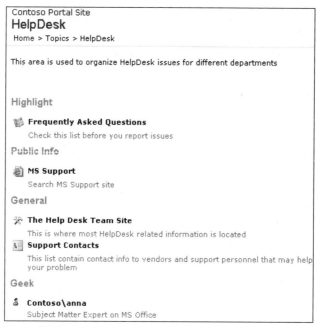

Figure 5-19

These group settings, including their name and position, are local for each area page. In other words, if you want to have a group called Public Info available on any other area, you need to re-create it there.

The News Area Page

The purpose of the News area is to offer a place to enter news items and similar information for easy access by all portal users. This area page has by default three subareas for organizing news into different categories:

- ❑ Company News
- ❑ Press Announcements
- ❑ External News

These subareas are very similar to the subareas under the Topics area page. Each of these subareas contains a news web part, identical to the news web part located on the top News area page. These three subareas are just examples of what you can do; you most likely will want to change them and add new ones.

News listings from one area can be displayed in other areas. For example, you previously saw how the Home area page used a News web part to display the news listed in the News area. In this situation SharePoint refers to the source listing as the "anchor" area. In other words, the Home area displays a news list, taking the information from the News area, which is the anchor area. These subareas of the News area can also be used as anchor areas, if you want. But the News area page uses another method to display listings from its subareas: It uses a special web part of the type *News Areas* that is configured to list the three latest news items from all subareas. That is why the News Area web part on the News page does not use the anchor area technique and still manages to display the news items on its subareas. Did you get confused? Yes, I agree that it is a bit complicated, but if you play with the settings for this News Area web part, you will soon become comfortable with how it works.

The Default News Subareas

By default, all news listings in these subareas are empty; therefore they don't show up on the News Area web part. To help you understand how they work, create one news item in each subarea, like this:

Try It Out   **Create News Listings in Subareas #1**

1. Open the News area page.

2. Click Add News under Actions.

3. This opens a web form where you enter the details about this particular news listing. You have seen this earlier in this chapter, but now you will get more details about these settings:

   a. **Title: "More profit for our company":** You can enter up to 100 Unicode characters, but you should be aware that this text will all be written on a single line. Therefore, using too many characters may look bad on the page.

   b. **Description: "This is company news":** Use this setting to describe this news item in more detail. You can enter up to 991 Unicode characters. Note that for shorter news items, this may be the only information needed.

   c. **Content:** This section lets you choose between entering a link to the news body or activating the text editor in this web part. There are some things to know about using links to information: You can link to any type of information, much like the links for a Topics area described earlier. See the text following this list for more details about the options for links and editor.

> **If you do not want to use the news body, make sure to select "Text Editor" instead of the option "Link to existing content." Otherwise, you will get a warning.**

d. **Dates:** In this example, do not change these settings. Use this section to define when this new item should be visible and when it should be expired (removed from the list); it will be archived, not deleted. You can still search for it.

e. **Group:** In this example, do not change this setting. These are the same types of groups discussed in the Topics area previously. By default the same three groups exist: General, Expert, and Highlight. You can change or add new groups for this news area listing, if needed. The purpose of this group setting is to enable you to organize information into groups. Note that you must configure the News web part to sort by groups before you will see this type of listing.

> **If you change the location for this item, the list of groups available will show all available groups for that location.**

f. **Image:** In this example, do not change this setting. Use this setting to enter a link to an image file. This image will be rescaled and placed next to the title. It will also show up on top of the body text if you use the text editor mentioned in step c. The same rules as before apply: You can skip initial references to the portal server (`http://spsrv2`) for references to local information in SharePoint or any of its virtual IIS directories (`/_layouts/images`). If you link to external pictures, make sure every portal user with access to this news listing is allowed to read that source.

g. **Location:** Click the link Change Location and then select Company News only. This setting defines in what area this news item will show up. By default you have four news areas: the News top area and its three subareas, Company News, Press Announcements, and External News. However, you can choose any portal area, as long as it has a news listing or topics listing. By default the location will be the news listing on the News area page (indicated by Home > News); click Change location to select another area. On this web form you can select one or more areas where this news item will be listed. If you just want to display this news item on Company News, expand the News node and check Company News. Make sure to uncheck News, unless you want it listed there too.

If you select more than one location for a news item, it will split in multiple copies, one for each location. There will be no connection or relation between these copies. If you later modify one of them, it will not affect the others!

h. **Audience:** In this example, do not change this setting. This setting allows you to filter the news items. For example, you may want to hide technical news items from everyone except the IT department. Later in this chapter you learn a lot more about audiences. By default the News part does not use the audience filtering; you must configure the web part first. So now it does not matter what audience, if any, you are choosing.

i. Click OK to save this news item in the Company News area.

As you can see, a number of settings are available when adding news. Some of them are very straightforward; others are a bit hard to understand or can do more than you at first may think. For example, the Content section lets you choose to link to existing information or use the Text Editor. Now look more closely at these two options:

❑ **Linking to existing information:** This allows you to link this news item to any type of object that can display information, such as MS Office documents, SharePoint team sites, MP3 music files, or public web sites pages. You can also link to a person, but you must use a special technique. For example, say you want to link to the user Anna on the portal SPSRV2. You would write this link: `http://spsrv2/personal/anna`. This assumes that Anna has what SharePoint calls a *personal site*. You learn more about personal sites in the next chapter. Note that this news link can point to any of these three standard URL formats, as the following table shows. It's a pity that URLs of type FTP, Telnet, and News aren't supported at this time, but hopefully that will come later.

Type of link	Example
Files	`\\Server1\share1\example.txt` links to a specific file. `\\server1\share\public` links to a folder.
Mailto	`mailto:Diana@contoso.com` creates an e-mail addressed to Diana. `mailto:Diana@contoso.com?subject=Book me for this training` creates an e-mail addressed to Diana with a given subject.
http	`http://www.microsoft.com links to a web page.` `http://spsrv2/doc/quote.doc links to a Word file.`

❑ **The Text Editor:** This second option is for when you add a news item and you need to add more text than fits in the description field. When selecting this option, the page is refreshed to activate the text editor button. Click this button to open a new page for entering the body text of this news. This editor supports most of the standard formatting features, such as fonts, size, color, and bulleted lists.

It also has buttons for adding links and pictures. Note that any standard link, for example `www.humandata.se`, will automatically be recognized as a web address, which is good. However, the feature for adding pictures into this text block is a bit strange. If you click it, a dialog box is displayed and you can enter the link address to the picture or use its Browse button. However, the Browse button does not work as expected. True, you can browse to anywhere, but when you save this link it gets converted to a link to the local web browser's directory for temporary files, which certainly will not do! The link must go to a picture that all users will be able to view, and that is most certainly not true for your temporary Internet files (I hope). So in the end you must manually enter the link. The simplest solution is therefore to view the picture, copy its URL address, and paste it into this image link, exactly like you did when adding icons to the topics listings previously.

Figure 5-20 shows this text editor and a picture that was manually added. Note that the text uses different fonts and bold characters.

If you remove any of the sources, the link will be broken. However, you will not notice this until you try to open it. Some tools are available on the Internet that will help you check for broken links and sometimes even try to repair them. A very nice tool is SPSTATUS (`www.james.milne.com/SPStatus`).

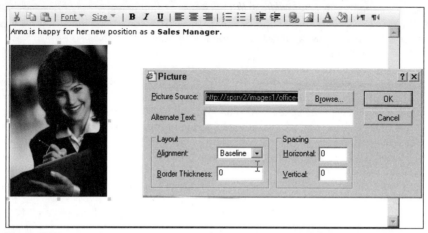

Figure 5-20

Now that you know the options available when creating news items, create two more: One for each News subarea, and this time you will only see the settings you need to change.

Try It Out   Create News Listings in Subareas #2

1. Open the News area page.

2. Click Add News under Actions.

3. In the following web form, enter these values to use a link to external information:

    a. **Title:** "Our Customer Wins a Prize."

    b. **Description:** "The Washington Post is publishing an article about our customer. Click the link to read it all."

    c. **Content / Link Address:** http://www.washingtonpost.com.

    d. **Location:** External News (make sure to uncheck all other areas).

    e. Click OK to save this new item.

4. The new link will be visible. Test it to make sure it really opens the external link.

5. Click Add News again, to add the third and last item in this example.

6. In the following web form, enter these values to use the Text Editor:

    a. **Title:** "Our New Sales President".

    b. **Description:** "Anna has accepted to be the new President for the Sales department. Click the headline to read more...".

    c. **Content / Add News listing by entering text:** Click the Open Text Editor button.

    d. Enter any text here. Test the different formatting features available. If you feel brave, add a picture by clicking the Insert Image button; in the following dialog box, enter the URL address to a picture. There will be no resizing, so choose a picture with a reasonable size.

You must enter the complete link address; this part does not accept the shortcuts that work for link icons and other objects.

    e.   **Location:** Press Announcements (make sure to uncheck all other areas).

    f.   Click OK to save this news item.

7.   Go to the News area page and look at the News Area web part. You will now see one news item for each of the subareas: External News, Press Announcements, and Company News.

Remember that if you want to edit any existing link, you must first click "Edit Page" to enable the menus for each item, and then choose Edit from that menu.

Note that none of these news items are listed on the larger News web part on this page. The reason is that you unchecked that news list (in steps 3d and 6f). If you now look at the Home area page, they are missing from that list too. Do you know why? Yes, it depends on the settings for the News web part on the Home area. It is configured to show only the first level of its anchor area, which is the News area; its subareas will not show up. That is easily fixed. Just follow these steps:

Try It Out   **Display More Area News on the Home News Part**

1.   Open the Home area.

2.   Choose Edit Page⇨Modify Shared Page / Modify Shared Web Parts⇨News to open its web part properties.

3.   Locate the setting Subarea Layers. Change the value from 0 to 1. This will list all news on the first level of subareas.

4.   Click OK to save and close the web part properties.

5.   Verify that you now can see all news items, including these on the subareas.

Managing News Subareas

By now you know how to work with existing areas and their news web parts. But you will most likely add your own subareas and maybe delete some existing ones. Remember that if you delete an area, it will also remove all its news items. Therefore, first make sure there is nothing left you want to save. If there is a news item that you want to keep, it is easy to move it to another area first:

Try It Out   **Move a News Item to another Area**

1.   Open the area page where the link is now.

2.   Click Edit Page, open the menu connected to this item, and select Edit.

3.   Click Change Location and select another area. Notice that you can select only one area (you can only move, not copy, news items). Avoid moving news listings to an area without any News web part, such as the Sites area. To move such an item back, open the area (for example, the Site area), choose Manage Content⇨Portal Listings, locate the news item in this list, and select Move to move the item to another area.

4.   Click OK to save and close. Make sure the news item has been moved to the new area.

It is very easy to add or delete a News subarea page. You use the same basic steps as for the Topics subareas. For example, say you need one new subarea named Research Results:

Try It Out	Add a New News Subarea

1. Open the News area page (if you want to create a subarea directly under this area).

2. Click Create Subarea under Actions.

3. In the following web form, enter the settings for this new subarea:

    a. **Title:** Research Results.

    b. **Description:** News about our Research.

    c. **Publishing Dates:** Because you want to see the new subarea now, you accept the defaults.

    d. **Location:** Make sure it points to the right parent area for this new subarea.

    e. Click OK to save and close this form. This will take a few seconds because SharePoint needs to create this area. You may recall that each area is in fact a site, so give it some time to do its job.

The new subarea should now be visible in the upper-left pane of the News area page. It will not be displayed in the News Areas web page until it contains news items.

How do you change a subarea? It is easy too! For example, say you want to change the description for the new subarea you just created. This is how you would do it:

1. Open the subarea you want to change (in this example, the Research Results).

2. Under Actions, click Change Settings. It will open a web form with all settings for this subarea.

3. Note that there are a number of tabs in this form, and a lot more information than you entered in the first place, as Figure 5-21 shows. Some of these settings that may need some explanation:

    a. **Tab General / URL name:** This defines the URL address for this subarea. Even though you can use non-English characters here (such as Å, Ä, and Ö), you should avoid them like the plague because they will be converted to 7-bit ASCII representations. For example, the URL "gås" will be converted to "g%c3%a5s", which is not the easiest URL to enter by hand. For the same reason you should avoid using the space character here because this will be converted to "%20%".

    b. **Tab General / Contact Information:** This setting is used in a web part at the top of the subarea page that lists the name of the person responsible for this page. If this is a user with a personal web site, including a photo, just make sure this setting lists the complete domain user name (for example, Contoso\Administrator). You can also add a user who does not have a personal website and add a link to her e-mail address and photo.

    c. **Tab Publishing / Listing Approval:** These two settings control whether a user with contributor permissions will be allowed to publish news item that will be displayed directly or if some other user with at least List Approval permission must approve (or reject) the news item first. By default all items will be published directly.

    d. **Tab Page / Subarea Templates and Area Templates:** These templates control the initial look of the page (what web parts it should contain). Note that the default setting is to use the News area template that you have seen some examples of already.

e. **Tab Display / Exclude from portal site navigation:** This setting makes it possible to hide a subarea without deleting it. This could be used in situations where you want to hide a subarea that you are not sure should be deleted. You can also use this setting to hide subareas used for special purposes; you can make a link to this subarea on another area. Or maybe you are developing a new subarea and do not want to show it until it is ready.

f. **Tab Search / Topics Assistant:** If you add links to a page of a special type that SharePoint can recognize automatically, the Topics Assistant will find them and suggest they get added to the same subarea as the others. By default this feature is turned off.

4. Click OK to save and close this web form.

5. Add a new link to this area page. Make sure it also shows up on the News area page and on the Home page.

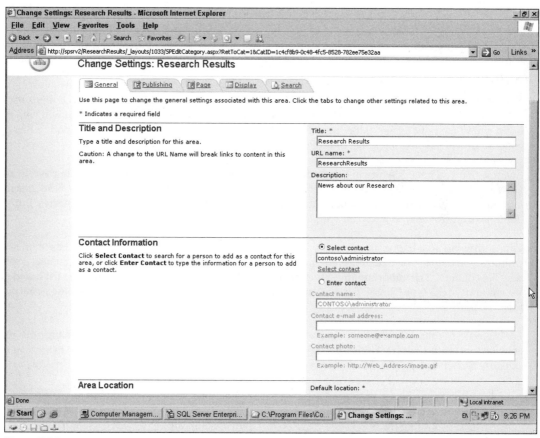

Figure 5-21

The Site Area Page

The fourth and last of the default area pages on the portal is the Site area. The purpose of this area is to help the users quickly find the right team site and to create new team sites. You may recall that the team sites are WSS sites, and most, if not all, work performed by the ordinary user takes place in these sites. So it is important that users can navigate easily to these team sites.

This area is a bit different from the other area and subarea pages in the portal:

❑ It does not have any Modify Shared Page link like the rest, and therefore you cannot easily add or modify its web part. Using FrontPage 2003 you can configure these web parts.

❑ It does have links to Views that will affect how the team sites are listed and sorted.

❑ It has a special Search for sites web part that will help the user find a specific team site easier.

❑ It has a web part that organizes team sites in Divisions and Regions to make it easier to find the right team site fast.

❑ It has two other web parts that list the newest sites and the sites you have added.

The Browse Site by Web Part

This is a standard SharePoint list that is used for storing information about team sites. It contains list columns to keep track of the site name, responsible person, link, and other properties that will help the users to find the right team site. Because this is a standard list, you can add, delete, and modify these list columns at will, just like any other SharePoint list.

Imagine that you have 500 files in one folder and you quickly realize you need to organize them to help you find the right files faster. You will create subfolders and move files into these folders. Now imagine that you have 500 team sites instead; for the same reason you need to organize these team sites. But you don't have any folders, so what can you do?

This is why this area uses a special web part that allows you to organize these team sites based on list columns you define. The default list columns that exist can be modified or deleted; you can also create new list columns. The important thing to remember is that this web part will organize the list based on list columns of the type Choice. For each such column you will see a category with the same name on this web part.

For example, say that you want to add a new category named Projects. You also want to change the available options for the existing Division to be Sales, Research, and IT only. Finally, you want to remove the category Region completely. This is how you do it:

Try It Out   Managing the Site List

1. Start by adding the new category Projects. Open the Sites area and click Customize List under Actions.

2. The web form for configuring this list is displayed. What you need to do is to create a new column. Click Add a new column and enter these settings in the following web form (see also Figure 5-22):

   a. **Column name:** Projects.

   b. **The type of information in this column is:** Choice. (The form will now be updated to offer new options.)

c.   **Optional Settings for Column/Type each choice on a separate line:** Internal, and External (one per line).

d.   Clear the field Default Value. The user will select the value.

e.   Click OK to save and close this form. You are returned to the previous form.

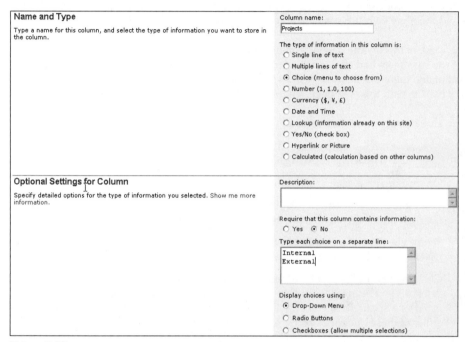

Figure 5-22

3.   The next task is to modify the choice options for the Division. You just want these options available: Sales, Research, and IT. Still on the Customize Sites page, in the Columns section, click the Division column to open its configuration web form:

a.   Modify the entries in the "Type each choice on a separate line" field to list only Sales, Research, and IT; make sure to enter only one option per line.

b.   Click OK to save and close.

4.   The final task is to remove the category Region. To do this, you must delete the column with the same name. Also in the Columns section of the Customize Sites page, click the Region column. At the bottom of this page, click Delete, and in the following popup window click OK. This column is now removed from this list.

5.   Click Go Back to "Sites" at the top of the form. Click the Summary link under "Select A View." Verify that you now have two categories and that each choice is listed beneath them, as Figure 5-23 shows.

Figure 5-23

The Spotlight Site Web Part

Returning to the previous analogy of the 500 files, assume that of these files, a few are much more used than others. It would be nice if these files could show up at the top of this list any time you look at this folder. This is exactly what the Spotlight Site web part does! When creating a team site, you get asked whether this will be a Spotlight Site; the default setting is no. If you say yes, it will show up in this web part; in other words, regardless of how many sites there are, this team site will always be listed on this page and therefore be much easier to access than others.

But the value of this feature depends on how many spotlight sites you define. Here is an anecdote for you: One of my customers had a sales manager who created at least 50 sites; she decided that all of them where important and therefore defined them as spotlight sites. Believe me, if you have 50 spotlight sites, it will be very hard to read this area page, so don't do this. Keep it below 10 to get the most out of this feature.

You can also change an existing team site listed as a spotlight site by using these steps:

Try It Out   Configuring Spotlight Sites

1. On the Sites area page, click Manage Sites.

2. You should see at least one site, the HelpDesk Team Site, created earlier in this chapter; click to the right of its name to display its edit menu and select Edit.

3. Set the check box for Spotlight site. Also note that this site has no settings for the two columns Divisions and Projects. Set any value for these columns just to see how it will affect the list of sites.

4. Click Save and Close. You will return to the previous page; click the view Summary under the Select a View heading to display the default page view. The HelpDesk Team Site will now be listed as a Spotlight Site. If you also changed the values for Division and Projects in step 3, click either of these categories and you should find this site listed here too.

The Newest Site Web Part

This web part is very similar to the Spotlight Site; the difference is the configuration of the web part setting *Query Type*. Note that you cannot see or change this setting unless you open this web page in FrontPage 2003 and review the web part properties.

The purpose of this web part is to list the five newest team sites. It will also sort this list in respect to when the site was created, such as Today, Yesterday, Last Week, and so on. The idea is that newly created team sites are more frequently used and therefore should be easier to find. It will also help everyone in the company be aware of newly created team sites.

The Sites I Have Added Web Part

This is also the same type of web part as the two previous web parts, but it is configured with another Query Type setting. The purpose of this web part is to list the team sites you have added. This list is therefore different for each user. It will show you a maximum of 10 sites at the time; if you have created more than 10 sites, click the Next button at the bottom of this page.

This list will also group these team sites into two categories: Approved and Pending. Approved means that this site link (not the team site itself) is approved for being listed in the site list; Pending means that somebody with at least List Approval permission must approve (or reject) this link to be listed. Regardless of the answer, the team site exists, and if you know its URL link you can open it.

The reason for this approval feature is to have control over this list. For example, if you have 400 users and everyone has permission to create team sites, there is a risk that the site list will become harder to use. The whole idea behind the site list is to make life simpler for the portal user. Therefore, to make sure only site links with proper values will be listed, this list requires approval. However, you do not have to approve the sites you create because as the administrator you have List Approval permissions.

If you want to remove the requirement of approving lists, you can do it this way:

Try It Out   Managing the Approval Setting of the Site Lists

1.   On the Sites area page, click Customize List.

2.   Click Change General Settings.

3.   Set Require content approval for submitted items to No; click OK on the following dialog box that warns you that all pending and rejected links will now be listed.

4.   Click Go back to Sites; click Summary to see the default view for this page. Note that the category Approved will no longer be displayed in The Sites I Have Added web part.

Creating New Team Sites

Previously in this chapter you got a crash course on how to create a team site (the HelpDesk Team Site). Here you get more details about this very important process. As described several times, every team site is actually a WSS site; so when you are going from the portal site to any team site, you are indeed moving from SPS to WSS. These two types of sites are different in appearance and behavior, such as security settings, how to deal with lists, and user permissions. If you need to refresh your memory, Chapter 3 presents the details for how WSS sites behave. In Chapter 7 you learn the differences between SPS and WSS.

When you create team sites this way, you are not just creating any site; you are creating a top site in a new site collection. You may recall from Chapter 3 that a site collection consists of one top site and an unlimited number of subsites. The owner of this top site (its creator) will have full access to all subsites in this site collection, regardless of their individual security settings. This is a very good reason for regulating which users can create or modify top sites.

Many organizations have a few people, often the administrators or HelpDesk, who create any new top site. Then they grant the user permissions to modify this top site and create subsites.

Now you will create some team sites; in this example you need to create one team site for each department: Sales, Research, and IT. Follow these steps to do it:

Try It Out   Create Team Sites Using the Site Area

1.   Open the Sites area page.

2.   Click Create Site under Actions. This opens the first of three configuration pages; this one is named New SharePoint Site (see Figure 5-24). Enter the following settings to create the Sales team site:

     a.   **Title:** Sales. This will be the name for this team site. It can be changed later.

     b.   **Description:** This is the Sales team site. This field can also be changed later.

     c.   **URL name:** Sales (making the complete name `http://spsrv2/sites/sales`). This name cannot be changed later.

d. **E-mail Address:** By default this will be the address of the creator. SharePoint will use this address to send reports and warnings regarding this site collection.

e. **Select Language:** English. This setting will only show up if you have installed language template packs, as described in Chapter 3.

f. **Create:** This creates the site and goes on to the next configuration page. Note that even if you abort the process after clicking Create, the site will be there but it will not be fully configured. You can open the site by entering the URL address manually, and it will show the third and last configuration page. So what happened to the second page? Well, that page is for configuring the settings you want for this team site in the Site area list. You can add these values later, if you want.

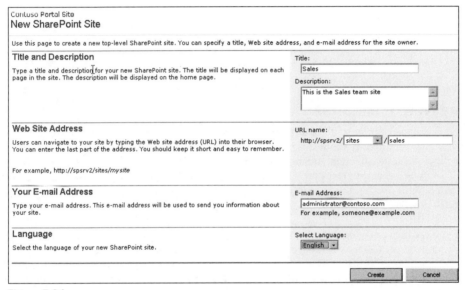

Figure 5-24

3. The second configuration page is named Add link to site and is the same page that you will see if you click Add Link to Site on the Site area page. The purpose of this page is to set the values for this site link on the Site area list. Continue the example and enter the following settings:

a. **Owner:** Anna Filippa. This can be any name; there is no check that this matches the name of the site creator or that this name exists. You can change this setting later.

b. **Division:** Sales.

c. **Spotlight Site:** No.

d. **Projects:** Internal.

e. **Include in search results:** Yes. This tells SPS to index all information in this site, thus making it searchable from the portal site.

f. The rest of these settings are inherited from the previous configuration page; normally you don't need to change them. Click OK to go on to the next page.

4. The third and last page is the Template Selection page; this page is used to select the default look and feel of this team site (for example, the color of the site, its web parts, and lists). Chapter 6 gives you more information about these templates. Continue with the example and enter the following settings:

    a. Select the Team Site template.

    b. Click OK to save this setting.

5. The new Sales team site will open. But you need to add two more top-level team sites; go back to the portal site by clicking the link in the top-right corner: Up to Contoso Portal Site.

6. Open the Sites area page again; click Create Site and enter these settings (following are only the settings you need to change):

    a. **Title:** Research.

    b. **Description:** This is the Research team site.

    c. **URL name:** research.

    d. Click Create.

7. On the page Add link to site, enter these settings:

    a. **Owner:** Albert Einstein.

    b. **Division:** Research.

    c. **Projects:** External.

8. Finally, on the Template Selections page, click OK to use the default Team Site template.

9. The new Research team site will open. Click Up to Contoso Portal Site to return to the portal site.

10. Open the Sites area page again; click Create Site and enter these settings:

    a. **Title:** IT.

    b. **Description:** This is the IT team site.

    c. **URL name:** it.

    d. Click Create.

11. On the page Add link to site, enter these settings:

    a. **Owner:** Bill Gates.

    b. **Division:** IT.

    c. **Projects:** Internal.

12. Finally, on the Template Selections page, click OK to use the default Team Site template. Click Up to Contoso Portal Site.

You are done! As you can see it is very easy to create new top-level team sites. If you look at the Sites area, you will now see four team sites listed on both Newest Sites and Sites I Have Added. Click Internal to see the two team sites in this category. To open any of them, just click their names. Click Summary to see the default view again. Click Research and you will only see the Research team site link.

Sometimes it is easier to see all site links listed, instead of organized in categories. This is what the All Items view is used for. Click it now, and you will see all four site links, including their settings. Some organizations want to have this as the default view for this area page. The problem is that this area does not allow you to change its default view; but this is easily fixed. While viewing the All Items view, notice that the URL address ends with `Allitems.aspx`; this is the information you need. It tells you that the name for this view is `Allitems.aspx`. Switch back to the Summary view and check the URL again. Now it says `Summary.aspx`. What you need to do is to change the `Default.aspx` page for this area to use `Allitems.aspx` instead of `Summary.aspx`. You can do it with FrontPage or even more simply with Notepad, using these steps:

Try It Out   Change the Default View for the Site Area

1. Open Windows Explorer.

2. Navigate to the same folder structure you worked with before when customizing the portal site: `C:\Program Files\Common Files\Microsoft Shared\web server extensions\60\ TEMPLATE\1033\SPSSITES.`

3. Open `Default.aspx`.

4. Replace `Summary.aspx` with `Allitems.aspx`. (Be sure to spell it correctly.)

5. Save and close Notepad.

6. Open the Sites area page and make sure it uses the All Items view by default.

7. If you want to restore to the old view, change `Allitems.aspx` back to `Summary.aspx` again.

As you have seen, this Site area page is easy to modify and adjust to the needs of your organization. Be aware that only top-level sites will be listed here, not subsites in a site collection. For example, if you create a subsite named Projects under the IT team site, it will not be listed here. If you absolutely want to also list a subsite, you can just add a link manually to that site. What you will need is the complete URL to that site; for example, the Project site under IT may have this URL: `http://spsrv2/sites/it/ projects`. Enter that link and your users will have fast access to that subsite from the Sites area.

Managing Access to the Portal Site

There are almost, but not exactly, the same procedures to manage users in the portal site as in the WSS site; you can add users and groups from the domain or the local server account database. Each user must belong to a site group in order to get access to any part of the portal site. Remember that the Home area site is the top-level site in the site collection that constitutes the portal site. Any permission settings for the Home area will by default be inherited by all other areas, such as News and Topics, including their subareas.

Managing Users and Groups

When you created the portal site, you also became its first user and administrator. To add a user or a group you perform the following steps. They can be done from any computer, as long as you have administrative rights on the portal.

Try It Out   **Adding Users to the Portal Site**

1. Open the portal site; any area page will do.

2. Click Site Settings at the upper right of the page. This opens up the general administration page for the portal site. From here you can also reach the administrative pages for WSS. It is actually rather hard in the beginning to understand whether you are in the SPS part or the WSS part, but don't despair; you will soon get the hang of it.

3. Click Manage Users. Because this is such a common task, it is placed on the first administrative page. Do not be surprised to see a link to the exact same Manage Users in another admin page; it is quite common that SharePoint has links to the same page in several places!

4. This is exactly the same page for adding users as in the WSS environment. Here is the complete list of all users and groups with access to this portal site. (You should see Anna listed here because you added her during a previous exercise in this chapter.) However, you may remember that members of the local Administrator group on the SharePoint server will have access, even if they are not listed here; the same goes for members of the SharePoint Administrators Group, which you learn more about in the next chapter. Click Add Users.

5. You can now enter one or more user names or groups in the Users text field; or click Select users and groups to display a web form where you can search the Active Directory domain for users and groups. You must enter at least one character in the "Starts with" field to start searching! Note that contrary to WSS, you cannot use the Global Address List when adding users to the portal site, even if you have Outlook installed.

   Use whatever you get and select one or more users and groups. Click OK to return to the previous page.

6. By now you should see one or more users and groups; select the Site Group for all these users (for example Reader) and click Next. You may remember from Chapter 3 that some of these groups have cumulative rights, for example a Contributor can do everything a Reader can do, so there is no need for making users members of several groups.

7. On the following page you will have the same options as when adding users to WSS sites; you can send an e-mail to the users (if they have an e-mail address) that will inform them about this new permission. This message will automatically include a link to the site and the membership granted by you. Click Finish to send the message.

8. You will return to the list of users. You can now add more users. Click any area link to leave the administration page.

As mentioned earlier, these settings will by default be inherited by all area pages. For example, open the Topics area and click its Manage Security link. It will look like Figure 5-25.

This page says that users and groups who belong to any of these site groups will have the same permissions on this particular area. You don't have to accept that. For example, if you do not want the Site Group Readers to be able to view the Topics area, check the Reader box and click Remove Permissions. This site group will now be removed from this page.

> *To restore all inherited permissions, click the link "Inherit permissions from the parent area" in the text segment at the top of this page.*

Contoso Portal Site > News

Manage Security Settings for Area News

Use this page to manage security settings for site groups, users, or groups for this area.

All users can see this area on the navigation hierarchy. Only show to users with View Area right.

These permissions are inherited from the parent area. If you change these permissions, this area will no longer inherit permissions from the parent area.

🗐 New User | ✖ Remove Permissions | 🗐 Edit

Select	Site Group	Permissions for this Area
☐	Reader	View listings
☐	Contributor	Can add content to existing document libraries and lists.
☐	Web Designer	View, insert, edit, delete listings; change area and list settings
☐	Content Manager	Can create and manage areas, lists, libraries, and sites.
☐	Member	Can view and personalize portal site content and create sites.
Select	User	Permissions for this Area

Figure 5-25

You can also change the default permissions inherited. For example, if you want to limit the group Contributors to only view permissions, check the Contributor box and click Edit. This will open a web form with all the detailed permissions this site group has. If you want to make it correspond to a Reader site group, remove all permissions except the View Area and View Page.

An easier way to set permissions is to click the link "Simple rights" at the bottom of the page with the detailed permissions; this will display a list of permissions that corresponds to each Reader, Contributor, and so on.

In the next chapter you learn more about the detailed permissions available for the portal areas. They are similar to but not the same as the permissions for WSS sites. For example, there are several new permissions that relate to areas.

You can also add a user or group directly to this security page. The result will be that whatever permissions this user will have on other parts of the portal, she will have special permissions on this particular area. For example, say that you want to grant the user Anna, who is a member of the Reader site group, Web Designer permissions. Click New User. On the following page, add Anna and select rights: view, insert, edit, and delete listings. Click OK to save and close this page. Her name and new permissions are now listed on the following page.

Site Groups

Just like WSS, SPS uses site groups for controlling access to the portal sites. All of the site groups you previously saw in WSS will be here, and some more. You can see the total list of default site groups if you click these links: Site Settings➪Manage Security and Additional Settings➪Manage Site Groups.

❑ **Reader:** These members can read, copy, and print, but not modify or delete information. Note that these members will not have access to personal sites, nor will they be able to define alerts anywhere in the portal site content.

❑ **Contributor:** These members can do the same as the Reader plus create, modify, and delete items in document libraries and lists. This group can also create News items and Topic links, but not modify or delete them! This group can also use personal sites and create team sites, but the site links must be approved by a Content Manager or Administrator before they are displayed in the Site area site list.

❏ **Web Designer:** These members can do the same as the Contributor plus create new lists and document libraries, including their columns and views, modify the area pages, and change Style Sheets.

❏ **Administrator:** These members have full access to every area, including permission settings.

❏ **Content Manager:** These members can modify, delete, and create new areas; they can also approve items like new or modified site links and documents.

❏ **Member:** These members can do the same as the Reader, plus Add Topic links and News items; use personal views of area pages; and have access to a personal site.

You cannot modify the administrator, if this is the last administrator listed. There must always be at least one user with this permission.

You can change the permissions for the default site groups, but as stated in Chapter 3, this is a bad idea. It is much better to create a new site group. However, in SPS you cannot copy an existing site group and use it as a template for a new site group, as you can do in WSS sites. (Hopefully, this glitch will be fixed in the next release of SPS.)

For example, say you want to add a group similar to the Contributor but that can edit and delete Topic links and News items. To create a new site group, follow these steps:

Try It Out **Create a New Site Group for the Portal Site**

1. On the portal site, choose Site Settings⇨Manage Security and Additional Settings⇨Manage Site Groups.

2. Start by checking what permissions the Contributor group has, because your new group will have some extra permissions. Choose Contributor⇨Edit Site Group Permissions. By default the permissions will be

    a. View Area

    b. View Page

    c. Add Items

    d. Edit Items

    e. Delete Items

    f. Manage Personal Views

    g. Add/Remove Personal Web Parts

    h. Update Personal Web Parts

    i. Browse Directories

    j. Create Personal Sites

    k. Create sites

    l. Use Personal Features

    m. Search

3. Return to the Manage Site Groups page. Click Add a Site Group.

4. Enter a descriptive name, for example Contributor Plus and a description.

5. Check all the settings from step 2 plus Manage Area, which will allow these group members the right to edit and delete News items and Topic links.

6. Click OK to save and close this page. The new site group will be listed among the others. It is now ready to be used like any other site group.

One of the most important things when planning your portal site is to analyze which users and groups need access and what permissions they need. Think about every area page. Is it okay that the default security setting is inherited from the Home page (the one defined by the Site Settings link)?

Contrary to WSS, there are no Cross-Site Groups in the portal site!

Anonymous Access

It is possible to open the portal site for anonymous access, but think really hard before you do this. This is especially important if you are concerned about the licensing model in SPS; unlike WSS you have to pay for each user accessing the portal site (but not its team sites, because they are WSS sites). Instead of allowing anonymous access, you can grant Reader access to all authenticated users, by utilizing the following built-in security group in Active Directory: Authenticated Users. Every user who logs on to the domain will automatically be a member of this group as long as they stay logged on.

To grant the group Authenticated Users access to SharePoint, follow these steps:

Try It Out   Open the Portal Site to All Authenticated Users

1. Open any area in the portal site as an administrator.

2. Choose Site Settings⇨Manage Users.

3. Click Add Users.

4. In the Users field, enter **Authenticated Users**. Set the permission you want for all users, for example Reader, and click Next. You will not be able to send an e-mail to each user, because the Authenticated Users groups do not have an e-mail address. Click Finish to save and close this page.

If you actually want to open the portal server for anonymous access, these are the steps to follow:

Try It Out   Open the Portal Site for Anonymous Access

1. First you must open the virtual IIS server for anonymous access. These are the same steps as for WSS described in Chapter 3. To begin, log on to the server as an administrator.

   a. Start the IIS Manager (Start⇨Administrative Tools⇨Internet Information Service (IIS) Manager).

   b. Right-click the virtual IIS server used by WSS (for example, Default Web Site, and select Properties).

    c.   Switch to the Directory Security tab.

    d.   In the Authentication and access control section, click the Edit button.

    e.   Check Enable anonymous access. Note that the account IUSR_SPSRV2 (assuming that the server is named SPSRV2) will be listed in the User name box. This account will be used by IIS whenever someone tries to access anything in this virtual IIS server. If you prefer, you can use your own account instead. The IURS_SPSRV2 user is a member of the built-in Active Directory group Guest, but is not a member of Authenticated Users.

    f.   Click OK until all pages are closed. Note that if you have web applications other than SPS active on the same virtual IIS server, you will be asked whether you want to apply the settings of anonymous access to their virtual directories. If this happens, just click OK again to close, without selecting any virtual directory in that dialog box.

    g.   Close the IIS Manager. You do not need to reset IIS!

2. Open any area in the portal site.

3. Choose Site Settings⇨ Manage security and additional settings⇨Change Anonymous Access Settings.

4. Select what rights the anonymous users will have on the portal site and all its areas, unless you change the inherited permission. You have these options:

❑   **Areas and content:** Can access every area in the portal, including all lists and libraries and their contents.

❑   **Areas, content and search:** Like areas and content, plus can search for information.

❑   **Nothing:** The default choice. Nothing in the portal can be accessed.

Click OK to save and close this web form. This setting will immediately be active.

Summary

In this chapter you learned the following:

❑   When you install SPS you also get WSS.

❑   SPS uses the portal site and WSS uses team sites.

❑   Branding and customization of the portal is possible, but you must edit the aspx files on the file system.

❑   SharePoint uses virtual IIS directories (such as _layouts) that point to the folder tree where all SharePoint files are stored.

❑   Every area page has its own folder structures; all team sites use the same folder structure (STS).

❑   LCIDs are language code identifiers; for example 1033 is U.S. English.

❑   The Home area page consists of both information that originates from other areas and locally stored information, such as Events and linked lists.

❑ The Topics area page is the top area for a number of subareas; each of these subtopics can be used to group links to information and people that are related. This will make it very easy for users to find the right information very fast.

❑ The News area page is used to list news items. There can be any number of subareas for news. News items in one area can be displayed in one or more other areas.

❑ The Site area page lists all top-level team sites (WSS sites under the portal site). It also contains a link for creating new team sites.

❑ You can add users or groups to the portal; they must belong to one or more site groups before they can access any area in the portal.

❑ The portal area uses site groups, much like WSS does, but there are two extra site groups in the portal. You can also modify these default groups, or create new ones.

❑ The portal can be opened for every user by making Authenticated Users a member of a site group or allowing anonymous access.

In the next chapter you learn more about advanced administration of the portal site.

Advanced Administration

So far you have seen how to install both WSS and SPS, and in the last chapter you learned how to configure and customize the portal site. But the fun does not stop there—there are lots of other interesting configuration settings for the SharePoint environment, including settings to target published information to specific groups. In this chapter, you also learn about how personal sites work, more about the security settings, and how to automatically remove unused team sites.

This chapter tells you a lot more about more advanced administration tasks for both SPS and WSS. Before you read this chapter, you should have a pretty good understanding of the basic administration. Be sure to read Chapters 3 and 5 before reading this chapter, because that will make it much easier to understand the information in this chapter.

SPS-Related Administration Topics

To take advantage of the many interesting and cool features of the portal site, you need to know more about its functionality and how to use it in an optimal way. The following sections give you this knowledge—just remember that this is about the portal site, not the team sites. Later on in this chapter you will learn a lot of stuff related to team sites as well. If you are running SPS, you should read all of this information. If you just implement WSS, read the parts about SPS so you will understand what you are missing!

Managing Portal Area Templates

In Chapter 5 you learned that all pages in the portal are referred to as areas. Some areas also have subareas, like Topics and News. You also learned how to create new top areas. Each area is in fact a web site of its own, although the portal does not say so. If you look closer at these area pages, you will notice some signs; for example, note that all area pages have the link "Manage Content" where all the local lists and libraries for this area (or site) are located. This section talks a little about what you can do with these areas.

A common request from users of the portal site is to have special area pages, such as one page per division or team. This is no problem; it is easy and you did exactly that in Chapter 5. But what you must understand is that these portal areas are not designed for collaboration, such as projects and other activities that require a number of people creating and sharing documents, contacts, and other information; this is what you have team sites for. The basic idea behind the portal is to be the starting place where users find frequently requested information, such as news, common contact lists and documents, and using smart navigation features and searching. The typical portal user is a consumer of its information, not a producer!

When creating several new portal area pages, you can choose from a list of templates. These templates are specifically for area pages, and cannot be used anywhere else, such as for team sites. It is hard to see the point in creating new area templates if all you want is to create a few new areas. Still, there may be situations in which this feature is required. By default SPS has these area templates available:

❑ **Content area template:** The default area template for any new area under Home.

❑ **Topic area template:** The default template used for the Topics top area.

❑ **News area template:** The default template for News subareas.

❑ **News Home area template:** The default template for the News top area.

❑ **Site Directory area template:** The default template for the Site area.

❑ **Community area template:** Not used by any area default.

❑ **Inherit Parent's template:** This template will make a subarea inherit its parent template.

Depending on where you create the new area, you will be able to choose among these templates, but in most places you will not be able to choose, or even see, which template to use for this new area. The reason for this is that the default settings for all new areas directly under the Home area will build upon the Content Area Template and look like Figure 6-1.

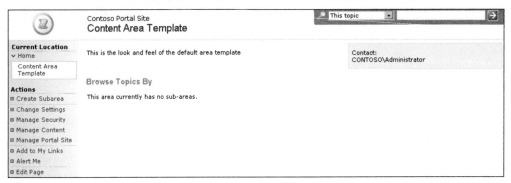

Figure 6-1

It may not be the most exciting page you have seen, but you can take it from here and add whatever web parts you may need. Two web parts are added by default to this list. One is the Area Detail Part, which describes more info about this page and a contact link and picture to its owner. The other web part is Browse Topics By, which will list the content of future subareas topic links. Every subarea created under this area will also build upon the same area template.

You can configure SharePoint to offer you a choice of templates. You change the settings depending on where you want to have this choice. The options are as follows:

❑   Configure the Home area to allow any top-level area under it to choose a template.

❑   Configure a specific area to allow its subarea to choose a template.

❑   Configure a specific subarea to inherit the same template setting as its parent area.

The third alternative is not used as a default by any area. The two top areas, News and Topics, have been configured to force all their subareas to use the "News area template" and "Topics area template," respectively.

To choose an area template when creating top areas, that is, any area directly under Home, perform the following steps:

Try It Out   Enable Area Templates for Top Areas

1.   Open the portal site as an administrator.

2.   Click Manage Portal Site under Actions. This link is available on most area pages.

3.   Hover the mouse above the Home link. Then click directly to the right of the Home area to display its edit menu and select Edit.

4.   Switch to the Page tab.

5.   Change from "All subareas will use the following template" to "Subareas can use any template."

6.   Click OK to save and close this page. You will return to the previous page.

7.   Test this now: Click Create Area under Actions (or use the Home edit menu and select Create subarea). This will display a web form where you configure the new area (see Figure 6-2). Enter some information, for example:

   a.   **Title:** HR.

   b.   **Description:** Local Intranet page for Human Resource.

   c.   **Template:** This is the new and magic part. You can now choose any available template. Try the Community area template.

   d.   Click OK to save and close this web form.

8.   Click the name of this new area (in the area tree, or directly on the header of this page). Inspect the selected template to see how it differs from the previous default Content area template.

That was easy, right? And if you now create a subarea for the HR area, it will also allow you to choose an area template.

Sometimes you want to use the exact same template for the subarea as for the parent area. If you know the template name used by the parent, then it's easy. But there is even an easier way that also offers a smart feature — using the Inherit Parent's Template option for the subarea. If you ever change the parent site template, the template for the subarea will also change. This is especially practical if you have an extensive area tree with lots of subareas where all are using the same template as the parent.

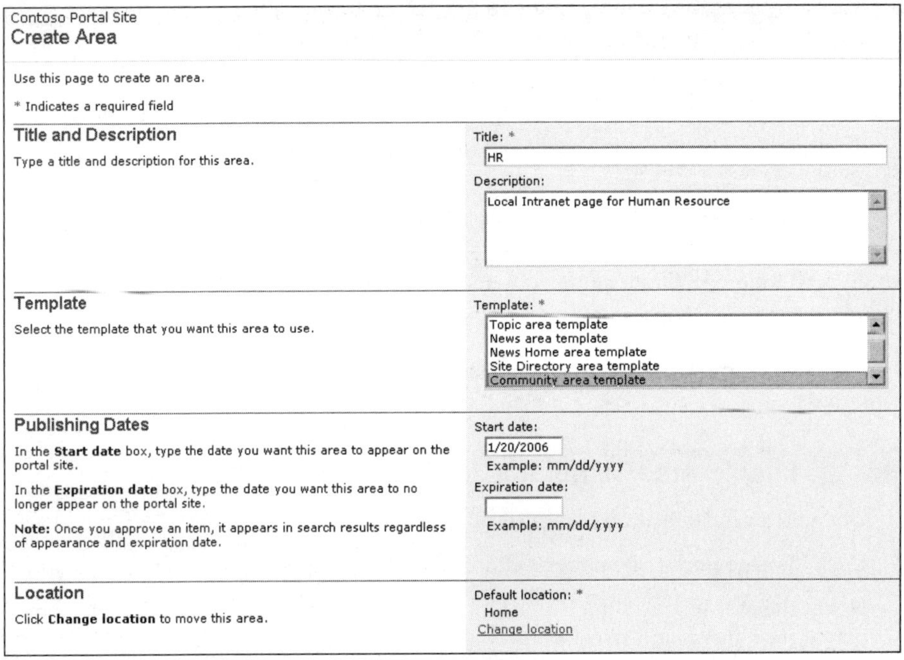

Contoso Portal Site
Create Area

Use this page to create an area.

* Indicates a required field

Title and Description

Type a title and description for this area.

Title: *

HR

Description:

Local Intranet page for Human Resource

Template

Select the template that you want this area to use.

Template: *

Topic area template
News area template
News Home area template
Site Directory area template
Community area template

Publishing Dates

In the **Start date** box, type the date you want this area to appear on the portal site.

In the **Expiration date** box, type the date you want this area to no longer appear on the portal site.

Note: Once you approve an item, it appears in search results regardless of appearance and expiration date.

Start date:

1/20/2006

Example: mm/dd/yyyy

Expiration date:

Example: mm/dd/yyyy

Location

Click **Change location** to move this area.

Default location: *
Home
Change location

Figure 6-2

The option "Inherit Parent's Template" will only be visible if the subarea has a different template than its parent area!

The other option mentioned in the previous bullet list is to enable a choice of area templates from a particular area. For example, say you created a top area named HR, and under it you want five subareas, all with different templates. The following example shows how you do it:

Try It Out   Enable Area Templates for Subsites

1.   Open the portal site and the specific area you want to use (in this example, HR).

2.   Click Manage Settings under Actions to view its configuration settings.

3.   Switch to the Page tab.

4.   Set the option Subareas can use any template.

5.   Click OK to save and close.

Note that any area, both top areas and any of their subareas, is the parent area for those areas immediately under it. The preceding steps can therefore be executed from anywhere in the area tree, not only from its top area.

Another interesting thing with areas is that you can change the template for an existing area. Just click the Change Settings link on the page, and switch to the Page tab. The section marked Area Templates provides three options:

❑ **This area uses the same template as the parent area:** Use this when you want to change the template used by a subarea to the same template used by its parent.

❑ **This area uses the template originally specified for this area:** Use this if you want to restore the original template for any site that has had its template replaced once. You do not need to know the name of the original template; SharePoint remembers that (it is stored in the configuration settings for this area).

❑ **This area uses the following page as template:** Use this option if you want to copy the template used by any other existing areas. For example, if you want the HR area you created previously to use the same template as some of the default areas, enter any of these links:

   ❑ **Home area template:** / (yes, just a slash! Home is the root area, as you may recall).

   ❑ **Topics area template:** /Topics.

   ❑ **News area template:** /News.

   ❑ **Site area template:** /SiteDirectory.

After you have created a number of areas and subareas, you will soon discover that their URL addresses will soon begin with /C1, /C2, and so on instead of just /HR, for example. SharePoint refers to these URL addresses as *web buckets*; these areas are not special in any way except in how the URLs are named. The reason for this special URL address format is the architecture of the portal site, and its functionality to allow you to move one area page to another part of this hierarchy. All web buckets follow this name standard: C1, C2, and so on. The logic behind this URL name format is this:

❑ The portal will allow the 20 first areas under the root area Home to have the same URL name as the area, preceded by the portal address. For example:

   ❑ `http://spsrv2/news`: The News area page.

   ❑ `http://spsrv2/Topics`: The Topics area page.

   ❑ `http://spsrv2/Divisions`: The subarea Division under Topics.

❑ When you need more areas than this, the web buckets address format will step in. For example, the 21st, 22nd, and 23rd area, regardless of where they are located in the portal area tree, will get names like these:

   ❑ `http://spsrv2/C1/Hobby`: The 21st area page named Hobby (regardless of its position in the area tree).

   ❑ `http://spsrv2/C2/Salary`: The 22nd area page, named Salary.

   ❑ `http://spsrv2/C3/Interest`: The 23rd area page, named Interest.

❑ The maximum number of URL addresses for each level of web buckets is 20. Whey you get more than C20, SharePoint will begin a second level of web buckets, thus using URL addresses like C1/C1, C1/C2, and C1/C3 for the first three areas created after the first web bucket level is filled.

❑ The URL address for areas will not indicate its position in the area tree, regardless of whether the area is among the 20 first that are using the same URL as its name, or using web buckets. The reason for this is to allow any area to be moved around without the need to change its URL address.

In other words, do not be surprised if the URL address contains C1 or even C3/C5—it only indicates that you have more than 20 areas in the first place and that you can freely move any of these areas or subareas to another location.

If you delete an area using web buckets, the deleted area's URL will be used when the next area is created. No new web buckets will be created as long as there is at least one available.

So how do you move area pages? It's easy! For example, say you have the subarea HelpDesk under the Topics area, and you want to move it so it is listed directly under Home (this will also make it listed in the top header menu, next to Topics and News and so on). The following steps show you how to do it:

Try It Out   Move an Area to Another Position in the Area Tree

1. Open any page in the portal.

2. Click Manage Portal Site under Actions. This displays the area tree.

3. Locate the area you want to move. In this example you will move it to HelpDesk, located under Topics.

4. Using the mouse, drag HelpDesk to its new location, for example next to News. The area tree will immediately get updated, and if you drag this area to the top level it will also now be visible on the top menu next to News. If the position is wrong, just do it again until you are satisfied.

5. Test the new location: Open this area and note that its URL address has not changed. If the area you moved had any subareas, they will also be moved.

This concludes the discussion about areas. You should now have a good understanding about areas and how to use them. To sum it up, areas give you a tool to build an easy-to-use navigation to documents, workspaces, and information used by your users for their everyday activities.

Managing User Profiles

When working together in any type of organization, you often need to get more information about a particular user. For example, you may read a document written by a user, and you need to ask this author for more information, or you need to send an e-mail to a project manager responsible for developing a solution that is related to your own work. So how do you find more information about people today? Most likely you are doing things like checking the address list in Outlook, looking at the Employee List on the intranet, or contacting the switchboard to ask for the person's phone number. The most commonly requested information is as follows:

❑   **E-mail addresses:** What is this person's e-mail address?

❑   **Phone Numbers:** What is this person's office phone, mobile phone, and so on?

❑   **Organizational information:** What department, group, or team does the user belong to?

❑   **Responsibilities:** Who is the manager for this department? Who is the project leader?

❑   **Expertise:** Who can I ask about a specific subject?

SharePoint solves this in a much smarter way! Whenever you see a name listed as a user, such as the author of a document or the last person who modified the Customer address list, simply click the user's name and you will get all publicly available information. If you don't see the name listed, you can search for this user; simply enter the name of this person in the search box at the top right of any portal area page. This will save any organization a lot of time, not to mention the frustration of chasing around the network resources or finding anyone with the information you need.

So where is this information stored? A good guess would be the Active Directory, right? And yes, this is often, but not always, true. Because SharePoint will also work in the Windows NT 4 environment, there may not even be a place for storing this type of user-related information. Microsoft solved this by adding a special database to SharePoint Portal Server for storing user profiles; this database can import information from the Active Directory. Note that this database does not exist in pure WSS environments, regardless of the type of server operating system.

User Profiles in a Windows NT 4 Environment

This configuration is easy to describe — there is nothing stored in the Windows NT 4 user account database that can be imported into the User Profile database! Everything you want to store about users, from their e-mail addresses to their phone numbers, must be entered manually. SharePoint does not enable importing from any other directory, so you are looking at a lot of manual work. Every time there is a change, such as adding a new employee or updating an existing user's e-mail address, it must be manually updated in the User Profile database. The procedure for this update is exactly the same as when running SharePoint in an Active Directory environment, which is described in the next section.

User Profiles in an Active Directory Environment

The most common configuration is SharePoint in an Active Directory (AD) environment; this enables SharePoint to regularly import information from AD to the User Profile database, typically once every 24 hours. This is only interesting if AD actually contains information worth importing, so there may still be situations where manual update may be the preferred solution for keeping the User Profile database updated. In reality you will often see a mix of these two; that is, some information is imported from AD, and the rest is manually updated.

SharePoint allows the administrator to control exactly what user properties to import from AD, what properties need to be manually edited, and whether users will be allowed to do this editing themselves. This last option is very handy for information you may not want to store in Active Directory, such as subject-matter expertise, home phone numbers, and descriptions of the users.

Configuring the User Profile Properties

All the settings that control the properties in the User Profile database are accessed through SharePoint's administration web pages. To see the options available, perform the following steps:

Try It Out   Manage the User Profile Database

1. Open the portal site as an administrator; click Site Settings in the top-right corner of the page.

2. Click Manage Profile Database in the section User Profile, Audiences and Personal Sites; you will see a summary of the current status, similar to Figure 6-3.

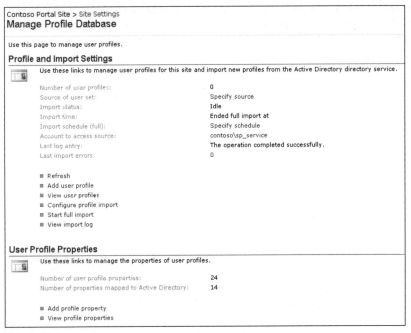

Figure 6-3

In Figure 6-3 you can see a lot of interesting things. At the top you will find a summary of all settings related to the import from Active Directory, such as the following:

❑ **Number of user profiles:** The current number of profiles. For a newly installed system you will see the number 0 here; if you see 1, you have probably tested the My Site feature of the portal site.

❑ **Source of user set:** What Active Directory domain will be imported. Specify Source means this setting is not yet configured. Click this link to configure this setting.

❑ **Import status:** Idle means there is no import process active at the moment.

❑ **Import time:** Gives the date for the last import process. "Ended full import at" means that there has not been any import process yet.

❑ **Import schedule (full):** Gives the date for the next import process. "Specify schedule" means no schedule is defined at this moment. Click this link to configure this setting.

❑ **Account to access source:** The listed user account will be used when the import process connects to the Active Directory database. Note that this user account must be granted read access in AD; by default this account will be the same as the account used by SharePoint when communicating with the MS SQL Server. Click this link to configure this setting.

❑ **Last log entry:** This is the latest status message regarding the import process.

❑ **Last import errors:** Should normally be zero. Click this number to see the latest log messages.

In the middle of this page are a number of text links that are self-explanatory. For example, to configure the import settings, click Configure profile import. This will open the same page as when clicking the Specify Source link, where you configure what domain to import, what account to be used, and the import type and schedule; see Figure 6-4.

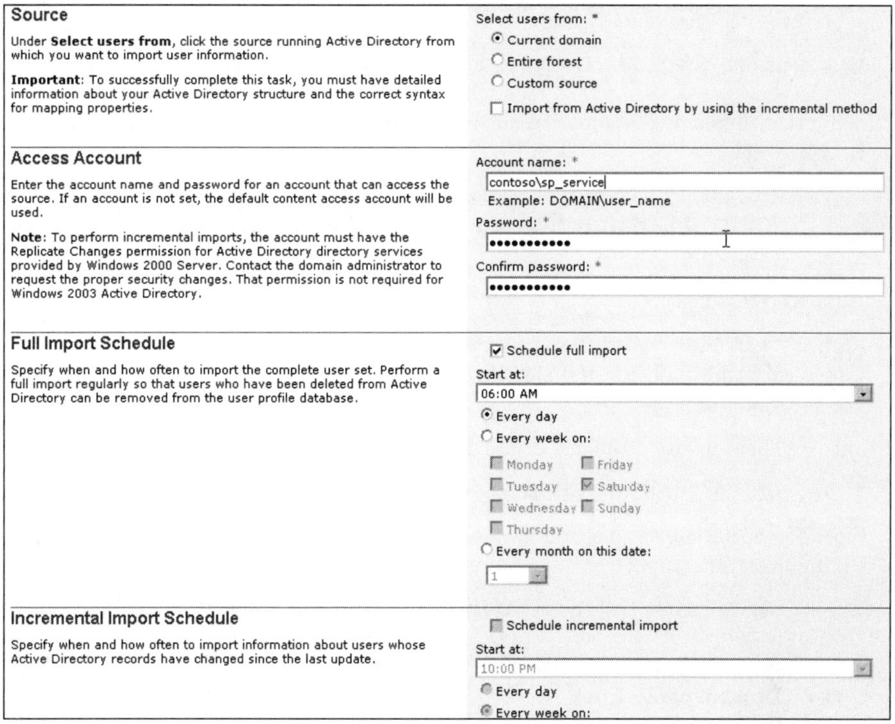

Source

Under **Select users from**, click the source running Active Directory from which you want to import user information.

Important: To successfully complete this task, you must have detailed information about your Active Directory structure and the correct syntax for mapping properties.

Select users from: *
- ○ Current domain
- ○ Entire forest
- ○ Custom source

☐ Import from Active Directory by using the incremental method

Access Account

Enter the account name and password for an account that can access the source. If an account is not set, the default content access account will be used.

Note: To perform incremental imports, the account must have the Replicate Changes permission for Active Directory directory services provided by Windows 2000 Server. Contact the domain administrator to request the proper security changes. That permission is not required for Windows 2003 Active Directory.

Account name: *

`contoso\sp_service`

Example: DOMAIN\user_name

Password: *

`•••••••••••`

Confirm password: *

`•••••••••••`

Full Import Schedule

Specify when and how often to import the complete user set. Perform a full import regularly so that users who have been deleted from Active Directory can be removed from the user profile database.

☑ Schedule full import

Start at:

`06:00 AM`

- ○ Every day
- ○ Every week on:
  - ☐ Monday ☐ Friday
  - ☐ Tuesday ☑ Saturday
  - ☐ Wednesday ☐ Sunday
  - ☐ Thursday
- ○ Every month on this date:
  - `1`

Incremental Import Schedule

Specify when and how often to import information about users whose Active Directory records have changed since the last update.

☐ Schedule incremental import

Start at:

`10:00 PM`

- ○ Every day
- ○ Every week on:

Figure 6-4

Use these setting to configure the import process that fits the needs of your organization. Avoid choosing a time when other activities may be running, such as the backup process or antivirus scanning. In Figure 6-4, the domain to be imported is listed as the Current domain (the same domain this SharePoint server belongs to). If you have more than one AD domain, and your users belong to any domain other than the SharePoint server, you can choose Entire forest.

> *If you have another AD domain name than your NetBIOS name, SharePoint may fail to identify the correct domain to be imported. This is common for domains upgraded from NT 4 to AD. To solve this, choose "Entire forest" even if you have just one domain.*

One consequence of importing the complete domain is that you will also import a number of system accounts. It may or may not be a problem, depending on the size of your domain and how sensitive you are about getting non-standard users listed in the User Profile database. In reality these extra accounts do not require that much space and no one will see them, except the SharePoint administrator when looking at this page. Still, you may want to control this import in more detail, especially if you have lots of accounts in your domain that never will be SharePoint users, such as test accounts or multiple organizations.

For example, say you have an Organizational Unit (OU) in Active Directory that contains SharePoint users. Why not just import that OU? You ask yourself; how hard can it be? What you need to do is to create a *Lightweight Directory Access Protocol* (LDAP) query filter. For example, the default LDAP filter that SharePoint uses is the following:

```
(&(objectCategory=Person)(objectClass=User))
```

This string says that all objects of class `Users` of the category `Person` will be imported.

The following steps explain how you do a custom import of the OU "SPUsers." I will let you be the judge of how hard it is:

Try It Out   Import a Custom Source from Active Directory

1. Use the Active Directory Users and Computers tool; select the View menu and its option Advanced features.

2. Right-click SPUsers, select Properties, and switch to the Object tab. Note the value of the Canonical name of object; in this example it will be `Contoso.com/SPUsers`. This string tells you the following:

   a. The domain attributes, or DC, are the com and contoso.

   b. The OU attribute is SPUsers.

3. Open the portal site as an administrator; click Site Settings, Manage Profile Database, and then Configure profile import.

4. Check Custom Source and click OK. This will open the Manage Connections page.

5. Click New Connection and enter the following values for this example (see Figure 6-5):

   a. **Domain name:** Contoso.com.

   b. **Select a domain controller:** Enter its name in the text box below. You can also choose the option "Auto discover domain controller" or select a specific DC.

   c. **Search base:** `OU=SPUsers,DC=Contoso,DC=com` (which is the default setting).

   d. **User filter:** `(&(objectCategory=Person)(objectClass=User))`.

   You can exclude disabled users by using this filter string instead: `(&(objectCategory=person)`
   `(objectClass=user)( !(userAccountControl:1.2.840.113556.1.4.803:=2)))`.

   e. **Scope:** Subtree. (This will include any sub-OU under SPUsers. You can also choose "One level" to ignore any sub-OU under SPUsers).

   f. Do not change any of the other values. They are fine for most import scenarios. Click OK to save this connection configuration.

6. You are returned to the Manage Connections page again. It is now possible to add other custom import sources, but in this example you are now done.

7. Click Manage Profile Database to return to this earlier page. The Source of user set is now listed as Custom source.

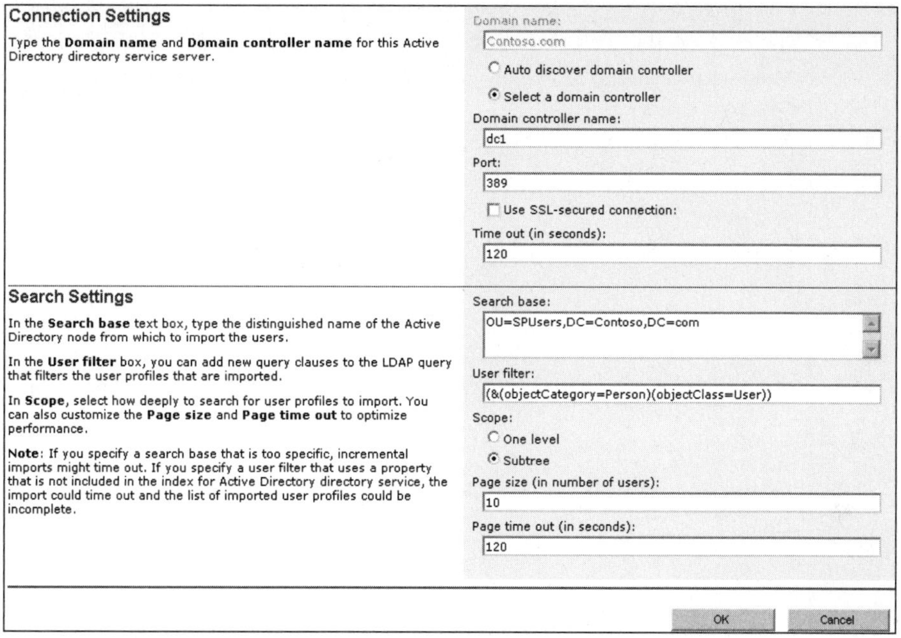

Figure 6-5

Regardless of whether you configure any custom source or use the default domain setting, the next thing to configure is the schedule for this import, if you did not do it previously. You can also force an import manually by clicking "Start full import." This will immediately start the import. You will see the page get refreshed once every minute, and the Import status changes to Importing. When it changes to Idle, the import is done. If this is the first time, you will see that the number of profiles has increased.

To set up the import schedule, click the link "Specify Schedule" on the Manage Profile Database page. It opens the same page where you previously configured the import source. Check the option "Schedule full import" and select a time and day for this import. It is also possible to configure an incremental import, but in order to do that you must first check the option "Import from Active Directory by using the incremental method" near the top of this page. Then you can check the option "Schedule incremental import" in the same way as for full import. The difference between full and incremental importing is that the latter will only import changed user accounts compared to the most recent import process. Click OK to save and close this page.

Click the "View user profiles" link to see a list of all the imported user profiles. You can delete any of these users, or change its imported settings; it will not affect the Active Directory information, because all of this is a one-way import. To view the imported settings, click to the right of the user name to display its edit menu and select Edit. This will display all the imported information about this particular user, as Figure 6-6 shows.

Note that any attribute with a disk icon indicates that this information was imported from Active Directory. You can change it now, but if you do it will be overwritten the next time the import process runs.

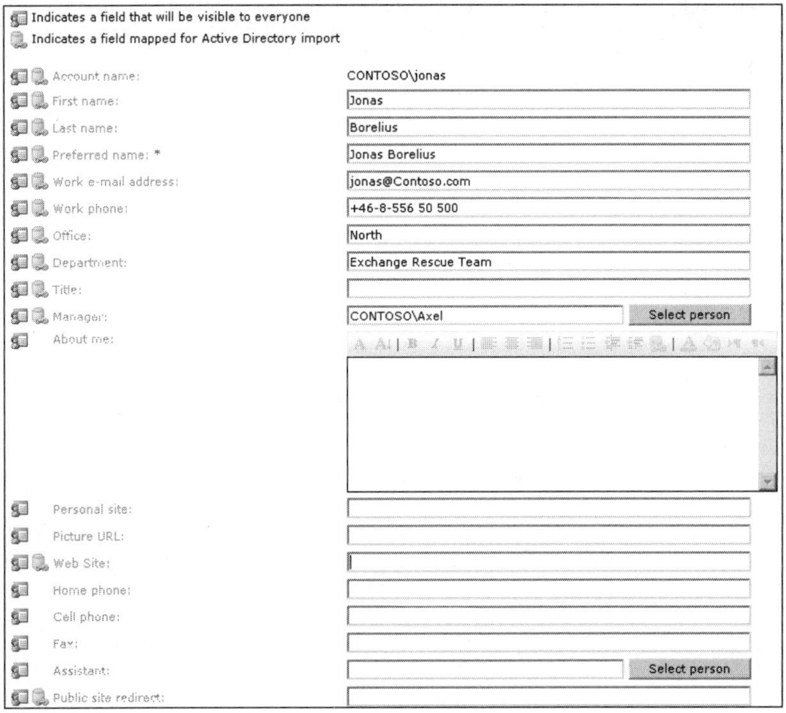

Figure 6-6

All attributes that do not have this disk icon, such as About me and Picture URL, must be set manually, either by the SharePoint administrator using this page, or possibly by the user. This is controlled on another page. If you changed any of these values, click Save and Close now to return to the View user profile page. Click the Manage profile database link to go back to the first page, shown previously in Figure 6-3.

There is more interesting information under the User Profile Properties section on this page. You can see the total number of user profile properties (24 by default), and how many of them are mapped to Active Directory attributes (14 by default). There are also two links that allow you to manage the profile properties:

❑ **Add profile property:** Use this link when you need to add more properties to the user profile. You can configure the new property in many ways, including any mapping to the Active Directory.

❑ **View profile properties:** Use this link to view and modify existing properties; for example, if you want to map an existing property to an Active Directory attribute.

The best way to understand these settings is, as usual, to test with an example. Say you want to add a new property named Expertise. You don't want to map this value to any Active Directory attribute, but you want to enable users to set this value by themselves. The following shows you how to do it:

Add a New Property to the User Profile

1. Open the portal site as an administrator; click Site Settings⇨Manage Profile Database⇨Add profile property. This opens a web form. Enter the following values (see Figure 6-7):

    a. **Name:** Expertise. The name for this property.

    b. **Display name:** Expertise. The name as displayed for the user.

    c. **Type:** string. Defines what type of information you can store in this property.

    d. **Length:** 32. Sets a maximum of 32 characters for this property.

    e. **View Settings:** Public. Every user will be able to see this setting.

    f. **Edit Settings:** Allow users to edit this property. Self-explanatory.

    g. **Display Settings:** Check both "Show in the Details section of the user profile" and "Show on the Edit My Profile page." This setting is important to make this property configurable by the user.

    h. Leave the rest, making sure this property is not mapped to Active Directory. Click OK to save and close this web form.

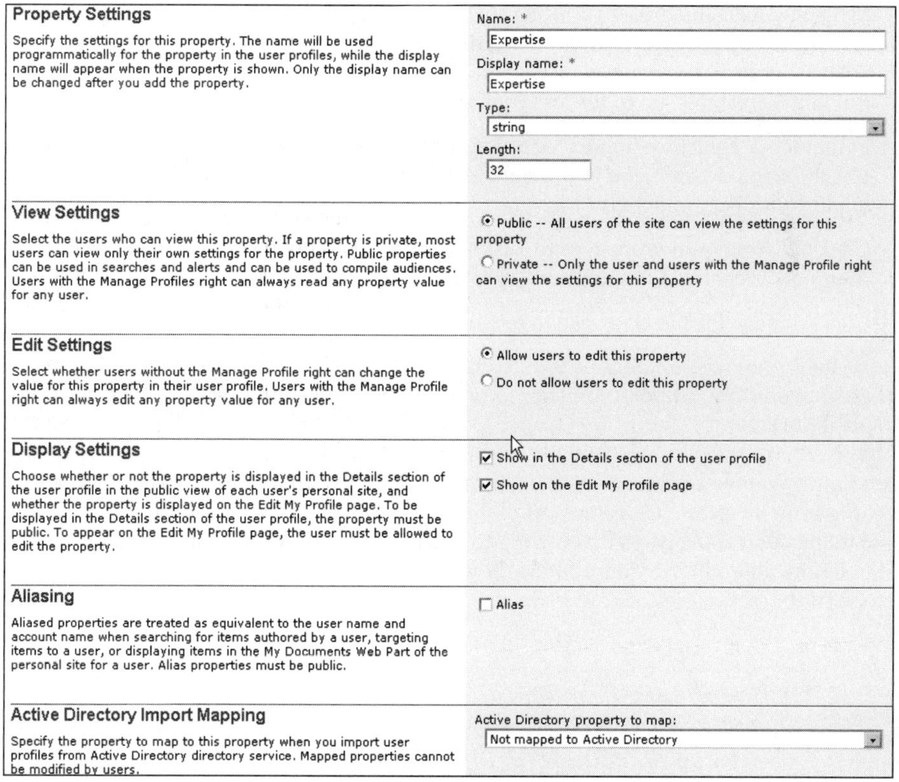

Figure 6-7

2.   You are returned to the list of available properties. Verify that the new Expertise property is listed and configured in a proper way. The arrow in the Change Column for the Expertise property allows you to move this property in this list. This affects the order in which these properties will be listed in the user's public view of their personal site (My Site).

3.   Test to set this value for a user listed in the user profile, click Manage Profile Database (note that the number of properties now have increased by one). Click View user Profiles and edit any user listed there. Enter a value, for example "SharePoint," and click Save and Close. Later on you will see how this value shows up on the My Site page.

The other item listed on the preceding bullet list was for modifying existing properties. For example, say that you want to map the attribute for the mobile phone number in Active Directory to the existing user property CellPhone. The following Try It Out shows how you would do this:

Try It Out   Map a User Property to an AD Attribute

1.   Open the portal site as an administrator; click Site Settings⇨Manage Profile Database⇨View profile properties. This opens a web form with all existing properties and their settings.

2.   Locate the property CellPhone. Note that the Active Directory Property column is empty. This is an indication that there is no mapping to any AD attribute. Hover the mouse over the CellPhone to display its menu arrow and then select the Edit menu for the CellPhone property. All current settings for this property are now listed. Note that you can set many things here, for example, whether or not this property will be editable by the user and if this property should be public. But in this example, go to the last part of this page.

3.   In the Active Directory Import Mapping section, note that it says Not mapped to Active Directory. Use the scroll-down menu to the right and locate the attribute "mobile" (type M to scroll directly to attributes beginning with M).

4.   Click OK to save and return to the list of properties. Note that the Active Directory Property column now is changed to mobile.

5.   Click Manage Profile Database to return to that page.

6.   If you cannot wait until the scheduled import starts, click Start Full Import. If you check the user profiles after this import, you should now see the mobile number listed for each user with that attribute set.

You have now seen how to manage user profiles, and how to add and modify new properties. You also learned how to do a custom source import of the Active Directory. It was not that hard, was it? Well, if you want to import just the users that belong to a distribution list or anything similar, you will need to understand more about LDAP query filters. Lots of sources with good information about LDAP are available, including examples of how to do more advance filtering for SharePoint's custom source import.

Use your favorite search engine and search for "SharePoint custom source import" to find a number of good links.

Managing Audiences

One of the main problems with sharing information between many users is that there will always be a lot of information collected, but the average user is only interested in parts of that information. A common way of solving this problem is to create specific places for each type of information or interest group, such as local intranets for each department. However, this creates a new problem: Now each user must know where to look, or even worse, information is stored multiple times, maybe in different versions. This is clearly something to avoid.

SharePoint Portal Server has a solution for this: Targeting. Almost every piece of information in the portal site can be targeted for a specific audience. The following is a list of examples using targeting:

❑ **News:** This list can be configured to only show sales-related news items for the sales team, IT-related news for the IT department, and both sales and IT news for other users.

❑ **Lists:** You can target any list in the portal site for a given audience. For example, the Sales department wants to see all sales meetings on the Home page of the portal site, whereas others do not want this displayed. The trick here is to use the web part instance that every list gets automatically. You cannot actually target the list itself, but you can target its web part.

❑ **Links:** The links displayed on the Topics areas can also be targeted. The user will therefore see only the links that apply to his or her specific tasks. SharePoint also has a feature called *Targeted Links* that the administrator can use to create links that show up on the user's personal site. You learn more about that in the next section.

❑ **Web Parts:** Practically all web parts available on the portal site have a targeting option; it is usually in the Advanced section of the web part configuration. Even the web parts on the Sites area page that lists sites can be targeted for a specific audience. However, you will need to use FrontPage in order to open the web part properties.

More about Audiences

It is easy to confuse audiences with security. Let's make this very clear: The audience feature is not a security feature. It is a filter that displays or hides information based on membership in audience groups. For example, if you know the URL to a news item that is hidden for you by this audience feature, you can type it manually to still get access to the item. The item is not restricted from you; it's just not easily visible.

Audiences are built upon rules that identify users based on properties and memberships. For example, you may have an audience named Sales where all users with the property Department = Sales are members. A user may be a member of multiple audience groups, so this user will see all information targeted for any of these groups.

You can have as many audience groups as necessary, but when you have a lot of these groups it will be easy to get confused. Make sure you plan your audience groups and take a note of why you created them. It is easy to forget that, after a while. Audiences are like fruit — it is great to have when it's fresh and tastes good, but old fruit only attracts flies.

By default there is always one audience group: All Portal Users. As it says, it will contain all users with access to the portal. You cannot remove or modify this audience.

Creating Audiences

In the previous section you learned about user profiles. Now it is time to use some of this knowledge. The information in the user profile is often used for selecting members for an audience. For example, say you want to create the audience group called Sales based on the Department property. If you import the user properties from Active Directory into the user profile, you have two places with this property. So the big question is which one will SharePoint use when compiling the audience group? The answer this time is the user profile. Actually, most of the time SharePoint will use the content stored in the user profile.

Follow these steps to create the Sales audience group, based on the Department property setting in the user profile:

Try It Out   Create an Audience

1. Make sure you have at least some users in Active Directory with the Department property set to "Sales."

2. Make sure this information has been imported into the user profile.

3. Open the portal site and click Site Settings.

4. Click Manage Audiences at the bottom of this page. This is the start page for all settings and management related to audiences. It will list the current status; for example, the number of audiences, when to run the compilation process (that is, rebuild the audience groups), and any errors encountered.

5. Click the Create Audience link. This opens the first of a series of web forms where you define this audience group by filling in values like the following:

    a. **Name:** Sales. This will be the name for this audience. It will be visible anywhere audiences are listed, so give it a good name.

    b. **Description:** "People from the sales department." Make sure to enter a clear description here, so other administrators 12 months from now understand its purpose.

    c. **Include user who:** Satisfy all of the rules. As long as you only have one rule, this setting is not important. But if you want to build a more complex rule you must be very sure if you want "all" or just "any" of the rules. For example, assume you create two rules: Department=Sales and Department=Finance, and choose the default "Satisfy all of the rules." Do you really have any user that has both Sales and Finance in their Department property? If not, this audience will not find any matching members.

    d. Click OK to open the next web form.

6. The Add Audience Rule page lets you choose between two types of operands: User or Property. Depending on what you select the rest of this page will adjust to the options available for that particular operand; see Figure 6-8. For this example, you must choose the following settings:

    a. **Operand:** Select one of the following: Property.

    b. **Operand:** scrollbar: Department. All of these are fetched from the user profile. If you previously completed the example of creating the new user profile property Expertise, it will be listed here.

    c.   **Operator:** = (equal sign). The four choices are "=", "Contains", "<>", and "Not contains".

    d.   **Value:** Specify Sales. This value is not case-sensitive.

If the property is not always spelled in the same way, such as "Sales" and "Sales Dept" and "Sales Department," choose the Operator "Contains" and set the value "Sales."

    e.   Click OK to save and close this first rule. You will return to a page with the current settings for this audience group. If you need to modify the rule, click its operand value. If you need to create a second rule, click Add rule. But for this example you are now done.

For a brand new audience it may feel tempting to click the "View membership" link on this page. Unfortunately it will tell you there are no matching users found. The reason, as listed, is that this audience is not yet compiled.

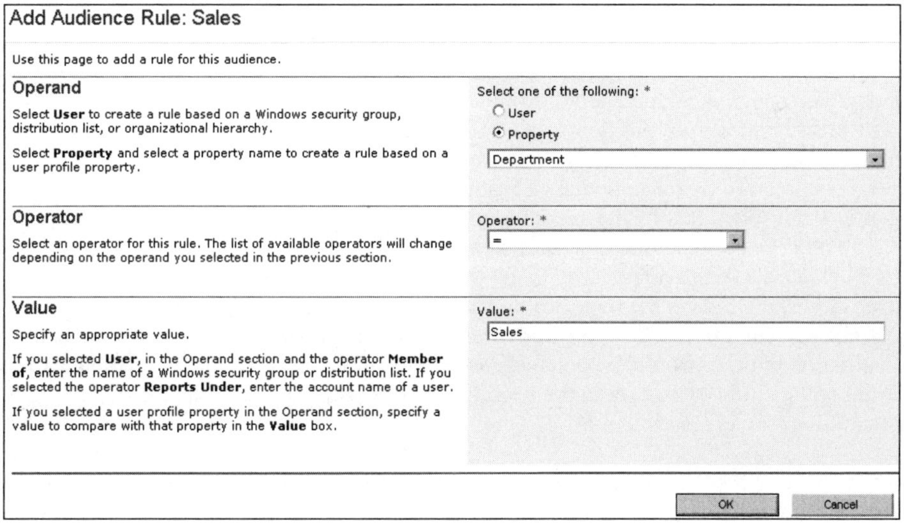

Add Audience Rule: Sales

Use this page to add a rule for this audience.

Operand	Select one of the following: *
Select **User** to create a rule based on a Windows security group, distribution list, or organizational hierarchy. Select **Property** and select a property name to create a rule based on a user profile property.	○ User ◉ Property [Department ▾]

Operator	Operator: *
Select an operator for this rule. The list of available operators will change depending on the operand you selected in the previous section.	[= ▾]

Value	Value: *
Specify an appropriate value. If you selected **User**, in the Operand section and the operator **Member of**, enter the name of a Windows security group or distribution list. If you selected the operator **Reports Under**, enter the account name of a user. If you selected a user profile property in the Operand section, specify a value to compare with that property in the **Value** box.	[Sales]

          [OK] [Cancel]

Figure 6-8

7.   Click the Manage Audience link at the top of the page to return to start page for audience management.

8.   Note that the status says Uncompiled audiences = 1. This is a clear indication that the last step is to compile the audience. This will start a process in SharePoint that will look for users that match the audience rules. Normally you would schedule this process, but because you are impatient you can click Start compilation. Just wait until this process is done (check the Compilation Status). You can also click Refresh occasionally to reduce the adrenaline level.

9.   When the Compilation Status is idle and the number of uncompiled audiences is 0, everything is completed. To view the membership of this group, click View audiences to list all existing audiences. Locate Sales, click to the right of its name, and from the menu select View membership. Verify that all the users you expected are here; if not, check the properties in the Active Directory, then the properties in the User Profile database, and finally check the rule for this property (use Edit in the menu, or click the View Audience Properties link on the top of this page).

This was rather straightforward, right? If you want to create an audience based on membership of a distribution list or a security group you will do the exact same steps as previously shown, except for step 6, which will look like this:

6.   At the page Add Audience Rule:

a.   **Operand:** Select User.

b.   **Operator:** Member of. (Note that for the operand User you will only have these operators to choose between: "Reports Under" and "Member of.")

c.   **Value:** Specify Contoso\Sales Team (the complete name for this group).

d.   Click OK to save.

e.   Click "Manage Audiences" in the breadcrumb trail; then click "Start compilation" to make sure your new rule has been compiled

So where did SharePoint go to find out the membership of this security group? Remember, the User Profile database contains nothing about groups, only user accounts. That leaves only Active Directory, which is the case in this example. So if you want to create audiences based on groups, you don't need to update the User Profile database. The other option for the operand User is "Reports under." Use this operand if you want to create an audience based on people working for a given person, such as the Sales manager. This time SharePoint will look at the settings in the User Profile database, not in Active Directory, so now you must be sure that the profile database is updated. This property is imported from Active Directory by default, so the correct way to get these settings updated is to enter this value in Active Directory, import the data to the User Profile database, and then compile the audience. Note that the user account you enter in the "Reports under" field for this audience rule will automatically be added to this audience. In other words, if you create an audience based on the fact that Anna is the manager, SharePoint will include every user in the profile database with the "Reports under" setting equal to Anna, including Anna herself.

> If this group contains other groups, they will also be included, as long its group members can be viewed in the current domain. If you have multiple domains you must use Universal Groups to be sure SharePoint will see the members in the remote domain.

Just as the user profile import can be scheduled, so can the compilation of audiences. The important thing to remember here is that the compilation of audiences should be scheduled to run after the user profile import, to make sure the User Profile database contains the most recent values. Use the administrative page "Manage Audiences" and click its link "Specify compilation schedule." Then check the option "Enable scheduling" and set the time and day for running the audience compilation.

Applying Audiences

Now comes the fun part: testing that targeting of information for given audiences actually works. Before you continue with the following steps, make sure you have at least one audience group besides the default All Portal Users.

Try It Out   **Target Information to Specific Audiences**

1.   Open the portal site.

2.   The first example is to create a news item targeted to the Sales audience only:

   a.   Open the News area page; click Add News.

   b.   Fill in the following form, as described earlier in Chapter 5. For example, enter a title that says "Only for the Sales People." The important stuff is at the end of this page.

   c.   In the Audiences section, double-click Sales to add it the Selected audience pane. Make sure it's the only one.

   d.   Click OK to save and close this news item.

3. Repeat step 2 but make a news item for the audience All portal users only.

4. Look at the News area page. Can you see these two news items? Yes, indeed. Is it because you are the administrator? No! The reason is that by default this new listing will not care about audiences. So you must change that setting:

Choose Edit page⇨Modify Shared Page⇨Modify Shared Web Part⇨Latest News. This will open the property page for the news web part.

5. Change the field Group by to Audience and click OK. Will you see anything? Yes, you should see the two new news items you added. But wait — the page is still in edit mode (look at the last Action link). If you click View page, the page will be displayed in a normal way. Suddenly all you see are news items targeted for the All portal users audience. In other words, it does not matter how powerful the user is; if you don't belong to an audience, you will not see it!

6. And now to something very strange (at least until you think about it): Switch to the Home area page that has a news web part connected (or *anchored*) to the News area. It will display all news items, regardless of the target settings. The reason is of course that the Home area has its own web part, and it has its own property settings. If you want that one to filter news items in the same way as the News area web part, you must repeat steps 5 and 6 for the Home area web part. Every web part, regardless of whether or not it is using an anchor, can be configured individually regarding its Group by setting.

The next practice is to target complete web parts. For example, make the Event calendar list displayed on the Home area page visible for the Sales audience only. The following Try It Out shows how you target that web part:

Try It Out   **Target Web Parts to Specific Audiences**

1. Open the portal site and the Home area page.

2. Choose Edit page⇨Modify Shared Page⇨Modify Shared Web Part⇨Events. This will open the property page for this web part.

3. Expand the Advanced section. At the end, click the Select button under Target Audiences. This will display a list of all available audiences, much like the one displayed when creating News items. Add Sales to the Selected Audiences pane and click OK. Click OK again to close the web part property pane. You will still see the Event list. Click View page to skip the edit mode and the list will disappear. Any time you switch to the edit page mode, all web parts, including this one, will be visible to make it possible for you to edit their web part property settings.

So the natural question now is can anyone see these targeted news items and the event list? Sure, just log on as a user that is a member of the Sales audience (and has at least read access to the portal) and this user will suddenly see this targeted information. Do you see how elegant and powerful this feature is?

It will help you create a portal site that automatically (some would say "automagically") adjusts its content to the current user. This is indeed a very useful feature of the portal site. Remember that this feature is exclusive to the portal; on the team sites (that is, the WSS sites) you will not find this targeting functionality.

But try the last type of objects that are audience-aware: Links. These links show up in one of two places:

- ❏ On a Topics area page.
- ❏ On the personal site's Links For You.

All the links you created in any of the Topics areas in Chapter 5 are audience-aware. This means that you can create all the links your organization needs, and still be sure that every user will still only see the links that apply to him. Try an example: you have a lot of links on the HelpDesk area page and you want to add some new ones and make sure these show up only for members of the Sales audience:

Try It Out   Target Links on Topics Areas

1. Open the HelpDesk area page. (If you followed the earlier example in this chapter, it will be under Topics.)

2. Click Add Person. On the next web form, fill in these values.

    a. **Account name:** Contoso\Alex (or whatever name you have).

    b. **Description:** "Expert on Sales Topics."

    c. Leave the Group and location as they are.

    d. **Audience:** Add Sales to the Selected audiences pane.

    e. Click OK to save and close.

3. Make sure the Grouped Listings web part is grouped by audience to see the effect of this audience setting. Go to Edit Page⇨Modify Shared Page⇨Modify Shared Web Parts⇨Grouped Listings and set the "Group by" value to Audience; then click OK to save and close.

4. Look at the HelpDesk. If your current user account is not a member of the Sales audience, you will not see the "Expert on Sales Topics" link listed. But if you log on as another user in the Sales audience, you will see it.

The second type of link is a feature in the portal site called "Links For You." What many administrators often get confused by is the fact that there is also a general web part named "Links For You" that you can add to all area pages on the portal site. But these web parts have nothing to do with the "Links For You" feature discussed here, because this type is only displayed on each user's personal web site, also known as *My Sites*. (You will learn more about them shortly.)

SharePoint also refers to these links as *targeted links.* The purpose of these targeted links is to offer the portal administrator the possibility of creating links on the users' personal sites, without needing access to these sites in the first place. For example, say that you need to add a link to an Excel file containing sales statistics for all the Sales people. Instead of adding this link to a Topic area, you can perform the following actions:

Try It Out   **Add Targeted Links to Personal Sites**

1.   Open the portal site.

2.   Choose Site Settings⇨Manage targeted links on My Site.

3.   Click Add Listing and a web form will open. Note how similar it looks to the Topics links web form, except for the missing section about Location. This section is not necessary here, because this link is predestined for the My Site location. Enter the following values:

   a.   **Title:** Sales Statistics.

   b.   **Description:** You can leave this empty; it does not show up on the user's My Site.

   c.   **Existing listing address:** `http://spsrv2/sites/Sales/Shared Documents/ Statistics.xls`. (This is just an example. Add your own address here.)

   d.   **Group:** General.

   e.   **Audience:** Add Sales to the Selected audiences pane. Click OK.

4.   The new link will be listed on the following page. You can now add more links. Note that it says clearly that the location for this link is My Site.

5.   Log on as a Sales user and click My Site. This link should be listed on that user's personal site, similar to Figure 6-9, which shows two links, one for the Sales audience and one for All portal users.

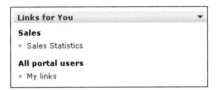

Figure 6-9

Managing My Sites

This is another feature exclusive to the portal site; there is no similar functionality in the WSS team site environment. Its purpose is to offer the perfect start page for the user, where all the information that is relevant for the user is collected in one place, such as the following:

❑   **Targeted news items:** Shows only news for your specific audience groups.

❑   **Targeted links:** The web part "Links For You" as described in the previous section.

❑   **Summary of Alerts created in the portal site:** Note that WSS alerts will not be visible here!

❑   **Manage Alerts:** This web part will list and make it possible to edit all alerts the user has defined on the portal site. Note that this web part will not list any alerts in the WSS team sites.

❑   **Personal Links:** Links that the user has created for team sites, documents and folders, as well as any external web site or file server, and so on. This feature is very similar to Favorites in your web browser, except that it is stored on your personal site instead of your local client computer. You can therefore access these links regardless of what client computer you are using.

❑ **Private Document library and Picture library:** Can only be accessed by the owner by default.

❑ **Public Document library:** Its content can be accessed by any portal user; this can be changed.

❑ Any web part listing you may find interesting, such as RSS news feeds, weather forecasts, and other information collected from an external source.

In other words, My Site will make sure users have access to most of their everyday information. Your users will love this page, as soon as they understand its meaning and the power they have over it. This site is actually a slightly customized WSS top site, that is, the start of a site collection that the user administrates. All the things you have learned about WSS team sites will also apply here, except for some small differences. For example, to create a new list you must click the Documents and Lists link, and then click Create. The user can create a subsite at any time for things like small projects, meetings, and personal purposes. Each of these subsites can have their own security setting, exactly like any other team site.

Just like a coin, there are two sides to My Sites. In addition to the personal site, there is also a public view with information about the user, including a photo and links to the public document library and more. Later in this chapter you learn more about this public view of My Site.

Activating My Site

By default all users except members of the Reader site group will have access to their own My Site, also known as the personal site. This can easily be changed. In Chapter 5 you learned how to manage site groups. The two permissions that control the settings to create and use My Site are the Create Personal Site and Use Personal Features; enable these settings for the Reader site group if you want everyone to have access to a personal site. If a user is not allowed to view his personal site, he will not see the link My Site on the portal site. To change these two permission settings, click Site Settings in the portal site, then choose Manage security and additional settings➪Manage site groups➪Reader➪Edit Site Group Permissions.

The first time a user clicks the link My Site (in the top-right corner) a process that creates the personal site starts. During this time a progress bar will be displayed, and then the site shown in Figure 6-10 will open.

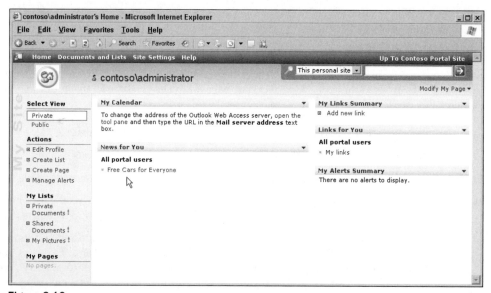

Figure 6-10

It contains the information mentioned in the preceding bullet list, including a web part that is not configured yet. One of the first things that will happen is that the user is prompted about creating links from MS Office to this personal site; see Figure 6-11.

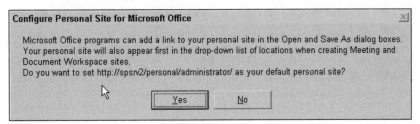

Figure 6-11

You have two options — at least in theory: Yes or No. But if you answer No, you will be prompted again the next time you open My Site. So give up and answer Yes. You may even like what it will do for you! The result will be that all MS Office programs will now display a quick link to the document and image libraries on your personal site, thus making it very easy to save and open documents; see Figure 6-12.

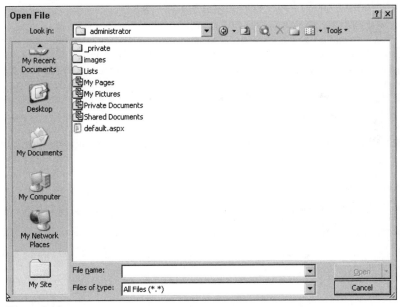

Figure 6-12

Configuring My Site

Look at Figure 6-10 again; there is a My Calendar web part that needs to be configured, in case the user wants it. If not, just click the arrow icon on the web part menu and select Close. This works with any visible web part on this page. But for now, configure it to display your Outlook calendar.

This web part will only work with a mailbox stored on an MS Exchange Server.

Try It Out   Configure the My Calendar Web Part

1. Open My Site as an ordinary portal user. Remember that readers by default don't have access to this site.

2. Locate the My Calendar web part; in the text of this web part, click its "open the tool pane" link.

3. The following configuration pane contains two very important settings:

    a. **Mail Server Address:** Must be configured to the same address that the *Outlook Web Access* (OWA) client uses for accessing the MS Exchange server. Typically it looks something like this: `http://mailserver.contoso.com/Exchange` assuming the fully qualified domain name for that server is `mailserver.contoso.com`. If it does not work, talk with your mail administrator and ask about the OWA address.

    b. **Mailbox:** This is the first part of your e-mail address, up to but not including the @ sign. You can also use your logon name here.

    c. Click OK to save. The calendar web part will now display the user's current calendar.

4. As a test, add an appointment for today using MS Outlook; then refresh the page and make sure you see the appointment in this web part too.

Cool, right? So why not add a web part to display the users' inbox too? But hold on — assume you have 450 users. It would be great if you could preconfigure the general settings for all of these users, including adding extra web parts. This is possible because the page you have just been working with is a shared page, but working in a personal view. The easiest indication of this is that the ordinary user will see the link Modify My Page, not Modify Shared Page. Only a member of the site group Web Designer or an administrator will be able to switch to the shared page view.

For example, say you want to preconfigure the existing My Calendar web part to have the correct URL to the MS Exchange server. Then you also want to add My Inbox for everyone, also preconfigured with the correct URL to the mail server. The following Try It Out shows how to do it:

Try It Out   Update My Site for All Users

1. Log on as an administrator or Web Designer, and then open My Site.

2. Click Modify My Page (far upper-right on the page) and select Shared View. Any modification now will apply to all users' My Site immediately.

3. The first task is to preconfigure the My Calendar settings: Click the arrow on the web part menu, select Modify Shared Web Part to open its configuration pane, and then change the following settings:

    a. **Mail server address:** `http://mailserver.contoso.com/exchange` (the same address most likely as to your OWA client; if not you must ask your mail administrator).

    b. **Mailbox:** You must leave this setting empty, because all users have their own mailbox name. This means that the user must enter this setting manually the first time.

    c. Do any other modification you may need. For example, change the Title for this web part under the Appearance section from My Calendar to Outlook Calendar.

    d.   Click OK to save and close the configuration pane. The page will be refreshed and the web part now says that the user must open the tool pane and change the mailbox name — a much easier task for most users than configuring both the mail server address and their mailbox name.

4. The second task is to add the web part that displays the mailbox, plus preconfigure it the same way as the My Calendar web part. Choose Modify Shared Page➪Add Web Parts➪Browse.

5. Locate the web part My Inbox and drag it to any position you like on the page. Click the web parts menu arrow and select Modify Shared Web Part to open its configuration pane. Change the following settings:

    a.   **Mail server address:** `http://mailserver.contoso.com/exchange` (the same as for the My Calendar web part in the preceding step). Make sure to enter the correct link here. It will then be copied to all users' My Inbox settings. If you then again modify this mail server address using the shared view, it will no longer be copied to the users' My Inbox, because they now have a mail server address value set!

    b.   **Mailbox:** You must leave this setting empty because all users have their own mailbox name. This means that the user must enter this setting manually the first time.

    c.   Do any other modifications you may need.

    d.   Click OK to save and close the configuration pane.

The page will be refreshed and the web part will now say that the user must "open the tool pane" and change the mailbox name — a much easier task for most users than configuring both the mail server address and their mailbox name.

These global modifications are now active. Log on as any user with access to My Site and see the new settings.

So now all users will have access to their Outlook calendar and inbox. But there is more you can do besides these two web parts; you also have the following two Outlook-related web parts to work with:

❏   **My Tasks:** Displays the personal tasks for this user.

❏   **My Mail Folder:** Displays any type of personal folder, including custom mail folders, contacts, and calendar folders.

Use the exact same steps as previously to add My Task. If you want to use the My Mail Folder web part, you need to configure more settings, because this is a general view of any type of folder. For example, say you need to give users a list of their personal contacts. Following is how you do it:

Try It Out   **Display Personal Contacts in My Site**

1. Log on as an administrator or Web Designer and then open My Site.

2. Click Modify My Page and then select Shared View to make this modification visible to all users.

3. Choose Modify Shared Page➪Add Web Parts➪Browse.

4. Locate the web part My Mail Folder and drag it to any position you like on the page. Click the web parts menu arrow and select Modify Shared Web Part to open its configuration pane. Change the following settings:

a. **Exchange folder name:** Contacts. This is the folder name to be displayed. Note that if you are using Outlook with local language names, you must enter the name exactly as in the ordinary Outlook folder tree. Remember that this language setting is local to the client, so there may be two users in your organization that use different languages. If so, they will have different names. For example, with a Swedish Outlook setting you type "Kontakter" instead of "Contacts."

b. **Mail server address:** `http://mailserver.contoso.com/exchange` (the same as for the other two web parts in the preceding sections).

c. **Mailbox:** You must leave this setting empty because all users have their own mailbox name. This means that the user must enter this setting manually the first time.

d. **Title:** My Contacts. This setting is under the Appearance section.

e. Click OK to save and close the configuration pane.

The page will be refreshed and the web part now says that the user must open the tool pane and change the mailbox name — a much easier task for most users than configuring both the mail server address and their mailbox name.

My Mail Folder can also display Public Folders in Outlook, using a little trick.

There is a trick to make this web part display any Outlook Public Folder, as long as the user has at least read access. If you want to use this trick, make sure that all your users have access to that public folder; otherwise they will receive an error message every time they open their personal site.

For example, say you have a top-level public folder named Statistics that all users have access to. To display this public folder you can use the following steps:

Try It Out   Display a Public Folder with My Mail Folder

1. Log on as an administrator or Web Designer; open My Site.

2. Click Modify My Page and then select Shared View to make this modification visible to all users.

3. Choose Modify Shared Page⇨Add Web Parts⇨Browse.

4. Locate the web part My Mail Folder and drag it to any position you like on the page. Click the web parts menu arrow and select Modify Shared Web Part to open its configuration pane. Change these settings:

    a. **Exchange folder name:** `<space>`. You can type anything here, as long as it is not empty. A space character will do fine.

    b. **Mail server address:** `http://mailserver.contoso.com/public/statistics/` `?cmd=contents&part=1`. This is the trick! This line says that you want to view the public folder Statistics, and that it be formatted as Content. The part of the line after the folder name must exist; otherwise this web part will only display an error!

    c. **Mailbox:** `<space>`. As long as the user has access to that public folder, you do not need any mailbox name here, but again it must not be an empty field because this will force the web part to ask the user for it.

    d. **Title:** `Statistics`. This setting is under the Appearance section.

    e. Click OK to save and close the tool pane for this web part.

For more information about formatting the folder content in step 4b, check this link: `http://` `blogs.technet.com/kclemson/archive/2003/11/04/53886.aspx`. *It describes, among other things, how to format a calendar folder in a weekly view.*

5. The content of this public folder will be displayed immediately. Log on as a user and make sure it works as expected.

A common request is to have any of these mail-related web parts on pages other than My Site. Yes, you can add them to any area page in the portal site, but not in WSS team sites. However, because almost all of these web parts require the individual mailbox name in its configuration settings in order to work, you will have a problem: For example, say you want to display the user's Inbox on the Home area page on the portal. You can add the My Inbox web part, but what mailbox name should it be configured to display? There can only be one mailbox name defined in this web part, so it will only work for that particular user; if another user opens the Home page, she will get an error when displaying the My Inbox web part because she doesn't have access to read that specific mailbox. Do you see the problem? If there was a way to automatically adjust the mailbox name for the My Inbox web part based on the current user, it would work. But the 2003 version of this web part does not support that feature, unfortunately. It may be fixed in SharePoint 2007.

A final web part you may want to use for the My Site page is My Workspace Sites. This web part will list all sites created directly under the users' personal site. A common default location for sites created using Office and Outlook is My Site; with this web part in place it will be easy for the users to see a list of these team sites and workspaces.

Team sites created from within MS Office 2003 and Outlook 2003 are called Workspaces. Everything is the same, only the look and feel of the site is different.

Adding Information to My Site

A SharePoint user will soon need a place to add links to often visited locations, such as documents, folders, and team sites. One option is to use the web browser's Favorites, as described earlier, but this information will then be stored locally on that particular client computer. A better method is to store these links in a server-based list, easily available when needed. Because every user needs his or her own list of links, the best place to store them is on My Site. By default, My Site has a web part visible for this very purpose, but you must understand how to add links to that list.

You will find a link named Add to My Links in numerous places, such as the following:

❑ On all Topics area pages, including any one you created.

❑ On all News area pages.

❑ On the Sites area page.

❑ On any new area page.

❑ On any list, document library, or picture library on the portal site.

❑ On individual documents or pictures in the portal.

❑ On individual links in topic areas (switch to edit mode first).

❑ On any list, document library, or picture library on a team site.

❑ On individual documents and pictures stored in a team site.

It is almost easier to say where you will not find Add to My Links. For example, there is no direct way of adding a link to a given team site. And there is no support for adding a link to an individual contact or other list item. Still it can be done, but you need to enter the URL address manually. Following are some examples of how to add links to different types of objects:

Try It Out   Add to My Links

1. Open the portal and choose any user with permission to use My Site.

2. Go to the Topics area page. Click Add to My Links under Actions in the left pane. This will open a web form (see Figure 6-13). Enter these values for this example:

    a.   **Title:** Topics. (The default name is copied from the object. Change it if needed.)

    b.   **Address:** This is listed as information only. It cannot be changed.

    c.   **New group / Existing group:** This is a method to organize all links. By default, all added links will belong to the General group. If you need to save the link under another group name, choose New Group and enter its name. The next time this group will be listed under the list of Existing group.

    d.   **Share on public view of My Site:** Check this option if you want others to see this link. This is a very handy way of listing links to objects that other users often ask you about.

    e.   Click OK to save and close. You return to the location you started from.

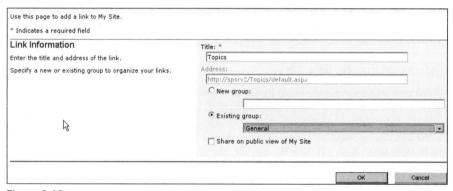

Figure 6-13

3. Go to any topic area with links, such as the HelpDesk created in a previous example. Click Edit Page under Actions to change to edit mode.

    a.   Locate an existing link on this page, such as Support Contact.

    b.   Hover the mouse above the link and click the arrow to the right of the link to display its menu.

    c.   Select Add to My Links.

    d.   Enter the values you want for this link, as described in more detail in step 2.

4. Add a link to a document library in the Home area:

    a.   Open the Home area page.

    b.   Click Manage Content.

    c.   Select Document Library.

    d.   Click Add to My Links in the left pane.

    e.   Enter the values you want for this link, as described in step 2. Note that the default name for this link will not indicate that the document library belongs to the Home area. You may want to change this name to something more descriptive.

5. Add a link to a specific picture in the Home area Image Library:

    a.   Click Manage Content.

    b.   Select Image Library.

    c.   Click Details under "Select a view." This will list all images as files.

    d.   Click the menu arrow to the right of any image file. Select Add to My Links from the menu.

    e.   Enter the values for this link.

6. Add a link to the team site IT. This description works with every object, and must be manually entered. It is often easier to open the specific object (or the IT team site in this example) and copy the URL address, and then create the link manually using the following steps:

    a.   Open the team site IT. Open the portal area Sites and then locate and click IT.

    b.   Copy the URL address; in this example: `http//spsrv2/sites/it`. You can skip the `default.aspx` part in the end of this URL, or copy that too; there will be no difference.

    c.   Open your My Site page.

    d.   Locate the web part My Links Summary. Click Add new link in this web part.

    e.   The following web form is exactly like Figure 6-13, but with no preset values. Enter the title and paste the URL into the address field. Select or create a proper group for this link and click OK.

7. The final example is to add a link to some external information, such as the MS Office SharePoint web site:

    a.   Open My Site.

    b.   Click Add new link under My Links Summary.

    c.   **Title:** SharePoint Homepage.

    d.   **Address:** `http://www.microsoft.com/sharepoint`.

    e.   Select a proper group, or create a new one now. Click OK.

The result of these examples will look like Figure 6-14.

If you need to modify or delete any of these links, click Manage Links on this web part; it will open a new page with all the links listed and buttons for managing them. You can also change group belongings. To edit a link, click to the right of the name and select Edit from the menu that shows up.

Figure 6-14

The Public View of My Site

So far you have only used the personal view of My Site. Every personal site will also have a public view, which lists public information about this user stored in the User Profile database discussed earlier. It is easy to assume that all users have their own web site for this public view because it contains personal information, but that is not true. There is only one web site for the public view. However, its content will depend on what person's My Site you are accessing at the time.

The best indication for this is that there is no way of configuring the web parts for this page, and there is no shared or personal view. But this page can be modified, either by editing the site definition file for the site, or using FrontPage 2003; you learn more about that in Chapter 12. This page has these web parts and content lists displayed by default:

❑ **Shared Links:** Any links added by this user where the option Share on public view of My Site is activated.

❑ **Recent Documents:** Lists up to the ten most recent documents this user has edited and that the current user looking at this page is allowed to read. This web part is actually a search result, using SPS standard search functionality. Click the web part heading to see all the documents created or modified by this user, and that you are permitted to read.

❑ **Shared Workspace Sites:** A list of team sites and workspaces under the user's personal site.

❑ A contact card with all publicly available information stored in the User Profile database, such as name, e-mail address, phone number, and optionally a picture.

❑ **Shared Documents:** A document library that every portal user is granted read access to by default.

❑ **Private Documents:** This document library can only be accessed by users with explicit permission. By default only the owner can view and use the contents of this library.

❑ **My Pictures:** A picture library that every portal user by default is granted access to.

You can create new lists and libraries for documents and pictures in My Site; if these are configured to allow access for anyone except you, their content will be possible to reach or even update, using the public view of My Site.

The detailed information about the user is retrieved from the User Profile database, as said before, but some of the information may not be complete. For example, a picture of the user, his home phone number, and his area of expertise may be missing. If the user is allowed to modify these settings, following is how to do it:

Update Your User Properties on My Site

1. Open your My Site.

2. Click Edit Profile under Actions.

3. All fields without a yellow warning sign are now editable by the user (see Figure 6-15). This warning sign indicates that the content of this field will be overwritten the next time the user profile import process runs. Enter the following values:

    a. **About me:** Enter a description; make sure to follow the policy, if any.

    b. **Picture URL:** Enter a URL to any publicly available picture of you.

    c. **Home phone:** Enter a phone number.

    d. **Cell phone:** Enter a phone number. Note that this may be marked with a yellow warning sign due to the previous example where you mapped this field to the Active Directory property "mobile"!

    e. **Fax:** Enter a fax number, if applicable.

    f. **Assistant:** Type the complete name, including the domain; for example, Contoso\Lasse, or click the Select Person to search for this user's account.

    g. **Expertise:** Any extra attribute you may have added to the user profile will be listed here, if you requested that. In this example Expertise is such an attribute.

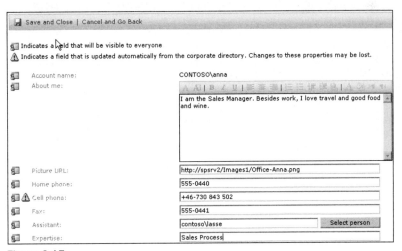

Figure 6-15

4. Click Save and Close.

5. Click Public under Select a view, and the result will look something like Figure 6-16.

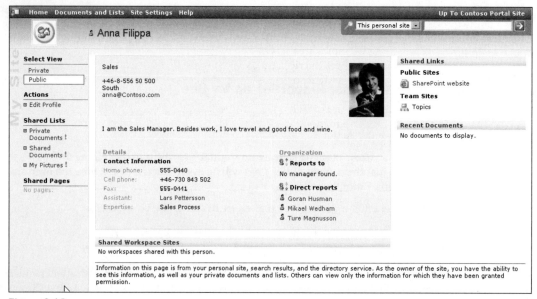

Figure 6-16

Note that every name listed on this page (for example, in the Organization section) will lead to the public view of that person's My Site. This is very handy if you need to get in contact with any of these other people. The Edit Profile link will only be visible when you look at your own public My Site page.

As you have seen, there is more to My Site than meets the eye. It makes the individual user more effective and reduces the time spent searching for important information, regardless of whether it is business oriented or more personal. Microsoft recommends that organizations replace the traditional Home directory with the document libraries in the personal site. One of the greatest benefits of using document libraries in My Site instead of a traditional Home directory is that you can have access to these files even when connecting to your portal site over the Internet (assuming your firewall configuration allows it). Note that if you don't have online access to SharePoint, you will not be able to access any of its document libraries. There is no built-in offline synchronization in SharePoint 2003.

> *Several tools are available that offer two-way synchronization between document libraries and the local client disk. One very nice and affordable tool is Revelation (*`http://www.digi-link.com`*).*

The other great use of My Site is that in all places you will see a name, such as the author of a document, news, or link, and by just clicking this name you will see that user's personal site. Thus no more hunting down the typical Employee List on traditional intranets, or searching Outlook's address list. Just click the name and you will have every piece of information available about this user in a few seconds, such as e-mail addresses, phone numbers, and a picture.

Security in the Portal Site

You have already seen how to add users and groups to site groups, such as Readers and Contributors, in the portal site. One important aspect about the security in the portal site is how SPS manages security on individual lists and document libraries. To sum it up, it is not possible to set individual permissions on lists and libraries; all these objects will inherit the security settings from its area page. In other words, if you have two document libraries on the same area page, you cannot have different security settings for these libraries. In fact, the only place you can modify the permissions is on the area page itself.

For example, say that you have a Topics area page named HelpDesk. On that page you have a document library. You want to enable some users the right to create and modify these documents, but nothing else on this page — this will not work! Is Microsoft sloppy, you ask? No! The portal site is designed to be a starting point, where you will see information targeted to lots of people, and to be a navigation vehicle. The team sites (the WSS part of SharePoint) is the place the users are supposed to use when working and collaborating with any type of information.

If you want to see that there are no security settings for any type of individual list or library, perform the following steps:

1. Open any area page on the portal.

2. Click Manage Content to see all the lists and libraries for that area.

3. Click Document Library (or any list you want to check).

4. Click Modify settings and columns.

5. The link to the security settings is normally listed among the top links, next to Change general settings, but as you can see there is no such link here.

Because the portal site has several special features not available in WSS team sites, it also has some other extra rights. To view the complete list of rights available for the portal site, you can just check any existing site group, such as Reader, or start creating a new site group, as in the following example:

Try It Out   **List Available Rights for the Portal Site**

1. Open any area page on the portal.

2. Choose Site Settings⇨Manage security and additional settings⇨Manage site groups.

3. Click Add a Site Group.

4. This will give you all 32 rights available for the portal site, as listed in the following table. Click Cancel to return to the previous pane.

All Rights	Description
View Area	View an area and its contents.
View Pages	View pages in an area.
Add Items	Add items to lists, add documents to document libraries, add web discussion comments.
Edit Items	Edit items in lists, edit documents in document libraries, edit web discussion comments in documents, and customize web part pages in document libraries.
Delete Items	Delete items from a list, documents from a document library, and web discussion comments in documents.

Table continued on following page

239

All Rights	Description
Manage Personal Views	Create, change, and delete personal views of lists.
Add/Remove Personal Web Parts	Add or remove web parts on a personalized web part page.
Update Personal Web Parts	Update web parts to display personalized information.
Cancel Check-Out	Check in a document without saving the current changes.
Add and Customize Pages	Add, change, or delete HTML pages or web part pages, and edit the web site using a Windows SharePoint Services–compatible editor.
Create Area	Create an area on the portal site.
Manage Area	Delete or edit the properties for an area on the portal site.
Manage Area Permissions	Add, remove, or change user rights for an area.
Apply Style Sheets	Apply a style sheet (.CSS file) to an area or the portal site.
Browse Directories	Browse directories in an area.
Create Personal Site	Create a personal SharePoint site (My Site).
Create Sites	Create SharePoint sites by using Self-Service Site Creation.
Use Personal Features	Use alerts on portal content, and personal sites (My Site).
Manage Alerts	Change alert settings for the portal site and manage alerts for users.
Manage User Profiles	Add, change, or delete user profile information and properties.
Manage Audiences	Add, change, or delete audiences.
Manage Portal Site	Specify portal site properties and manage site settings.
Manage Search	Add, change, or delete index and search settings in the portal site.
Search	Search the portal site and all related content.
Manage List Permission	Grant, deny, or change user permissions to access a list.
Manage Lists	Approve content in lists, add or remove columns in a list, and add or remove public views of a list.
View Items	View items in lists, documents in document libraries, view web discussion comments, and set up e-mail alerts for lists.
Manage Site Groups	Create, change, and delete site groups, including adding users to the site groups and specifying which rights are assigned to a site group.
View Usage Data	View reports on web site usage.
Manage Web Site	Grants the ability to perform all administration tasks for the web site as well as manage content and permissions.
Apply Themes and Borders	Apply a theme or borders to the entire web site.
Create Cross-Site Groups	Create a group of users that can be granted access to any site within the site collection.

Note the number of rights related to the area concept, which does not exist in the team sites. For a more complete comparison between the rights in the portal and team sites, see Chapter 7, but just check one site group, the Reader. Its default rights might surprise you! See the following table:

Reader Rights	Description
View Area	View an area and its contents.
View Pages	View pages in an area.
Search	Search the portal site and all related content.

Compare that to the complete list above. What is says is that members of the Reader site group will be able to view and search, but not create personal sites, and not use alerts on any object at all.

Another site group that may not work as you first expect it to is the Contributor group. If you check its rights, there seems to be everything a contributor, sometimes referred to as an author, might need. For example, add a document to any library and then delete it. It works fine. Then try this: Add a news item to the News area. Then try to edit or delete it. You cannot do this! So a contributor might add news or a link, but cannot correct a spelling error, for example. This is a bit annoying. The reason you cannot edit or delete is that news and links in the area are regarded differently from the content of document libraries and other lists. The rights required for editing news and other links are in the Manage area. Its description says "Delete or edit the properties for an area on the portal site." In other words, the links and news items on an area page are regarded as property.

The ability for a Contributor to add links and news at all depends on whether the Add Items right is in place. Although its description says "Add items to list, add documents to SharePoint document libraries, add web discussion comments" it also controls the permission to add area properties such as links and news items. Using this logic, one would assume that the rights Edit Items and Delete Items are also affected area properties—but they are not! You just have to know this.

Searching

One of the greatest time savers is search engines. Just look at how often you use MSN Search or Google, just to mention a few of them. On the Internet, searching is absolutely critical, because you have no idea where the information is stored, and there may be new sources of this information appearing minutes from now. That is why you search all the time. Your internal network is the same way. True, the volume of information is much less in your network, and you know where at least some of it is stored because you created it. Still, it does not take much activity within an organization to create so much information that the average user loses track of where things are stored. You start looking around to find the file, document, or whatever you are looking for, and after a few minutes, you find it. The question now is whether this is the latest version, or is there a newer version somewhere? Then when you have what you looked for, you most likely want to be notified if that document gets updated later on. What you need is a solution that:

❑ Finds information regardless of where it is stored.

❑ Makes sure it is the latest version.

❑ Sends a notification to you when this information gets updated.

SharePoint has solutions for the first bullet item, but there is a great difference in what SPS is offering compared to the WSS environment, as the following section covers in more detail. The second bullet is covered by the built-in version management of documents and list content in both SPS and WSS, and the third bullet item is the alert feature, also a built-in feature in SPS and WSS. So let's focus on the search functionality.

Searching in WSS

A quick summary of the search feature in WSS is this: None! End of story. But there is a remedy to this lack of functionality, even for the WSS environment. If WSS is using an MS SQL Server database, instead of the WMSDE version, you can take advantage of the Full-Text Indexing feature in SQL Server. However, it also has its limitations; it will only allow the user of a team site to search the current site — no subsites or any other site collections, just the current site. Still, this is better than nothing, but it means that the user must know in what site the information is stored before searching it. The following list summarizes the search functionality in WSS, when combined with SQL Server:

❑ Finds information of any type, as long as it is stored in the current team site.

❑ Performs free text search in documents, files, and list content.

Remember that the Full-Text Indexing feature in SQL Server must be installed before you can use this feature in WSS. Note that this indexing feature will use the Microsoft Search (MSSearch.exe) service in Windows 2003. This service must be running before WSS can use it for indexing and searching. The next step is to configure WSS to use this full text indexing:

Try It Out   **Activate Full-Text Search in WSS**

1. Log on as an administrator.

2. Start the SharePoint Central Administration tool. Use either the portal sites Site Settings⇨ Go to SharePoint Portal Server central administration and click Windows SharePoint Services in the left pane or use Windows by going to Start⇨Administrative Tools⇨SharePoint Central Administration.

3. Click Configure full-text search in the Component Configuration section.

4. Check the option "Enable full-text search and index component." A process starts that creates and populates a Full-Text Catalog index in the SQL Server, and configures it for the needs of WSS. This may take a long time if there is a lot of information stored in this content database. There is no need to modify these settings in SQL Server — do not touch them unless instructed by MS Support.

   The index catalog file is created under the content database; if the content database is named Contoso, the index will get the name ix_STS_contoso in a pure WSS environment; in SPS the same file will be ix_Contoso_SITE.

5. When the process is done, all documents and lists are also indexed and ready to be searched. Open any WSS team site and use the yellow search field at the top-right corner of the page. Type a text string you know exists in any of the lists or inside any documents stored in this team site.

If there is a problem with the full-text index, try to disable the full-text search, and then enable it again. This will re-create the index file and populate it.

Understanding the Search Feature in WSS

When searching is activated in WSS, there is nothing more to configure. The search engine in SQL Server is fast and stable; its behavior is controlled by stored procedures in SQL Server. You may find tips on how to optimize these stored procedures, but before you do that you must understand that this will violate the conditions for getting help from Microsoft's support team! It may also create problems when you install the next service pack or upgrade to the next release.

The objects indexed by this full-text indexing are these:

- ❑ **List items:** Such as individual names in a Contact list.
- ❑ **Documents:** Of these types: .doc, .xls, .ppt, .txt, and .html.
- ❑ **Lists:** Such as Announcements.

There are also objects that will not be indexed, and therefore not searchable:

- ❑ Non-text columns in lists (for example, Lookup fields, currency, Yes/No).
- ❑ Attachments to list items.
- ❑ Survey lists.
- ❑ Hidden lists.

The process of re-indexing new or modified information is automatic in WSS, and there is no scheduled process to manage. This process will detect any new information within a few minutes and then index it. As soon as this process is done, users can search for it.

The yellow search field is visible in all team sites; enter the string you are searching and press Enter or click the green arrow to the right of the search field. Note that if you enter more than one text string, it will match any object with either or both of these strings, also called a Boolean OR search. The SQL search engine is using a type of search called FREETEXT, which uses stemming (meaning that it includes plural forms and other word variations of the search text). For example, if you search for the word "Run" it will also match "Running" and "Ran." But you must enter the complete word; stemming will not work with abbreviations. For example, you cannot search for "admin" to find references to "administrator."

All of these constraints and behaviors are due to the way the stored procedures are defined. If you absolutely must change this, be sure to make a backup of the original stored procedure and make thorough notes of what you did and why, so anyone later on can restore or remove this customization, if necessary.

The Internet is full of tips on how to enhance the search functionality in WSS; for example, `http://wss.collutions.com/Lists/FAQ/Offline.aspx`. *Just keep in mind the information in this section.*

Indexing New File Types

You can use the MS Search service in SQL Server to index more file types than default. The most common request is Adobe's PDF files. What MS Search needs to index any file type is a program that can open that file and read its text; such a program is called an *Index Filter* or *IFilter* for short. So to index PDF files you need an IFilter for PDF. The good news is that this IFilter is free to download from Adobe's web site:

```
http://www.adobe.com/support/downloads/detail.jsp?ftpID=2611
```

Note that this IFilter is regularly updated, so make sure you get the latest version. After you download this program, install it on the SQL Server, if you are using a separate WSS and SQL server.

> *This is only true if you are running a pure WSS environment! If you are running an SPS server, this IFilter must be installed on all SharePoint servers with the Index role.*

After the installation, you must reactivate the full-text search again, in order to index all PDF files that existed in the content database before this IFilter was installed. If you don't do this, only new PDF files will be indexed:

1. Start SharePoint Central Administration.

2. Click Configure full-text search.

3. Clear the option "Enable full-text search and index component" and click OK. Wait for the SharePoint Central Administration page to return. Now the indexing component is removed.

4. Set the "Enable full-text search and index component" again and click OK; this will force a re-indexing of all documents. When this is done, all existing and future PDF files will be searchable.

Searching in SPS

This is one of the strongest features in SharePoint Portal Server! It has its own search engine, completely independent of the Full-Text Indexing service in SQL Server. In fact, you may want to have both of them running simultaneously, because the SQL search will also allow your portal users to search inside individual team sites. Here is a summary of the search features in SPS:

❑   Searches everywhere in SharePoint (any portal area, team site, and workspace site).

❑   Searches any source outside SharePoint, including file servers, MS Exchange servers, Lotus Notes, and other web servers, including any public web site on the Internet.

❑   Searches all MS Office file types by default, plus all neutral file formats, such as TXT, HTML, and so on.

❑   Can be extended to search any file type. An IFilter is needed for each file type.

❑   You can control what file types to be indexed, even if there is an IFilter installed for it.

❑   You can set the schedule for full and incremental indexing; you can also force a full indexing anytime.

This indexing and search feature is activated by default for all information stored in SharePoint, both portal areas and team sites; there is no special configuration needed to activate this. Because this feature is much more advanced than the full-text search in SQL Server, there are also a lot more configurations you can make; this also requires more management. You, as an administrator, must understand how this feature works in SPS and what you can do to optimize it. This is especially true when some problem arises, such as when the search results are not as expected, or when a content source fails to be indexed. The following sections tell you all you need to know for the everyday work as an administrator, and how to extend and adjust this very important feature.

For an in-depth description of the Search and Indexing feature, see "Microsoft SharePoint Product and Technology Resource Kit."

The Basics

Two SPS roles are engaged in this feature:

❑ **Indexing:** Responsible for crawling content sources and building index files.

❑ **Search:** Responsible for finding all information matching the search query by searching the index files.

This is important: all searching is performed against the index files. If they don't contain what the user is looking for, there will not be a match. So the index files are critical to the success of the search feature of SPS. In fact, practically all configuration and management are related to the indexing service. The search functionality can be described in its simplest form as a web page where users define their search query.

The index role can be configured to run on its own SPS server, or run together with all the other roles, as discussed in Chapter 4. It performs its indexing tasks following this general workflow:

1. The Windows program Scheduled Tasks stores the time and activities for the indexing service.

2. When activated, Index will look in SharePoint's databases to see what content sources to index, and what type, such as a full or incremental indexing.

3. The index service will start a program called the *Gatherer*, a program that will try opening the content that should be indexed.

4. For each information type, the Gatherer will need an IFilter that knows how to read text inside this particular type of information. For example, to read an MS Word file, an IFilter for .doc is needed.

5. The Gatherer will receive a stream of Unicode characters from the IFilter. It will now use a small program called a *Word Breaker;* its job is to convert the stream of Unicode characters into words.

6. The Gatherer will now compare each word found against a list of *Noise Words*. This is a text file that contains all words that will be removed from the stream of words. These include words that do not need to be stored in the index, such as "the," "a," and numbers.

7. The remaining words are stored in an index file, together with a link to the source. If that word already exists, only the source will be added, so one word can point to multiple sources.

8. If the source was information stored in SharePoint, or a file in the file system, the index will also store the security settings for this source. This will prevent a user from getting results that he is not allowed to open.

Pretty straightforward, if you think about it. But the underlying process is a bit more complex. Fortunately you do not need to dive into these details, unless you have a very good reason. By default, SPS will create two index files for its use:

❏ **Portal Content:** Everything stored in the portal site, including any area and its content, such as document libraries, lists, and news links.

❏ **Non-Portal Content:** Everything stored outside the portal site, such as all the team sites, workspaces, and by default all the external content sources you may add later.

The typical SPS environment will have most of its content in the team sites, which will make the non-portal content index file the largest. If you also configure SPS to index external content sources, it may grow a lot more. These index files are not stored in the SQL Server, like the rest of SharePoint's information. Instead they are stored in the file system on the server configured to run the Index role in the SharePoint farm. These index files are stored in separate folders under the following location:

```
<Drive:>\Program Files\SharePoint Portal Server\DATA\<Application GUID>
```

The "Application GUID" is a unique hexadecimal string that identifies a specific portal site, such as ae0cd4fe-ed29-418f-aa0f-eecfd7956b4f. If you have more than one portal site installed on the same server you can check the following registry key to see exactly what portal this Application GUID is pointing to:

```
HKEY_Local_Machine/Software/Microsoft/SPSSearch/Applications
```

Its Display Name property will tell you what portal site it is. The number of files and folders stored in each index folder may surprise you, but indexing is a complex process and this shows here. You do not need to configure these files, because everything is managed by SharePoint's administration pages.

The Gatherer process keeps a log of all its activities; these log files are also stored in this folder structure, but the easiest way to view these log entries is to use SharePoint's administrative web pages.

Configuring Searching and Indexing

By default SharePoint takes care of configuring the search and index feature. Still, there are a lot of things to do for an administrator, especially when you want to extend the information indexed, such as add new content sources and new file types, or just force a full re-indexing. To open the start page for all these activities, open the portal and choose Site Settings⇨Configure Search and Indexing. The resulting page is divided into three sections:

❏ **General Content Settings and Indexing Status:** Contains the status of the index, the number of documents found, and when the index was last indexed. You can also force a re-indexing from this section; see Figure 6-17.

❏ **Site Directory:** Contains the index status of team sites. You can see how many sites are indexed, if any are excluded from this indexing, and configure how often these sites will be indexed. See Figure 6-18.

❏ **Other Content Sources:** Contains a list of all sources. By default you will only see People there, which is the User Profile database, and Portal, which is the portal site itself. If you add new content sources to be indexed by SPS, they will show up in this list. See Figure 6-19.

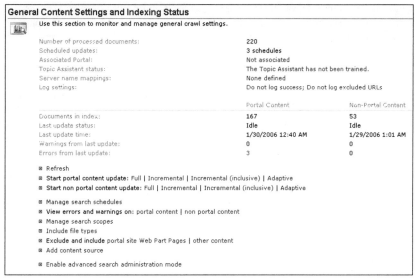

Figure 6-17

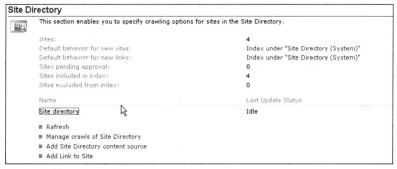

Figure 6-18

Figure 6-19

You will see a note in a red text font at the top of this page, saying "For enhanced security, portal site Web Part Pages are currently excluded from the index. To include this content in the index, click Exclude and include portal site Web Part Pages in the General Content Settings and Indexing Status section."

It simply means that the specific web part pages used for defining the look and feel of the portal area pages are not indexed. In other words, you cannot search for content in these web part pages. This is not a problem, because your users are more interested in the content of a page than its definition.

Checking Errors and Warnings

With this information in mind, you can work with the indexing feature now. For example, say you want to check for any errors or warnings listed in the General Content Settings and Indexing Status section previously mentioned. Look at the lines Warnings from last update and Errors from last update; if you see something other than 0 here, you may have a problem. In Figure 6-17 there are 3 errors from last update of the Portal Content. Click the number to see exactly what the error is, or use the link "View errors and warnings on," which will open the Gatherer log details, as shown in Figure 6-20.

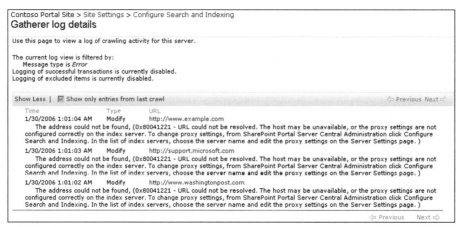

Figure 6-20

In this example the problem seems to be that the crawler process cannot access the following public sites: `www.example.com`, `www.microsoft.com`, and `www.washingtonpost.com`. In this particular case the trouble is caused by a problem accessing the Internet. But why would SharePoint try to index these sites in the first place? The answer is simple: they are listed as links in the portal sites. You may remember that in some earlier examples, you created news items and topic links pointing to these sites. SharePoint will try follow any link added to the portal areas, including sites on the Internet—but only their first web page (thank you for that!)

Forcing an Update

Still on the General Content Settings and Indexing Status page, you can see when the index was rebuilt last time. If you need to force an update very easily, just click the type of update you want next to the Start portal content update or Start non-portal content update. There are four different types of updates, each with their special focus and purpose:

❑ **Full:** This will index everything, including previously indexed information. It will also remove deleted items from the index. Note that this will not perform a total reset of the index; this is described later in this chapter. This may take a very long time, depending on the data volume indexed, also known as the *Corpus*. Select this type of update in special cases, such as the following:

❑   If this is the first time you update the index for this content source.

❑   A new file type is included or excluded for indexing.

❑   The Noise Word file is updated.

❑   An area changes name.

❑   Problems such as power outage.

❑   **Incremental:** This will index all items not previously indexed, but will not remove deleted items from the index nor index existing information. This is a very fast process compared to a Full update.

❑   **Incremental (inclusive):** This will index all new items not previously indexed, including updated web part pages. It will also remove any deleted items from the index. This process is not as fast as the Incremental update.

❑   **Adaptive:** This will index only items that are likely to be changed regularly and is a very fast process. This knowledge is based on statistical analysis; SharePoint must run for some time before this statistic is available. The idea is that frequently modified files will be indexed often, whereas static information can be skipped. To be sure not to miss any update of an infrequently modified file, SharePoint will index these files every two weeks.

Managing the Indexing Schedules

SharePoint uses different indexing schedules for different content sources. You need to know exactly when the index is updated to understand when you can expect updated information to be searchable. These are the default schedules used by SPS:

❑   **Portal Content:** All portal content will be indexed using two types of updates:

      ❑   **Incremental:** Every 10 minutes.

      ❑   **Incremental (Inclusive):** Every night at 3:00 a.m.

❑   **Non-Portal Content:** This applies to team sites.

      ❑   **Incremental:** Every night at 1:00 a.m.

The consequence of this default schedule is that new and updated information on the portal area will be discovered within 10 minutes, whereas updates in team sites will not be discovered until the next day, or 1:00 a.m. to be exact. This is probably acceptable in most cases, but if needed the schedule can be modified. Click the "Manage search schedules" link in the General Content Settings and Indexing Status section to view or modify these schedules; see Figure 6-21.

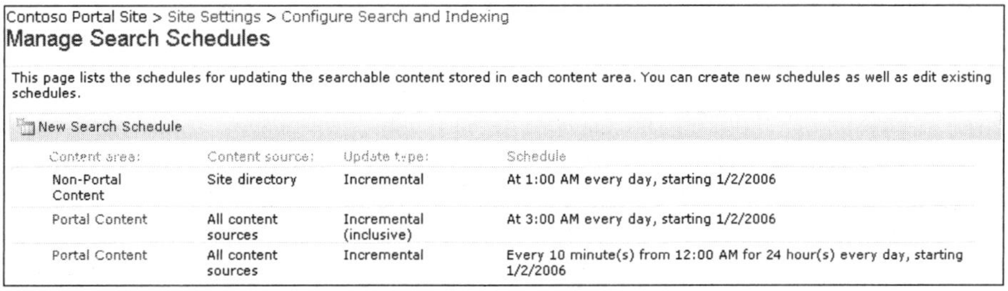

Contoso Portal Site > Site Settings > Configure Search and Indexing
Manage Search Schedules

This page lists the schedules for updating the searchable content stored in each content area. You can create new schedules as well as edit existing schedules.

New Search Schedule

Content area:	Content source:	Update type:	Schedule
Non-Portal Content	Site directory	Incremental	At 1:00 AM every day, starting 1/2/2006
Portal Content	All content sources	Incremental (inclusive)	At 3:00 AM every day, starting 1/2/2006
Portal Content	All content sources	Incremental	Every 10 minute(s) from 12:00 AM for 24 hour(s) every day, starting 1/2/2006

Figure 6-21

Note that these settings will be stored as tasks in the Windows Scheduled Tasks application. You can change the schedule in either location; the Manage search schedules web page is just a web display of SharePoint-specific scheduled tasks.

There is one special type of update that is scheduled to run every 60 minutes that will not be listed as a scheduled task. This process will check the People content, which means that the User Profile database and all personal sites are incrementally indexed. This allows the portal user to discover updated information about other users within one hour. This scheduled process will also affect what documents will be listed on the public view of a user's personal site, in the web part Recent Documents, and update the index for private documents stored in this site.

Controlling What Files to Index

When the indexing process is running, as described earlier in this chapter, the Gatherer process will open the files found in the content sources. But exactly what file types will it open? This is controlled by a list of file types accessed by the "Include file types" link on the Configure Search and Indexing page. The information in this list shows two things:

❑ What file types the Gatherer will try to open.

❑ If there is any icon defined in SharePoint for this file type.

The last bullet is interesting. If a file type does not have an icon next to it in this list, this file will not have a specific icon when listed in a document library. Instead it will have the icon used for unknown file types. This can be modified. Later in this chapter you will learn how to add an icon for the PDF file, and the same technique can be used for any file types.

Look at the list — if you are missing one file type, you can add it now by clicking New File Type. But this will not be enough; the Gatherer also needs the specific IFilter for this file type. But some file types actually are managed by the default IFilters, and still are not listed here, for example RTF files. To add that file type, click New File Type, enter **rtf**, and click OK. Note that it now is listed, and that it automatically got the MS Word icon associated to it.

> *You can use this feature to temporarily stop indexing a specific file type; just remove it from this list. Then add it when you want to index the file type again.*

Managing Search Scope

SharePoint allows you to limit the search scope, in order to make it easier for the user to find the information they are searching for. This is especially handy when the index file contains information from several content sources. For example, if the user knows that the document she is looking for is stored somewhere in the file system, set the search scope to the file system only. This will make the search faster and more focused and will generate less CPU load on the SharePoint server.

By default there is one search scope: All Sources. Use the "Manage search scopes" link on the Configure Search and Indexing page (or at the Site Settings page) to view and manage these search scopes. Edit All Sources and you will see that it is defined to include all content; everything that exists in the index files. Search scopes can be based on topics and areas, by source groups, or both. A source group is a method to group together several content sources under one name. For example, say you are indexing three file servers on your network. You need a way to refer to all three of these when creating a search scope. Creating a source group with these three content sources as members will fulfill your needs.

Depending on what scope you want to use, this is either easy or may require some planning. For example, say that you want to create a search scope that only matches information in the portal areas, but not team sites. Following is how you would do it:

Try It Out   Add a New Search Scope

1. Open the "Manage search scopes" page.

2. Click New Search Scope.

3. Enter these values:

   a. **Name:** Areas Only. This is the name for this scope.

   b. Select the option "Limit the search scope to items in the following topics or areas." Then click "Change areas." This will open the portal area tree. Check the Home area and this will cover all subareas.

   c. Select the option "Exclude all content sources."

   d. Click OK to save and close.

Another common request is to limit the search scope to team sites only. To do that you follow these steps:

1. Click New Search Scope.

2. Enter these values:

   a. **Name:** "Team Sites only."

   b. Select the option "Include no topic or area in this scope."

   c. Select the option "Limit the scope to the following groups of content sources," and then check Sites in the site directory.

   d. Click OK to save and close.

There is more to say about search scope, but first you must understand how to add new content sources, and to use the advanced search administrative mode. You learn more about that next.

Managing Crawls of the Site Directory

All team sites under the portal site will by default be indexed. If need to you can change what team sites are indexed by clicking Manage crawls of Site Directory on the Configure Search and Indexing page (or at the Site Settings page). At first it will list all sites awaiting approval (they are created but not yet published). Click Approved sites in the left pane to list all such top-level sites. Next to each site is the Crawling Behavior. If it says "Crawl this site," then this site is indexed.

The term "Site" here means "Site Collection," that is, the top site and all its subsites and workspaces.

Adding New Content Sources

When installing SharePoint the organization will have most, if not all, of its information stored in locations other than SharePoint. Even after some time, a lot of information will be kept in the old locations, often because you don't want to move old data into SharePoint, but you do not want to delete it either. An elegant solution to make this information available to the portal user is to add it to SharePoint's index files. This will enable users to search for both old and new information, without requiring them to know exactly where this information is stored.

To add external information to SharePoint's index files, you create new content sources. You may recall from a previous section in this chapter that SharePoint can index the following sources and locations: SharePoint's own database, any file server, MS Exchange folders, Lotus Notes databases, other web applications, and external web applications. The way to do that is to create content sources.

For example, say you want to index a specific file share: \\dc1\projects. Following is how to do it:

Try It Out   Add a Content Source

1. Open the Configure Search and Indexing page.

2. Click "Add content source" (the same link is listed in two places; choose either).

3. On the Content Type page, select File share. Click Next.

4. On the next page, enter these values.

   a. **Address:** \\dc1\projects.

   b. **Description:** The Projects File Share on DC1.

   c. Accept the other default settings to index this and all subfolders. Click Finish.

5. On the next page, you can set the update schedule, configure exceptions (for example to avoid indexing a given subfolder, or use a specific user account when crawling this source), and force a full update now. Normally you only need incremental updates after a full update has been performed. In this example you will configure this content source to run incremental updates every morning at 6:00 a.m. Do the following:

   a. Click "Specify incremental update schedule." Use the drop-down menu for the Schedule type and set it to Daily. The page gets updated.

   b. Set the Starting time to 6:00 AM.

   c. Click OK to save and close. You are returned to the previous page.

6. Check "Start full update" and click OK to save, and start the full update of this content source.

On the Configure Search and Indexing page you will see that the "Non-Portal Content index" changes from Idle to Crawling. Because all content sources outside the portal site are regarded as non-portal content (and right that is!), its index needs to be updated. You can also see that the number of documents in this index is increasing. When the status is idle again, the new content source is indexed and is ready to be searched.

Also look at the end of this page; the new content source is listed in the section Other Content Source. If you need to change an existing content source, just click its name and its configuration page opens. You can also force a full update again, if needed.

Click "Manage content sources" to open a page with all existing content sources. For each of these sources you see the current update status, and when it was last updated. Each content source has a menu for editing or deleting this source, or to force an update. You can also open the Gatherer log for this particular content source.

Before you can add a Lotus Notes database as a content source you must install a Lotus Notes client on the SharePoint server. The Gatherer will use this client to read the Notes database. Unless this client is installed, there will be no option to install Lotus Notes content sources.

Adding New File Types

In addition to the default file types indexed, you can add almost any other well-known file type. In fact, you can add your own type, if necessary, but this will require that you write some code to do it. You must do two things to make the Gatherer index a new file type:

❑   Make sure the file type is listed in the Include File Type list, as discussed before.

❑   Make sure there is an IFilter installed that can read this type of file.

The trick, of course, is to find the IFilter. But the good news is that there are lots of sources on the Internet. These IFilters are not specific for SharePoint's index engine, but most will also work for the SQL Server full-text indexing and other MS Search–based engines. Following is a list of the most common IFilters and at least one source. Some are free, others are commercial, but most often with a low price:

File Type	Download Source	Price
PDF	http://www.adobe.com/support/downloads/detail.jsp?ftpID=2611	Free
ZIP	http://www.citeknet.com	Free
RAR	http://www.citeknet.com	Free
HLP	http://www.citeknet.com	Free
CHM	http://www.citeknet.com	Free
MHT	http://www.citeknet.com	Free
CAB	http://www.citeknet.com	Free
EXE	http://www.citeknet.com	Free
StarOffice	http://www.IFilter.org	Free for personal use
OpenOffice	http://www.IFilter.org	Free for personal use
MindManager	http://www.IFiltershop.com	299 USD per server
MS Project	http://www.IFiltershop.com	299 USD per server
MS Visio	http://www.microsoft.com/downloads	Free
OneNote	Install MS OneNote on the SharePoint server	
Audio/Video files: MP3, WMA, WMV, ASF	http://www.aimingtech.com	Free for personal use
DWG AutoCad	http://www.cadcompany.nl	250 Euro

This list is long, and it grows constantly. Remember that each new file type indexed will increase the CPU load and the size of the index files; be sure you really need to search files, like MP3, before you add it, even if it is cool!

> www.citeknet.com *has a very nice (and free) IFilter explorer. Use it to see all IFilters installed on the server.*

If you need to remove an IFilter, just uninstall it like any other program, using the Add/Remove Programs applet in the Control Panel.

So now add PDF as an indexed file. The download link to the IFilter is listed in the preceding table, and you know how to add PDF as a file type to index. But in this case, and some others too, there will be one thing missing — users will not see the familiar PDF icon next to PDF files in SharePoint's document libraries, so you must also download this icon and install it in the proper way. Following is how to do it:

Try It Out   Index PDF Files in SPS

1. Download the IFilter for PDF as listed in the preceding table. Install the IFilter on the SharePoint server — if you are running a SharePoint farm, it must be installed on the SPS server running the Index role!

2. Open the following page in the portal site: Site Settings⇨Configure Search and Indexing⇨ Include file types.

3. Click New File Type and enter **PDF**. Click OK to save and close. Check that PDF is now listed among the indexed file types. Also note that it does not have any icon. This is a cosmetic but nevertheless important problem.

4. Download the file `pdf16.gif` from the Internet; for example `http://sps.terradigitalis .nl/download/pdf16.zip`. Save the `pdf16.gif` file in the following location on the SharePoint server: `C:\Program Files\Common Files\Microsoft Shared\web server extensions\ 60\TEMPLATE\IMAGES`.

   Do not change the name. It must be `pdf16.gif` *or else you will not see the icon in every place there is a PDF file!*

5. The next step is to teach SharePoint to display this icon for each PDF file: Open the following file with Notepad: `C:\Program Files\Common Files\Microsoft Shared\web server extensions\60\TEMPLATE\XML\DOCICON.XML`.

   > **Note: Make a backup of the original** `DOCICON.XML` **just to be safe.**

   a. Add the line `<Mapping Key="pdf" Value="pdf16.gif"/>` anywhere in the `<ByExtension>` section in this file. The exact location is not important, but why not add it before the "png" to get it in a nice order?

   b. Save and close this `DOCICON.XML`.

6. Open the SharePoint administrative page "Include file types" again—you should now see that the pdf file type has its well-known icon next to it! If not, you did something wrong.

7. Everything is now done. If you don't want to add some more file types, while you are at it, force a full update of both the portal content and non-portal content, to be sure that all existing pdf files get indexed.

Advanced Search Administrative Mode

The configuration setting discussed so far will be enough for everyday management of the search and indexing features. But some things cannot be done in this default administration mode, such as resetting an index or creating a new search index. You need to switch to the advanced search administrative mode for that. You can start using the default administration mode, and if the need comes to do more advanced search administration, you can change it at that time. It is also common to switch to the advanced mode directly after the installation of SPS, just to get used to that administrative page. There is really nothing hard or complicated to administrating the search features in advanced mode, so don't be afraid to do it.

Try It Out   **Switch to Advanced Search Administration Mode**

1. Open the Configure Search and Indexing page in the portal site.

2. Click "Enable advanced search administration mode" in the General Content Settings and Indexing Status section. This will open a new page, warning you that this can never be undone (similar to switching to Native Mode in Active Directory, for example). After taking a deep breath, click OK.

3. You return to the Configure Search and Indexing page, but it looks a bit different. Everything you know and love about this page is there, but some things are hidden behind new links.

Seriously, do not be afraid of switching to this advanced search mode; this simply gives you more options, and it is not harder to manage or configure. The following sections describe the new features in more detail.

Resetting an Index

Sometimes an index may get messed up, and the normal Full update will not fix it. The thing to do then is to delete the old index and rebuild it from scratch. Follow these steps to rebuild an index:

Try It Out   **Reset an Index Completely**

1. Open the Configure Search and Indexing page in the portal site (in advanced search mode).

2. Click "Manage content indexes." The two current indexes are listed. If you want to reset the non-portal content index, use its menu (displayed when hovering the mouse over its link) and select Reset Content Index; click OK to confirm this operation.

3. Wait until the status says that Documents in Index = 0. Using the menu for this index again, select Start Full Update. Wait for this update to be complete. Note that it may take many hours, depending on how much information it need to index.

You don't need to wait for this process to complete. Close this page and it will still run in the background.

Creating a New Index

In some situations it may be advantageous to create more index files, for example, if you have lots of content sources and you want to keep them in a separate index. Note that this will in some way create a new problem for you. This is due to how the search process lists the results from search queries.

Say that you are searching for the word "Zappa" and there are several files and locations containing this word. SharePoint will now rank the list of matching files using the following logic:

1. Any person with this name will always be listed on top — people are regarded most important in SharePoint's search logic.

2. The document containing the most instances of Zappa will be listed next.

3. Documents containing Zappa in the beginning will be on top of other documents with the same number of instances, but with the word appearing further down in the document.

The logic is actually more complex than this, but it is enough to understand how it works. The problem is that this logic only works within a given index. Each index has its own ranking. In other words, even if there is a file containing Zappa 50 times, this file may be listed further down in the total result list because another index ranking is listed first. So the more indexes you have, the greater risk that the result list is not sorted in the way the user expects. If you still want to create an index, following is how you do it:

Try It Out   Create a New Index

1. Open the Configure Search and Indexing page in the portal site (in advanced search mode).

2. Click "Add content index" (which is also available on the page "Manage content indexes").

3. On the following page, enter the following to create a new index that you will use for external content:

   a. **Name:** External-Index. This name can only contain characters, numbers, and hyphens.

   b. **Description:** External Content only.

   c. **Source Group:** External Content Only. Use an existing group name or create a new one.

   d. **Server:** SPSRV2. Select an SPS server configured to run the Index role.

   e. **Address:** If you want to store the index files for this new index in location other than default, check Use a different local address.

   f. Click OK to save.

4. Verify that this new index is now listed together with the others in the Content Indexes section.

The new index is ready to be used. When creating a new content source you can configure it to use this new index. Existing content sources cannot be modified to use another index; you will need to delete that content source and create it again.

To move existing indexes to a new location, see `ToolsHowTo.txt` *in the Support\Tools directory on the SharePoint Portal Server CD.*

Some Tips about Searching

The search and index functionality in SPS is full of features, as you have seen so far, and still there are more things you can do. This last section about searching and indexing describes two tips that may become handy. Let's start with the first one.

Enabling Wildcard Searching

Yes, this is correct—a rather simple modification in the configuration files will allow the user to do a wildcard search, so that "Admin*" will match "Administrator." Following is how you activate it.

Try It Out   **Enable Wildcard Searching**

1. Open the portal site.

2. Type in this URL address: `http://spsrv2/search.aspx?Mode=Edit&PageView=Shared`. This will display the default search results web parts. Your mission is to modify these web parts to allow full-text searching. So far you will not see much on this page.

3. Choose Modify Shared Page⇨Design this Page. Now you see the two web parts that list the search results.

4. Use the Search Results web part menu and select Export; see Figure 6-22.

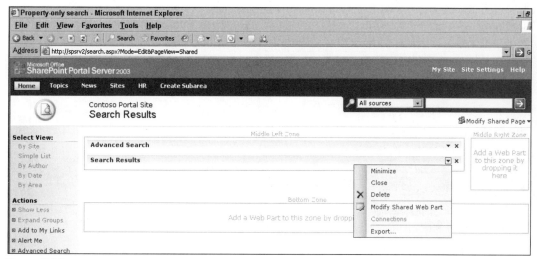

Figure 6-22

5. Click Save and store the `Search Results.dwp` on the local disk. This is a text file with all the configuration settings for this web part. The next step is to modify this file, to make it manage full-text searching.

6. Save a copy of `Search Results.dwp`, just to be safe, and then open this file using Notepad.

7. At the end of this file, locate the following code lines:

```
OR FREETEXT(#WeightedProps, '%__keywordinput__%') )
AND (%__sourcegroups__%) %__morewhereCondition__%
</QueryTemplateWherePart>
```

8. Add the following text marked in gray near the end of this web part:

```
OR FREETEXT(#WeightedProps, '%__keywordinput__%') )
AND (%__sourcegroups__%) %__morewhereCondition__%
OR CONTAINS('"%__keywordinput__%"')
</QueryTemplateWherePart>
```

9. Save and close this file.

10. Finally, replace the current web part with the new version: You are back to step 3. Use the menu for the search web part you previously exported, and delete it. Click Yes to confirm this operation.

11. Import the modified web part: Choose Modify Shared Page⇨Add Web Parts⇨Import. Use the Browse button and select the modified web part file. Click Upload.

12. Place the imported web part directly under the Advanced Search web part, that is, the same position as before.

13. Click any area page, for example Home, to leave the design mode. Search for "Admin," note the number of results, then search for "Admin*" and you will see a lot more results (probably).

Using a Custom User Account for Searching

You may remember from Chapter 4 that the Default Content Access Account is the user account used by default when the Gatherer crawls external information. If this user account doesn't have at least read access to these sources, it will generate an access error in the Gatherer log (see Figure 6-23). If you can use another account with read access granted for this particular source location, it will succeed.

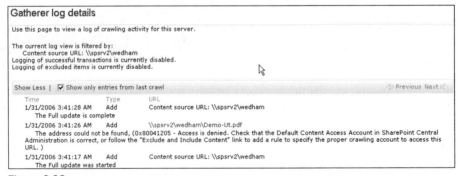

Figure 6-23

To make the content source use a special account, you must configure *Exclude and Include* rules for the content index file used by this content source. Follow these steps to set another search account when using advanced search mode:

Try It Out   **Configure a Custom Search Access Account**

1. Open the Configure Search and Indexing page. (Note that this page is also available in the default search administration mode, and you can configure a custom search account in this mode too, but some of the following steps will be slightly different).

2. Click the content index name, for example Non-Portal Content.

3. In the Status section, click View the Gatherer log. It will describe the problem as in Figure 6-23.

4. Click "Exclude and Include Content" in the left pane. This will open a page will all the rules that define how this content index manages its content sources. You must add a new rule that tells the Gatherer to use a specific account when searching one given folder path.

5. Click New Rule and enter these values to add a specific user account for the \\spsrv2\wedham file share:

    a. **Path**: \\spsrv2\wedham*. (This will be converted to "file://spsrv2/wedham/*" in the list of content for this rule).

    b. Select the option Include all items in this path.

    c. Select the option "Specify crawling account" and enter the account name and its password twice. Do not allow Basic authentication.

    d. Click OK to save this new rule. The new rule will be listed along with the other rules now, as in Figure 6-24.

Figure 6-24

6. Force an incremental update now. When ready, check the Gatherer logs to see if the content source could be indexed this time.

With this knowledge about the search and indexing process you will be able to set up the most common search scenarios, as well as solve most problems that may arise.

Summary

In this chapter you learned the following:

❏ Portal areas are built on area templates.

❏ You can create new templates, or use existing ones when you create a new area page.

❏ You must configure the portal to enable the choice of area template.

❏ Web buckets, such as C1 and C5, are URL addresses that point to area pages.

❏ Areas can be moved to any part of the portal tree without losing anything.

❏ The User Profile database stores information about portal users.

❑ SharePoint can import user properties from Active Directory to the User Profile database.

❑ User properties in the User Profile database can be added, deleted, or modified anytime.

❑ Using LDAP queries you can import only specific Organizational Units from AD.

❑ SPS uses audiences for targeting of information.

❑ Only SPS has this audience feature; team sites cannot use it.

❑ An audience is defined by creating rules, for example, "Department = IT".

❑ Almost all types of rules for compiling audiences use the User Profile database; the exception is group membership.

❑ Audience is a filtering mechanism, not a security mechanism.

❑ My Site is a personal site available for all portal users. By default members of the Reader group will not have access to any personal site.

❑ My Site has a public view that lists information and properties for each user. Some of this information may be managed by the users themselves.

❑ The security in area pages will apply to all objects belonging to that area.

❑ The number of rights is bigger for SPS than WSS, due to the more complex environment.

❑ To search in WSS you will need the MS SQL Server Full-Text Indexing engine.

❑ WSS allows only searching in the current site.

❑ Searching and Indexing will save users a lot of time. By default only content in the portal database will be indexed.

❑ SharePoint can add content sources to file servers, MS Exchange, Lotus Notes, and internal and external web sites.

❑ Besides the default file types that the index engine understands, you can add new ones.

❑ The Gatherer is the process that the Index process calls to perform crawling of content sources.

❑ The Gatherer needs an IFilter to open and read a specific file type.

❑ There are two index files by default: Portal Content and Non-Portal Content.

❑ All team sites and by default all external content sources will use the Non-Portal Content index.

❑ The portal is updated every 10 minutes, and the team sites once every night.

❑ Use Search Scopes to limit the volume to be searched.

❑ Only in Advanced Search Administration mode can you reset and delete index files.

❑ You can extend the search functionality without programming, for example to enable wildcard searches.

❑ If needed, a given source location can utilize a specific user account when crawling.

In the next chapter you learn more about the differences between SPS and WSS and understand when one or the other is the better choice.

Comparing WSS and SPS

So far you have learned a lot about what WSS can do and also what SPS offers. It can be difficult to understand when WSS or SPS would be a better choice. Many features are similar in WSS and SPS, but they do not work exactly the same way. Some web parts are only available in SPS but not in WSS. And so on. If you are new to SharePoint, you can get confused at times, but this is natural. This chapter helps clarify the differences and similarities between WSS and SPS. It summarizes information listed in other parts of this book, plus describes several other features not previously discussed.

The History of SharePoint

For many years Microsoft and other software developers focused on making products with more and more features. For example, look at MS Word 2003 — a fantastic program, so full of features and functionality that nobody understands them all or even knows they exist. Microsoft always asks MS Office users what they want to see in the next release; more than 90 percent of the requests already exist. This is one of the driving forces for changing the interface of the coming version of MS Office 2007, to ensure that users find more features and understand how to use them.

Anyone working on a team sharing information knows the challenge: to find the information you need without having to look in several places and be sure it is the latest version. Users don't need more features now; they need help organizing and sharing information, such as documents, contacts, news, and calendars. This is the reason Microsoft started to build not one, but two products to satisfy this need.

SharePoint Team Services (STS)

This web-based application was similar to what WSS looks like today. Its goal was to offer a web page where the team or group could share information, such as documents, contact lists, and announcements. It was released in 2001 and used an MSDE database to keep track of its configurations and lists. All documents were stored in the file system, but their properties, or metadata, were stored in the database.

STS was free and came bundled with FrontPage 2002. It was based upon the FrontPage Server Extensions, and most configurations and customizations required FrontPage. This SharePoint version was integrated with MS Office XP, thus enabling easy access of documents and files stored in SharePoint.

Many large companies used STS installations, including Microsoft and the former Digital Equipment Corporation (DEC), which used STS to keep track of documentation of its products. More than 50,000 users around the world used this system for more than two years.

SharePoint Portal Server 2001 (SPS)

This product focused mainly on document management, allowing the user to create custom properties and categories. It had a very powerful search engine and stored both data and configurations in its database. This product was licensed per server and per user. Some of its features competed with STS, but basically it was a completely different product, using a different database type: MS Exchange!

Initially this SharePoint version, also known as "Tahoe," was planned to be an add-on to MS Exchange Server 2000. However, during the beta testing phase, many customers told Microsoft they would never allow such a large application to run on their MS Exchange server because the e-mail system was too important for this! So when SPS 2001 was finally released, it contained its own private MS Exchange 2000 database, also known as the Exchange Information Store. More than one SPS administrator was surprised to find messages in the Event Log file that related to Exchange because they thought no Exchange database was installed on their server.

SharePoint Portal Server's strength was its document management. Combined with the features that the Exchange engine offered, it had alerts, document workflow, individual settings of folders, and even to some extent individual documents. The problem with SPS 2001 was its limited capacity to manage large volumes of data and users. It was never built to be used by large and demanding companies.

The Road Ahead from 2001

Both STS and SPS 2001 were successful; these programs were installed by many organizations, and Microsoft got a lot of feedback. Clearly it was confusing that Microsoft offered two applications with a name that indicated some sort of relationship, but if you tried to install both of them on the same server, you quickly got into trouble. It was also clear that although the MS Exchange engine offered some very nice features, it could not handle the volume of data that larger companies demanded.

The solution was to build a new generation of SharePoint products. This time, STS was enhanced with lots of new features, especially document management. The new STS was also built to store all data, both configuration and document, in its SQL Server–based database. An enhanced version of MSDE, called the WMSDE, was also developed and could be used as an alternative to the full SQL Server.

Under the hood of STS, many things also happened. No longer was this new version based on FrontPage Server Extensions; everything was rewritten to use the new ASP.NET programming environment. It was re-engineered to cope with extremely large volumes of data and to be used by millions of users. This new version was renamed rather late in the development process. Instead of STS 2.0 it was called Windows SharePoint Services, or WSS. But you can still see many references to STS 2.0 in documentation and utilities.

The largest modification was of the new SPS version. It was not just rewritten; it was totally transformed. True, they shared some resemblance, but they were definitely different. The new SPS did not have its own database. It no longer had any document management, but it did have its search engine. And the rest of its features were completely new, compared to the first version.

The new version of SPS was then redesigned to be an add-on to the new WSS. It could no longer be installed by itself. The SPS development team started building the new SPS version by copying the new WSS; they continued by adding new features not to be found in WSS and by removing some things that WSS would have. In other words, the new SPS was based on the new WSS, but many important things were changed. The goal of integration was achieved, at least when looking from the outside. This is why today's SPS 2003 looks so similar, but still different, compared to WSS 2003.

Comparing the Objectives

Both of these products contain the word "SharePoint," and this is exactly what they do: They create a point where users can share information. The name really suits the products. But Microsoft designed these two products with different objectives regarding how to enable this sharing point and what is to be shared. Remember that WSS comes free with Windows 2003, whereas SPS it not free. You can come a long way with just WSS, but in the end you will need more features, and that is where SPS comes in.

The SharePoint Philosophy

Often when people see SharePoint for the first time, they wonder why Microsoft did not add a site tree view, listing all the subsites and enabling the user to jump directly to a specific site. Microsoft did not forget to put it there. They had a clever plan when designing WSS and SPS: to make WSS attractive to small- and medium-sized teams for sharing their internal information. When these users later have created a lot of team sites, they will need a way to organize information so that users can quickly navigate to or search for what they need. This is what SPS does.

Compare this to the file system. For decades people have structured and organized shared files in such a way that users could find the file they needed. The administrators create the overall structure for these shared file systems, and sometimes even a user may be allowed to create some subfolders. Often, average users have difficulty understanding this elegant file structure and finding what they are looking for. So much difficulty, in fact, that once they find a file, they store it on their local drive (and even there they can lose it at times).

What I am trying to say is that folder trees are excellent and easy to use, especially if you created them. They are also easy to use if you are a computer-literate user who understands how the hierarchical structure works. But other users generally have a hard time navigating these folder structures. The average user doesn't want to see folder structure; he only wants to see the documents that interest him. All of them. Collected together, if possible. And — this is important — without having to know exactly where these files actually are stored. If you think about it, most users find Windows Explorer to be a nerdy tool, even though most administrators could never survive without it.

Okay, so you love tools like Windows Explorer, and now you are the SharePoint administrator. Your job is to set up an environment based on SharePoint that will be used to share files and other information among users. It sounds similar to the basic idea of the shared file system, doesn't it? So why not create a hierarchical structure with one top site, and then a number of subsites? You can do this in SharePoint; in fact, you will most likely create such a structure. And guess what? The same users who did not understand the file tree will have a hard time understanding the site tree. And it will be even harder for these users in WSS, because WSS does not come with a site tree view.

Now you ask what your users actually need — real users like sales personnel, marketing people, and HR team members. They are the users who will read, create, and modify documents, contacts, and other types of information. Here are what some common answers will be:

❑ **The average user:** "Give me one page that contains a list of all the important files, links, and information that I need."

❑ **The project leader:** "Show me a list of all my project sites."

❑ **The project member:** "Show me a status list of all current tasks that I am responsible for."

❑ **The salesperson:** "Show me a list of all information regarding this customer."

❑ **Every user:** "Give me a tool that can find any information I am interested in."

You will not hear these users saying "Give me a tool so I can go up and down the team sites in SharePoint and find the information I need." So why should you give them such a tool and even require that they must use it to find the information they need?

You shouldn't. That is why Microsoft did not ship WSS with a site tree viewer. They did not expect you to build the same type of hierarchical structure as in the file system. Instead, they gave you the team sites for collecting information about a specific subject. To make it easier for the large user community to find what they need, you can create topic areas in the portal site that contain links to information; using the audience targeting features to make sure users see only relevant information. If the users still need to find anything not listed in the area page, they can search for it.

Still, there are times when a site tree view is very valuable, and in version 3.0 of WSS you will indeed find such a tree view. If you need it today, the world is full of such tools: some free, some commercial; some very basic, others very intelligent. Following is a list of some of the most popular site tree views as of today:

❑ **SharePoint Explorer (**www.thedotnetfactory.com**):** A very smart tree view that displays all team sites, areas, and document libraries that you are allowed to use. If you right-click any node, you can directly do things that are specific for this type of node; for example, right-click a document library and you can create a new document or customize its property settings. This cool tool is not free, and it is licensed based on the number of clients. Check the vendor's web site to find out the exact price.

❑ **Universal SharePoint Manager (**www.idevfactory.com**):** A very advanced tool with complete tree views of sites, areas, and their content. It also has a lot of management features for content and users. The administrator and power users who create and manage sites and areas will find this tool very interesting. This nice tool is also licensed per user client.

❑ **Site Navigator** and **Area Navigator** (`sharepoint.advis.ch`): Two very nice tree view web parts that also display lists and libraries, plus a lot more. For roughly $200 you get a lot of functionality. This company also has many other interesting web parts and tools for SharePoint.

❑ **Microsoft.Sharepoint.menu** (`www.gotdotnet.com`): A free site tree viewer that displays all the subsites, lists, and libraries. It also works for portal areas. To find this tool in this very rich web site, type **Microsoft.SharePoint.Menu** in the search field.

The Primary Objective for WSS

Microsoft designed WSS to be the perfect place to share information between a limited number of users, such as a project team, a sales group, or a small department. It is not meant to be the intranet for a large group of users, because it cannot target information or hide objects that the user cannot open. Use WSS for things like these:

❑ **Managing project information:** Store everything about the project in this site, including documents, contact lists, project calendars, and issue lists.

❑ **Product management:** Store everything about a specific product in this site, such as documentation, price lists, customers, issues, and frequently asked questions.

❑ **Local intranet for the Sales department:** Post news and announcements, list customer information, store templates for quotes and purchase orders, and link to partners and vendors.

❑ **Meeting sites:** Store everything about the meeting details here, such as decisions, tasks, activities, protocols, and agendas.

The idea is that the information in one team site is focused on one specific subject. All members in this site will quickly find the information they need about this subject. They will also add and update documents, lists, and other information for this team site.

The Primary Objective for SPS

The portal site has a different objective from that of WSS. It is designed to be a smart intranet for any size organization and to enable you to build navigational structures based on topics and areas. As explained in the previous section, SPS enables you to create area pages with links to the information needed by users. The nice thing with this feature is that the user does not have to know exactly where the underlying information is stored. And using the audience targeting feature in SPS, these pages and their links will only be visible for the right group of users.

Areas should not be used as workspaces. They are meant to be used to access information. Most likely there will be only a limited number of users with write access to the portal areas, whereas the majority of users will be consumers of this information. One clear indication of this is the default names for the document libraries:

❑ **Shared Documents:** The default name for document libraries in WSS team sites.

❑ **Document Library:** The default name for the same type of library in the portal areas.

The portal area is also the place to find information not listed in the usual places visited by the user. Its search functionality is very powerful, and you can find almost anything you look for, regardless of where it may be stored.

The personal sites (called My Site) in SPS are also a very powerful method of giving the users information about people, including their contact information, organizational location, and much more. The private view of a personal site is also the perfect starting page for any user, because it contains targeted information, such as news, links, and his inbox and calendar. The user also has access to private document and picture libraries that can replace the traditional home directory most organizations are using today.

To summarize the objectives of the portal site: This is a shared place for all users in the organization; still, it may only show targeted information for each user. It is also the place to go when the user needs to navigate to information. The portal site is all about informing and navigation — consuming information, not creating it!

Comparing Security

Even though SPS is built on the WSS technology, it has very different security settings because it has a different purpose and usage. To summarize, these are the most important differences:

- ❏ List security
- ❏ Site security and rights
- ❏ Visibility of objects
- ❏ Cross-site groups

List Security

When working with lists, document libraries, and picture libraries in WSS team sites, it is important to be able to define exactly what each user can do. For some lists you may also need to grant access to users outside this team site without granting them access to the whole site. WSS gives you this control. Every list inherits the team site's general permission settings, but if necessary these settings can be customized. For example, say that the user Axel is a member of the Reader site group for this team site, and he needs full access to all the documents in the Shared Documents library. Just add this user to this particular document library, as Figure 7-1 shows.

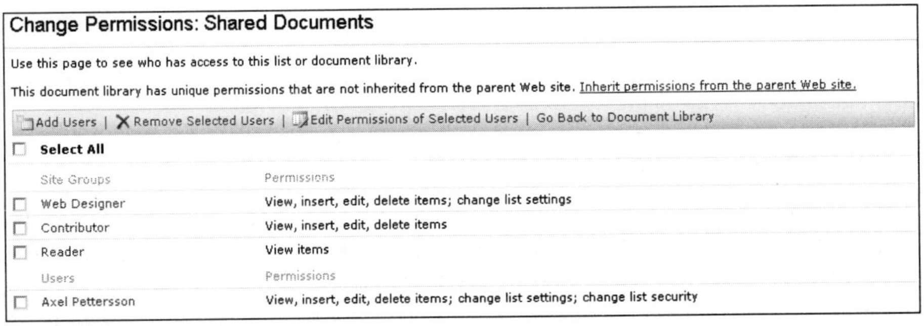

Change Permissions: Shared Documents	
Use this page to see who has access to this list or document library.	
This document library has unique permissions that are not inherited from the parent Web site. Inherit permissions from the parent Web site.	
☐Add Users | ✖ Remove Selected Users | ☐Edit Permissions of Selected Users | Go Back to Document Library	
☐ **Select All**	
Site Groups	Permissions
☐ Web Designer	View, insert, edit, delete items; change list settings
☐ Contributor	View, insert, edit, delete items
☐ Reader	View items
Users	Permissions
☐ Axel Pettersson	View, insert, edit, delete items; change list settings; change list security

Figure 7-1

This is not possible in the portal areas. The lists and libraries just don't have the option to configure permission rights. The security settings for these lists are inherited from the area page itself, and these settings are not possible to customize for individual lists. Compare Figure 7-2, which shows the configuration page for a document library in WSS, with Figure 7-3, which is the same type of document library but in a portal area page. Notice that the link "Change permissions for this document library" is missing here.

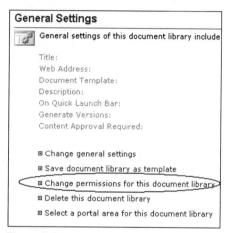

Figure 7-2

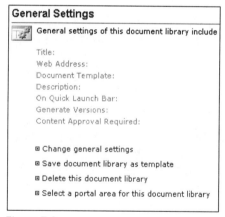

Figure 7-3

This is a very good reason to use WSS team sites and not portal areas for collaborations.

Site Security and Rights

The portal site and team sites share a lot of rights, but each site type also has its own set of rights. This is because of the differing functionality between WSS and SPS; for example, only the portal site has rights related to areas. The following table lists all the rights that exist in SPS and WSS:

Rights	Where	Description
View Area	SPS	View an area and its contents.
View Pages	SPS	View pages in an area.
Manage List Permission	WSS	Grant, deny, or change user permissions to a list.
Manage Lists	WSS	Approve content in lists, add or remove columns in a list, and add or remove public views of a list.
Add Items	SPS/WSS	Add items to lists, add documents to document libraries, and add web discussion comments.
Edit Items	SPS/WSS	Edit items in lists, edit documents in document libraries, edit web discussion comments in documents, and customize web part pages in document libraries.
Delete Items	SPS/WSS	Delete items from a list, documents from a document library, and web discussion comments from documents.
View Items	WSS	View items in lists, documents in document libraries, and web discussion comments; set up e-mail alerts for lists.
Manage Site Groups	WSS	Create, change, and delete site groups, including adding users to the site groups and specifying which rights are assigned to a site group.
View Usage Data	SPS	View reports on web site usage.
Create Subsites	WSS	Create subsites such as team sites, meeting workspace sites, and document workspace sites.
Manage Web Site	WSS	Grant the ability to perform all administration tasks for the web site as well as manage content and permissions.
Manage Personal Views	SPS/WSS	Create, change, and delete personal views of lists.
Add/Remove Personal Web Parts	SPS/WSS	Add or remove web parts on a personalized web part page.
Update Personal Web Parts	SPS/WSS	Update web parts to display personalized information.
Cancel Check-Out	SPS/WSS	Check in a document without saving the current changes.
Add and Customize Pages	SPS/WSS	Add, change, or delete HTML pages or web part pages; edit the web site using a Windows SharePoint Services–compatible editor.
Apply Themes and Borders	WSS	Apply a theme or borders to the entire web site.
Create Area	SPS	Create an area on the portal site.
Manage Area	SPS	Delete or edit the properties for an area on the portal site.

Rights	Where	Description
Manage Area Permissions	SPS	Add, remove, or change user rights for an area.
Apply Style Sheets	SPS/WSS	Apply a style sheet (CSS) to an area or the portal site.
Browse Directories	SPS/WSS	Browse directories in an area.
View Pages	WSS	View pages in a web site.
Create Personal Site	SPS	Create a personal SharePoint site (My Site).
Create Sites	SPS	Create SharePoint sites by using Self-Service Site Creation.
Use Personal Features	SPS	Use alerts on portal content and personal sites (My Site).
Manage Alerts	SPS	Change alert settings for the portal site and manage alerts for users.
Manage User Profiles	SPS	Add, change, or delete user profile information and properties.
Manage Audiences	SPS	Add, change, or delete audiences.
Manage Portal Site	SPS	Specify portal site properties and manage site settings.
Manage Search	SPS	Add, change, or delete index and search settings in the portal site.
Search	SPS	Search the portal site and all related content.
Create Cross-Site Groups	WSS	Create a group of users who can be granted access to any site within the site collection.

Besides the differences in rights in WSS and SPS, there are also differences in the permissions for the default site groups. These differences may be a source for confusion at first, but when you know they exist it is easy to cope with them. Chapter 5 discusses site groups and how to manage them. The following table summarizes the differences for the three default site groups for both WSS and SPS:

Site Group	WSS	SPS
Reader	Can read, copy, and print informa- and create alerts.	Can read, copy, and print information. tion Can search, but cannot create alerts.
Contributor	Can create, modify, and delete list itemsand documents. Can use personal views and web parts in sites. Can create cross-site groups. Cannot create subsites.	Can view areas. Can create, modify, and delete list items and documents. Can create News items and topic links, but not change or delete them. Can use personal views and web parts in sites. Can create sites, including My Site.
Web Designer	Can do everything except manage list settings, manage site groups, create subsites, and manage this web site.	Can do everything except manage area permissions and configure Audience, User profiles, Alert settings, and Search settings.

Visibility of Objects

WSS and SPS also treat protected objects differently. This is one of the great confusions for users of SharePoint. Luckily this is fixed in the SharePoint 2007. The rules are these:

❑   **SPS:** Objects that you don't have at least read access to are hidden.

❑   **WSS:** Objects that you don't have read access to are visible; but if you try to open or click on these objects, you will be asked to enter a user account and password.

This is how it works: A user with at least read access to a team site can see all links, lists, and libraries, even to those that they do not have access to. If the user tries to open such a link or list, she will be prompted for a user account and password. The reason is that MS Internet Information Service (IIS) discovers that the user is trying to access a resource without the proper permissions. It is not WSS that prompts the user for the user account and password; it is IIS! You can actually see an entry in the IIS log file when this happens.

For example, at 5 p.m. the user Anna tries to create a site. But she is just a member of the Contributor site group, and these members cannot create subsites. Anna gets prompted three times. After that, the control is returned to WSS, which offers the user a chance to send a request to the owner of this site. See Figure 7-4.

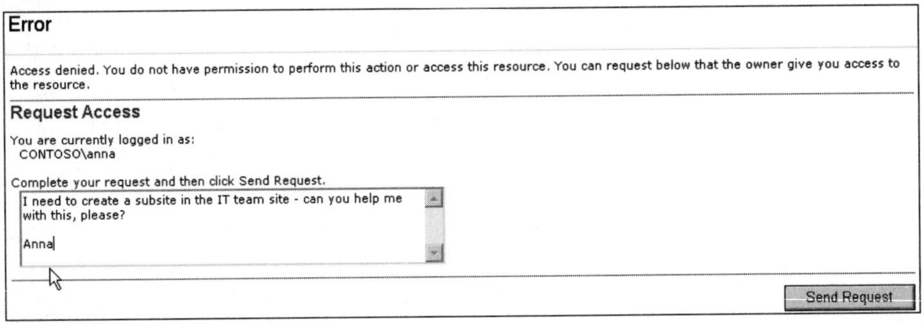

Error

Access denied. You do not have permission to perform this action or access this resource. You can request below that the owner give you access to the resource.

Request Access

You are currently logged in as:
   CONTOSO\anna

Complete your request and then click Send Request.

I need to create a subsite in the IT team site - can you help me with this, please?

Anna

Send Request

Figure 7-4

Anna enters a message and then clicks Send Request. This message is now sent to the owner of this team site. He receives the message in Figure 7-5.

Note that the message is sent from the default SharePoint sender address that is described in more detail in Chapter 2. This message contains a link that allows the owner of the site to quickly find the web page used to manage this request.

Now look at the log file: Because Anna tried to access something she was not allowed to read, IIS will store this event in the log file. Use Windows Explorer and open the following folder on the SharePoint server:

```
C:\WINDOWS\system32\LogFiles\W3SVC1
```

Use Notepad and open the latest file in this folder; it will have a name similar to `ex060202.log`, where the current date is part of the file name. In this file, locate the time when this happened. Note that IIS uses GMT time zone, regardless of what regional setting is used by the server. In this file you will see something like this:

```
2006-02-02 16:00:31 W3SVC1 192.168.15.241 POST /_layouts/1033/newsbweb.aspx - ⤸
80 contoso\anna 192.168.15.241 Mozilla/4.0+(compatible;+MSIE+6.0; ⤸
+Windows+NT+5.2;+SV1;+.NET+CLR+1.1.4322;+InfoPath.1) 401 5 0
2006-02-02 16:00:33 W3SVC1 192.168.15.241 POST /_layouts/1033/newsbweb.aspx - ⤸
80 - 192.168.15.241
```

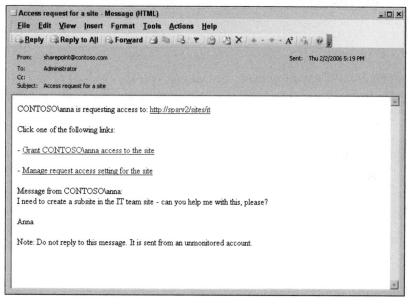

Figure 7-5

It says that at `16:00` GMT (5 p.m.) `contoso\anna` tried to access `newsbweb.aspx` (new sub-web) from a computer with the IP number `192.168.15.241`. The response was error `401` with the sub-error code 5. The question is: What does error `401 5` mean? There are lots of places where you could find the answer; one place is on the server. Open the following folder:

```
C:\WINDOWS\Help\iisHelp\common
```

Look for a file with the same name, or in this example `401.5`. Open it and read the description; see Figure 7-6.

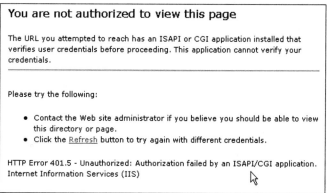

Figure 7-6

It tells you that the user Contoso\Anna was not authorized to view this `newsbweb.aspx` file. The best solution would be if Anna did not see this link unless she was allowed to use it, but this is something you will get with WSS 2007.

Cross-Site Groups

WSS has the concept of local groups, similar to security groups in Active Directory. These groups can be very handy when you need to group a number of users but don't want to create a new security group in Active Directory. These are called *cross-site groups* in WSS.

A cross-site group is only visible within its own site collection. You cannot export or copy a cross-site group to another site collection. This is one of several good reasons to keep the number of site collections to a minimum.

SPS does not have anything that corresponds to cross-site groups. If you need to work with groups in the portal site, you must create them in Active Directory.

Comparing Web Parts

Another area where SPS differs from WSS is web parts. To sum it in two lines:

❑   All web parts that work in WSS will also work in SPS, except for Members.

❑   The majority of web parts in SPS will not work in WSS.

One reason that some web parts work only in SPS is that they are *target-aware*, meaning that you can use audiences to control who will see this web part. Because WSS does not support audiences, these web parts will not work in team sites. A web part designed for portal areas is also exclusive for SPS.

Another reason is that SPS supports a feature called *Single Sign-On* (SSO). This feature makes it possible to create connections from SharePoint web parts to other web-based applications that use their own proprietary authentication mechanism; some typical examples here are Siebel and SAP. The SharePoint administrator can store the logon account and password in a special database in SharePoint, called SSO. The web parts that can take advantage of this SSO database will work only in SPS.

The web parts that work only in SPS are listed in the following table:

Web Part	Description
Area Contents	Use to display content of subareas
Area Details	Use to display area details, such as description and contact information
Grouped Listings	Use to display listings in an area displayed in groups
Links for You	Use to display links targeted to you
My Alert Summary	Use to display your alerts and alert results
My Calendar	Use to display your Outlook Calendar

Web Part	Description
My Inbox	Use to display your Outlook Inbox
My Links	Use to display your links
My Mail Folder	Use to display any Outlook folder
My Tasks	Use to display your Outlook tasks
My Workspace Sites	Use to display your workspace sites
News	Use to display the five latest news items in an area
News Areas	Use to display listings grouped by area
News for You	Use to display News targeted for you
Portal Owner QuickStart	Use for QuickStart links
Topic Assistant Suggestions	Use to display Topic Assistant suggestion for an area
Your Recent Documents	Use to display recent documents authored by you

A web part that many organizations look for is something that lets users view their Outlook content also in WSS. Because the web parts My Inbox and My Calendar are exclusive for SPS, you cannot use them in WSS. However, there are some products that solve this need; for example, look at My Workplace for Outlook (www.corasworks.com). It is a very nice web part that displays all the personal Outlook folders, including all their standard functionality. This web part is actually better than the Outlook web parts that come with SPS; see Figure 7-7.

But you can also write your own code to display Outlook folders; see the next chapter for more information about managing web parts.

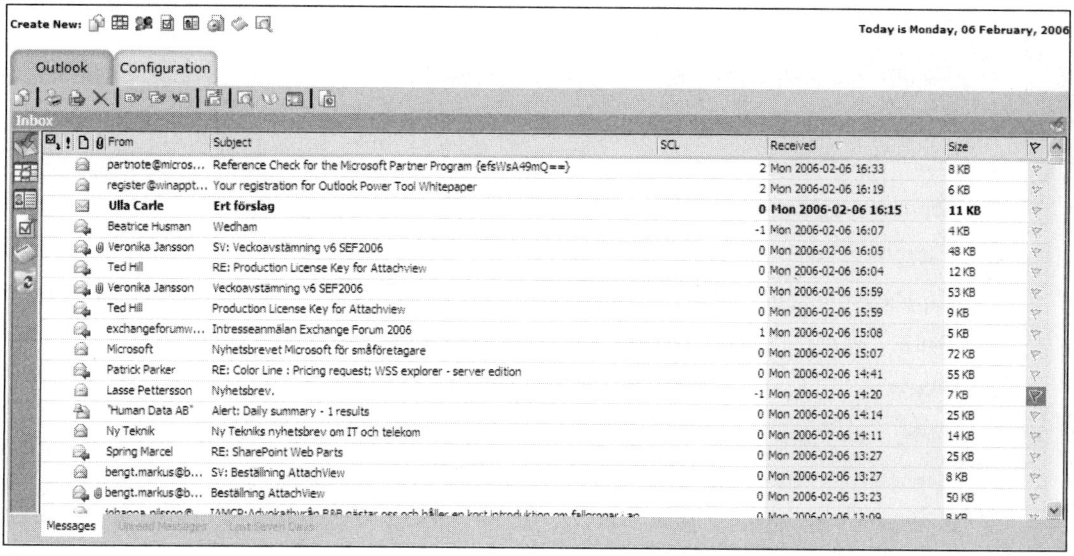

Figure 7-7

Comparing Customization

The methods for customizing SPS are very different from those for customizing WSS in several important aspects. It is fair to say that it is easier to change at least some parts of WSS sites. For both products you will need FrontPage to do some customizations, such as adding and modifying web part zones. Note that there is no other web design tool that understands how SharePoint and its web parts work.

With Visual Studio 2005 .NET, you as a developer can do most, if not all, the customization that previously only FrontPage allowed you to do.

Customizing Colors and Styles

With WSS you can use themes to set colors, background pictures, and styles for a give team site. These themes are really FrontPage themes, and you can create or modify any theme if necessary. In Chapter 12 you learn more about creating new themes with FrontPage. Following is a list of the default themes available in every team site:

- ❑ **Default theme:** Also referred to as "No Theme" because it uses the CSS files instead of themes. This gives the team site the default blue look.
- ❑ **Afternoon:** A yellow theme.
- ❑ **Arctic:** A light gray theme.
- ❑ **Blue Calm:** A dark blue theme, designed for users with sight disabilities.
- ❑ **Breeze:** A very dark blue theme, for users with sight disabilities.
- ❑ **Canyon:** A dark green theme, for users with sight disabilities.
- ❑ **Compass:** A light gray theme.
- ❑ **Concrete:** A gray theme.
- ❑ **Deep Blue:** A dark blue theme, for users with sight disabilities.
- ❑ **Evergreen:** A dark green theme, for users with sight disabilities.
- ❑ **Ice:** A light blue theme.
- ❑ **Iris:** A lilac theme.
- ❑ **Journal:** A light gray theme with red text.
- ❑ **Papyrus:** A green/brown theme.
- ❑ **Ripple:** A dark blue theme, for users with sight disabilities.
- ❑ **Satin:** A dark red theme, for users with sight disabilities.
- ❑ **Sky:** A gray/blue theme.
- ❑ **Slate:** A dark gray/black theme, for users with sight disabilities.
- ❑ **Sonora:** A brown/orange theme.
- ❑ **Spring:** A light yellow theme.
- ❑ **Water:** A blue theme with white text.

SPS does not support themes; the only way to change colors is by modifying a Cascading Style Sheet (CSS) file. You can also use CSS files to control how WSS sites look and feel, instead of using templates. The CSS files used by SharePoint are these:

- ❑ **OWS.CSS:** The base style sheet, used by all SPS team sites.

- ❑ **SPS.CSS:** A special style sheet for SPS pages only.

Both of these files are stored in the following folder location on the SharePoint server:

```
C:\Program Files\Common Files\Microsoft Shared\web server ⤴
extensions\60\TEMPLATE\LAYOUTS\1033\STYLES
```

You can modify these style sheet files directly, but this is neither easy nor smart, because an update may overwrite your modification. It is smarter to create a custom CSS file and then instruct SharePoint to apply its settings after the default CSS file. This custom CSS file will have precedence over the default one. To make SharePoint use the custom CSS file, do this:

1. Open the portal site.

2. Choose Site Settings⇨Change portal site properties and SharePoint site creation settings.

3. In the section Custom Cascading Style Sheet, enter the location, for example: `/_layouts/1033/styles/MyStyle.css`. This example assumes that the custom CSS file is named `MyStyle.css` and is stored in the default Styles directory, as listed previously.

The only problem with this method is that it works only with the portal site. WSS does not have any interface where you can apply a custom CSS file. If you want to change the WSS style sheet, you must either modify the `OWS.CSS` file directly or (recommended) create a new template using FrontPage. These templates are in fact CSS files in disguise.

Customizing the Site Layout

The methods to do this are similar on both WSS and SPS sites. You either modify the .aspx files that define the layout of the sites (usually the `Default.aspx` file) or modify the page directly with FrontPage 2003. Both of these methods have their issues:

- ❑ **Modify the .aspx files directly:** This modification will apply immediately on all sites using this file, but it requires that you know exactly what you are doing. If you make an error, the page will not be displayed. Even worse, an update or service pack for SharePoint may overwrite this file.

- ❑ **Modify the site page with FrontPage 2003:** This is easier, because you will see what you are changing. However, because you now are modifying the layout of the site, SharePoint can no longer use the default .aspx file stored in the file system. The layout of this site will now be stored in the content database, and therefore it may take longer to open this page. This is also known as *un-ghosting*. This may (or may not) be a problem, depending on how large a SharePoint environment you are running. For organizations with fewer than 3,000 users, you will not notice any difference in the time it takes to load the page. Even for larger organizations it may be hard to notice any delay. Maybe the real issue with this method is that all sites are now individually stored. Say that you want to move a menu on 50 team sites that are un-ghosted; you must now open every one of these sites with FrontPage and change them individually.

For more information about these .aspx files, see Chapter 5 and its section about customizing sites.

Site Definitions for WSS

Both SPS and WSS allow you to create new site layouts in the file system without any need to un-ghost them. For WSS this is known as creating new *site definitions*. A site definition consists of several files and is similar to themes in the way that it is used to define both the layout of a site and its look and feel. There are several advantages to using this method:

1. It is not affected when applying service packs or upgrades.

2. Any modification is immediately effective.

3. Modifications of the site definition apply to both existing and new sites.

The drawback to this method is that it is harder than using FrontPage. You must understand how the .aspx files are constructed. It is not at all impossible, but make sure to test this method before modifying your production environment!

There is much to learn about creating a site definition; fortunately a lot of information is available on the Internet that describes what you can do, and how. A very good resource is the web site `http://www.sharepointcustomization.com`, which is hosted by Microsoft's FrontPage team in Redmond. The best way of understanding this is to create a simple site definition. Follow these steps to create a new site definition named Projects:

Try It Out   Create a Site Definition

1. By default you have one site definition named STS used by all WSS sites. Copy all the files and subfolders for this site template folder in the following location:

```
C:\Program Files\Common Files\Microsoft Shared\Web Server ⊃
Extensions\60\Template\1033\STS
```

2. Create a new folder in the same folder level with the name Project.

```
C:\Program Files\Common Files\Microsoft Shared\Web Server ⊃
Extensions\60\Template\1033\Project
```

3. Paste all the files and subfolders from step 1 into the Projects folder.

4. Copy the `WEBTEMP.XML` file and save it with the new name `WEBTEMPPROJECT.XML` in the following folder. Note it is important that the file name begins with `WEBTEMP` and ends with same name as the new site definition:

```
C:\Program Files\Common Files\Microsoft Shared\Web Server ⊃
Extensions\60\Template\1033\XML
```

5. The `WEBTEMPPROJECT.XML` file contains a list of all the templates available for this site definition. Because you copied the default WSS site definition, it will contain all the familiar templates you have used so far. Now clean it up a bit. Remove everything except these lines:

```xml
<?xml version="1.0" encoding="utf-8" ?>
<Templates xmlns:ows="Microsoft SharePoint">
    <Template Name="PROJECT" ID="10111">
        <Configuration ID="0" Title="Contoso Project Site" Type="0"
            Hidden="FALSE"
            ImageUrl="/_layouts/images/stsprev.png"
```

```
            Description="This template provides the lists for projects">
        </Configuration>
    </Template>
</Templates>
```

6. The next file to modify is ONET.XML. This file defines the top link bar and the Quick Launch bar on the left side of the page. It also defines what lists and default documents are available for this site. For each list and library, it also defines their default columns and settings. Open ONET.XML in your new site definition folder PROJECT\XML and look at the following code snippet. It defines the standard links on all sites, such as "Documents and Lists" and "Site Settings." Now add a link at the top that points to the portal site address http://spsrv2 using the gray line in the following code:

```
<NavBarLink Name="Documents and Lists"
    Url="_layouts/[%=System.Threading.Thread.CurrentThread.CurrentUICulture.LCID%]/
    viewlsts.aspx">
</NavBarLink>

<NavBarLink Name="Create"
    Url="_layouts/[%=System.Threading.Thread.CurrentThread.CurrentUICulture.LCID%]/
    create.aspx">
</NavBarLink>

<NavBarLink Name="Site Settings"
    Url="_layouts/[%=System.Threading.Thread.CurrentThread.CurrentUICulture.LCID%]/
    settings.aspx">
</NavBarLink>

<NavBarLink Name="Go to Portal" Url="http://spsrv2"> </NavBarLink>

<NavBarLink Name="Help"
    Url='javascript:HelpWindowKey("NavBarHelpHome")'>
</NavBarLink>
```

7. Finally, there is one more important file for the site definition: SCHEMA.XML. This is stored in each folder under PROJECT\LISTS\<list name> (for example, PROJECT\LISTS\CONTACTS). The SCHEMA.XML file defines the columns, views, and content of this particular list. To keep this example simple, you don't change these SCHEMA.XML files this time. Just open one of them with Notepad to see what they contain.

8. Restart IIS by going to Start⇨Run⇨IISRESET.

9. Test the new site definition. Create a new site. Make sure to select the PROJECT template, as in Figure 7-8. When the site is created, click the Go to Portal link and verify that it works.

10. Just for fun, open ONET.XML and change the URL address for the Go to Portal link to http://www.microsoft.com. Run IISRESET and refresh the team site. Note that the link now points to the new URL address. This type of modification that affects existing team sites is unique for site definitions. It is not possible for modifications done with FrontPage 2003.

As you can see, it is rather easy to create a site definition. The hard work is understanding how to configure the ONET.XML and the SCHEMA.XML files. A good source to start with is this article: http://dotnet.sys-con.com/read/48162_1.htm. Another excellent source is of course Microsoft's own msdn.microsoft.com site; search for Site Definition and you will get a list of several documents.

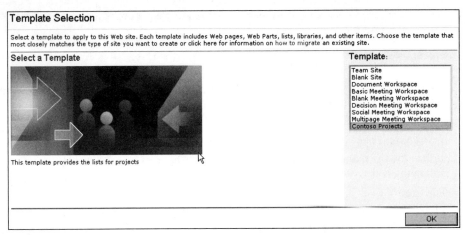

Figure 7-8

Area Templates for SPS

With SPS it is possible to create a layout configuration similar to the site definition in WSS. In SPS you use what are called *area templates*. You use area templates when you need to create a new layout with specific settings for your organization. The steps for creating area templates are similar to those for creating site definitions, and the level of understanding and knowledge needed to configure these area templates are the same.

All existing area templates are stored in the same root folder structure as the WSS site definitions:

```
C:\Program Files\Common Files\Microsoft Shared\web server ⮌
extensions\60\TEMPLATE\1033
```

You may recall that 1033 is the LCID code for U.S. English. If you are installing another SPS language, it will have another LCID number; see more about this in Chapter 5.

The folders in the preceding structure contain all the default area templates. All of them begin with SPS:

- ❑ **SPS:** The Home area page of the portal site.
- ❑ **SPSCOMMU:** The Community area page of the portal site.
- ❑ **SPSMSITE:** The My Site home page of the portal site.
- ❑ **SPSPERS:** The team sites under My Site on the portal site.
- ❑ **SPSNEWS:** The News area page of the portal site.
- ❑ **SPSNHOME:** The News home page of the portal site.
- ❑ **SPSSITES:** The Site Directory page of the portal site.
- ❑ **SPSTOC:** The Topics home page of the portal site.
- ❑ **SPSTOPIC:** The area pages under the Topics home page.

To create a new area template, follow these steps. In this example, you copy an existing template and modify it to suit your needs:

Try It Out   Create Area Templates

1. Use Windows Explorer and navigate to the TEMPLATE\1033 root folder. Create a new directory named SPSMYTMPL on the same level as all the other area template folders.

2. Copy all the files and subfolders from SPSNEWS and paste them into SPSMYTMPL. In other words, you are copying the existing area template.

3. To make SharePoint aware of this new template, you must add a new WEBTEMP*.XML file. Open the TEMPLATE\1033\XML folder. Copy the WEBTEMPSPS.XML file and paste it as the new file WEBTEMPSPSMYTMPL.XML in the same folder.

4. Edit the WEBTEMPSPSMYTMPL.XML file so it contains these lines only. Note that the Template Name must be equal to the folder name for this area template. It must also be in capital letters:

```
<?xml version="1.0" encoding="utf-8" ?>
<Templates xmlns:ows="Microsoft SharePoint">
    <Template Name="SPSMYTMPL" ID="10102">
        <Configuration ID="0" Title="My Template" Type="0"
        Hidden="TRUE"
        ImageUrl="/_layouts/images/spshome.gif"
        Description="This is a demo of area templates" />
    </Template>
</Templates>
```

5. Run IISRESET. After that, the new template is available when creating portal areas, as Figure 7-9 shows.

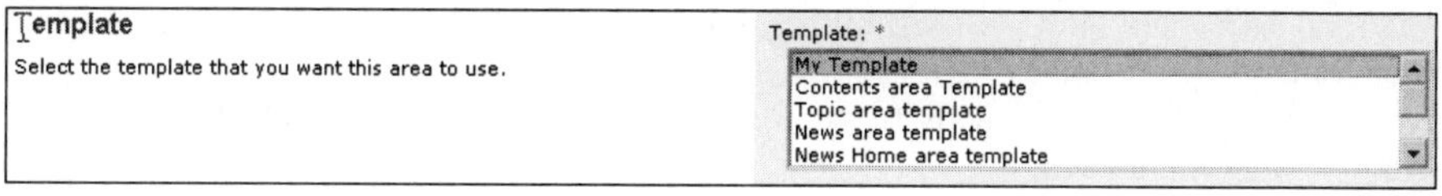

Figure 7-9

This new area template is a copy of the News area. The next logical step is then to customize it for your needs. There are two methods to do this:

❑   Edit Default.aspx with Notepad and do things such as adding web part zones and adjusting the look and feel of this page. This file is stored in the SPSMYTMPL folder. Changes will immediately affect all new and existing area pages, based on this template. No IISRESET is necessary.

❑   Edit the XML configuration files for this area template. The most important file is ONET.XML, and it works the same way as the ONET.XML file for WSS site definitions, in that it assists SharePoint when building the page using the Default.aspx file. You must run IISRESET to activate the updated configuration.

> Some changes in ONET.XML, such as adding new web parts, apply only to new areas, not existing areas! This is the most important drawback of this method.

The challenge here is to understand how the ONET.XML file works and what you can do with it. In general, the different sections in this file describe this information in the following order:

❑ **NavBars:** This section describes the layout of the navigation bar at the top of this page.

❑ **ListTemplates:** This section creates the templates for all the lists to be used by the configurations. It uses the BaseTypes section to control the basic fields and other detail information. It also describes global settings for the list, including its ID, descriptive text, and an image.

❑ **DocumentTemplates:** This section defines what document templates the user can select as the default document template in Document Libraries.

❑ **BaseTypes:** This section defines the columns and views for a created list. The ListTemplates section uses the BaseTypes section to create a completely formed list.

❑ **Configurations:** This section maps the configurations referred to in the WEBTEMP*.XML file in the XML directory directly under the 1033 folder. The configuration section defines what things to include in a configuration, including Web Parts, Web Part pages ("Modules"), and Lists ("ListTemplates").

❑ **Modules:** This section describes what files are to be added to the SharePoint site and their configuration. Every Web Part page in SharePoint is a file. This section describes what web parts to display on that file. It also controls the layout of the navigation bar on those pages.

Comparing Templates

SharePoint allows you to create templates for several types of objects, such as team sites, lists, and document libraries. Just open an existing object and save it as a template. This is a very handy when you need to re-create any of these objects with a customized look and feel. For example, say that your company decides that all document libraries used for legal documents must contain the columns Security Class and Client Name. Instead of adding these two columns every time a new document library is created, you can create a template with exactly this configuration. The user simply selects this template when creating a new document library.

It can be hard to understand the difference between a site template and a site definition. A site definition is the basic description of how a site should look and feel, and a site template is a deviation from that site definition. Site definitions are stored in the file system, whereas site templates are stored in SharePoint's content database.

However, SPS and WSS support this template feature in different ways:

❑ **Site Templates:** Can only be created in WSS team sites.

❑ **Document Library Templates:** Can be created in both SPS and WSS, but only templates in WSS will be available in all the subsites in the current site collection. Templates in SPS will only be available in the area page where it was created.

❑ **Image Library Templates:** Same logic as for Document Library Templates.

❑ **List Templates:** Same logic as for Document Library Templates.

Templates are important features in SharePoint that make it much easier to use customized lists, libraries, and team sites. Make sure to understand them and get the most out of them.

Creating Site Templates

Assume your company designs a team site especially for a project, using a number of customized lists and document libraries, maybe even some extra web parts and a special theme. Wouldn't it be nice if this design could be saved so the next time someone needs to create a project site, they could make it look exactly like the first one? This is what site templates are for.

Note that only WSS allows you to create site templates in this way, without requiring any changes to the `Default.aspx` or `ONET.XML` files. All you need is to use the built-in features of SharePoint. If you need to do more advanced customization, you may need FrontPage 2003. Still, all of this customization and design work is possible to save in a site template.

In the following example, you create a site template for all future IT projects. It needs one document library named Project Documentation, one customized list named Time Reports, one Project Contact list, and one Project Calendar. It also uses the Afternoon theme. You can use any existing site as the base for a site template, but in this example you will create it from scratch. Follow these steps to create this site template:

Try It Out   **Create a Site Template**

1. The first thing to do is to create a site exactly the way you want the new site template to be:

   a. Open the Site area page in the portal.

   b. Click Create Site.

   c. Give it a Title: **Project Template**.

   d. Give it an URL name: **ptemp**.

   e. Click Create.

2. The "Add link to site" page opens. Enter the Description: **A template site for projects**. Click OK to go on to next page.

3. On the Template Selection page, select Blank Site and click OK. After a few seconds you will see the new (and rather empty) site.

4. It is time to make this site look exactly like the project template sites should look. Use the Create link at the top menu and create the following lists and library:

   a. Choose Create⇨Document Library. In the Name field, enter **Project Documents**. Click Create.

   b. Choose Create⇨Custom List. In the Name field, enter **Time Reports**. Click Create. Click Modify settings and columns. Click Add a new column and name it **Name**. Click OK. Click Add a new column and name it **Date**; select Date and time and click OK. Click Add a new column and name it **Hours**; select the type Number and click OK.

   c. Choose Create⇨Contacts. In the Name field, enter **Project Contacts**; click Create.

d.   Choose Create⇨Events. In the Name field, enter **Project Calendar**; click Create.

e.   Click Home. You will see your four new lists and library on the left side of the page.

f.   Choose Modify Shared Page⇨Add Web Parts⇨Browse. In the Web Part List, locate the four lists you created in steps a–d. Drag them to the web part zones so it looks like Figure 7-10. Click Home to get out of the design mode for this page.

g.   You are almost done. You just need to set the theme as well. Choose Site Settings⇨ Apply theme to site. Select the Afternoon theme and click Apply. Click Home to see your new site. It will look similar to Figure 7-10.

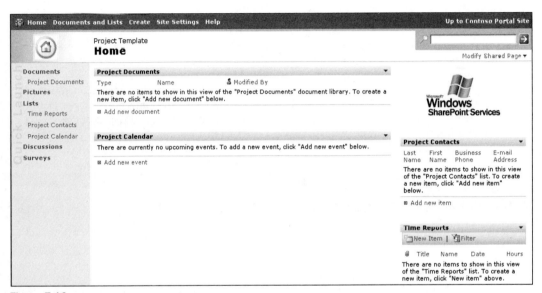

Figure 7-10

5.   To create a site template based on this site (or any other existing site), choose Site Settings⇨ Go to Site Administration⇨Save site as template. On the following page, enter these values:

a.   **File name:** IT Projects.

b.   **Template title:** IT Projects. This name will be listed in the template list.

c.   **Template description:** "Use this template for all IT projects." This text will be displayed when you select this template from the template list.

d.   Click OK. The next page says Operation Completed Successfully; click OK.

This template is now ready to be used. Note that it has some constraints: It will only be visible within the site collection where it was created; it also will only be visible when you create new sites using the same language as the template site.

To test the new site template, follow these steps:

1. Open the site "ptemp" that you used when creating the site template in the previous steps. (The reason you must use that site is because the template was stored within this particular site collection.)

2. Choose Create⇨Sites and Workspaces. You can now see the web form where you define the name and URL for this new subsite of "ptemp". Enter these values (except the quotes):

    a. **Title:** "Project XYZ".

    b. **Description:** "Testing the new site template".

    c. **URL name:** "xyz".

    d. **User Permission:** Accept the default.

    e. Click Create.

3. On the next page you can select the site template. In the Template list, select "IT Projects," then click OK. Verify that the new site looks exactly like the template site, except for the URL address, the name, and the description.

There is no live link between the original team site used when creating the template and any team sites created based on this template. In other words, if you change the original site or the site template, it will not affect existing team sites! If you need a way to modify the existing web pages, then create site definitions instead of using site templates, because these files can be modified after they are created.

Creating Lists and Library Templates

It is also a very common request to have several preconfigured lists and libraries using customized columns and views. As with the site templates, you can create list templates very easily. You can start with any existing list or library or create a new one to be used as the base for the new template.

In this example, you need a customized document library that has two extra columns: Security Level and Client Name. You also want an extra list view that groups all items based on the security level. Follow these steps to create this document library from scratch and do the modifications. Then create the library template based on this document library.

Try It Out	Create a Document Library Template

1. Open any team site (for example, the IT Projects site).

2. Create the new document library to be used for the template:

    a. Choose Create⇨Document Library. Enter the Name **DL-template** and click Create.

    b. Click Modify settings and columns; click Add a new column, named **Security Level**; select the type Choice and enter these values in the "Type each choice on a separate line" box: **Open**, **Internal**, and **Secret**. Click OK.

    c. Click Modify settings and columns; click Add a new column and name it **Client Name**; click OK. The two extra columns are now created.

    d. The next task is to create the new list view. Click Create a new view, select Standard View, and enter the name **Security Levels**. Check the column File size. Sort by "Name (for use in forms)." Expand "Group by" and select the column Security Level. Set the Grouping options to Collapsed. Click OK.

3. To make a template based on a list, open Modify settings and column. Click Save document library as template. Enter the following values:

    a. **File name:** "DL-Type1". This is the internal name for this template. It is not visible to users.

    b. **Template title:** "DocLib Type 1". This text is visible to the users.

    c. **Template Description:** "This library has two extra columns and one extra view". This is also visible to the users.

    d. Click OK to save and then OK again.

4. Click Home to return to the team site.

5. To use this new template, go to any team site in this site collection and click Create; your template should be listed under the section Document Libraries. Click this template and give it a name. When the new document library shows up, make sure it has the same columns and views as the template.

The preceding example uses a document library, but the exact same steps are used when creating templates from any list or image libraries. Remember that all templates, including site templates, are language dependent; if you create a list template on an English site, you will not see this template when creating a German team site.

Copying Templates

Templates are very easy to create, but they are only visible in their own site collection. So how do you copy a template from one site collection to another? The technique is identical, regardless of whether it is a site template or a list template. The trick is to save the template on the file system and then import that file into the new site collection. Follow these steps to copy the library template "DocLib Type 1" to the Sales site collection:

Try It Out	Copy a Template to Another Site Collection

1. Open the top-level site IT Projects that contains the document template to be copied.

2. Choose Site Settings⇨Go to Site Administration.

3. Under the section Site Collection Galleries, click Manage list template gallery.

4. You should see the library template here. If not, you are in the wrong site collection or not in the top-level site. Click the name DL-Type1.stp and click Save. Select a folder to store this template file and click Save again. Click Close.

5. Open the top-level site in the site collection where you want to import this template (in this example go to the Sales team site).

6. Choose Site Settings⇨Go to Site Administration.

7. Under the section Site Collection Galleries, click Manage list template gallery.

8. Click Upload Template; use the Browse button and select the template file stored in step 4. Click Save and Close to start importing. When done, you will see the new document template listed.

9. Test it: Click Create and verify that the template is listed under the section Document Libraries. Select it, and give it a name. Then the new document library opens. Verify that the extra columns and the extra view are there.

This was rather straightforward. The only strange thing is that you must export the template to a file. Because it has a file type of STP, it would be easy to assume that the template is stored in the file system by default. This is not true, however. It is stored in SharePoint's content database, which is why you need to export it manually.

You may recall that SPS does not inherit list and library templates between portal area pages. The only area page that allows an import of any list or library template is the Home page. If you need to add templates to other area pages, you must customize the ONET.XML file.

> *SPS cannot import list or library templates from WSS team sites, because these lists are not completely identical. For example, the SPS list does not have a link for permission settings, as the WSS list does.*

If you need to copy a site template instead, you use the preceding steps, except that you use Manage site template gallery instead of the Manage list template gallery. Remember that site templates are only visible when creating new team sites. These templates are not listed on the page displayed when you click Create, as with the list templates.

But this technique requires that the site collection already exists — how do you use a site template when creating a new site collection? The trick here is to use the STSADM.EXE program; it has features that will load any site template into a global gallery that is used when new site collections are created. Follow these steps to add the IT Projects site template you created before into the global site template gallery:

Try It Out   Add a Site Template to the Global Gallery

1. Open the top-level site Project Template that contains the site template to be copied.

2. Choose Site Settings⇨Go to Site Administration.

3. Under the section Site Collection Galleries, click Manage site template gallery.

4. Click the template name IT Projects and select Save. Select a folder to store this site template in. Then click Close. The site template is now stored in the file system. The next step is to import it to the global template gallery.

5. Open a command prompt window. Go to the folder where you stored the IT Projects.stp file.

6. Type **STSADM** and press return. If this gives an error message, you must enter the complete path to this tool, which is `C:\Program Files\Common Files\Microsoft Shared\web server extensions\60\BINSTSADM`; but if you see a list of options, you will only need to type **STSADM**:

```
STSADM -o addtemplate -filename "IT Projects.stp" -title "IT Projects" ⤵
-description "Use this template for IT Projects"
```

7. If this command says Operation completed successfully, you are now done. If you instead get a list of all the options for STSADM, you have typed something wrong. Make sure you are in the right folder where the template file is stored.

8. The next step is to reset IIS in order to activate this new global template: Open a command prompt and type **IISRESET**. Wait for it to complete, and then open the portal site. (It will take some time because you have emptied the cache, so be patient.)

9. Test this new template:

    a. Open the Sites area and click Create Site.

    b. Enter any name and URL for this site and click Next.

    c. On the next page enter the description of this site and click Next.

    d. On the following page in the list of templates, you should see IT Projects listed. Select this and click OK.

You have just created a new top site, using your site template.

The great advantage with the global template library is that you can use these site templates anywhere in any site collection. If you ever need to remove a site template from this global gallery, you can do it with STSADM and its option DeleteTemplate.

Comparing Administrative Web Pages

SharePoint comes with one graphical administrative tool, the web-based SharePoint Central Administration tool. This tool is used for administering both the WSS and the SPS environment. You can activate this tool from the Site Settings link in SPS or from Start➪All Programs➪SharePoint Portal Server or Start➪All Programs➪Administrative Tools. There are many differences between SPS and WSS regarding configuration and management, due to their very different functionality, as described earlier in this chapter. It is important that you understand whether you are configuring the portal site or you are configuring a team site when using this administrative tool. When installing SPS you also get an extended set of administrative web pages that allows you to configure both SPS and WSS settings.

You can see the different administrative web pages if you do this:

1. Open the portal area and click its Site Settings. The settings on this page control the portal site only.

2. On the Site Settings page, click the link "Go to SharePoint Portal Server central administration." This is a mixture of WSS and SPS settings. For example, the "Set SharePoint administrative group account" is a typical WSS feature, whereas "List and manage portal sites" belongs to SPS.

3. In the top-left corner of this page, click Windows SharePoint Services to open the administrative tool that will display only the WSS configuration settings.

4. Click "SharePoint Portal Server" in the left pane to open the page "SharePoint Portal Server central administration" regardless of what page you have opened in the administrative tool.

5. Click "Configure virtual server settings from the Virtual Server List page." Then click the virtual IIS server used by this SharePoint installation, typically the Default Web Site. The page that now opens is only for WSS settings. But some things you configure on this page will also affect the portal site, such as Configure Self-Service Site Creation. If you disable this feature, no new top-level sites can be created, not even from the portal area Sites and its Create Site link.

The administrative tools are not the most intuitive management tools that Microsoft has developed. It will take time to learn and master them. Make sure to take some time to look around and experiment. Don't be surprised if you find more than one way to open a specific administrative page, such as Add Users. You must also get used to the lack of consistency regarding how to return to a previous page: Sometimes you will find a Cancel button, sometimes there will be a breadcrumb trail, and you can always click the Internet browser's Back button. Experienced SharePoint administrators quickly learn to create Favorites links that point to places, such as the portal Home, the central administration page, and other frequently used administrative pages.

Comparing Backups

The backup is yet another part that differs between SPS and WSS. If you install just a pure WSS server, you will have these options for taking backups:

- ❑ **STSADM.EXE:** Can back up a complete site collection but not single sites. This tool cannot back up a portal site, but it can back up the portal's My Sites.

- ❑ **SMIGRATE.EXE:** Can back up a single site or any site and all its subsites in the site tree.

These tools only have a command-line interface, which is great if you want to create a script. Both of these tools are stored in this folder location:

```
C:\Program Files\Common Files\Microsoft Shared\web server extensions\60\BIN
```

If you install SPS you will also get a third backup tool: SPSBACKUP. It will back up a complete portal environment (including any WSS team sites or all team sites). The folder location for this tool is:

```
C:\Program Files\SharePoint Portal Server\Bin
```

But there is an easier way to start the SPSBACKUP tool: go to Start➪All Programs➪SharePoint Portal Server➪SharePoint Portal Server Data Backup and Restore. This tool has both a graphical interface and a command-line interface, so you can run it in an interactive mode or create a script that runs the backup procedure.

In Chapter 13 you learn all the ways to perform backups and restores. This section was only about the different backup tools for WSS and SPS. Chapter 13 also tells you about third-party tools that make it a lot easier to perform backup procedures.

Summary

In this chapter you learned the following:

- ❑ The previous version of WSS was called SharePoint Team Services, or STS. It used an MSDE database but stored all documents on the file system.

- ❑ The previous version of SPS was SPS 2001. It used an Exchange database and was a separate product compared to STS.

- ❑ SharePoint 2003 wants to go away from the traditional tree view used in file systems; the average user doesn't find that tree view easy to use or understand.

- ❑ Users want all their information accessible in one place, regardless of where it is physically stored. This is possible to some extent in WSS.

- ❏ The area pages and topics in the portal site are the perfect places for grouping the user's information in one place. Using targeting you can filter this information so users see only what they need.

- ❏ Lots of great tools are available if you need to use a tree view of all sites.

- ❏ The objective for WSS is to collect all information for a specific subject in one place (for example, a project site or a meeting workspace).

- ❏ The objective for SPS is to create a place where large groups of users can view news and similar information.

- ❏ The portal site is also the place where users can find all the information they need collected in one place, even when the information is stored in a large number of team sites.

- ❏ The security for a portal site is defined for each individual area page. There are no separate security settings for the lists and libraries on these area pages.

- ❏ The security for a WSS sites allows each individual list and library to have a unique setting that differs from the WSS site itself.

- ❏ WSS will display links that the user is not allowed to use; SPS will hide such links.

- ❏ SPS has many more rights than WSS, due to its area features.

- ❏ The default site groups do not have the exact same rights in WSS as in SPS.

- ❏ SPS does not have the concept of cross-site groups. Use security groups in AD instead.

- ❏ SPS has many more web parts than WSS (for example, the ability to view the Outlook Inbox and Calendar).

- ❏ SPS-specific web parts cannot be used in WSS.

- ❏ WSS web parts can be used in SPS, except for the Member web part.

- ❏ WSS allows the user to define colors, styles, and fonts using Themes.

- ❏ SPS cannot use Themes; you must use Cascading Style Sheets (CSS files).

- ❏ The site layout for both WSS and SPS can be modified using the `Default.aspx` file.

- ❏ Instead of modifying the default team site configuration files, create Site Definitions.

- ❏ For customizing the portal area pages, create area templates.

- ❏ Create templates for lists, libraries, and team sites when you need an easy way of re-creating customized lists or sites.

- ❏ Templates in WSS are visible within their own site collection, but you can copy templates to other site collections.

- ❏ To make site templates available when creating new site collections, you must add the template to the global template gallery using STSADM.

- ❏ The administrative tools are a mixture of WSS and SPS features.

- ❏ Backup and restore procedures are different for WSS and SPS. There are three tools: STSADM, SMIGRATE, and SPSBACKUP.

In the next chapter you learn more about web parts: what they are, how to add new web parts, and many tips on smart third-party web parts.

Working with Web Parts

This is a fun chapter, with lots of tips and tricks that will help you build an interesting SharePoint environment. Every standard page in the portal site and team sites is constructed of web parts. These building blocks can display any type of information, including internal SharePoint information such as document lists, contacts, and news lists, and external information such as the current weather in your area, stock market listings, and product information retrieved from a non-Microsoft database. They can also show an application such as SAP and your old intranet on a SharePoint page.

A number of web parts come with Windows SharePoint Services, and several more come with SharePoint Portal Server. You can download even more web parts from Microsoft, both from an online gallery and from Microsoft Office Resource Kit. More and more Microsoft applications now come with SharePoint web parts (for example, MS Project, MS CRM, and MS Business Scorecard Manager). When you install SharePoint in your organization, you also create a foundation for collecting information from a lot of sources. SharePoint will soon be the primary source of information for your organization, almost regardless of type, and web parts play a very important role in making this possible.

Introduction to Web Parts

A web part is a special type of ASP.NET server control; it must be added to a special type of web page, called a *smart page*. These server controls differ from ordinary ASP.NET server controls by offering a richer end-user experience, such as allowing a user to add, delete, and configure web parts, if given the proper permission. The user can do this using her standard web browser. There is no need for her to have a web developer or administrator to do this.

A web part will display information in HTML or XML format. The information is usually retrieved from a source outside the web part, such as a database list, a document, or an external application. In other words, a web part seldom contains the information it displays. A web part is a small application that reads or receives information and converts it to a format that can be displayed on a web page. Almost any type of web-based application can end up as a web part.

To create a web part you need ASP.NET programming skills. The best environment is MS Visual Studio .NET 2005, which contains a lot of functionality for developing web parts. This is not a simple task; you will also need programming skills for Visual Basic .NET or C# .NET, as well as an understanding of how SharePoint's object model works.

A web part can also connect to another web part. For example, in one web part you may select a specific customer; this selection will be sent to another web part that uses this customer name to retrieve and display sales statistics for this particular customer from a SQL database.

Web parts also allow users to perform personal configurations that will not affect other users using the same web page and web part. This is a very powerful feature that allows each user to create his or her own view of the content presented by web parts.

> *Older web parts for SPS 2001 and STS cannot be used with SPS and WSS 2003. That is also true for web parts designed for the old Digital Dashboard environment.*

Web Part Zones

Every smart page that hosts web parts must have one or more web part zones. These zones operate as a layout manager for web parts and set the boundaries for where a web part can exist and how much space it can use. There are many types of zones in SharePoint. For example, the Catalog Zone lets you browse the available web part galleries, and Editor Zones are used when you configure a web part. Both of these zones are hidden until you activate them when browsing or configuring a web part. See Figure 8-1 for an example of a smart page with two web part zones, named Left and Right.

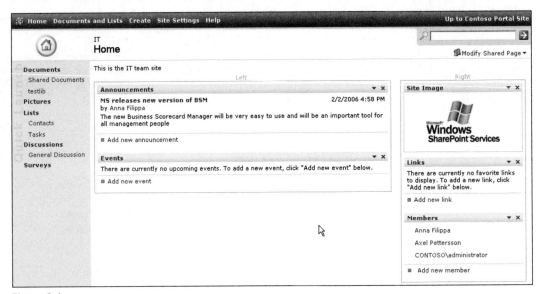

Figure 8-1

The pages in WSS and SPS use different web part zones by default. WSS has a different number of web part zones for each type of web site. All pages in the portal site use the same web part zone layout. The default settings are these:

- ❑ **WSS Team Sites:** Two web part zones: left and right (see Figure 8-1).

- ❑ **WSS Meeting workspace:** Three web part zones: left, center, and right.

- ❑ **WSS Document workspace:** Three web part zones: left, right, and top.

- ❑ **SPS area pages:** Four web part zones: top, middle left, middle right, and bottom.

Default Web Parts

There are different types of web parts. All lists and libraries created in a WSS or SPS site are also listed as web parts, thus making it possible to display the content of these lists directly on the web page. There are also what are called true web parts. WSS has just a few of these true web parts; SPS has more. The following sections give you more information about each default web part and how to use it.

Content Editor Web Part

The Content Editor web part, also known as the CEWP, will display text, HTML code, or the content of a file. For example, you can use the rich text editor in this web part to display static text, such as an instruction or help text. If you copy formatted text from a Word file, it will retain its formatting when pasted into this editor. This editor also allows you to enter pictures and tables.

The CEWP also allows you to enter HTML or JScript code, which presents a lot of opportunities. You can do practically everything that is possible with HTML and JScript. For example, to open the current user's mailbox within a team site, you could paste this code into the CEWP "Source Editor":

```
<object classid="clsid:0006F063-0000-0000-C000-000000000046"
id="ViewCtlFolder" width="100%" height="200" codetype="application/x-oleobject"
codebase="http://activex.microsoft.com/activex/controls/office/
outlctlx.CAB#ver=9,0,0,3203"
border="0">
<param name="Namespace" value="MAPI">
<param name="Folder" value="//Inbox">
<param name="Restriction" value="">
<param name="DeferUpdate" value="0">
</object>
```

If you instead want to display the content of the public folder "Sales," you would change the "Folder" line to this:

```
<param name="Folder" value="//Public Folders/All Public Folders/Sales
```

Or you could show the current date and time with this JScript code in the CEWP Source Editor:

```
<!-- Clock Part 1 - Holder for Display of Clock -->
<span id="tP"> </span>
<!-- Clock Part 1 - Ends Here -->

<!-- Clock Part 2 - Put Anywhere AFTER Part 1 -->
<script type="text/javascript">

    // Clock Script Generated By Maxx Blade's Clock v2.0d
    // http://www.maxxblade.co.uk/clock
    function tS()
    {
        x=new Date();
        x.setTime(x.getTime()),
        return x;
    }

    function lZ(x)
    {
        return (x>9)?x:'0'+x;
    }

    function tH(x)
    {
        if (x==0)
        {
            x=12;
        }
        return (x>12)?x-=12:x;
    }

    function y2(x)
    {
        x=(x<500)?x+1900:x;
        return String(x).substring(2,4);
    }

    function dT()
    {
        window.status=''+eval(oT)+'';
        document.title=''+eval(oT)+'';
        document.getElementById('tP').innerHTML=eval(oT);
        setTimeout('dT()',1000);
    }

    function aP(x)
    {
        return (x>11)?'pm':'am';
    }

    var dN = new Array('Sun','Mon','Tue','Wed','Thu','Fri','Sat'),
        mN = new
Array('Jan','Feb','Mar','Apr','May','Jun','Jul','Aug','Sep','Oct','Nov','Dec'),
        oT="dN[tS().getDay()]+' '+tS().getDate()+' '+mN[tS().getMonth()]+
' '+y2(tS().getYear())+' '+':'+':'+' '+tH(tS().getHours())+':'+
```

```
lZ(tS().getMinutes())+':'+lZ(tS().getSeconds())+' '+aP(tS().getHours())";

    if (!document.all)
    {
        window.onload=dT;
    }
    else
    {
        dT();
    }
</script>
<!-- Clock Part 2 - Ends Here  -->
```

This clock code was generated by Maxx Blade's JavaScripts Clock Script Generator (see also www.maxxblade.co.uk/clock). Figure 8-2 shows how this clock will be displayed.

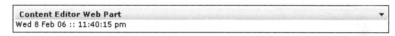

Figure 8-2

The Content Editor web part can also display the content of a given file stored in SharePoint or externally. Note that external files must be reachable by all users who use this page and its web part; if not, they will see an error message here. Just enter the URL address for this file, and SharePoint will load and display it.

The Content Link must start with HTTP:// *or* HTTPS://. *No other URL formats are supported.*

Make sure the file is in HTML format. CEWP cannot display other file types, such as .doc or .PDF. However, all MS Office programs can store their documents in .HTML format. For example, you can create an Excel spreadsheet and save it to a document library in SharePoint as a "web page (*.htm, *.html)" file type. Then link this file name to the Content Link in CEWP; see Figure 8-3 for an example.

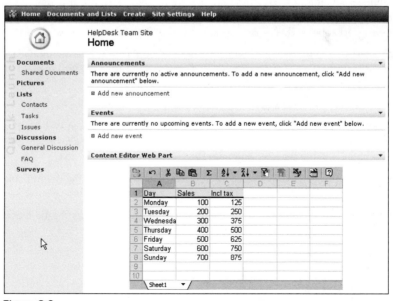

Figure 8-3

As you can see, this CEWP is very powerful and can be used in a number of situations. Search the Internet to see what others have done with this cool web part.

Form Web Part

The Form web part is used to request input from a user; then this input is used to filter the content in another web part. For example, say that you have a document library with extra columns, such as Security Class (see Figure 8-4). If you only want to view the documents with the Security Class equal to Secret, you could do this with the Form web part.

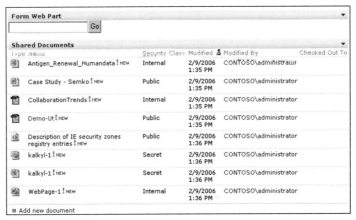

Figure 8-4

Start by installing the document library and the Form web part on this page and then configure it to connect to the document library, using these steps:

1. In this example you will use the "Shared Documents" library. Place the web part for this document library on the web page by doing the following: Go to Modify Shared Page⇨Add Web Parts⇨Browse. Locate the document library in the Web Part list and use the mouse to drag it to any web part zone on this page (for example, the "Left" zone). Do not close the Web Part list yet.

2. Continue by locating the Form web part in the Web Part list. Use the mouse to drag the Form web part to a location directly above the document library. This will make it easier for the user later to understand they are related.

3. Choose Modify Shared Page⇨Design this Page.

4. Use the quick menu (the blue arrow on the title bar) for the "Form Web Part" and select Connections⇨Provide Form Values To⇨Shared Documents. This instructs the Form web part to send whatever value the user enters to the "Shared Documents" list.

5. In the dialog box (Edit Connections⇨Web page Dialog), accept the default column T1 and click Next.

6. On the next form set the Column value equal to Security Class in Shared Documents and click Finish.

The connection between the Form web part and the Shared Document web part is now complete. Test it by typing an existing security class value in the Form web part. Now you will only see documents with this particular security class; see Figure 8-5.

Figure 8-5

This Form web part can connect to any type of list-based web part and the columns in that web part's list. It can also connect to several other web parts, such as the Image web part. If you want to reset the list so it does not filter anything, just click any other page or link and then return again.

Image Web Part

The Image web part displays a picture or graphics. A common use for this web part is to display a company logo or a picture of the manager (yes, this is true!). It accepts most of the well-known graphical file types, such as the following:

- ❑ Windows Bitmap (BMP)
- ❑ Windows Enhanced Metafile (EMF)
- ❑ Graphical Interchange Format (GIF)
- ❑ Joint Photographic Experts Group (JPG, JPEG)
- ❑ Portable Network Graphics (PNG)

You can configure the properties of this web part to alter the picture it displays, such as its size, alignment, and background color. The picture to be displayed can be defined in several ways:

- ❑ Enter a static URL address to the file. Make sure this file is accessible for all users and that they have at least read access to this picture.
- ❑ Connect the Image web part to another web part or list that contains an URL address that links to a picture.

The last option is interesting. Say that you have a list of products with one column of URL addresses that link to pictures of products. Connect the Image web part to this list and the picture column. Now select a product in the list, and its picture is displayed! See an example in Figure 8-6.

Products
New Item | Filter
Product name
Item No
Description
Picture
Mamba ! NEW
10066
Green and mean!
http://spsrv2/Images1/33193.wmf
Black Jack ! NEW
33193
What to wear when dating
http://spsrv2/Images1/33193.wmf
Necken ! NEW
32233
Play like the Devil
http://spsrv2/Images1/32233.wmf
Magic ! NEW
98221
The touch you need
http://spsrv2/Images1/98221.wmf
Okeido ! NEW
22331
Anything goes
http://spsrv2/Images1/22331.wmf

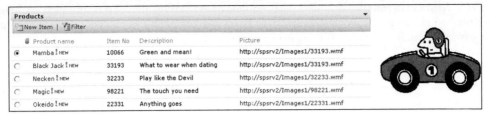

Figure 8-6

Members Web Part

The Members web part is a very handy web part for users. It displays the names of the users and groups with access to this web site. Using its web part properties, you can set things such as the title, the number of members to display, height and width, and so on.

This web part also contains a link for adding new members. You need to be an administrator for this team site to add members using this web part. If you click the Add new member link, this opens the standard web page for adding users that you have used several times before.

The Member web part cannot be used in the portal site!

Page Viewer Web Part

The Page Viewer web part is similar to the Content Editor web part discussed before. It can display any web page, folder, or file. You install it in the same way as every other web part (by going to Modify Shared Page➪Add Web Parts➪Browse, locating the Page Viewer Web Part in the Web Part list, and dragging it to a web part zone). Technically, this web part will display its content in an IFrame tag. Here are some things you can use this web part for:

- **Display an Outlook Public Folder:** Set the type to Web page and enter the link `http://dc1/public/statistics/?cmd=contents&part=1` to display the public folder Statistics on the Exchange server DC1. The last part configures the display to show the content of this public folder.
- **Display another web application in your company:** Set the type to Web page and enter the URL to the other web application.
- **Display a file folder on any server in your network:** Set the type to Folder and enter the UNC name to the folder. For example, to display the shared folder Projects on the server DC1, you would enter this link: `\\dc1\projects`. Double-click any of these files to open them. See Figure 8-7.

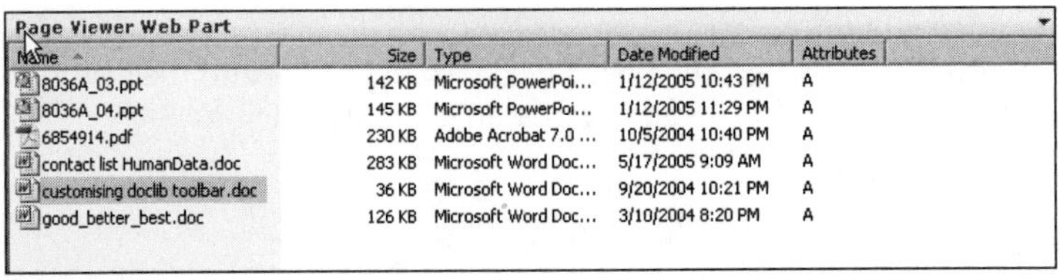

Page Viewer Web Part
Name
Size
Type
Date Modified
Attributes
8036A_03.ppt
142 KB
Microsoft PowerPoi...
1/12/2005 10:43 PM
A
8036A_04.ppt
145 KB
Microsoft PowerPoi...
1/12/2005 11:29 PM
A
6854914.pdf
230 KB
Adobe Acrobat 7.0 ...
10/5/2004 10:40 PM
A
contact list HumanData.doc
283 KB
Microsoft Word Doc...
5/17/2005 9:09 AM
A
customising doclib toolbar.doc
36 KB
Microsoft Word Doc...
9/20/2004 10:21 PM
A
good_better_best.doc
126 KB
Microsoft Word Doc...
3/10/2004 8:20 PM
A

Figure 8-7

❑ **Display the content of a file in this web part:** Set the type to File and enter the UNC name for the file. You can enter all file types that are possible to view within a web client, for example .doc, .xls, .txt, and .pdf. See Figure 8-8.

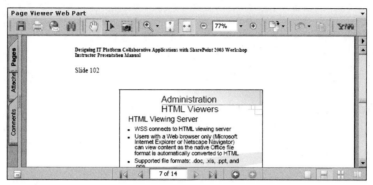

Figure 8-8

Note that if your web client prompts you to save or open a file type, such as .doc or .ppt, this still happens when you display that file type in the Page Viewer web part. By saving the file in HTML format, you can avoid this problem.

XML Web Part

eXtensible Markup Language, or *XML*, is a way to describe and structure any type of data. XML is based on a standard and can be used by anybody. Compare that to the .doc or .xls file formats that are owned by Microsoft. If you need to move an .xls file to another program, it must understand the XLS file format, or it will not work. If the source file is stored in XML format, any XML-aware application can read this file. An XML file can use an *eXtensible Stylesheet Language Transformation*, or *XSLT*, instruction to transform an XML file into another XML document.

SharePoint has the XML web part, which understands how to use XML-formatted information. This web part also allows you to enter an XSLT definition to translate the XML information if necessary. You can use this XML web part for a number of things, for example to display the content of *Really Simple Syndication* (RSS) information. RSS is used for reporting new content at a web site. RSS defines rules for listing information about new content added to a web site, such as the title, link, and a short description, which the source site publishes as an XML file at a specific URL. This file, often called a news feed, can then be read and combined with feeds from other sites by news aggregators, which display the consolidated information on a web site. RSS is widely used by news sites and weblogs. As of today, four versions are in widespread use: 0.91 (Netscape), 0.92 (Userland Software), 1.0, a variation based on *Resource Description Framework* (RDF), and 2.0, presented in September 2002 by Userland's Dave Winer.

A lot of information sources on the Internet today offer their content as RSS news feeds. Note that these URL pages should be accessed with RSS readers to be readable; if you open these pages using a web browser, all you will see is XML code. Following are some examples of these RSS sources:

❑ **MSDN blogs about SharePoint:** `http://blogs.msdn.com/sharepoint/rss.xml`

❑ **USA Today News:** `http://www.usatoday.com/repurposing/NewslineRss.xml`

❑ **MS Security Bulleting:** `http://www.microsoft.com/technet/security/bulletin/secrss.aspx`

To use the XML web part as an RSS feed reader, follow these steps:

Try It Out   **Use the XML Web Part as an RSS Feed Reader**

1. Add the XML web part to a SharePoint web page. This works with both WSS and SPS sites.

2. Switch the page to Edit mode and open the properties for this web part.

3. Paste the URL to the RSS source in the XML Link.

4. Open the XLS Editor. Paste the following code in the editor and then click OK to save and close:

```xml
<?xml version="1.0" encoding="UTF-8" ?>
<xsl:stylesheet version="1.0" xmlns:xsl="http://www.w3.org/1999/XSL/Transform">
<xsl:template match="/">
<html>
<body>
<xsl:for-each select="rss">
<xsl:for-each select="channel">
<xsl:for-each select="item">
<xsl:for-each select="title">
<a>
<xsl:attribute name="href">
<xsl:value-of select="../link" />
</xsl:attribute>
<B>
<span style="color:navy; font-family:Tahoma; font-size:8pt; font-style:normal;">
<xsl:apply-templates />
</span>
</B>
</a>
</xsl:for-each>
<br />
<xsl:for-each select="pubDate">
<span style="font-family:Tahoma; font-size:8pt;font-style:italic;">
...
<xsl:apply-templates />
</span>
</xsl:for-each>
<br />
</xsl:for-each>
</xsl:for-each>
</xsl:for-each>
</body>
</html>
</xsl:template>
</xsl:stylesheet>
```

5. Expand the Appearance section for the XML web part and enter a description of this RSS feed into the Title field.

6. Click OK to close the web part configuration pane.

Your XML web part should now display the RSS feed. Every time this page is refreshed or opened, this XML web part will connect to the RSS source and download its latest updates. See Figure 8-9.

Figure 8-9

Area Content Web Part

The Area Content web part only works in the portal site. Use it to display the subareas and their content. To see an example of this web part, look at the Topics area page, which displays this web part by default with the title "Browse Topics By." In addition to all the standard configurations for web parts, such as size, location, and so on, the Area Content web part also has several special properties to control exactly what and how it will display:

❑ **Number of Top Level Columns:** Defines how many columns to display; the default is two.

❑ **Number of areas shown by default:** Defines how many levels of subareas to display; the default is 20. For example, if this value is 0 you will only see the subareas directly under the current area page. If this value is 1, you will see the first level under these subareas.

❑ **Number of listings shown by default:** Defines how many links, documents, and other listings to display for each subarea; the default is 20.

❑ **Use vertical layout for areas and listings:** Organizes all subareas and their lists to display one per line. The default is to display several objects on the same line.

❑ **Align areas horizontally:** Aligns areas horizontally.

❑ **Show top-level area listings:** Displays all listings, such as links and documents, from the top-level area.

❑ **Show Sub Title:** Displays the sub title for this area page, if any.

❑ **Show Listings:** Displays the listings, such as links and documents, for this area and all subareas listed on this web part. Note that if you have a lot of links on the subareas, this may not look so good, although it makes it possible for the user to use a link on any area listed here without the need to open that particular area first. If you use this option, you may also want to combine this with the "Show listing icons" and "Use vertical layout for areas and listings" properties to make it easier to read these links.

❏ **Show area icons:** Displays the specific area icon for each subarea listed here. This option makes it easier to see what listings on this page are subareas, especially if you also display subarea listings.

❏ **Show listing icons:** Displays an icon for each listing, such as links and documents, on the sub-areas. If these listings have customized icons, they will be displayed here. This option must be combined with Show Listings, or no icon will be displayed.

❏ **Show descriptions:** Displays the Description field for each subarea listed on this web part.

❏ **Description Text Trim Size:** Sets a limit on how many characters to display for each area description. The default value is 100 characters.

Area Details Web Part

The Area Details web part displays a description of this area, including the name and picture of the contact person for this area. This name is taken from the Contact Information settings for this area. (Click Change Settings to configure this setting.) If this name has a personal web site, the user can click this name to open it. If there is no personal web site, but an e-mail address is defined for this contact, the user can click this name to open an e-mail with this address automatically set. A picture of the contact will be displayed if the User Profile settings for this user have a picture defined (which also will be displayed on the personal site for this user). This web part is also displayed by default at the top of the Topics area page; see Figure 8-10.

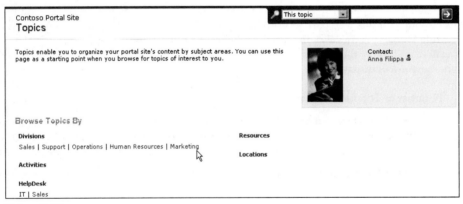

Figure 8-10

This Area Details web part has a few extra properties:

❏ **Show Sub Title:** Display the subtitle for the area where this web part is used.

❏ **Fixed image width / Fixed image height:** Set the size in pixels for the picture for this contact. The default size is 50 pixels for both these settings. You may want to increase this to make it easier for the users to see this picture.

❏ **Display Contact Picture:** Check this to display the picture of this contact.

Grouped Listings Web Part

Use the Grouped Listings web part to display the listings for an area in groups. By default all areas have three groups: General, Expert, and Highlight. You can create new groups or modify the default groups, as described in more detail in Chapter 5. This web part is typically used on area pages to group related links, documents, and other information. For example, you may have an area page for the sales team. On this area page you have the groups Quotes, Partners, and Customers; each group lists the links and documents related for this type of group.

The purpose of the grouped list is to make it easy for the user to quickly find the information related to a given subject. To add listings in this web part, use the links "Add Listing" or "Add person" in the left side of this page. By default you will see this web part on the Topics subareas (see also the previous example in Chapter 5 about creating subareas for the Topics area).

There are some special properties for this web part:

❑ **Maximum Number of Listings:** Sets the number of listings for each group. For example, a value of 4 only displays the first four listings for each group. A value of 0 displays all listings for each group.

❑ **Fixed image width:** Sets the size in pixels for the image for a link. The default value is 60 pixels. Note that this setting does not have any effect unless you configure this web part to display pictures; see the Display Template in this list.

❑ **Fixed image height:** Sets the size in pixels for the image for a link. The default value is 0, which means that it will be automatically adjusted to the ratio for this image, based on the Fixed image width. If you change the Fixed image height value, be careful not to distort the picture.

❑ **Ignore Listings in Anchor Area:** If this web part is connected to another area (the "anchored area"), this setting controls whether or not the links in that anchored area will be displayed. By default, this setting is not set.

❑ **Subarea Layers:** Defines how many levels of subareas are to be displayed here. For example, a value of 2 includes all the links in the first and second subareas along with the links on this area page. The user does not see what areas the links actually belong to; they all are listed together.

❑ **Display Template:** Controls what and how these links will be displayed. There are five templates by default:

  ❑ **Minimum:** Displays the links in a bullet list. No icons, images, or descriptions are displayed.

  ❑ **Compact:** Is the same as Minimum, but displays only the links' names and no bullets.

  ❑ **Normal:** Displays the links and their descriptions, but no images or icons.

  ❑ **Topic Items:** Displays the links, descriptions, and icons.

  ❑ **Expanded:** Displays the links, descriptions, and images, if any.

When you create a link, you can define the image URL. This image will be displayed when using the Expanded template. A standard link, typically the web icon, will be displayed when using the Topic Items template. To display a custom image, you must edit the existing link and set the URL to the icon image.

- ❑ **Group by:** Controls how these links will be grouped. There are six options:

  - ❑ **None:** Shows all listings without any groupings. Use "Sort Listings By" to control the order in which to display these listings.

  - ❑ **Area:** Shows all listings sorted by area. Use this setting together with Subarea Layers to show the user what area these links really belong to.

  - ❑ **Creation Date:** Sorts the listings based on when the links were created. The actual creation date will be displayed.

  - ❑ **Last Modified Date:** Sorts the listings based on when the links were modified. The actual modification date will be displayed.

  - ❑ **Audience:** Sorts the listings based on audience. The user will see only the links that are targeted to the audience he or she belongs to.

  - ❑ **Group:** Sorts the listings based on their group membership. This is the default setting for this Grouped Listings web part.

- ❑ **Sort Listings By:** Defines how these listings will be sorted. There are four options:

  - ❑ **Title:** Sorts by the link title, in alphabetic order.

  - ❑ **Creation Date:** Sorts by the creation date.

  - ❑ **Last Modified Date:** Sorts by the last modified date.

  - ❑ **Order:** Sorts by the order you define, using the Manage Grouping and Ordering link that is visible at the bottom of this web part when this page is in edit mode and this web part is grouped by "Group." This is the default setting.

- ❑ **Sort Direction:** Defines if the sort order should be Ascending (default) or Descending.

- ❑ **Display Columns:** Defines how many columns to use for the listings in this web part. The default is 1. If you have lots of links, it may be much easier to view them when using two or more columns.

- ❑ **Highlights Visibility:** Defines how the listings that belong to the group Highlights will be displayed:

  - ❑ **All Listings:** Shows all listings, regardless of whether they are members of the Highlights group. This is the default setting.

  - ❑ **Highlight Listings Only:** Shows only the links in the Highlights group.

  - ❑ **Non-highlight Listings Only:** Shows all but the links in the Highlights group.

- ❑ **More Info Link Text Label:** Is supposed to show a link with the text you enter in this field, but does not work in this web part.

- ❑ **More Info Link URL:** Shows the link that opens when the user clicks More Info Link Text Label.

- ❑ **Description Text Trim Size:** Defines how many characters are to be displayed for each link description. The default value is 0, which shows all characters.

- ❑ **Show Sub Title:** By default this web part does not show its title. Check this box if you want to display the web part title. To set the title, use the Title field in the Appearance section.

> This web part also has some cache settings in the Miscellaneous section that may be used if this web part is configured to use cached information. To read more about cache settings in SharePoint, see the SharePoint Products and Technology Resource Kit.

Links for You Web Part

This is the basically same web part as the "Grouped Listings" described in the preceding section. The only difference is that Links for You is by default configured differently:

- ❑ **Display Template:** Minimum.
- ❑ **Group By:** Audience.
- ❑ **Sort listings By:** Creation Date.
- ❑ **Sort Direction:** Descending.
- ❑ **Title:** Links for You.

The purpose of this link is to display all links that are targeted to the current user, based on their audience membership. To add links to this web part, do exactly as you do to add links to the Grouped Listings web part (click "Add Listing" or "Add Person" under Actions in the left pane of this page and make sure to set the Audience property).

My Alert Summary Web Part

The My Alert Summary web part lists all portal alerts for the current user. By default, this web part is added to the user's personal web site ("My Site"). However, it may also be added to any other portal area page. It also contains the link Go to My Alerts page, where users can manage all their portal links.

My Calendar Web Part

The My Calendar web part can be configured to display the Outlook calendar for the configured user. It is by default added to the user's personal web site. You should not add this web part to a portal area, because it must be configured to show a particular calendar. The exception is a calendar that all users with access to this area are allowed to see, such as a resource calendar; for example, a conference room mailbox. Note that a resource configured as an Outlook public folder cannot be displayed using this web part.

Use these web part properties in the Mail Configuration section to configure what Outlook calendar is displayed:

- ❑ **Exchange Folder Name:** The name for the calendar folder, by default "Calendar." Note that this folder name must match the current user's Outlook folder name. For example, if the user's calendar is named "Kalender" you must use that name instead. Open the user's MS Outlook to see the correct name to be used.
- ❑ **Mail server address:** The URL to the mail server, for example http://mailsrv1/exchange.
- ❑ **Mailbox:** The name for the mailbox that contains this calendar.
- ❑ **Title** (in the Appearance section): The name for this web part; by default it will be "My Calendar."

My Inbox Web Part

The My Inbox web part lists the Outlook inbox for the configured user. The most common place for this web part is the user's personal site, but you can use it on any area page as long as everyone with access to that area will also have at least read access to that inbox. A typical example here is a resource mailbox, such as Support or Helpdesk.

Use these web part properties in the Mail Configuration section to configure what Outlook inbox is displayed:

❑   **Mail server address:** The URL to the mail server, for example, `http://mailsrv1/exchange`.

❑   **Mailbox:** The name for the mailbox that contains this inbox.

❑   **Title** (in the Appearance section): The name for this web part; by default it will be "My Inbox."

My Links Web Part

The My Links web part is your own SharePoint version of your web browser's "Favorites," enabling you to add your own favorite links to this list. The advantage of using this for saving links is that it is stored in SharePoint's database, whereas Favorites are stored on your local client. You can use the links in the My Links web part regardless of what client you are using, as long as you have access to SharePoint.

This web part is by default added to the user's personal site. It can also be added to any other portal area page, and it will still show the same content. It will be organized in the groups you define for these links. These groups are specific for My Links and have no connection to the groups used for other listings (for example, the content in Grouped Listings). There are some specific properties for this web part:

❑   **Specifies the maximum number of items to display:** This long headline says it all! The default value is 1,000 items.

❑   **Widths of columns:** Defines how much of the web part zone width this web part will use; the default is 100%.

❑   **Display text for no result:** Defines what this web part will display if there are no links; the default is an empty field.

My Mail Folder Web Part

The My Mail Folder web part displays any Outlook mailbox folder the user may have. It is most often used in the user's personal web site, because its property settings are configured to display a specific mailbox user account. As for the My Calendar and My Inbox, this web part can also be used to display shared mailbox folders (typically resource mailboxes such as Helpdesk and Support).

This web part may be used to display a public folder, using the instructions in Chapter 6 in the Try It Out "Display a Public Folder with My Mail Folder."

It has the same type of web part properties in the Mail Configuration section as My Inbox and My Calendar, plus one extra where you define what folder to display:

❑   **Exchange folder name:** The name in Outlook for the mailbox folder to be displayed in this web part.

❑   **Mail server address:** The URL address to the mail server, for example `http://mailsrv1/exchange`.

❑ **Mailbox:** The mailbox account to be displayed.

❑ **Title:** (in the Appearance section). Enter the title for this web part. By default it is "My Mail Folder."

My Tasks Web Part

Again, the My Tasks web part is very similar to the other Outlook-related web parts. It displays the Tasks for a given mailbox. It is usually used in the user's personal site but can also be used on any area page to display the tasks of a shared mailbox. Its properties are as follows:

❑ **Mail server address:** The URL address to the mail server, for example
`http://mailsrv1/exchange`.

❑ **Mailbox:** The mailbox account to be displayed.

My Workspace Sites Web Part

The My Workspace Sites web part displays all subsites directly under the user's personal site. It cannot be used on a portal area page. If you try to use it on a portal area page, the page will say "This web part is intended for use with personal sites, and does not work on other pages. Please remove the web part from this page."

This web part displays only sites or workspaces directly under the personal site; if there are more levels of sites, they will not be listed here.

News Web Part

The News web part is exactly the same web part as Grouped Listings, described earlier in this chapter. Its purpose is to display news items created on this area page. The only differences are the settings of these web part properties:

❑ **Maximum Number of Listings:** 5. Lists the five most recent news items from this area.

❑ **Display Template:** Expanded. Shows the title, description, and picture of each list item.

❑ **Group By:** None. Instead it is sorted in a special way.

❑ **Sort Listings By:** Creation Date.

❑ **Sort Direction:** Descending. The latest news is listed at the top of this list.

❑ **Title:** News (in the Appearance section).

News Areas Web Part

The News Areas is also the same web part as Grouped Listings. Its purpose is to display news items grouped by area. Its specific web part settings are these:

❑ **Maximum Number of Listings:** 3. Lists only the three latest news items from each area.

❑ **Subarea Layers:** 1. Displays the news links in the current area page, plus the news links on the first subarea under this page.

❑ **Display Template:** Minimum. Shows only the link item title.

❑ **Group By:** Area. The content is grouped based on what area page the news belongs to.

❑ **Sort Listings By:** Creation Date.

❑ **Sort Direction:** Descending. The latest news is listed at the top of this list.

❑ **Title:** News Areas (in the Appearance section).

News for You Web Part

Once again, this is a web part based on Grouped Listings. Its purpose is to display a news item that is targeted to the audience of the current user. The specific web part settings used here are as follows:

❑ **Maximum Number of Listings:** 0. Shows all news items.

❑ **Subarea Layers:** 9. Displays the news links in the current area page, plus the news links on the nine subarea layers under this page.

❑ **Display Template:** Minimum. Shows only the link item title.

❑ **Group By:** Audience. The content is grouped based on the current user's audience membership.

❑ **Sort Listings By:** Creation Date.

❑ **Sort Direction:** Descending. The latest news is listed at the top of this list.

❑ **Title:** News for You (in the Appearance section).

Page Viewer Web Part

The Page Viewer web part is very useful and is discussed in more detail in Chapter 7. Use it to display a web page, a folder on the file system, or the content of a file of a type that the web browser can display (for example. .html, .txt., or a .pdf file).

Topics Assistance Suggestions Web Part

This web part is only of interest if you have activated the Topics Assistance. This feature is only available on the portal site. For more information about this feature, see http://office.microsoft.com/en-us/assistance/HA011649111033.aspx. The purpose of this web part is to list all the links that the Topics Assistance has found during the last indexing process that match the criteria of existing links on this area page. It is basically the same web part as My Links, but with special settings:

❑ **Specifies the maximum number of items to display:** The default value is 50 items.

❑ **Widths of columns:** Defines how much of the web part zone width this web part will use; the default is 90% or 95 pixels.

❑ **Display text for no result:** "No links have been suggested"; displays this text when no links have been found by the Topics Assistance.

Only users with Manage Area rights will be able to accept or decline the suggestions of the Topics Assistant. By default this right is included for the site groups Content Manager, Web Designer, and Administrator.

Finding More Web Parts

The web parts are what make SharePoint so great! You have now seen all the default web parts for SPS and WSS. The real fun starts when you add new web parts. The question is where do you find them? The answer, of course, is on the Internet! Start your favorite web search engine and search for SharePoint web parts. You will be surprised by the number of hits you will get. In fact, there are so many that you may need some hints about where to find good web parts. This section describes some of the best known web parts available. Of course, this is an area that is developing very rapidly; it seems as if every day there are new web parts.

What are the chances that the web part you are looking for really exists? Well, if you need to display something in SharePoint, then most likely somebody else has already had this same need. This is a great business opportunity for creative people! Search the Internet for the key feature you are looking for, such as "site tree," "task rollup," or whatever you may need.

Free Web Parts

There are a surprisingly large number of web parts that a developer provides for free or humbly asks you for an optional donation. I suggest that if you download such a web part and find yourself really using it, send a donation; this will encourage this developer to continue to develop this and other web parts. The following sections offer free web parts.

GotDotNet

Use the following URL to go to the GotDotNet site: `http://www.gotdotnet.com/workspaces/directory.aspx`.

This site is full of interesting web parts for SharePoint, and new parts are constantly being added. Open the URL and search for "SharePoint" at the top of this web site. If you know the name of a specific web part, you can also search for that name directly. There are more than 90 SharePoint web parts and tools; to see them all, change the "Items per page" to 100. Click "Title" to sort the list in alphabetic order. Following are some of these web parts:

- ❑ **ReGhost.NET:** Now you can easily reghost those unwanted pages that are being served from the database without needing to access the SharePoint databases directly with Enterprise Manager or installing any web parts. This simple desktop application can run locally on the front-end web server or anywhere else that has appropriate access to the SharePoint databases. The tool presents a list of unghosted pages and allows you to safely reghost them with ease.

- ❑ **cBlog:** This is a custom site definition used to create a Blog in SharePoint.

- ❑ **SharePoint Reports:** This is a reporting tool for analyzing the contents of SharePoint sites and portals. It works with both WSS and SPS.

- ❑ **SharePoint Site Permissions Manager:** This SharePoint portal 2003 utility shows all portal sites and manages site users and roles globally in one common interface. It will eventually also manage SharePoint portal areas, area users, site groups, and cross-site groups globally in that common interface. The Site Permissions System provides integrated SharePoint management that can help you address your company's business needs and increase productivity by helping with the time-consuming and cumbersome tasks of permissions management. With one common interface, administrators can delegate Active Directory permissions to their sites easily and quickly, whether they have one site or 20. Site Permissions Manager can also provide "Top-level Site Administration" for each of the sites listed, cutting down management time with other SharePoint administrative tasks.

- ❑ **WSS/SPS Recycle Bin for Document Libraries (WSS/SPS):** Microsoft SharePoint Document Library does not support Recycle Bin functionality, so this project is designed to solve this simple issue and provide you with a framework to handle it.

❏ **SharePoint Web Part: Drop-Down Navigator:** The Drop-Down Navigator provides administrators with the ability to add a web part capable of providing navigation via the selection of a value in a drop-down box to any SharePoint Portal or Windows SharePoint Service page. This type of functionality is commonly used to present end users with the ability to quickly accomplish a number of frequently performed tasks performed on different pages.

❏ **Wrap Up Web Part:** The Wrap Up web part for SPS aggregates lists in the areas and subareas beneath them. Lists are "wrapped up" by aggregating them based on their name. For example, a wrap up list for all lists named "Policies" could be placed at the root of the portal in order to display all policies in one location.

❏ **SharePoint Web Part: Finder:** The Finder web part provides Administrators with the ability to add a custom search box to any SPS web part page. In addition to this, it provides the ability to filter searches based on a specific type of content. For example, a search could be restricted so that the search includes only "People."

❏ **SharePoint Cleaner:** This is a tool for "cleaning" SharePoint of data that is no longer relevant. This release starts by cleaning the User tables on team sites after an account has been removed from the AD.

MSD2D

Use the following URL to go to the MSD2D site: `http://www.msd2d.com`.

This site is a very interesting discussion forum for SharePoint topics, with lots of tips on web parts, both free and commercial. To use it, you must create an account, free of charge. Go to this site, click the SharePoint tab, and select the SharePoint Web Parts tab. Here, you see a list of categories; click a category to see all its web parts. Following are some free web parts from this site:

❏ **CorasWorks User Display (Category: Tools):** The CorasWorks User Display web part is designed to return the user who is currently logged in and viewing the web part page where the web part is instantiated. The selectable return will be "Currently Logged In As," "Currently Logged In As ()," "", or "()." The view that is returned is selectable by the user via the Display Properties within the web part. If the user is an Anonymous user, the selectable return will be "Currently Logged In As Anonymous" or "Anonymous."

❏ **CorasWorks WSS Search (Category: Tools):** This web part performs a search of a WSS site and its subsites and then displays the search results based upon a user's entry. It allows the user to search within lists (such as tasks, announcements, and events), libraries (such as document libraries), or both. It requires that WSS is using an MS SQL Server with full text indexing.

CorasWorks also provides web parts for a fee; they are described later in this chapter.

❏ **Mailing List (Category: Tools):** The Mailing List can be placed on a site or area together with any kind of a contacts list view. It allows you to quickly send an e-mail to all currently shown contacts (filtered or unfiltered) in the connected list view.

Trinity Expert Systems

Use the following URL to go to the Trinity Expert Systems site: `http://www.tesl.com/TESL/SharePoint+integration+tool/`.

Some tools are so cool that they need to be described in more detail. This company has a free add-on to the MS Outlook client that allows the user to copy e-mail to any document library in SharePoint. Trinity calls this tool the "SharePoint Uploader for Outlook" and it works like this:

1. You install "NavStructure web services" to the SharePoint server. This web service comes with the "SharePoint Uploader for Outlook" package. It will tell the client tool what sites exist in the SharePoint environment.

2. You install this Outlook add-on to each client. It adds a button to Outlook; click it and it shows up as a free-floating window.

3. The first time it must be configured with the URL to the SharePoint portal site or WSS top site, depending on whether you have SPS or only WSS installed.

4. This window is now populated by all the sites and their document libraries. You do not see other types of lists, because you can only drag e-mail into a document library.

5. Pick any e-mail in your mailbox and drag it to the document library of your choice. The mail, including any attachments, is now copied to that document library. See Figure 8-11.

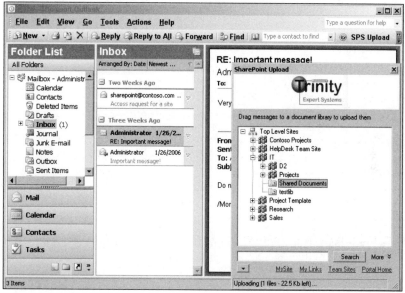

Figure 8-11

This company can also enhance this tool so it automatically creates the properties for this e-mail when stored in the document library (for example, you may want to have columns for Sender, Receiver, Attachments, and so on). For this they will charge a reasonable fee.

MS Office Web Parts

Use the following URL to go to Microsoft's Web parts page in its Download Center: http://www
.microsoft.com/downloads/details.aspx?familyid=38BE67A5-2056-46A1-84B1-337FFB549C5C
&displaylang=en.

The MS Office developer team also has some cool and free web parts for SharePoint. To download them, go to the preceding link and download the STSTPKPL.EXE file. Make sure to select the same language as your portal site or WSS installation. After this package is installed, you will find seven new web parts in the Virtual Server Gallery that is available in all portal areas and all team sites:

❑ **Office Datasheet:** Connect this web part to an external source or another web part, and it displays that source. This web part can connect to almost any external source, including standard ODBC connections, MS SQL Server, Oracle, and SharePoint lists. Test and use its "Connect to an external data source" feature, select New SQL Server Connection, enter the name and logon credentials, and then select a database and a table. You can also select SharePoint's content database option if you want to explore it a little; choose, for example, the Docs table to see how SharePoint stores documents. See Figure 8-12.

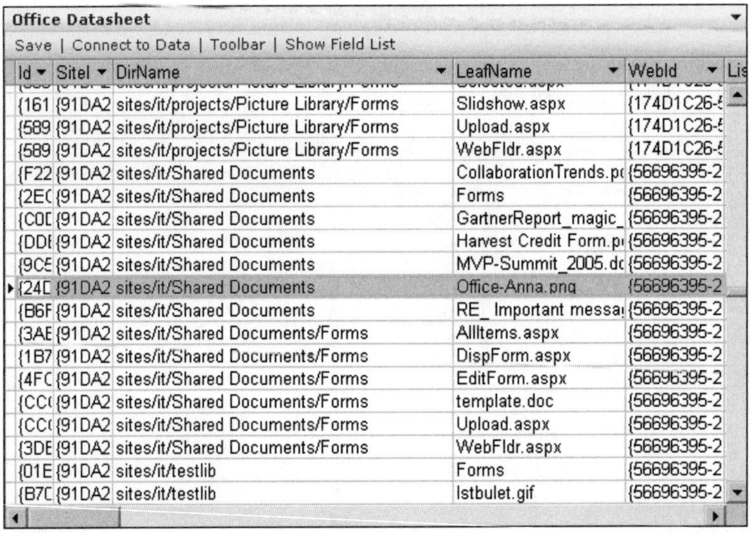

Figure 8-12

❑ **Office PivotChart:** This web part is similar to the Office Datasheet but with another default view, configured in the web part properties and its Pivot View settings. It has therefore the exact same possibilities to connect to almost any data source. The Office PivotChart displays a chart with Pivot capabilities (meaning that you can move the columns and rows around freely to present and group the content in this web part). See Figure 8-13, which displays both the graphic picture and the Chart Field List.

❑ **Office PivotTable:** Use this web part to display a table with Pivot functionality. You can drag and drop lists from the Pivot Table Field List.

❑ **Office Pivot View:** This is very similar to the Office Datasheet web part; use the folder list to add the column to be displayed.

❑ **Office Spreadsheet:** This is a special view that looks very similar to Excel 2003. You can connect external data to this web part, and you can also add new data into this spreadsheet.

❑ **Quick Quote:** This is a web part that allows the user to enter a standard stock quote, such as US:MSFT, to see its current stock value and some statistics. If you don't know the abbreviation for a given stock quote, click the "Look up" link, which opens the URL address http://

`moneycentral.msn.com/investor/common/find.asp` where you can search for the names. Note that this web part also works with non-U.S. stock markets; for example, you can search for the Swedish Telecom company Ericson by entering their abbreviation SE:ERIC-B.

❑ **Web Capture:** This web part is very cool. It allows you to connect to any web site in the world, including your internal web sites, and select to view just one or a few elements from that source. Click Create to define what this web part will capture. It opens a new window. Enter the URL address for the web application. Then click the yellow arrow next to each element that you want to display in this Web Capture web part. You can also use it to display lists and libraries from other portal areas or team sites. For example, see Figure 8-14, which displays the News listing from the portal area on the team site IT.

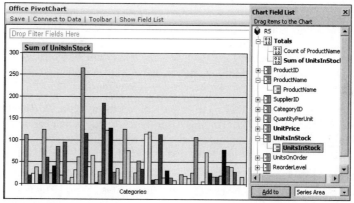

Figure 8-13

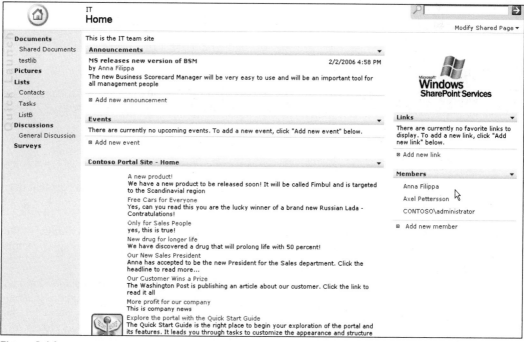

Figure 8-14

SharePoint Customization

Use the following URL to go to get web parts from Microsoft FrontPage's Customization Kit: `http://www.sharepointcustomization.com/resources/webparts.htm`.

This site is managed by Microsoft's FrontPage team and focuses on SharePoint-related topics. The preceding link displays a list of free web parts, like these:

❏ **Breadcrumb Site Navigation:** The Breadcrumb Site Navigation web part is to be used for displaying the hierarchical location of a WSS site collection. This breadcrumb trail will continue all the way down to the site that the user is currently on.

❏ **MS Office Live Meetings:** The Live Meeting 2005 web parts integrate Live Meeting with SharePoint (both WSS and SPS) to aggregate information within a single portal. By integrating with Live Meeting, SharePoint users can seamlessly view their upcoming Live Meetings or recently made recordings without having to log in or remember any passwords. Not only do the web parts provide a view into Live Meeting from SharePoint, they also allow a user to conveniently publish meetings and record information in a shared event calendar so that team members can interact more effectively by having everything in one place.

❏ **Rate This Page:** The Rate This Page web part allows users to provide feedback on the value of pages inside sites based on WSS or SPS. Users can rate pages that contain the web part by clicking a number. The ratings are stored in the Page Ratings list, so you can add the Page Ratings web part to the site to expose the top-rated pages.

❏ **Remote Desktop:** The Remote Desktop web part establishes a Remote Desktop connection on a Web Part page. The part can be used for two different scenarios. The first is when users know which server they would like to connect to and can establish the connection themselves. The other scenario allows a web administrator to preconfigure the connection to automatically connect to the remote machine. See Figure 8-15.

To make this web part work, you must install this ActiveX component on the server: `http://www.microsoft.com/windowsxp/downloads/tools/rdwebconn.mspx`.

Miscellaneous Web Parts

These free web parts are coming from different sources. Very often a company will give away web parts as a way of increasing the interest in its other products. Some of these web parts are really worth trying:

❏ **Hello Web Part** (`store.bamboosolutions.com`)**:** Welcome users to your portal by displaying a personal welcome message that includes the user's name. The standard message changes depending on the time of day.

❏ **Flash Slideshow** (`www.flexnetconsult.co.uk`)**:** This is an easy-to-use web part that displays the contents of a local SharePoint picture library using Macromedia Flash Version 6 or greater. Just set a few simple properties, and the web part will show a rotating display of all the pictures in the picture library with a fade transition between each picture. You can set the size of the picture window along with display time and transition time. It's a great way to display picture sets of your products, employees, social events, and so on.

❏ **Events For You** (`http://sharepointsolutions.blogspot.com/2006/02/free-sharepoint-portal-ser_113980953585198810.html`)**:** The Events for You web part functions in a manner very similar to the Links for You web part that can be found on the Home Page and personal My Site page of SPS. With this free web part, Event Items from the Events List located in the portal's root web are presented to portal users based on their Audience membership. The Events for You web part can also be configured to override a user's Audience membership, targeting Events to a definable set of one or more Audiences.

❑ **Calendar Web Part** (`http://programsunlimited.com/webparts.htm`): The Programs Unlimited Inc. Calendar web part is much more flexible than the Microsoft offering. It can grow and shrink depending on the zone in which it is dropped. You can set a specific a country to display its local holidays in the calendar. When a list is used as a source for the calendar, the description of the list item appears in the calendar. Clicking the description in the calendar will take you directly to the list item.

❑ **cMySites** (`http://dev.collutions.com/Beta/pages/Web%20Parts.aspx`): This is a web part that provides a list of subsites in which the current user is a member. Optional settings display an image showing the type of SharePoint site (Team Site, Doc Workspace, or Meeting Workspace).

❑ **Gantt Charts** (`http://www.teuntostring.net/blog/2006/01/web-part-for-rendering-gantt-charts.html`): This displays a Gantt chart for a list that contains a starting and ending WSS Date field. Manual installation procedure (description is on this web site).

❑ **SPToolbar** (`http://james.milne.com/SPPageToolBar/Demo`): To enhance the usability and look and feel of your SharePoint pages, you can add the Page Toolbar web part to your pages. The toolbar adds a number of common features to your page quickly and easily: Print Friendly Version, Send This Page, Add to Favorites, Comment, Alert Me, and Add to My Links.

❑ **UserAlerts** (`http://weblogs.asp.net/jan/archive/2004/03/27/97335.aspx`): Many site administrators want to be able to create alerts on behalf of other users. SharePoint 2003 does not allow you to do this, so this web part allows an administrator to create alerts for any user.

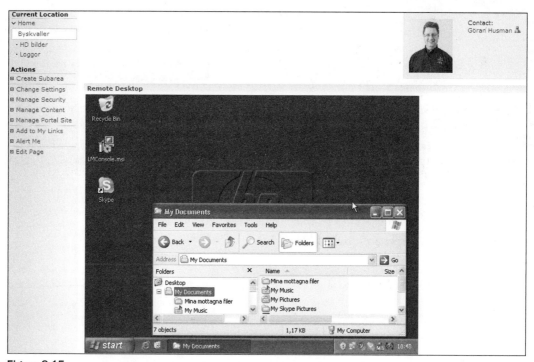

Figure 8-15

Not-So-Free Web Parts

If you are prepared to pay for a web part, there is almost no end to what you can find. It is interesting to note that an increasing number of companies are completely focused on developing web parts for SharePoint. The chance to find what you are seeking is very good. And of course you can always develop your own web parts. (See the end of the chapter for more on this.)

In the following sections you will find a number of companies that focus solely on SharePoint web parts. These are by no means the only ones. Many other talented companies might have the special web part you are looking for.

ADVIS AG

Use the following URL to go to ADVIS: `http://sharepoint.advis.ch/`.

This Swiss company is known in the SharePoint community for its affordable and high-quality web parts; some of them are even free. The company also customizes web parts if needed. Following are just two of the commercial web parts it offers:

❑ **Area Navigator:** This is a customizable, Explorer-like portal area navigation web part (see Figure 8-16). The current area is highlighted, "hidden" areas and areas where the current user has no access are not displayed in this list. This is a very handy web part when working with lots of portal area pages. It replaces the simple Topics area navigation tree displayed on the portal Home area. This web part has a number of interesting properties; following are just some of them:

   ❑ **Anchor Area:** Sets the start (or root) of the area tree to something other than the Home area.

   ❑ **Show Hidden:** Controls whether areas marked as "Exclude from portal site navigation" are visible in this tree view.

   ❑ **Home Area Icon:** Defines what icon is to be displayed for the Home (or root) area.

   ❑ **Subarea Icon:** Defines what icon is to be displayed for all subareas in this tree view.

   ❑ **Navigation Icon for Collapsed Areas:** Defines what icon is to be displayed next to collapsed areas in this tree view. (The default is "+".)

   ❑ **Navigation Icon for Expanded Areas:** Defines what icon is to be displayed next to expanded areas. (The default is "-".)

Figure 8-16

❑ **Site Navigator:** This is a similar web part to the Area Navigator, but for WSS team sites only. It has a very large number of custom properties and satisfies most organizations' needs for a site navigation tool. Among all these properties you will find the following:

    ❑ **Navigation Anchor:** By default, this web part displays a tree view based on the current site collection. You can also configure it to display all site collections in this virtual IIS server. See Figure 8-17.

    ❑ **URL Filter:** Enter the URL for sites that should not be displayed in this tree view.

    ❑ **Show Libraries and Lists:** Control if and how lists and libraries will be displayed. You can configure this to show the lists of only the current site or all sites.

    ❑ **Show hidden Libraries and Lists:** Use this to control whether lists and libraries that are not displayed on the team site's quick launch bar will be displayed in this tree view.

    ❑ **Show Folders in Libraries:** Use this to control whether folders in libraries will be displayed.

    ❑ **Show Search Box:** Type the name of the team site to be displayed. You can enter a complete name, a word, or just a part of a word. Only team sites that match this search criterion will be displayed.

    ❑ **Open in New Window:** Check this box to open all links in this tree view in a separate window.

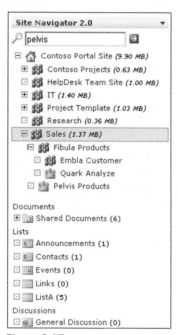

Figure 8-17

SPSDev

Use the following URL to go to SpsDev.Com: `http://www.spsdev.com`.

This U.S.-based company has several very interesting web parts with reasonable prices. Some of these web parts are solving common SharePoint problems in a unique way, such as the Pocket Portal, which adjusts the SharePoint layout to fit the screen of a Pocket PC and similar devices.

❑ **Area Menu:** This web part displays all subareas, including top-level team sites, as a drop-down menu on the portal header links instead of the classical tree view. You can save a lot of space with this technique.

❑ **Bulk Upload:** This is a special tool for importing multiple files from a file system and setting their document library properties at the same time. This will save you a lot of time when importing existing files from the old file system into SharePoint's document libraries.

❑ **Group at a Glance:** The Group at a Glance web part provides an easy way to determine the availability of your virtual team members in your team web sites. It can automatically determine who all of your site's members are, retrieve their calendar information, and display their availability in a rich graphical interface. It also includes an aggregate view of everyone's calendar so you can quickly see the times of day when everyone is available for a quick meeting, conference call, or chat. Group at a Glance provides a number of other features to help you show the information you want to see, exactly like you want to see it. It includes options for viewing calendar information in 30- or 60-minute blocks, rendering the calendar in standard or military time, adding other users who aren't part of your site to the group calendar, changing the starting time and length of day for the calendar, controlling the colors used, and more. Note that this web part requires an MS Exchange mail server.

❑ **Pocket Portal:** Pocket Portal allows you to browse through virtually all of your data, whether it's on an SPS site or a WSS site. It provides an easy-to-use navigational structure that allows you to quickly move between different areas of information in your portal site. Within each site you can view all the document libraries and lists, as well as the individual items they contain. If you have a device that supports the document types stored in SharePoint, you can open them right on your mobile device. There is even a special version of Search built into Pocket Portal. Now you can search through all of the content you have across your organization, external sites, Exchange public folders, Lotus Notes databases, and so on, all from your mobile device. Pocket Portal makes it quick and easy to find your important data, while leveraging the valuable investment you've made in Microsoft SharePoint Technologies and Products. See Figure 8-18.

❑ **Web Manager:** This is a tool that will perform statistical analysis of the SharePoint environment and its usage. With Web Manager you can use a special crawler to gather loads of statistical information about what sites you have, who owns them, who's using them, and what they're accessing. The Web Manager application comes predefined with several important and interesting reports about the SharePoint data in your organization, such as the "Ten biggest Webs," the "Ten biggest users," and several more reports.

The Dot Net Factory

Use the following URL to go to The Dot Net Factory: `http://www.thedotnetfactory.com`.

Figure 8-18

Yet another U.S.-based company that develops really smart web parts for SharePoint. These tools are very sophisticated, and their prices reflect that. Some of the great tools that TDNF has include:

❑ **EmpowerID Web Manager:** This tool is a completely web-based user and group administration tool allowing granular delegation of user and group management. Its flexible architecture employs a unique LDAP query-based technology. This easy to use search-like delegation mechanism allows any information in your Active Directory to be used as the basis for delegating and restricting account management activities. Common scenarios include delegation to Helpdesk, Business Partners, Divisional Admins, Department Managers, HR, and more. The detailed SQL reporting greatly enhances compliance efforts by auditing all provisioning and account management activities.

❑ **EmpowerID WhitePages:** The Dot Net Factory's EmpowerID WhitePages is a completely web-based corporate directory application designed with the non-technical user in mind. Its familiar Microsoft Office 2003 look and feel makes it easy and secure for employees to find information, update their personal data, and change their passwords. EmpowerID WhitePages enables the Active Directory to serve as your most up-to-date, cost-effective, and easily accessible directory of employee information for your enterprise. Readily available and accurate directory information increases productivity by simplifying employee communications and collaboration. With EmpowerID WhitePages users can easily find detailed information, navigate and explore relationships, access resources and services, and publish information and links to resources for others to use and share, all subject to your defined security policies.

❑ **SharePoint Explorer:** SharePoint Explorer Server Edition is a client-free global navigation pane providing end users the richest possible SharePoint usage and navigation experience. SharePoint Explorer Server Edition provides a friendly tree-based navigation pane that allows novice and expert users alike to see all of their SharePoint Sites, document libraries, and lists at a glance with right-click menus for all common functions. This tool saves the power user and administrator a lot of time and frustration when performing common tasks such as creating new document libraries, adding users, or configuring alert settings. Simply right-click the site, folder, or file, and it displays a menu with specific options for this type of object. See Figure 8-19.

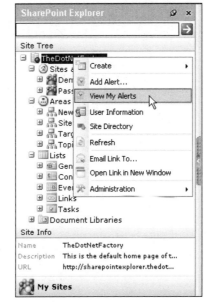

Figure 8-19

Nintex

Use the following URL to go to Nintex: `http://www.nintex.com`.

This is an Australian-based company focusing on one thing: developing an enhanced form of document library including a workflow engine. This product is called SmartLibrary and has a reasonably low price compared to other products on the market with workflow engines.

After installing SmartLibrary to the SharePoint environment, you can enhance any document library with these new features:

- ❑ **Advanced Workflow:** SmartLibrary provides advanced workflow for SharePoint through an easy-to-use graphical interface. Workflow features include serial and parallel approval at document or folder level, progress reporting, reviewer comments, and customizable e-mail alerts.

- ❑ **Activity Monitoring and Reporting:** SmartLibrary provides monitoring and reporting of activities within document libraries and throughout the workflow approval process. Users can monitor statistics such as the average time a document takes to complete the workflow cycle.

- ❑ **Document Undelete:** SmartLibrary provides an undelete facility for documents and folders that have been accidentally deleted. Administrators have the ability to permanently delete items either manually or once a deleted item has reached a predetermined age.

- ❑ **Publish to Other Systems:** Workflow-approved documents can be automatically published at the completion of the workflow to other systems including Web Servers, SharePoint Servers, File Servers, and Web Service–compatible systems.

CorasWorks

Use the following URL to go to CorasWorks: `http://www.corasworks.com`.

This U.S.-based company is one of the big players in the SharePoint web part world! It has a multitude of web parts that are designed for stand-alone use or for working together. These web parts enhance common tasks in SharePoint (for example, project management, designing Helpdesk applications, and creating Executive dashboards). These high-quality web parts are far from free, but the return-on-investment is worth it, and you know that these web parts continually will evolve and expand. Some of the web parts made by CorasWorks are also free; they are described earlier in this chapter. Following are just a few of these SharePoint solutions that CorasWorks offers:

- ❑   Asset Tracking
- ❑   Change Request Tracking
- ❑   Customer Service
- ❑   Document Management
- ❑   Executive Dashboard
- ❑   Help Desk
- ❑   My Workplace for Outlook
- ❑   Partner Extranet
- ❑   Travel Expenses Approval

CorasWorks also has special solutions for the U.S. Air Force, local governments, and manufacturers. Its web site has a very nice demo page where you can test all these solutions before buying them.

Installing Web Parts

There are several ways to install a web part, depending on how the web part is delivered. There are basically three different installation procedures:

- ❑   Use a separate setup program or if the web part is delivered in an .MSI package, just run the program or .msi file.
- ❑   Use the STSADM program to install the web part. Web parts you install this way most often have the file type .CAB.
- ❑   Manually import the web part and configure SharePoint so it will be aware of this new web part.

The first method does not need any more explanation; just run the setup program or the .msi file. Be sure to do this on the SharePoint server itself!

The second method is very common. Using the STSADM.EXE file that installs automatically on the SharePoint server (WSS or SPS) is easy when you know the syntax for adding web parts. This is a command-line tool, so you must run it in a command prompt window (previously called a DOS window).

This STSADM tool is very rich in functionality, but for this discussion you need only to know two of these functions: `addwppack` and `deletewppack`. Enter the following command using a command prompt to get more information about their settings:

❑ **STSADM –o addwppack:** This adds a web part package to the SharePoint server.

❑ **STSADM –o deletewppack:** This removes a web part package from SharePoint.

The easiest way of learning how to use STSADM is by following an example. Say that you have a web part called "Install-FlashSlide.cab" (see "Flash Slideshow," mentioned earlier in this chapter, for more information about this web part), and it is stored in the folder `C:\tmp` on the SharePoint server. You type the following command to install it:

```
stsadm.exe -o addwppack -filename Install-FlashSlide.cab -force -globalinstall
```

The argument `-force` is used to overwrite any previous web part with the same name. The argument `-globalinstall` adds this web part to the global web part gallery for this virtual IIS server so that it can be used in any team site or portal area.

See Chapter 2 to see how to update the PATH system variable to contain the path to the STSADM folder.

Using the same example, to remove the globally installed web part from SharePoint, you type this command (make sure to do this directly on the SharePoint server):

```
Stsadm -o deletewppack -name Install-FlashSlide.cab
```

The last installation method is seldom used for web parts you find on the Internet; it is more often used for a web part developed by you or a colleague. If you need to install a web part using this method, you should request a detailed description of the installation process from the developer. It is very easy to miss a step and fail to install the web part.

You can find a good source regarding this manual installation procedure at Bamboo Solutions: http:// store.bamboosolutions.com/productspecs/SharePoint%20WP-CAS%20FAQ.pdf.

Developing Web Parts

If you decide that you want to develop your own web parts, you can create solutions for almost anything, and it will be great fun! However, this is not an easy task even for an experienced programmer. The challenge is to understand how SharePoint web parts work and what the rules are when creating new web parts. Fortunately, lots of good online sources and books are available on how to do this. Microsoft also has a course (MOC number 2014) to help you get started. But remember this: Make sure you are at least a bit experienced in Visual Studio .NET development, either VB.NET or C#.NET. Only then are you prepared to jump into the wonderful world of web part development.

When using Visual Studio .NET 2005, you will have a lot more built-in functionality for web part development than in previous versions of Visual Studio .NET. So when you read instructions on the Internet on developing web parts, make sure they are referring to the same version of Visual Studio .NET that you have!

Following are some good introductions to web part development:

- ❏ `http://www.devx.com/dotnet/Article/17518/1954?pf=true`

- ❏ `http://www.webbuildermag.com/dotnet/Article/17518/0/page/6`

- ❏ `http://www.sharepointcustomization.com/search.htm` (search for "develop web parts" to see all links).

In most cases you will need a local SharePoint server when developing web parts. Install a local WSS environment for this purpose; avoid developing directly on the production server in case something bad happens. (Bad things eventually do happen, even to the best of us!)

Summary

In this chapter you learned the following:

- ❏ Web parts are the building blocks of SharePoint.

- ❏ A web part is really an ASP.NET server control.

- ❏ A web part must reside in a web part zone.

- ❏ Quite a few web parts come with WSS and SPS.

- ❏ Many web parts for SPS cannot be used in WSS, but almost all web parts for WSS can also be used in SPS.

- ❏ To create or change web part zones, you need FrontPage 2003.

- ❏ Many web parts can be used in ways that are not intuitive; for example, the XML web part can be configured to operate as an RSS feed reader.

- ❏ RSS = Really Simple Syndication.

- ❏ A number of web parts in SPS are in fact the same web part, but configured differently (for example, the Grouped Listings, Links for You, and the News web parts).

- ❏ The Internet is full of free web parts, but the commercial web parts are often, but not always, more advanced.

- ❏ Installing web parts is most often done by installation programs or .msi packages. However, web parts can also be installed using the command-line function `STSADM -o addwppack - filename web_part.cab`.

- ❏ To develop web parts you need some Visual Studio .NET experience, but it is worth it!

In the next chapter you learn more about how to use SharePoint for effective file and document management.

More Effective File and Document Management

Every computer user is managing files and documents every day. It is an important and often frustrating task to find the needed file quickly and to be sure it is the correct version. Every step you can take to make this task easier will be received by standing applause from your users. If you also can make it just a bit more fun, they will cheer. File and document management is this important! SharePoint can help you make this happen. And this chapter is all about how to help users find their files more quickly and easily.

Traditional File Chaos

To understand what SharePoint can do requires that you analyze how things work traditionally. These are the typical tasks a user performs with files and documents every day:

Common File Tasks	Challenges/Problems
Create a file	Where will this file be stored so it can be found later by me and my colleagues? What name should I give this file so it is clear what it contains?
Update a file	How do I find the file to be updated? How can I save the new version without overwriting the old file? How can I update a public file over a period of days and avoid someone seeing the document before it is fully updated? How can several people cooperate when updating a file?
Open a file	How do I find the file? How can I be sure it is the latest version? How can I contact the most recent author if necessary?
Delete a file	How can I be sure there is no other copy of this file still existing?

These are the challenges that your users deal with every time they work with a file or document. Face the reality: Users solve these challenges in several ways, and the consequence is that you soon have file chaos. No one is sure where all the files are stored, no one is sure that the file they found is the latest version, and all these files make the backup and restore procedures unnecessarily complicated and time-consuming.

Document Management Systems

There are some great tools for creating documents and files, with MS Office being the premium example. Some of these tools have built-in features for organizing and locating files. This is good, but the problem is that this solution only works within each tool; there is no global solution for managing all types of documents and files. So the traditional document management solutions may be good to some extent, but they are not enough. That is why all, not some, but *all* organizations have a more or less chaotic system for managing their files. Even so, users have learned to live with this situation. Can you imagine how much time you would save your company if you could reduce this file chaos, or even eliminate it altogether?

One partial solution for this file chaos is a *document management system*, or *DMS*. These types of products have existed for many years, and people love the idea of them when they read about what they can do. A DMS costs a lot of money, but if all these promises are fulfilled, the improved efficiency and productivity of your users can quickly result in a good ROI (return on investment). Although this is a pleasant idea, the reality is not always that positive. What most often happens is that some users love the new DMS and start working with it to its full extent. Others start to use it grudgingly, but after some time they go back to the old routine, which they are more familiar and comfortable with, despite the problems it causes them. And some simply never even start using the new DMS. Period. The result is even worse than before. Now you have some files stored in the old way (usually in a mix of file shares, local disks, and mailbox attachments), and other files are stored in the fancy DMS. And the organization is paying an expensive license every year to keep its DMS working.

What does the manager or other person who is responsible for the DMS purchase do now? That is right; they continue to work with the DMS, to pay its annual fees, and maybe even invest some more in it. Isn't this strange? At first glance, it might even seem foolish, but that depends who you are. If you were the person who convinced the CEO that you needed this DMS and that the ROI for this $50,000 per year was no problem, you are now faced with the prospect of either telling the CEO you have problems and most likely get sacked or trying to fix it somehow, while praying to whichever God that pleases you that the users will somehow get the idea and start using the system.

How can something like this happen? The basic idea is excellent: Get a system that will help users to manage their documents in a more sophisticated way. So why does it go wrong? The usual reasons are one or more of these:

❑ **The system is too complex to use:** Having too many features makes it hard for the average user to understand how to use it.

❑ **The system is not integrated into MS Office:** If users must produce the document in MS Word and then move to another application for entering document properties and so on, it is easier for users to store the file in the same file system as they have always done.

❑ **The system slows down the user:** If the DMS is slow or requires several extra steps for users to complete, users will see this as an obstacle that has a negative effect on their performance.

❏ **The user is expected to learn the system without training:** This may not be a problem if there are just a few new features to learn that are intuitive and well integrated into MS Office. If not, this is definitely a show-stopper.

❏ **The user refuses to learn anything new, ever!** This is more common than one first may expect. And the reason for this strange opinion is often fear: fear that the user will not understand the new system, fear that it will be a more complicated process and take more time than before, and general fear of any type of change, regardless of what it is.

That last bullet is not something to ignore. If you can make such a user accept the new solution, you can get the results you hope for when investing in this DMS solution. So try to find these users and use them as indicators of how successful your new DMS solution is.

Traditional File Management Systems

Without a DMS solution, the need to organize files and documents must be solved another way. This organizational need is most often solved this way:

1. Create a hierarchical folder tree in a file server. The user has a mapped disk drive to that file share.

2. Name each file so it is easy to understand what it contains (for example, "Budget_Q3_2006_V1.XLS").

This method has been with us since MS DOS 2.0 was released in 1983, when the user for the first time could create hierarchical file structures. It was a great feature at that time; taken from the UNIX operating system, of course. A typical traditional file system looks something like this:

```
C:\Public
      \Projects
            \IT
                  \AD-migration
                  \Exchange
                  \DMS
            \Sales
                  \Marketing
                  \Customers
                        \HM
                        \Ericson
                        \Ford
                  \Products
      \Customers
            \HM
                  \Contracts
                  \Quotes
                  \Products
            \Ericson
                  \Contracts
                  \Quotes
                  \Products
            \Ford
                  \Contracts
                  \Quotes
                  \Products
```

With this hierarchical folder tree, it is very easy to find all project documents for AD migration done by IT and all quotes for Ford. But what if a user wants to see all quotes, regardless of the customer? Then this user must look into three different folders, and if there are 300 customers, the user must look in all 300 Quote folders. In this situation it is very common that the users will copy these quotes to their local client, just to make them listed together and easier to work with. Now you have the same files in two places. This happens all the time and is one of the major reasons you end up with file chaos.

Why is the folder's structure arranged by customers and then document types? The answer is probably that someone thought that was a great idea when it was created, based on whatever limited criteria they were using at the time. If this is not true any more, you can of course rearrange this structure; it will take some time, but it certainly can be done. But your users must be informed about this change, or they will become very confused when the folder structure has changed. The point here is that a file system is almost static out of necessity. The folder structure will stay like this for a long time, even if some people want to change it. This is something you have to accept when using a file system.

What about the file names, such as "Budget_Q3_2006_V1.XLS"? Is this really a good name? Well, sort of. It is easy to see what type of content it has (Budget), what period it is from (Q3 2006), and what version it is (V1). The problem here is that there is nothing that will force another user to use the same file name format. The next user may call an updated version of that file "2006-Q3_Budget-2.xls." It is still rather easy to guess that this is the second version of the previous file. But the third update gets this name: "Q3-6-3-BG.xls." If these three files are stored in different places, it really starts to get messy. The problem is that you cannot describe the file using anything other than its name. You can of course create a new folder named Budget and then store files with names like "Q3-2006-v1.xls" in it. Imagine that you copy that file to another place now. How will you know it's a budget file in its new location?

Another common problem is keeping track of updates: For example, when a specific file you depend on gets updated by another user, how do you get this information? Or, if there is a new quote sent out to the customer H&M, how will you know this?

As you can see there are lots of problems and limitations with the traditional file structure as we know it. Fortunately, solutions are available to address all of this, as you will see in the following sections.

What You Really Need

You need a new method to organize and group files without using folders, something that will be easy to change, or will even change automatically for each user looking at these files. For example, a project manager might want to see project documents presented in one way, but each project member may need to organize this information in another way, maybe even hiding everything but the files the project member works with.

All these problems with file names could be solved if you were allowed to create your own properties for a file or document, such as Document Type, Year, and Period. Then you could store this information in the properties instead of building it into the actual file name. If the system also could keep track of versions automatically, you would not have this mess anymore either, right?

You also need a mechanism that will tell you when something gets changed. Because each user knows best what files they are interested in, they must be able to define for themselves which files to monitor and how to monitor them. In addition to files, users may need to monitor folders as well.

Another common need is to have a feature that will enable a user to update an existing document stored in a shared file resource without any risk that other users may see what they are doing until the work is complete. This method must be able to lock the file for editing to a specific user regardless of whether they are actively editing the file. If there is more than one user who will update this document during this editorial period, there must be a way that allows several users to collaborate without somebody else seeing what is happening until the work is completed and published.

To summarize the entire situation, what you need are features like these:

- ❏ A way to organize, sort, and group files, based on file properties.

- ❏ A file structure that is easy for the user to directly modify at any time.

- ❏ A way to describe the files other than using the file name.

- ❏ A way to force all users to follow this new naming standard.

- ❏ An automatic version history that keeps track of every modification to the file.

- ❏ A way to monitor individual files and folders that notifies you when something happens.

- ❏ A way to lock the editing of a shared file to a specific user, regardless of whether this user is working with the file.

- ❏ A way to handle the situation where more than one user will edit a shared document during a period. When all of these editorial users are done, this file should be published so everyone can see it in this shared location.

And all of this must be easy to use and integrate into the MS Office products as much as possible. It must also be fast and reliable. Can it be done, you ask? You bet!

The SharePoint Way

The solutions described in the previous section can be provided with the WSS version of SharePoint (that is right, the free version). To make the solution complete, you need MS Office 2003, but even with earlier Office versions, you can come a long way. The recommendation is that users who work actively with updating documents have at least MS Office 2003, but users who read and act on these documents can do so with MS Office 2002 or even MS Office 2000.

The features described in this section are available for both SPS and WSS, meaning this can be done in both the portal areas and team sites. But you may remember from previous chapters that collaborating should be done in team sites, so even if you have SPS installed, you will most likely end up implementing these solutions in a team site.

The basic structure for file and document management is SharePoint's document libraries. It provides you the following built-in features:

- ❏ **Storing any type of file:** Note that there is a global setting in SharePoint that controls what file types SharePoint does not allow; see the following section on how to change that setting.

- ❏ **Built-in version history:** This is disabled by default, but when enabled it automatically keeps track of all updates of each file in this document library.

Chapter 9

❑ **Add custom file properties:** You can add any number of columns to a document library to describe properties or any type of information you want about each file.

❑ **Add custom views:** You can create definitions on how to sort and present the files in this document library; these views can be personal or publicly available.

❑ **Built-in file locking:** Using the standard type of Check-out/Check-in capabilities found in all DMSs, the user can lock a file for any period of time.

❑ **Create Document Workspace:** This automatically makes a copy of a file and builds a subsite around it. This site, or workspace, may then have one or more users allowed to work with this file. When done, the new version of this document will be published back to its original location.

❑ **Send alerts when updated:** Use this feature to send an e-mail when a specific document or folder is modified.

❑ **Fully integrated with Office 2003:** All of these features can be used with the web client interface or an MS Office 2003 tool, such as MS Word, MS Excel, or MS PowerPoint.

So there you have it: everything you need to build a solution for more effective document management. And remember that all of this is available not only for MS Office documents, but for any file type (for example, PDF files, ASCII text files, and CAD files).

Allowed File Types

There is a global setting that will affect what file types users are allowed to store in any document library. Note that there is no way to control an individual document library in SharePoint 2003. To view and manage these file types you do this:

Try It Out   **Manage Disabled File Types**

1.   Depending on whether you run the full SPS or only WSS, you start like this:

   ❑ **WSS:** Start SharePoint Central Administration.

   ❑ **SPS:** On the portal site go to Site Settings⇨Go to SharePoint Portal Server central administration.

2.   Click Manage blocked file types.

3.   On the following page, you will see a list of 76 blocked file types; see Figure 9-1. If users try to add a file of any of these file types, they will receive this error message: "The following file(s) have been blocked by the administrator: <file name>.<blocked file type>."

4.   If you want to enable a blocked file type, just mark that line and press Delete. If you want to block a new file type, add it to a new line. When done, click OK to save and close this page.

The 76 file types that are blocked by default are these:

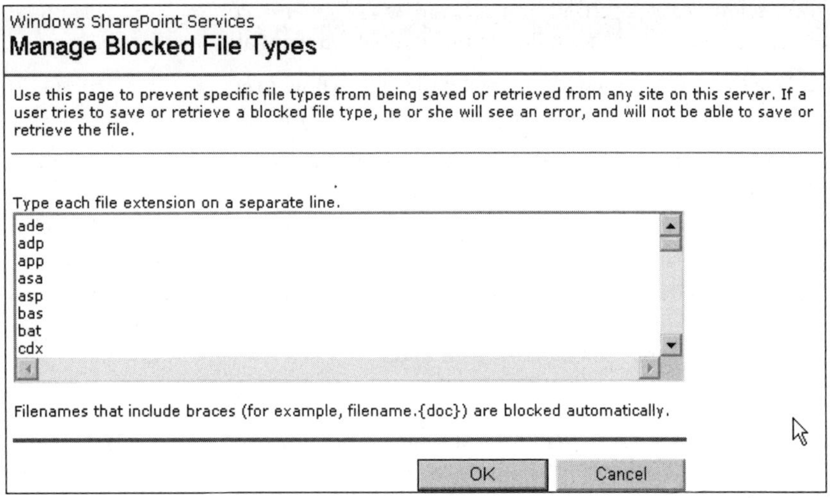

Windows SharePoint Services
Manage Blocked File Types

Use this page to prevent specific file types from being saved or retrieved from any site on this server. If a user tries to save or retrieve a blocked file type, he or she will see an error, and will not be able to save or retrieve the file.

Type each file extension on a separate line.

```
ade
adp
app
asa
asp
bas
bat
cdx
```

Filenames that include braces (for example, filename.{doc}) are blocked automatically.

| OK | Cancel |

Figure 9-1

File type	File type	File type	File type
ade	adp	app	asa
asp	bas	bat	cdx
cer	chm	class	cmd
com	cpl	crt	csh
dll	exe	fxp	hlp
hta	htr	htw	ida
idc	idq	ins	isp
its	jse	ksh	lnk
mad	maf	mag	mam
maq	mar	mas	mat
mau	mav	maw	mda
mdb	mde	mdt	mdw
mdz	msc	msi	msp
mst	ops	pcd	pif
prf	prg	printer	pst

Table continued on following page

File type	File type	File type	File type
reg	scf	scr	sct
shb	shs	shtm	shtml
stm	url	vb	vbe
Vbs	wsc	wsf	wsh

The reason these file types are blocked is security. They can each be used to activate some sort of malicious action, such as a virus, Trojan horse, or worm. If you want to replace the shared file system with SharePoint's document libraries, you may need to unblock some or all of these file types.

> **Before you unblock these file types, it is strongly recommended that you implement a SharePoint-enabled antivirus solution, just as you would do in an ordinary file system.**

Creating Document Libraries

To start with, you need a document library. Some team site templates, such as Team Sites, already contain one document library named "Shared Documents." Either you start with this or you create a new one, using these steps:

Try It Out   **Create a New Document Library**

1. Go to the site where the new document library will be created.

2. Click the Create link at the top of this page.

3. To create a standard document library, click Document Library and enter its properties in the following page (see Figure 9-2):

   a. **Name:** Enter a name for this document library that is unique in this site.

   b. **Description:** Enter a description of this document library.

   c. **Navigation:** Select Yes if you want this document library to be listed in the left pane of this team site; this pane is referred to as the quick launch bar. If you select No you can find it by clicking the Documents and Lists link on the team site. You can also add it as a web part to display its content directly to the team.

   If you create a document library in a portal area, this Navigation setting has no meaning, because there is no quick launch bar. To see the library, either click the Action link "Manage Content" or display the web part for this library.

   d. **Document Versions:** Select Yes to activate version history for all documents in this library or No to save only the latest version of each document. You can later change this setting for existing libraries.

   e. **Document Template:** Select the document that will be used as a template when a user clicks the New Document button on the document library page.

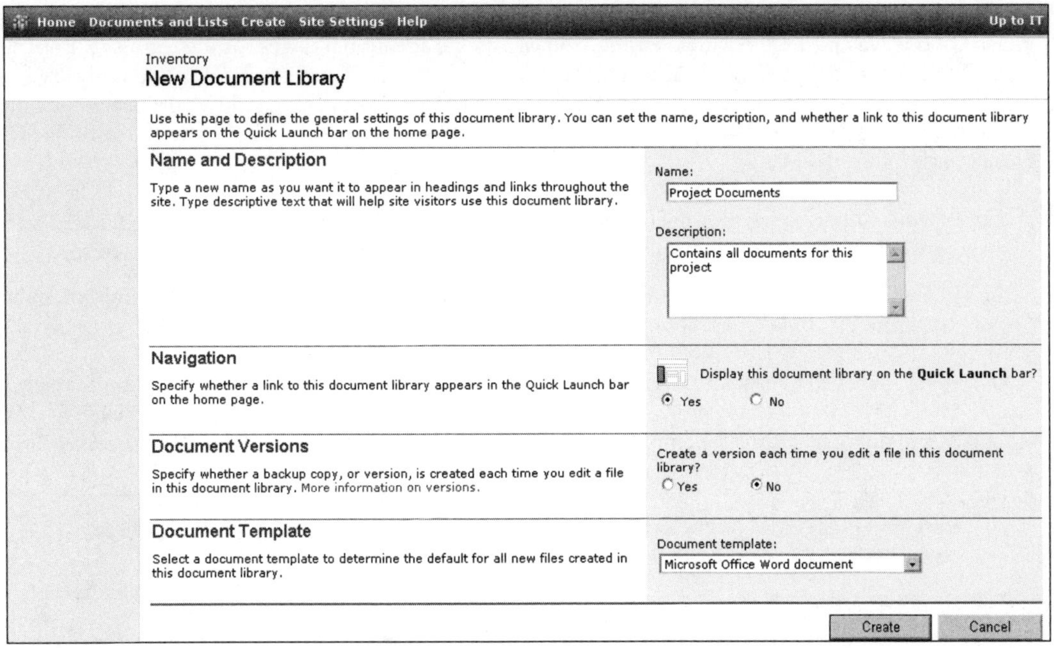

Figure 9-2

By default a document library can only contain one document template. There are several ways to this change limitation, and you will find more information about this in Chapter 12. The available default templates are listed here. Note that the actual template files are stored in the subfolder Forms in the document library.

❑ **None:** Click New Document to start MS Word with an empty document (the same one you get when starting MS Word by itself).

❑ **MS Office Word document:** Click New Document to start MS Word based on the content of the file Template.doc. Edit Template.doc if you want all new files to start with a specific content.

❑ **MS Office FrontPage Web page:** Click New Document to start MS FrontPage based on the content of the file Template.htm. Edit Template.htm if you want all new files to start with a specific content.

❑ **MS Office Excel spreadsheet:** Click New Document to start MS Excel based on the content of the file Template.xls. Edit Template.xls if you want all new files to start with a specific content.

❑ **MS Office PowerPoint presentation:** Click New Document to start MS PowerPoint based on the content of the file Template.pot. Edit Template.pot if you want all new files to start with a specific content.

❑ **Basic page:** Click New Documents to create a new basic web page in this site. Note that all extra web pages for a SharePoint site will be stored as files in a document library. This page will have the Content Editor web part added to allow you to enter information on this page in rich text format, including tables and pictures.

❑ **Web Part Page:** Click New Documents to create a new web part page with a specific layout in this site. Just like basic pages, these web part pages must be stored in a document library.

The last two options, Basic page and Web Part Page, may need some extra clarification. All team sites consist of one web part page named Home. You can create additional pages for the team site, both standard HTML pages and web part pages; these extra pages are stored as files in a document library in this team site. To actually display a page on the site, the user must open its page file. In order to make it easier for the user to see what extra pages exist and open them, you can use either of these methods on the Home page for this team site:

❑   Display the web part for the document library where these pages' files are stored. Make sure to give these page files descriptive names so the user understands what they are used for.

❑   Display the Links web part and create links to these page files. Use descriptive link titles so the user understands what these pages are used for.

Adding extra pages to a team site makes it possible to extend the information displayed on that site, while still using all its security settings, lists, and libraries. An alternative is to create a subsite to this team site, but doing so creates a completely new site with its own content and possibly security settings.

> **Note that these extra pages will not be displayed in a tab view. You can use page layers and tab buttons to create this view, as described in Chapter 12.**

A relevant question now is "How many document libraries do I need?" And the answer is: Start with one library and use it for everything until one of the following scenarios happens:

❑   **You need to have different permission settings for some files:** For example, if Adam needs Contributor permissions to some but not all files in a document library, you can create two separate document libraries and set different permissions for each one.

❑   **You need different columns or views for different files:** If it is important that users will see only the views and custom columns related to a given set of files, you may have to create a separate document library.

❑   **You need to activate version history for some, but not all, files:** Because this feature is set per folder, not per file, you must create a separate document library for each set of files, unless you don't mind having version history active even for those files that don't really use it. The price will be that more disk space is required on the SQL Server.

❑   **You need content approval for some, but not all, files:** This feature is also set per folder. If only some of the files need this feature, create a separate document library for them.

One document library can host more than one million files. When you get these kinds of numbers, you may also need to divide them into several libraries to ensure the optimum performance when opening and updating these files.

Understanding Columns and Views

The most common mistake is to create one document library for each main file share structure; for example, in the file system depicted earlier in this chapter you would end up with one library named "Projects" and another named "Customers." That might sound like a good idea, but test if you can store all files in one library first using columns and views to sort them into Projects and Customers. To do this, you need to create custom columns and then build views that use these columns to sort and filter the list of files.

Document Library Columns

This feature makes it possible to describe the file's content without using the file name. Actually, when you start using these columns, you may even start to wonder why you need file names at all. When you add columns to a document library, you have a number of types to choose from. It is important to use the correct column type because it will affect what you can to with the column, especially when creating views. The following table displays all the column types and how to use them:

Column Type	Description	Examples
Single line of text	Allows the user to enter one text line with up to 255 characters.	Can be used for short descriptions or comments.
Multiple lines of text	Allows the user to enter up to 1,000 lines of text of 80 characters each.	Can be used for longer descriptions.
Choice	Allows the user to select from more than 100 predefined choices.	Create a list of Document Types, such as "Info, Quote, Contract" or Customers, such as "Ericson, H&M, Ford."
Number	Allows the user to enter a number with or without decimals or in percent.	Enter the number of products in stock, the weight of a patient, a zip code, and so on.
Currency	Allows the user to enter a number that will be treated as currency. You can define what format to be used.	Use for prices, income, net results, and so on.
Date and Time	Allows the user to enter a date and optional time value.	Use for contract dates, defining time periods, birthdays, and so on.
Lookup	The value displayed in this field will come from another list or library on this site.	Use for displaying a list of all members for this site, a customer name retrieved from a Customer Contact list, or a Product List on this site.
Yes/No	The user can select Yes or No.	Use it for binary options, like "This document is public," "There are optional add-ons," or "Quote is active."
Hyperlink	The user can enter an HTML URL address; this address can be displayed as a link or formatted as a picture.	Use this to add links to external information or to display pictures of products or people.
Calculated	This field is automatically filled with a calculated value. The user will not enter anything in this field. You can use mathematical formulas and logical operators.	Calculate the total sum based on two other "Number" columns; or the date 30 days from now.

The last column type, Calculated, is similar to a calculated cell value in MS Excel. For example, say that you have two columns named "Price" and "Pieces" and you want a third column that calculates the total sum based on Price × Pieces. A reference to another column is defined by entering the name within [ ]; for example, [Price] and [Pieces]. The formula would then be:

```
[Price]*[Pieces]
```

Another example would be to display text based on a given limit. For example, if the column Sales is higher than Expenses, you want a third column to display "Nice business"; if not it should display "You are losing money!" The formula for this will look like this:

```
IF([Sales]>[Expenses],"Nice business","You are losing money!")
```

The result would then look like Figure 9-3.

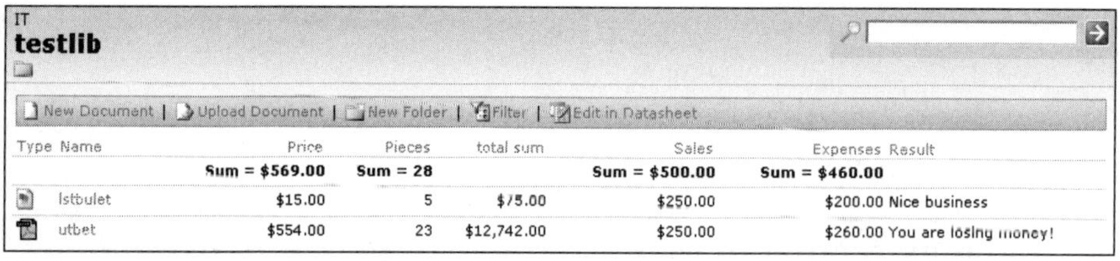

Figure 9-3

You can find a lot more information about calculated columns using the link "Show me more information" next to where you define the calculated column; see Figure 9-4.

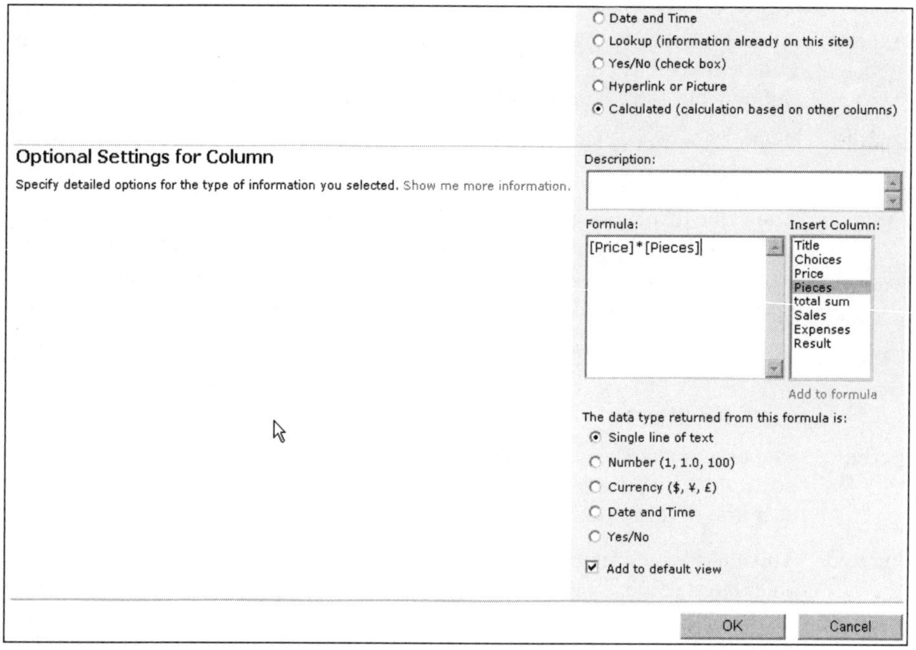

Figure 9-4

As usual, examples are the best way of demonstrating how to work with columns in document libraries. Say that you have a list of files and you need to describe the document type (Quote, Order, and Contract) and security class (Public, Internal only, and Secret) for each of these files. Instead of creating files with names such as Quote_Internal_Ford.doc, you want to do it the SharePoint way:

Try It Out   **Create Columns for Document Libraries**

1. Log on as a user with Web Designer or Administrator rights for this site.

2. Click the document library name (for example, "Shared Documents") and it opens a new page with all the features available for this document library.

3. Click Modify settings and columns in the quick launch bar. A new page opens where you can configure this document library.

4. Scroll down to the Columns section. Click Add a new column. On the following web form (see Figure 9-5), enter these settings:

    a. **Column name:** Doc Type. This will be a column for storing the document types.

    b. **The type of information in this column is:** Choice.

    c. **Description:** "This column is used to define the document type."

    d. **Type each choice on a separate line:** Make sure to enter one choice per row: Quote; Order; Contract.

    e. **Display choices using:** Drop-Down Menu.

    f. **Allow "Fill-in" choices**: No.

    g. **Default value:** Clear this text box; you don't need a default value this time.

    h. Click OK to store and save this web form. The first column is now done!

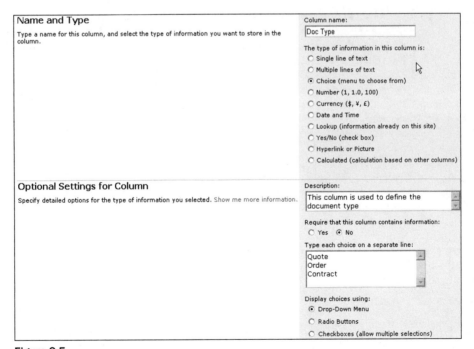

Figure 9-5

5. You need a second column as well; click Add a new column again and enter these values:

    a. **Column Name:** Security Class.

    b. **The type of information in this column is:** Choice.

    c. **Description:** "This column is used to define the security class for this document."

    d. **Type each choice on a separate line:** Public; Internal only; Secret.

    e. **Default value:** Clear this box.

    f. Click OK to store and save this web form. The second column is now done!

If you need to modify a column, just click its name to open its configuration page.

6. Near the top of the page, click Go back to "Shared Documents" to return. Note that the two new columns are listed to the far right side of the header line. All new columns will show up like this.

7. It is time to add some documents. Click Upload Documents, and a web form is displayed with these two new columns. Select Doc Type = Contract and Security Class = Internal only. Then click Browse and locate a file to which you want to add to this document library. Click Save and Close.

8. The new file is listed with the values you selected for these two columns. But what about any existing files? There are two ways to set these column values for existing files:

    a. Use the quick menu (hover the mouse over the file name, and click the menu arrow to the right). Select Edit Properties and set the value for Doc Type and Security Class; then click Save and Close.

    b. Click Edit in Datasheet. This feature requires that the user has Excel 2003 locally installed. Click a cell in the Doc Type column, and you will see a scroll-down menu that allows you to easily select any of the preconfigured choices. Set the values for your files and then click Show in standard view to leave the Datasheet mode.

When updating these new property settings using "Edit in Datasheet" you may sometimes get a question saying "You have pending changes or unresolved conflicts and errors. Do you want to wait for this operation to complete?" Click Yes if this happens. The reason this may happen is that the Datasheet is an ActiveX component that does its synchronization in short intervals; if you are too fast, it might have not automatically synchronized the modifications yet.

The first method is fine if you just want to change the properties for a single document; the second method is very handy when you want to modify several documents' properties at the same time. Use whichever method you find convenient.

This is fun, don't you agree? It is so easy to add a new column if there is a need to keep track of a new property. Now try some more: Say you want to list the person who is responsible for each document. You also want to display the company name that each file is connected with. Now (and this is very nice), if you already have a contact list that contains all the customers, you can use that list in this document library.

To make this exercise more fun, before you continue, add some company names to the contact list for this site. Click Home to return to the start page for this web site. Click Contacts to view the list. To add some extra contacts, click New Item. Make sure to add a company name for each contact, because you will use this column next.

1. Click the Shared Documents link to open a new page with this library.

2. Click "Modify settings and columns" in the quick launch bar. A new page is open where you can configure this document library.

3. Scroll down to the Columns section. Click Add a new column. On the following web form, enter these settings:

   a. **Column Name:** Doc Manager. This column will store the name of the user responsible for this file. Note that, because this person must have access to this site. (How else would he/she else be responsible for a file here?)

   b. **The type of information in this column is:** Lookup. Instead of adding a choice list of possible document managers, you can utilize the fact that these users must have access to this site. With the column type Lookup, you can ask SharePoint to look for a value in another list.

   c. **Description:** "Enter the responsible user for this document."

   d. **Get information from:** User Information.

   e. Click OK to store. Your third column is done.

4. The next and final column will get its content from the customer contact list. What you need is just the company name. Click "Add a new column" and fill in the following values (as shown in Figure 9-6):

   a. **Column Name:** Company. This column displays the company that this file is connected to.

   b. **The type of information in this column is:** Lookup.

   c. **Description:** "This column gets its value from the Contact list."

   d. **Get information from:** Contacts (the name for this list).

   e. **In this column:** Company.

   f. Click OK to store. Your fourth column is done.

5. Click Go back to "Shared Documents."

6. Use the quick menu for any file and select Edit properties.

   a. In the Doc Manager drop-down menu, note that it lists all users who are members of this site (who have been granted any level of permission); select any of these names.

   b. Then use the Company drop-down menu, and note that it will contain the names in the Contacts folder; select any company name in this list.

   c. When ready, click Save and Close.

   Repeat this for at least five other documents to prepare for later exercises.

As you have seen, adding new columns is very easy and makes it much easier to understand what a specific file is used for. To sort the list of documents, click the column names. For example, if you want to sort the files based on document types, click the Doc Type name; click one more time if you want to reverse the sort order. Even if the column feature is very nice, it will be hard to find what you are looking for when the list contains hundreds or even thousands of files. What you need is a way of grouping and filtering the file names.

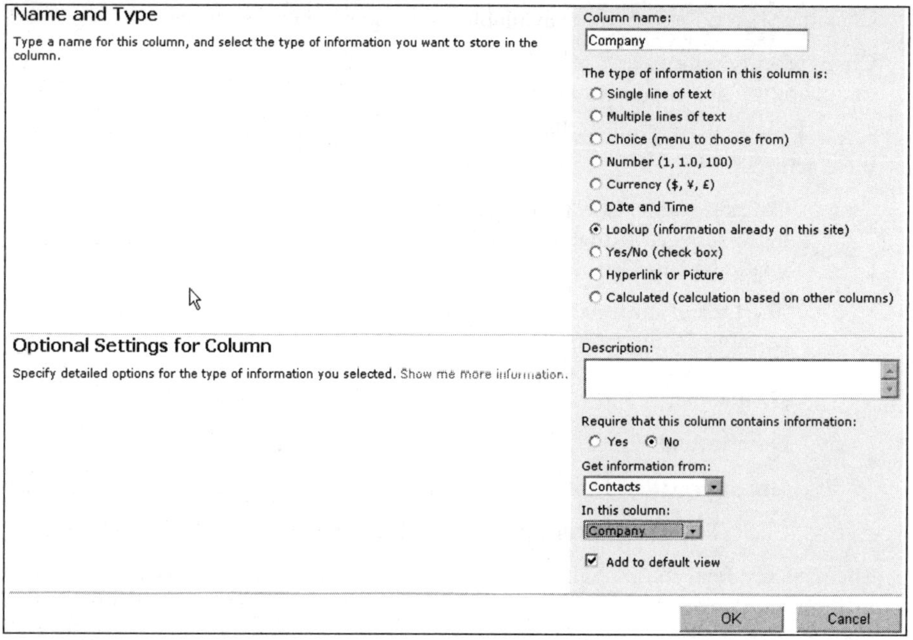

Figure 9-6

Working with Views

A document library with custom columns is so much easier to use than a standard file system. But you can also use these columns to something more; they can be the base for sorting, grouping, and filtering the files presented in the document library. SharePoint calls this a *view*. You can create a view that only displays documents where the Security Class is equal to Secret or a view that groups all documents and files based on company, or a view that only displays the files of which you are the Document Manager.

A document library can have any number of views. Each view can be either public or personal. Note that views are not security definitions; if someone knows the URL address for another user's personal view, he can use it by typing in the URL address manually.

The real beauty with columns will show up when you start creating views. Note that end users are supposed to create their own views, after some training, without any assistance from the administrator or a web developer. Views are an important feature and a key to achieving effective document management.

Now do some examples, again. The previously mentioned views will do fine. Use these steps to create these views, and remember that they are dependent on the columns made in the previous examples:

Try It Out   **Create Views in Document Libraries**

1. Log on as an administrator or a member of the Web Designer site group.

2. Open the document library where the new views will be created (in this example, "Shared Documents").

3. Click Modify settings and columns. Scroll down to the Views section. Click "Create a new view."

4. You will select one out of three available types of views: Standard View, Datasheet View, or Calendar View. In this example, select Standard View.

5. Now you see a web form asking about how this view is to be configured. The first example is a view that only displays a document with security class equal to Secret:

    a. **Name:** Secret Documents. This is just a label for this view.

    b. **Make this the default view:** No (the default value).

    c. **View Audience:** "Create a Public view" (the default value). A personal view will only be displayed for the user who created it.

    d. **Columns:** Check each column to be displayed in this view. You can also change the order by using the Position from Left option.

    e. **Sort:** Name (for use in forms). This setting will present all documents in a list sorted by the file name.

    f. **Filter:** Under "Show the items when column," set "Security Class" equal to "Secret." Note that this automatically sets the filter option "Show items only when the following is true." Now you have created a filtered list. Click OK at the end of this page to close and store this page.

6. Click Go back to "Shared Documents." This displays all the documents using the default view.

7. Look at the top-left corner of the picture; your newly created view is listed here, named Secret Documents. Click this view link. You should only see files with the security class Secret. Click All Documents to display the default list view again.

8. To create another view that will group all files based on Company name, click "Create a new view" and select Standard View. Enter these values:

    a. **Name:** Companies.

    b. **View Audience:** Create a Public view.

    c. **Columns:** Define what columns to display and in what order.

    d. **Sort:** "Name (for use in forms)".

    e. **Group by / First group by column:** Company.

    f. **Group by / By default, show groupings:** Collapsed.

    g. Click OK.

9. Click Go back to "Shared Documents"; click the new view Companies. It should display a view similar to folders with no files listed, as in Figure 9-7. Note that the numbers in parentheses indicate how many files match this company name.

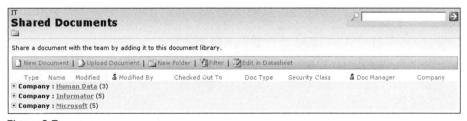

Figure 9-7

10. To create a third view that only lists documents where you are the Document Manager is almost as easy; the only difference is that you must in some way tell the view who you are. SharePoint has a special variable for this: [Me]. Note that these variables are translated into your local language if you install anything other than U.S. English. Click "Create a new view" and select Standard View. Enter these values:

    a. **Name:** My Documents.

    b. **View Audience:** Create a Public view.

    c. **Columns:** Define what columns to display, and in what order.

    d. **Sort:** "Name (for use in forms)".

    e. **Filter:** Set "Show the items when column" Doc Manager equal to [Me]. (Note that you have to enter [ME] manually).

    f. In the Totals section, set the column Name to "Count." This will calculate and display the number of files over the "Name" column.

    g. Click OK.

You can also combine multiple columns (for example, if you need a view that lists all public files that you are responsible for). It is also possible to display slightly more advanced calculations. For example, say that you have one column that displays the date when a contract ends. You want a view that lists all documents with fewer than 30 days to the end of the contract. This is not possible to define with just a view, but you can create an extra column that contains the date 30 days before the end of the contract and then use both of these columns when creating a view like this:

Try It Out   **List Documents with Less Than 30 Days to a Date**

1. Open the document library; click Modify columns and settings.

2. Click Add a new column with these settings:

    a. **Name:** End Date.

    b. **Type:** Date and Time.

    c. Click OK.

3. Enter the end dates for each file in this new column. Make sure some have dates more than 30 days away and some have dates less than 30 days away, to make the search results more interesting.

4. Click Add a new column with these settings:

    a. **Name:** 30 Days.

    b. **Type:** Calculated. Use the formula "=[End Date]-30" and set the returning data type as Date and Time.

    c. Click OK.

5. Now you have the two limits you need. The next step is to create a view that compares today's date with these limits. SharePoint has the special keyword [Today] that you will use in this example; it allows you to compare dates with the current date. If the current date is within the limits defined in steps 2 and 4, this document should be listed; if not, do not list it. Click Create a new Standard View with these settings:

    a.   **Name:** Check these documents.

    b.   **View Audience:** Create a Public view.

    c.   **Columns:** Define what columns to display and in what order.

    d.   **Sort:** "Name (for use in forms)".

    e.   **Filter:** "30 Days is less than or equal to [Today]" and "End Date is greater than [Today]".

    f.   Click OK.

Working with Alerts

One of the coolest features is alerts. An alert is your own private servant that checks all documents and other information types; if something you are interested in changes, you will get an e-mail from SharePoint. This is known as an alert, and it exists for both SPS and WSS, even though they are different beasts that use different modules. Here are the most common alerts:

❑   **A single file:** Sends you an e-mail if any specific folder gets changed.

❑   **A complete folder:** Checks a folder; if it is modified or if a file is added, modified, or removed, you are notified.

❑   **A list item:** Checks a specific list item in any type of list; if the item is modified, you are notified.

❑   **A complete list:** Checks a specific list; if the list is updated (for example, if a list item is added or modified), you get an e-mail.

❑   **A news item:** Lets SharePoint's alerts govern the News list on the intranet; when something happens with this list, you will get an e-mail.

❑   **Search query:** Gives you an option when creating a search query (under the Action section) to define a persistent SQL query, meaning that your search query can be saved and used again later.

A common question when discussing SharePoint alerts is how to add an alert for somebody else. This is contrary to what Microsoft defined SharePoint for. According to Microsoft's extensive research, users say they need more control without the assistance from an administrator to help them. That is why Microsoft did not add this feature from the beginning. However, some products can help you with this, such as these:

❑   **Alert Manager:** www.sharepointsolutions.com ($495 per server).

❑   **UserAlerts:** weblogs.asp.net/jan/archive/2004/03/27/97335.aspx (by Jan Tielens; a free web part).

❑   **csegAlertsWebPart:** www.ideseg.com (by Carlos Segura Sanz, a free web part).

In the following example you add an alert for a single file and for a complete document library, by following these steps:

Try It Out   **Add Alerts to Files and Document Libraries**

1. Log on as a member of the Web Designer site group or as an administrator.

2. Open the site and click the document library to view it on a separate page.

3. To add an alert:

    ❑   **For a separate file:** Use the quick menu for any file; select Alert Me.

    ❑   **For a document library:** Click Alert Me under Actions in the quick launch bar.

4. Verify what e-mail address these alerts will be sent to. It is copied from the AD.

5. Set what modification you want to trigger an alert. The default is All changes.

6. Define how often you want SharePoint to check for modifications. The recommended frequency is Send a daily summary. This will group all alerts into one e-mail message per day.

7. Click OK to save and close this web form.

8. A summary of your alerts is listed in three places. Note that each summary does not show the same information:

    a.   **All alerts for a specific team site:** Choose Site Settings⇨My alerts on this site.

    b.   **All alerts on the portal site:** Go to My Site and check the "My Alerts Summary" web part; note that alerts in team sites will not be listed there.

    c.   **All alerts in both the portal site and any team site:** In Outlook 2003: Tools⇨Rules and Alerts⇨the Alerts tab. Note that this is the only way to display a total summary of all alerts!

The alert feature is available almost everywhere in SharePoint, both in the portal site and in team sites. Learn how to use alerts. They can save you a lot of time and make sure you know about important changes in the sites.

Checking Out and Checking In

So far you have learned how to work with custom columns and views, as well as alerts. Now look more closely at how the actual document gets updated. When you open an MS Office document stored in a file share, it automatically opens the document in edit mode, even if your intention is only to read it. If someone else tries to open the same document while you have it open in edit mode, it will not work, because you have locked it; the other user can now use a copy of that document or wait for you to close the document (also closing the edit mode). It would have been better if documents were automatically opened in read-only mode instead of edit mode. SharePoint does this, and you actually must use the document's quick menu to select "Edit with MS Office Word" or whatever file type you are opening.

Assume that you need to update a specific document that is stored on a public file share; you know that it will take more time than you have today, so what do you do? One solution is to copy the file to a local computer and while doing this make sure only you can update this file. The problem with this very common solution is that someone else may start modifying the original file, unaware that you are making updates to a copy of this file; when you are done with your editing, you copy the file back to the original storage. What will happen if the original file has been updated during this time, without your knowing this? Well, your file will overwrite the updated copy stored on the file share.

A much better way is to lock the file so only one person can edit this document. This is a standard feature of WSS team sites. It is called Check Out when a user locks the editing process on a file; from that point on only this user is able to update that document. When this user is done, he or she performs a Check In, which saves the current version and removes the editing lock. The file is now available for others to edit.

So what happens when a user checks out a file? It actually splits into two separate versions: one that the editor sees and works with and another that other users see, which is the same as the most recent public version. When the editor later checks in the file, that version replaces the previous public version. What happens with the previous file depends on the setting for version history. If version history is activated, the file is saved but hidden; if version history is not activated, the file is overwritten.

When a user checks out a file, her name will be listed in the default column "Checked Out To" that all document libraries have. If another user tries to open that file in edit mode, she will be warned that this file is checked out by the first user. There is no way a checked-out file can be edited by more than one user.

When opening MS Office files, such as Word and Excel files, without any previous check out, it also works as if the file is checked out. In other words, SharePoint does a silent and implicit check out when opening an Office document; when this document later is saved and closed, a silent check in occurs. No listing is created in the "Checked Out To" column, but it works the same way, except that it only works as long as the user has this document opened in her MS Office application. This feature will work with MS Office 2000 or later.

Try It Out   Check Out and Check In Documents

1. Go to any document library where you have at least Contributor rights.

2. Choose an existing file. Use its quick menu and select Check out. Note that your name now is listed in the Checked Out To column (as in Figure 9-8), regardless of whether you have the file opened in MS Office.

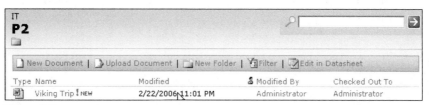

Figure 9-8

3. Log on as another user. Try to open the same document: Quick Menu⇨Edit in Microsoft Office Word. You get a warning that this document is checked out by another user (see Figure 9-9). Close that warning and the MS Office program again.

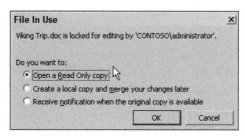

Figure 9-9

4. Go back to your first account. Try to open the same document using its quick menu command "Edit in Microsoft Office Word", and it will work just fine. Do some modifications and close down MS Word. You will now be prompted (see Figure 9-10) asking if you want to:

   a. **Save changes and check in:** Choose this if you are done editing this file. It will no longer be checked out to you any more.

   b. **Save changes only:** Choose this if you want to continue editing this file at a later time. It will remain checked out.

   c. **Discard changes and undo check out:** Choose this if you want to discard all the changes you have made. This will restore the previous version.

   d. **Discard changes only:** Choose this if you want to discard all changes you have made during this editing session but keep the file checked out. You can continue editing this file at a later time.

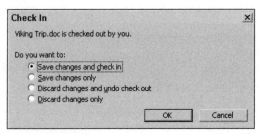

Figure 9-10

5. Choose Save changes only and click OK. The file is closed and your name is still listed in the Checked Out To column. It is perfectly fine if you want to go home for the night and continue to edit this file tomorrow.

When the editing is done, you must check in the file.

6. You can choose Save changes and check in as in step 4, or you can do it with your web browser.

7. Use the quick menu for this file, and select Check in. This will bring you a web form where you can select alternatives similar to step 4 (see Figure 9-11).

8. You can, and should, enter a short description of the modifications done in the "Check In comments" field; it will make it so much easier later, when you display the version history for this file.

9. Click OK. Note that the Checked Out To column is now empty for this file.

A commonly asked question is whether the administrator can break or undo a check-out lock. The answer is Yes! The administrator simply goes to the same document library, uses the quick launch bar, and selects Check in. Because it is a user other than the one who first did the Check out, SharePoint gets suspicious. You will then see the warning depicted in Figure 9-12.

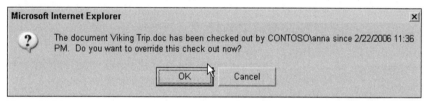

IT
Check In

Use this page to check in a document that you have currently checked out.

Document Check In

The changes you make to a document can be made available to other users when you check in changes or the document to this Web site.

◉ Check in document

◯ Check in changes saved to this document, but keep the document checked out

◯ Discard changes and undo check out

Check In comments:

Added a new paragraph

| OK | Cancel |

Figure 9-11

Microsoft Internet Explorer ☒

❓ The document Viking Trip.doc has been checked out by CONTOSO\anna since 2/22/2006 11:36 PM. Do you want to override this check out now?

| OK | Cancel |

Figure 9-12

Document Version History

By default SharePoint will not store previous versions of any document. It is possible to activate the version history feature, but only for document libraries, XML libraries, and picture libraries. You cannot create version history for other types of lists, such as a Customer list or Task list.

The reason version history is disabled by default is that once you activate it, SharePoint will store a complete copy of every version throughout the history of this file, which can require a lot of extra disk space for the content database. If you have version history active and later revert back to no version management, it will in effect delete all prior versions of all documents except the latest version.

Try It Out   Enable Version History

1. Log on as a user with full permissions.

2. Click the document library (for example, Shared Documents) to view it on a separate web page.

3. Choose Modify settings and columns⇨Change general settings.

4. Click Yes in the section Document Versions.

5. Click OK and then Go Back To "Shared Documents."

Another way of enabling version history is this:

1. Use the quick menu for any file, and select Version History.

2. Click Modify Versioning Settings in the upper-left corner of this page; this will bring the same web form as in the previous step 4.

Regardless of how you enabled this version history, it is now active, but only for this current library! If you have more document libraries and want a version history of them all, you must enable this for all of these libraries. Test it now:

1. Edit any MS Office document in this list and then save and close this file.

2. Use the file's quick menu in Internet Explorer and select Version History. If you changed an existing file once, you should now see a list of two files, but with different times and dates. These two versions also have a quick menu. You can use it to view, restore, or delete this version (see Figure 9-13).

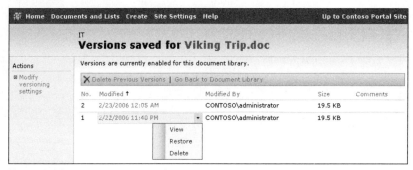

Figure 9-13

If you choose to restore a previous version, the current version will simply be the second newest version, so if you want to undo this restore, you can restore the second newest version. In other words, using the preceding example, you now have three versions, where 1 and 3 are identical.

> *SharePoint 2003 does not have any minor version number schema, such as 4.1 and 4.2. A clever program- mer can fix this with a custom web part; SharePoint 2007 will have this type of version schema built-in.*

Document Management with MS Office

So far you have worked exclusively with a web browser, typically MS Internet Explorer. A user using MS Office 2003 will also find a lot of SharePoint-related features integrated into products like MS Word, MS Excel, and MS PowerPoint. The integration will make it possible for a user who works a lot with MS Office products to use and set SharePoint information without having to start up the web browser. Using any edition of Office 2003, you can do the following SharePoint-related tasks:

❑ **Check Out / Check In:** Lock and unlock editing for a file.

❑ **View version history:** Display a list of all previous versions, including all comments. You can also view, restore, and delete previous versions.

❑ **Manage Alerts:** Set an alert for the current document.

❑ **Manage other files in the library:** Set alerts and delete and open other files. You can also add new documents and create folders in the current library.

❑ **Manage Document Workspace:** Create and delete a workspace for the current document; see more about workspaces later in this chapter.

❑ **View membership:** See what members have access to this team site and if they are online, add new members, edit their Site Group membership, and remove members.

❑ **Manage Tasks:** View, modify, delete, and add new tasks, and create alerts for a task. This information will be stored in a task list on the site where this document library is stored. For more information about working with task lists, see Chapter 10.

❑ **Manage Links:** View, modify, delete, and add new URL links; and create alerts for a link. This information will be stored in a link list on the site where this document library is stored.

❑ **Manage Document Properties:** All properties (including column settings) for this document are available here and can be changed and used in the Office document (for example, in a document header or footer). If you change a column value in Office, this will be replicated back to the document library when you store the changes.

❑ **Manage the team site:** From within Office, you can open this site, change its title, and open its site settings.

None of these features is available for earlier versions of MS Office. It is therefore important that at least the users who produce documents have MS Office 2003 in order to have an optimal working environment.

To see how all these features work, look at some examples. Use the following steps to get familiar with this MS Office integration:

Try It Out   MS Office 2003 Integration

1. Log on as a user with at least Contributor rights to a team site. Open any of its document libraries. Use the quick menu for any MS Office document (for example, an MS Word file), and select Edit in Microsoft Office Word.

2. In MS Word, make sure that you have the Task Pane visible on the right side of the page; if not, check View➪Task Pane. It should look something like Figure 9-14.

3. Click the yellow attention icon to the left of the task pane. It will display important status information about this document, such as if someone has checked out this document. The number under the icon indicates the number of current status information.

4. Click the user icon (second from the left): the number under the icon indicates how many users and groups have access to this library. You will also see the names of these users and groups and their current online status, in case you are using a local MS Live Communication Server in your network or the public MSN instant messaging service. Point the mouse to any of these users; a quick menu will be available that allows you to manage this user, assuming you have the administrative rights in this team site to do this. You will see more information about these users, such as calendar status, phone numbers, mail addresses, and other Outlook properties. At the bottom of this pane tab is a button to add new members and to send e-mail to all members. This last feature is very handy when you want to inform all users about an important update and you do not know if everyone has created an alert for this document.

Figure 9-14

5. Click the task icon (third from the left): the number indicates the total number of tasks in this list. Note that some of these may have been added directly to the task list on the team site. Using the links at the bottom of this tab you can add new tasks and request alerts about tasks. If there is any existing task, it will be listed. Point to a task to see all its details; use its quick menu to edit, delete, or create an alert for this particular task. If a task is completed, set the check box in front of the task and this information will directly be updated on the team site. Use tasks when working with documents as a reminder or to delegate things to do to other members. This is much better than sending an e-mail to team members to delegate tasks to do.

6. Click the document icon (third from the right): the number indicates the total number of documents in this library. Below these documents are listed, unless the number is too high; if so you will see a link to open this list in a browser instead. The reason for this is to avoid long download of information to the MS Office program. There is a drop-down menu for sorting this document list, for example based on creation date or file name. Every document listed has a quick menu that can be used to open or delete it, or to create an alert for this specific document. At the bottom of this tab are links for adding new documents, adding folders to this library, and creating an alert for the current document.

7. Click the link icon (second from the right): The number indicates the current number of URL links available in the linked list in the team site. The actual URL links are listed below; use the Sort by menu to change the sort order for this list. For each URL there is a quick menu that can be used to edit or delete this link, and to create an alert for this particular link. At the bottom you will find buttons for creating new links and managing alerts for these links.

8. Click the information icon (far right): Note that there is no number here. This tab will display all properties, or column settings, for this particular document. You can view or modify these settings, and you can also add these settings to the content of this page, as described in the Try It Out section below. At the bottom of this tab you will find links to restrict permissions using MS Information Rights Management, IRM (implemented in Windows Server 2003 using "MS Rights Management Service," or "RMS"). Note that you must install the IRM client before you can use this cool feature (see http://www.microsoft.com/rms for more information about this). At the bottom of this tab you will also find links for creating an alert for the current document, to check out (or check in), and to view the version history for this document.

9. Click the drop-down menu for the team site link at the top of this pane; it will display a number of options:

   a. **Open Site in Browser:** Starts your web browser and goes to this team site.

   b. **Change Site Title:** Allows you to modify the title for this team site.

   c. **Change Site Settings:** Opens the administrative page for this team site.

   d. **Disconnect from Workspace:** Removes the existing link for this document to a document workspace.

   e. **Delete Workspace:** Deletes the current workspace for this document.

One very handy feature is the propagation of document properties from SharePoint's document library into MS Office. This makes it possible to view and display these properties inside the content of this document. For example, say that you have a column in the document library that defines the customer name for a document. You can use this information to display the customer name in the document header, by following these steps:

Try It Out   Display Properties Inside Office Documents

1. Open an MS Office document in edit mode from the document library, which has custom properties, such as the "Doc Type" column you created in the "Create Columns for Document Libraries" Try It Out.

2. Set the cursor where this information will be displayed, such as in a document header. Type a label to describe the property to be displayed.

3. Place the cursor where you want the property to be displayed. Click the menu Insert↷Field and select DocProperty in the Fields names list. This will display a list of all the properties for this document. You will also find your custom column properties here. Select the property to be displayed and click OK. The property setting will now be visible on this page.

Note that Word documents by default have a number of properties, such as Author and Customer. If you have created a column with the same name, you will find two properties with the same name. For example, if you created the column "Customer" you will find both "Customer" (the standard property found in all Word documents, and "Customer0" (which is your column).

4. Use the Task Pane to the right, and the information tab; change the value for this column you used in step 3. Right-click the old value in the Office document and select Update field, and the new value will be displayed. The reason it does not automatically show updated column values is that MS Office is only configured to always react to changes. This is something you can instruct this MS Office program to do automatically; for example, every time this document is opened or closed. When you have several values you need to update, you can also use Control+A to select all text in the document and then press the F9 key, which will update all field values.

This last feature of displaying column settings inside an MS Office document is very handy when using the document header or other structured documents. Instead of adding values like document type, customer name, or project number manually in the document, you can create columns for this document library and allow the user a much easier way to both view and set these values.

Note that all columns do not work well with this technique. For example, displaying a column of type "Lookup" (displaying an item stored in another list, as described earlier in this chapter) will only display the index number for the item, not its actual value.

Working with Datasheets and MS Excel

For document libraries with custom columns, you can use MS Excel for adding or editing the setting of these columns. Instead of updating the settings one document at a time, it is possible to update all documents at the same time. For example, look at Figure 9-15; it shows a typical document list with some custom columns.

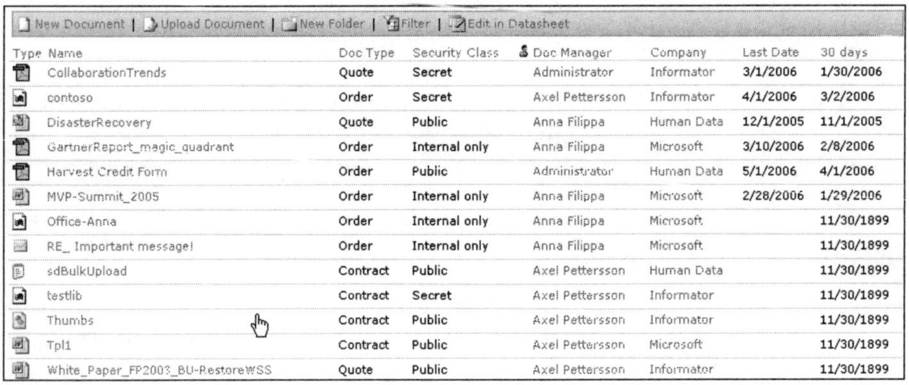

Type	Name	Doc Type	Security Class	Doc Manager	Company	Last Date	30 days
	CollaborationTrends	Quote	Secret	Administrator	Informator	3/1/2006	1/30/2006
	contoso	Order	Secret	Axel Pettersson	Informator	4/1/2006	3/2/2006
	DisasterRecovery	Quote	Public	Anna Filippa	Human Data	12/1/2006	11/1/2005
	GartnerReport_magic_quadrant	Order	Internal only	Anna Filippa	Microsoft	3/10/2006	2/8/2006
	Harvest Credit Form	Order	Public	Administrator	Human Data	5/1/2006	4/1/2006
	MVP-Summit_2005	Order	Internal only	Anna Filippa	Microsoft	2/28/2006	1/29/2006
	Office-Anna	Order	Internal only	Anna Filippa	Microsoft		11/30/1899
	RE_ Important message!	Order	Internal only	Anna Filippa	Microsoft		11/30/1899
	sdBulkUpload	Contract	Public	Axel Pettersson	Human Data		11/30/1899
	testlib	Contract	Secret	Axel Pettersson	Informator		11/30/1899
	Thumbs	Contract	Public	Axel Pettersson	Informator		11/30/1899
	Tpl1	Contract	Public	Axel Pettersson	Microsoft		11/30/1899
	White_Paper_FP2003_BU-RestoreWSS	Quote	Public	Axel Pettersson	Informator		11/30/1899

New Document | Upload Document | New Folder | Filter | Edit in Datasheet

Figure 9-15

Using the Edit in Datasheet button, you can display the same list in a view very similar to MS Excel, as Figure 9-16 shows.

It sure looks like MS Excel. In fact, it is MS Excel! To use this view, the client computer must have MS Excel installed. If so, SharePoint will use an ActiveX component that comes with MS Excel to display this view. Using this view makes it very easy to edit several document settings at the same time; you can also copy cell content to another cell in the same column by using the little black square that is displayed for the currently active cell. If a column has choice values defined, you will see a menu that displays all available choices for this particular column.

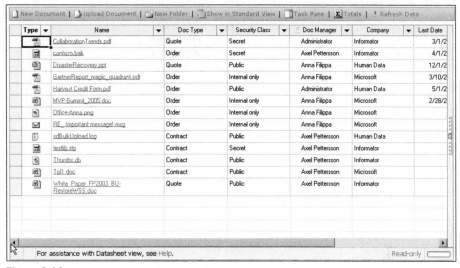

Figure 9-16

You can right-click the column name to get a list of options, such as these:

- ❏ **Copy:** Copy this column.
- ❏ **Paste:** Paste a previously copied column to this position.
- ❏ **Add Column:** Create a new column for this document library.
- ❏ **Edit/Delete Column:** Self-explanatory.
- ❏ **Column width:** Define the width of the column. You can also drag the horizontal line for this column to a size required. If you define a column width of 0, it will be hidden.

To the right of each column name is a black arrow. Use it to filter the document list. Using its Custom Filter, you can define more advanced filtering, such as "Show only documents of type Quote or Contract" or "show document with a size greater than 450KB."

You can also right-click any cell, for example the document name. It will display another quick menu with these options:

- ❏ **Cut:** Cut this document.
- ❏ **Copy:** Copy this document.
- ❏ **Paste:** Paste a previously cut or copied document.
- ❏ **Delete Document:** Remove this document permanently.
- ❏ **Add Column:** Create a new column for this document library.
- ❏ **Edit/Delete Column:** Self-explanatory.
- ❏ **Fill:** Fill the setting of the current cell with the same value as above, or auto-calculate, if possible, such as Days or Months.

❑ **Pick From List:** Pick a value from a list.

❑ **Document:** This choice has three options:

    ❑ Open Document (Read-Only)

    ❑ Check Out Document

    ❑ Document Versions

❑ **Discuss:** Use the built-in feature of SharePoint's document library to allow users to discuss a document without editing the actual document. This information will be stored in SharePoint's SQL database separately. (It is possible to delete this discussion without affecting the document.)

❑ **Alert Me:** Create an alert for this document.

❑ **Help:** Open SharePoint's help manual pages for this menu.

There is a cleverly hidden button at the far right side of the Datasheet view. It looks like a part of the right frame. Click it, and a task pane will be displayed. Another way of displaying this pane is to click on the Task Pane button at the top of the document list (see Figure 9-17).

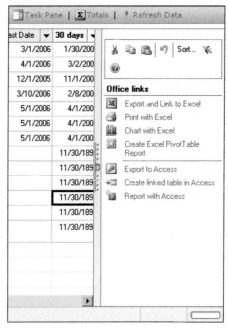

Figure 9-17

Using this task pane, a user can activate these features:

❑ **Export and Link to Excel:** Note that this option is also available directly under Actions on the left quick launch bar, called Export to spreadsheet. Use this option to open the list of documents and its column values in MS Excel. In this program, you can update values (if so, make sure to click the Synchronize List button that will show up in the List toolbar). You can also start working on the settings for this list; maybe doing statistical analysis and similar things. Note that any changes in this MS Excel view will be lost unless you click Synchronize List. When closing this spreadsheet MS Excel asks if you want to save—select yes if you need to save a copy of the modifications done, but be aware that this operation will not send any updates to SharePoint. In other words, if the purpose was to use MS Excel as a temporary edit tool, you click Synchronize List to save the modifications, and say no when asked to save the actual spreadsheet.

❑ **Print with Excel:** Because SharePoint is a web application it has poor printing functionality. Use MS Excel if you want a better control of the print process, such as the formatting, fonts, and colors.

❑ **Chart with Excel:** If you have columns with a numerical or date format you can use these values in MS Excel to create charts, such as histograms and pie charts.

❑ **Create Excel Pivot Table Report:** Use the column properties to create a dynamic summary of these cell values, typically for pivot tables.

❑ **Export to Access:** Use this feature if you want to create a table in MS Access with the same values as this list. It can be used for creating reports and presentations.

❑ **Create linked table in Access:** This feature will build a table in MS Access with a live link back to this document library; if you change any of the settings for this document library, it will also show up in the MS Access table.

❑ **Report with Access:** Use this to create reports based on the settings for this document library.

❑ You will also find buttons for tasks like cut, copy, and paste documents or columns.

Managing List Access

Each document list will by default inherit the security settings of the team site. In other words, if Axel is a member of the Contributor site group for this team site, he will also be a contributor for any document library in this team site. This can be changed in a team site, contrary to a portal area, which is one of the strongest arguments for using team sites instead of portal areas for collaborations.

In SharePoint 2003 you cannot set individual rights for a document; all security settings are on the library level and will be valid for all documents stored in this library. If you must have individual security settings for a document, also referred to as "Item-level security," you should look at the IRM client. Using this Rights Management Service feature, you can define security settings such as these:

❑ Axel can read the document, and Anna can modify it.

❑ This document cannot be printed.

❑ This document will cease to exist on Friday at 5 p.m.

All of these settings will be valid regardless of how a user gets a copy of this document, whether it is by the file system, by e-mail, or by a document library in SharePoint. If you want to know more about IRM and RMS, look at this page: http://www.microsoft.com/rms.

Sometimes you need a security setting in a way other than inherited from the team site settings. For example, a user named Beatrice who works in another department may need access to these documents but should not be able to read anything else on this team site. This is managed like this:

Add Custom Rights to a Document Library

1. Open the document library using an account with administrative rights for this team site.

2. Click the Modify settings and columns link under the Actions section.

3. Click the link Change permissions for this document library. This will display the inherited settings (what rights each site group member has).

4. Click Add user to open a web form very similar to the page when adding users to the team site. The only difference is that the user you add will get specific rights instead of membership to a site group. You can either use the grouped rights that are listed, such as View items, or you can click Advanced permissions to display the six different rights available for a document library:

   a. **Manage Lists:** Can approve or reject updated documents awaiting approval.

   b. **Manage List Permissions:** Can define or modify the rights for this document library.

   c. **Manage Personal Views:** Can add and modify personal views of this library.

   d. **Cancel Check-Out:** Can cancel an active check-out process.

   e. **Add List Items, Edit List Items, and Delete List Items:** Self-explanatory.

   f. **View List Items:** Self-explanatory.

5. After entering the name or group to be added and selecting the rights, click Next. A form opens where you can send a message to this user, telling Beatrice her new rights for this document library, including a link to this document library. Click Finish to close this form.

The preceding example was about adding the user Beatrice as a reader to this library, but she should not get access to anything else on this team site. This goal is accomplished using the preceding steps, but how will Beatrice be able to see a list inside a team site that she has no access to? SharePoint solves this by adding this user as a "Guest" to the team site; this will allow her to read a specific list or library but nothing else on this team site.

Managing Document Workflow

For some types of documents, the author is not allowed to publish the document by herself. If so, you must configure this document library to activate Content Approval. The effect will be that every added or modified document will be hidden until a user with Manage Lists rights has approved the document. If the author has this right, the document will automatically be approved.

Activate Content Approval in a Document Library

1. Log on as an administrator for the team site where this document library is stored.

2. Open the document library.

3. Click the Modify settings and columns link under the Actions section.

4. Click Change General Settings.

5. Select Yes for the option Require content approval for submitted items?

6. Click OK to save and close.

7. Click Go back to "Shared Documents" or whatever the name for your library is.

The approval process is now activated. Log on as a user that is a member of the Contributor site group. This group does not have the Manage Lists rights, and so every update from these members will need to be approved by a user with this right (for example, the Web Designer or Administrator).

> Note that if a user with Manage Lists rights adds or modifies a document, it will automatically be approved.

Try It Out   Test the Content Approval Process

1. Log on as a member of the Contributor site group.

2. Update any existing document. Note that when you save it, it will disappear! The reason for this strange behavior is perfectly logical; a modified document should not be visible until it is approved. If it is not approved, the document continues to be hidden. This information is also displayed for the author so they understand what will happen next.

3. A user with the Manage Lists right must now check the modification. When the Content Approval process is activated for a document library, you will find two new views: Approve/Reject items and My Submissions. The first of these two views is not available unless you have Manage Lists rights; the second view will list all documents that you have submitted to this document library and list what status they have. When the user with the Manage List right uses the view Approve/ Reject Items, he or she will see all documents awaiting approval or that have been denied (see Figure 9-18).

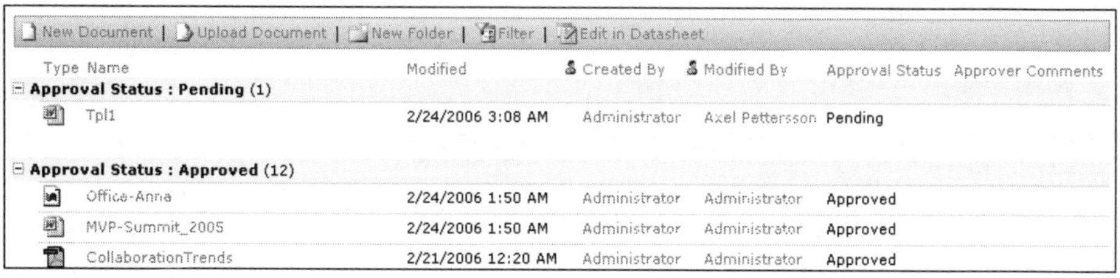

Type	Name	Modified	Created By	Modified By	Approval Status	Approver Comments
	New Document | Upload Document | New Folder | Filter | Edit in Datasheet					
Approval Status : Pending (1)						
	Tpl1	2/24/2006 3:08 AM	Administrator	Axel Pattersson	Pending	
Approval Status : Approved (12)						
	Office-Anna	2/24/2006 1:50 AM	Administrator	Administrator	Approved	
	MVP-Summit_2005	2/24/2006 1:50 AM	Administrator	Administrator	Approved	
	CollaborationTrends	2/21/2006 12:20 AM	Administrator	Administrator	Approved	

Figure 9-18

4. Before you approve or reject the modification, you must view the document. Open the document in a normal way, and read its column settings. To approve or reject it, use the quick menu for this document and select Approve/reject. It will open a web form where you select to approve or reject; you can also enter a description that will be stored along with this document.

355

When the document is approved, it will be public; if rejected the document continues to be hidden. There is no feature in SharePoint 2003 that will inform the author about the result of the approval process.

To summarize this: The content approval process is very handy for some types of documents where a specific user, such as a manager, must approve a document before going public. The problem with this process in SharePoint 2003 is that neither the user who must approve or reject the modification nor the author will receive any e-mail saying what is going on! This is clearly not good and has opened up a great business opportunity for several talented companies that make add-ons for SharePoint to solve this problem.

One of these vendors is the Australian company Nintex (www.nintex.com), which bases its company solely on such an add-on named SmartLibrary. This is a reasonably priced tool that enables workflow functionality to SharePoint's document library. Using SmartLibrary you can define exactly which people are responsible for this approval process, in serial or parallel; each person will automatically get an e-mail stating what is expected of them ("Please go and approve or reject this document"). When the process is done, the document can be simply published in the document library, copied to another library, or stored anywhere else. This add-on also contains an undelete waste basket.

Working with Document Workspaces

When you are alone and updating a public document, you will be doing fine with the check-out feature that the document library offers. But what do you do when you are working collaboratively with one or more other people? Or you may be just one person, but you need the input from two other colleagues during the development of an updated document version. This is clearly not something that can be solved with the check-out procedure. This is what you use document workspaces for. A document workspace is a team site that initially contains only one thing: a document copied from another site, usually the parent site.

To create a document workspace, you have two options:

❑   Use the quick menu for a document and select Create Document Workspace.

❑   Inside MS Office, use the Task Pane and the Documents tab (on the "Shared Workspace" pane); use the quick menu here for the currently opened document and select Create Document Workspace.

When creating a document workspace, a copy of this document will be stored in the new workspace. Initially, only the user who created the workspace will have access, so the next step is often to add one or more users to this workspace. Note that even in a document workspace the same rules apply; only one user at a time can update a document. If necessary you can also use the check-out/check-in feature in this workspace.

Why do you need a new site just for one document? Well, it is simple. If the document is so important that you need several people to be able to update it, you will most likely want to have your own private playground for this work. This workspace will also allow this group to share ideas, links, tasks, and maybe other supporting documents by storing all this information in the workspace.

When the document update is done, it should be copied back to the original location. This is taken care of by SharePoint's "Publish back to source location" feature. Use the following steps to create a workspace, update the copy of the document, and finally publish it back to the source location:

---

1. Log on as a user with at least Administrator membership for this team site. This is necessary in order to be able to create subsites. If you want to enable authors to create document workspaces, you must either make them members of the Administrator site group or add the right "Create Subsites" to the Authors site group. For more information about site groups, see Chapter 3.

2. Open the document for editing in MS Word (assuming it's a Word file).

3. In the Task Pane, on the Documents tab (on the "Shared Workspace" pane) locate the currently open document (it will be listed) and using its quick menu, select Create Document Workspace. Accept to create it, when asked. Word now automatically switches to the document copy stored in the workspace. The workspace will get its name based on the document title.

4. Add some more users to this workspace. Click the Member tab and click Add new members. Enter their name (user account or e-mail address) and set their site group membership; click Next and accept to send an e-mail to these users, stating their new rights and where to go to start collaborating on this document. If you don't send this e-mail to these users, you must give them the URL to this workspace in another way. Otherwise they will not know where to find this workspace.

5. Use the standard procedure to open, edit, and close this document, using the user accounts that are granted permissions to this workspace. At some point, you are done with all the editing. It is time to send the updated version back to its original location.

6. You can either use the Task Pane / Document tab in MS Office and the quick menu for this document to select Publish back to source location or use the quick menu in the document library for this document and select the same command. When done, MS Office will close the document version stored in the workspace and open up the same document stored in the source location.

Note that the document workspace will still remain after you have copied the document back to its source location. The reason for this is that you may later be interested in going back to this workspace and see what users were active in developing the new version and view the other information used during that development.

Using SharePoint as a File Share

So far you have used the web client to view and open documents. But SharePoint can display its information just like any file share, using either the traditional file share (for example F:) or by your defining a web folder. The main difference between these two options is that file shares only allow you to use one character for this share, whereas web folders allow you to type a name including blank spaces. This is much easier to read and understand, but not all programs understand how to use a web folder. You have to test it to see whether web folders work in your environment. All recent MS Office products understand web folders.

To create a traditional file share link to a document library, you do this:

Try It Out   Create a File Share Link to a Document Library

1. Assume you have a document library named "Shared Documents" in the team site `http://spsrv2/sites/it`. You want to access that library using the F: disk label.

2. Start Windows Explorer.

3. Choose Tools⇨Map Network Drive.

4. Set the Drive = F.

5. Enter the following address:

```
\\spsrv2\sites\it\shared documents
```

Now you will find an F: in Windows Explorer and any program that has an "Open" and "Save" feature. Note that this will only work directly for Windows XP clients; if you do this on a Windows 2003 server, including the SharePoint server itself, it will fail. The reason is that Windows XP has a service running that is needed for this functionality, whereas Windows 2003 does not.

Just open the Start⇨Administrative Tools⇨Services; locate the service WebClient; open its properties and switch to Manual or Automatic, click Apply to activate this setting, and finally click Start.

The second method is to use web folders. It works the same way, except that you can have a longer and better description of what the link is pointing to. Follow these steps to create the web folder:

Try It Out   Create a Web Folder to a Document Library

Assuming the same document library and team site, do this:

1. Start Windows Explorer.

2. Choose Tools⇨Map Network Drive.

3. Click Sign up for online storage or connect to a network server. This link is on the same page as the one used in step 4 in the previous steps.

4. The Add Network Place Wizard will start up. Click Next. On the following page, make sure that "Choose another network location" is selected and click Next again.

5. Type the following network address (see Figure 9-19):

```
http://spsrv2/sites/it/shared documents
```

6. Type a good name for this web folder, such as "Shared Documents on IT"; then click Next.

7. Click Finish. Your new web folder is now created.

8. Test it: Start MS Word, select File Open, click My Network Places, and your web folder should be listed here. Click it and you will see all Word files in this folder.

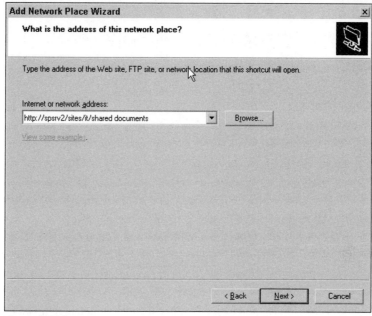

Figure 9-19

Both the traditional disk label and the newer web folders can be used directly from Windows Explorer (for example, to copy files from the file system into a SharePoint document library or to copy files from one library to another).

Note that when you copy or move files using web folders or disk labels, only the latest version of the document will be copied or moved, not previous versions. However, if you open and update files using these web folders or disk labels, the version history gets updated, exactly as when using the web client interface.

SharePoint will automatically create web folders for any document library that you have stored documents into. They are seldom cleverly named, so to give them better names or just check where they point to by right-clicking the web folder and selecting Properties. There you will see the URL address, and you can enter another name for this link.

For each document library there is a system folder named Forms that contains aspx files for default views and specific web forms. It also contains all custom views created by users. When using Windows Explorer you will see this Forms folder. Normally users will not be able to delete or modify any of its files, but just to be safe, you should instruct your users to avoid changing anything in that folder or deleting that folder itself.

Summary

In this chapter you learned the following:

- ❑ The traditional file system is not enough any more. It is much too easy to create file chaos, where few, if any, have control of the information stored.

- ❑ Traditional document management systems, DMSs, are often very advanced and hard to use, which may be an obstacle when implementing DMS in an organization.

- ❑ Traditional DMSs are not always so well integrated into MS Office.

- ❑ SharePoint enables you to create new columns for document libraries that contain metadata or properties for these documents.

- ❑ Using SharePoint's views, documents can be sorted, presented, and grouped in a large number of ways, based on the column settings for the document library.

- ❑ SharePoint does not allow all file types to be stored in a document library, but that is easy to fix. However, be sure to protect your document library with SharePoint-enabled antivirus solutions.

- ❑ Each document library may have individual permission settings. All settings will be valid for all documents in that library.

- ❑ Create alerts when you want to be notified that a specific document or a folder is updated.

- ❑ Lock a file for editing using Check-Out; this will be active until the user does a check-in.

- ❑ An administrator can break an active check-out.

- ❑ SharePoint supports version history. However, by default it is disabled; when activated it will store any number of versions for all documents in the folder.

- ❑ SharePoint stores complete copies of each document version, not only the modified information in the document.

- ❑ Using MS Office 2003 a user will have access to a lot of SharePoint-specific features, such as check-out/check-in, version history, and document properties.

- ❑ Use Datasheet for fast editing of document properties and for managing columns and their position on the page.

- ❑ SharePoint supports content approval but will not send e-mail to the person who should approve any modification. Solve this by purchasing add-ons.

- ❑ Document Workspace is a team site that contains a copy of a document; this copy may be updated by several users. When done, you will publish this document back to its source location.

- ❑ Create network drives, such as F:, or web folders, such as "Shared Documents on IT" to make it possible to view information in SharePoint as a file share.

In the next chapter you learn more about using SharePoint for more effective meetings.

More Effective Meetings

Meetings are one of the most common activities in any type of organization. Meetings are important for many reasons, such as making sure that everyone on a team is working toward the same goal, managing issues with customers, and keeping projects on track, to mention just a few. The problem with meetings is how they are managed before, during, and after the actual meeting. Ask any member of an organization about what annoys them the most, and a majority of them will put meetings on top of that list, with arguments such as these:

- ❑ Meetings are boring.

- ❑ They don't lead to anything meaningful.

- ❑ Too often the members do not understand the objective of the meeting.

- ❑ Participants are poorly prepared for the meeting.

- ❑ It is very hard to follow up on decisions made in a meeting.

Everything that you can do to address these issues is good. SharePoint is not a magic wand, but it does offer a number of features that may help to manage the meeting process more effectively. Note that everything described in this chapter requires only WSS. You do not need SPS for this to work!

The Typical Meeting Process Today

Before you start using the features that SharePoint offers for meetings, you should analyze what the issues are in order to better understand how to address them. A meeting process can be split into three different parts: before, during, and after the meeting. This is true regardless of whether it is a meeting where people come together or a meeting using video and telephony devices to connect participants.

One situation in which SharePoint cannot help is when meetings are held regularly simply because they always have been. I am sure you recognize the typical reoccurring meeting where people get together without any clear understanding of why. These types of meetings should be questioned: Why do you have these meetings? Can the reason be managed in another way, for example by creating a team site to share and discuss the issues covered during these meetings? It can take some nerve to question meetings that have questionable value, but the rewards can be big, especially if you provide an alternative that will save everyone time and money.

Before the Meeting

Look at what happens before the meeting takes place. Except for meetings that are routinely scheduled without question, you will find that the typical meeting prologue is something like this:

1. A person, the meeting organizer, needs to discuss a topic with some other people. It might be a new project, a problem at the mill, or planning the Christmas party. Regardless, the topic is the objective for this meeting.

2. The meeting organizer needs to determine which people to invite and when they are available.

3. An invitation to this meeting needs to be distributed. If someone cannot attend, the time for the meeting might have to be changed and new invitations sent out.

4. The meeting organizer also needs to find a place for this meeting that is available and has the proper prerequisites (the size of the room, whether it has an Internet connection and a video projector, and so on).

5. The meeting organizer must come up with an agenda and an estimate of the total time needed for this meeting.

6. Before the meeting takes place, some information may need to be prepared and distributed to all participants.

You may come up with many more tasks and steps to prepare for the meeting, but the preceding ones are sufficient for the discussion here. The real problem here is time: It may take a while to find a place and a time for this meeting that are acceptable for all participants. It may also be a challenge to distribute information that the participants need to read before the meeting.

During the Meeting

When the actual meeting takes place, it often looks like this:

❑ Someone important did not show up, so a final decision cannot be made during this time.

❑ Some participants came 10 minutes late.

❑ Two participants forgot the meeting agenda.

❑ Only a few prepared for this meeting by reading the distributed information.

❑ During the meeting some parts of the agenda took more time than expected.

❑ During the meeting one participant misunderstood what part of the agenda was being talked about.

❑ Someone had to leave early for another meeting, so no more decisions could be made.

❑ The meeting minutes that were taken were sparse, but the meeting organizer hoped that everyone took notes about their tasks.

Maybe not all of these things are happening every time, but most of them occur with disturbing regularity. The result is a meeting that does not start on time and takes longer than expected. It might not be possible to arrive at final decisions, and participants might not be clear about what tasks they have been delegated.

After the Meeting

When the meeting is over, it might be difficult to know exactly what was said, what decisions were made, and what tasks were delegated and to whom. The reason for this is bad or even non-existent meeting minutes. If you trust that all participants not only took notes of the tasks delegated to them, but also will perform them on time, you are going to be disappointed. What's more, if you don't have good documentation of the delegated tasks and decisions, it will be very hard to follow up on them. To summarize, the problems after the meetings are often these:

- ❑ Some tasks were not performed at all, because the people assigned to them did not understand what they should do.

- ❑ Some tasks were done but not on time.

- ❑ It is hard to say exactly what was said during this meeting and by whom because the meeting minutes were so sparse.

- ❑ Parts of the meeting minutes are inaccurate, because the person taking these minutes misunderstood what was said.

- ❑ There is no practical place to save documents created as a result from this meeting. If there is a follow-up meeting later, it will be hard to find these documents.

The Problems of Today

When looking at all these issues, it is easy to understand why meetings are sometimes ineffective and can feel meaningless. Some of the more important show-stoppers are these:

- ❑ It is hard to find a time for the meeting that is suitable for all attendees, plus an available conference room.

- ❑ It is hard to send out updates about the meeting and be sure the attendees will have their calendars updated.

- ❑ It might be difficult to distribute information and documentation to all attendees in advance, especially if there is a lot of information. Also, if the materials are large enough, you might need to increase the mailbox size for the attendees.

- ❑ It is hard for the participants to influence the agenda before the meeting takes place.

- ❑ It is easy to miss something when writing the meeting minutes, because no one is checking the minutes' content until after the meeting.

- ❑ It is cumbersome to document the decisions made and the tasks delegated during the meeting.

- ❑ After the meeting it may be hard find documents created during or after the meeting.

What You Really Need

To be realistic, you cannot fix all the problems and issues previously mentioned, such as making sure that people respect the meeting time and come well prepared, unless you are a fantastic boss who can mix promises and threats in a convincing way. But you can do a lot about the other issues if you have the right tools. What you really need are tools that can help you before, during, and after the meeting, as described in the following sections.

Before the Meeting

You need tools that will help you, as the meeting organizer, to accomplish many things. You must organize and invite attendees, and you must locate and reserve resources, such as conference rooms and video projectors. All attendees' responses must be easy for you to collect and read. You also need to distribute information, such as documents and figures, to the attendees so they can prepare for the meeting. The attendees must also be able to create or update information that will be easily available to all attendees. The attendees must be able to view the agenda, including the details of each item, such as estimated time, description, and who is responsible for it. The meeting organizer must be able to describe the objective of this meeting, to make clear to everyone why this meeting is taking place. You must be able to change the time for the meeting, move it to another conference room, and add or remove attendees, easily and with full control. All this information must be available in one place so that all attendees, including the meeting organizer, can have easy access to and an overview of this information.

During the Meeting

During the actual meeting, attendees should have access to all information collected, such as the meeting's objective, the agenda, and the invited attendees and their status (such as whether they are attending and, if not, why they could not come).

It must also be easy to see and open the documentation created for this meeting, even for people who forgot to bring their own copy with them (unless there is another way of viewing this information in real time so the attendees would not need to bring their own copy, such as a projected PowerPoint presentation of the same material).

All decisions made, tasks assigned, and notes created during the meeting must be documented. You need a better way of doing this than writing it down on paper, and then later writing traditional meeting minutes that must be verified by some other member of that meeting. You know how fun that is, right?

You need a way to present all these documents, decisions, notes, and pieces of information so everyone sees the same thing in real time. This ensures that everyone knows exactly which item is discussed at the moment, even if they fall asleep for a short while.

After the Meeting

A meeting usually, but not necessarily always, leads to a number of decisions, tasks, and other types of activities. If the expectations of these decisions and tasks are not fulfilled in the appropriately determined time, the meeting was a failure. One common reason people fail to execute a decision or task is that they forget about it, because the documentation (the meeting minutes) is hard to get or simply gets lost. Face it: Meeting minutes are a pain! If you can replace minutes with something better, do it!

Another common need that often arises after the meeting is to find the documents and other information that belong to the meeting. It is also sometimes very interesting to see who attended a specific meeting, especially if important decisions where made at that time.

A meeting is very seldom a one-time event. Most often it is part of a series of meetings, for example to track the development of a project or monitor an important customer relationship. Each new meeting instance continues where the old meeting ended. In other words, all information from one meeting must be easily available in the next meeting. Sometimes it is very important to be able to go back to any instance in a meeting series, even if there have been 20 or more of these meetings. If so, traditional meeting minutes are not sufficient. You need something more advanced that allows you to go back to any previous meeting, sometimes even during the current meeting.

How to Do This with SharePoint

So now you know that the traditional meeting methods are insufficient if you want to have more effective meetings. One solution is to use SharePoint to keep track of everything about the meetings. But some things, such as sending meeting invitations and keeping track of people's calendars, are handled better with other tools. For these things you should use MS Outlook 2003. This mail client is fully integrated with SharePoint and is the preferred way of creating meeting invitations and workspaces at the same time. Your users don't have to learn a completely new way of managing these meetings; everything they know about checking the calendar status for attendees and resources, managing invitations, and moving meetings, is exactly like before. However, there are some new features related to creating a common place to store all the meeting details; this place is known as a *meeting workspace*.

A meeting workspace is a common team site, built on a specific site template. It has a number of preconfigured lists for storing information such as the meeting agenda, decisions, a list of attendees, and a list of tasks. Just like any other team site, it can be modified to suit your needs for this particular meeting. You can also create a series of meeting workspaces that are connected to each other; this will make it very easy to go back to any previous meeting instance to view its details.

> *You can use a meeting workspace just as a place to store everything about a meeting, but the best way to use it is to display its content in real time during the meeting, using a video projector. This makes sure that everyone focuses on the same thing.*

> *Another smart move is to enter the decisions and tasks in their lists, and take notes directly in SharePoint during the meeting. This way all attendees who are still awake will see what is documented and can comment if something is wrong.*

The following sections list the logical steps for using SharePoint's meeting workspaces for managing meetings and using a video projector during the actual meeting. Later you will see the steps for doing this in MS Outlook and SharePoint. This is what you will need to work with meeting workspaces as described:

- ❑ **Windows SharePoint Services:** SharePoint Portal Server will also do fine.

- ❑ **MS Outlook 2003:** Earlier Outlook versions do not have the integration needed.

- ❑ **MS Exchange Server:** To view calendars of the attendees and resources.

If you don't have MS Outlook and MS Exchange, it is still possible to create meeting workspaces, but it is not anywhere near as easy and effective a process as if you have these programs.

Before the Meeting

In this example, you are the meeting organizer who needs to discuss a new project that will start next week. You have five project members, and all of them must participate in this first meeting:

1. You create a meeting agenda, including an estimation of how much time each item will take and who will be responsible for it. The total estimated meeting time seems to be about 60 minutes.

2. Using MS Outlook 2003, you look for a time when all five project members seem to be available.

3. Using MS Outlook you also look for a conference room that is equipped with a video projector and a network connection and is available for this meeting.

4. You create, but do *not* yet send, the meeting invitation for all project members, plus the conference room, which happens to be a resource mailbox in this case (but a public folder mailbox will also do fine).

5. Still having the meeting invitation open, you create the meeting workspace in SharePoint.

6. You add a description of this meeting and then send the invitation to the attendees and the resource mailbox.

7. Using your calendar, you open this new meeting workspace and start adding the agenda items, the objective, and some documents that will be discussed during this meeting.

8. All attendees except Bill accept the invitation. Because Bill must be there in order to make decisions, you reschedule this meeting using Outlook. A new invitation is sent out. There is no need to change or update the meeting workspace.

9. Bill sends you an e-mail saying that he needs to add two items to the agenda. You tell him to use the link in his meeting invitation to open its workspace and add these items. Because Bill is an attendee, he is automatically granted the rights to write and update any list in this workspace.

10. Everyone (including you) seems satisfied with the meeting preparations so far. Just relax and await the actual meeting.

During the Meeting

It is time for the meeting. You take your laptop to the conference room and connect it to the network to make sure you can open the meeting workspace. Then, you connect your computer to the video projector. Everything is now ready for your meeting:

1. When all attendees have arrived, you display the meeting workspace using the video projector. You give a quick overview of the meeting workspace so everyone understands what is displayed.

2. You point to the meeting objective described on the workspace and tell the attendees what this meeting is all about.

3. You point to the meeting agenda and show the attendees the short title, the longer description, the name of the person responsible for each item, and finally how much time each item is supposed to take. Make sure people understand that they must stick to the estimated time or the meeting will take longer than planned, which is something nobody wants.

4. The first item on the agenda is to greet everyone, welcome them to this meeting, and explain what this meeting is about. You have just done that so you continue with the next item on that list.

5. The next item is to discuss the project plan. Instead of handing out paper, you open the document that describes this plan: Everyone can see this document now, and you can all start discussing this plan.

6. You all agree that Bill should be the Project Leader. This is entered in the Decision list in the meeting workspace.

7. You go on with the next agenda item. Marina is given the task of ordering new software tools that will be needed during this project. This information is entered in the Task list on the workspace.

8. Marielle comments on the number of project members. She thinks it will be hard to meet the deadline with just five people. This comment is entered in a list normally used for announcements.

9. For each item on the agenda, a number of decisions, delegated tasks, and comments are made; all of these are entered in their respective lists. When the meeting is over (on time because everyone tried to keep to the expected time slot for each agenda item), you will have full documentation of everything important that happened at this meeting.

10. You end this meeting, reminding all attendees that they can go back to this workspace whenever they need to read what was said and done.

After the Meeting

Because a meeting normally results in a number of tasks that need to be accomplished in due time, it is interesting to revisit the workspace for some time after the actual meeting. SharePoint stores this information until you actively delete this workspace; if necessary you can reuse this information in later meetings. Following are some typical activities after a meeting:

1. Marina wants to check some details about the task assigned to her, so she looks at her Outlook calendar to find the booking for that meeting, which contains the link to the meeting workspace.

2. Because Bill is the project leader, he also wants to see the complete list of tasks and their due date to check if anybody is behind schedule.

3. The manager for your department says he wants a copy of the meeting minutes. You open the meeting workspace and add the manager as a Reader, using the built-in feature of SharePoint to send an e-mail to the user who has been granted access to a site. You add some descriptive text in that e-mail and explain that you don't use meeting minutes anymore but instead use SharePoint's workspaces.

4. Marielle wants to find out who the project members are today. She also uses her Outlook calendar and the link in the booking for this meeting to quickly access that meeting workspace and read its list of attendees.

5. One important partner wants to view the details from this meeting. Because he does not have any user account on your network, you cannot ask him to open the workspace for this meeting. And because there are no meeting minutes, you have nothing to send him. Instead you start an MS Live Meeting session, sharing your web browser to display the workspace for this partner. This way, you also can be sure this partner will not see anything other than what is required.

Integrating Outlook and SharePoint

MS Outlook plays a very important role when managing meetings in SharePoint. It is used to send out invitations and to quickly open the meeting workspace before, during, and after the meeting. MS Outlook is also used to create the meeting workspace, although you can create this workspace from within SharePoint, just like any other team site. Remember that a workspace is just an ordinary team site but uses a special meeting site template.

Only MS Outlook 2003 is integrated with SharePoint. Previous versions of Outlook cannot create a meeting workspace, nor can they see its properties.

In order to create a meeting workspace, the user needs to be assigned the right "Create Subsites" on the web site that is the parent of this workspace. Members of the portal site have this right on their personal web sites (My Site). Members of team sites need to be an administrator to have this right, unless you have changed the default settings. In other words, team sites you have created and personal sites are locations you can use to create meeting workspaces. Regardless of where the meeting workspace is created, all users who are invited are automatically assigned the right to join that workspace, even if it is created in a personal workspace. Typically a project manager (who uses a team site for his project information) will create all related meeting workspaces under that project team site, and other users who just need to create an ad hoc meeting workspace will use their own personal site.

After the workspace site is created, no meeting workspace or other subsites can be created under the new meeting workspace site!

Managing Integration Features in Outlook

The features integrated with Outlook are stored in the Windows Registry settings. These settings can be controlled by the deployment tool that comes with the MS Office 2003 Resource Kit or by the Group Policy Objects (GPO) in Active Directory.

Use the GPO templates "Office11.adm" and "Outlk11.adm" to control these SharePoint-related features. See Chapter 18 in the MS Office Resource Kit for more information about using these settings.

The following table lists the key registry entries; all of them are in the HKEY_CURRENT_USER \ Microsoft\Office\11.0 key:

Key	Value	Type	Description
Common\DWS	PollingInterval	DWORD	The number of minutes before checking for updates of Document Workspace (default 10, allowed values are 1–999).
Common\ MailSettings	DisableSharingOptions	DWORD	1 = disable; 0 = enable: Shared Attachments option in Outlook messages.
Common\Security \ Trusted Alert Sources	All	DWORD	0 =do not allow; 1 = allow: users to use Outlook to manage all SharePoint alerts (default = 0).

Key	Value	Type	Description
Common\Security \ Trusted Alert Sources	AllIntranet	DWORD	0 = disallow; 1 = allow: users to use Outlook to manage alerts from all SharePoint sites within Outlook (default = 0).
	AllTrusted	DWORD	0 = do not allow; 1 = allow: users to use Outlook to manage alerts from all intranets (default = 1).
Meetings\Profile	EntryUI	DWORD	1 = disable; 0 = enable: Meeting Workspaces button on Outlook meeting requests.
	ServerUI	DWORD	2 = disable that user can enter values to server list. If so: publish default, disallow others.
	MRUInternal	String	Set a limit of 5 servers available for Meeting Workspace sites. See more about this following this table.
Outlook\ Preferences	DisallowSTS	DWORD	1 = disable; 0 = enable: the feature of linking SharePoint contacts and events lists with Outlook.
	STSSyncInterval	DWORD	The number of minutes before the next update process for linked SharePoint contacts and events lists in Outlook (default is 20 minutes). Set any value between 1 and 1430.
SharePointTracking\ Name#	Name	String	(# = 1 - 4) The display name of SharePoint site that will be listed in the "Select A Location list."
	URL	String	The URL of SharePoint site to be listed in the "Select A Location list."

The settings for the key "SharePointTracking\Name#" and the values "ServerUI" and "MRUInternal" for the "Meetings\Profile" key control what options the user sees listed in the menu "Select a location" when creating the meeting workspace. The default is to show these sites:

❑　My Site.

❑　Sites listed in the MRUInternal value.

❑　Up to five of the most recently used sites listed in the SharePointTracking\Name key.

❑　Up to five of the most recently used sites. This list is built from cookies stored when users visit a site, where they have the right "Create Subsite."

❑　"Other," which allows the user to enter any SharePoint URL.

You can create up to five SharePointTracking\Name# (#=0-4) to have these sites listed for the user when creating the meeting workspace.

The five default meeting workspace templates are listed in the following table.

TemplateName	TemplateID
Basic Meeting Workspace	Mps#0
Blank Meeting Workspace	Mps#1
Decision Meeting Workspace	Mps#2
Social Meeting Workspace	Mps#3
Multipage Meeting Workspace	Mps#4

Meeting Workspace Templates

Just like any other team site, meeting workspaces are built upon a site template. By default there are five different meeting workspace templates:

❑ **Basic Meeting Workspace:** Contains four lists: Agenda, Attendees, Objectives, and Document Library.

❑ **Blank Meeting Workspace:** Contains no lists or web parts.

❑ **Decision Meeting Workspace:** Contains these lists: Agenda, Objectives, Attendees, Document libraries, Tasks, and Decisions.

❑ **Social Meeting Workspace:** Contains three tabs, or pages: Home, Discussions, and Photos. These three pages contain these lists: Attendees, Directions, Things to Bring, Discussions, and Picture Library. You can add new lists to any of these pages. You can also create new pages using the Modify This Workspace link.

❑ **Multipage Meeting Workspace:** Contains three pages: Home, Page 1, and Page 2. They contain the following lists on the Home page: Objectives, Attendees, and Agenda. The other pages are empty until you add one or more lists to them. You can also create new pages, using the Modify This Workspace link.

As with team sites' workspaces, you can save any customized meeting workspace as a site template. This makes it available when creating new meeting workspaces in the same site collection. You may recall from previous discussions that a site collection is all the team sites created under a specific top-level team site, including the top-level site itself.

Creating a Meeting Workspace

Creating a meeting workspace is very easy. This process is fully integrated with the Outlook process to send invitations to users. For example, say that you want to create a meeting workspace for yourself, Anna, and Axel. This workspace should use the basic workspace template and have the name Project ALPHA. Because you are the administrator for the IT team site, you will create it under that site. Use these steps to do this:

Try It Out Create a Basic Meeting Workspace under IT

1. Log on as an administrator for the IT team site.

2. Start MS Outlook and pick a date and time for the meeting with Anna and Axel.

3. On the Outlook Calendar page, choose New⇨Meeting Request. Enter the attendees, subject, and location like this (see Figure 10-1):

    a. **To:** Anna Filippa; Axel Pettersson.

    b. **Subject:** Project ALPHA.

    c. **Location:** Room 302.

    d. **Description:** Welcome to our project meeting!

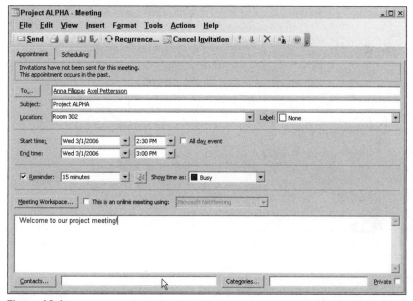

Figure 10-1

4. Normally you would now click Send, but not this time. Now you create the meeting workspace! Click Meeting Workspace. This opens a new pane at the right of this window (see Figure 10-2).

   If you don't see the Meeting Workspace button, you are creating an appointment instead of a meeting request. Click Invite Attendees to change the type.

5. The default setting is to create a meeting workspace using the Basic Meeting Workspace template in the current site (if you are the administrator). All this is listed in this workspace pane at the right. Click Create to create the meeting workspace. You can see a progress bar at the top of the pane; this process takes 5–30 seconds, depending on how fast your computer environment is. After the workspace is created, you can see that a link has been added in the description; its name is taken from the subject for this invitation. Note that the pane gives you some important tips: that all invited attendees now will have Contributor access to this site and that you should now open the workspace to create the agenda and add information to it (see Figure 10-3).

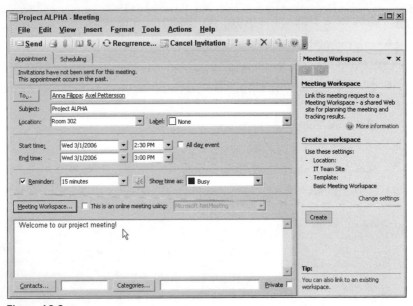

Figure 10-2

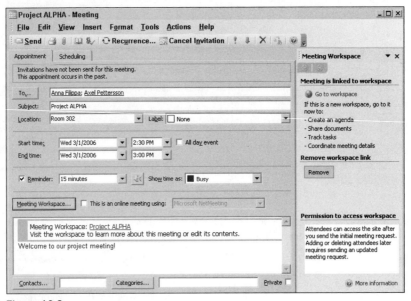

Figure 10-3

6. The invitation is ready, and the workspace and its link are created. Click Send to send this invitation to all attendees. They will also see this link, and they will automatically be added as Contributors to this site. This gives them the right to add agenda items, documents, and tasks. However, they will not be able to add new members to this workspace site.

The meeting is now added to the Outlook calendar. If you open this meeting, it will display the link to this site. You can also right-click this meeting and select View Meeting Workspace, as Figure 10-4 shows.

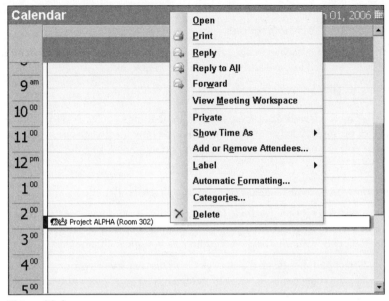

Figure 10-4

Modifying a Meeting Workspace

When you open the new workspace, it displays the four lists: Objectives, Attendees, Agenda, and Document Library. The next logical thing to do is to add information to this workspace, such as the objective and the agenda. Note that you do not need to add attendees, because this list is automatically populated based on the invited users for this meeting. The list also displays each user's status regarding this invitation, for example Accepted, Declined, or No response so far.

Try It Out   **Modifying a Meeting Workspace**

1. Adding an objective is very simple: Click Add New Item under the Objectives list, and type in the objective.

2. Adding items to the agenda is also very simple. Click Add new item and enter the following values:

   a. **Subject:** Enter a short description for this agenda item.

   b. **Owner:** Enter who is responsible for this item.

   c. **Time:** Enter how much time this item will take.

   d. **Notes:** Enter a longer description of this item. Note that you can also attach a file to this item using the Attach File button on the headline.

   e. Click Save and Close when done. You can now add the next agenda item the same way.

After doing this for a while, you might want a faster way of adding agenda items. The simplest way is to use the Datasheet view. To do that, follow these steps:

1. On the start page for this workspace, click the Agenda header to open this list on its own page.

2. Click the Edit in Datasheet button.

3. Enter the values for each item, as if this was an Excel spreadsheet. Note that the user must have Excel 2003 installed to have access to this Datasheet view.

4. When done, click Show in Standard View.

This was an easier method, right? But there are still some things you can do to improve the management of the agenda. For example, you can summarize the total time for this meeting, and you can add a new column that you can use to indicate that an item is completed. Use the following steps to fix these features:

1. Make sure you have the Agenda page open. Click Modify Settings and Columns.

2. To calculate the total time, you need to change the column type for the Time column. In the Columns section, click Time to open its settings. Note that it is defined as "Single line of text." SharePoint cannot summarize text columns, so you must change this:

   a. Select Number instead and click OK. This displays a warning: Changing the type of this column may result in a loss of data. Are you sure that you want to change this field from Single line of text to Number? Click OK.

   b. Scroll down to the bottom of this page. Click the view All items (which is the default view for this agenda list). You can now see the configuration settings for this view. Scroll down until you see the Totals section. Expand this section and change the Total setting for the Time column from None to Sum. Then click OK at the bottom of this page. This view will now display the total time for this meeting.

3. The second feature, to create a check box for each item, is also accomplished using the Modify Settings and Columns page. Scroll down to the Columns section and click Add a new column. Enter the following values:

   a. **Column Name:** Done.

   b. **Column Type:** Yes/No (check box).

   c. **Default Value:** No.

   d. Click OK to save and close.

   e. You want this check box at the beginning of each line, so click All Items again. In the Columns section, change the Position from Left setting for the Done column from 6 to 1 and click OK at the bottom of this page. Click Go Back to "Agenda" to return.

This enhanced list is now ready to be used. Note that the Done column is the first column on this list. Also note that the total sum for the Time column is displayed on top of the Time column (see Figure 10-5).

Figure 10-5

The Done column is not that easy to use in the default view. It is much easier to switch to the Datasheet view, because you can simply check each item as it is completed. Compare Figure 10-6 to Figure 10-5.

Basic				
Agenda				
Use the Agenda list to outline topics and a timeline for your meeting.				
New Row	Change Order	Show in Standard View	Task Pane	Totals	Refresh Data

	Done	▼	◎	▼	Subject	▼	Owner	▼	Time	▼	Notes	▼
	☐				Welcome to this meeting		Jack		5		Explain the objectives for this meeting.	
	☐				Project organization		Jack and Alex		10		Define what each project member will do during this project.	
*	☐											
	Total								15			

Figure 10-6

Because the Datasheet view is so much easier to see and modify items in, it is the recommended view to use when holding this meeting with the attendees. You could also create a new view based on the Datasheet view and use that view on the first page for this meeting workspace. Use the following steps to do that:

Try It Out   Create a Datasheet View for the Agenda List

1. Log on as an administrator for this team site.

2. Open the Agenda list on its own page.

3. Click "Modify settings and columns" and scroll down to the Views section. Click Create a new view.

4. Select Datasheet view and enter the following values on the web form:

   a. **View Name:** Datasheet View.

   b. **First Sort by the column:** ID.

   c. **Totals / Set Time:** Sum.

   d. Click OK and then click Go Back to "Agenda." Note that you have the new view listed under Views on the left pane of this page. Click Home to go back to the default start page for this team site.

5. You must change the default view that the Agenda web part list is using: Click the arrow to the right of the Agenda web part heading and select Modify Shared Web Part.

6. Use the scroll-down menu for the Selected View part; change it to Datasheet View (the name given in step 4a.). You get a warning that this modification will break any web part connections, but this is fine for now. Click OK and then OK again. The new Agenda is displayed using the Datasheet view (see Figure 10-7).

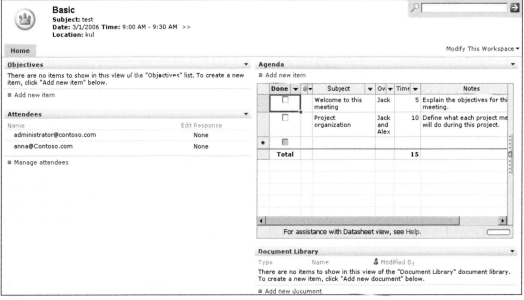

Figure 10-7

The meeting workspace is starting to look good now, but some things are still missing. There is no place to add notes or comments from the meeting, and there is no way to store decisions and tasks created during this meeting. You fix this easily like this:

Try It Out   Add Extra Features to the Meeting Workspace

1. You can use any of several standard lists for taking notes (for example, Announcements and Discussions), or you can create your own list from scratch. In this example you will use the Announcements list. Choose Modify This Workspace⇨Site Settings⇨Modify site content⇨ Create new content⇨Announcements. Fill in this information:

    a. **Name:** Meeting comments.

    b. **Description:** Comments from this meeting instance.

    c. **Change items into series items:** No.

    d. Click Create. The new list opens.

2. Click Home to go back to the start page for this workspace. Note that the new list is automatically added to this page to make it easier to use.

This new list has the same columns as the Agenda list. In fact, they are identical. It is a very handy tool for taking notes and comments directly during the meeting. Another way is to write an MS Word file, but the advantage with the Agenda list is that everyone can see these notes directly without opening a document.

The other feature needed is a place to write down decisions and tasks. SharePoint has preconfigured lists for this type of information. Use these steps to add these lists to the workspace:

1. Go to the start page for this workspace.

2. Choose Modify This Workspace⇨Add Web Parts. This displays all specific web parts for meeting workspaces.

3. Locate the Decisions list; using the mouse, drag it to the web part zone where you want to store it.

4. Locate the Tasks list; drag it to a web part zone.

5. To exit the design mode, click Modify This Workspace and unselect Design this page.

6. Test these two new lists. Click Add new item for the Decision list and for the Tasks list. Make sure they are listed on the start page for this workspace.

What do you say? Isn't this a very easy way of documenting comments, decisions, and tasks during the meeting? By adding the lists you need and modifying their columns, you can control what and how information is entered in this workspace, thus making sure nobody forgets about adding important information. It sure beats the traditional meeting minutes!

Managing Pages

Did you notice that all lists you add to the workspace immediately are displayed on the web page? Compare that to ordinary team sites where you can choose to add these lists and libraries as a link on the quick launch bar or add them to the web page. This choice is not available for workspaces, because they do not have the quick launch bar. For more complex meetings you may need more than one page for your list. This is a very easy task to accomplish with workspaces, but team sites do not have the same functionality. Another difference between workspaces and team sites is that you will automatically create a new list or library when adding web parts in workspaces, whereas in team sites the same operation will create a copy of that list or library. This is demonstrated in the following example.

For example, say that you have a workspace for a project meeting with several lists on the Home page and you also have a large document library. You discover that this library will make the Home page very long and hard to use, so you decide to create a second page on this workspace and move these documents there, using these steps:

Try It Out   **Add a New Page to a Workspace**

1. Log on as the administrator for the workspace and open its Home page.

2. Choose Modify This Workspace⇨Add Pages:

   a. **Page Name:** Add a short name for this page. It will be displayed next to Home.

   b. Click Add to continue.

3. The new page is displayed, but the problem is that your list of documents is stored in the Home page and you want them listed on the second page. Because there is no easy method to move or copy a list or library from one page to another in a workspace, you must do it this way:

   a. Go to the second page. Choose Modify This Workspace⇨Add Web Parts.

   b. Drag the web part Document Library to the place of your choice on this second page. Its name will be "Document Library1" because this is the second document library created on this workspace and the first was named "Document Library." (Remember that adding web parts in a workspace will create new libraries instead of copying them, so the new library must have a unique name.) If the first document library had custom columns, you need to either re-create them in this new document library or create a template from the first library and create this new document library based on that template (if so, click Show All Lists under the web part list to see the new template). If you don't do this, you will lose all custom columns when moving the documents to this new library.

   c. Go back to the Home page and click the title name for this document library. Switch to the Explorer view. Click any existing document and press Ctrl+A and then Ctrl+C to copy all these documents.

   d. Go to the document library on the second page. Click its title name. Switch to the Explorer view. Select any free space on that page and press Ctrl+V to paste all files.

   e. When you are absolutely sure all the files are copied to the new document library, go back to the Home page. Click the title name for the document library. Choose Modify settings and columns⇨Delete this document library⇨OK to execute this delete instruction.

4. Click Home to display this page. Make sure that the old document library is gone. Open the second page. All files should be visible in this new library, including their custom columns.

   You can also make a template of the original document library and include all documents, but only if their total size is less than 10 MB.

You can move, rename, or delete a page, except for the Home page. To move a page, choose Modify This Workspace⇨Manage Pages. Note that you cannot move the Home page, nor can you move a page to the left of the Home page.

To change the name of an existing page, choose Modify This Workspace⇨Manage Page and click the line with the title Order. It displays a menu with different options, as in Figure 10-8. Click Settings and enter the new name for this page.

Deleting the page also removes all its content. Because there is no way to undo this operation, make sure you copy the page's lists before you delete it! Use Manage Page and its menu as depicted in Figure 10-8. Then select Delete. This displays a list of all pages except Home. Select the page to be removed and click the Delete button at the bottom to remove this page from the workspace. Click OK on the warning page.

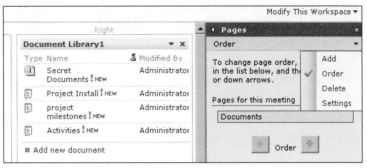

Figure 10-8

Managing a Series of Meetings

It is very common to have a series of meetings. For each of these meetings, it is important to have easy access to the information from previous meetings. Using SharePoint's meeting workspaces, this is a breeze. One of my customers complained that their project meetings were almost too complicated to perform, due to their constant need to go back to previous meetings to see things like who was responsible for a specific task or when a certain decision was made. When they started to use SharePoint's meeting workspaces, they told me that all this was now much easier; in fact, their meetings were now both fewer and shorter.

The support for a series of meetings in SharePoint is a very strong feature! This can save you a lot of time and energy, compared to using traditional meeting minutes on paper. It makes it possible to go back and forth between the meeting dates and see everything that happened in them. You can even search all the meeting instances for a given text string, as long as the SQL Server has installed the Full-Text Indexing feature.

Joining an Existing Meeting

After the first meeting workspace has been created as described previously, you can join, or link, new meeting instances to that first workspace. This creates a new page that looks like an individual workspace, but in fact it is a part of the first workspace, cleverly disguised behind smoke and mirrors. "Behind smoke and mirrors" might not be completely true; you will soon see that the workspace gets one enumerated folder for each meeting instance in this series to store the information from that meeting.

For example, say that the first project meeting you created in the previous example will be followed by a number of other meetings related to that project. Now you need to create the second meeting, and you must make sure to link it to the first meeting workspace instead of creating a completely new one. Follow these steps to do this:

Try It Out   Link to an Existing Meeting Workspace

1. Use the Outlook calendar and create a meeting request (any time after the first meeting will do fine); enter the following settings:

    a. Enter all attendees as recipients of this meeting request. Don't forget to add a room reservation on the same request, if needed.

    b. Enter a Subject for this meeting. This will be the instance name of this workspace.

    c. Click the Meeting Workspace button.

    d. Click "You can also link to an existing workspace."

    e. Use the pull-down menu "Link to an existing workspace" in the "Select a workspace" section, and select the previous meeting name. If you don't see the meeting name, you may have the wrong team site selected. If so, change the site using "Select a location" at the top of this pane.

    f. Click OK and then Link to create the second meeting instance.

    g. Click Send to send this meeting request to all attendees.

2. Right-click this meeting in the calendar and select View Meeting Workspace to open this workspace. Note that it contains exactly the same lists, libraries, and layout as the first workspace. The reason for this is that it *is* the same workspace. However, all list content is stored in separate subfolders to avoid mixing it with the content from the first workspace.

3. Note that there are now two dates listed in the left pane. To view the content from the first meeting, click the date for that meeting. Using these dates, you can go back and forth to any meeting and view its content. As you later add more meetings to this series, the list of dates will grow.

Managing List Content for a Series of Meetings

The ability to link a series of meetings to the same workspace is a real time-saver. You can easily find any information about an earlier meeting just by clicking a meeting's date. However, sometimes it would be great if the content from one list could be available in any meeting instance. For example, say that you have a list named "Tasks"; it contains a list of actions to be performed, each action's due date, and the name of the person responsible for each action. Assume you have this list on a project meeting workspace; when performing each meeting, you want to see all actions remaining from earlier meetings. To do this, you need to change the way a list is managed by SharePoint, as the following steps describe:

Try It Out   Change a List to a Series Object

1. Open the workspace as the administrator.

2. Click the name of the list to be converted to a series object (in this example, Tasks).

3. Choose Modify settings and columns⇨Change general settings.

4. Set Change items into series items to Yes.

5. Click OK and then click Go Back to "Tasks." Click Home to see the start page for this workspace.

6. Test by adding an item to the Tasks list. Click Add new item. Add anything you like and click OK. Then select any other meeting date; note that the Tasks list still contains the same items.

In other words, by making a list contain "series items," you make it one single list for all meetings in this series.

This works fine as it is, but sometimes you want to filter the list to prevent it from showing all items. For example, the Tasks list displays all actions, including the ones that have been completed. It would probably be more interesting to see only items that are not completed. This is easily solved by using a view that filters the Status column that the Tasks list contains in this example. The good news is that there already exists such a view for this list, named "Active Tasks." You just have to use it as the default view for the Tasks web part:

1. Click the arrow to the right of the Tasks web part and select Modify Shared Web Part.

2. In the Selected View pull-down menu, select Active Tasks. Click OK to refresh the page, and click OK to save and close this web part configuration setting.

3. Note that the Tasks list shows only items where Status is not equal to Completed.

Now you have a general idea of how to use lists and views for series of meetings. You have the tools for creating a very powerful and time-saving workspace for meetings.

Tips about Series of Meetings

Adding new meetings to an existing series is easy, but sometimes there is a need to change or manage these meetings. In the following table you get some tips about these situations:

Situation	Comment	Solution
You, the meeting organizer, delete an existing meeting request in Outlook that has an associated workspace.	This will make the specific meeting instance in the workspace an orphan. Its data remains in SharePoint, but there is no connection to Outlook.	Open the workspace. There is a red exclamation mark next to the orphaned meeting date. Click this exclamation mark and it displays a menu (see Figure 10-9). You can select to Move the workspace's data to another existing meeting instance (overwriting any of its content; see Figures 10-10 and 10-11); Keep (data remains in the workspace, but no Outlook appointment is associated); or Delete (this instance of the workspace and all its data is removed).
You want to remove one meeting instance from a series of meetings.	For example, say that you planned one meeting, but it was canceled, and you don't want to move it.	Use the previous technique: Delete the meeting request in Outlook. Open the workspace and its date will have the red exclamation mark. Use its menu to Delete the workspace. Instead of deleting the meeting appointment in Outlook, you can also open its properties and click the Remove button in the Meeting Workspace pane.

Table continued on following page

Situation	Comment	Solution
You want to connect one meeting instance to a new date.	Say that you have an existing meeting instance with lots of data and that you want to associate it with a new meeting request and a new date.	1. Go to the original meeting request in Outlook. Delete it or remove its workspace link (as described earlier). 2. Create a new meeting request in Outlook. Join the workspace for this series of meetings, but do not add any information to that workspace instance. 3. Open the workspace. Use the menu next to the red exclamation mark for the old meeting date you initially deleted. Select Move and select the new date you just created. This will move all existing information to the new meeting date.

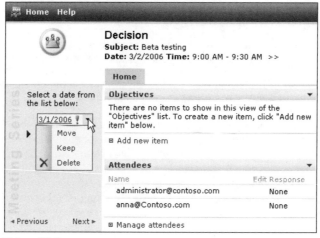

Figure 10-9

Figure 10-10

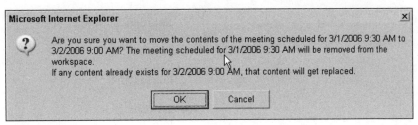

Figure 10-11

Meetings with Other Users

The procedures described in the preceding sections work very well for internal users who have access to your SharePoint environment and have been invited using Outlook's meeting requests. But sometimes you need to allow other users to view the meeting workspace. This section describes the options you have to handle these situations.

Allowing Additional Internal User Access

Sometimes there will be people in your organization who aren't invited to your meetings but who need to access the meeting workspace. The typical example is a manager who wants to know what you do in these meetings. Before you started using meeting workspaces in SharePoint, he got a copy of the meeting minutes. Because you don't have these anymore (and frankly, you don't miss them), you must provide him with this information in another way. The easiest way is to add this manager to the list of users with access to this workspace site; making the manager a member of the Reader site group is sufficient to enable him to view and copy all the content of this workspace.

> *When you have a series of meetings, all invited users have Contributor access to all meeting instances, regardless of when they were invited! There is no way to limit access to just one meeting because the series is sharing the same workspace, and therefore the same list of users. The same is true when you add additional users; they also have access to all meeting instances. But you can set a unique right for any user to a specific list or library by using its security settings in the "Modify settings and columns" link.*

To add an extra user to an existing meeting workspace without making him or her a meeting attendee, you can do this:

Try It Out   Grant Extra Users Access to the Workspace

1. Open the workspace as an administrator.

2. Click Modify This Workspace and select Site Settings.

3. Click the Manage Users link.

4. Click the Add Users button.

5. Enter the name of the new user to be granted access to this meeting. Grant the user the rights needed (for example, Reader) and click Next.

6. Enter descriptive text in the mail body to be sent to this user and click Finish. The user now gets the link to this workspace and a description of granted permissions.

Another solution would be to manually create meeting minutes from the data in the workspace. One way of making this task easier would be to export the list for the Agenda and Decisions to Excel and copy that information into the meeting minutes.

> *I have not seen any tool that does this automatically, although it may be possible using MS SQL 2005 Reporting Services.*

Allowing External User Access

Another common request is to allow people outside your organization access to the information stored in the meeting workspace. The problem here is that these users do not have access to anything inside your network, because they don't have a network user account. Following are some options to handle this situation:

❑ **Create a user account:** If you make this external person a member of your network, you could grant him or her access the same way as any internal user, as for the previous example about the manager. This solution will be of interest if this a reoccurring request.

❑ **Create meeting minutes manually:** Again, as the previous section discussed, you can manually create a document with the meeting minutes. This is acceptable for a one-time request with a limited amount of data in the workspace.

❑ **Use MS Office Live Meeting:** This program is designed to allow anyone with an Internet connection to see and participate in any meeting, not only SharePoint's meeting workspaces. One way of using this program is to invite the external user ahead of time to join the Live Meeting. You can also allow a user who has not previously been invited to the Live Meeting session to simply join it at the time it starts by displaying the workspace on the MS Live Meeting panel and sending the user this URL link in an e-mail. Either way, you can give this user real-time access to the meeting and allow him or her to participate and discuss matters like any attendee of this meeting.

The last option may also be of interest for internal users, when they need to attend meetings while working from home or from an Internet café when on vacation.

> *For more information about MS Office Live Meeting, visit* `http://office.microsoft.com/en-us/FX010909711033.aspx`.

Summary

In this chapter you learned the following:

❑ You can make meetings much more effective using SharePoint.

❑ Meeting workspaces enhance and optimize most tasks and activities before, during, and after the meeting.

❑ A meeting workspace is just a team site using a special site template and some specific lists, such as Agenda, Objectives, and Decisions.

❏   You can create a meeting workspace just like creating any site in SharePoint or using MS Outlook 2003.

❏   You can also create a meeting workspace when entering new events using the "Event" type of list.

❏   The most effective way is to use MS Outlook, because it will allow you to create a meeting request, book resources, and create the meeting workspace at the same time.

❏   To find the workspace for specific meeting requests, right-click it and select "View Meeting Workspace."

❏   Using meeting workspaces, you don't have to write meeting minutes anymore.

❏   To create a meeting workspace, the user must have "Create Subsite" rights on the parent site. By default it requires the user to be the Administrator for this parent site, unless this right is granted to another site group.

❏   By default all users are able to create meeting workspaces under their own personal site. (Remember that only SPS allows users to create personal sites.)

❏   Lots of settings in the Windows Registry are related to the integration between MS Outlook 2003 and meeting workspaces. Use Group Policy Objects to manage these settings for all or some of the users.

❏   By default there are five meeting workspace templates. All of them can be customized, like any team site.

❏   Change the Agenda list to make it easier to use in real time (for example, add a column to note when each item is done and use the Datasheet view to more easily update the list content).

❏   Add extra pages when you need extra space for lists and libraries.

❏   Create a series of meetings by joining meeting instances to the same workspace. All meetings are listed by date, thus making it very easy to go back to any previous meeting.

❏   Change a list to a series of list items if you need to see the content of a list in all the instances of a meeting series.

❏   Allow non-attendees access to the workspace by adding their user account to the workspace.

❏   External users can participate in the meeting using MS Office Live Meeting, or you can later show them a particular meeting instance using the same program.

In the next chapter you see an example of how to build an intranet with team sites. This will give you insight on how to use all SharePoint features discussed so far in the book.

Case Study: Building an Intranet

You are getting close to the end of this book. So far you have seen a lot of what SharePoint can do and how you can extend its functionality. This chapter gives you a recap of the most important topics in the book and discusses what things to do and in what order. You will do this by following two case studies: one that uses WSS as a simple but useful intranet and one that builds an intranet based on SPS. After that you will find several examples on how to create team sites for common tasks such as projects, meetings, and other collaboration workspaces.

This chapter assumes that you have a default SharePoint server installed, using the full MS SQL Server. Each case study starts with an analysis of the needs and objectives for this intranet. It then continues with a technical analysis of how to build the solution and then finally describes how to actually build it.

Analyzing the Needs

When building a software solution, you need to know two things: what the current situation is and what your objective is. To know that, you must analyze what you have today and what the needs of your users are. The more time and energy you put into this analysis, the greater the chance that you will make the right decisions and avoid costly mistakes. A golden rule when analyzing is to ask the right people and never accept a vague answer, like "I think we have enough free disk space for your new SharePoint server." If you have even the slightest doubt about some answers, make sure to conduct a thorough investigation to get the facts. This does not necessarily mean that you have to do everything yourself; you can delegate tasks to reliable people.

Another golden rule when you start designing the SharePoint environment is KISS — Keep It Simple, Stupid! If you can make it with one server, then do so; if the intranet will work with just three site groups, then do that; if one document library will be enough for storing all documents, then use one library. Every time you add more servers, more site groups, and more document libraries, you also add to the complexity of this SharePoint solution. And more complexity means more time for administration and management, plus a more complex environment to analyze if something goes wrong. So please, remember KISS. It will make your life easier!

WSS or SPS?

The boss comes to you and tells you that the company needs an intranet, and fast! You need to get something up and running within one week, if possible without spending any money. So your mission is to build an intranet, and you start wondering what to do next. You should get answers to some questions before you start, like these:

Question	People to Ask	Comment
Do you need an intranet for the whole organization?	Top-management, people responsible for managing organization-wide information.	For a small company with fewer than 50 users, WSS may be sufficient. But if there is a lot of information, SPS can fill your needs much better.
Do you need a local intranet for your department or teams?	Middle management, team leaders.	WSS is a good choice if the department or team needs to share information.
Do you need an easy and fast way of navigating your information, regardless of its storage location?	Subject-matter experts, project leaders, power users, end users.	SPS offers *topics* to solve this need. You can build similar functionality in WSS, but it requires much more work.
Do you want to be able to search for information stored both inside and outside SharePoint?	All types of users.	Only SPS offers global search functionality.
Is searching inside SharePoint enough for your needs?	All types of users.	This is a complementary question to the previous one; if the answer is yes, you can fulfill this need by using WSS and MS SQL Server together.
Do groups of users need to share and update different information?	All types of users.	If yes, this need is fulfilled with the WSS site. If only a few people need to update the information, an option would be to use SPS areas.
Do you need a way of presenting more information than just the e-mail addresses and phone numbersfor some or all of your users?	Middle management, team leaders, project leaders.	SPS has its "My Site" feature, which presents much more information about users than the typical "Employee List."

If the answers to these questions indicate that WSS will be sufficient, then by all means build the intranet using Windows SharePoint Services. It is indeed a very good platform for sharing information within your organization. If you use MS SQL Server and its Full-Text Indexing, it also offers some basic search capabilities.

But if you need more than WSS can provide, don't hesitate to go with SharePoint Portal Server. Its features are very nice, and it gives you the best intranet and collaboration environment that Microsoft can offer today. If you are unsure what to choose, why not use the free SPS 2003 evaluation copy that works for 120 days? It will give you a fair chance to see what SPS can do for your users.

Analyzing an Intranet

The intranet as we know it has been around for more than 10 years now. But what is an intranet? Here are some common definitions, which, although similar, demonstrate subtle differences:

- ❏ An intranet is a web application for sharing information that only internal users can access.
- ❏ An intranet is a secure web-based environment where local users can access information.
- ❏ An intranet is a web-based solution for sharing news, links, and documents with internal users.

An older definition states that an intranet is a TCP/IP-based local network, but this type of definition is not what this book is discussing. So the general consensus is that an intranet is a web site where the local users will find the information they need, much like an internal news paper. Now stop for a moment and think again: Is this really what your users need? The answer is most likely both yes and no! Who is asking for this intranet? Everyone, you say. This is true, but when I ask my clients this question, I often find out that:

- ❏ The management wants to publish information about the company and its activities.
- ❏ The users want to find information related to their work.

One of the reasons management wants to publish information is to ease the burden on some internal groups. If the intranet contains all the news and links to internal standards, handbooks, and forms, then it is up to the user to find the information. For example, if a user wants to request a vacation, he uses the intranet to find the proper form and procedure. After a while, the users do indeed learn how to find the information they need.

However, there is another consideration that it is important to not overlook. If you have an intranet in your organization today, how many of your users have this site as the start page for their web browser? How many of the users are checking the intranet every day, or at least once per week? I don't know the exact answer in your case, but the traditional intranets I have seen give depressing answers, maybe 10 percent, if you are lucky. How can this be? Here is a hint: Look at what the users are using as the default start page for their browsers. It is usually a search site, such as Google, or a news site on the Internet. Why is this? Easy, because it gives the users what they want! This is something you should have in mind when designing your intranet. If you don't, why bother to build it at all?

If you give the users something they are interested in, you don't need to force them to check the intranet. But to be fair, all types of intranets cannot be that interesting for all users. In such cases it is great if the users can be notified whenever there is something new and interesting. Another valuable tool you can use in intranets is pictures. Compare the intranet to some popular newspapers. Pictures make articles much more interesting. Your intranet should learn from newspapers.

To summarize, an intranet should contain the following things to be interesting to your users:

- ❏ Company news that relates to the current user, with pictures when possible.
- ❏ External news from a site the current user is interested in.
- ❏ Information related to the user's personal tasks and interests, such as:
  - ❏ Notifying the company's receptionist about absences and meetings.
  - ❏ Filling in time cards.
  - ❏ Listing today's menu in the local restaurant.
  - ❏ Providing the weather forecast for the user's local area.

❑ Information related to the user's work, such as documents, contacts, and project information.

❑ Information about co-workers, such as their e-mail addresses, phone numbers, responsibilities, and pictures.

One could argue whether information such as external news and weather forecasts should be listed on the intranet, but in my experience this type of extra information makes the site interesting enough that users may even use it as the start page for their web browsers. In the following section you will try to follow these rules when building an intranet using a WSS environment.

An Intranet Based on WSS

The team sites in Windows SharePoint Services are really meant to be a place to collaborate. But that does not stop you from using WSS as a simple intranet. You have the basic features available for building an intranet, such as the following:

❑ A news list (text only, and no pictures; but you can add an extra column for pictures).

❑ An RSS news feed from a site on the Internet, using the XML web part.

❑ A list of links that point to any place inside SharePoint, the Internet, or to a file.

❑ The content of a public Internet site using the Page Viewer web part.

❑ Lists for storing documents, contacts, and tasks related to specific projects or activities.

❑ A list of employees, including e-mail addresses, phone numbers, and pictures.

❑ A web part that displays a picture (one at the time).

These are just some of the tools for building the intranet. You can also find more advanced web parts on the Internet; some are free, and others are commercial products. One problem is that you cannot filter any information in a list; either you see the list content or you don't. WSS has no feature similar to the audience targeting that exists in SPS. So you must think hard before you create one intranet for all users in your organization. One way to solve this problem is to create a top site of this WSS-based intranet that contains more general information, and from that follow links to local intranets for departments, teams, or other smaller groups.

General Features of the Intranet

Your job is to create a WSS-based intranet for a company with 80 users. This company has these departments: Sales, HR, Finance, and IT. There is also the important Board of Directors team for management. All of them need a place to share internal information, and it is important that the Finance department and the Board of Directors team have their own security.

First you analyze the current situation in your organization:

❑ You have a fresh WSS site, built on the clean site template that does not have any lists from the beginning. This WSS server is using MS SQL Server, which has the Full-Text Indexing feature activated.

❑ Users save some documents in the common file share "P:" and sometimes on their local disk.

❑   Common calendar and contact lists are stored in Outlook's public folders.

❑   Important news about the company or its customers is distributed using e-mail.

❑   Information about co-workers is found in Outlook's global address list.

Then you summarize the objectives for the new intranet, based on the analysis you performed in your organization:

❑   There should be one start page on the intranet that displays this info:

   ❑   Common news with pictures for the company and its customers.

   ❑   Links to often-requested information, such as company policies, HR documents, and local intranets.

   ❑   A list of external news from the Internet news site `http://www.usatoday.com/repurposing/NewslineRss.xml`.

   ❑   A weather forecast.

   ❑   A list of employees, including their data and pictures.

❑   On each local intranet the user will find:

   ❑   Local news for this department.

   ❑   A local list of contact information for customers and vendors.

   ❑   Links to folders, documents, and team sites used by this local department.

❑   The Board of Directors and Finance groups also need their own team sites, but the access permission must be set so only the proper people can view or modify that information.

So now you know your starting point, and you also know where to go. Make sure to keep an eye on the objectives during this implementation to make sure not to miss any important features.

Building an Intranet Using WSS

You have one empty top web site, based on the Blank Site template, to start with in this example with the URL address `http://filmportalen`. Follow these steps to create the intranet in this example:

> **For more information about installing WSS and creating team sites, see Chapter 2.**

Try It Out   Create a Basic Intranet

1.   Log on as the administrator to the existing site `http://filmportalen`.

2.   Create a list of pictures to be used in the News listing:

   a.   Click Create and select Picture Library.

   b.   **Name:** Pictures for News.

   c.   **Display this picture library on the Quick Launch bar:** No.

   d.   Click Create.

   e.   The new picture library is displayed; click Add Pictures and add all the pictures you will need for the news items. Make sure to use reasonable sizes no larger than 160 × 160 pixels, because these pictures will be displayed in their actual size!

3.   The next step is to create a list for displaying the three latest news items, including pictures; make sure the picture is displayed to the left of each news article.

   a.   Click Create and select Announcements.

   b.   **Title:** Company News.

   c.   **Display this list on the Quick Launch bar:** No.

   d.   Click OK to save and close.

   e.   Click Modify columns and settings.

   f.   In the Columns section, click "Add a new column." Give it the name "Picture." Set the Type to "Hyperlink or Picture." Set "Format URL as" Picture. Click OK.

   g.   In the View section, click All Items. Change the "Position from Left" to 1 for the column Picture; to 2 for the Title; and to 3 for the Body. Make sure to check "Body" so it will be displayed. Go down to the section "Item Limit"; set the "Number of items to display" to 3, and select "Limit the total number of items returned to the specified amount." Next click OK.

   h.   Click Go Back to "Company News."

   i.   Add the News list to the Home page: Open the Home page for this team site. Choose Modify Shared Page⇨Add Web Parts⇨Browse. Locate the list "Company News" and drag it to the top position in the Left web part zone.

   j.   To refresh the modified "All Items" view for this Company News list, choose Modify Shared Page⇨Company News and change the Select View from "Current view" to "All Items." Click OK on the popup window and then OK again to save and close the property page for this web part.

   k.   Click "Add new announcement" to add one news item; make sure to include a URL to one of the pictures you added in step 2e.

The easiest way of copying the URL to any of these pictures is to open the picture library in a separate web browser, click a picture to display it, then right-click the picture, and select Copy Shortcut, as in Figure 11-1.

   l.   Repeat step 3f. After adding at least three items, you should have a news list that looks similar to Figure 11-2.

4.   The intranet also should have the current weather listed on the Home page. There is a free web part for this named MSNBC Weather:

   a.   Choose Modify Shared Page⇨Add Web Parts⇨Browse⇨Online Gallery. Drag MSNBC Weather to the top of the right web part.

   b.   Click "select a location," enter the city you live in, and click Go. If there is more than one city that matches this name, use the menu below and select the right city and country.

   c.   Choose Fahrenheit or Celsius and click OK to save.

5.   You don't need the default picture at the left top. Use its quick menu and select Delete to remove it from this page. (You can still take it back by dragging it from the web part site gallery.)

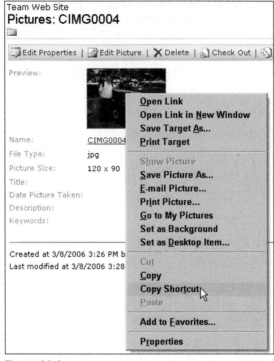

Figure 11-1

Figure 11-2

6. To make this page more interesting for your users, add an RSS feed from the latest news from the web publication of *USA Today*.

When setting up an RSS feed, it is always a good idea to check the policies and requirements of the provider.
To review USA Today's policies, go to `http://asp.usatoday.com/marketing/rss/index.aspx`.

    a.   Choose Modify Shared Page⇨Add Web Parts. Drag the XML web part to a position directly under the Company News web part.

    b.   Open the tool pane for this XML web part and enter the following URL in the XML Link field: `http://www.usatoday.com/repurposing/NewslineRss.xml`.

    c.   Expand the Appearance section and set the Title to USA Today.

    d.   Then click XSL Editor and enter the following code to make it understand RSS feeds:

```xml
<?xml version="1.0" encoding="UTF-8" ?>
<xsl:stylesheet version="1.0" xmlns:xsl="http://www.w3.org/1999/XSL/Transform">
<xsl:template match="/">
<html>
<body>
<xsl:for-each select="rss">
<xsl:for-each select="channel">
<xsl:for-each select="item">
<xsl:for-each select="title">
<a>
<xsl:attribute name="href">
<xsl:value-of select="../link" />
</xsl:attribute>
<B>
<span style="color:navy; font-family:Tahoma; font-size:8pt; font-style:normal;">
<xsl:apply-templates />
</span>
</B>
</a>
</xsl:for-each>
<br />
<xsl:for-each select="pubDate">
<span style="font-family:Tahoma; font-size:8pt;font-style:italic;">
...
<xsl:apply-templates />
</span>
</xsl:for-each>
<br />
</xsl:for-each>
</xsl:for-each>
</xsl:for-each>
</body>
</html>
</xsl:template>
</xsl:stylesheet>
```

    e.   Click OK to save and close this web part.

7.   Next, you want to make a list of all employees. Start by creating a contact list; then add all employees, and display the web part for this list:

    a.   Click Create on the Home page.

    b.   Select the Contacts list and give it the name Employees.

    c.   Add all the employees to this list, either by manually entering their name, phone number, and so on or by using the Import Contacts feature, which allows you to import names from your Outlook address book.

d. Go to the Home page and choose Modify Shared Page⇨Add Web Parts. Browse for the Employee list and then drag its web part to the Home page.

8. Now make it possible to display only employees with specific last names. Use the Form web part for this:

a. Choose Modify Shared Page⇨Add Web Parts. Browse for the Form web part and drag it to the position directly above the Employees list.

b. Next you will create a lookup field that a user can use to find a specific employee: Choose Modify Shared Page⇨Design This Page to open the page in design mode. Using the quick menu for the Forms web part, select Connections⇨Provide Form Values To⇨Employees.

c. **Select a Column:** T1; click Next.

d. **Select a Column:** Last Name; this will make it possible to find employees, using the field Last Name in the Employees list. Then click Finish.

e. To make it more obvious what the Form web part is for, you should give it a descriptive name. Use the quick menu to open the properties for this Form web part; in the Appearance section, change Title to "Search for Last Name." Then click OK.

f. Click Home to exit from the design mode.

Test the Form web part by entering a last name you know exists. The Employees list now displays only the names that match your search string.

The page now has some basic features that a simple intranet usually has. It should look similar to Figure 11-3.

Figure 11-3

Creating Local Team Intranets

It is time to create the local intranets for the departments and the teams. Remember that two of them require their own security settings. Because the current intranet is the top site, it also rules all the sub-sites under it, such as the administrator settings and templates for lists and sites. If the Finance and the Board of Directors teams need their own settings, you must create a new top site each for them; the other local intranets for HR, IT, and Sales can be located under the current intranet site. You can set unique permission settings for these three sites (as you will do in the following example), but the administrator of the top site will still be able to access these sites regardless of their permission settings, because they are part of that site collection. You can start by creating the last three intranets:

Try It Out   **Create Local Departmental Intranets**

1. Log on as an administrator for the current top-level site `http://filmportalen`.

2. Choose Create⇨Sites and Workspaces. Enter these values to create the intranet for the IT department, using the standard Team Site template:

    a. **Title:** IT.

    b. **Description:** Intranet for IT.

    c. **URL name:** it (so the total address will be `http://filmportalen/it`).

    d. **User Permissions:** Use unique permissions.

    e. Click Create to go to next page.

    f. **Template:** Team Site.

    g. Click OK.

    This brings you to a standard team site. Change it now as you see fit. When you are done, you need to adjust the permissions and make it easy to find this IT intranet from the company intranet.

3. In the new IT intranet, choose Site Settings⇨Manage users; then:

    a. Click Add Users and add the user names and/or groups that will have access to this site.

    b. Select the rights for these users and groups and click Next.

    c. Fill in the mail body (if these new users have an e-mail address) and click Finish.

    d. Click Home to return to the start page for this IT intranet.

4. Click "Up to Team Web Site" in the top-right corner of this page. This will take you back to the intranet page on the top site (`http://filmportalen`).

5. Repeat steps 2, 3, and 4 and add a local intranet for the HR and Sales departments. When all this is done, you will have three subsites under the top-level intranet site.

6. To make it easier for your users to open these local intranets, you can add a link to each of them or you can use a web part that lists all subsites. Because these three local intranets will be fairly static, it is probably best to use static links this time. Go to the general intranet (`http://filmportalen`) and choose Create⇨Links and enter these values:

    a. **Name:** Local Intranets.

    b. **Description:** Links to local intranets.

    c. **Display this list on the Quick Launch bar?:** No.

d.   Click Create. The new list will be displayed.

e.   Click New item and enter the URL `http://filmportalen/it`. Enter the Description IT and click Save and Close.

f.   Repeat this step and add the links to HR and Sales, using their respective URL addresses.

7.   Click Home to go back. Choose Modify Shared Page⇨Add Web Parts⇨Browse. Locate the new list Local Intranets and drag it to the location directly under the Weather web part. Then click Home to leave the design mode.

8.   The list with its three links will be displayed. Click any of these and make sure they open the correct intranet. If not, click the heading Local Intranet to open the list on its own page, and change any errors.

Creating Top-Level Local Intranets

Now you have two more local intranets to create for the Finance and the Board of Directors teams. These must be top-level sites in order to have their own security settings and other features that are local for a site collection. Both of these intranets require a more elaborate design. Fortunately, Microsoft has released several complete SharePoint applications you can use:

Try It Out   **Create Finance and Board of Directors Intranets**

1.   Open a web browser and go to the Microsoft site where these applications are stored: `http://www.microsoft.com/technet/prodtechnol/sppt/wssapps/default.mspx`.

2.   Locate and download the Board of Directors application. Unpack the two files and save them on the SharePoint server. There are two site templates, a basic one and a more elaborate version called "custom," which is what you will use. To make this custom site template available for new top-level sites, you must add it to the global site template gallery using the STSADM program:

   a.   Open a CMD window.

   b.   Change the current file directory to the one where the two new site templates are stored.

   c.   Type the following:

```
STSADM -o Addtemplate -filename BoardofDirectors_Custom.stp -title ↵
"Board of Directors"
```

   d.   Run IISReset in the CMD window.

   e.   Close this window.

3.   The other web application for the Finance is stored on another web site: `http://www.sharepointcustomization.com`. Choose Working With⇨Microsoft Windows SharePoint Services; then scroll down to Finance and click "Download this site's Web package." Save it to the same location as the previous site template.

4.   To use these two new templates, you must use two different techniques because they are two different file types. One is a standard SharePoint site template (.STP), and the other is a FrontPage 2003 Backup Site (.FWP). But first you need to create two empty top-level sites that you later will brand with these two site templates:

   a.   Start the SharePoint Central Administration tool (located in Start⇨Administrative tools).

   b.   Click Create a top-level Web site.

    c.   Click the IIS site used by SharePoint (usually Default Web Site).

    d.   Select Create site under this URL and enter **finance**.

    e.   Add the user name and mail address for the owner.

    f.   Make sure the Language is English (otherwise you cannot use the custom site template because it was made using an English team site). Click OK when ready.

    g.   Repeat steps b through f and create a second top-level site named Board of Directors.

5.   Next, brand the first of these two top-level sites with the Board of Directors template. It is easy; just open its URL address and the new site template is listed. Select the Board of Directors template and click OK. The new site opens and is ready to be used (see Figure 11-4).

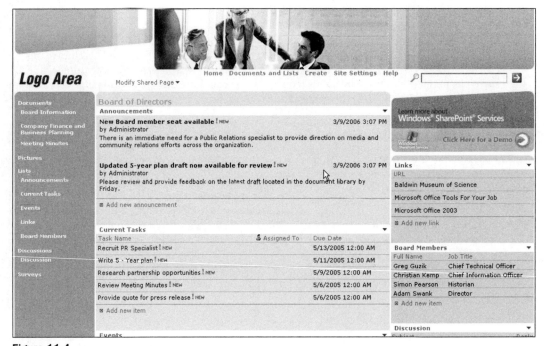

Figure 11-4

6.   The second branding must be done differently because this file is a FrontPage backup file:

    a.   Start FrontPage 2003.

    b.   Choose File⇨Open Site. Enter the name `http://filmportalen/sites/finance` and click Open. The empty top-level site opens.

    c.   Select Tools⇨Server⇨Restore Web Site⇨finance2_sharepoint_v2.fwp. Click Open and then OK. The restore of this site starts.

    d.   Close FrontPage.

    e.   Open the new Finance site: `http://filmportalen/sites/finance`. It looks like Figure 11-5.

Figure 11-5

7. Almost done! You only have to add links from the company intranet to these two new local intranets. Go to `http://filmportalen`:

    a. Click Add new links. Set the URL to `http://filmportalen/sites/board` and the Description to Board of Directors. Click Save and Close.

    b. In the "Local Intranets" area, click Add new link. Set the URL to `http://filmportalen/sites/finance` and the Description to Finance. Click Save and Close.

The next logical step would be to configure the user access list to the Finance and Board of Directors sites and then to start adding information to it. With WSS you also have the perfect tool for managing projects, activities, and meetings. One way of meeting this need is to create a subsite structure under each local intranet (IT, Finance, and so on). Such a site tree might constantly be growing with more and more subsites. If you need to have a link to each of these subsites on the intranet page it will be hard to manually update the list to these sites. Another way of solving this is to add a web part for listing subsites on the local intranet so when you look at the IT site, you can see all its subsites, and when you look at the Finance site, you see all its subsites. In Chapter 8 you saw several samples of such web parts. A personal favorite of mine is the Site Navigator web part from `sharepoint.advis.ch` because of its many configuration settings and its ability to hide subsites that you are not allowed to use.

An Intranet Based on SPS

In the previous section you saw that a simple but useful intranet could be based on WSS. However, you were forced to make several adjustments just to make the lists suitable for containing news. There also was no way to hide some of the news for some users; they saw either everything or nothing.

The full SharePoint Portal Server 2003 has a lot more features for building a smarter intranet with less hassle. SPS also makes it possible to search everywhere for information, regardless of location and type. Using WSS you can only search the current site for information.

This section uses the same example as for WSS (to build one company-wide intranet and then several local intranets for HR, IT, and so on). Comparing the two case studies will give you a better understanding of the differences between WSS and SPS.

The Portal Site Overview

This is the company-wide intranet that all users will have read access to, regardless of their department or position. When using SPS it is common to use the term "the portal site" for this intranet. It consists of several pages, also known as *areas*. There are two types of areas: topics areas and general areas. The primary use of the topics areas is for navigation (to make it easier for the users to find the information they are searching every day). The primary uses for the general areas are for sharing information such as reference material and for departmental intranets. One of the differences between a topics area and a general area is the built-in actions that are available: Only the topics area has "Add Listing" and "Add Person" capabilities. This is something that should guide you when creating area pages in the portal.

In this example you start with a default configured SharePoint Portal Server 2003. You have the same organizations as in the previous WSS example. You also have the same goal: Build an intranet for the company, plus some local or departmental intranets for HR, IT, Finance, Sales, and the Board of Directors teams. Because this version is built on SPS, you will use its standard features as much as possible. Later, you may need to do some branding (change the colors and look-and-feel), but for now that is not important.

You start by configuring the default portal site to meet the objectives for the general intranet, as listed by the project leader for the intranet. The Home page should contain these features:

❑ Links to projects and workspaces, complete with pictures.

❑ General news items, but filtered for each department.

❑ A company calendar.

❑ Weather information.

❑ News items from an Internet-based news site.

❑ The personal calendar for the current user.

❑ Search capabilities for employees.

❑ The lunch menu for today.

❑ Links to departmental intranet pages. Only the members of a department should see the link to their local intranet.

Creating Picture Libraries

One thing to start with is to create a picture library for news items, personal web sites, and listings. SharePoint allows you to add a link to a picture wherever it may be (for example, on another server in your network environment or on a public web site on the Internet). It is important that this link is available to anyone using the portal site, regardless of their current location. For example, say that you add a picture link to a news item, and this link points to a local file server. This works for everyone working at the local network (in the office), but a user temporarily working from home cannot see this picture unless she has a virtual private network (VPN) set up on her local workstation.

In this example you add some pictures to a picture library in the portal site. These pictures will be used later when creating news items and personal sites:

Try It Out   Create a Picture Library

1. Log on as the portal site administrator.

2. Open the Home page of the portal site (your new intranet) that was created by default when you installed SPS, as described in Chapter 4.

3. Choose Manage Content⇨Create⇨Picture Library. Configure it like this:

    a. **Name:** Pictures.

    b. **Description:** Pictures for news items and personal web sites.

    c. **Display this picture library on the Quick Launch bar?:** No. (This setting actually does not matter, because there is no quick launch bar in the portal site; only team sites have the quick launch bar.)

    d. **Create a version each time you edit a file in this picture library?:** No.

    e. Click OK.

4. The new library opens. Click Add Picture and add a few pictures of your choice, but add some portraits too. You may want to rescale them if they are high-resolution pictures, because they will be adjusted to fit the pictures of news items and similar places.

Targeting Audience Groups

The next thing is to create the target groups for the general news and the departmental intranets. You can use the audience groups for targeting, and you can use security groups in the Active Directory to control the access and visibility of the departmental intranets. However, these audience groups are most often based on property settings in the User Profile database, and not based directly on the Active Directory properties.

So you must begin by configuring the User Profile procedure:

Try It Out   Configure the User Profile Database

1. Log on as the SharePoint administrator and open the portal site `http://filmportalen`.

2. Choose Site Settings⇨Manage profile database.

3. Click Configure profile import.

4. Select the scope to be imported; in this example you will use Current Domain.

5. Check "Schedule full import" and set "Start at" to a time when the backup process is not running; in this example use 05.00AM and Every Day. Then click OK to save and close this form.

6. Force the import now by clicking the Start full import link. Wait until the status says Idle again.

All the properties that have been configured to be imported from the Active Directory are now stored in SharePoint's own User Profile database.

The next step is to create the audiences for each department: HR, IT, Sales, and Finance:

Try It Out   Create Department Audiences

This example expects that each user has the Department property set in the Active Directory.

1. Open the portal site `http://filmportalen`.

2. Choose Site Settings⇨Manage audiences.

3. Click Create audience; then enter this information to create the IT audience:

    a. **Name:** IT.

    b. **Description:** Members of the IT department.

    c. Click OK.

    d. **Operand:** Property; **Operator:** "=".The result is "Property=Department".

    e. **Value:** IT.

    f. Click OK and then the "Manage Audiences" breadcrumb trail.

4. Repeat step 3 to create an audience group for HR, Sales, and Finance as well. Use the respective name of each specific department (HR, Sales, and Finance) when you define the Value property in step 3e.

5. These audience groups will not be activated until compiled. (SharePoint needs to scan its user list for all members that match the filter criteria defined in step 3.) You can either start the compilation manually or schedule this process, as shown here:

    a. Click Specify compilation schedule.

    b. Check Enable scheduling.

    c. Set "Start at" to a proper time; remember to make this time *after* the User Profile import! For this example, set the time 06.00AM and select Every Day. Click OK to save and close this form.

    d. Force a manual compilation now by clicking the Start compilation link. Wait for the Compilation status to be listed as Idle again.

6. Click "View audiences" to see the list of compiled audiences, including how many members each group contains. Make sure the number in the "Members" column is what you expect; if not, you have most likely defined the rules in the wrong way.

These audience groups can now be used to filter the News list on the Home page. The result is that each user only sees news items targeting the audience group they belong to. You may remember that a user can belong to several audience groups, and if a news item is targeted to more than one audience group, the same news item will show up for each audience. The following steps activate the audience filtering for the News listing:

Try It Out   Filter Audiences

1. Open the Home page of the portal site.

2. Choose Edit Page⇨ Modify Shared Page⇨Modify Shared Web Parts⇨News. This opens the property pane for the News web part.

3. Change "Group by" from None to Audience. Click OK to save and close. Click Home to exit the design mode.

Now you will not see any news items at all! The reason is that the two default news items do not have any audience defined. If you want to display them, go to the News page where they belong and click Edit Page. Then use the quick menu for each news item and edit their property settings. The audience setting is listed on the Display tab.

Now test the new audience filtering by adding one news item for each audience group:

1. Open the News page.

2. Create a news item for the IT department:

    a.   Click Add News.

    b.   **Title:** For IT only!

    c.   **Description:** This news item is only visible for members of the IT audience group.

    d.   Select "Add news listing by entering text." (You must do this even if you don't intend to add any more text, because the default option requires that you add a link.)

    e.   **Image:** /Pictures/<the picture file>. Add a link to any of the pictures you have in the picture library. Use the same technique as described earlier in this chapter in the WSS section to copy a picture link. Note that the link does not need to start with `http://filmportalen`; the relative address `/Pictures` will work fine too.)

    f.   Scroll down this form. Add the IT to the Selected Audience pane.

    g.   Click OK.

3. Repeat step 2 for each department, making sure to adjust the title, description, and audience group to use the right department.

4. Note that all four of these news items are visible on the News page, because the News web part is not configured to filter by Audience at this time. Switch to the Home page, and it will show you only the news item targeted to the audience group your current logon account belongs to; in other words, the Home page and the News page have different settings. Test and log on with user accounts that belong to any of the other audience groups to see that the targeting works as expected.

5. One thing that makes an intranet more interesting is pictures. The News web part is by default configured to show one of the two picture types a news item can have: an icon or a larger picture. When you add a new news item, you are only allowed to enter one picture link, which is a large picture. To add an icon to a news item, open its properties and add the icon link on the Display tab. The size of the large picture is set by the properties for the News web part:

    a.   Open the Home page. Make sure the page is in design mode (Edit page⇨Modify Shared Page⇨Design this Page).

    b.   Use the quick menu for the News web part and select Modify Shared Web Part.

    c.   Set the size for this picture in "Fixed image width (in pixels)" at 120. Note that if you leave the value for the "Fixed image height (in pixels)" at 0, it will automatically adjust the height of the picture.

Now you have completed the first task: to activate the targeting of news items and make them more attractive by setting a larger picture size.

Hiding Links from Users

Look at the Home page. It contains several links that ordinary users should not see, such as Links for You with the help links for the administrator, and the Portal Owner QuickStart Guide. You can hide these lists from your users either by targeting them for a special audience group for Administrators (you must create that group first) or by removing them completely. You may remember from Chapter 5 that the Portal Owner QuickStart Guide is a special web part. If you remove this one, you cannot get it back again.

In this example, you remove Links for You and hide the Portal Owner QuickStart Guide for all but the IT audience group:

Try It Out   Remove Links

1.   Open the Home page.

2.   Choose Edit page⮕Modify Shared Page⮕Design this Page.

3.   Use the quick menu (to the right of the list name) for Links for You, select Delete, and then click OK.

4.   Use the quick menu for Portal Owner QuickStart Guide and select Modify Shared Web Part.

   a.   Expand the Advanced section.

   b.   Click Select under Target Audiences, add IT to the Selected audiences, and click OK.

   c.   Click OK to save and close this web part property pane. Now this list is only visible for members of the IT audience.

Adding Calendars

The next task is to add a common calendar for the company. Because there already is one calendar named Events on the Home page, you just have to rename it:

Try It Out   Rename the Events List

1.   Use the quick menu for the Events list and select Modify Shared Web Part:

   a.   Expand the Appearance section.

   b.   Change the Title from Events to Company Activities.

   c.   Click OK.

2.   Move the Company Activities web part from its current position in the bottom of the Middle Left Zone to the top of the Middle Right Zone.

Weather Reports

Add the same Weather web part as in the WSS example. Put it at the top of the middle right zone:

Try It Out   **Add a Weather Web Part**

1. Choose Edit page⇨Modify Shared Page⇨Add Web parts⇨Browse.

2. Click the Online Gallery.

3. Drag the MSNBC Weather web part and place it at the top of the Middle Right Zone (just above the Company Activities list).

4. Click the link Select a location in this web part, set the city, and select how to display the temperature.

External News Reports

The next task on your list is to make this page more interesting by adding a list of news items from an external source, such as *USA Today*. This is the exact same technique used in the WSS example:

When setting up an RSS feed, it is always a good idea to check the policies and requirements of the provider. To review USA Today*'s policies, go to* `http://asp.usatoday.com/marketing/rss/index.aspx`.

Try It Out   **Add External News Stories**

1. You still have the web part galleries listed. Select Filmportalen Gallery (the name for this portal site).

2. Drag the XML web part to a position directly under the News web part.

3. Open the tool pane for this XML web part and enter the following URL in the XML Link field: `http://www.usatoday.com/repurposing/NewslineRss.xml`.

4. Expand the Appearance section and set the Title to "News from USA Today."

5. Click XSL Editor and paste the following code to make it understand RSS feeds; then click OK to save and close this web part.

```xml
<?xml version="1.0" encoding="UTF-8" ?>
<xsl:stylesheet version="1.0" xmlns:xsl="http://www.w3.org/1999/XSL/Transform">
<xsl:template match="/">
<html>
<body>
<xsl:for-each select="rss">
<xsl:for-each select="channel">
<xsl:for-each select="item">
<xsl:for-each select="title">
<a>
<xsl:attribute name="href">
<xsl:value-of select="../link" />
</xsl:attribute>
<B>
<span style="color:navy; font-family:Tahoma; font-size:8pt; font-style:normal;">
<xsl:apply-templates />
```

```
</span>
</B>
</a>
</xsl:for-each>
<br />
<xsl:for-each select="pubDate">
<span style="font-family:Tahoma; font-size:8pt;font-style:italic;">
...
<xsl:apply-templates />
</span>
</xsl:for-each>
<br />
</xsl:for-each>
</xsl:for-each>
</xsl:for-each>
</body>
</html>
</xsl:template>
</xsl:stylesheet>
```

Personal Calendars

The next task is to add the personal calendar of the current user. This will require that all users have Outlook 2003 installed on their computer, because it will use an ActiveX component in Outlook to display the content of that folder. The difference between using this method and using the My Calendar web part is that the ActiveX method automatically displays the current user's calendar, whereas the My Calendar must be preconfigured with a specific user name and the URL to the Exchange server. For more information regarding this technique, see Chapter 8.

Try It Out **Create a Personal Calendar**

1. Open the Home page.

2. Choose Edit page⇨Modify Shared Page⇨Add Web Part⇨Browse.

3. Drag the Content Editor web part to the location directly under the Weather web part; then configure it like this:

   a. Open the tool pane for the Content Editor web part. Click Source Editor, enter the following code into that editor, and then click Save:

```
<object classid="clsid:0006F063-0000-0000-C000-000000000046"
id="ViewCtlFolder" width="100%" height="400" codetype="application/x-oleobject"
codebase=⤵
"http://activex.microsoft.com/activex/controls/office/outlctlx.CAB#ver=9,0,0,3203"
border="0">
<param name="Namespace" value="MAPI">
<param name="Folder" value="//Calendar">
<param name="Restriction" value="">
<param name="DeferUpdate" value="0">
</object>
```

   b. Adjust the width and height in the second line of code if the calendar does not look good. If you are using a non-English version of Outlook you may have to change the folder name "//Calendar" to whatever name you are using for your calendar in your Outlook.

c. Expand the Appearance section; change the Title to Your Calendar.

d. Click OK to close and save these changes.

4. Click Home to exit from the design mode. Verify that the calendar and the rest of the web parts look good; if not, make whatever changes are necessary to them now.

At this stage, your intranet will have a targeted list of news items, weather information, the current user's personal calendar, and a news listing from an external web site; Figure 11-6 shows what a member of the IT audience group will see.

Figure 11-6

Searching with SPS

It is also important to be able to search for employees on the intranet. Fortunately, this is a standard feature in SPS. You simply use the general search field at the top-right part of the portal site and enter a name. Any matching user is listed on top, because SharePoint regards people as high-priority objects when ranking search results.

Displaying Web Content

Another item this intranet should contain is the lunch menu for today. Depending on how this information is stored, you have different options for displaying it:

❑ **It's an HTML file:** Use a Content Editor web part to display the content of this file.

❑ **It's an e-mail:** Store the mail as an HTML file and use the preceding method.

❑ **It's displayed on the restaurant's public web site:** Use the Web Capture web part.

407

Before you can use the Web Capture web part, you must download and install MS Office 2003 Web Parts and Components. This web part displays only a part of a web page, not the complete web page. It is very handy when you need to present just the lunch menu and nothing more from the restaurant. See the following steps:

Try It Out   **Use the Web Capture Web Part**

1. Download and install the MS Office 2003 Web Parts and Components package from this location: `http://www.microsoft.com/downloads/details.aspx?familyid=38be67a5-2056-46a1-84b1-337ffb549c5c&displaylang=en`. It adds seven new web parts to the virtual server web part gallery. (See Chapter 8 for more information about this package.)

2. Open the Home page on the portal site.

3. Choose Edit page⇨Modify Shared Page⇨Add Web Part⇨Browse. Click Virtual Server Gallery.

4. Drag the Web Capture web part to the location where you want to display the lunch menu (for example, the Bottom Zone).

5. Click its Create Web Capture link.

6. Click the Create button. This opens a new window. Enter this information:

    a. **Address:** Enter the URL to the restaurant and press Return. This displays that web site and a yellow indicator for each part of it.

    b. Click the yellow indicator for the part that lists the lunch menu. This area is now marked.

    c. Click OK to save and close this window.

7. Click OK again to close the web part property pane. The selected part of that external web page is now displayed in this Web Capture web part.

This concludes the first page of the intranet. Is this all there is to intranets? No! This is just the foundation to help you get started. You can accomplish much more than this. But for some modifications you will need FrontPage, which is covered in the next chapter.

Departmental Intranets

The project leader for the intranet in this example also wanted local intranets for some departments in your company. Before you go to the trouble of creating local intranets, you should ask your project leader why these departments need them. If the answer is that they need a separate place for their news, you don't need to do anything, because the targeting of news based on audience groups has already solved this need. But these departments may have more information that they want to display for their local employees only. Again, this can be solved by adding lists of information to the Home page and targeting these to specific audiences.

However, sometimes it is better to give these departments their own pages. If you determine this is the case, you have two options:

❑   Use a team site for each department. This is the same type of solution as when building the WSS-based intranet earlier in this chapter.

❑   Create a separate portal area page for each department and configure its security settings so its pages are available only to members of the respective department.

The following steps describe how to do the second option. In this example you need to create two area pages in the portal site, one for HR and one for Finance. You also need to set the security so only HR employees can see the HR page, and so on.

Try It Out   Create Departmental Intranets

1. Log on to the portal site as an administrator.

2. Click Manage Portal Site. This page shows a tree view of the portal site (but not the WSS sites). Create the two new portal areas like this, starting with the HR page:

    a.   Hover over the Home link and use its Create Subarea menu.

    b.   **Title:** HR.

    c.   **Description:** Local intranet for the HR department.

    d.   Click OK.

    e.   Repeat steps a–d and create a new page for the Finance department.

3. The two new area pages show up at the top menu on the portal site. At this stage, everyone who has access to the portal site also has the same access to these pages. Change that like this:

    a.   Go to the portal area for HR.

    b.   Click Manage Security.

    c.   Remove all inherited security settings.

    d.   Click New User.

    e.   Enter the names of all employees at HR; or (much better) enter the name for a security group that contains the names of these employees. Use the Select rights settings to grant these users or groups the proper permission to this area page. For example, if you want to make sure HR employees can only read this HR area page, then make them members of the Reader site group. Click OK when ready.

4. Repeat step 3 to set the security for the Finance area page. Note that you must at least be a member of the Reader site group in order to have access to either of these two area pages to see their names in the top heading. That is a good thing; it makes sure the users can only see pages they have access to. But remember that the SharePoint administrator will have access to all area pages, regardless of their security settings!

    If you add new topics area pages instead of general pages, their names will be listed on the Home page, although you may not have access to them. To hide these topics pages completely, click the link "Only show to users with View Area right" at the top of their "Manage Security" page.

5. Start configuring these area pages as these departments require. You can use all web parts discussed previously, but one of them that might be particularly interesting is the News web part. If the department requires having a private News listing, it can be done by adding the News web part to their departmental intranet page. Tell the contributors of that intranet page to use the Add Listing link at the Home page when adding news items to the News listing on their local intranet page. Make sure they change the Location setting when creating the news item to match their departmental page only, and to remove the default Home location to make sure the news will be listed on their local intranet page only.

Smarter Navigation

Because all SPS installations also have WSS installed, you should instruct people to use the team sites when needing a place for sharing documents, calendars, contacts, and other types of information. As described earlier, portal areas do not allow individual security settings for lists and libraries because they inherit these settings from the area page itself. This is one of the main reasons why it is better to use team sites than portal areas for sharing information and collaborating.

You have already seen a lot of examples of how to use team sites for this type of use. But when using SPS you have a much better way of making the information in these team sites available to the user. The old rule that says that no information should require more than three mouse clicks to get to is still very much true. Using the portal site's topics will make it possible to follow this rule, instead of requiring users to browse a team site tree to find the information they need.

The best way of explaining this is by example. Say that the project leader for the intranet tells you that a recent poll among the users showed that more than 70 percent wanted an easier and faster way to find the information they needed for their everyday work. You are asked to find a better solution. Now, what do you do?

The solution is topics! See these pages as a place to group links to documents, lists, and information used by specific users or groups. When the intranet is providing news and information about what is happening, the topic is providing links to the user's daily work. Does it not require a large number of topics? Maybe, but what's the problem? These topics pages can be made visible for only the users who work with them by configuring the security settings for these pages. You can also target links and information on a topics page to a specific audience, just like you did for news items previously. And you don't have to use this technique to navigate to all information; in some cases it is still easier or more logical to browse the team site tree.

Now continue with the example. You have a group of salespeople and they need access to information such as the following:

❏ **Customer contact list:** Stored in the "Contacts" list in the team site "Customer Info."

❏ **Quote Instructions:** Stored in the team site "Sales Info."

❏ **Quote templates:** Stored in a document library in the team site "Sales Info."

❏ **Order History:** Stored as a custom list in the "Sales Info" site.

❏ **Price lists:** Stored at your partners' extranet sites.

Of course there is more, but you get the idea. The information they need is spread out, so when a new sales guy starts, he must learn where to find each of these lists and documents. Surely, it would be much better if the sales manager could instruct the new sales guy to simply open the intranet and click the Sales Topic to find everything he needs to do his job. This is how you make it happen:

Try It Out   Create Topics-Based Navigation

1.   Open the portal site as a user with permission to create a topics area page.

2.   Switch to the Topics page.

3.   Click Create Subarea; enter these values:

      a.   **Title:** Sales.

      b.   **Description:** This page lists all information needed by sales employees.

      c.   Click OK to save and close. The new Topic page is created.

4. Open the Sales page. Note that it has two ways of adding information: Add Listing and Add Person. If you know the exact URL to the information to be listed on this page, you can use Add Listing. But a much easier way is to go to the source, and from that location add a link to this portal page. For example, to add a link to the customer contact list you would do this:

      a.   Go to the team site "Sales."

      b.   Click the "Contacts" list to open it.

      c.   Click Modify settings and columns.

      d.   Click Select a portal area for this list.

      e.   If needed, change the Title and Description for this list.

      f.   Click Change location. Expand Topics and select Sales. Clear the default check mark for Home, and then click OK.

      g.   If needed, change the Group and/or Audience settings.

      h.   Click OK to save and close this link.

5. Repeat step 4 to add a link to the Quote Template library and the Order History list.

6. To add a link to the "Quote Instructions" document, do this:

      a.   Go to the team site "Sales Info."

      b.   Open the document library storing the "Quote Instructions."

      c.   Use the quick menu for the Quote Instructions document and select Submit to portal area.

      d.   If needed, change the Title and Description for this list.

      e.   Click Change location. Expand Topics and select Sales. Clear the default check mark for Home, and then click OK.

      f.   If needed, change the Group and/or Audience settings.

      g.   Click OK to save and close this link.

7. Finally, to add a link to the price list on your partner's web site you would do this:

      a.   Open the Sales topic page.

      b.   Click Add Listing.

      c.   **Title:** Price Lists.

      d.   **Description:** Customer Price Lists.

      e.   **Existing Listing/Address:** `http://www.avepoint.com/website/pricelist.html`.

      f.   If needed, change the Group and/or Audience settings.

      g.   Click OK to save and close.

8. Test it now. Open the Home page of the portal. Click Sales in the top-left list, and you see all the links you just created. Click one of them to make sure it works.

Surely this is much easier to use, especially when you need to do it several times per day. One advantage with this method is that the underlying data could be moved to new locations, without the user having to know this (as long as you update the link). You could make the links on this page more appealing by adding your own icons and using groups to organize these links, as described in more detail in Chapter 5.

Summary

In this chapter you learned the following:

- ❑ It is very important to analyze needs before you start building the intranet.
- ❑ Remember KISS — Keep It Simple, Stupid.
- ❑ Try to understand what the users really want. Create a list of "must have," "should have," and "nice to have" features. Put your time and money into the features in the "must have" list before doing anything else.
- ❑ An intranet today is often a web-based newspaper, no more interesting than a list of extinct insects. The problem is that the information very seldom is what a user needs to know every day.
- ❑ Make the intranet more personal:
    - ❑ Use the targeting feature of SPS.
    - ❑ Add information such as an external news list, weather information, lunch menus, and so on.
    - ❑ Make sure to use a lot of pictures, when possible. It makes the information more interesting to read and more attractive.
- ❑ Using WSS allows you to build a basic intranet with all the standard features.
- ❑ Using SPS allows you to build an intranet with global search features, targeted news items and lists, topics-based navigation, and personal web sites.

In the next chapter you learn more about using MS FrontPage for more advanced design of SharePoint sites.

Designing with FrontPage

SharePoint is built to allow an ordinary user with the proper permissions to easily change the layout of sites without any extra tools besides the web browser. This feature is very important because it makes it possible for non-developers to quickly adjust a portal site or a team site to their own needs. No web designer or administrator is required for this task. The key to this feature is the use of web parts and their web part zones; just add any new web parts needed and drag them to the preferred location on the page. In order to allow this, SharePoint has specially constructed web part pages (also known as smart pages), and every portal site and team site is built upon such web part pages.

However, sometimes it may be necessary to perform more modifications than possible using a web browser. This is where FrontPage 2003 comes in. This program was especially designed with SharePoint in mind and has a lot of features for enhancing the look-and-feel of SharePoint sites. No other design tools for web sites have this functionality, so you will need to use FrontPage when it comes to SharePoint. Fortunately, whether you are inexperienced or are accustomed to using other design tools, you will find that FrontPage is relatively easy to use.

> *Only FrontPage 2003 has SharePoint integration. Earlier FrontPage editions do not have this functionality.*

This integration between FrontPage and SharePoint becomes even stronger in the SharePoint 2007 release. In fact, FrontPage is changing its name to "SharePoint Designer 2007" and ceasing to exist as a general design editor for web sites. Because this book was written before the actual release of SharePoint Designer 2007, throughout this chapter it is referred to as FrontPage. The good news is that most of the steps and features described in this chapter are still valid in SharePoint Designer 2007, so it is definitely worth your time to learn how FrontPage 2003 works.

Why FrontPage?

The big question is of course why you need FrontPage. What does it allow you to do that cannot be done using a web browser? The answer is: A lot! In fact, most of the things you can do with the web browser, such as adding and managing web parts, can also be done in FrontPage, and more. Some things that FrontPage allows you to do with SharePoint are the following:

❑ Add new web part zones.

❑ Add special web parts.

❑ Apply more advanced formatting of lists.

❑ Add extra links in the quick launch bar and the title bar.

❑ Add buttons and tabs.

❑ Add background pictures.

❑ Create new site themes.

❑ Install special SharePoint packages.

❑ Backup and restore individual team sites.

And there is more. Note that only FrontPage 2003 has this SharePoint integration. There is no similar functionality in earlier FrontPage editions. The current version is also much better behaved than its predecessors; you don't have to worry about FrontPage adding extra codes and comments without telling you about it, as earlier versions did. So try it; you may even like it!

A Quick Guide for FrontPage

Even though FrontPage 2003 (from now on referred to as "FrontPage") is a general design tool for standard web sites, it has special features when editing a SharePoint site. You will need a basic understanding of FrontPage in order to start using it with SharePoint. The following sections describe the basic features of FrontPage and how to work with them. Later you will see detailed steps on how to add to and modify the site with FrontPage.

Opening Sites with FrontPage

FrontPage is like all other editors in that you either open an existing file and modify it or create a file from scratch. However, when using FrontPage for editing SharePoint sites, you don't start by creating a site. It is much easier to create the SharePoint site the normal way and then open it in FrontPage and start editing. You have two options for opening the existing SharePoint site:

❑ Start FrontPage with Start⇨All Programs⇨Microsoft Office⇨Microsoft Office FrontPage 2003, and connect it to a SharePoint site using File⇨Open Site and entering the full URL to that site.

❑ Open the site you want to modify in Internet Explorer, and then use its File⇨Edit menu with MS Office FrontPage.

The second method is of course easiest because you don't have to enter the site URL, but it requires that FrontPage is the default web editor in your computer. Either way, FrontPage will load the SharePoint site and display its content, displaying many more details than even the design mode using Internet Explorer will show; see Figure 12-1 as an example.

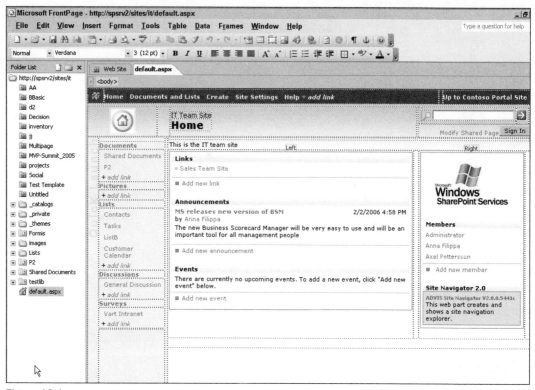

Figure 12-1

FrontPage's Display Modes

When working with a design tool like FrontPage, sometimes you need to see the code behind a page or the page layout. FrontPage fulfills this need by having several display modes that can present different types of content. Whenever needed, you can easily switch among these display modes by selecting their buttons at the lower-left corner of the screen. Look at the bottom line of Figure 12-2; it lists these display options:

❑ **Design:** Shows the graphical presentation of the current site in real time. It will also show the content of many web parts and lists. Figure 12-1 uses this mode to display the IT team site.

❑ **Split:** Shows both the graphical design and the code behind it. If you select an object in the graphical part, FrontPage marks the code for that object. For example, look at Figure 12-2 where the description "This is the IT team site" is selected and automatically its code is marked.

❑ **Code:** Shows the code behind the page.

❑ **Preview:** Displays this page as it will be shown when opened in a web browser.

The two most useful modes are design and split. The design mode is very handy when you want to see exactly what part of this page you working with, but the code part in the split mode gives you control of the exact location when managing objects on the page while still seeing the graphical representation of the page.

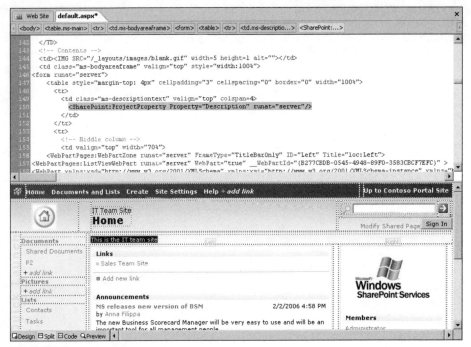

Figure 12-2

Modifying the Site

Use the menus and toolbar buttons to add, delete, and modify the SharePoint site. For example, if you want to add a web part, you select the web part zone in the design mode and then click the top menu Data⇨Insert Web Part. Using the Task Pane will give you easy and fast access to most of the things you will need while working with SharePoint sites. To display the Task Pane view, either click the top menu View⇨Task Pane or press Ctrl+F1. The Task Pane shows up in the same location as the Task Pane in all MS Office 2003 products (at the right part of the page).

You can also modify the code directly. For example, if you want to change the watermark text "Quick Launch" that is listed vertically on the Quick Launch pane, you can search for this text using Find (F2) and change it directly in the code. The graphical part will automatically be updated to show the new text you added. If you know HTML and ASP.NET programming, you will have full control of this page. However, you must in this case also understand how SharePoint's object model works, in order to make some changes. To add your own code, use the split or code display mode.

Saving Your Work

When working with a SharePoint site, you are only working with a copy. You can do and test whatever modifications you want on this site, but it will not be stored in SharePoint until you save these changes, in any of these ways:

❑   File⇨Save.

❑   Click the Save button on the toolbar.

❑ Press F12. This saves the current modifications and also displays the results using Internet Explorer.

As long as you don't close FrontPage, you can use the Undo command (Edit⇨Undo or Ctrl+Z) to undo all of the changes and then save the site once again. This way you can restore a site from most types of modifications that you happened to make but don't want to keep anymore.

Differences between SPS and WSS

When using FrontPage for editing SharePoint, you must be aware that there is a difference between the portal site and team sites. Even though the portal site is built upon team sites, it has several features not available in team sites, such as targeting, a topics tree view, and action menus that are sensitive to the current user's rights. That is why a portal site will behave differently than a team site when using FrontPage, in ways such as the following:

❑ **Web Parts:** In team sites you see live content, but in portal sites it is a static view.

❑ **Backup & Restore:** You cannot use the backup/restore features in FrontPage on portal sites as you can with team sites.

❑ **Areas:** Do not use FrontPage to delete or add areas in the portal; they will look like sites, but they are special for the portal sites.

❑ **My Site:** This is actually one and the same site for all users. If you change My Site for one user using FrontPage, it changes for all users.

❑ **Styles:** It is not possible to use FrontPage themes on the portal site; you must use CSS files for this.

❑ **Navigation:** It is not possible to add FrontPage link bars or navigation bars to a portal site.

Ghosting and Un-ghosting

As described in Chapters 5 and 6, every SharePoint page is defined by one or more files stored in the file system on the SharePoint server, such as `Default.aspx`. For example, every Home page for all WSS team sites is built upon this file:

```
\Program Files\Common Files\Microsoft Shared\Web Server ⤵
Extensions\60\TEMPLATE\1033\STS\Default.aspx
```

Even if you have 300 team sites, all of them build on this `Default.aspx` file. This makes it fast to open these team sites and make global changes to all of the team sites, and it also saves a lot of space because there is just one copy of this site definition. This is called *ghosting*, because these sites don't actually exist as the "real" independent entities that they appear to be.

When you modify one of these team sites, SharePoint must store the complete site definition (including all its content) in the SQL content database. This site now is *un-ghosted*. The consequence of un-ghosting SharePoint sites is that such a site requires more space in the database and takes slightly longer to load, compared to a ghosted site. But in reality you must have a lot of SharePoint sites and/or a lot of users before anyone will ever notice any difference. I have never met a SharePoint administrator who actually had any real problem because of un-ghosting, so please do not hesitate to use FrontPage for editing these SharePoint sites.

Still, some organizations want to be sure that nobody can use FrontPage for modifying SharePoint sites, not even the administrator. If you need to prohibit anyone from modifying SharePoint team sites with FrontPage, you can edit the `Onet.xml` file in the STS\XML structure like this:

Try It Out   **Prohibit FrontPage from Editing SharePoint Sites**

1. Log on to the SharePoint server as an administrator.

2. Navigate to this folder:

```
\Program Files\Common Files\Microsoft Shared\Web Server ⤴
Extensions\60\TEMPLATE\1033\STS\XML\Onet.xml
```

3. Edit Onet.xml with Notepad.

4. Locate a line near the top that looks like this:

```
<Project Title="Team Web Site" ListDir="Lists" xmlns:ows="Microsoft SharePoint">
```

5. Add the text DisableWebDesignFeatures=wdfopensite at the end of that line:

```
<Project Title="Team Web Site" ListDir="Lists" xmlns:ows="Microsoft ⤴
SharePoint" DisableWebDesignFeatures=wdfopensite>
```

6. Reset IIS with Start⇨Run: IISRESET.

7. Test by opening any team site in FrontPage. It displays a dialog stating that FrontPage cannot
    edit this site; see Figure 12-3.

Figure 12-3

Basic Design

Using FrontPage for editing SharePoint sites allows you to do almost anything. To give you an idea of
what you can do, this section describes often requested modifications that are easy to do. Remember to
keep FrontPage open while testing these modifications; if anything goes wrong you can use the undo
feature in FrontPage and then save again.

Adding Text Outside Web Parts

There are a lot of web parts for displaying text on the SharePoint site, but sometimes you need to add a
text block without relying on a web part. For example, you may want to add an instruction at the top of
the site where there is no web part zone:

Try It Out   **Add Text to Any Part of a Site Page**

1. Log on to SharePoint as a member of the Web Designer or Administrator site group.

2. Open the site to be modified.

3. Start FrontPage by choosing File⇨Edit with Microsoft Office FrontPage.

4. Make sure FrontPage is using the Design view.

5. Place the cursor where you want to enter the new text block, for example next to the site header.

6. Enter the text.

7. Save this page; then test it using a browser (see Figure 12-4). If it does not look good, go back to FrontPage, use the Undo feature under the Edit menu, and save the page again.

Figure 12-4

Adding Links to Team Sites

This feature is not possible in portal sites but works very well in team sites. With FrontPage you can add extra links to the top link bar and to the quick launch bar. You don't have to do anything special; when opening a team site in FrontPage, you see "+add link" in several places. For example, say that you want to add a link to the Outlook Web Access client at the top of a team site. You do this:

Try It Out   Add Extra Links to Menu and Action Bars

1. Open the site to be modified in FrontPage as previously described.

2. Click the +add link on the top menu bar. The Add to Link Bar dialog box appears. (See Figure 12-5.)

3. **Text to be displayed:** OWA.

4. **Address:** `http://dc1.contoso.com/exchange` (the same URL as when using a browser to start your OWA client).

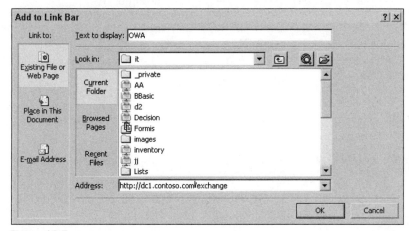

Figure 12-5

5. Click OK.

6. Note that the new link OWA and a new +add link are displayed.

7. Save this modification, but don't exit FrontPage. Test this link in a web browser to see that it works as expected.

Adding a Background Picture

Because team sites use themes for controlling the style of the page, you cannot add a background picture to the whole page, but you can add it to a table or cell on this page. For example, say you want to add a photo as a background picture to a web part zone in a team site; right-click a free part of that zone and edit the cell:

Try It Out   Add a Background Picture to a Web Part Zone

1. Open the site to be modified in FrontPage as previously described.

2. Right-click a free part of the web part zone; select Cell properties.

3. Check Use background picture and enter or browse the picture. Make sure every user will be able to access this picture, or they will get an error when opening this site! If the picture needs to be adjusted, right-click the picture and select Picture Properties.

4. Click OK to save and close; the picture is immediately visible.

To add a background picture to all web part zones, select "Table properties" in step 2.

Changing the Team Site Logo

The logo at the top left on the Home page of every team site is the same, because the team sites all use the same site definition. You can replace that default logo with a special logo for a specific team site like this:

Try It Out   Replace the Team Site Logo

1. Add the file with the new logo to a SharePoint image library (for example, in the portal site). It is important that this image file is available for all members of this team site, or they will get an error when opening the Home page.

2. You need the URL to this image file. It is easiest to open that image library, click the logo to open all its details, right-click the logo, and select Copy Shortcut; now you have the URL. Close that image library.

3. Open the site to be modified in FrontPage as previously described.

4. Mark the current logo and paste the copied link. The new logo is immediately displayed.

Interactive Buttons

Many of my customers have requested a button on the Home page that performs an action or opens another page. This is very easy to do with FrontPage. Also, you have a lot of different looks for these buttons, which makes it easy to find just the right button for your site.

Try It Out   **Add Interactive Buttons**

1. Open the site to be modified in FrontPage as previously described.

2. Place the cursor where you want the button. Note that you cannot place the button inside a web part zone!

3. Choose Insert⇨Interactive Button; then do the following:

    a. Scroll the Buttons list field and select the type of button you want. There is a preview of this button above this field. Then enter the following values for that button:

    b. **Text:** Enter the text for this button, for example "OWA".

    c. **Link:** Enter the link to be activated for this button (for example, `http://Filmportalen/News`) to make this button open the News area page.

    d. Click OK to save and close.

4. Save this modified page. Then test the new button to make sure it works as expected. See Figure 12-6, which has three different types of buttons added.

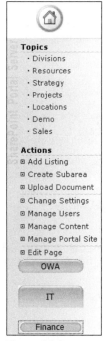

Figure 12-6

If you add a button with rounded corners on a shaded background, you will see the default white background color just outside the corners of this button picture; this will not look good, unless you placed the button on a white area. To change this, right-click the button and select "Button Properties." Switch to the Image tab and either change the background color or make the button a GIF image so it can use a transparent background.

Hiding Fields on a Web Form

Sometimes it is necessary to change the way a web form works so that the user filling in this form has access to only some of the fields, while the user reading this form is able to work with all fields. This is possible because there is one separate form for filling in the values and another form for opening an existing entry. Using FrontPage you can hide some of these fields for the first form but let them be visible in the second form.

For example, say that you have a list for Helpdesk Issues. You tell all users to fill in a new entry in this list whenever there is an issue that the Helpdesk team should attend to. But you don't want the users to set some of the values, such as what person will be assigned to this issue. Here is how to do this:

Try It Out   **Hide Some Fields on a Web Form**

1. Log on as an administrator and open any team site. Create the Helpdesk Issue list for this example like this:

   a. Choose Create⇨Issues.

   b. Enter the name **Helpdesk Issues**.

   c. Click OK to create the list.

   d. Click Home to open the default page for this site.

2. Click the Helpdesk Issue list to open it in a full page.

3. Click New Item. This is the web form that all users will use when entering new issues; its name is NewForm.aspx.

4. When the web form is visible, open it in FrontPage as previously described.

5. Right-click the web form in the Design window; select Customize SharePoint List Form.

6. Select the complete lines (both the title and field) you want to hide. The easiest way is to click just to the left of each row title; to select more than one line, press the Ctrl key for the following lines. Then right-click one of these selected rows and click Delete Rows. For example, delete the lines for Assigned to, Status, and Priority.

7. Save this modified page in FrontPage.

8. Update your web browser and click New Item. Note that it does not include the three deleted fields this time; see Figure 12-7. Click Save and Close.

9. Open the newly created item. Notice that these three fields will be visible this time.

   This modification would not be so interesting if all users could edit an existing item, because that form displays all the fields. So the next step is to make sure ordinary users can create, but not edit or delete, an item in this list.

10. Open the Helpdesk Issue list.

11. Click Modify settings and columns.

12. Click Change permissions for this list.

13. Click any of the existing user or site groups that should have write access but not edit or delete access (for example, Contributor); then click Advanced permissions. Make sure that the user only has View List Items and Add Lists Items permissions.

14. Click OK to save and close.

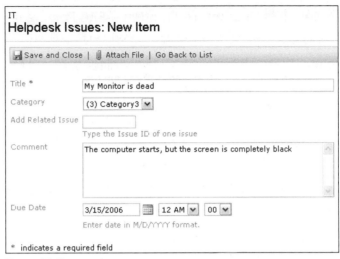

Figure 12-7

Managing Site Templates

You may recall that any team site can be stored as a site template. This is a very handy way of creating templates for sites, including content if necessary. The problem is that you can only store 10 MB of content on a SharePoint team site. Using FrontPage you can save a complete site, including all its content, in a backup file and then restore it anywhere, including other SharePoint environments. This is very handy if you have a test environment and need to copy sites from that environment to the production server.

One good example of this is the sites that are known as *web packages*, which you can find on the start page of the site www.sharepointcustomization.com. This site contains three different web package sites of this type:

- ❑ **Finance:** A complete site with all the usual features that a financial department works with, including a blog and a form for expenses, based on MS InfoPath.

- ❑ **Sales & Marketing:** A complete site with lots of features and web parts adjusted for this group, a Weekly Report form based on InfoPath, and a Visio organizational chart.

- ❑ **Human Resource:** A complete site with features for users working in the HR department; it contains interactive buttons, a list of books from Amazon web services, and an InfoPath form for applicant rating.

To download one of these sites, go to www.sharepointcustomization.com and click the "Microsoft Windows SharePoint Services" link. On the following page you can see the descriptions of these three sites, including the link "Download this site's web package"; click that link and save the file on your computer. Note that it does not have to be on the SharePoint server; you can use this from any client as long as you have the owner permission on the team site where you want to import this web package. These sites contain everything you need to get going, except the site itself and its users. So before you can install any of these site packages, you must create a team site and eventually also add users to it.

In this example you see how to do all of the steps to get the Sales and Marketing site installed:

Try It Out   Create a Site and Import FrontPage Site Packages

1. Log on as an administrator.

2. Go to the team site that will be the "parent" for this new site. You can also create a new top-level team site, using SPS or the WSS central administration tool.

3. Create the team site as usual, but when asked to select a site template, exit from that page! The reason for this is how FrontPage handles site template packages. The package allows you to brand a site, but not to create it. That is why the site must be created but not branded with any standard site template.

4. Start FrontPage with an empty page. (Do not start FrontPage by opening a site this time.)

5. Select File➪Open Site. Enter the URL to the site you created in step 3. When it opens, there is not much in this site, because it has never been branded. But the next step is to brand the site.

6. Select Tools➪Server➪Restore Web Site. Browse until you find the file `Sales2_sharepoint_v2`
   `.fwp`. Select Open and then click OK. This starts the restore process of this site package. It may take some minutes, depending on how much data it contains. When done, FrontPage displays a dialog box saying "Web site restore completed successfully." Click OK.

7. You don't have to save anything in FrontPage. Just open this new site in SharePoint, and it will have a lot of interesting features; see Figure 12-8 for an example.

You may notice that this site does not have a link back to the portal site, but this is easy to fix. Open the site in FrontPage, click +add link in the top-right corner, and then add a link to the start page of the portal (if your installation has SPS installed, that is).

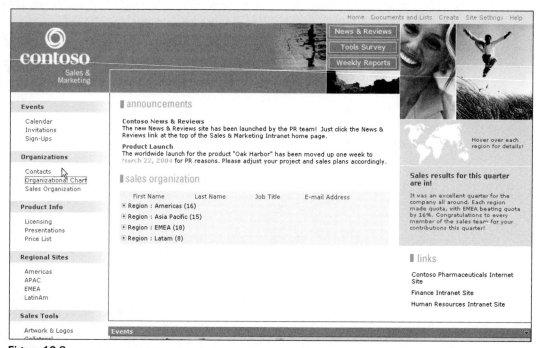

Figure 12-8

Page Transitions

A feature in SharePoint that may seem cool at first, but irritating later on, is page transitions. Using this technique you can configure a specific page to open in a special way, for example sliding into or blending with the current page. For some types of SharePoint sites, this is very nice, but be sure to check that this is really acceptable for the end users working with this site.

Try It Out   Create Page Transitions

1.   Log on as an administrator.

2.   Go to the page to which you want to add page transitions, for example `http://filmportalen/sites/it`.

3.   Open this page in FrontPage.

4.   Choose Format⇨Page Transition.

5.   Select the type of transition and the duration. For example, select Virtual Blinds and a Duration of 2 seconds. Click OK to save and close this window.

6.   Save this page in FrontPage.

7.   Test this page now. Go to any SharePoint site; then switch to the page you changed. Note that it is using the selected transition when opened (but not when you leave this page).

Managing Web Part Zones

You already know that a web part must be stored in a web part zone. But sometimes you need to add a web part to another part of the page. A common example is when you want to add a site tree web part to the quick launch bar in a team site. To do that you need to create a new web part zone. Only FrontPage allows you to create such a zone.

Try It Out   Create a New Web Part Zone

1.   Log on as an administrator.

2.   Go to the page to which you want to add the web part zone, for example `http://filmportalen/sites/it`.

3.   Open this page with FrontPage.

4.   Place the cursor where the new zone will be. For example, to create the zone in the quick launch bar, click in the empty cell in the right column, and you can see the cursor jump to the right of the cells above. Then press Space (or Enter) to get a new row in the empty cell.

5.   Choose Data⇨Insert Web Part Zone. The new zone is directly added to this location.

6.   The next step is adding a web part. Choose Data⇨Insert Web Part or use the Click to insert a Web Part link in the new web part zone.

7.   When all the web parts you need are added, save this page in FrontPage. Then open this page in the web browser and make sure it works as expected. If not, open this page in FrontPage again and drag it to a new position.

8.   To delete a web part zone, select it by clicking its name and then press the Delete key.

Note that you can create any number of web part zones, and they will resize automatically when you add new web parts to them.

You can edit web part properties directly in FrontPage. Right-click and select "Web Part Properties."

Adding an IFrame

There is one standard web part that comes with SharePoint that displays the content of another web page: the Page Viewer. It works very well, but it can only be used within a web part zone. Sometimes you may need to display an external web page without the constraint of a web part zone; then you should add the IFrame (Inline Frame). It works very similarly to the Page Viewer but can be placed anywhere in a SharePoint page, except for a web part zone.

In Figure 12-9, a Page Viewer and an IFrame are displaying the same page: the Start page of another team site; note that they both are identical.

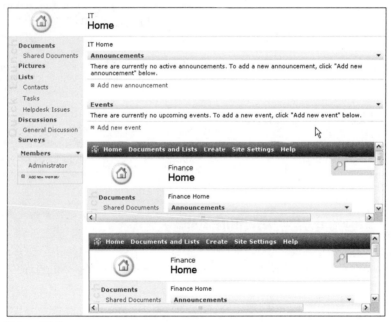

Figure 12-9

Because the IFrame can be added to any page, you can use it to display content on non–web part pages, such as the Shared Documents page or the web form for adding new contacts. In the following example you add an IFrame to the Shared Documents page of the IT team site. This IFrame displays the documents in the Finance team site.

Try It Out   Add an IFrame to a SharePoint Page

1. Click Shared Document on the IT team site so it will open in a full page.

2. Open this page with FrontPage.

3. Place the cursor below the list of files on this page.

4. Choose Insert⇨Inline Frame.

5. Click Set Initial Page and enter the URL in the Address field. Then click OK.

6. Save this page.

7. Open the page with a browser. Make sure it displays both the documents in this library and the documents in the Finance team site in an IFrame, as Figure 12-10 shows.

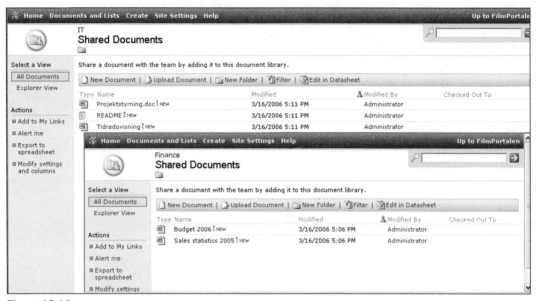

Figure 12-10

Retrieving a SharePoint Summary

Because FrontPage knows how SharePoint works, it can also present a lot of information for a given portal or team site, such as a list of all files, links, and pictures. It can run a test to see what pages are slow to load and much more.

Try It Out   **Create a Summary for a Site**

1. Open the site in FrontPage.

2. Choose View⇨Reports and select the following:

    a. **Site Summary:** A summary of the current site; see Figure 12-11.

    b. **Files:** Lists all files, new files, old files, and so on.

    c. **Shared Content:** Style sheets, themes, dynamic web templates, and so on.

    d. **Problems:** Unlinked files, slow pages, hyperlinks, component errors, and so on.

    e. **Workflow:** Lists all checked-out documents, review status, and published documents.

    f. **Usage:** Displays statistics about this site. It requires that you have activated logging (WSS Central Administration⇨Configure usage analysis processing).

One analysis that the site summary can present is to test the speed of your pages. For example, if you link a lot of external information to your SharePoint pages, you must make sure it does not take too long to open these pages. Control this either by using Site Summary, which displays slow pages, or by using Problems⇨Slow Pages and testing them. Note that this page allows you to set the limit in seconds to define what a "slow page" really is.

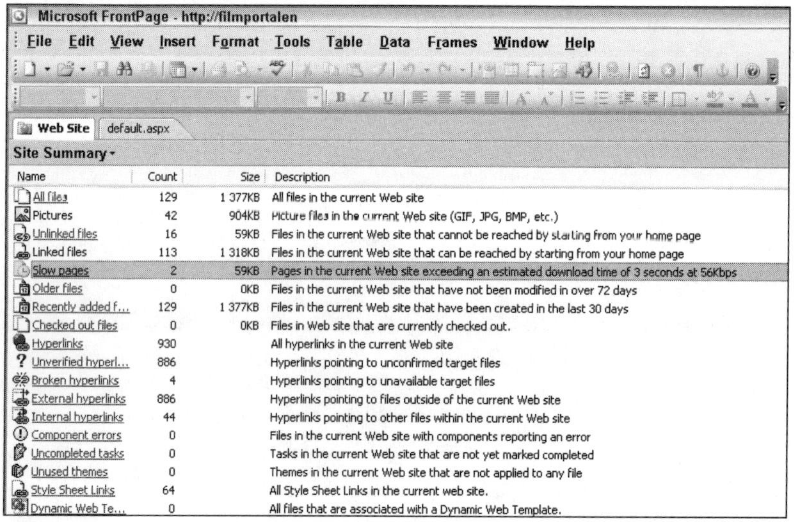

Figure 12-11

Extended Design

The previous section described several modifications that are easy to do on any SharePoint site page. In this section you see more advanced modifications that FrontPage allows you to do.

Managing Themes

The look-and-feel of a portal site in SPS is completely controlled by Cascading Style Sheets (CSS). But team sites in WSS have another technique called *themes* to define what fonts, sizes, and colors are to be used by different parts of a page. By using preconfigured themes, a team site owner (its "administrator") can directly change the site's look-and-feel using the web browser. Using the link Site Settings⇨Apply theme to site, the owner can select from 21 different themes. Note that many of them are especially high-contrast themes for visually impaired users, and these are hard to see for people with normal eyesight.

Creating FrontPage Themes

Even WSS team sites are using CSS files because these themes are also built on CSS. Themes are overriding the color settings for fonts, menus, and backgrounds of the ordinary CSS files. You may want to create your own theme; you can do this easily with FrontPage, because the themes in SharePoint are indeed FrontPage themes.

Try It Out   **Create New SharePoint Themes in FrontPage**

1. Log on to the SharePoint server as an administrator.

2. Open a team site in FrontPage.

3. Choose Format⇨Theme. A list of FrontPage themes is displayed.

4. Select a theme in this list to start with. Use one that is as close to what you want to do as possible so you don't have to change too much. In this example, select "Afternoon." Hover the mouse over that theme and click the arrow at the right of the image to display a menu. Select "Apply as default theme" and then click OK when the display box appears.

5. Click "Create new theme" at the bottom of the theme list. This displays a configuration editor, as shown in Figure 12-12.

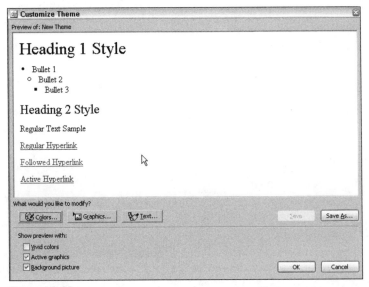

Figure 12-12

6. Click Save As and give this theme a new name (for example, My Theme). You now have a theme that you can start customizing. Following are just some of the customizations you can do.

7. To change the colors in this theme, click the Colors button:

    a. Switch to the Custom tab.

    b. Select the Item to be Background and select a color. You see a preview of the result to the right. If you don't like it, change it to another color.

    c. Select the Item to be Banner and select a color.

    Instead of using the "Custom" tab, use the "Color Schemes" tab, which has a number of preconfigured colors that are tested by professional designers.

    d. Click OK when done.

    e.   To change the text style, click the Text button: Use the Item, select the type of test to be changed, and then select a new font for that text type. Note that SharePoint does not use all the text types; so you have to figure out what types to change. Click OK to save and close this window.

The challenge is to find out what types SharePoint uses. A good way is to use the pictures at the following link, which tells you the name for each "element" of the SharePoint page: http://www .sharepointcustomization.com/wss/articles/themes-custom2.htm.

    f.   Finally you can add a picture for this theme, for example as a background. Click Graphics and enter the picture name or click Browse.

    g.   Make whatever changes you want. When done, click OK, then OK again, and then Save. The new theme is now applied (if not, double-click your theme in the list).

8.   Use the menu for your theme. Select "Apply as default theme" if you want to use this theme for all pages in this site, or select "Apply to selected pages" if you only want to use this theme on the current page. Open the page in a web browser and be amazed at the results. It may look nice; however, it is also very easy to overdo things with a tool like this, as shown in Figure 12-13.

Figure 12-13

A more professional layout using this technique is demonstrated in the site template packages Finance, Human Resource, and Sales & Marketing at www.sharepointcustomization.com, which were discussed earlier in this chapter. See them as an example of how and what you can do with FrontPage's themes in a more tasteful and professional manner.

See this article on how to change the menu bar in team sites: `http://www.sharepoint customization.com/wss/articles/themes-gradients.htm`.

Adding New SharePoint Themes

The themes created and customized within FrontPage are not visible in SharePoint's list of preconfigured themes. However, you can add your own themes to this list. This makes it possible to apply the theme to new sites without using FrontPage. Although this chapter is about FrontPage, this section also applies to SharePoint themes in general.

All of the 21 preconfigured themes in SharePoint are stored in the file system on the SharePoint server. Each theme consists of a number of CSS and GIF files. Instead of creating all of them from scratch for your new theme, you can copy an existing theme folder and modify these files as necessary.

Try It Out   Create New Standard SharePoint Themes

1. Log on to the SharePoint server as an administrator.

2. Open this folder:

```
C:\Program Files\Common Files\Microsoft Shared\web server ⊃
extensions\60\TEMPLATE\THEMES
```

3. Note that it contains a number of folders, each with a name that matches the themes listed in the team sites administrative page. Start by copying one of these folders (for example, ICE) and pasting it into the same THEMES folder. Rename this new folder using capital letters only (for example, DEMO).

4. Open that new folder. Locate the INF file with the same name as the folder you copied (in this example, ICE.INF). Rename it to match your folder exactly: DEMO.INF.

5. Edit DEMO.INF with Notepad. Change the Title to the same name as your folder; note that you don't have to use capital letters here. When finished, save the file.

```
[info]
title=Demo
```

6. Next, open this file in Notepad:

```
C:\Program Files\Common Files\Microsoft Shared\web server ⊃
extensions\60\TEMPLATE\LAYOUTS\1033\SPTHEMES.XML
```

7. Each theme has a section in this XML file (for example, the default ICE):

```
<Templates>
  <TemplateID>ice</TemplateID>
  <DisplayName>Ice</DisplayName>
  <Description>Description</Description>
  <Thumbnail>../images/thice.png</Thumbnail>
  <Preview>../images/thice.gif</Preview>
</Templates>
```

8. Copy this section and paste it back. Then edit the copied section to match the name of your theme. The TemplateID must match your folder name, but with small letters! Also change the DisplayName and the Description field because they are displayed in SharePoint's theme list.

```
<Templates>
  <TemplateID>demo</TemplateID>
  <DisplayName>Demo</DisplayName>
  <Description>My Demo Theme</Description>
  <Thumbnail>../images/thice.png</Thumbnail>
  <Preview>../images/thice.gif</Preview>
</Templates>
```

9. The new theme is now active. Make sure to refresh the cache in your web browser (Ctrl+F5) or you may get an error stating that this theme already exists. So far you have created an exact copy of the ICE theme. If you want, you can apply the new theme to convince yourself that it is a copy of ICE.

10. The next step is to change this theme so is does not look the same as the one you copied. Open the THEME.CSS file in your newly created Theme folder. Change whatever elements you need in this CSS file and then save the file.

In order to see the modification you must: a) first select another theme, then b) apply your new theme, and then c) refresh the browser (Ctrl+F5).

It is not so easy to understand the THEME.CSS file and what elements to modify to get a specific result. Luckily there are some good resources that describe what each element does:

❑ This article by Microsoft describes each locator and an image of each object so you can more easily see what it does:
http://msdn.microsoft.com/library/default.asp?url=/library/en-us/odc_SP2003_ta/html/ODC_SPSCustomizingSharePointSites3.asp.

❑ This article by Shane Perran not only offers a good explanation of how to create your own theme, but also offers a package of 10 free themes, each of which contains descriptive comments so you can understand what it does. This is an excellent tool for learning the fine art of creating themes: http://www.graphicalwonder.com/2005/11/sharepoint_site_creation_stepb_6.html.

Adding Pages to SharePoint

You may have noticed that each team site consists only of one single web part page. The other pages for document libraries and lists are not web part pages and cannot be modified with a standard web browser. Sometimes you may need one or more extra pages, maybe because there is a lot of information to be displayed for this site. This may also be true for a portal site, even though it is easy to create new area pages.

SharePoint allows you to create two types of pages: standard HTML pages and web part pages, either by using the browser or FrontPage. This section describes how to add an extra page of each type to the Home page of a team site. Each page, regardless of type, must be stored as a file in a document library on this site. The trick is not to create these extra pages, but to easily and seamlessly integrate them in the Home page. You will see how to do that in some of the following examples.

Adding Web Part Pages

This type of page is exactly like the Home page of a team site. It has one or more web part zones, which you add web parts to. It also displays the same header and menus as the Home page.

In this example you add one new web part page using the web browser to the following team site: `http://filmportalen/sites/crm`. This new page also has some web parts added to it. At this stage you just create the page; later you will create buttons to make this page easier for the user to use.

Create a New Web Part Page Within the Browser

1.   Open the team site in a web browser.

2.   Choose Create⇨Web Part Page (at the bottom of this page).

3.   Select the layout of the web part zones and enter the name for this file. (All extra pages are stored as files, remember?)

    a.   **Name:** WP-Page.

    b.   **Layout Template:** Header, Footer, 3 Columns.

    c.   **Document Library:** "Shared Documents." This is where the file will be stored. You may want to create a new library just for pages.

    d.   Click Create.

4.   The new page opens. Take some web parts and add them to the web part zones (for example, Members and Shared Documents).

5.   Click Home to return to the default start page for this team site.

The big question now is of course how to display it again. The answer is as simple as it is surprising: Open the document library and click the WP-Page file. This was easy but not so intuitive, right? You will soon see some ways to make it more intuitive.

Adding Standard HTML Pages

Now create the other type of pages. The difference here is how this page behaves. It will not contain any web part zones, so you cannot add web parts to it. But it is the perfect place to add any standard HTML formatted information, such as the IFrames you created earlier.

In this example you will use FrontPage to add this page. Now you will have the flexibility of being able to choose whether to add pages with the browser or FrontPage. The task is to add a new page to the same document library as the previous page:

Create an HTML Page Using FrontPage

1.   Open the team site in FrontPage.

2.   Choose File⇨New and select More page templates in the Task Pane.

3.   This displays a list of preconfigured standard HTML pages. If you want an empty page, select the Normal Page. But to make this example more fun, select the template Frequently Asked Questions. This page is now displayed. Normally you would make changes to this page, but just click Save in FrontPage. Make sure to save this new page in the same Shared Documents as the previous web part page.

4.   Open the Shared Documents and click the new HTML page, which opens. Click Back on your web browser to return to the Home page for this team site.

Making Pages Easier to Open

Creating extra pages is easy and opens up interesting opportunities. As stated before, the challenge is to make them work seamlessly with the rest of this team site. Several options are available:

❑ **Create a link in a list:** Requires that you create a SharePoint list for links. This is very easy but may not be the most intuitive way of opening these added pages.

❑ **Create a link in the Quick Launch bar:** Requires FrontPage. The result is easy for the user to understand and use.

❑ **Create a button:** Requires FrontPage. This option is also easy to use and may be more intuitive because you can design the buttons to make them more attractive.

❑ **Create a list of tabs:** Requires FrontPage. You can use buttons shaped as tabs and place them near each other to make an impression of a number of tabs instead of pages. The best result is when using web part pages, because they also use the same top header and color as the Home page.

In the following example, you use a simple list of links and then build a tab view.

Try It Out   Make It Easier to Access Added Pages

The first task is to create a list for these links:

1. Open the team site with a browser.

2. Choose Create⇨Links.

3. **Name:** More Information.

4. Click Create. The new list is displayed.

5. Click New Item.

6. To make it easier for you to add the URL links to these pages, you start a new browser connected to the same team site. One way of doing this is to press Ctrl+N, which opens a new browser window with the same URL. Use this second browser to open Shared Documents, right-click the file for the first added page, and select Copy Shortcut.

7. Go back to the first browser with the New Item form and paste the shortcut into the URL field. Enter a descriptive name for this page. Click Save and Close.

8. Repeat steps 5–7 for the second page file.

9. Open the Home page.

10. Add the web part More Information to this page.

11. Click any of the links in this list to make sure it works as expected.

The second task adds tab buttons to give the impression that this it is a pages view. The challenge here is that you must add these tab buttons on all the pages and in the same position to make it seamlessly integrate in this team page. This can be tricky at times, but if you are careful it can be very nice.

FrontPage has a nice feature called *layers*. A layer is a transparent type of page that lies on top of the ordinary web page. You can add objects such as buttons and images to these layers, and these objects look as if they are placed on the web page. You can then choose whether a specific layer should be hidden or visible. A layer can also be copied and applied to another web page. You can use this technique here. Instead of adding single tab buttons on each page, you can create a layer that contains these tab buttons and then copy this layer to each page. Here is one way of doing this:

1. Open the Home page with FrontPage.

2. Use the Insert menu and select Layer. Locate the layer where you want these tab buttons (for example, just under the top menu). You may need to adjust the size of this layer to fit all the buttons you will add.

   If the Layer option is grayed when you select it, you have located a part of the page that does not allow you to create a layer; if so go to the top of the code for this page and try again.

3. Make sure the cursor is inside the layer and then add the first tab button:

   a. Choose Insert⇨Interactive button.

   b. Select the tab button you prefer; note that there are several types and colors to choose from. In this example, use Glass Tab 1.

   c. **Text:** Home. Because you will add this layer to several pages, you should also have a button that takes you to the Home page. This is especially important when you add standard HTML pages, because they will not have the default team site top menu.

   d. **URL:** Click Browse and select `Default.aspx`, which is the Home page for this team site.

   e. Click OK to save this button.

4. Add the second button next to the first one. Instead of creating the button from scratch, select the existing one; right-click and select Copy.

   a. Place the cursor directly to the right of the first tab button.

   b. Right-click and select Paste.

   c. Double-click the new button. Its configuration pane opens.

   d. Change the Text to whatever you want to call the second page.

   e. Click Browse for the URL field. Open the document library where these added page files are stored and select the second page. In this example it is Shared Documents and the file `WP-page.aspx`.

   f. Click OK to save and close this page.

5. If you have more pages, add a tab button for each of these to the layer. When you are done, adjust the position and size of this layer so it will look good on every page. Make sure to save this page in FrontPage (click OK to save the images for these buttons) but do not yet close FrontPage.

6. Right-click the frame around this layer and select Copy; you will now paste this layer on all other pages:

   a. Open the second page in FrontPage.

   b. Select Edit⇨Paste. This will place the layer in the same location as on the first page.

   c. Save this page in FrontPage.

   d. Repeat steps a–c for all added pages to this team site.

7. Make sure you have saved all modifications in FrontPage. Open the team site with a browser and click one of the tab buttons. It should open that page that also contains the same buttons. Make sure it works and that it looks good. See Figure 12-14, where the second page is displayed with its three buttons.

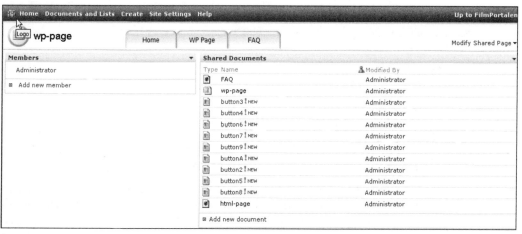

Figure 12-14

If you choose to add tab buttons to these pages, you may want to remove the text Home from the start page for this team site to make that page look better. Use FrontPage to do this.

Creating a Blog Package

FrontPage is not only a very nice editor for SharePoint pages; it also contains some preconfigured site packages that you can use in the SharePoint environment. One request that I get often from my customers is to add a *web log* site (more commonly known as a *blog*). Instead of creating one from scratch, you can use the preconfigured blog that comes with FrontPage. Because a blog is by its nature often very personal, it is logical to place it under the user's personal site (My Site). This requires that you have SPS installed. But a WSS environment can also use this FrontPage block. Just make sure it is configured to allow other people to read this site.

In the following example, you add a blog to the user Steve's personal site. It also allows every SharePoint user access to this site. Note that you must manually enter the URL address for this new blog site. You may remember from earlier chapters that all personal sites in SPS have this generic URL by default:

```
http://<portal site>/personal/<user logon name>
```

The URL to Steve's personal site is `http://Filmportalen/personal/steve`. Finally, when creating a blog using this FrontPage package, you must also manually enter the name for this site (for example, "blog"), so in Steve's example the complete URL to this blog is:

```
http://Filmportalen/personal/steve/blog
```

Follow these steps to create this blog site for Steve:

Try It Out   **Create a Blog Site**

1.   Log on as an administrator and then start FrontPage.

2.   Choose File⇨New.

3.   In the Task Pane, select Web package solutions.

4.   Make sure the Package tab is open, select Web Log, and then do the following:

     a.   Specify the location of the new Web Site as `http://filmportalen/personal/` `steve/blog`.

     b.   Click OK.

     c.   In the next window you are asked if you want to import this package to the given URL. Click Import.

     d.   If you get a security warning about trusting this package from Microsoft, click Yes (or Run, if the warning asks you whether you want to run the process).

     e.   After a short period you will get a dialog box stating Web Package "Weblog" Deployment complete. Click OK to close.

5.   The blog is now created and ready to be used, but you will probably want to configure it first. Log on as the user Steve and open his personal site. If this site has the web part Shared Workspace Sites, it now displays this blog. If not, click Documents and Lists and then click Sites in the quick launch bar, and you see the blog. Open this blog and it looks like Figure 12-15.

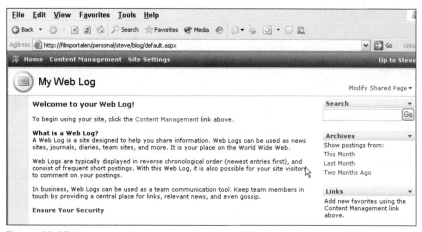

Figure 12-15

6.   The next step is to set the permissions for this blog site. By default it inherits the permissions from its parent site (Steve's personal site in this example). This blog works as any SharePoint site, so do this:

     a.   Choose Site Settings⇨Go to Site Administration.

     b.   Choose Manage permission inheritance⇨Use Unique Permissions.

     c.   Click OK.

    d.   On the Site Settings page, click Manage users.

    e.   The inherited settings are displayed. Make whatever changes you need now and make sure that the right group of users can read and write to this blog.

    f.   Click Home to exit from this administrative page.

7.   Finally, Steve should now start adding information to his site:

    a.   Choose Content Management⇨Make a new Web Log posting.

    b.   Enter a Title and a Body. Notice that you can use standard formatting features, like fonts, sizes, and links.

    c.   Click OK.

8.   If necessary, use FrontPage to change the design of this page. You may have noticed that his is a web part page, so you can add any web parts available to this blog (for example, images, calendars, and document libraries).

9.   To make it easy for other users to access this blog site, you should create a link to it. This could be a link on the portal site; for example, you can create a list of links to all blog sites. Another way is to add this blog to the public view of this site, like this:

    a.   Logged on as Steve, open his personal site.

    b.   Under My Links Summary, click Add new link.

    c.   **Title:** Steve's Blog.

    d.   **Address:** `http://filmportalen/personal/steve/blog`. This address must be entered manually.

    e.   Select or create the group for this link.

    f.   Check Share on public view on My Site.

    g.   Click OK.

10.   Make sure the link is displayed. Log on as another user and open Steve's site. (For example, search for Steve. Users are always on top of the search results.) Follow the link to Steve's blog and test entering comments to a posting. Click the little yellow icon; then click Post a new comment.

This blog can be used not only for internal use, but it can be configured to allow anonymous access to make it available from the Internet. Use the steps described in Chapter 3 to configure this blog site to accept anonymous access. Make sure that any firewall, for example, MS ISA Server, allows anonymous access to this site from the Internet.

Data Sources and Data Views

A very common request is to make content in one site available in another site. Most of the SharePoint installations I have worked with use team sites for managing projects, and after some time the need for a shared view of tasks in different sites emerges. Another similar request is to have one team site that displays the document libraries in other sites. Finally, a third request may be to display content in an external database, for example a product database in an MS SQL Server.

SharePoint has at least one web part that can display external content: the Web Capture web part that comes with the MS Office 2003 Resource Kit. See more about that web part in Chapter 8. But this web part can only display HTML-based content; it cannot display a table in an external database.

This section describes how you can use two special types of web parts that come with FrontPage:

❑ **Data Source:** Define what source to read.

❑ **Data View:** Define how this source will be displayed.

Both of these are integrated in the same package in FrontPage: the Data View. This is not a standard web part and cannot be installed in a web part zone. You must add it to another part of the page. In the following examples you see how to display a document library in another team site and how to display a table in an external MS SQL database.

Displaying Content in Other Sites

The first example uses the team site `http://filmportalen/sites/info` to display a document library stored in `http://filmportalen/sites/it`. This example can easily be extended to display any type of list, and it works for both SPS and WSS environments.

Try It Out	Display Content in Another Site

1. Log on as an administrator.

2. Open the team site `http://filmportalen/sites/info in FrontPage.`

3. Using the Design mode, place the cursor directly under the Left web part zone.

4. Use the menu Data⇨Insert Data View. This opens the task pane and displays all the data sources in the current team site, as in Figure 12-16.

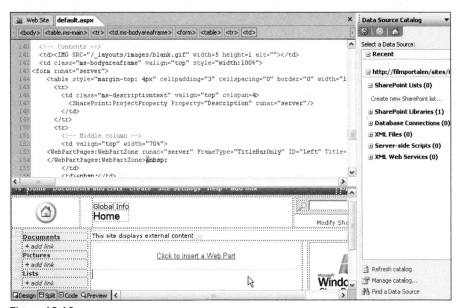

Figure 12-16

5. The data source you need is not listed. Click Manage catalog at the bottom of the Task Pane, and then:

    a. Click the Add button and enter the following:

    b. **Display Name:** IT Team Site.

    c. **Location:** `http://filmportalen/sites/it`.

    d. Click OK twice. Note that the Data Source Catalog now lists IT Team Site.

6. Expand the IT Team Site (click its plus sign). All lists and libraries in this site are now listed. Expand the SharePoint Libraries to see the Shared Documents library. Add this library to the page like this:

    a. Click the name Shared Documents. A menu is presented.

    b. Click Insert Data View. A table is displayed on the page, and a list of all available columns for this library is presented in the Task Pane.

    c. Verify that the content is displayed. If you are happy with this view, save this page in FrontPage.

7. You can also change the view of the table, for example what columns to display, the sort order, and formatting. It is similar to creating views for any SharePoint list, but more powerful. Here are some of the things you can do, starting with how to add more columns:

    a. To display more columns, you must first create a new column. It can be tricky to do this the first time, so make sure you get it right: In the new data view, hover the cursor at the top edge above the column header you want to move to the right; when you see a black arrow pointing down, you are in the right position. Right-click and select Insert Column; a new column is displayed in the table. Note that it is very narrow, because it does not contain any data yet.

    b. Set the cursor inside the new column for any of the data rows. Because it is so small, it is actually easier to use the arrows on the keyboard to place the cursor in this cell. Make sure not to set the cursor in the title row!

    c. In the Task Pane's Data View Details, you can see all the columns for the document library you have added as a Data View. Right-click the column to be added. Select Insert as <Text/Number/Currency> and choose whatever type is appropriate for this column.

    d. Place the cursor in the title row for this column; type a name for this column.

8. Another thing you probably want to do is to create a link to these documents so they can be opened. By default only their names are displayed, but you cannot click them to open as you could in a normal document library. Use these steps to replace the existing URL column with the same content but with hyperlinks:

    a. Select the URL Path for the first document (not the title row, please).

    b. Right-click the URL Path in the Data View Details pane; select Insert as Hyperlink.

9. Another way to do this is to make the document names hyperlinks. By clicking a name it will first open the web form for the document, where the user can open the actual document.

    a. Select any of the existing file names.

b.   Right-click and select Format item as⇨Hyper link to⇨Display Form.

10.   To change the sort order and group items, you can do this:

a.   Under Manage view settings in the Task Pane, click Sort & group.

b.   Select the column to sort by; click Add. If necessary add more columns. Check Show group header if you want to group these documents.

c.   Click OK to save and close.

11.   This data view also allows you to create conditional formatting. For example, if you want to display files larger than 10,000 bytes with a red text font, do this:

a.   Start by adding an extra column that displays the file size. To do this, follow the previous instructions in step 7.

b.   Select the size for any of the documents.

c.   Right-click and select Conditional Formatting. This opens the Task Pane for Conditional Formatting.

d.   Click Create. (Tip: If the create button is not active, you have not selected a value in the table.)

e.   Select Apply formatting. A dialog window for this is displayed.

f.   Select Click here to add a new clause. The first row now allows you to set the criteria for this formatting.

g.   Set the first row to: Field name = File Size; Comparison = Greater Than; Value=10000; then click OK.

h.   Click Format⇨Font; set the Color to red and click OK twice. The list is displayed and all documents with a file size greater than 10,000 bytes now have this size in red.

You can do a lot more, but by this point you have the general idea of how to use and customize this list.

You can also drag fields directly from the field list in the Task Pane to the Data View. You can also insert more than one field into a column, and you can combine these fields into one single column.

Displaying External Info

The second use for the Data View is to display content in sources outside SharePoint. It is capable of connecting to many type of sources, such as:

❑   MS SQL Databases

❑   XML files

❑   Web Services

In this example, you connect to the demo database Northwind that is included by default in all MS SQL databases. By coincidence it happens to be the same database that SharePoint uses, but you can use these steps to connect to any database. You will display the Products table on the same team site as in the previous example.

Try It Out   Display Content in an External Database

1. Log on as an administrator.

2. Open `http://filmportalen/sites/info` in FrontPage.

3. Use the Task Pane and choose Data➪Insert Data View to display the Data Source Catalog. Look at the listing under this site name. It shows you all the sources available for this team site (lists, libraries, but also database connections, XML files, server-side scripts, and XML web services).

4. Expand the Database Connections.

    a. Click Add to Catalog. A dialog window opens.

    b. Click Configure Database Connection.

    c. Enter the server Name for the SQL database. You must also define what user account to use when reading this information. You could choose Windows Authentication, which uses the current user's account and permission to this database, as in Figure 12-17, or you can define a specific account that you know has access to this database and table. Click Next to continue.

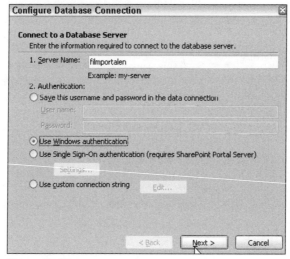

Figure 12-17

    d. All databases in this MS SQL Server are listed; select Northwind. A list of all tables for this database is listed. Select Products and click Finish.

    e. A list of options for filtering and formatting this table is displayed; don't change anything now. Click OK.

    f. Select the location where you will add the Products data view.

    g. In the Data Source Catalog under Database Connections, you now see Products on Northwind. Click it and select Insert Data View.

5. This table is now listed on the SharePoint page. You can now start formatting this list the same way as described in the previous example.

Connecting Web Parts

Look at the result from the previous example; it shows you the product names and the Supplier ID. What if you want to see the full name for this supplier? You can do it by adding the table for suppliers and then connecting these two listings. It works like this: When the user clicks one of the products, the details of the corresponding supplier are displayed in their own list.

Try It Out   Connect Web Parts

1. Open the same team site as in the previous example.

2. Use the previous steps and add the Suppliers table under the Products list on this team site page.

3. Right-click the Products table and select Web Part Connections:

   a. Make sure the Action is "Provide Data Values to" and click Next.

   b. Make sure to select "Connect to a Web Part on this page" and click Next.

   c. Change the "Target Web Part" to "Supplier in Northwind"; make sure the Target Action is "Filter View Using Data Values From"; then click Next.

   d. Select SupplierID in both list boxes and click Next.

   e. Change "Create a hyperlink on" to ProductName and click Next.

   f. Click Finish.

4. The connection is now active. Save this page in FrontPage. Open this team site in a browser and click any product. The supplier for this product will be listed below. Note that several products have the same supplier; see Figure 12-18.

Again you could use the formatting features of these data views to make everything more attractive. One thing you may want to do right away is to delete the SupplierID column in the Product list, because the details about the supplier get listed below; another thing may be to group each product based on CategoryID.

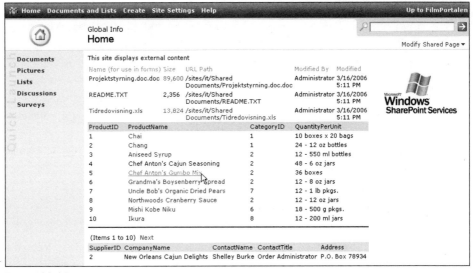

Figure 12-18

Summary

In this chapter you learned the following:

❑ A smart page is another name for a web part page in SharePoint.

❑ More advanced customization requires MS FrontPage.

❑ Only FrontPage 2003 (SharePoint Designer 2007) knows how SharePoint works; no other web designer tool has the features required to customize SharePoint 2003.

❑ The behavior of FrontPage is different in SPS than WSS; for example, only in WSS will FrontPage display live content.

❑ Ghosting is the default way site definitions work; all the settings and layout for every page in the portal site and team sites are based on files stored on the SharePoint Server's file system.

❑ Un-ghosting is when a page is customized by FrontPage and SharePoint must store this page in the database. No longer is the site definition on the file system used for this page; everything is stored in the content database.

❑ Use the DisableWebDesignFeatures keyword in the Onet.xml file to prohibit a site page from being edited by FrontPage.

❑ Examples of basic customization with FrontPage include things like adding extra text, extra buttons, and extra links on a team site.

❑ Using FrontPage you can hide some fields in a web form from the user who creates a new item; the same fields may later be visible for the user who reads this web form.

❑ FrontPage allows you to install complete site packages with unlimited size; this is a very handy way of copying a large site to another SharePoint environment.

❑ Using FrontPage's Report feature, you can get a summary of a given SharePoint site, including a list of broken links and pages that are slow to open.

❑ FrontPage allows you to customize an existing theme in great detail. You can also create new themes.

❑ Use FrontPage to add extra pages of web part type or standard HTML pages to any SharePoint site.

❑ FrontPage has a web log, or blog site package, based on a web part page. Add it to the SharePoint site, and you can have a nice blog up and running in no time.

❑ FrontPage's Data Source and Data Views are very powerful tools. They allow you to display content stored in other SharePoint sites and in external sources, such as SQL databases, XML files, and Web Services.

❑ The formatting features of Data View are much more advanced than the views available for lists and libraries in SharePoint.

❑ Connect one or more lists with FrontPage to filter information in other lists.

In the next chapter you learn more about backup and restore procedures for SharePoint and how you can move content between different SharePoint environments.

Backup and Restore

By now I am sure you agree that SharePoint is a great product and a fantastic tool for managing information for your complete organization, regardless of what types of tasks or activities you need to perform. When your SharePoint project goes from being a test phase into a production environment, it suddenly contains important information—a lot of it, and growing every day. Sooner than you might expect, SharePoint becomes a mission-critical application in your environment. How can you protect it? By making backups, of course! As the old SharePoint geek joke goes: "What do you call a SharePoint administrator who does not make backups? Unemployed!"

This chapter tells you how to keep your job as a SharePoint administrator. It starts by describing what information you need to protect and then lists all available options. You learn how to perform backup and restore procedures. You also read about other options, such as MS SQL backups and third-party backup tools.

Just remember this: If you do not regularly verify that your backup solution works (that it actually is possible to restore data with your backup plan), you can save a lot of time and effort by skipping the backup process completely. During my 28 years in the computer business, I have seen a large number of backup solutions that do not work when you actually need them! A lot of IT administrators seem to think it is good enough to come up with some sort of backup solution, manage to get it running (at least one time), and then relax. In my experience as a consultant, the number of restore failures is close to 50 percent, so please make sure you don't join this group. Regularly restore the data and make sure you can read it; you will be surprised how often it will fail. By performing these fire drills regularly, you and your team become experienced at doing a quick restore that actually works. This will help you all sleep better at night, and it will help you retain your jobs.

What Data Should You Protect?

This is a good question to start with. What data is it that you need to back up in order to be sure you can survive a catastrophic situation? The answer is that the information that relates to SharePoint is stored in a lot of places, not only the databases as one may at first believe. This section describes what you need to know in order to protect the SharePoint environment. There is one golden rule when it comes to SharePoint backups:

> **Rule #1: What you back up is what you can restore!**

In other words, if you make a backup of a site, you will be able to restore that site, and nothing but that site. For example, you will not be able to restore a list or a single document in that site. The consequence is that you will most likely develop a strategy consisting of several backup procedures that all work together, in order to make it possible to restore whatever data has been lost.

The SharePoint Database

All information in all SharePoint sites is stored in the SQL database, including data, configurations, and customizations. SharePoint will use these types of databases, depending on if it is SPS or WSS:

Database	Content
Content Database (SPS and WSS)	All documents, news, links, contacts, calendars, and so on. All web parts and their settings. All customization of sites done with FrontPage.
Config Database (SPS and WSS)	All team site names and their configuration properties. All site collections. All portal sites including portal areas. All general configuration settings of the SharePoint server.
User Profile Database (SPS only)	All user properties entered manually or imported from Active Directory.
Service Database (SPS only)	Data for the indexing and search service, plus information about alert settings in the portal site. This is also known as the "Component database."

The two most important database types are the Content database and the Config database. Lose them and you are in big trouble. If you lose either of the other two, it is also a problem, but maybe not that big: You can recover them by importing the user profiles again from AD, or you can reconfigure the search settings and ask people to reenter their alerts.

Note that SharePoint may have more than one content database. Therefore, make sure that all of these databases will be backed up by your procedure in case you will perform pure SQL-based backup procedures instead of using any of the special backup tools that exist for SharePoint.

> **Rule #2: Make sure all of SharePoint's databases are backed up.**

SharePoint Files

If all databases are backed up, you will be able to restore all data and configurations, as listed in the table in the previous section. But in the case of a total server disaster, you will still lose SharePoint information, because some of it is stored in the file system on the SharePoint server. You may recall from Chapter 4 that there are different types of SharePoint servers, with different roles:

❑ **Front-End Server:** A SharePoint server responsible for one or more roles; see the following table.

❑ **Back-End Server:** The server running the MS SQL database (MSDE, WMSDE, or MS SQL Server).

If you are using separate front-end and back-end servers, you will have to take steps to back up both of them, because both contain vital SharePoint information. The previous section described the information stored on the back-end server (the SQL Server). The front-end sever can also contain information depending on what role it has in the SharePoint farm, as listed in the following table:

Front-end Role	Data stored in the file system of this server
Web	General SharePoint binary files. Default site definitions, CSS files, and WSS themes. Customized site definitions. Customized CSS files. Customized WSS themes. Customized web part files. Customized IIS Metabase settings, including virtual servers.
Search	General SharePoint binary files. Copy of index files (used by the search engine).
Index	General SharePoint binary files. Index files generated by the crawler process.
Job	General SharePoint binary files.

The conclusion is that the SharePoint server running the Web role is very important, in case you have customized your environment. If this is lost, you will have to redo all branding and customization, which requires that all these changes have been documented. (I am still waiting to see a SharePoint environment that is completely documented, including the IIS settings. Promise me that you will make the first one, okay?)

If the Search server crashes, there is no real worry; just reinstall the SharePoint binaries, and the index files will be copied from the Index server again.

If the Index server crashes, it may be a problem, depending on how important the search process is for your users. The solution in case there is no backup is to rescan all data sources. This may take a long time if there is a large volume of data, and during this time users cannot trust that the search results they get are complete, because all data may not yet have been crawled.

If the Job server crashes, just reinstall the SharePoint binaries; there is no specific data stored on this server.

> **Rule #3: Make sure to back up the file system and the IIS Metabase on the front-end servers.**

Backup Options

As you understand from the previous sections, you should think carefully about how to design your backup plan. It is more complicated than you at first may expect. Still, it is a very easy and manageable task when you know how to do it and what tools to use. SharePoint comes with several tools that you can use to back up the most important SharePoint information:

❑   **Smigrate:** Will back up and restore single sites and nested sites.

❑   **Stsadm:** Will back up and restore complete site collections only.

❑   **Spsbackup:** Will back up and restore complete portal sites including all WSS sites.

You should learn to use all of these three tools because they focus on different backup scenarios, but remember that they will only serve to back up data in the SQL database, plus in the case of Spsbackup, the index files. These tools are covered in more detail in the following sections.

In addition to these free tools that come with SharePoint, there are also several commercial backup solutions for both WSS and SPS. You learn more about some of these at the end of this chapter.

Moving and Copying Information

Sometimes you need to move or copy information, such as a site, a list, or a single document. One example is when you develop a team site on a test server and upon determining that it works as expected, you want to move it to the production environment. Another example is when you want to restore a single document that accidentally was deleted. There are several methods for doing these things, and almost all of them use these backup and restore procedures.

The exceptions occur when you want to move or copy a list or library, a list item, or a single document between two sites. In these instances you have these options:

❑   To move or copy single documents (for example an MS Word file), use any of these methods:

   ❑   Open the document library in SharePoint and select the Explorer View. Now you can right-click a document, select Copy, open the destination library in an Explorer View, and select Paste.

   ❑   Use Web Folders mapped to each library. Copy and paste between these folders like you do with any standard file folders.

   ❑   Open the document in MS Word and save it in the destination library.

> **Rule #4: You can only copy the latest version of a document, not its complete version history**

❑   To move or copy single list items (for example, a Customer Contact), use this method:

   1.   Open the Contact list using the Datasheet View.

   2.   Right-click the contact and select Copy.

   3.   Open the destination list in Datasheet View.

   4.   Right-click the asterisk (*) and select Paste. If you select an existing item in the destination list, it will be overwritten.

❑　To move or copy a complete library (for example, a Document Library), use these methods:

   ❑　**To move a library to another site in the same site collection:** Click Modify settings and columns for the library to be moved. Select Save document library as template, give it a name and description, make sure to check Include content, and click OK. Open the site where this library will be copied. Click Create in the top menu bar, select the template, and give it a new name.

   ❑　**To move a library to another site collection:** Click Modify settings and columns for the library to be moved. Select Save document library as template, give it a name and description, make sure to check Include content, and click OK. On the following page, click the "list template gallery" link, click the template name for this list, and select Save. Next, open the top-level site for the site collection where this list will be copied. Choose Site Settings⇨Go to Site Administration⇨Manage list template gallery⇨ Upload Template. Select the previously saved file, and click Save and Close. Then go to the site where you want this library and click Create. Your copied library is listed in the Document Library section.

   ❑　**To move a library with more than 10 MB of content to another site collection:** Save the library as a template as just described, but do not check Include content. Continue to import that template in the other site collection. Now use the previous technique to move single documents and move (or copy) all documents from the old library to the new one.

> **Rule #5: A template for a list or library can only contain up to 10 MB of content. To view the size of a list or library, choose Site Settings⇨Go to Site Administration⇨ View storage space allocation (in the Site Collection Administration section).**

❑　To move or copy a complete list (for example, a Task list), use these methods:

   ❑　**To copy lists with less than 10 MB of content:** Use either of the first two options for moving and copying a complete library.

   ❑　**To copy a list with more than 10 MB of content:** Create a view that shows all the columns you want to move with this list, and then open the list using this new view. Click Export to spreadsheet. In Excel save this list as an Excel file. Go to the site where you want this list. Click Create in the top menu, and then select Import Spreadsheet. Give this new list a name, enter the saved file in the File location, and click Import. In Excel, for the Range Type field use "List Range" and for the Select Range field pick the only option available; then click Import. The complete list, including column definitions, is copied. Note that this method will not copy any special views. You will have to re-create them (or save the list as an empty template, create the new list using this template, and then use Excel to export and import the list content).

> **Rule #6: Use Excel for moving or copying lists greater than 10 MB.**

Third-party tools are also available that may help you move single documents and lists, such as XPlica from Vyapin (`www.vyapincom`), which can copy a single document, complete lists, and complete libraries, including the full version history. Similar capabilities are provided by the backup tool DocAve from AvePoint (`www.avepoint.com`). SMove from Triplewood (`www.triplewood.com`) can copy and move lists and libraries, including document versions, between sites and portals.

Backing Up with Stsadm

The same tool as you have seen described in this book when discussing site templates and web parts can also be used for backup and restore procedures. It is a fast and *full-fidelity* procedure, meaning that it will do a restore that will be exactly like the sites you backed up, including security settings and personal site views.

This tool has some limitations and behaviors you must be aware of, such as the following:

- ❑   It can only back up and restore complete site collections, not single sites.
- ❑   The result will be stored as a file. Stsadm cannot write to other backup media.
- ❑   It must be executed on the SharePoint server.
- ❑   You must be a SharePoint server administrator to run Stsadm.
- ❑   This is a command-line tool. You can schedule it using Windows Tasks.

Because it will only back up complete site collections, you will need to run it once for each site collection in your SharePoint environment. This may be okay when you have a limited number of site collections, but if you have hundreds of them, it starts to get hard. There are tools that can help you with this problem, as described in the later section "Tools for Stsadm."

The number of switches available for the Stsadm tools is impressive. In fact, there are most likely a lot of switches that you never will use; then again, there are some that you will use frequently. Following is a list of just a few of the most common switches, but if you want to see them all, simply open a command prompt window and type **Stsadm** without any switches.

Switch	Example	Description
-o backup	`Stsadm -o backup -url http://spsrv1/sites/finance -filename C:\bkup\Finance.bkp`	This will back up the complete site collection finance to the file `Finance.bkp`.
-o restore	`Stsadm -o restore -url http://spsrv1/sites/finance -filename C:\bkup\Finance.bkp -overwrite`	This will restore the content in the file `Finance.bkp` to the listed site URL. If there is anything previously stored in that site collection, it will be overwritten.
-o enumsites	`Stsadm -o enumsites -url http://spsrv1`	List all top team sites under the portal spsrv1.
-o addtemplate	`Stsadm -o addtemplate -filename "C:\abc\projtemp.stp -title "Project template" -description "This is our standard site template for projects"`	Import the site template `projtemp.stp` into the global site template gallery.

Preparing for Stsadm

Stsadm.EXE is stored deep in the file system, or to be exact in this folder:

```
C:\Program Files\Common Files\Microsoft Shared\web server extensions\60\BIN
```

As described in Chapter 2, you should add this folder's file path to the system path variable to avoid having to type this long path every time you run Stsadm. This is how to add the path to Stsadm to this system variable:

Try It Out   Update the PATH System Variable

1. Start Windows Explorer and navigate to the path for the Stsadm as given in the preceding text.

2. Right-click the file path in the Address field and select Copy.

3. Click Start to see the Windows Start menu.

4. Right-click My Computer and select Properties.

5. Switch to the Advanced tab and click the Environment Variables button.

6. In the lower pane named System Variables, locate PATH and click Edit.

7. Go to the end of the current list in Variable value (use the END key or the right arrow on the keyboard). Type in a semicolon (;) as a separator, and paste the path you copied in step 1. Then click OK three times to save this modification and close all the dialog boxes.

Test it by opening a command window (Start⇨Run and type **Cmd**); type **Stsadm** in this command window. If you get a long list of options, you did it right. If not, repeat these steps and make sure to follow them exactly as described.

Running the Stsadm Backup

What if you want to back up the site collection for the IT department with the following URL to the top-level site: http://filmportalen/sites/it? You do this:

Try It Out   Back up with Stsadm

1. Log on to the SharePoint server as the administrator.

2. Locate a file folder where the backup file generated by Stsadm will be stored; in this example, you will use C:\Bkup.

3. Open a command window and run the following command:

```
Stsadm -o backup -url http://filmportalen/sites/it -filename c:\bkup\sites#it.spb
```

4. When the backup is completed, you will find the file sites#it.spb in the folder C:\bkup.

Later in this chapter, in the section "Restore Procedures," you learn how to restore the backup file created by Stsadm and the other tools mentioned in this backup section.

Tools for Stsadm

Two add-ons are available for Stsadm that you should know about. For example, there is one that assists you in creating a backup procedure. Another add-on gives a graphical user interface on top of Stsadm that makes it much easier to use, especially for an inexperienced SharePoint administrator. The following table describes these two add-ons:

Name	URL for more info	Description

STSAdmWin-2Go	`http://download.microsoft`
	`.com/download/1/6/8/16887e30-`
	`897e-4d6c-afce-3e85a43e6eaa/`
	`stsadmWin-2go.zip`
		A free graphical user interface for Stsadm.

SPBackup.exe	`http://www.microsoft.com/` `mspress/books/6454.asp`	Comes with the SharePoint 2003 Resource Kit. Creates a backup script using Stsadm for modified site collections.

Using the graphical STSAdmWin-2Go tool for doing the same backup as described previously looks like Figure 13-1. Just select the backup operation, and its command switches URL, Filename, and Overwrite are displayed. Enter the values for the switches and then click either Submit to execute this command or Compose to see the complete command, as depicted in Figure 13-1.

Figure 13-1

This tool is also an excellent way of learning all the commands of Stsadm. Just select an Operation, and you will see its command switches. If you play with this tool a little, you will be surprised how much Stsadm can do for you.

The other tool, SPBackup (not SPSBackup), is more interesting when you need to design a backup strategy. It will help you with analyzing which sites have been modified. You can create a script file with the

Stsadm command to make a backup of these site collections. By using this tool you can save a lot of time because only modified site collections will be backed up. You run this tool once every night to create the backup script, which is then executed. The available command switches for SPBackup.exe are as follows:

- ❑ **SPBackup –a:** Generates a script that will back up all modified site collections.

- ❑ **SPBackup –d:** Generates a script that will back up all modified site collections the past day.

- ❑ **SPBackup –w:** Generates a script that will back up all modified site collections the past week.

- ❑ **SPBackup –f <file name>:** Sets the name of the resulting script. The default name is Spbakout.bat.

   SPBackup must be installed in the same folder as Stsadm unless the system PATH variable is updated to include the path to Stsadm.

If you run this command on an SPS server, it will automatically make a backup script for all team sites, all document and meeting workspaces, and all personal sites in the portal.

For example, say that you have three site collections: IT, Sales, and HR. They contain a lot of information but are not always updated every day. To save time and disk space, you decide to use the SPBackup.exe tool to generate a script with all the modified site collections from the past day. The following steps show how you can do this:

Try It Out   Run SPBackup to Create a Backup Script

1. Log on to the SharePoint server as an administrator.

2. Make sure that SPBackup.exe is stored in the same file folder as Stsadm.exe.

3. Open a command prompt window and select a file folder to store the script and the backup files (for example, C:\Bkup). Open that folder.

4. Run this command and it will create a backup script for all site collections modified the last day only (because there is no -f switch, the script is named Spbakout.bat by default):

```
SPBackup -d
```

5. Inspect the Spbakout.bat script. Note that it will give each backup file a name that indicates what type of site collection it is. (For example, an ordinary team site named IT gets the backup file name "sites#IT.spb", while the personal folder for Steve has the name "personal#steve.spb".)

6. Run the script by typing **Spbakout.bat**. All site collections in this script are backed up to the current folder.

7. If the Spbakout.bat works as expected, configure the Windows tool Scheduled Tasks to first run SPBackup.exe to create a new Spbakout.bat file, and then add a second scheduled task to run the Spbakout.bak once every night:

   a. Select the menu Start⇨All Programs⇨Accessories⇨System Tools⇨Scheduled Tasks.

   b. The Windows Scheduler starts. Click Add Scheduled Task and click Next.

   c. Click Browse and select SPBackup.exe.

   d. Select when to perform this task (normally it will be Daily) and click Next.

e. Select what time to run this task (for example, 06:00). Avoid running this command at the same time as other tasks, such as the profile import or audience recompilation. Then click Next.

f. Enter the user account this script will run under. It must have administrative rights to the SharePoint server. In this example choose the domain administrator. Then click Next.

g. Click Finish to close and activate this scheduled task.

h. Right-click this new task, select Properties, and add the switch –d to make this script look for sites modified the last day only. The complete line in the Run field will then look like this: SPBackup.exe –d. Click OK.

i. Enter the password for the user account associated with this task.

j. Test the script by right-clicking its name in the task list and selecting Run. You should see a command prompt window that runs the script and then closes.

k. Repeat steps b–g to add a scheduled task to run Spbakout.bat a few minutes after the first task generated it (for example at 06:05).

l. Verify that the Scheduled Tasks window looks similar to Figure 13-2. Then close the Scheduled Tasks tool.

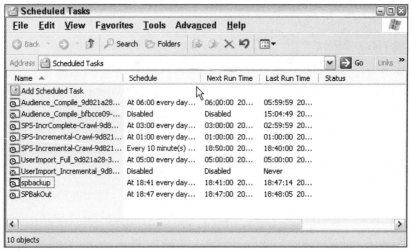

Figure 13-2

Backing Up with Smigrate

Another tool that also has been mentioned earlier in this book is Smigrate.EXE. It is stored in the same file folder as Stsadm, and it can also be used to make backups of sites. However, it differs from Stsadm in several important ways:

❑ It can back up single sites or any site including its subsites. It does not have to be the top-level site in the site collection.

❑ It cannot make backups of portal sites.

❑ It is not a full-fidelity backup. For example, it will not restore user permissions or personal site views.

❑ The result will be stored as a file. Smigrate cannot write to other backup media.

❑ It can be executed from any computer with access to the site to be backed up.

❑ You must be the administrator *for this site* to run this command.

❑ This is a command-line tool. You can schedule it using Windows Tasks.

This tool is great when you need to make a backup of a single site (for example, when you want to move or copy a site to another SharePoint environment or when you want to move a site from one site collection to another in the same SharePoint server). Its backup file format is identical to the files generated by FrontPage 2003 when running backups of sites. In fact, FrontPage can restore a file that was backed up with Smigrate, and the other way around.

At first it may sound strange that Smigrate does not restore all settings, as Stsadm does. But the explanation is very simple: It was designed to be used for migrating sites to other SharePoint environments, and because they may have different users and permissions, you must reconfigure these settings anyhow. This solves a problem that you have with Stsadm backups; they expect that the restore server is more or less identical to the original SharePoint server this site collection belonged to previously. So the name Smigrate ("SharePoint Migrate") is very descriptive indeed.

Preparing for Smigrate

Smigrate, just like `Stsadm.EXE`, is stored in this folder on the SharePoint server:

```
C:\Program Files\Common Files\Microsoft Shared\web server extensions\60\BIN
```

If you added this path to the system PATH variable as described in the previous section, it will also be possible to execute Smigrate in any folder; no other specific preparation is necessary.

The command switches for Smigrate are these:

❑ **Smigrate –f:** The file name for this backup. Use `.fwp` as the file type.

❑ **Smigrate –e:** Excludes subsites during backup.

❑ **Smigrate –r:** Restores the given file name in `-f`.

❑ **Smigrate –w:** The web site URL that will be backed up or restored to.

❑ **Smigrate –x:** Excludes security during the restore procedure when migrating sites from the previous version SharePoint Team Services to Windows SharePoint Services.

❑ **Smigrate –y:** Indicates yes to overwrite the existing backup file.

❑ **Smigrate –u:** The administrator's username for this site. You do not need to enter this switch if the current user logged on has administrative access to this site.

❑ **Smigrate –pw:** The password for this user. Enter * to be prompted about this password.

Only the -f and -w switches are required. The exception is when the site is configured to use Basic Authentication; then you must also enter the -u switch. For example, to back up the site http://intranet/hr but no other sites to the file C:\Bkup\Site-HR.fwp, you enter:

```
smigrate -f c:\bkup\site-hr.fwp -w http://intranet/hr -e
```

Another example: To restore the file C:\Bkup\Site-HR.fwp to the site http://test/hr, you enter this command line:

```
smigrate -r -f c:\bkup\site-hr.fwp -w http://test/hr
```

Running the Smigrate Backup

For example, say that you want to back up just the site Project, which is a subsite under the top-level site IT, with the URL http://filmportalen/sites/it/project, and save the backup file as C:\Bkup\project.fwp. You do this:

Try It Out   Back up with Smigrate

1. Log on to the SharePoint server as the administrator.

2. Locate a file folder to store the backup file in; in this example, C:\Bkup.

3. Open a command prompt window and run the following command:

```
smigrate -f c:\bkup\project.fwp  w http://filmportalen/sites/it/project -e
```

Tools for Smigrate

Smigrate also has some tools that make it easier to use. "GUI Smigrate" (created by Renaud Comte) is especially popular because it helps the administrator to both run backups and create scripts for backups. You can find a download link to this excellent and free tool here:

```
http://blog.spsclerics.com/articles/436.aspx
```

To use this tool to back up the site in the previous example, you would do the following:

1. Log on as a user with administrative rights to this site.

2. Start GUI Smigrate.

3. Enter the URL to the site to back up (http://filmportalen/sites/it/project).

4. Enter the BackUp Filename (for example, GUI-Projects.fwp).

5. Enter the Storage Folder (C:\Bkup). See Figure 13-3.

6. Click Start Process. A new window is displayed, showing the same type of information as when running Smigrate manually.

Instead of executing the backup process, this tool can also just create the script file for this backup. To do this, click the "Generate the .bat file only" button. Then you can add this script as a scheduled task, as described earlier for Stsadm.

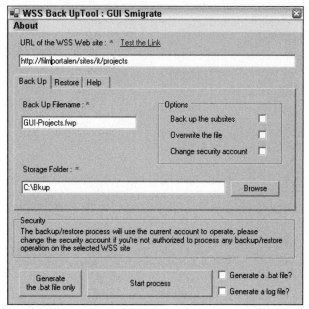

Figure 13-3

Backing Up with Spsbackup

This tool comes only with SPS. Its focus is to create complete backups of SharePoint's portal sites, including all WSS sites, personal sites, and workspaces. It is also the only backup tool that can back up the index files created by the crawler process. The features and limitations of Spsbackup.EXE are these:

❑ It can back up complete SharePoint portals including WSS sites, but not specific site collections or single sites.

❑ It must be executed on the SharePoint server.

❑ It requires that the MS SQL Server Client Tools are installed on the SharePoint server (including the latest service pack for MS SQL Server).

❑ It requires Administrative rights to the SharePoint server.

❑ This is a full-fidelity backup tool.

❑ It has both a command-line interface and a graphical user interface.

This tool is the most complete backup utility that ships with SharePoint. It makes a backup of all the database files in the MS SQL Server and the index files. The only thing it does not back up is any customization of SharePoint files such as site definitions, CSS files, and XML files stored on the SharePoint server's file system. As with the other backup tools, it has a number of command switches available when running Spsbackup using the command-line interface; to see these switches, run the command Spsbackup /? to display a graphical window with all available options listed:

- ❑ **/all:** Back up all portal sites and all WSS sites in this farm.

- ❑ **/teamdbs:** Back up all WSS sites but no portal sites.

- ❑ **/ssodb:** Back up the Single Sign-On database.

- ❑ **/doclib:** Back up the SPS 2001 backward-compatible document library.

- ❑ **/portal:** Define the URL address for the portal site; the default is the current portal site.

- ❑ **/service:** Define type of service to backup: Must be either sitedbs or index.

- ❑ **/file:** Define the file name for this backup.

- ❑ **/backupfilepath:** Define the path to the file folder that will contain the backup files.

- ❑ **/fileprefix:** Define the file name prefix for all generated backup files. For example, if the file prefix is "Full," then all backup file names will begin with "Full."

- ❑ **/overwrite:** Use this to overwrite any previous backup file with the same name.

- ❑ **/DMLocalPath:** The local path on the SPS 2001 compatible Document Library for temporary storage of backup files.

If you don't enter any of these command switches and instead just type Spsbackup, the graphical user interface is activated, as depicted in Figure 13-4. The program is by default installed in the following folder on the SharePoint server: `C:\Program Files\SharePoint Portal Server\Bin`.

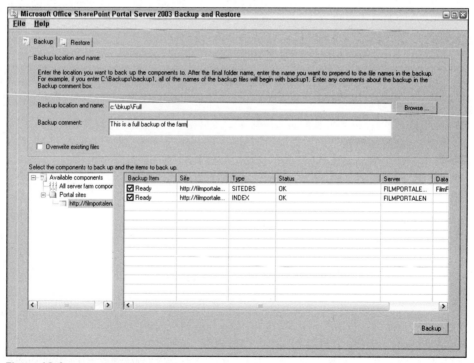

Figure 13-4

Making Backups Using the Graphical Interface

This graphical interface can be used for running backup and restore procedures. You can select what to back up by selecting the components listed in the left pane of the backup window. It displays the name of the portal site and also lets you choose to back up the team sites ("SITEDBS") and index files ("INDEX"). For example, say you want to make a complete backup of the SharePoint farm, including the portal site, all WSS sites, and the index files. This is how you do it:

Try It Out	Run a Complete Backup Using Spsbackup

1. Log on to the SharePoint server as the administrator.

2. Start the Spsbackup tool by choosing Start⇨All Programs⇨SharePoint Portal Server⇨SharePoint Portal Server Data Backup and Restore (or enter **Spsbackup** in a command prompt). Now this tool starts up using a graphical user interface.

3. Enter the "Backup location and name." This is the location where the backup files will be stored, and it determines the prefix for each file name. For example, if you type **\\Srv2\bkup\Full**, it will store all backup files in the location \\srv2\bkup and all file names will begin with Full. You should save the backup files on a server other than the SharePoint server to avoid the risk of total disaster in the event that the disk gets corrupted!

4. Enter any Backup comment you wish. This will help you later on to understand what type of backup this is.

5. In the left pane, expand Available components and then Portal sites. Select the URL for the current portal site. It will display the service options available for this portal, typically SITEDBS and INDEX.

6. Check both the SITEDBS and INDEX services. See also Figure 13-4 for an example.

7. Click the Backup button. This will start the backup process. The time it takes to run the backup is dependent on the data volume.

8. When the process is done, a dialog window will pop up that says "All backup operations completed successfully." Click OK to close this window.

9. Close the Spsbackup program.

Open the folder you entered in step 3. Look at the files this program generated. Their names depend on the file prefix defined in step 3. In this example you will find the following files:

```
Full.XML
Full-FilmPort1_SERV.SPB
Full-FilmPort1_PROF.SPB
Full-FilmPort1_SITE.SPB
Full-FilmPort1.SPB
```

All files of the type SPB contain data of some sort. Exactly what this type of file contains is described in more detail in Chapter 4. The file ending with .XML is called the *manifest file*. It contains information about how these SPB files relate to each other and to the SharePoint environment they belong to. When you later perform a restore from these files, it is the manifest file you will use. In other words, do not lose this file or it will be difficult or impossible to restore the data, even though the data will still exist.

Making Backups Using the Command-Line Interface

Spsbackup's graphical user interface is very nice when you want to run in interactive mode, but it cannot be used for scheduled tasks. However, the same program can also be used in command-line mode, as described earlier. To perform the same type of backup as in previous example, you do this:

Try It Out   **Run a Backup Using the Command-Line Interface**

1. Log on to the SharePoint server as the administrator.

2. Open a command prompt window and navigate to this folder:

```
C:\Program Files\SharePoint Portal Server\Bin
```

3. Type the following command line to start the backup process, using the fact that the default URL points to the portal site on this server:

```
Spsbackup /All /File C:\Bkup\Full /overwrite
```

4. Press Enter to activate the preceding command. It will not display any information about the current backup procedure; you need to check the destination folder to see that it works.

5. After verifying that the Spsbackup command works like expected, you can add this line to the Scheduled Task application, using the same steps as described for the Stsadm earlier in this chapter. Remember to open the properties for this task and add the exakt same Spsbackup command as listed in step 3 above.

If you compare the results from this command-line backup with the backup files from the graphical user interface, you can see that they are exactly the same. Basically, you can make a backup with the command-line interface and restore these files with the graphical interface. And this is the way you will do it, because the command-line interface does not allow you to restore files. It can only be done through the graphical interface.

Restore Procedures

Now you know how to make backups of the SharePoint data. You also know that some information such as customization of site definitions, CSS files, and XML files is not covered by the standard backup tools that SharePoint provides. These files need to be backed up with the usual file backup procedures (for example, the Windows Backup tool that comes free with Windows 2003 Server, also known as "NTBackup").

But the big question is how to restore data from these backups in the event of a disaster. The answer to that question depends on what you need to restore and what type of backup you have. Remember the first golden rule: "What you back up is what you can restore." If you only run Spsbackup and make full backups of the SharePoint environment, you cannot restore just a specific site or library from that backup set. In that event, you must first restore to a temporary server and then move the data to the production environment.

The following sections describe how to restore different types of data, such as single documents, a site collection, or a complete portal server. Remember that all these descriptions are based on the backup tools that come with SharePoint. Later in this chapter you learn more about what third-party backup tools can do.

Restoring a Single Item

This type of backup may sound simple but in fact may be the hardest one to perform. SharePoint 2003 does not have an undelete feature. This is a fact that you must take into account when planning your backup strategy. There are ways to restore single list items and single documents, but you must perform this recover following special steps, as shown in the following Try It Out. However, you cannot restore the complete version history for documents using these steps.

> **Rule #7: You can only restore the current version of a document.**

The only way to do a complete restore of a document including all its previous versions is to restore the complete site directly to the production environment (unless you are using any of the previously mentioned third-party tools such as XPlica, because they will allow you to restore the site to another location and then move the document including all its versions to the production site). Note that this operation will overwrite everything in this production site, so make sure this is okay first!

For example, say that one of your users accidentally deletes a document in one of the team sites. You check what backups you have and realize that you must use a temporary restore location, and then move the document from that location to the production site. In this example assume that you have previously prepared for this by creating a separate site collection with the URL address `http://filmportalen/sites/temp`. To restore the document, you then create a temporary subsite named projects under temp to be used in this restore process.

The way you restore backup files created with Smigrate is different than the other restore tools mentioned here. Before you can run the restore procedure, you must create an empty site (a site with no site template). In this example it is named "projects." A simple way of creating an empty site is to follow these steps:

Try It Out   Create a Site Without a Site Template

1. Log on as a user with permission to create a new team site.

2. Open the URL `http://filmportalen/sites/temp` and do the following:

   a. Choose Create⇨Sites and Workspaces.

   b. Enter any Title.

   c. Enter the URL name "projects" (the complete URL address will be `http://filmportalen/sites/temp/projects`).

   d. Click Create.

3. When asked to select a Site Template, abort this process! *Do not click OK;* just close the web browser or jump to another page. (If you happen to select a site template, you must then delete the site (see Chapters 2 and 3) and then repeat these steps.)

Now you have created a site without a template, and you can use it one time for restoring a backup performed with Smigrate.

Try It Out   **Restore a Single Document from an Smigrate Backup**

1. Find the latest backup file containing this document; in this example, this file is stored in `C:\Bkup\Projects.fwp`.

2. Because you have used Smigrate to back up individual sites, you just have to restore that site, but to a temporary site. (See the section about Smigrate earlier in this chapter about how to create a site without any site template.) In this example this site has the URL `http://filmportalen/sites/temp/projects`.

3. Open a command prompt window and enter the following:

```
Smigrate -r -w http://filmportalen/sites/temp/projects -f c:\bkup\projects.fwp
```

4. The temporary site is now active. Open this site in a web browser, locate the missing document, and copy it to the production site, as described in the section "Moving and Copying Information" earlier in this chapter.

5. When the document is restored to the production environment, this temporary site `projects` can safely be deleted.

What happens if the only backup you have is made by Stsadm? If so you can restore the complete site collection in this backup file to a new site collection in the production server and then move the data the same way as in the previous example. Follow these steps for this type of restore process:

Try It Out   **Restore a Single Document from an Stsadm Backup**

1. Find the latest backup file containing this document; in this example this file is stored in the backup for the site collection IT: `C:\Bkup\sites#it.spb`.

2. Because the backup file contains a complete site collection, you most likely don't want to restore this information back to the original name, but you can restore it to another site collection. However, you must first create a new content database that the restored site collection can use. In this example you will create the URL address `http://filmportalen/sites/restore`, which you later will overwrite with the backup file from Stsadm. Open a command prompt window and enter the following command (on one line):

```
Stsadm.exe -o createsiteinnewdb -url http://filmportalen/sites/restore ↩
-ownerlogin "contoso\administrator" -owneremail administrator@contoso.com
```

3. You now have a content database for restoring any site collection to the URL address above. The next step is to run the restore procedure: Open a command prompt and type (on one line):

```
Stsadm -o restore -url http://filmportalen/sites/restore -filename ↩
c:\bkup\sites#it.spb -overwrite
```

4. The temporary site collection is now active and has the exact same settings as the original site collection. Use a web browser and open the site in this collection where the document is stored, locate the missing document, and copy it to the production site, as described in the section "Moving and Copying Information" earlier in this chapter.

5. When the document is restored back to the production environment, this temporary site collection `projects` can safely be deleted. A quick way to do this is to use Stsadm (see the following line of code). Just make sure to delete the right site collection! Note that you don't need to delete this site collection; you can still restore new site collections to this site URL, as long as you use the switch `-overwrite` in step 3.

```
Stsadm -o deletesite -url http://filmportalen/sites/restore
```

The next time you need to restore a site collection, you don't have to create a content database first (you can omit step 2). It can be used to restore any site collection in the future.

What if you only have a backup set created with Spsbackup and need to restore a single document? This requires a separate server; there is no way to restore that information to a temporary location on the production server, as you could for Smigrate and Stsadm backups. Use the following steps to restore a single document from an Spsbackup:

Try It Out Restore a Single Document from a Backup Made with Spsbackup

1. Find a temporary server that you can use as a temporary SharePoint server. Note that you can use MS Virtual PC or VM-Ware when creating this server; it does not have to be a physical server.

2. Install the same SharePoint release, including service packs, as the production server. You can use a local SQL Server in this temporary environment, regardless of how the production server is configured. Make sure to install the MS SQL Server Client Tools and apply the same MS SQL Server service pack as in the production environment. Avoid using the same MS SQL Server as the production environment, because you may overwrite the production databases!

The temporary server doesn't need to have the same name as the production server!

3. Locate the latest backup files (in this example, in C:\Bkup).

4. Start SharePoint Portal Server Data Backup and Restore tool and then do this:

    a. Switch to the Restore tab.

    b. Use the Browse button and locate the manifest file (the backup file that ends with .XML).

    c. Expand the Available components in the left pane, and then click the URL address for this portal site. The services SITESDBS and INDEX will show up. (There may be more, for example, if you have installed the Single Sign-On feature.)

    d. Select the first service SITESDBS and click the Edit button. Make sure to enter the correct values for the IIS virtual server, URL, and database server. Click OK to close.

    e. Check Ready at the far left for SITEDBS.

    f. Select the next service INDEX and click Edit. Make sure the correct server name is selected. Click OK to close.

    g. Check Ready for INDEX.

    h. When all services are checked Ready, you can start the restore procedure by clicking the Restore button to the right of this page. You will be warned that existing data will be overwritten; click OK to accept. Now the restore procedure starts. Depending on how much data will be restored, this will take anywhere from one minute to one day.

    i. When the restore is done, close this tool.

5. Open the temporary SharePoint server; locate the file to be restored and move it using the steps listed earlier in the section "Moving and Copying Information."

Each of these three examples describes how to restore a single document. Use the same steps when restoring single pictures in image libraries, XML files in forms libraries, and single list items.

Restoring a Single Site

When you want to restore a single site, you follow almost the same steps as when restoring single items. The only difference is that you can restore directly to the production server if you have a backup of individual sites using Smigrate. If not, you must restore to a temporary storage location and then move the site. All scenarios are described in this section.

For example, say that you accidentally deleted the subsite `Projects` in the IT site collection and its URL was `http://filmportalen/sites/it/projects`. You must now restore that site including all its content. Depending on what type of backup you have available, you will follow different steps, as listed in the following Try It Out sections:

Try It Out   Restore a Single Site Using Smigrate Backups

1. Locate the backup file for this site (in this example, `C:\Bkup\projects.fwp`).

2. Because Smigrate requires a new site without a template, you must first create this site:

    a. Open the parent site for the site to be restored with a web browser.

    b. Choose Create⇨Sites and Workspaces.

    c. Enter any Title (it will later be replaced) but make sure to enter the correct URL name as the original site. Select the same type of User Permission as the original site.

    d. Click Create.

    e. On the Site Template page, click Abort! Jump back to any other page or close the browser.

3. Open a command prompt window and enter the following command.

    ```
    Smigrate -r -w http://filmportalen/sites/it/projects -f C:\bkup\projects.fwp
    ```

4. Open the restored site with a web browser; make sure to manually update all security settings. The site is now restored and ready to be used.

If you only have backup sets made with Stsadm, you cannot restore a single site, because the backup contains a complete site collection. In this case you must first create a temporary site collection, then use Smigrate to back up the site to be restored, and finally use the previous method.

Try It Out   Restore a Single Site Using Stsadm Backups

1. Find the latest backup set containing the site to be restored. In this example this site is stored in the backup for the site collection IT: `C:\Bkup\sites#it.spb`.

2. As described before, a site collection needs a new content database before it can be restored. If you have not done so before, open a command prompt and enter the following command. This will create a content database and associate it with the site collection `http://filmportalen/sites/restore`.

    ```
    Stsadm.exe -o createsiteinnewdb -url http://filmportalen/sites/restore↵
      -ownerlogin "contoso\administrator" -owneremail administrator@contoso.com
    ```

3. You now have a content database for restoring any site collection to the preceding URL address. The next step is to run the restore procedure. Open a command prompt and type the following (on one line):

```
Stsadm -o restore -url http://filmportalen/sites/restore -filename ⤶
c:\bkup\sites#it.spb -overwrite
```

4. The temporary site collection is now active and has the exact same settings as the original site collection. The next step is to make a backup of the site to be restored. Open a command prompt and type the following:

```
Smigrate -f c:\bkup\projects.fwp -w http://filmportalen/sites/restore/projects -e
```

5. Now you have a backup of the single site Projects. Follow the steps for restoring a single site using an Smigrate backup to copy it back to the production environment.

Finally, if all you have is a backup made by Spsbackup, you need to follow a similar procedure as the previous example: First restore the backup to a temporary SharePoint server; then make a backup with Smigrate of the single site to be restored, and then restore that site to the production environment.

Try It Out   Restore a Single Site Using Spsbackup Backups

1. Find a temporary server that you can use as a temporary SharePoint server. Note that you can use MS Virtual PC or VM-Ware when creating this server; it does not have to be a physical server. In this example this server is named restore-srv.

2. Install the same SharePoint release, including service packs, as the production server. You can use a local SQL Server in this temporary environment, regardless of how the production server is configured. Make sure to install the MS SQL Server Client Tools and apply the same MS SQL Server service pack as in the production environment.

3. Locate the latest backup files (in this example, in C:\Bkup).

4. Start the SharePoint Portal Server Data Backup and Restore tool and then do the following:

    a. Switch to the Restore tab.

    b. Use the Browse button and locate the manifest file (the backup file that ends with .XML).

    c. Expand the Available components in the left pane and then click the URL address for this portal site. The services SITESDBS and INDEX will show up. (There may be more, for example, if you have installed the Single Sign-On feature.)

    d. Select the first service SITESDBS and click the Edit button; make sure to enter the correct values for the IIS virtual server, URL, and database server. Click OK to close.

    e. Check Ready at the far left for SITEDBS.

    f. Select the next service INDEX and click Edit. Make sure the correct server name is selected. Click OK to close.

    g. Check Ready for INDEX.

    h. When all services are checked Ready, you can start the restore procedure by clicking the Restore button to the right of this page. You will be warned that existing data will be overwritten. Click OK to accept, and the restore procedure starts. Depending on how much data will be restored, this will take anywhere from one minute to one day.

    i. When the restore is done, close this tool.

5. Open the temporary SharePoint server and make sure it works.

6. Open a command prompt and run the following command to make a backup of the site to be restored:

```
Smigrate -f c:\bkup\projects.fwp -w http://restore-srv/sites/it/projects -e
```

7. Now you have a backup of the single site Projects. Follow the steps described earlier for restoring a single site using an Smigrate backup to copy it back to the production environment.

Restoring a Single Site Collection

If you need to restore a complete site collection, you need a backup by Stsadm or Spsbackup. You can also restore the data in case you only have Smigrate backups, as long as you have a backup of all sites in that site collection, but you need to manually reconfigure all security settings. This section focuses on the scenarios where you have Stsadm or Spsbackup backups available.

For example, say you accidentally delete the complete site collection http://filmportalen/sites/it. You must now restore it. Depending on what type of backup files you have available, you will follow one of these procedures:

Try It Out   Recover a Site Collection Using Stsadm

1. Find the latest backup set containing the site to be restored. In this example this site is stored in the backup for the site collection IT: C:\Bkup\sites#it.spb.

2. Because you need to restore the complete site collection, you can do it directly to the production server. Open a command prompt and enter the following:

```
Stsadm -o restore -url http://filmportalen/sites/it ⤸
-filename c:\bkup\sites#it.spb -overwrite
```

This was simple, because the backup set contained exactly what you needed to restore.

If you only have a backup made with Spsbackup, you first need to restore the complete portal site to a temporary server, then make a backup of that site collection, and finally restore that site collection to the production server.

Try It Out   Recover a Site Collection Using Spsbackup

1. Find a temporary server that you can use as a temporary SharePoint server. Note that you can use MS Virtual PC or VM-Ware when creating this server; it does not have to be a physical server. In this example this server is named restore-srv.

2. Install the same SharePoint release, including service packs, as the production server. You can use a local SQL Server in this temporary environment, regardless of how the production server is configured. Make sure to install the MS SQL Server Client Tools and apply the same MS SQL Server service pack as in the production environment.

3. Locate the latest backup files (in this example, in C:\Bkup).

4. Start the SharePoint Portal Server Data Backup and Restore tool and then do the following:

   a. Switch to the Restore tab.

   b. Use the Browse button and locate the manifest file (the backup file that ends with .XML).

   c. Expand the Available components in the left pane and then click the URL address for this portal site. The services SITESDBS and INDEX will show up. (There may be more, for example, if you have installed the Single Sign-On feature.)

   d. Select the first service SITESDBS and click the Edit button. Make sure to enter the correct values for the IIS virtual server, URL, and database server. Click OK to close.

   e. Check Ready at the far left for SITEDBS.

   f. Select the next service INDEX and click Edit. Make sure the correct server name is selected. Click OK to close.

   g. Check Ready for INDEX.

   h. When all services are checked Ready, you can start the restore procedure by clicking the Restore button to the right of this page. You will be warned that existing data will be overwritten. Click OK to accept and now the restore procedure starts. Depending on how much data will be restored, this will take anywhere from one minute to one day.

   i. When the restore is done, close this tool.

5. Open the temporary SharePoint server and make sure it works.

6. Open a command prompt and run the following command to make a backup of the site to be restored:

```
Stsadm -o backup -url http://restore-srv/sites/it/ -filename c:\bkup\IT.spb
```

7. Now you have a backup of the site collection IT. Because you need to restore a complete site collection, you can do it directly to the production server. Open a command prompt and enter the following:

```
Stsadm -o restore -url http://filmportalen/sites/it ↵
-filename c:\bkup\IT.spb -overwrite
```

Restoring a Complete Portal Server

The final scenario is when you have lost a complete SPS portal site and need to get it back fast. This requires that you have a backup set made by Spsbackup. Neither of the other two tools (Smigrate or Stsadm) will work because they cannot back up portal sites. However, using other tools such as the MS SQL Server backup or third-party backup solutions for SharePoint will also work, and they are described later in this chapter.

For example, say you have a portal with the URL http://filmportalen. It contains a large number of WSS sites as well. Something happens and the portal gets corrupted beyond repair. Now you must restore the complete SharePoint environment. Luckily you have a full backup made with Spsbackup last night. Restore it by following these steps:

Try It Out Restore a Complete SharePoint Environment Using Spsbackup

1. Install the same SharePoint release, including service packs, on the same server. Make sure to install MS SQL Server Client Tools and apply the same MS SQL Server service pack as in the production environment.

2. Locate the latest backup files (in this example, in C:\Bkup).

3. Start the SharePoint Portal Server Data Backup and Restore tool and then follow these steps:

    a. Switch to the Restore tab.

    b. Use the Browse button and locate the manifest file (the backup file that ends with .XML).

    c. Expand the Available components in the left pane and then click the URL address for this portal site. The services SITESDBS and INDEX will show up. (There may be more, for example, if you have installed the Single Sign-On feature.)

    d. Select the first service SITESDBS and click the Edit button. Make sure to enter the correct values for the IIS virtual server, URL, and database server. Click OK to close.

    If the fields for database file names are empty, the old databases might still exist in the SQL database. Use SQL Enterprise Manager and delete all the old databases before you restore them again using the same names.

    e. Check Ready at the far left for SITEDBS.

    f. Select the next service INDEX and click Edit. Make sure the correct server name is selected. Click OK to close.

    g. Check Ready for INDEX.

    h. When all services are checked Ready, you can start the restore procedure by clicking the Restore button to the right of this page. You will be warned that existing data will be overwritten. Click OK to accept and the restore procedure starts. Depending on how much data will be restored, this will take anywhere from one minute to one day.

    i. When the restore is done, close this tool.

4. Open the restored portal server and make sure it works.

The important thing to remember when restoring complete portals is that SharePoint will not allow you to restore the portal as long as the old portal exists. The Spsbackup tool will tell you if this is the case. If so, you must first remove the remains of the old portal using the following steps before restoring it from the backup set:

Do not follow these steps unless you really want to delete the portal site!

1. Log on as an administrator to the SharePoint server.

2. Choose Start➪All Programs➪SharePoint Portal Server➪SharePoint Central Administration.

3. Click List and manage portal sites.

4. Hover with the mouse to the right of the current portal; use its quick menu and select Delete Portal Sites.

5. Check Delete all databases and click OK. Now this portal and all its WSS sites will be completely removed.

Your SharePoint server is now ready to be restored, following the steps from the previous list.

Making a Backup Plan

A backup plan is very important and something you should make before using SharePoint in a production environment. Exactly how this plan should look depends on a lot of parameters, like these:

❑   Which SharePoint edition are you using? Stand-alone WSS or WSS including SPS?

❑   How important is the data stored in SharePoint?

❑   Which sites will be most important to protect?

❑   How often are the sites updated?

The description you get here is just general guidelines that you can follow to make your own backup plan. Remember the statement at the beginning of this chapter: If you don't regularly verify that the backups are being properly made, you cannot be sure that your backup plan is working! It is very important that you run fire drills now and then, to see that you actually can restore data. I suggest that you do a test every month and verify that you and your fellow SharePoint administrators can do a restore of the following:

❑   A single document.

❑   A single site.

❑   A site collection.

❑   The complete portal environment (if you are running SPS).

Use the following guidelines to write your own backup plan:

1.   Document your SharePoint environment, such as:

   a.   The name of the SharePoint Server(s).

   b.   The name of the MS SQL Server.

   c.   The URL for the SharePoint environment.

   d.   The IIS settings (virtual server and application pool settings).

   e.   The Search and Index settings (if SPS).

   f.   The Audience groups (if SPS).

   g.   Any customization of the User Profile settings (if SPS).

   h.   The security settings for the portal site areas (if SPS).

   i.   All customization of portal sites (if SPS).

   j.   A list of all site collections and their owners.

   k.   Any non-default configuration settings of SharePoint.

   l.   A list of all added web parts, including where you found them.

   m.   A description of all modified SharePoint files, such as ASPX, CSS, and XML files.

2.   Decide if and when to run Smigrate to protect important sites (such as your boss's site), thus making it very easy and fast to restore specific sites and items.

3. Decide if and when to run Stsadm to make it easier to restore site collections, sites, and specific items.

4. Decide how often to run a full backup using Spsbackup. Once per night is the recommended frequency.

5. Decide where to store the backup files, and whether you should overwrite them every time or move them to another location before the next backup process runs.

6. Decide how often to run a file backup on the SharePoint server, including a System State backup that also covers the IIS Metabase. This will make it possible to recover from a complete disk crash.

7. Document the restore procedures and who is responsible for them, including the responsible people's contact information.

8. Document the fire drills: what to test, how often to run them, and who is responsible for them.

I am sure you can think of more things to describe in this backup plan. Just remember that this is a "living" document; it needs to be constantly updated (for example, whenever you add a new web part, change any configuration settings, or create new site collections).

The first place you might think of to store this backup plan is of course in SharePoint, but this is not a good idea because you will need it in the event of a SharePoint disaster. Make sure to have not one but at least two copies of this backup plan in different locations in case of fire or flooding and similar disasters. You should also have this plan stored in various ways (on hard drives, on disks, even printed out) for the greatest possible flexibility when you need it.

Third-Party Backup Tools

Lots of alternatives are available for the backup tools that come with SharePoint; both specific SharePoint backup programs, and SharePoint agents for general backup applications. The difference between these two types is that specific backup programs do one thing only: create backups of SharePoint (although they do usually have a lot of options for restoring the data, such as restoring a site, a list, or a single document). The backup agent used by general backup programs often has just a few restore options, such as a complete restore of the portal, a site collection, or a single site. They will often make it easier to perform backups and in some cases make it possible to restore things that SharePoint cannot restore by itself, such as the complete version history for a document.

The purpose of this section is to give you a general overview of these third-party tools to make you aware that they exist and how they can be a useful alternative to SharePoint's own tools. This is not a complete list of everything that is available. You will discover that there are many other wonderful tools out there as well.

General Backup Agents

Practically all popular backup applications available today know how to back up SharePoint sites besides the file system, MS Exchange, and other applications. Generally, you will need to purchase a special "SharePoint Agent" to enable these applications to back up and restore SharePoint information. Following is a table with the most common backup tools, their SharePoint implementation compatibility, and their restore capabilities:

Backup Programs	SharePoint Agents	Comments
Veritas BackupExec	For WSS and SPS 2003	Can restore single sites, site collections, and portal sites
Veritas NetBackup	For WSS and SPS 2003	Can restore single sites, site collections, and portal sites
Commvaults Galaxy	For WSS and SPS 2003	Can restore sites, site collections, portal sites, and individual documents
SynSort Backup Express	For WSS and SPS 2003	Can restore sites, site collections, and portal sites
Brightstore ArcServe	For WSS and SPS 2003	Can restore sites, site collections, and portal sites

Note that only one of these general backup products allows you to restore individual documents, but none of them allow you to restore the document's version history or web discussions, list items, or entire lists. To get this type of functionality, you need to look at backup tools specifically designed for SharePoint, such as DocAve and NSE tools, which are discussed in the following sections.

MS SQL Backup Tools

Because SharePoint is using MS SQL as data storage, it is only natural to think about using the standard backup tools for MS SQL for SharePoint backups. And this is definitely possible. You can use these SQL tools for SharePoint data. But there are some things you need to be aware of:

❑ MS SQL Enterprise Manager only comes with MS SQL 2000 Server, not MSDE or WMSDE. You therefore need a special tool for backups of those two database types.

❑ When using SQL backup tools, you must restore all databases in the event of data loss. In other words, you cannot restore a single site or site collection. Only a complete restore is possible with these tools.

❑ SQL backup tools does not back up files on the SharePoint server, such as the Search and Index files. You may still need to use another backup tool as a complement.

❑ When using Spsbackup you don't need to use SQL backup tools. All SharePoint data in the SQL database is secured by SharePoint's own tool, and it works for MSDE databases too.

It is easy to solve the first issue: Several tools on the market can be used for backing up MSDE and WMSDE databases, such as CiberSQL, Laplas Soft, and MSDE.biz. You can find a list on Microsoft's web site for SQL partners:

```
http://www.microsoft.com/sql/msde/partners
```

The remaining issues in the preceding list are harder to solve. I recommend that you combine any SQL-based backup tool with one or more of the SharePoint tools, like Stsadm and Smigrate, to enable you to restore single items, lists, or sites when needed. Today the hardware is most often very reliable and there is very seldom a disk crash. Almost all recovery situations are about restoring single documents, list items, or sometimes complete lists, and the SQL Backup tool does not help you with that. The biggest advantage with SQL backups is that they back up all data in the SQL Server, including SharePoint's databases. So it is convenient when doing backups, but it is not the best solution when it is time for a restore.

AvePoint Tools

One of the absolute first vendors that developed backup solutions specifically for SharePoint was AvePoint (http://www.avepoint.com). Its main product DocAve is today one of the most popular tools, because of its very advanced restore options. It is often recommended by Microsoft as the solution for organizations that require a way to recover single documents including the complete version history. Note that DocAve by itself is not a substitute for a complete SharePoint backup. Its objective is to offer the administrator the ability to restore the following objects to their original location or to another SharePoint farm:

❑ Restore a single document, including all its previous versions and web discussions.

❑ Restore a specific version of a document instead of all versions.

❑ Restore a single list item.

❑ Restore a single list or library.

❑ Restore a single site.

❑ Restore a single personal site.

❑ Restore a single portal area.

The current version of DocAve does not back up the complete SharePoint structure, so you still need to use a tool like Spsbackup, a SQL backup tool, or DocAve's own SharePoint Disaster Recovery tool. However, because DocAve protects all data, it most likely is enough to run tools like Spsbackup once per week or even once per month, depending on how often you change the structure of your SharePoint environment. The SharePoint Disaster Recovery tool replicates the complete SharePoint environment to another server; if a total disaster happens, you simply rebuild the basic structure on the old server and click the Recover button, and all data is replicated back to that server again.

There is also a very handy complement to DocAve called TrashBin that allows a user to undelete any document, list item, or list directly from within the site, without any assistance from the administrator. TrashBin uses the backups made by DocAve, which gives the user the same type of restore options as the administrator (all the options previously listed). Compare that to other Undelete tools that cannot restore documents deleted from the file system or using the Explorer View. This is no problem for TrashBin.

NSE Tools

Another company that focuses on SharePoint backups is NSE (http://www.nse.com) with its product SPManager. It is also a complete backup solution for SharePoint environments, both WSS and SPS. It has been around for several years now and is easy to use for both backup and restore tasks. The main uses of SPManager are these:

❑ Restore single documents.

❑ Restore single list items.

❑ Restore web parts.

❑ Restore single sites.

❑ Restore complete SharePoint environments.

All these restore operations can be performed on the original SharePoint server or on another SharePoint server. This can also be used as a migration tool or when you need to create a test environment of your production server.

Summary

In this chapter you learned the following:

❑ You should follow the rules for backing up and restoring:

Rule #1: What you back up is what you can restore!

Rule #2: Make sure all of SharePoint's databases are backed up.

Rule #3: Make sure to back up the file system and the IIS Metabase on the front-end servers.

Rule #4: You can only copy the latest version of a document, not its complete version history.

Rule #5: A template for a list or library can only contain up to 10 MB of content.

Rule #6: Use Excel for moving or copying lists greater than 10 MB.

Rule #7: You can only restore the current version of a document.

❑ You should know the following things about Stsadm:

❑ Stsadm can only back up and restore complete site collections.

❑ Stsadm is a full-fidelity backup. All settings, including users and rights, will be restored.

❑ Use STSAdmWin-2Go for a graphical user interface for Stsadm.

❑ You should know the following things about Smigrate:

❑ Smigrate can back up a single site, or a site including all subsites.

❑ Smigrate is not a full-fidelity backup. You must manually re-create some settings, such as the user permissions and personal site views.

❑ Use GUI Smigrate for a graphical user interface for Smigrate.

❑ You should know the following things about Spsbackup:

❑ Spsbackup will create a backup script for all modified site collections.

❑ Spsbackup will back up the complete SPS farm, including all WSS team sites.

❑ Spsbackup is a full-fidelity backup tool. It will restore everything in the SQL database and all index files.

❑ Spsbackup can be used as a graphical tool or as a command-line utility.

❑ Use Windows built-in "Scheduled Tasks" to schedule Stsadm, Smigrate, or Spsbackup backups.

❑ Make sure to devise a Backup Plan, also known as a Disaster Recovery Plan.

❑ Do fire drills to make sure the backups are working and that you know how to do a restore.

❑ For easier recovery procedures and a way to restore single items including version history, look at third-party backup tools that focus on SharePoint.

In the next chapter you learn more about what is new in SharePoint 2007.

SharePoint 2007

SharePoint 2007 is being released together with MS Office 2007, which continues to grow with new products. It is very exciting from a SharePoint perspective because all these Office products and a number of other Microsoft products either use SharePoint as the preferred database for storing information or integrate with SharePoint in a seamless way. In short, you have made a smart choice to start working with SharePoint now, because the time and effort you invest now will be rewarded as the foundation you build on becomes upgraded in the future. Those organizations that haven't yet seen the light will have a lot more to learn, because Microsoft will make SharePoint a necessity for getting the most out of at least 15 new or updated programs.

One way of looking at SharePoint is to compare it with MS Exchange Server: This mail server is the foundation for the advanced e-mail and calendar functionality in products such as MS Outlook, MS SharePoint, all typical MS Office products like Word and Excel, and the list goes on. MS Exchange is designed by Microsoft to be the primary messaging tool for all Microsoft products. If you choose another mail server, you will lose a lot functionality and integration. SharePoint 2003 is designed in the same way; it is already today extending the functionality of a lot of products, and in the next release it is mandatory for releasing the full power of a lot of programs. Where MS Exchange is the primary communication vehicle, MS SharePoint is the primary system for working with and sharing information of all kinds.

This final chapter describes some of the most important features in SharePoint 2007 and what you can do to prepare for this version. As of this writing, MS Office 2007 (with SharePoint as a member) is not yet released, so the information here is based on the beta material. Still, the information in this chapter focuses on features that most likely will be available in the final version of SharePoint 2007.

Although SharePoint 2007 introduces many interesting new features, a lot of organizations will be happily running SharePoint 2003 for several years to come. After all, it is always an investment in money and time to upgrade to a new version, which must be balanced against an organization's needs and available resources. If you don't need the new features in SharePoint 2007, you should ask yourself if it is worth the investment to upgrade at this time.

Why a New Version?

My hope is that after reading this book, you will not walk, but run, to the server room and install SharePoint 2003! It has so many great features and it will empower every computer user, especially those running MS Office 2003. So why would Microsoft create a new version? There are several reasons for this:

- ❑ SharePoint can benefit even more from some important features, like these:
    - ❑ A workflow engine.
    - ❑ A way to limit the number of versions stored.
    - ❑ The ability to store partial documents when saving previous versions.
    - ❑ An easy way to customize web forms for entering data.
    - ❑ A built-in replication engine between a client and the server.
    - ❑ An undelete feature.
    - ❑ Support for automatically adjusting the language of a site.
    - ❑ SPS support for the new features in MS SQL 2005.
    - ❑ Seamless integration between SPS and WSS.
- ❑ Fifteen new or updated Microsoft programs can use new features in SharePoint.
- ❑ Users want even more enhanced features. Their appetite is growing for things like these:
    - ❑ Improved document management features.
    - ❑ More support for sharing information with external partners.
    - ❑ Improved replication features.

For several years creative people have run companies focusing on enhancing SharePoint in these ways. So whatever need you may have today, it seems there is at least one product that can fulfill that need. Still, in many cases it is best for Microsoft to enhance SharePoint itself. For us customers it means that Microsoft knows the solution works with other MS products and is supported. Besides, some of these features should have been built-in from the start, to be honest.

Of course Microsoft is aware of the areas where improvements can be made. Microsoft has talked with a lot of customers; they are reading blogs and news discussions on the Internet, and they do a lot of internal research. Don't forget that Microsoft is one of the world's largest SharePoint users. Microsoft knows very well how SharePoint works and what can be done to make it better. But they also wanted to build the greatest engine for an information system the world has seen, at least for users running the other MS Office products. So instead of releasing new service packs with enhanced SharePoint features, Microsoft decided to rewrite a large part of SharePoint in order to meet or exceed the expectations from the user community, and the result is SharePoint 2007.

The Next Generation

This section describes the overall picture of the new MS Office Server products, and especially the new SharePoint release. The objective here is to show you what to expect in general to help you prepare for the next generation of Microsoft products and to give you a good idea of new features in SharePoint. Following is a list of the new or updated products that are being released during 2007:

- ❏ MS Windows SharePoint Service 2007
- ❏ MS Office SharePoint Server 2007
- ❏ MS Word 2007
- ❏ MS Excel 2007
- ❏ MS PowerPoint 2007
- ❏ MS Access 2007
- ❏ MS Outlook 2007
- ❏ MS Publisher 2007
- ❏ MS InfoPath 2007
- ❏ MS OneNote 2007
- ❏ MS Project Server 2007
- ❏ MS Office Project Portfolio Server 2007
- ❏ MS SharePoint Designer 2007
- ❏ MS Expression Web Designer 2007
- ❏ MS Content Manager Server 2007
- ❏ MS Office Groove 2007
- ❏ MS Visio 2007
- ❏ MS Office Forms Server 2007

And several interesting products were released at the end of 2005, such as MS SQL Server 2005, MS Dynamics CRM 3.0, MS Communicator, and MS Business Scorecard Manager. As you can see from this list, Microsoft has been very busy. Its challenge is not only to develop new versions of software, but to make them integrate with other products and especially SharePoint. So now it's just up to you to learn all these products. But then again, how hard can it be, right?

One of Microsoft's top priorities for the new version of SharePoint is improved performance. As good as performance is with SharePoint 2003, all initial tests indicate that SharePoint 2007 performs even better. As long as you follow the recommended guidelines for building a SharePoint farm (see Chapters 2 and 4) the performance with SharePoint 2007 will surpass even what you have today, which is especially important for large organizations with large farms.

The MS Office 2007 Suites

Due to the increased number of products, the number of MS Office Suites is growing to seven. With the new version of Office, you can choose between the packages listed in the following section. All of them can use either MS Office SharePoint Server 2007 or MS Windows SharePoint Services 2007. The new features in SharePoint 2007 are integrated into the Office 2007 products when appropriate, but you can still use a web browser to take advantage of most of these features if you are running pre-Office 2007 applications.

Microsoft Office Enterprise 2007

This is a completely new package that focuses on sharing and collaboration both inside the company and with external partners. It consists of the following products:

- ❏ Microsoft Office Excel 2007
- ❏ Microsoft Office Outlook 2007
- ❏ Microsoft Office PowerPoint 2007
- ❏ Microsoft Office Word 2007
- ❏ Microsoft Office Access 2007
- ❏ Microsoft Office InfoPath 2007
- ❏ Microsoft Office Communicator 2005
- ❏ Microsoft Office Publisher 2007
- ❏ Microsoft Office OneNote 2007
- ❏ Microsoft Office Groove 2007
- ❏ Solutions for Enterprise Content Management, and Rights Management Service

Microsoft Office Professional Plus 2007

This is an upgraded version of the suite with the same name. It consists of the following products:

- ❏ Microsoft Office Excel 2007
- ❏ Microsoft Office Outlook 2007
- ❏ Microsoft Office PowerPoint 2007
- ❏ Microsoft Office Word 2007
- ❏ Microsoft Office Access 2007
- ❏ Microsoft Office InfoPath 2007
- ❏ Microsoft Office Communicator 2005
- ❏ Microsoft Office Publisher 2007
- ❏ Solutions for Enterprise Content Management, and Rights Management Service

Microsoft Office Professional 2007

This is also an upgraded version of the previous suite with the same name and consists of these products:

- ❏ Microsoft Office Excel 2007
- ❏ Microsoft Office Outlook 2007
- ❏ Microsoft Office PowerPoint 2007
- ❏ Microsoft Office Word 2007
- ❏ Microsoft Office Access 2007

❑   Microsoft Office Publisher 2007

❑   Microsoft Office Outlook 2007

Microsoft Office Small Business 2007

This version is focusing on smaller organizations and consists of these products:

❑   Microsoft Office Excel 2007

❑   Microsoft Office Outlook 2007

❑   Microsoft Office PowerPoint 2007

❑   Microsoft Office Word 2007

❑   Microsoft Office Publisher 2007

❑   Microsoft Office Outlook 2007

Microsoft Office Standard 2007

This is a very basic Office suite and consists of these programs:

❑   Microsoft Office Excel 2007

❑   Microsoft Office Outlook 2007

❑   Microsoft Office PowerPoint 2007

❑   Microsoft Office Word 2007

Microsoft Office Home and Student 2007

This is a suite especially targeting the home market and students; it consists of these programs:

❑   Microsoft Office Excel 2007

❑   Microsoft Office PowerPoint 2007

❑   Microsoft Office Word 2007

❑   Microsoft Office OneNote 2007

Microsoft Office Basic 2007

This is the most basic Office suite and consists of these programs:

❑   Microsoft Office Excel 2007

❑   Microsoft Office Outlook 2007

❑   Microsoft Office Word 2007

The "Enterprise Content Management," or ECM, that is included in the first two packages listed above is referring to a much more advanced management of information than anything preceding it. For example, it allows an organization to define a policy that will move documents older than 6 months to a secondary archive or to delete e-mail from a given resource after 1 year. The ECM is dependent on features of SharePoint 2007.

All of these products have a bunch of new features, not the least of which is the completely redesigned user interface for Word, Excel, Power Point, and Outlook. For more details and examples of the new look-and-feel for these products, be sure to check out Jensen Harris's blog:

```
http://blogs.msdn.com/jensenh/default.aspx
```

Jensen is the Lead Program Manager on the Microsoft Office "User Experience" team, and he describes a lot of background information about the new interface. One of the reasons for this dramatic change to the user interface is interesting. Up until this time, most of the requests that Microsoft received for new features in Office products were features that already existed! It was obvious that the current user interface did not work very well if people wanted features and didn't realize they already had them. For a long time, Microsoft has been evaluating a number of different look-and-feel designs, both internally and with external customers, in its usability labs. The result is what you will see in Office 2007. It may look strange at first, but it will make it much easier for users to find the features they need. Bill Gates told the audience at the MS Office Developer Conference 2006 that "the learning curve is about 20 minutes," but his colleague Steven Sinofsky (Senior Vice President, Office) said that he thinks it will take about one day. Do you remember Windows 3.1 and your reaction when moving on to Windows 95 and then going to Windows XP? Most people had a hard time finding things on the new interface, but if you return to any of the previous versions, I am pretty sure you will wonder how on earth you ever could work with the old interface.

Early in 2005 Microsoft acquired the company Groove from the former founder of Lotus Notes, Ray Ozzie. The Groove product is known for its excellent replication features, allowing a team of users to share and collaborate on documents, contacts, calendars, and other types of information. Every user in the Groove workspace has their own copy of the information, and Groove takes responsibility for replicating any updates to all other members in this workspace. This replication mechanism is now available in SharePoint 2007 and enables any team to collaborate using SharePoint sites, regardless of whether they have access to the local SharePoint environment. The replication feature of Groove is not relying on Active Directory accounts, so it is possible to share the information with people outside your organization, without creating new user accounts for these external users.

Windows SharePoint Services

WSS 2007, also known as WSS 3.0, contains a ton of features, including enhancements of existing features in WSS 2003 and completely new features. This section describes some of these features.

Enhanced User Interface

WSS 2003 is easy to use, but there is always room for improvement. Some of the enhanced features of the new user interface in WSS 2007 are these:

❑ **Current user:** The name of the current user is always displayed at the top of the page. There is also a drop-down menu that allows you to temporarily log on as another user. This is perfect when you want to view how a site layout will be displayed for a non-administrator. When you log out as that user (using the same menu), the previous user account will be activated.

❑ **Permission-aware links:** If a user is not allowed to see a list or use a specific link, it will be hidden. For example, a user with read access will not see any links for changing the settings for the site. The same is also true for lists and libraries; a user without at least read access to a list will not see the name of this list in the quick launch bar. This also works for menus; it will only show the actions the current user is allowed to use.

❏ **Design Mode:** Instead of having a list of web part galleries to the right and the web part zones to the left, you will now see only web part zones on a site page in the design mode. At the top of each zone is a link named "Add web part"; click this and you will see all available web parts.

❏ **Administration:** The former layout of administrative pages in WSS 2003, with one start page for the Site Settings that lead to another page, that also lead to another page, and so on, is now gone. Instead you will see one page with a lot of links, organized into columns based on focus and activity (see the following list). Select the link you want to modify and that page is displayed. It is much easier and faster to find what you are looking for.

 ❏ **User and Permission:** Add and manage users and permissions.

 ❏ **Look and Feel:** Configure the layout of the site and its lists.

 ❏ **Galleries:** List all web parts, site templates, and list templates.

 ❏ **Site Administration:** Configure the current site.

 ❏ **Site Collection Administration:** Configure the complete site collection.

❏ **Create a site:** WSS 2003 requires at least two pages to create a site (or three, if you create the site from the portal site). With WSS 2007 all these settings are aggregated into one single page, which gives you a better overview and makes it faster to create a new WSS site.

❏ **Bread-crumb trail:** All pages now have a bread-crumb trail at the top. It shows the user exactly what page he is using and how it relates to others in the site hierarchy. It is also easy to jump to any previous page; just click any of the links in the bread-crumb trail and that page opens.

❏ **Navigation:** WSS 2007 allows the administrator of the site to choose what type of navigation view to use for a given site. For example, you can choose to see only the lists and libraries in the current site (much like the view of WSS 2003), or you can display a site hierarchy that will display the sites above and below the current site.

❏ **Menus:** The layout of the page connected to a list or library is also enhanced. The "New Item" button in WSS 2003 is now a drop-down menu that lists the options available. For example, when looking at a Task list page, it will have a new menu called "Actions" that contains options such as these:

 ❏ Edit in datasheet

 ❏ Open in Outlook

 ❏ Export to Excel

 ❏ Create Visio diagram

 ❏ View RSS Feed

 ❏ Alert me

❏ **RSS Feeds:** This is a new and very smart feature that is an alternative to creating alerts. For example, say that you want to keep track of what is happening with a list of tasks. If you use the Actions menu and its option "View RSS Feed," it will create a folder in your Outlook that automatically will synchronize with this task list. This will make it possible for you to keep track of any modifications just by reading this list under the "RSS Subscriptions" folder in Outlook (online or offline). This new feature is one of my personal favorites in WSS 2007.

❏ **Filtering:** Instead of opening a new page for filtering and sorting a list, all column headers now have a drop-down menu that allows the user to define a filter. The result is a very fast and intuitive layout.

❑ **Customize Quick Launch:** It is now possible to add or change the menus listed on the quick launch menu without FrontPage. This increases the ways a user who creates a site can customize it to suit his needs, without any extra tools or assistance.

❑ **Mobile View:** There is a new view adjusted for small devices such as Personal Digital Assistants (PDAs), smart phones, and other devices that can browse Internet pages. The URL address to this view is `http://<SharePoint server>/m` ("m" as in "mobile"). You can also define how each list and library will look like when using this view. There is a new section for mobile display in the settings for the list where you configure how this particular list will look.

Document Management

Among the enhancements for WSS 2007 are much stronger document management features. For example it will be possible to define how the version history will work. Either you can have it as it works in WSS 2003, using a time and date stamp, or you can define a version history based on "Major" and "Minor" versioning numbers (getting document versions like 2.1 and 6.3, where the number to the left of the decimal point (6) is the major version number and the number to the right (3) is the minor number).

Another important change is that you can ask SharePoint to save just a limited number of versions. WSS 2003 either doesn't save any version at all or saves every version. Although there are scripts to be found on the Internet that will delete all versions except the most recent five, for example, it will be much easier when you can define a document library to save only the five most recent versions automatically.

Every version of a document in SharePoint 2003 is a complete document. In other words, if you have a 1-MB document and change one letter, SharePoint 2003 stores another 1 MB again. This is not the best way to use your disk resources, but it makes it easy to go back to previous version. In WSS 2007 Microsoft has changed this so only the modification is saved (the modified letter in this example). This dramatically lowers the load on the disk server.

With SharePoint 2007 it is possible to define individual security settings for documents, which many users have asked for. It is also possible to define how SharePoint treats documents that are checked out. You can select among these options:

❑ Everyone with read access to this document can see the draft.

❑ Everyone with write access to this document can see the draft.

❑ Only users with Approval permission can see this draft.

In WSS 2003, you set the security for the document library, and these settings apply to all documents in that library. The result is that you create one separate document library for each specific security setting needed. Although in practice this feature for individual security settings is not used so much (just look at a file system), it is still an important feature that is appreciated by many.

WSS 2007 has the same options for checking out and checking in documents as in WSS 2003, with one exception: It is now possible to enforce that a document must be checked out before it is edited. Users of the old SPS 2001 will recognize this setting, because it was mandatory in that version. In WSS 2003 you can switch this setting on or off, as appropriate.

If you use Outlook 2007, you can also replicate a document library to the client. This gives the user access to these documents when offline. If the user changes a document, it is not automatically synchronized back to SharePoint's document library; but the user can manually check in this document.

Everything described here is also valid for document libraries in the new Office SharePoint Server (OSS). With the new OSS you also get a lot of exciting new features regarding enterprise content management; read more details about that in the OSS section.

Enhanced Lists Features

In WSS 2003 you can create list for storing information, such as Tasks or Contacts. It is also possible to track changes and activities in these lists by creating alerts, either for a specific item or for the complete list. In WSS 2007 this functionality has been enhanced with these features:

❑ **Item versioning:** Just like for document libraries, now lists also keep track of changes made to them. This is a very important feature for many types of lists where it is important to see who made a change and when.

❑ **Append-only fields:** Now you can create a field in the list that users can use only for appending data, not modifying or deleting it.

❑ **Workflow:** The new workflow engine that comes with SharePoint 2007 can be used for building applications that trigger on modified or added items in the list.

❑ **Individual permissions:** The same types of individual permissions available for document libraries in WSS 2007 (as described earlier in this chapter) are now also available for lists.

❑ **Alerts:** It is now possible to define the exact time for when you want these alerts. You can define in greater detail exactly what will trigger the alert. You can also configure the list to send alerts to other users than yourself.

❑ **E-mail enabled:** Every list can now have an e-mail address associated with it.

The new item versioning feature not only stores who and when an item was modified; it also stores what was modified. For example, say that you have a contact list for customers and somebody changes the office phone number for a customer. Using the new versioning feature, it is now possible to see who did the change, when it was done, and that it was the office number that was changed. This type of auditing also opens up a lot of interesting possibilities for building smart applications without any coding.

The Append-only feature makes it possible to add information to a field but not change the content already stored there. Again, using the Helpdesk application as an example, you can create a field for comments where different people at the Helpdesk department type in what they have done; all these comments are stored in the same field, along with the name and date of the author.

These new features are now a core part of all types of lists in WSS 2007, and they make it possible to build a smart tracking application that uses a list as a repository for the data without any code. For example, you can build a Helpdesk application where a user can fill in an issue report, which will trigger the workflow to send an e-mail to the Helpdesk department, where they can see and update fields that the user could not use. Microsoft will even ship an Issue Tracking list template to make it really easy to get started with this type of application. The MS Access developer team at Microsoft has even created a tracking template that will interact with this Issue Tracking list, so you can use MS Access as a front-end for applications using this tracking list.

To e-mail–enable a list, you use the same page for this list as all other configuration settings; SharePoint automatically creates this e-mail address in Active Directory, and you can use a specific Organizational Unit for these addresses, if needed. If you later delete this list, the e-mail address also gets deleted. This feature makes it possible to send an e-mail directly to any type of list, including document library lists. Users of Public Folders in MS Outlook and MS Exchange environments will recognize this feature; it works exactly like an e-mail–enabled public folder. An example of when this feature can be very handy is in a project where you also want to save important e-mail conversations along with project documents. Another example is to create events in a SharePoint Calendar by inviting the e-mail address for this list when creating this invitation in Outlook. This way you can have a calendar in SharePoint that shows all the project meetings.

> *Using Visual Studio it is easy to extend the e-mail features of lists to automatically map properties in the message to list columns. You can find more information on how to do this in MSDN for the WSS 2007 release.*

Workflows

Ever since SharePoint 2003 was released in October 2003, there has been one major request from the user community: "Give us document workflows in SharePoint!" At last it is included in SharePoint 2007, not only for documents, but for all types of lists. Now it is possible to build really advanced tracking applications (for example, Issue tracking, Customer Relations Manager (CRM) tracking, and tracking for other types of applications that require some sort of workflow).

Some basic types of workflows are built into SharePoint that the user can actively direct within the browser; a typical example of this is workflows for document approval. For more advanced workflows you need the new Microsoft SharePoint Designer (SD), which is the customized version of FrontPage specifically designed for working with SharePoint sites. Using SD you can define a workflow for all lists and even InfoPath forms.

For example, you could create an application that does the following:

1. It displays an InfoPath form on a web page. (Yes, IP forms can now be displayed as web forms.)
2. A user fills in this form and clicks "Submit," and the workflow gets activated.
3. The workflow sends an e-mail to the person responsible for this form, who takes some actions.
4. Depending on the actions, the workflow may send an e-mail to the user who filled in the form.
5. The form is then stored in a specific SharePoint library, and the workflow ends.

Note that workflows defined in SD require no code, but you still have a large set of options when defining the workflow. If you want to create an even more advanced workflow, you have to use Visual Studio 2005, which has built-in features for managing workflows in SharePoint.

The New Gantt View

When working on a project, it is often important to see what activities are planned and when they are scheduled. When you have a number of activities, it may be hard to get an overview of all of them, especially if they also are dependent on each other. One way of making this easier to view is to create a special type of diagram called Gantt (invented by the engineer Henry Laurence Gantt), which is frequently used in project applications, such as MS Project.

Using WSS 2003 you can add third-party web parts for Gantt schemas, but with SharePoint 2007 they are included as a native view, not a web part. You can use the new Gantt web part in SharePoint 2007 on any type of list with a start and end date and present the items in this list using the new Gantt view. Note that this is not as advanced as the Gantt schemas in MS Project; for example, you cannot define relationships and dependencies. Still, it can be very useful for some types of lists. For example, say that you have a list where users can book a conference room; using this Gantt view, it is very easy to see when this room is available and which user has done the booking.

Because every type of list now also has access to a workflow engine, it is possible to build smart applications for tracking and activating processes while presenting information in a Gantt view. If the list is based on the Task list template, it will also be possible to synchronize this list to the user's Outlook 2007 client, thus making it easier for the user to see tasks assigned to him or her.

A good resource for more information about tasks and time management is `http://blogs.msdn.com/` `melissamacbeth.`

Improved Synchronization

One of the common complaints about WSS 2003 is about its synchronization of list and library content. It makes it hard to use the information in these lists when offline. Look at how WSS 2003 treats contact and calendar lists; you can synchronize these lists *from* SharePoint *to* Outlook, but not the other way around. Although that makes it possible to see the content in these lists when offline, it does not allow the user to update this content in Outlook. And a task list is not at all possible to replicate to Outlook.

In WSS 2007 all this is changed. You can update information in Outlook and it is replicated back to the original SharePoint list. For example, you can drag a meeting from your ordinary calendar in Outlook and drop it onto the replicated SharePoint calendar, and it is synchronized back to the original SharePoint list. The same goes for contacts: Drag any contact from your ordinary Outlook contacts and drop it onto the replicated SharePoint contact list, and it is synchronized back to SharePoint.

You can also replicate task lists. Even better: Instead of the user keeping track of a lot of different task lists in SharePoint, all these lists where the user has been assigned a task are replicated to Outlook and aggregated on the same page. The user now has a much better overview of all these tasks. All tasks replicated from SharePoint are stored in Outlook in a separate subfolder under the general SharePoint folder. If you open this list, you will see all tasks, including the usual Outlook tasks.

Another new list type that can be synchronized is Discussions. For example, say that you have a project site where the members are using a discussion list to share ideas and comments. With WSS 2003 you need online access to read and write comments, but with WSS 2007 you can choose to synchronize this list to your Outlook 2007 client, thus making it possible to both read and write when offline. It is also stored as a subfolder under the SharePoint folder, like the other synchronized lists.

In case anything goes wrong during the synchronization process, Outlook makes an entry in the synchronization log file. For example, if you change the status for a task in Outlook at the same time somebody else changes the same field in the original SharePoint list, you will have a conflict. This will be discovered by Outlook during the next synchronization process, which will take place immediately after an object has been updated in Outlook. In the event of a conflict, the following will happen:

1. SharePoint makes a note of this conflict in the synchronization log.
2. The user is notified that it is a conflict.
3. The modification in SharePoint always takes precedence, overwriting the modification in Outlook.
4. The user can then open a Conflict subfolder in Outlook's SharePoint folder, where the modification from Outlook is stored; the user can reapply this modification without the need to redo the complete modification and resynchronize.

This conflict handling is very important when you have two-way replication of data. It works very well, and you can safely start working with synchronized lists in your WSS 2007 environment.

New Security

You can still define exactly what users and groups have access to the WSS 2007 sites, but you can also see three different default user groups:

❑ **Visitors:** Can only read information in this site.

❑ **Members:** Can read, write, and delete information.

❑ **Administrators:** Have full access to this site.

These three groups are defined on the same page where you define the name and other settings when creating a new site. The Site Settings page also allows you to update these security settings, as in WSS 2003.

In WSS 2003 you have cross-site groups, which work like a substitute to Active Directory groups (they contain one or more users and can be granted permissions to sites and lists). The problem with the cross-site group is its scope. It can only be used in the site collection in which it was created. SharePoint 2007 allows you to create "SharePoint Groups." They work the same as cross-site groups, but they can be used anywhere, including in the portal site, and not only in a specific site collection.

The SharePoint Group can also be associated with a mail distribution list (DL). The name for this DL is defined on the same page where you set the group name and its members. SharePoint automatically creates this DL in Active Directory, and it is then listed in the Global Address List in Outlook. If you later delete this SharePoint Group, the DL is automatically deleted from Active Directory.

Improved Printing

Because SharePoint is a web application, its printing capability is as good or bad as the web browser it runs in. In other words, you normally don't print SharePoint pages or lists from within the browser. SharePoint 2007 has been extended so that it can know if you are printing a page. It removes all the menus, the logo, and so on (also known as the *chrome*) before sending the page to the printer. Still, you need to export lists to MS Excel or MS Access before printing to get full control of the print layout.

The New SharePoint Portal Server

The new version of SPS is called Microsoft Office SharePoint Server, abbreviated as MOSS (or sometimes OSS). It contains a lot of new features and behavior, as described in the following sections.

The New User Interface

The user interface is totally redesigned compared to SPS 2003. In SharePoint 2003 the layout of SPS is different from WSS. In SharePoint 2007 both OSS and WSS look the same; in fact, you must look carefully if you want to know if you are working in a WSS site or an OSS site. And this is good! It prevents you from confusing the SharePoint user with different navigation and layout; these two products are now seamlessly integrated from a user's perspective.

Following are some of the features in the new user interface; for more details about some of these, see the previous section about WSS 2007:

❑ **Bread-crumb trails:** These provide easier navigation.

❑ **Action Menu:** The menus to the left in portal areas are gone; you have a drop-down menu that looks the same as WSS 2007 pages.

❑ **Action Settings:** This is a new menu that lists the options and actions available at this moment. This menu only displays options that the current user is allowed to use.

❑ **Customization:** Using the "Look and Feel" option in the site settings allows you to customize this page to a greater extent than with SPS 2003 without tools like the new SharePoint Designer.

❑ **Current user:** The name for the current user is listed at the top of the page.

❑ **Sign in as Different User:** It is possible to temporarily login as another user and then return to the first user login.

❑ **My Links:** This is a new menu at the top of the page that displays the current user's links. This menu in SPS 2003 is located in the user's personal site (My Site).

❑ **A new Site list:** Your sites can be displayed in new ways: One is to configure the Sites link to work like a drop-down menu that displays the sites; another is to configure the navigation settings to display the site name with all the other portal areas at the top menu.

❑ **Page Layout:** If you have seen MS CMS 2002, you will recognize this new feature, because it actually is MS CMS added to OSS 2007. It allows you to define exactly how a page should look, including text, pictures, and so on. This web content management feature offers you much better control over how the intranet pages look and behave.

❑ **Mobile View:** This is the same feature as for WSS 2007. It makes it possible to view the portal site in a mobile device, like a Smart Phone.

Central SharePoint Administration

This administrative tool is now completely redesigned and looks and feels very much like any SharePoint 2007 site. The pages are much more logically organized, and the links and actions on each page are easier to find. This makes it much easier for the administrator to quickly find the page he or she needs to use for a specific configuration.

Enterprise Content Management

The Enterprise Content Management (ECM) feature in SharePoint 2007 helps organizations to keep track of their documents and other types of information. The usual life cycle for a document looks like this:

1. The document gets created.

2. It is published (for example, placed in a public file folder).

3. The document gets updated and then published again.

4. After some time, the document is obsolete and should be deleted.

SharePoint 2003 takes care of the different versions already, but the real improvement here is step 4. With SharePoint 2003, documents very seldom are deleted when obsolete; they are stored on the file server forever. (A disk crash now and then may be a good thing, after all.)

With the ECM feature you are able to define policies for the life cycle of any document, in every stage of its life. You can define a workflow that takes care of this routine and makes sure you don't have a number of documents floating around your IT environment. ECM will most likely be one of the most appreciated features of the new SharePoint and Office 2007 environment.

Record Management

Another important feature related to ECM is *Record Management*, which provides policies and procedures that govern how documents, e-mail, and other information types are managed during their life cycle. One very important reason for Record Management is to make SharePoint able to meet the requirements of governmental document regulations, like the *Sarbanes-Oxley Act* (SOX) and the *Health Insurance Portability and Accountability Act* (HIPAA). This defines how an organization should manage any type of information. For example, SOX states that an organization must be able to move a specific type of obsolete information to a message vault (a kind of data store that will prohibit anyone from modifying or deleting this information stored in this vault). This Record Management feature is also designed to allow auditing of any activities regarding these records; for example, it is possible to see who and when a document was updated, and who has read it. The administrator can generate reports for information in the auditing log.

In other words, for the first time it is possible to have complete control of information in the organization. This will most likely be applied to a limited number of documents, e-mail, and so on, but the important point here is that with OSS 2007 and Office 2007, you can build a world-class enterprise content management system that integrates in the user's normal working environment in such a way that you don't have to force all users to learn completely new ways of working. Instead, they will have an environment that allows them to work in a professional way without being worried about breaking any government regulations.

The developer team at Microsoft responsible for this Record Management feature studied all the most important regulations in the industry and designed this feature so it could meet or exceed the expectations of these regulations. Another important goal was to make it easy to extend or customize the policies that regulate the behavior of Record Management, if necessary. There was one more goal: People who work with documents and information seldom appreciate any kind of policy that forces them to work in a certain way. So Microsoft designed the Record Management to automate as much of the work as possible and to be integrated with MS Office 2007. Their first real test of this feature was when the Legal Department at Microsoft moved most of its manual management of more than 1.5 million documents to the new Record Management in OSS — and it worked as expected!

My Site

The personal sites (or "My Site") are still there in OSS 2007. My Site has been extended with several new features, but the basic idea is the same as in SPS 2003:

❑ **A private place** where the user can see targeted information, such as news, links, and e-mail.

❑ **A public place** where the details about the user are described, such as phone number, department, and e-mail address.

Microsoft has analyzed how My Sites are used in SPS 2003 and what other features organizations have asked for. This has resulted in the following new features in My Site:

❑ **OWA Auto configured:** Users do not need to configure the Outlook Web Access web parts for their Inbox and Calendar any more; SharePoint does that automatically now.

❑ **New properties:** There are properties that describe the areas of expertise of the user. This information is also displayed on the public view of this site. It is also possible to search for these. For example, you can search for a person who is an expert on SOX regulations.

❑ **My Colleagues:** This web part that displays a list of users you work with. This list can be manually updated by the user or automatically updated based on either the Buddies in your Instant Messaging client (MSN or Communicator) or the people you have e-mail conversations with.

- ❑ **Visibility:** The user can define how the public view of My Site looks for these groups of users:

  - ❑ **My Manager:** Based on the settings in the user profile.

  - ❑ **My Workgroup:** As defined in the user profile.

  - ❑ **My Colleagues:** As defined by the user in the "My Colleagues" web part.

  - ❑ **Everyone:** Anyone can see this information.

- ❑ **Social Networking:** This web part on the public view lists the relationships users have with each other. For example, if Adam looks at Anna's public site, he may see that he has the same manager as Anna, that he belongs to the same SharePoint Groups for some sites, and that he is a member of the same distribution lists as her. This will help Adam to quickly understand his working relationship with Anna.

- ❑ **Personal Roll-up:** This web part automatically lists all sites in a tab view where the user either has been assigned tasks or has created, modified, or checked-out documents. It gives the user instant access to the sites that he or she most likely is using frequently without the need to manually add a link to the "My Links" list. The user can also add links manually to this web part.

- ❑ **Site Roll-up:** This is a more generic version of the Personal Roll-up. The user adds frequently visited sites to this web part and then defines what information in that site to display in this roll-up.

People Profile Store

The database known as the User Profile database in SPS 2003 is enhanced, both in terms of the administration and the number of properties available for each user. Previously, there were 25 properties defined for each user in the profile database by default. In OSS you will find 41 properties. As in SPS 2003, you can easily add new properties when needed.

The most important change is that the profile database can retrieve data from more sources than the Active Directory that SPS 2003 supports; the new list of sources is this:

- ❑ **Active Directory:** The same as before.

- ❑ **LDAP v3 Directory:** Any directory that complies with version 3 of the LDAP directory; for example, Novel NDS.

- ❑ **Business Data Catalog:** Any database that SharePoint can read using the new BDC feature; for example, an MS SQL database.

As before, this replication is one-way: from the source to SharePoint, not the other way around. For example, if you want to update Active Directory from SharePoint, you need to develop some code for this. The good news is that you can use the new "Active Directory Management Web Services" interface for this. This is the same interface used by SharePoint when creating e-mail addresses for e-mail–enabled lists and SharePoint groups.

Audience

The Audience is enhanced, compared to SPS 2003. It has almost the same layout as its administrative pages, but there have been other important enhancements:

- ❑ **Better Scalability:** Can manage a lot more people and audience groups.

- ❑ **Increased Usability:** Can be used in more places in SharePoint.

- ❑ **Increased Depth:** Has more properties to define the audience.

Search

The search feature is enhanced in OSS. It is faster and the ranking of results is better, so there is now higher probability that the information you are searching for will be at the top of the result list. Any modifications of properties are now indexed immediately, instead of when the next indexing process runs. The result is that you can find updated documents much faster than before. The layout of the search page is also changed to make it easier to use and read:

❑ All keyword hits are listed separately, not together with the rest of the result list.

❑ There is a tab view for selecting to search for documents or people.

❑ Using the Advanced Search for documents is easy in OSS; when defining the search query, you have a number of additional fields where you can enter text to look for:

    ❑ **And:** This text phrase must also exist.

    ❑ **Exact phrase:** Look for exactly this text phrase.

    ❑ **Any of these words:** This is a logical OR search operand.

    ❑ **None of these words:** This is a logical NOR operand.

    ❑ **Scope:** Define in what area you want to search.

    ❑ **Language:** Define in what language you want to search. This requires that you have installed language packs. For example, if you have German installed on an English OSS, you can say that your search query should only look for documents written in German.

    ❑ **Result type:** Choose the type of document you are looking for: All results, Documents, Word documents, Excel documents, or Presentations (PowerPoint files).

❑ When searching for people, you also have a simple and advanced view. Click the Search Options link to define any of the following properties:

    ❑ **Name:** Any part of the name for the person, such as the first name or last name.

    ❑ **Departments:** The department person belongs to.

    ❑ **Title:** The title for the person.

    ❑ **Manager:** The manager for this person.

    ❑ **Skills:** The skills or expertise areas that are defined for this person.

    ❑ **Responsibility:** The duties that the person is responsible for.

Business Data Catalog

This is a completely new feature in OSS 2007. It builds upon the Data Source web part in FrontPage 2003, but it has been redesigned to allow the SharePoint administrator (you) to add one or more external databases as SharePoint's data sources. The Business Data Catalog (BDC) opens up a lot of new possibilities, such as the following:

❑ Searching for data in external databases, such as a Product database in MS SQL Server.

❑ Showing data in external databases in SharePoint lists.

❑ Using external data in SharePoint lookup tables.

❑ Using external data in InfoPath forms used in SharePoint.

And all this without writing any code or using tools like the SharePoint Designer. Of course this data can be used in code as well to create more advanced SharePoint applications. The BDC can read from any MS SQL database or any external data source that can expose its content by web services, such as SAP or Siebel. To make it easy for the user to work with and display the data sources in the BDC, SharePoint now has these four new web parts:

❑ **Business Data List:** For example, lists all customers or products in the data source.

❑ **Business Data Items:** For example, displays all the details about a specific customer.

❑ **Business Data Related List:** For example, displays all the products bought by a specific customer.

❑ **Business Data Action:** Shows all the actions available for a given "Business Data Item"; for example, sends an e-mail to a customer using the address listed in the data source.

It is also possible to connect these web parts to other web parts on the site (for example, to filter what information you want to present in a web part).

News for Developers

There are several important features for the SharePoint developer. One is that SharePoint 2007 builds on ASP.NET 2.0, which makes it possible to use any ASP.NET .2.0 controls on a SharePoint page. Another feature is the Microsoft Office SharePoint Developer 2007 editor, or SD. This is a much enhanced version of FrontPage 2003 that totally focuses on SharePoint customization. It is possible to use SD on SharePoint 2003 sites, but you do not have access to all the features, such as ASP.NET 2.0 controls or master pages, because these features are not supported by SharePoint 2003.

> *The previous performance penalty for un-ghosting sites in SharePoint 2003 is no longer a problem. A site will still be un-ghosted when using the SharePoint Designer, but it will not decrease the performance any more. It is also very easy to re-ghost a site if necessary, using the SharePoint Designer.*

Master Pages

One very interesting feature in SD is the concept of a master page. This page defines the branding for a SharePoint 2007 site, including:

❑ Colors

❑ Top menus

❑ Actions

❑ Navigation layout

❑ Logos

❑ Banners

Each SharePoint 2007 site has one master page associated with it. The same master page can be (and usually is) used by several sites. If this master page is modified, all these sites will then show the updated layout. This solves a problem in SharePoint 2003, where the only way of changing existing sites is to modify the site definition. You can still use site definitions in SharePoint 2007, but using master pages is much easier; it allows a SharePoint designer to change the look-and-feel for a site whenever needed. There is a Master Page Gallery that can contain any number of master pages. The administrator for the site can select any of these at any time.

Page Layout

Whereas the master page defines the branding of the site, *page layout* defines the content part of the page. This feature is inherited from MS CMS 2002 and works this way: A web designer defines the page layout for one or more content types, like News, Reports, and Product Description. This layout is stored in a file. When you define a new site page, you also select one of these page layouts. This way you have full control over how information is presented, regardless of which page the information is presented in. If you need to change the layout, you edit the page layout file, and all sites using this layout are updated.

Every page layout has one or more controls (for example, a picture control or a content editor control). You can add any type of SharePoint or ASP.NET 2.0 control to the page layout. You can also use new ASP.NET 2.0 controls or purchase controls from third-party vendors.

In other words, the master page and the layout page together control the look-and-feel of a site. It is easy to change existing pages and create new ones using SharePoint Designer 2007. This is not something the end user does, because it requires the technical understanding of how to work with SD, master pages, and page layouts. But this is a very fun and easy way of branding SharePoint 2007 sites.

Content Pages

The actual content that is displayed in the page layout is referred to as "Pages," also a concept inherited from CMS 2002. Each page is a file that is stored in a SharePoint library; to add new content you create new pages. By using a SharePoint library it will be possible to take advantage of version history, check in/check out and approval workflows, which offers a much better control of this information compared to News items in SPS 2003.

Because the layout pages are web part pages, the page editor can take advantage of audience targeting when publishing content. It is also possible to add any type of standard web parts to the layout pages that will then display its content on the final page.

The New Concept "Features"

In version 2003 of SharePoint you can add your own menus and actions to the sites by updating the site definition files on the SharePoint server. The problem is that you need to do this in several places if the site consists of multiple pages, so the maintenance is hard. If you want to change anything, you need to make sure to update the code in all places that are customized.

In SharePoint 2007 there is a new concept called "Features." At least this was the name that was being used in the beta version, as this book was being written. A "Feature" is like a kind of code snippet or a module. It usually does something very specific, such as adding a new option to the document menu in document libraries. This module can now be added to SharePoint 2007 by using STSADM.EXE (yes, the program is still there, and it has been extended) or the administrative pages in SharePoint. Then it can be used in one or more sites in the SharePoint environment.

A "Feature" is a number of files in the folder "FEATURES" that is stored in the same folder structure as all the other files and folders in a SharePoint server. By default there are a lot of "Features" installed in this file structure in a standard configured SharePoint server, and you can add as many new "Features" as you need. Each "Feature" can inherit properties from another "Feature," so you only write the code that is needed. It is like building with Lego blocks: Pick the pieces you like and put them together to build whatever you like.

Because a "Feature" is installed only once, it is easy to maintain and update; simply change the code you want, reactivate the "Feature," and the new settings become active. You can set different scopes for a "Feature," deciding where this "Feature" will be visible:

❑ **A Form:** Make the "Feature" visible only when uploading documents.

❑ **A Virtual IIS Server:** Make the "Feature" available in all the sites for a specific virtual server.

❑ **A Site Collection:** Make the "Feature" available only for a specific site collection.

❑ **A Site:** Make the "Feature" available only for a specific site.

Upgrading to SharePoint 2007

One of the most important questions is how to prepare an existing SPS or WSS 2003 environment for an easy upgrade to SharePoint 2007. The answer is that it will be an easy upgrade, as long as you have not done extensive customization. All the data in the lists and libraries will be upgraded without any particular migration process. (Compare that to the process of upgrading from SPS 2001 to SPS 2003, which was a real pain!)

Different Upgrade Scenarios

You have several ways to upgrade an existing SharePoint 2003 environment:

❑ **In-place upgrade:** Run the Upgrade command on the existing server. When it is finished, you have access to SharePoint 2007 and all its features. All data is updated. No new hardware is required.

❑ **Gradual site-by-site upgrade:** Install the new SharePoint program on the existing SharePoint servers and then move one or more sites from the old environment to the new. This upgrade process automatically updates all URL links so your environment will work during this migration period. No new hardware is required.

❑ **Gradual cross-farm upgrade:** Create a completely new SharePoint 2007 farm and then gradually migrate data from the old environment to the new farm. This requires more hardware, but it is a good choice if you want to change the hardware at the same time (as you often want to do).

I have been involved in a lot of migrations projects over the past 20 years, and the general lesson I have learned is that it is better to create a new environment and move the old data to it. The reason is that every time you do an upgrade, you will still carry a lot of the old stuff with you, such as registry settings and customized system and ini files. If something strange starts to happen after an in-place upgrade, you are never sure whether the problem is related to the new server version or there are some remains from the old environment that cause the problem. Obviously, because the new SharePoint version is not yet released at the time of this writing, I cannot tell from experience how the SharePoint upgrade process works, but I am sure I will most likely recommend that my customers choose the gradual cross-farms method when possible. I am sure the other methods will do a great job, but I have learned that it pays to be a little paranoid about these things at times.

A Default Site

If you have an existing SharePoint 2003 environment with no specific customization, you can just run the upgrade process. After this you have a SharePoint 2007 environment with the same data and the same look-and-feel. All existing lists in WSS 2003 continue to exist, including their content. All the new lists features of WSS 2007, such as workflows and enhanced version history, are now available for all upgraded lists and libraries. It is now possible to start branding these sites with the new techniques available in SharePoint 2007, such as master pages and layout pages, and all the new features. All the web parts used in SPS 2003 or WSS 2003 still work in SharePoint 2007, including the ones you have developed. But I recommend you look at the many new web parts that come with SharePoint 2007; if possible use them instead because they most likely will have enhanced functionality.

A Customized Site

Customizations of SharePoint 2003 sites using FrontPage 2003 will normally work without any modification. You may, however, want to take advantage of all the new features in SharePoint Designer and ASP.NET 2.0, such as master pages and layout pages. If so you will need to remove all current customization in the site and then reapply it using the new techniques. This may be a small or large task, but doing so will provide you all the benefits of the new design features, so you should really consider this.

I have seen several SharePoint installations with extensive customization, where a large number of SharePoint-specific files, including stored procedures in MS SQL Server, have been changed. These sites will most likely be hard, if not impossible, to migrate. The chances are high that you will need to redo all this customization from scratch. The good news is that it will probably be easier now to do the same branding using the new design features in SharePoint Designer.

A lot of the advanced SharePoint hacking I have seen will not be necessary in SharePoint 2007. For example, I have seen custom-developed web parts for "undelete," people-search, and basic roll-ups. All of these are now built into SharePoint 2007. All well-behaved web parts will continue to work, but some of the web parts I have seen using "smart short-cuts" will most likely not survive the upgrade process.

> *One way to test if a custom web part will work in SharePoint 2007 is to install a temporary WSS 2003 server with Service Pack 2, running ASP.NET 2.0 and install this web part there. If it works there, it will also work in your upgraded production environment.*

Summary

In this chapter you learned the following:

❑   WSS 2003 is replaced by WSS 2007 in SharePoint 2007.

❑   SPS 2003 is replaced by MS Office SharePoint Server 2007 (OSS) in SharePoint 2007.

❑   MS is releasing more than 15 new or updated MS Office Server products during 2007.

❑   Important new lists and library features are workflow, extended version history, individual security settings, and support for e-mail enabling.

- ❑ Important design enhancements include bread-crumb trails, customizable navigation, matching look-and-feel for WSS and OSS, smarter menus, and improved layout.

- ❑ Synchronization is two-way when using Outlook 2007.

- ❑ Layout is enhanced for the Central SharePoint Administration tool.

- ❑ There is support for Enterprise Content Management and Record Management.

- ❑ Functionality is extended in My Site; for example, new roll-up web parts.

- ❑ There is extended search functionality and an enhanced search page in SharePoint 2007.

- ❑ Business Data Catalog provides support for accessing external data.

- ❑ FrontPage 2003 has evolved into SharePoint Designer, which is now the dedicated design tool for all SharePoint 2007 sites.

- ❑ Dynamic updates of site branding and page layout are now possible using the new features of ASP.NET 2.0: master pages and layout pages.

- ❑ There is no performance penalty for un-ghosting sites.

- ❑ There are three ways to upgrade an existing SharePoint environment: in-place, gradual site-by-site, and gradual cross-farm.

Index

L